To

> *Dr. Abraham Fischler, President of Nova University and to*
> *Dr. Edward Simco, Dean of the Nova University Center for Computer and*
> *Information Sciences*

> *For their vision of an institution for advanced scientific and computer science education and research in South Florida, and for their indefatigable efforts in realizing that vision in this young university.*

> *H. M. D.*

To

> *My teachers at Lawrenceville and M.I.T.*

> *For instilling in me a love of learning and writing.*

> *P. J. D.*

Contents

Illustrations

xi

Preface

Welcome to C! This book is by an old guy and a young guy. The old guy (HMD; Massachusetts Institute of Technology 1967) has been programming and/or teaching programming for more than 30 years. The young guy (PJD; MIT 1991) has been programming for a dozen years and has caught the teaching and writing "bug." The old guy programs and teaches from experience. The young guy programs from an inexhaustible reserve of energy. The old guy wants clarity. The young guy wants performance. The old guy appreciates elegance and beauty. The young guy wants results. We got together to produce a book we hope you will find informative, interesting, and entertaining.

In most educational environments, C is taught to people who already know how to program. Many educators believe that the complexity of C, and a number of other difficulties, make C unworthy for a first programming course—precisely the target course for this book. So why did we write this text?

C has in fact become the systems implementation language of choice in industry, and there is good reason to believe that its object-oriented variant, C++, will emerge as the dominant language of the mid-to-late 1990s. Harvey Deitel has been teaching Pascal in university environments for 13 years with an emphasis on developing clearly written, well-structured programs. Much of what is taught in an introductory Pascal course sequence is the basic principles of structured programming. We have presented this material exactly the way HMD has done in his university courses. There are some pitfalls, but where these occur, we point them out and explain procedures for dealing with them effectively. Our experience has been that students handle the course in about the same manner as they handle Pascal. There is one noticeable difference though: The students are highly motivated by the fact that they are learning a language that will be immediately useful to them as they leave the university environment. This increases their enthusiasm for the material—a big help when you consider that C is considerably more difficult to learn.

Our goal was clear: Produce a programming textbook using C for introductory university-level courses in computer programming for students with little or no programming experience. But produce a book that also offers the rigorous treatment of theory and practice demanded by traditional C programming courses. To meet these goals, we produced a book larger than other C texts—this because our text also patiently teaches structured programming principles. Approximately 1000 students have studied this material in our courses.

The book contains a rich collection of examples, exercises, and projects drawn from many fields to provide the student with a chance to solve interesting real-world problems.

The book concentrates on the principles of good software engineering and stresses program clarity through use of the structured programming methodology. We avoid the use of arcane terminology and syntax specifications in favor of teaching by example.

Among the pedagogical devices of this text are the use of complete programs and sample outputs to demonstrate the concepts being discussed; a set of objectives and an outline at the beginning of every chapter; common programming errors (CPEs) and good programming practices (GPPs) enumerated throughout each chapter and summarized at the end of each chapter; summary and terminology sections in each chapter; self-review questions and answers in each chapter; and the richest collection of exercises in any C book. An instructor's manual is available on IBM PC format disks and Macintosh format disks with all the programs in the main text and with answers to all exercises at the end of each chapter. The exercises range from simple recall questions to lengthy programming problems to major projects. Instructors requiring substantial term projects of their students will find many appropriate problems listed in the exercises for Chapters 5 through 15. We have put a great deal of effort into the exercises to enhance the value of this course for the student. The programs in the text were tested on ANSI C-compliant compilers on a Sun SPARCstation, Apple Macintosh (Think C), IBM PC (Turbo C, Turbo C++, and Borland C++), and DEC VAX/VMS (VAX C).

This text specifically follows the ANSI C standard. Many features of ANSI C will not work with pre-ANSI C versions. See the reference manuals for your particular system for more details about the language, or obtain a copy of ANSI document X3.159-1989, "*American National Standard for Information Systems—Programming Language—C*," from the American National Standards Institute, 1430 Broadway, New York, New York 10018.

About this Book

This book is loaded with features to help the student learn.

Objectives

Each chapter begins with a statement of learning objectives. This tells the student what to expect and gives the student a chance, after reading the chapter, to determine if he or she has, in fact, met these objectives. It is a confidence builder and a source of positive reinforcement.

Quotations

The learning objectives are followed by a series of quotations. Some are humorous, some are philosophical, and some offer interesting insights. Our students have told us that they enjoy relating the quotes to the chapter material.

Outline

The chapter outline helps the student approach the material in top-down fashion. This, too, helps students anticipate what is to come and set a responsible pace.

Sections

Each chapter is organized into small sections, that address key areas. C features are presented in the context of complete, working C programs. Each program is followed by a window containing the output produced when the program is run. This enables the student to confirm that the programs run as expected. Relating outputs back to the program statements that produce the outputs is an excellent way to learn and reinforce concepts. Our programs are designed to exercise the diverse features of C. Reading the book carefully is much like entering and running these programs on a computer.

Illustrations

An abundance of line drawings and charts is included. The discussion of structured flowcharting, which helps students appreciate the use of control structures and structured programming, features numerous carefully drawn flowcharts. The chapter on data structures uses abundant line drawings to illustrate the creation and maintenance of important data structures such as linked lists, queues, stacks, and binary trees.

Helpful Design Elements

We have included four design elements to help students focus on important aspects of program development, testing and debugging, performance, and portability. We highlight scores of these in the form of *Good Programming Practices (GPPs)*, *Common Programming Errors (CPEs)*, *Performance Tips (PERFs)*, and *Portability Tips (PORTs)*.

Good Programming Practices (GPPs)

Good programming practices are highlighted it in the text with our GPP design element. This calls the student's attention to techniques that help produce better programs. These GPPs represent the best we have been able to glean from a combined four decades of programming experience.

Common Programming Errors (CPEs)

Students learning a language—especially in their first programming course—tend to make certain common errors. Focusing the students' attention on these common programming errors is an enormous help. It also helps reduce the long lines outside instructors' offices during office hours!

Performance Enhancement Tips (PERFs)

We find that writing clear and understandable programs is by far the most important goal for a first programming course. But students want to write the program that runs the fastest, uses the least memory, requires the smallest number of keystrokes, or dazzles in some other nifty way. Students really care about performance. They want to know what they can do to "turbo charge" their programs. So we have include *Performance Tips (PERFs)* to highlight opportunities for improving program performance.

Portability Tips (PORTs)

Software development has become complex and enormously expensive. Organizations that develop software must often produce versions customized to a variety of computers and operating systems. So there is a strong emphasis today on portability, i.e., on producing software that will run on many different computer systems without change. Many people tout C as the best language for developing portable software. Some people assume that if they implement an application in C, the application will automatically be portable. This is simply not the case. Achieving portability requires careful and cautious design. There are many pitfalls. The ANSI Standard C document itself lists 11 pages of potential difficulties. We include numerous Portability Tips (PORTs). We have combined our own experience in building portable software with a careful study of the ANSI standard section on portability, as well as two excellent books on portability (see references Ja89 and Ra90 at the end of Chapter 1).

Summary

Each of our chapters ends with a number of additional pedagogical devices. We present a detailed summary of the chapter in bullet-list fashion. This helps the students review and reinforce key concepts,.

Terminology

We include a Terminology section with an alphabetized list of the important terms defined in the chapter. Again, further confirmation. Then we summarize the GPPs, CPEs, PERFs, and PORTs.

Self-Review Exercises

Extensive Self-Review Exercises with complete answers are included for self-study. This gives the student a chance to build confidence with the material and prepare to attempt the regular exercises.

Exercises

Each chapter concludes with a substantial set of exercises spanning the range from simple recall of important terminology and concepts, to writing individual C statements, to writing small portions of C functions, to writing complete C functions and programs, to writing major term projects. The large number of exercises enables instructors to tailor their course to the unique needs of their audiences and to vary course assignments each semester. Instructors can use these exercises to form homework assignments, short quizzes, and major examinations. The text for the exercises is included on the IBM-PC-format and Apple-Macintosh-format disks available to instructors through their Prentice-Hall representatives.

A Tour of the Book

Chapter 1, "Introduction," discusses what computers are, how they work, and how they are programmed. It introduces the notion of structured programming and explains why this set of techniques has fostered a revolution in the way programs are written. The chapter gives a brief history of the development of programming languages from machine languages, to assembly languages, to high-level languages. The origin of the C programming language is discussed. The chapter includes an introduction to the C programming environment.

Chapter 2, "Introduction to C Programming," gives a concise introduction to writing C programs. A detailed treatment of decision making and arithmetic operations in C is presented. After studying this chapter, the student will understand how to write simple, but complete, C programs.

Chapter 3, "Structured Programming," is probably the most important chapter in the text, especially for the serious student of computer science. It introduces the notion of algorithms (procedures) for solving problems. It explains the importance of structured programming in producing programs that are understandable, debuggable, maintainable, and more likely to work properly on the first try. It introduces the fundamental control structures of structured programming, namely the sequence, selection (`if` and `if/else`), and repetition (`while`) structures. It explains the technique of top-down, stepwise refinement that is critical to the production of properly structured programs. It presents two program design aids, namely structured flowcharting and structured pseudocode. The methods and approaches used in Chapter 3 are applicable to structured programming in any programming language, not just C. This chapter helps the student develop good programming habits in preparation for dealing with the more substantial programming tasks in the remainder of the text.

Chapter 4, "Program Control," refines the notions of structured programming and introduces additional control structures. It examines repetition in detail, and compares the alternatives of counter-controlled loops and sentinel-controlled loops. The `for` structure is introduced as a convenient means for implementing counter-controlled loops. The `switch` selection structure and the `do/while` repetition structure are presented. The chapter concludes with a discussion of logical operators.

Chapter 5, "Functions," discusses the design and construction of program modules. C includes standard library functions, programmer-defined functions, recursion, and call-by-value capabilities. The techniques presented in Chapter 5 are essential to the production and appreciation of properly structured programs, especially the kinds of larger programs and software that system programmers and application programmers are likely to develop in real-world applications. The "divide and conquer" strategy is presented as an effective means for solving complex problems; functions enable the programmer to divide complex programs into simpler interacting components. Students enjoy the treatment of random numbers and simulation, and they appreciate the discussion of the dice game craps which makes elegant use of control structures. The extensive collection of 39 exercises at the end of the chapter includes several classical recursion problems such as the Towers of Hanoi.

Chapter 6, "Arrays," discusses the structuring of data into arrays, or groups, of related data items of the same type. The chapter presents numerous examples of both single-subscripted arrays and double-subscripted arrays. It is widely recognized that structuring data is just as important as using control structures in the development of properly structured programs. Examples in the chapter investigate various common array manipulations, printing histograms, sorting data, passing arrays to functions, and an introduction to the field of survey data analysis. The end-of-chapter exercises include an especially large selection of interesting and challenging problems. These include improved sorting techniques, the design of an airline reservations system, an introduction to the concept of turtle graphics (made famous in the LOGO language), and the Knight's Tour and Eight Queens problems that introduce the notions of heuristic programming so widely employed in the field of artificial intelligence.

Chapter 7, "Pointers," presents one of the most powerful features of the C language. The chapter provides detailed explanations of pointer operators, call by reference, pointer expressions, pointer arithmetic, the relationship between pointers and arrays, arrays of pointers, and pointers to functions. The chapter exercises include a simulation of the classic race between the tortoise and the hare, and card shuffling and dealing algorithms. A special section entitled "Building Your Own Computer" is also included. This section explains the notion of machine language programming and proceeds with a project involving the design and implementation of a computer simulator that allows the reader to write and run machine language programs. This unique feature of the text will be especially useful to the reader who wants to understand how computers really work. Our students enjoy this project and often implement substantial enhancements.

Chapter 8, "Characters and Strings," deals with the fundamentals of processing nonnumeric data. The chapter includes an extremely detailed walkthrough of the character and string processing functions available in C's libraries. The techniques discussed here are widely used in building word processors, page layout and typesetting software, and text-processing applications. The chapter includes an interesting collection of 33 exercises that explore text-processing applications. The student will enjoy the exercises on writing limericks, writing random poetry, converting English to pig Latin, generating seven-letter words that are equivalent to a given telephone number, text justification, check protection, writing a check amount in words, generating Morse Code, metric conversions, and dunning letters. The last exercise challenges the student to use a computerized dictionary to create a crossword puzzle generator!

Chapter 9, "Formatted Input/Output," presents all the powerful formatting capabilities of `printf` and `scanf`. We discuss `printf`'s output formatting capabilities such as rounding floating point values to a given number of decimal places, aligning columns of numbers, right justification and left justification, insertion of literal information, forcing a plus sign, printing leading zeros, using exponential notation, using octal and hexadecimal numbers, and controlling field widths and precisions. We discuss all of `printf`'s escape sequences for cursor movement, printing special characters, and causing an audible alert. We examine all of `scanf`'s input formatting capabilities including inputting specific types of data and skipping specific characters in an input stream. We discuss all of `scanf`'s conversion specifiers for reading decimal, octal, hexadecimal, floating point, character, and string values. We discuss scanning inputs to match (or not match) the characters in a scan set. The chapter exercises test virtually all of C's formatted input/output capabilities.

Chapter 10, "Structures, Unions, Bit Manipulations, and Enumerations," presents a number of important features. Structures are like records in Pascal and other languages—they group data items of various types. Structures are used in Chapter 11 to form files consisting of records of information. Structures are used in conjunction with pointers and dynamic memory allocation in Chapter 12 to form dynamic data structures such as linked lists, queues, stacks, and trees. Unions enable an area of memory to be used for different types of data at different times; such sharing can reduce a program's memory requirements or secondary storage requirements. Enumerations provide a convenient means of defining useful symbolic constants; this helps make programs more self-documenting. C's powerful bit manipulation capabilities enable programmers to write programs that exercise lower-level hardware capabilities . This helps programs process bit strings, set individual bits on or off, and store information more compactly. Such capabilities, often found only in low-level assembly languages, are valued by programmers writing system software such as operating systems and networking software. A feature of the chapter is its revised, high-performance card shuffling and dealing simulation. This is an excellent opportunity for the instructor to emphasize the quality of algorithms.

Chapter 11, "File Processing," discusses the techniques used to process text files with sequential access and random access. The chapter begins with an introduction to the data hierarchy from bits, to bytes, to fields, to records, to files. Next, C's view of files and streams is presented. Sequential access files are discussed using a series of three programs that show how to open and close files, how to store data sequentially in a file, and how to read data sequentially from a file. Random access files are discussed using a series of four programs that show how to sequentially create a file for random access, how to read and write data to a file with random access, and how to read data sequentially from a randomly accessed file. The fourth random access program combines many of the techniques of accessing files both sequentially and randomly into a complete transaction processing program. Our students in our industrial seminars tell us that after studying this material on file processing, they were able to produce substantial file-processing programs that were immediately useful in their organizations.

Chapter 12, "Data Structures," discusses the techniques used to create dynamic data structures. The chapter begins with discussions of self-referential structures and dynamic memory allocation. The chapter proceeds with a discussion of how to create and maintain various dynamic data structures including linked lists, queues (or waiting lines), stacks, and trees. For each type of data structure, we present complete, working programs and show sample outputs. Chapter 12 helps the student truly master pointers. The chapter includes abundant examples using indirection and double indirection—a particularly difficult concept. One problem when working with pointers is that students have trouble visualizing the data structures and how their nodes are linked together. So we have included a large number of illustrations that show not only the actual links, but the sequence in which they are created. The binary tree example is a superb capstone for the study of pointers and dynamic data structures. This example creates a binary tree, enforces duplicate elimination, and introduces preorder, inorder, and postorder recursive tree traversals. Students have a real sense of accomplishment when they study and implement this example. They particularly appreciate seeing that the inorder traversal prints the node values in sorted order. The chapter includes a substantial collection of exercises. A highlight of the chapter is the introduction to compiling via the study of infix notation and postfix notation. The exercises walk the student through the development of an infix-to-postfix-conversion program and a postfix-expression-evaluation program. Some of our students modify the postfix evaluation algorithm to generate the machine language code a compiler would typically produce. The students place this code in a file (using the techniques of Chapter 11) and then actually run their machine language programs on the software simulators they built in the exercises of Chapter 7!

Chapter 13, "The Preprocessor," provides detailed discussions of the preprocessor directives. The chapter includes more complete information on the #include directive that causes a copy of a specified file to be included in place of the directive before the file is compiled, and the #define directive that creates symbolic constants and macros. The chapter explains conditional compilation for enabling the programmer to control the execution of preprocessor directives, and the compilation of program code. The # operator that converts its operand to a string and the ## operator that concatenates two tokens are discussed. The five predefined symbolic constants (__LINE__, __FILE__, __DATE__, __TIME__, and __STDC__) are presented. Finally, macro assert of the assert.h header is discussed. assert is valuable in program testing, debugging, verification, and validation.

Chapter 14, "Advanced Topics," presents several advanced topics not ordinarily covered in introductory courses. Section 14.2 shows how to redirect input to a program to come from a file, redirect output from a program to be placed in a file, redirect the output of one program to be the input of another program (piping), and append the output of a program to an existing file. Section 14.3 discusses how to develop functions that use variable-length argument lists. Section 14.4 shows how command-line arguments can be passed to function main, and used in a program. Section 14.5 discusses compiling programs that exist in multiple files. Section 14.6 discusses registering functions with atexit to be executed at program termination, and terminating program execution with function exit. Section 14.7 discusses the const and volatile type qualifiers. Section 14.8 shows how to specify the type of a numeric constant using the integer and floating point suffixes. Section 14.9 explains binary files and the use of temporary files. Section 14.10 shows how to use signal handling library to trap unexpected events. Section 14.11 discusses the creation and use of dynamic arrays with calloc and realloc.

We are pleased to include Chapter 15, "Object-Oriented Programming and C++." There is a revolution occurring in software engineering today. Object-oriented programming (OOP) gives us an entirely new way to view the process of designing and building software. It offers us the opportunity for software reusability instead of constantly "reinventing the wheel." With OOP, organizations are discovering that they can substantially increase productivity. Our original goal was to write a brief introduction to C++. As we wrote the chapter, however, we saw a chance to offer computer science students a major opportunity to appreciate OOP early in their education. So we decided to present a much more substantial treatment. Because of time constraints, many courses will not be able to cover this chapter in depth, if at all. Regardless, students will have the material available in the same form as we presented C—a friendly approach with lots of learning aids and working programs. The chapter treats *both* major areas for which C++ was intended—enhancing C and supporting OOP. Among the C enhancements we discuss are single-line comments, local declarations, C++ stream-oriented input/output, inline functions, reference parameters, default arguments, and C++-style dynamic memory allocation with the `new` and `delete` operators. We then proceed with a discussion of object-oriented programming in C++. We discuss data abstraction, information hiding, classes, objects, software reusability with class libraries, the scope resolution operator, accessing class members, controlling access to data members and member functions, friend functions, constructor functions, destructor functions, inheritance, derived classes, operator overloading, function overloading, polymorphism, and virtual functions. A detailed case study on software reusability using C++ and object-oriented programming is included. The case study first converts our list processing program of Chapter 12 to C++ format. Then the program is encapsulated to form class `listclass`. We instantiate an object of that class and show that the object performs properly. Then we use inheritance to form derived classes for stacks and queues, instantiate objects of these classes, and show that these objects function properly. The reader will discover that Chapter 15 presents a solid treatment of C++ and OOP—much more than might be expected in a C textbook. We have loaded the chapter with C++ programs, execution outputs, and self-review exercises and answers, so even the student who does not have access to a C++ compiler will be able to learn a great deal. The exercises include some particularly challenging problems: using `stackclass` to create an OOP program implementing infix-to-postfix conversion and postfix evaluation algorithms, defining a string class, using OOP to develop a discrete-event queueing simulation that models the operation of a highway toll plaza, and using OOP to develop a simulation of the reader's favorite sport. The chapter includes extensive references for further study. The chapter concludes with an appendix that provides resources for the reader interested in further exploration of C++ and OOP. The appendix includes names and addresses for the Object Management Group—an industry consortium devoted to encouraging the use of OO-based techniques, publications about C++ and OOP topics, and companies that offer C++ products for the related OO-based languages Simula and Smalltalk. We hope our chapter will encourage the reader to pursue further study in C++ and object-oriented programming.

Several Appendices provide valuable reference material. In particular, we present the C syntax summary in Appendix A; a summary of all C standard library functions with explanations in Appendix B; a complete operator precedence and associativity chart in Appendix C; the set of ASCII character codes in Appendix D; and a discussion of the binary, octal, decimal, and hexadecimal number systems in Appendix E.

Acknowledgements

One of the great pleasures of writing a textbook is acknowledging the efforts of the many people whose names may not appear on the cover, but without whose hard work, cooperation, friendship, and understanding producing this text would have been impossible.

PJD would like to thank Professor Richard Wang of the Massachusetts Institute of Technology for his support and understanding, and for his interesting classes in C, UNIX, and SQL. PJD would also like to thank his Wellesley College friends Ms. Nancy Paz and Ms. Karin Monsler, and his MIT friends Will Martinez, Tim Nieto, Rich Wong, Mark Schaefer, Alex Hou, Goose (Brandt Casey) and last—but not least—Spike (Cliff Stephens).

HMD wants to thank his Nova University Colleagues Ed Simco, Clovis Tondo, Lois Simco, Ed Lieblein, Phil Adams, Raisa Szabo. Raul Salazar, Laurie Dringus, Pattie McCormick, and Barbara Edge.

We would like to thank our friends at the Corporation for Open Systems International (Bill Horst, David Litwack, Steve Hudson, and Linc Faurer), Informative Stages (Don Hall), Semaphore Training (Clive Lee), and Digital Equipment Corporation (Janet Hebert, Faye Napert, Betsy Mills, Jennie Connolly, Stephanie Stosur Schwartz, Barbara Couturier, John Ferreira, Gretchen Forbes, Debbie Barrett and Paul Sandore) who have made teaching this material in an industrial setting such a joy.

We are fortunate to have been able to work on this project with a talented and dedicated team of publishing professionals at Prentice Hall. Kathleen Schiaparelli did a marvelous job as production editor. Diana Penha and Jaime Zampino coordinated the complex reviewer effort on the manuscript, and were always incredibly helpful when we needed assistance—their ebullience and good cheer are sincerely appreciated.

We would like to thank Mr. James A. Cannavino, IBM Vice President and General Manager, Personal Systems, and Mr. Steve Ballmer, President of Microsoft Corporation for their friendship and for a photographic moment at Fall Comdex 1991 that we will never forget.

This book happened because of the encouragement, enthusiasm, and persistence of Marcia Horton, Vice President and Editor-in-Chief of Prentice-Hall's Computer Science and Engineering department. It is a great credit to Prentice-Hall that its top executives continue their editorial responsibilities. We have always been impressed with this, and we are grateful to be able to continue working so closely with Marcia even as her administrative responsibilities increase.

We appreciate the efforts of our reviewers

Gene Spafford (Purdue University)
Clovis Tondo (IBM Corporation and visiting professor at Nova University)
Jeffrey Esakov (University of Pennsylvania)
Tom Slezak (University of California, Lawrence Livermore National Laboratory)
Gary A. Wilson (Gary A Wilson & Associates—UNIX/C course consulting and instruction—and University of California Berkeley Extension)
Mike Kogan (IBM Corporation; chief architect of 32-bit OS/2 2.0)
Don Kostuch (IBM Corporation retired; now worldwide instructor in C, C++, and object-oriented programming)
Ed Lieblein (Nova University)
John Carroll (San Diego State University)
Alan Filipski (Arizona State University)

Greg Hidley (University of California San Diego)
Daniel Hirschberg (University of California Irvine)
Jack Tan (University of Houston)
Richard Alpert (Boston University)
Eric Bloom (Bentley College).

These people scrutinized every aspect of the text and made dozens of valuable suggestions for improving the accuracy and completeness of the presentation.

The authors would like to extend a special note of thanks to Ed Lieblein, one of the world's leading authorities on software engineering, for his extraordinary review of Chapter 15, "Object-Oriented Programming and C++." Dr. Lieblein is a friend and colleague of HMD at Nova University in Ft. Lauderdale, Florida where he is Full Professor of Computer Science. Dr. Lieblein was previously Chief Technical Officer of Tartan Laboratories, one of the leading compiler development organizations in the world. Before that, he served as Director of Computer Software and Systems in the Office of the Secretary of Defense. In that capacity, he managed the DoD Software Initiative, a special program to improve the nation's software capability for future mission critical systems. He initiated the Pentagon's STARS program for software technology and reusability, guided the Ada program to international standardization, and played an important role in establishing the Software Engineering Institute at Carnegie Mellon University. It is indeed a special privilege for us to be able to work with Dr. Lieblein at Nova University.

We would also like to extend a special note of thanks to Dr. Clovis Tondo of IBM Corporation and visiting professor at Nova University. Dr. Tondo was the head of our review team. His meticulous and thorough reviews taught us much about the subtleties of the C language and of teaching C properly. Dr. Tondo is the co-author of *The C Answer Book* which contains answers to the exercises in—and is widely used in conjunction with—*The C Programming Language,* the classic book on C by Brian Kernighan and Dennis Ritchie.

This text is based on the version of C standardized through the American National Standards Institute (ANSI) in the United States and through the International Standards Organization (ISO) worldwide. We have used extensive materials from the ANSI standard document with the express written permission of the American National Standards Institute. We sincerely appreciate the cooperation of Mary Clare Lynch—Director of Publications for ANSI—and her associates Kim Bullock and Beth Somerville for helping us obtain the necessary publication permissions. Figures 5.6, 8.1, 8.5, 8.12, 8.17, 8.20, 8.22, 8.30, 8.36, 9.1, 9.3, 9.6, 9.9, 9.16, 10.7, and 11.6, and Appendix A: C Syntax, and Appendix B: Standard Library have been condensed and adapted from *American National Standard for Information Systems—Programming Language—C, ANSI X3.159-1989,* copyright 1990 by the American National Standards Institute. Copies of this standard may be purchased from the American National Standards Institute, 11 West 42nd Street, New York, NY 10036.

Last, but certainly not least, we would like to thank Barbara and Abbey Deitel, for their love and understanding, and for their enormous efforts in helping prepare the manuscript. They contributed endless hours of effort; they tested every program in the text, assisted in every phase of the manuscript preparation, and proofread every draft of the text through to publication. Their sharp eyes prevented innumerable errors from finding a home in the manuscript. Barbara also researched the quotes, and Abbey suggested the title for the book.

We assume complete responsibility for any remaining flaws in this text. We would greatly appreciate your comments, criticisms, corrections, and suggestions for improving the text. Please send us your suggestions for improving and adding to our list of GPPs, CPEs, PORTs, and PERFs. We will acknowledge all contributors in the next edition of the book. Please address all correspondence to our email address:

> deitel@world.std.com

or write to us as follows:

> Harvey M. Deitel (author)
> Paul J. Deitel (author)
> c/o Computer Science Editor
> College Book Editorial
> Prentice Hall
> Englewood Cliffs, New Jersey 07632

We will respond immediately.

Harvey M. Deitel

Paul J. Deitel

1
Computing Concepts

Objectives

- To understand basic computer concepts.
- To become familiar with different types of programming languages.
- To become familiar with the history of the C programming language.
- To become aware of the C Standard Library.
- To understand the C program development environment.
- To appreciate why it is appropriate to learn C in a first programming course.
- To appreciate why C provides a foundation for further study of programming in general and C++ in particular.

Things are always at their best in their beginning.
Blaise Pascal

High thoughts must have high language.
Aristophanes

Our life is frittered away by detail ... Simplify, simplify.
Henry Thoreau

Outline

1.1 Introduction

Welcome to C! We have worked hard to create what we sincerely hope will be an informative and entertaining learning experience for you.

C is a difficult language that is normally taught only to experienced programmers. This book is unique in two important ways:

- It is appropriate for people with little or no programming experience.
- It is appropriate for experienced programmers who want a deep and rigorous treatment of the language.

How can one book appeal to both groups? The answer is that the common core of the book places an emphasis on achieving program *clarity* through the use of the proven techniques of "structured programming." The first four chapters of the book introduce the fundamentals of computing, computer programming, and the C language. The discussions are wrapped in an introduction to computer programming using the structured approach. People with little or no programming experience will learn programming the "right" way from the beginning. We have attempted to write in a clear and straightforward manner. The book is abundantly illustrated. Novices who have taken our courses tell us that they learn the material quickly and that they receive a solid foundation for the deeper treatment of C and C++ in Chapters 5 through 15.

Experienced programmers typically read the first four chapters quickly and then discover that the treatment of C and C++ in Chapters 5 through 15 is both rigorous and challenging. Experienced programmers who have taken our courses tell us that they really appreciate our treatment of structured programming. Often they have been programming in structured languages like Pascal or PL/1, but because they were never formally introduced to structured programming, they are not writing the best possible code in these languages. So whether you are a novice or an experienced programmer, there is much here to inform, entertain, and challenge you.

Most people are familiar with the exciting things computers do. In this course, you will learn how to command computers to do those things. It is *software* (i.e., the instructions you write to command the computer to perform actions) that controls computers (often referred to as *hardware*), and one of today's most popular software development languages is C. This text provides an introduction to programming in ANSI C, the version recently standardized in both the United States through the American National Standards Institute (ANSI), and around the world through the International Standards Organization (ISO).

Use of computers is increasing in almost every field of endeavor. In an era of steadily rising costs, computing costs have been decreasing dramatically because of exciting developments in electronics and other technologies. Computers that might have weighed many tons, filled large rooms, and cost millions of dollars 25 years ago can now be inscribed on the surfaces of silicon chips smaller than a fingernail, and that cost perhaps a few dollars each. Ironically, silicon is one of the most abundant materials on the earth—it is an ingredient in common sand. Silicon chip technology has made computing so economical that approximately 100 million general-purpose computers are in use worldwide helping people in business, industry, government, and in their personal lives. That number could easily double within five years.

1.2 What Is a Computer?

A *computer* is a device capable of performing computations and making logical decisions at speeds millions, and even billions, of times faster than human beings can. For example, many of today's personal computers can perform tens of millions of additions per second. A person operating a desk calculator might require years to complete the same number of calculations a powerful personal computer can perform in one second. (Point to ponder: How would you know whether the person added the numbers correctly?) Today's fastest *supercomputers* can perform hundreds of billions of additions per second—about as many calculations as one thousand people could perform in one year! And trillion-instruction-per-second computers are already functioning in research laboratories.

Computers process *data* under the control of sets of instructions called *computer programs*. These computer programs guide the computer through orderly sets of actions specified by people called *computer programmers*.

The various devices (such as the keyboard, screen, disks, memory, and processing units) that comprise a computer system are referred to as *hardware*. The computer programs that run on a computer are referred to as *software*. Hardware costs have been declining dramatically in recent years, almost to the point that personal computers have become a commodity. Unfortunately, software costs have been rising steadily as programmers develop ever more powerful and complex applications, without being able to improve the technology of software development. In this book you will learn software development methods that can reduce software development costs, namely structured programming, top-down stepwise refinement, functionalization—and in the last chapter of the book—object-oriented programming.

1.3 Computer Organization

Regardless of differences in physical appearance, virtually every computer may be envisioned as being divided into six *logical units* or sections. These are:

1. *Input unit*. This is the "receiving" section of the computer. It obtains information (data and computer programs) from various *input devices* and places this information at the disposal of the other units so that the information may be processed. Most information is entered into computers today through typewriter-like keyboards.

2. *Output unit*. This is the "shipping" section of the computer. It takes information that has been processed by the computer and places it on various *output devices* to make the information available for use outside the computer. Most information is output from computers today by displaying it on screens or by printing it on paper.

3. *Memory unit*. This is the rapid access, relatively low-capacity "warehouse" section of the computer. It retains information that has been entered through the input unit so that the information may be made immediately available for processing when it is needed. The memory unit also retains information that has already been processed until that information can be placed on output devices by the output unit. The memory unit is often called either *memory* or *primary memory*.

4. *Arithmetic and logic unit (ALU)*. This is the "manufacturing" section of the computer. It is responsible for performing calculations such as addition, subtraction, multiplication, and division. It contains the decision mechanisms that allow the computer, for example, to compare two items from the memory unit to determine whether or not they are equal.

5. *Central processing unit (CPU)*. This is the "administrative" section of the computer. It is the computer's coordinator and is responsible for supervising the operation of the other sections. The CPU tells the input unit when information should be read into the memory unit, tells the ALU when information from the memory unit should be utilized in calculations, and tells the output unit when to send information from the memory unit to certain output devices.

6. *Secondary storage unit*. This is the long-term, high-capacity "warehouse" section of the computer. Programs or data not actively being used by the other units are normally placed on secondary storage devices (such as disks) until they are again needed, possibly hours, days, months, or even years later.

1.4 Batch Processing, Multiprogramming, and Timesharing

Early computers were capable of performing only one *job* or *task* at a time. This form of computer operation is often called single-user *batch processing*. The computer runs a single program at a time while processing data in groups or *batches*. In these early systems, users generally submitted their jobs to the computer center on decks of punched cards. The users often had to wait hours or even days before printouts were returned to their desks.

As computers became more powerful, it became evident that single-user batch processing rarely utilized the computer's resources efficiently. Instead, it was thought that many jobs or tasks could be made to *share* the resources of the computer to achieve better utilization. This is called *multiprogramming*. Multiprogramming involves the "simultaneous" operation of many jobs on the computer—the computer shares its resources among the jobs competing for its attention. With early multiprogramming systems, users still submitted jobs on decks of punched cards and waited hours or days for results.

In the 1960s, several groups in industry and the universities pioneered the concept of *timesharing*. Timesharing is a special case of multiprogramming in which users access the computer through input/output devices or *terminals*. In a typical timesharing computer system, there may be dozens or even hundreds of users sharing the computer at once. The computer does not actually run all the users simultaneously. Rather, it runs a small portion of one user's job and then moves on to service the next user. The computer does this so quickly that it may provide service to each user several times per second. Thus the users *appear* to be running simultaneously.

1.5 Personal Computing, Distributed Computing, and Client/Server Computing

In 1977, Apple Computer popularized the phenomenon of *personal computing*. Initially, it was a hobbyist's dream. It became economical enough for people to buy computers for their own personal or business use. In 1981, IBM, the world's largest computer vendor, introduced the IBM Personal Computer. Literally overnight, personal computing became legitimate in business, industry, and government organizations.

But these computers were "standalone" units—people did their work on their own machines and then transported disks back and forth to share information. Although early personal computers were not powerful enough to timeshare several users, these machines could be linked together in computer networks, sometimes over telephone lines and sometimes in local area networks within an organization. This led to the phenomenon of *distributed computing* in which an organization's computing, instead of being performed strictly at some central computer installation, is distributed over networks to the sites at which the real work of the organization is performed. Personal computers were powerful enough to handle the computing requirements of individual users, and to handle basic communications tasks to pass information back and forth electronically.

Today, personal computers are becoming as powerful as the million dollar machines of just a decade ago. The most powerful desktop machines—often called *workstations*—provide individual users with enormous capabilities. Information is easily shared across computer networks where some computers called *file servers* offer a common store of programs and data that may be used by *client* computers distributed throughout the network, hence the term *client/server computing*. C has become the programming language of choice for writing software for operating systems, for computer networking, and for distributed computing applications.

1.6 Machine Languages, Assembly Languages, and High-level Languages

Programmers write instructions in various programming languages, some directly understandable by the computer and others that require intermediate *translation* steps. Hundreds of computer languages are in use today. These may be divided into three general types:

1. Machine languages
2. Assembly languages
3. High-level languages

Any computer can directly understand only its own *machine language*. Machine language is the "natural language" of a particular computer. It is closely related to the actual design of that computer. Machine languages generally consist of strings of numbers (ultimately reduced to 1s and 0s) that instruct computers to perform their most elementary operations one at a time. Machine languages are *machine-dependent*, i.e., a particular machine language can be used on only one type of computer. Machine languages are cumbersome for humans, as can be seen by the following section of a machine language program that adds overtime pay to base pay and stores the result in gross pay.

```
+1300042774
+1400593419
+1200274027
```

As computers became more popular, it became apparent that machine language programming was simply too slow and tedious for most programmers. Instead of using the strings of numbers that computers could directly understand, programmers began using English-like abbreviations to represent the elementary operations of the computer. These English-like abbreviations formed the basis of *assembly languages*. *Translator programs* called *assemblers* were developed to convert assembly language programs to machine language at computer speeds. The following section of an assembly language program also adds overtime pay to base pay and stores the result in gross pay, but more clearly than its machine language equivalent:

```
LOAD     BASEPAY
ADD      OVERPAY
STORE    GROSSPAY
```

Computer usage increased rapidly with the advent of assembly languages, but these still required many instructions to accomplish even the simplest tasks. To speed the programming process, *high-level languages* (HLLs) were developed in which single statements could be written to accomplish substantial tasks. The translator programs that convert high-level language programs into machine language are called *compilers*. High-level languages allow programmers to write instructions that look almost like everyday English and contain commonly used mathematical notations. A payroll program written in a high-level language might contain a statement such as:

```
GROSSPAY = BASEPAY + OVERTIMEPAY
```

Obviously, high-level languages are much more desirable from the programmer's standpoint than either machine languages or assembly languages. C is one of the most powerful and most widely-used high-level languages.

1.7 The History of C

C evolved from two previous languages, BCPL and B. BCPL was developed in 1967 by Martin Richards as a language for writing operating systems software and compilers. Ken Thompson modeled many features in his language B after their counterparts in BCPL and used B to create the first UNIX system at Bell Laboratories in 1970 on a DEC PDP-7 computer. Both BCPL and B were "typeless" languages—every data item occupied one "word" in memory and the burden of treating a data item as a whole number or a real number, for example, fell on the shoulders of the programmer.

The C language was evolved from B by Dennis Ritchie at Bell Laboratories and was originally implemented on a DEC PDP-11 computer in 1972. C is most widely known as the development language of the UNIX operating system. Over the past two decades, C has become available for most computers. C is hardware independent. With careful design, it is possible to write programs in C that are *portable* to most computers. C uses many of the important concepts of BCPL and B while adding data typing and other powerful features.

By the late 1970s, C had evolved into what is now referred to as "traditional C." The publication in 1978 of Kernighan and Ritchie's book, *The C Programming Language,* brought wide attention to the language (see reference Ke88 at the end of this chapter). This publication became one of the most successful computer science books of all time.

The rapid expansion of C over various types of computers (sometimes called *hardware platforms*) led to many variations. These were similar, but often incompatible. This was a serious problem for program developers who needed to develop code that would run on several platforms. It became clear that a standard version of C was needed. In 1983, the X3J11 technical committee was created under project 381-D of the American National Standards Committee on Computers and Information Processing (X3) to "provide an unambiguous and machine-independent definition of the language." In 1989, the standard was approved. The document is referred to as ANSI X3.159-1989. Copies of this document may be ordered from ANSI. The second edition of Kernighan and Ritchie, published in 1988, reflects this version called ANSI C, a version of the language now used worldwide.

1.8 The C Standard Library

As you will learn in Chapter 5, C programs consist of modules or pieces called *functions*. You can program all the functions you need to form a C program, but most C programmers take advantage of a rich collection of existing functions called the *C Standard Library*. Thus, there are really two pieces to learning the C "world." The first is learning the C language itself, and the second is learning how to use the functions in the C Standard Library. Throughout the book, we discuss many of these functions. Appendix B (condensed and adapted from the ANSI C standard document itself) enumerates all the functions available in the C standard library. The book by Plauger (Pl92) is must reading for programmers who need a deep understanding of the library functions, how to implement them, and how to use them to write portable code.

You will be encouraged in this course to use a *building block approach* to creating programs. Avoid reinventing the wheel. Use existing pieces—this is called *software reusability* and it is a key to the developing field of object-oriented programming as we will see in Chapter 15. When programming in C you will typically use the following building blocks:

- C Standard Library functions
- Functions you create yourself
- Functions other people have created and made available to you

The advantage of creating your own functions is that you will know exactly how they work. You will be able to examine the C code. The disadvantage is the time-consuming effort that goes into designing and developing new functions.

Using existing functions avoids reinventing the wheel. In the case of the ANSI standard functions, you will know that they are carefully written, and you will know that because you are using functions that are available on virtually all ANSI C implementations, your programs will have a greater chance of being portable.

1.9 Other High-level Languages

Hundreds of high-level languages have been developed, but only a few have achieved broad acceptance. *FORTRAN* (FORmula TRANslator) was developed by IBM Corporation between 1954 and 1957 to be used for scientific and engineering applications that require complex mathematical computations. FORTRAN is still widely used.

COBOL (COmmon Business Oriented Language) was developed in 1959 by a group of computer manufacturers and government and industrial computer users. COBOL is used primarily for commercial applications that require precise and efficient manipulation of large amounts of data. Today, more than half of all business software is still programmed in COBOL.

Pascal was designed at about the same time as C. It was created by Professor Nicklaus Wirth and was intended for academic use. We will say more about Pascal in the next section.

1.10 Structured Programming

During the 1960s, many large software development efforts encountered severe difficulties. Software schedules were typically late, costs greatly exceeded budgets, and the finished products were unreliable. People began to realize that software development was a complex activity that needed careful analysis. During the mid-to-late 1960s, a flurry of research activity resulted in the evolution of *structured programming*—a disciplined approach to writing programs that are clear, demonstrably correct, and easy to modify. Chapter 3 presents an overview of the general principles of structured programming. The remainder of the text discusses the development of structured C programs.

One of the more tangible results of this research was the development of the Pascal programming language by Nicklaus Wirth in 1971. Pascal, named after the seventeenth-century mathematician and philosopher Blaise Pascal, was designed to facilitate teaching structured programming in academic environments, and was rapidly accepted as the programming language of choice in most universities. Unfortunately, the language lacks many features needed to make it useful in commercial, industrial, and government applications, so it has not been widely accepted in these environments. History may well record that the real significance of Pascal was its selection as the base of the *Ada* programming language.

Ada was developed under the sponsorship of the United States Department of Defense (DOD) during the 1970s and early 1980s. DOD observed that hundreds of separate languages were being used to produce its massive command and control software systems. DOD wanted a single language that would fulfill most of its needs. Pascal was chosen as a base, but the final Ada language is quite different from Pascal. The language was named after Lady Ada Lovelace, daughter of the poet Lord Byron. Lady Lovelace is generally credited with writing the world's first computer program in the early 1800s. One important capability of Ada is called *multitasking*; this allows programmers to specify that many activities are to occur in parallel. The other widely used high-level languages we have discussed—including C—generally allow the programmer to write programs that perform only one activity at a time. It remains to be seen if Ada will meet its goals of producing reliable software and substantially reducing software development and maintenance costs.

1.11 The Basics of the C Environment

All C systems consist of three parts: the environment, the language, and the C Standard Library. In this section, we explain some of the elements that are generally common among environments. Figure 1.1 shows a C program development environment.

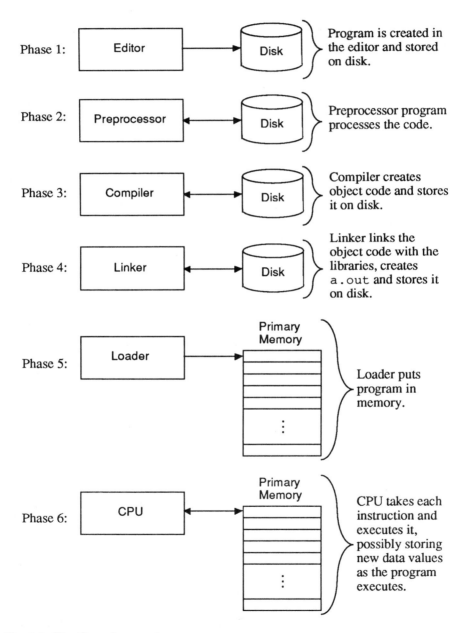

Fig. 1.1 The C environment.

C programs typically go through six phases to be executed (Fig. 1.1). These are: *edit, preprocess, compile, link, load,* and *execute.* We concentrate on a UNIX-based C system here. If you are not using a UNIX system, refer to the manuals for your system, or ask your instructor how to accomplish these tasks in your environment.

The first phase consists of editing a file. This is accomplished with an *editor program.* The programmer types a program with the editor and makes corrections if necessary. The program is then stored on a secondary storage device (usually a disk). All C program file names should end with the .c extension. Two editors widely used on UNIX systems are vi and emacs. C software packages such as Turbo C for IBM PCs and compatibles, and Think C for the Apple Macintosh have built-in editors that are smoothly integrated into the programming environment. We assume that the reader knows how to edit a program.

In the second phase, the programmer gives the command to *compile* the program. The compiler translates the C program into machine language code (also referred to as *object code*). In a C system, a *preprocessor* program automatically executes before the translation phase begins. The C preprocessor obeys special commands called *preprocessor directives* which indicate that certain manipulations are to be performed on the program before compilation. These manipulations usually consist of including other files in the file to be compiled and replacing special symbols with program text. The most common preprocessor directives are discussed in the early chapters; a detailed discussion of all the preprocessor features appears in Chapter 13. The preprocessor is automatically invoked by the compiler before the program is converted to machine language.

The third phase is called *linking.* C programs typically contain references to functions defined elsewhere such as in the standard libraries or in the libraries of a group of programmers working on a particular project. Thus, the object code produced by the C compiler typically contains "holes" due to these missing parts. A *linker* links the object code with the code for the missing functions to produce an *executable image* (with no missing pieces). On a UNIX system, the command to compile and link a program is cc. For example, to compile and link a program named welcome.c type

```
cc welcome.c
```

at the UNIX prompt and press the return key. If the program compiles and links correctly, a file called a.out will be produced. This is the executable image of our welcome.c program.

The fourth phase is called *loading.* Before a program can be executed, the program must first be placed in memory. This is done by the *loader* which takes the executable image from disk and transfers it to memory.

Finally, the computer, under the control of its CPU, executes the program one instruction at a time. To load and execute the program on a UNIX system, we type a.out at the UNIX prompt and press return.

Most programs in C input and/or output data. Certain C functions take their input from *stdin* (the *standard input device*) which is normally assigned to be the keyboard, but stdin can be another device. Data is output to *stdout* (the *standard output device*) which is normally the computer screen, but can be another device.

When we say that a program prints a result, we normally mean that the result is displayed on a screen. Data may be output to other devices such as disks and hardcopy printers. There is also a *standard error device* referred to as `stderr`. The `stderr` device (normally the screen) is used for displaying error messages. It is common to route regular output data, i.e., `stdout`, to a device other than the screen while keeping `stderr` assigned to the screen.

1.12 General Notes About C and this Book

C is a difficult language. C programmers often take pride in being able to pull off some weird, contorted, convoluted usage of the language. This is a poor programming practice. It makes programs more difficult to read, more likely to behave strangely, and more difficult to test and debug. This book is geared for novice programmers, so we stress writing clear, well-structured programs.

> ### *Good Programming Practice (GPP) 1.1*
> *Write your C programs in a simple and straightforward manner. This is sometimes referred to as KIS ("keep it simple"). Do not "stretch" the language by trying "weirdisms."*

Often you may hear that C is a portable language, and that programs written in C can run on many different computers. *Portability is an elusive goal.* Although it is possible to write portable programs, there are many problems between different C implementations and different computers that make portability difficult to achieve. Simply writing programs in ANSI C does not guarantee portability. The ANSI standard document (An90) lists 11 pages of portability issues, and complete books have been written that discuss portability in C (Ja89) (Ra90).

We have done a careful walkthrough of the ANSI C standard document and audited our presentation against it for completeness and accuracy. However, C is a very rich language, and there are some subtleties in the language and some advanced subjects we have not covered. If you need additional technical details on ANSI C, we suggest that you read the ANSI C standard document itself or the reference manual in Kernighan and Ritchie (Ke88).

We have limited our discussions to ANSI C. Many features of ANSI C are not compatible with older C implementations, so you may find that some of the programs in this text do not work on older C compilers.

> ### *GPP 1.2*
> *Read the manuals for the version of C you are using. Reference these manuals frequently to be sure you are aware of the rich collection of C features and that you are using these features correctly.*

> ### *GPP 1.3*
> *Your computer and compiler are good teachers. If you are not sure how a feature of C works, experiment and see what happens.*

1.13 Concurrent C

Two other versions of C have been developed through continuing research efforts at Bell Laboratories. Gehani (Ge89) has developed *Concurrent C*—a C superset that includes capabilities for specifying that multiple activities can be performed in parallel. Languages like Concurrent C will become popular in the next decade as the use of *multiprocessors*, i.e., computers with more than one CPU, increases. As of this writing, Concurrent C is still primarily a research language. Operating systems courses and textbooks (De90) usually include substantial treatments of concurrent programming.

1.14 Object-Oriented Programming and C++

Another C superset, namely *C++*, was developed by Stroustrup (St86) at Bell Laboratories. C++ provides a number of features that "spruce up" the C language. But more importantly, it provides capabilities to do *object-oriented programming*.

Objects are essentially reusable software *components* that model items in the real world. There is a revolution brewing in the software community. Building software quickly, correctly, and economically remains an elusive goal, and this at a time when demands for new and more powerful software are soaring.

Software developers are discovering that using a modular, object-oriented design and implementation approach is making software development groups 10 to 100 times more productive than is possible with conventional programming techniques.

Many object-oriented languages have been developed. It is widely believed that C++ will become the dominant systems-implementation language in the mid-to-late 1990s.

Many people feel that the best educational strategy today is to master C and then study C++. Therefore, we have provided Chapter 15, "An Introduction to Object-Oriented Programming and C++." We hope the reader finds this valuable, and that the chapter will encourage the reader to pursue a more in-depth study of C++ after completing this book.

Summary

- A computer is a device capable of performing computations and making logical decisions at speeds millions, and even billions, of times faster than human beings can.
- Computers process data under the control of computer programs.
- The various devices (such as the keyboard, screen, disks, memory, and processing units) that comprise a computer system are referred to as hardware.
- The computer programs that run on a computer are referred to as software.
- The input unit is the "receiving" section of the computer. Most information is entered into computers today through typewriter-like keyboards.
- The output unit is the "shipping" section of the computer. Most information is output from computers today by displaying it on screens or by printing it on paper.

- The memory unit is the "warehouse" section of the computer, and is often called either memory or primary memory.
- The arithmetic and logic unit (ALU) performs calculations and makes logical decisions.
- Programs or data not actively being used by the other units are normally placed on secondary storage devices (such as disks) until they are again needed.
- In single-user batch processing, the computer runs a single program at a time while processing data in groups or batches.
- Multiprogramming involves the "simultaneous" operation of many jobs on the computer—the computer shares its resources among the jobs.
- Timesharing is a special case of multiprogramming in which users access the computer through terminals. The users appear to be running simultaneously.
- With distributed computing, an organization's computing is distributed via networking to the sites at which the real work of the organization is performed.
- File servers store programs and data that may be shared by client computers distributed throughout the network, hence the term client/server computing.
- Any computer can directly understand only its own machine language.
- Machine languages generally consist of strings of numbers (ultimately reduced to 1s and 0s) that instruct computers to perform their most elementary operations one at a time. Machine languages are machine-dependent.
- English-like abbreviations form the basis of assembly languages. Assemblers translate assembly language programs into machine language.
- Compilers translate high-level language programs into machine language. High-level languages contain English words and conventional mathematical notations.
- C is known as the development language of the UNIX operating system.
- It is possible to write programs in C that are portable to most computers.
- The ANSI C standard was approved in 1989.
- FORTRAN (FORmula TRANslator) is used for mathematical applications.
- COBOL (COmmon Business Oriented Language) is used primarily for commercial applications that require precise and efficient manipulation of large amounts of data.
- Structured programming is a disciplined approach to writing programs that are clear, demonstrably correct, and easy to modify.
- Pascal was designed for teaching structured programming in academic environments.
- Ada was developed under the sponsorship of the United States Department of Defense (DOD) using Pascal as a base.
- Ada *multitasking* allows programmers to specify parallel activities.
- All C systems consist of three parts: the environment, the language, and the standard libraries. Library functions are not part of the C language itself; these functions perform operations such as input/output and mathematical calculations.

- C programs typically go through six phases to be executed: edit, preprocess, compile, link, load, and execute.
- The programmer types a program with an editor, and makes corrections if necessary.
- A compiler translates a C program into machine language code (or object code).
- The C preprocessor obeys preprocessor directives which typically indicate that other files are to be included in the file to be compiled, and special symbols are to be replaced with program text.
- A linker links the object code with the code for missing functions to produce an executable image (with no missing pieces).
- A loader takes an executable image from disk and transfers it to memory.
- A computer, under the control of its CPU, executes a program one instruction at a time.
- Certain C functions (such as `scanf`) take their input from `stdin` (the standard input device) which is normally assigned to be the keyboard,.
- Data is output to `stdout` (the standard output device) which is normally the computer screen.
- There is also a *standard error device* referred to as `stderr`. The `stderr` device (normally the screen) is used for displaying error messages.
- Although it is possible to write portable programs, there are many problems between different C implementations and different computers than can make portability difficult to achieve.
- Concurrent C is a C superset that includes capabilities for specifying that multiple activities can be performed in parallel.
- C++ provides capabilities to do object-oriented programming.
- Objects are essentially reusable software components that model items in the real world.
- It is widely believed that C++ will become the dominant systems implementation language in the mid-to-late 1990s.

Terminology

Ada	C
ALU	C++
ANSI C	central processing unit (CPU)
arithmetic and logic unit	.c extension
assembler	clarity
assembly language	client
B	client/server computing
batch processing	COBOL
BCPL	compile error
building block approach	compiler

computer
computer program
computer programmer
computer programming
Concurrent C
C Preprocessor
CPU
C Standard Library
cursor
data
define
distributed computing
editor
environment
executable image
executes
execution error
fatal error
file server
FORTRAN
functions
hardware
high-level language (HLL)
input device
input/output (I/O)
input unit
linker
linking
loader
loading
logical units
logic error
machine dependent
machine independent
machine language
memory
memory unit

multiprocessor
multiprogramming
multitasking
natural language of a computer
nonfatal error
object
object code
object-oriented programming
open systems
output device
output unit
output window
Pascal
performs
personal computer
portability
primary memory
programming language
registers
reserved words
runs
runtime error
screen
software
software reusability
standard error (**stderr**)
standard input (**stdin**)
standard output (**stdout**)
stored program
structured programming
supercomputer
syntax error
task
terminal
timesharing
translator program
workstation

Good Programming Practices

1.1   Write your C programs in a simple and straightforward manner. This is sometimes referred to as KIS ("keep it simple"). Do not "stretch" the language by trying "weirdisms."

1.2   Read the manuals for the version of C you are using. Reference these manuals frequently to be sure you are aware of the rich collection of C features and that you are using these features correctly.

1.3   Your computer and compiler are good teachers. If you are not sure how a feature of C works, experiment and see what happens.

Self-Review Exercises

1.1   Fill in the blanks in each of the following:
   a) The company that brought the phenomenon of personal computing to the world was _____.
   b) The computer that made personal computing legitimate in business and industry was the _____.
   c) Computers process data under the control of sets of instructions called computer _____.
   d) The five key logical units of the computer are the _____, _____, _____, _____, and the _____.
   e) _____ is a special case of multiprogramming in which users access the computer through devices called terminals.
   f) The three classes of languages discussed in the chapter are _____, _____, and _____.
   g) The programs that translate high-level language programs into machine language are called _____.
   h) C is widely known as the development language of the _____ operating system.
   i) This book presents the version of C called _____ C that was recently standardized through the American National Standards Institute.
   j) The _____ language was developed by Wirth for teaching structured programming in universities.
   k) The Department of Defense developed the Ada language with a capability called _____ which allows programmers to specify that many activities can proceed in parallel.

1.2   Fill in the blanks in each of the following sentences about the C environment.
   a) C programs are normally typed into a computer using an _____ program.
   b) In a C system, a _____ program automatically executes before the translation phase begins.
   c) The two most common kinds of preprocessor directives are _____ and _____.
   d) The _____ program combines the output of the compiler with various library functions to produce an executable image.
   e) The _____ program transfers the executable image from disk to memory.
   f) To load and execute a program on a UNIX system, type _____.

Answers to Self-Review Exercises

1.1   a) Apple. b) IBM Personal Computer. c) programs. d) input unit, output unit, memory unit, arithmetic and logic unit (ALU), and central processing unit. e) timesharing. f) machine languages, assembly languages, high-level languages. g) compilers. h) UNIX. i) ANSI. j) Pascal. k) multitasking.

1.2   a) editor. b) preprocessor. c) including other files in the file to be compiled, replacing special symbols with program text. d) linker. e) loader. f) `a.out`.

Exercises

1.3.   Categorize each of the following items as either hardware or software:
   a)   CPU
   b)   C compiler
   c)   ALU
   d)   C preprocessor
   e)   input unit
   f)   a word processor program

1.4.   Why might you want to write a program in a machine-independent language instead of a machine-dependent language? Why might a machine-dependent language be more appropriate for writing certain types of programs?

1.5.   Translator programs such as assemblers and compilers convert programs from one language (referred to as the *source* language) to another language (referred to as the *object* language). Determine which of the following statements are true and which are false:
   a)   A compiler translates high-level language programs into object language.
   b)   An assembler translates source language programs into machine language programs.
   c)   A compiler converts source language programs into object language programs.
   d)   High-level languages are generally machine-dependent.
   e)   A machine language program requires translation before the program can be run on a computer.

1.6.   Fill in the blanks in each of the following statements:
   a)   Devices from which users access timesharing computer systems are usually called _____.
   b)   A computer program that converts assembly language programs to machine language programs is called _____.
   c)   Which logical unit of the computer receives information from outside the computer for use by the computer _____.
   d)   The process of instructing the computer to solve specific problems is called _____.
   e)   What type of computer language uses English-like abbreviations for machine language instructions? _____.
   f)   What are the six logical units of the computer? _____.
   g)   Which logical unit of the computer sends information that has already been processed by the computer to various devices so that the information may be used outside the computer? _____.
   h)   The general name for a program that converts programs written in a certain computer language into machine language is _____.
   i)   Which logical unit of the computer retains information? _____.
   j)   Which logical unit of the computer performs calculations? _____.
   k)   Which logical unit of the computer makes logical decisions? _____.
   l)   The commonly used abbreviation for the computer's control unit is _____.
   m)   The level of computer language most convenient to the programmer for writing programs quickly and easily is _____.
   n)   The most common business-oriented language in wide use today is _____.
   o)   The only language that a computer can directly understand is called that computer's _____.

p)   Which logical unit of the computer coordinates the activities of all the other logical units? _____.

1.7.   State whether each of the following is true or false. Explain your answers.
a)   Machine languages are generally machine-dependent.
b)   Timesharing truly runs several users simultaneously on a computer.
c)   Like other high-level languages, C is generally considered to be machine-independent. _____.

1.8   Discuss the meaning of each of the following names in the UNIX environment:
a) `stdin`
b) `stdout`
c) `stderr`

1.9   What key capability is provided in Concurrent C that is not available in ANSI C?

1.10   Why is so much attention today focused on object-oriented programming in general and C++ in particular?

Recommended Reading

(An90)   ANSI, *American National Standard for Information Systems—Programming Language—C (ANSI Document ANSI X3.159-1989)*, New York, NY: American National Standards Institute, 1990.

This is the defining document for ANSI C. It specifies the C language and the various functions of the C Standard Library. An 11-page appendix discusses portability issues in detail. The document is available for sale from the American National Standards Institute, 1430 Broadway, New York, New York 10018.

(De90)   Deitel, H. M., *Operating Systems* (Second Edition), Reading, MA: Addison-Wesley Publishing Company, 1990.

A textbook for the traditional computer science course in operating systems. Chapters 4 and 5 present an extensive discussion of concurrent programming.

(De89)   Dewhurst, S. C., and K. T. Stark, *Programming in C++*, Englewood Cliffs, NJ: Prentice Hall, 1989.

A solid introduction to C++ for people who know C. Contains 30 pages of solved exercises. The authors are with AT&T Bell Laboratories, Summit, New Jersey.

(Ge89)   Gehani, N., and W. D. Roome, *The Concurrent C Programming Language*, Summit, NJ: Silicon Press, 1989.

This is the defining book for Concurrent C—a C language superset that enables programmers to specify parallel execution of multiple activities. The book is rich in interesting examples and discussions of the classic problems in concurrent programming. Also included is a summary of Concurrent C++.

(Ja89)   Jaeschke, R., *Portability and the C Language*, Indianapolis, IN: Hayden Books, 1989.

This book contains a thorough discussion of key issues in writing portable programs in C, i.e., C programs that will run with little, and preferably no modification on a variety of computers with different operating systems. Jaeschke served on both the ANSI and ISO C standards committees.

(Ke90) Kelley, A., and I. Pohl, *A Book on C (Second Edition),* Redwood City, CA: Benjamin/Cummings Publishing Company, Inc., 1990.

This book is an excellent ANSI C text and reference for established programmers.

(Ke88) Kernighan, B. W., and D. M. Ritchie, *The C Programming Language* (Second Edition), Englewood Cliffs, NJ: Prentice Hall, 1988.

This book is the classic in the field. The book is extensively used in C courses and seminars for established programmers, and includes an excellent reference manual. Ritchie is the author of the C language and one of the co-designers of the UNIX operating system.

(Kr91) Kruse, R. L.; B. P. Leung; and C. L. Tondo, *Data Structures and Program Design in C,* Englewood Cliffs, NJ: Prentice Hall, 1991.

This widely used university textbook introduces in a C context the fundamentals of important data structures such as linked lists, queues, stacks, and trees. The book includes detailed treatments of searching, sorting, recursion, and mathematical methods. The book places a strong emphasis on software engineering. Kruse is with Saint Mary's University in Nova Scotia, Leung is with the University of Illinois at Urbana–Champaign, and Tondo is with IBM Corporation and Nova University in Ft. Lauderdale, Florida.

(Li89) Lippman, S. B., *C++ Primer,* Reading, MA: Addison-Wesley Publishing Company, 1989.

A first course in C++ programming for programmers. Includes a particularly detailed discussion of multiple inheritance. The author is with AT&T Bell Laboratories.

(Pa91) Pappas, C. H., and W. H. Murray, III, *Borland C++ Handbook,* Berkeley, CA: Osborne McGraw-Hill, 1991.

An extensive introduction to C++ using Borland's C++ compiler package, one of the most successful commercial C++ products. The authors are on the faculty of the State University of New York at Binghamton.

(Pl92) Plauger, P. J., *The Standard C Library,* Englewood Cliffs, NJ: Prentice Hall, 1992.

Defines and demonstrates the use of the functions in the C standard library. Plauger served as the head of the library subcommittee of the committee that developed the ANSI C standard, and he serves as the Convenor of the ISO committee that is evolving C.

(Ra90) Rabinowitz, H., and C. Schaap, *Portable C,* Englewood Cliffs, NJ: Prentice Hall, 1990.

This book was developed for a course on portability taught at AT&T Bell Laboratories. The book is rich in insights into why portability is so difficult to achieve, and includes abundant examples of nonportable code and their portable versions. The authors introduce the C-World—an environment-independent C program execution model. Rabinowitz is with NYNEX Corporation's Artificial Intelligence Laboratory, and Schaap is a principal at Delft Consulting Corporation.

(Ri78)   Ritchie, D. M.; S. C. Johnson; M. E. Lesk; and B. W. Kernighan, "UNIX Time-Sharing System: The C Programming Language," *The Bell System Technical Journal,* Vol. 57, No. 6, Part 2, July–August 1978, pp. 1991–2019.

This is one of the classic articles introducing the C language. It appeared in a special issue of the *Bell System Technical Journal* devoted to the "UNIX Time-Sharing System."

(Ri84)   Ritchie, D. M., "The UNIX System: The Evolution of the UNIX Time-Sharing System," *AT&T Bell Laboratories Technical Journal,* Vol. 63, No. 8, Part 2, October 1984, pp. 1577–1593.

A classic article on the UNIX operating system. This article appeared in a special edition of the *Bell System Technical Journal* completely devoted to "The UNIX System."

(Ro84)   Rosler, L., "The UNIX System: The Evolution of C—Past and Future," *AT&T Bell Laboratories Technical Journ~', ~*ol. 63, No. 8, Part 2, October 1984, pp. 1685–1699.

An excellent article to follow (Ri78) for the reader interested in tracing the history of C and the roots of the ANSI C standardization effort. It appeared in a special edition of the *Bell System Technical Journal* devoted to "The UNIX System."

(Se90)   Sedgewick, R., *Algorithms in C,* Reading, MA: Addison-Wesley Publishing Company, 1990.

This book, widely used in universities and professional seminars, introduces various data structures and surveys several important classes of useful algorithms, all in the context of C. Sedgewick is a professor of computer science at Princeton University.

(St84)   Stroustrup, B., "The UNIX System: Data Abstraction in C," *AT&T Bell Laboratories Technical Journal,* Vol. 63, No. 8, Part 2, October 1984, pp. 1701–1732.

The classic article introducing C++. It appeared in a special edition of the *Bell System Technical Journal* devoted to "The UNIX System."

(St86)   Stroustrup, B. *The C++ Programming Language,* Reading, MA: Addison-Wesley Series in Computer Science, 1986.

This book is the defining reference for C++, a C superset that includes various enhancements to C, especially features for object-oriented programming. Stroustrup developed C++ at AT&T Bell Laboratories.

(To89)   Tondo, C. L., and S. E. Gimpel, *The C Answer Book,* Englewood Cliffs, NJ: Prentice Hall, 1989.

This unique book provides answers to the exercises in Kernighan and Ritchie (Ke88). The authors demonstrate an exemplary programming style, and provide insights into their problem solving approaches and design decisions. Tondo is with IBM Corporation and Nova University in Ft. Lauderdale, Florida. Gimpel is a consultant.

(Wi88)   Wiener, R. S., and L. J. Pinson, *An Introduction to Object-Oriented Programming and C++,* Reading, MA: Addison-Wesley Publishing Company, 1988.

A first course in C++ and object-orientation. A particularly strong feature of the book is an 87-page section with three highly detailed case studies. The authors are with the University of Colorado at Colorado Springs.

2

Introduction to C Programming

Objectives

- To be able to write simple computer programs in C.
- To be able to use simple input and output statements.
- To become familiar with fundamental data types.
- To understand computer memory concepts.
- To be able to use arithmetic operators.
- To understand the precedence of arithmetic operations.
- To be able to write simple decision-making statements.

*What's in a name? That which we call a rose
By any other name would smell as sweet.*

William Shakespeare
Romeo and Juliet

*I only took the regular course ... the different branches of
arithmetic—Ambition, Distraction, Uglification, and
Derision.*

Lewis Carroll

*Precedents deliberately established by wise men are enti-
tled to great weight.*

Henry Clay

Outline

2.1 Introduction

The C language facilitates a structured and disciplined approach to computer program design. In this chapter we introduce C programming and present several examples that illustrate many important features of C. Each example is carefully analyzed one statement at a time. In Chapter 3 we present an introduction to *structured programming* in C. We then use the structured approach throughout the remainder of the text.

2.2 A Simple C Program: Printing a Line of Text

C uses some notations that may appear strange to people who have not programmed. We begin by considering a simple C program. Our first example prints a line of text. The program and the program's screen output are shown in Fig. 2.1.

Even though this program is simple, it illustrates several important features of the C language. We now consider each line of the program in detail. The line

```
/* A first program in C */
```

begins with /* and ends with */ indicating that the line is a *comment*. Programmers insert comments to *document* programs and improve program readability. Comments do not cause the computer to perform any action when the program is run. Comments

```
/* A first program in C */

main()
{
    printf("Welcome to C!\n");
}
```

```
Welcome to C!
```

Fig. 2.1 Text printing program.

are ignored by the C compiler and do not cause any machine language object code to be generated. The comment A first program in C simply describes the purpose of the program. Comments also help other people read and understand your program.

The line

```
main()
```

is a part of every C program. The parentheses after main indicate that main is a program building block *function*. C programs contain one or more functions, one of which must be main. Every program in C begins executing at the function main.

Good Programming Practice (GPP) 2.1

Every function should be preceded by a comment describing the purpose of the function.

The *left brace,* {, must begin the *body* of every function. A corresponding *right brace* must end each function. The line

```
printf("Welcome to C!\n");
```

instructs the computer to print on the screen the string of characters contained between the quotation marks. The entire line, including printf, its arguments within the parentheses, and the *semicolon* (;), is called a *statement*. Every statement must end with a semicolon (also known as the *statement terminator*). When the preceding printf statement is executed, it prints the message Welcome to C! on the screen. The characters normally print exactly as they appear between the double quotes in the printf statement. Notice that the characters \n were not printed on the screen. The backslash (\) is called an *escape character*. It indicates that printf is supposed to do something out of the ordinary. When encountering a backslash, printf looks ahead at the next character and combines it with the backslash to form an *escape sequence*. The escape sequence \n means *newline*, and it causes the cursor to position to the beginning of the next line on the screen. Some other common escape sequences are listed in Fig. 2.2. The printf function is one of many functions provided in the *C Standard Library* (listed in Appendix B).

Escape Sequence	Description
\t	Horizontal tab. Move the cursor to the next tab stop.
\r	Carriage return. Position the cursor to the beginning of the current line; do not advance to the next line.
\a	Alert. Sound the system bell.
\\	Backslash. Used to print the backslash character in a printf statement.
\"	Double quote. Used to print the double quote character in a printf statement.

Fig. 2.2 Some common escape sequences.

GPP 2.2

The last character printed by a function that does any printing should be a newline (\n). This ensures that the function will leave the cursor positioned at the beginning of a new line. Conventions of this nature encourage software reusability—a key goal in software development environments.

The right brace, }, indicates that the end of main has been reached.

GPP 2.3

Indent the entire body of each function one level of indentation (three spaces) within the braces that define the body of the function. This makes the functional structure of a program stand out and helps make programs easier to read.

GPP 2.4

Set a convention for the size of indent you prefer and then uniformly apply that convention. The tab key may be used to create indents, but tab stops may vary. We recommend using either 1/4-inch tab stops or hand counting three spaces per level of indent.

The printf function can print Welcome to C! several different ways. For example, the program of Fig. 2.3 produces the same output as the program of Fig. 2.1. This works because each printf resumes printing where the previous printf stopped printing. The first printf prints Welcome followed by a space, and the second printf prints immediately following the space.

A single printf can print several lines by using newline characters as in Fig. 2.4. Each time the \n (newline) escape sequence is encountered, printf positions to the beginning of the next line.

2.3 Another Simple C Program: Adding Two Integers

Our next program uses the standard library function scanf to obtain two integers typed by a user at the keyboard, computes the sum of these values, and prints the result using printf. The program and sample output are shown in Fig. 2.5.

```
#include <stdio.h>

main()
{
   printf("Welcome ");
   printf("to C!\n");
}
```

```
Welcome to C!
```

Fig. 2.3 Printing on one line with separate printf statements.

```
#include <stdio.h>

main()
{
    printf("Welcome\nto\nC!\n");
}
```

```
Welcome
to
C!
```

Fig. 2.4 Printing on multiple lines with a single `printf`.

The comment `/* Addition program */` states the purpose of the program. The line

```
#include <stdio.h>
```

is a directive to the C preprocessor. Lines beginning with # are processed by the preprocessor before the program is compiled. This specific line tells the preprocessor to include the contents of the *standard input/output header file* (`stdio.h`) in the program. This header file contains various information and declarations used by the compiler when compiling valid standard input/output library functions such as `printf`. The header file also contains information that helps the compiler determine if calls to library functions have been written correctly. We will explain the contents header files in more detail in Chapter 5.

```
/* Addition program */
#include <stdio.h>

main()
{
    int x, y, z;

    printf("Enter first integer\n");
    scanf("%d", &x);
    printf("Enter second integer\n");
    scanf("%d", &y);
    z = x + y;
    printf("Sum is %d\n", z);
}
```

```
Enter first integer
45
Enter second integer
72
Sum is 117
```

Fig. 2.5 An addition program.

As we stated earlier, every program begins execution with `main`. The left brace {
marks the beginning of the body of `main` and the corresponding right brace marks the
end of `main`. The line

```
int x, y, z;
```

is a *declaration*. The letters x, y, and z are the names of *variables*. A variable is a location in memory where a value can be stored for use by a program. This declaration
specifies that the variables x, y, and z are of type *int* which means that these variables will hold *integer* values, i.e., whole numbers such as 7, -11, 0, 31914, and the
like. All variables must be declared with a name and a data type before they can be
used in a program. There are other data types beside `int` in C. Several variables of the
same type may be declared in one declaration. We could have written three declarations, one for each variable, but the preceding declaration is more concise.

GPP 2.5

Place a space after each comma (,) to make programs more readable.

A variable name in C is any valid *identifier*. An identifier is a series of characters
consisting of letters, digits, and underscores (_) that does not begin with a digit. An
identifier can be any length, but only the first 31 characters are required to be recognized according to the ANSI C standard. C is *case sensitive*—uppercase and lowercase
letters are different in C, so a1 and A1 are different identifiers.

GPP 2.6
---
*Use identifiers of 31 or fewer characters. This helps ensure portability and can
avoid some subtle programming errors.*

GPP 2.7

Choosing meaningful variable names helps make a program self documenting.

Declarations must be placed after the left brace of a function and before *any* executable statements. For example, in the program of Fig. 2.5, inserting the declaration
after the first `printf` would cause a syntax error. We will say more about this in
Chapter 4.

Common Programming Error (CPE) 2.1

Placing variable declarations among executable statements.

GPP 2.8
---
*Separate the declarations and executable statements in a function with one
blank line to emphasize where the declarations end and the executable statements begin.*

The statement

```
printf("Enter first integer\n");
```

prints the literal `Enter first integer` on the screen and positions to the beginning of the next line. This message is called a *prompt* because it tells the user to take
a specific action.

The statement

```
scanf("%d", &x);
```

uses *scanf* to obtain a value from the user. The `scanf` function takes input from the standard input file which is usually the keyboard. This `scanf` has two arguments, `"%d"` and `&x`. The first argument, the *format control string*, indicates the type of data that should be input by the user. The `%d` *conversion specifier* indicates that the data should be an integer. The second argument is an ampersand (`&`)—called the *address operator* in C—followed by the variable name. The ampersand, when combined with the variable name, tells `scanf` the location in memory the variable x is stored. The computer then stores the value for x at that location. The use of ampersand (`&`) is often confusing to novice programmers or to people who have programmed in other languages. For now, just remember to append the ampersand character to all variables in `scanf` statements. Some exceptions to this rule are discussed in Chapters 6 and 7.

When the computer executes the preceding `scanf`, it waits for the user to enter a value for variable x. The user responds by typing an integer and then pressing the *return key* (sometimes called the *enter key*) to send the number to the computer. The computer then assigns this number, or *value*, to the variable x. Any subsequent references to x in the program will use this same value. The `printf` and `scanf` functions facilitate interaction between the user and the computer. Because this interaction resembles a dialogue, it is often called *conversational computing* or *interactive computing*.

The statement

```
printf("Enter second integer\n");
```

prints the message `Enter second integer` on the screen, then positions to the beginning of next line. This `printf` also prompts the user to take action.

The statement

```
scanf("%d", &y);
```

obtains a value for variable y from the user. The *assignment statement*

```
z = x + y;
```

calculates the sum of variables x and y, and assigns the result to variable z using the *assignment operator* =. The statement is read as, "z *gets* the value of x + y." Most calculations are performed in assignment statements. The = operator and the + operator are called *binary operators* because they each have two *operands*. In the case of the + operator, the two operands are x and y. In the case of the = operator, the two operands are z and the value of the expression x + y.

GPP 2.9

Place spaces on either side of a binary operator. This makes the operator stand out and makes the program more readable.

The statement

```
printf("Sum is %d\n", z);
```

uses the `printf` function to print the literal Sum is followed by the numerical value of variable z on the screen. This `printf` has two arguments, "Sum is %d\n" and z. The first argument is the format control string. It contains some literal characters to be displayed, and it contains the conversion specifier %d indicating that an integer will be printed. The second argument specifies the value to be printed. Notice that the conversion specification for an integer is the same in both `printf` and `scanf`. This is the case for most data types in C.

Calculations can also be performed inside `printf` statements. We could have combined the previous two statements into the statement

```
printf("Sum is %d\n", x + y);
```

The right brace } informs the computer that the end of the function `main` has been reached.

CPE 2.2

Placing a \n outside the format control string of a `printf` statement.

CPE 2.3

Forgetting to include in a `printf` containing conversion specifiers the expressions whose values are to be printed.

CPE 2.4

Not providing in a `printf` format control string a conversion specifier when one is needed to print an expression.

CPE 2.5

Placing inside the format control string the comma that is supposed to separate the format control string from the expressions to be printed.

CPE 2.6

Forgetting to append an & to a variable in a `scanf` statement when that variable should, in fact, be preceded by an ampersand.

CPE 2.7

Appending an & to a variable included in a `printf` statement when, in fact, that variable should not be preceded by an ampersand.

2.4 Memory Concepts

Variable names such as x, y, and z actually correspond to *locations* in the computer's memory. Every variable has a *name*, a *type*, and a *value*.

In the addition program of Fig. 2.5, when the statement

```
scanf("%d", &x);
```

is executed, the value typed by the user is placed into a memory location to which the name x has been assigned. Suppose the user enters the number 45 as the value for x. The computer will place 45 into location x as shown in Fig. 2.6.

Whenever a value is placed in a memory location, the value overrides the previous value in that location. Since this previous information is destroyed, the process of reading information into a memory location is called *destructive readin.*

Returning to our addition program again, when the statement

```
scanf("%d", &y);
```

is executed, suppose the user enters the value 72. This value is placed into location y, and memory appears as in Fig. 2.7. Note that these locations are not necessarily adjacent in memory.

Once the program has obtained values for x and y, it adds these values and places the sum into variable z. The statement

```
z = x + y;
```

that performs the addition also involves destructive readin. This occurs when the calculated sum of x and y is placed into location z (without regard to what value may already be in z). After z is calculated, memory appears as in Fig. 2.8. Note that the values of x and y appear exactly as they did before they were used in the calculation of z. These values were used, but not destroyed, as the computer performed the calculation. Thus, when a value is read out of a memory location, the process is referred to as *nondestructive readout.*

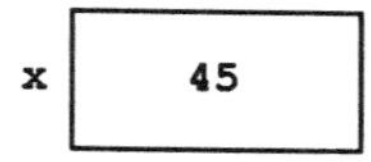

x | 45

Fig. 2.6 A memory location showing the name and value of a variable.

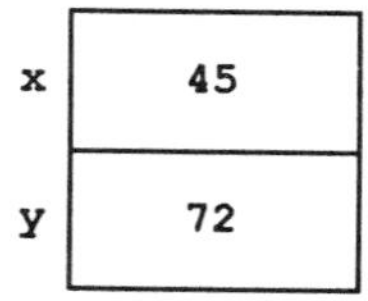

x | 45
y | 72

Fig. 2.7 Memory locations after both variables are input.

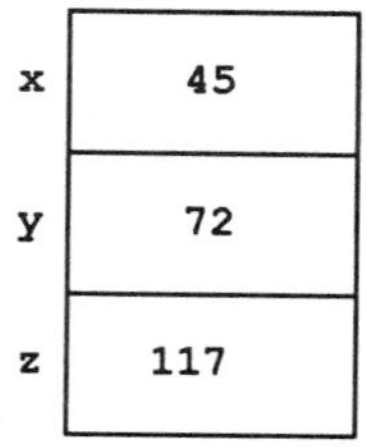

x | 45
y | 72
z | 117

Fig. 2.8 Memory locations after a calculation.

2.5 Arithmetic in C

Most C programs perform arithmetic calculations. The C *arithmetic operators* are summarized in Fig. 2.9. Note the use of various special symbols not used in algebra. The *asterisk (*)* indicates multiplication, and the *percent sign (%)* denotes *modulus* operator which is introduced below. The arithmetic operators are all binary operators. For example, the expression 3 + 7 contains the binary operator + and the operands 3 and 7.

Integer division yields an integer result. For example, the expression 7 / 4 evaluates to 1, and the expression 17 / 5 evaluates to 3. C provides the modulus operator, %, which yields the remainder after integer division The modulus operator is an integer operator that can be used only with integer operands. The expression x % y yields the remainder after x is divided by y. Thus, 7 % 4 yields 3, and 17 % 5 yields 2. We will discuss many interesting applications of the modulus operator.

Arithmetic expressions in C must be written in *straight-line form* to facilitate entering programs into the computer. Thus, expressions such as "a divided by b" must be written as a / b so that all constants, variables, and operators appear in a straight line. The algebraic notation

$$\frac{a}{b}$$

is generally not acceptable to compilers, although some special-purpose software packages do exist that support more natural notation for complex mathematical expressions.

Parentheses are used in C expressions in much the same manner as in algebraic expressions. For example, to multiply a times the quantity b + c we write:

```
a * (b + c)
```

C evaluates arithmetic expressions in a precise sequence determined by the following *rules of operator precedence,* which are generally the same as those followed in algebra:

1. Expressions or portions of expressions contained within pairs of parentheses are evaluated first. Thus, *parentheses may be used to force the order of evaluation to occur in any sequence desired by the programmer.* Parentheses are said to be at the "highest level of precedence." In cases of *nested,* or *embedded,* parentheses, the expression in the innermost pair of parentheses is evaluated first.

2. Multiplication, division, and modulus operations are evaluated next. If an expression contains several multiplication, division, and modulus operations, evaluation proceeds from left to right. Multiplication, division, and modulus are said to be on the same level of precedence.

3. Addition and subtraction operations are evaluated last. If an expression contains several addition and subtraction operations, evaluation proceeds from left to right. Addition and subtraction also have the same level of precedence.

C operation	Arithmetic operator	Algebraic expression	C expression
Addition	+	f + 7	f + 7
Subtraction	–	p – c	p – c
Multiplication	*	bm	b * m
Division	/	x / y	x / y
Modulus	%	r mod s	r % s

Fig. 2.9 C arithmetic operators.

The rules of operator precedence are guidelines that enable C to evaluate expressions in the correct order. When we say evaluation proceeds from left to right, we are referring to the *associativity* of the operators. We will that some operators associate from right to left. Fig. 2.10 summarizes these rules of operator precedence.

Now let us consider several expressions in light of the rules of operator precedence. Each example lists an algebraic expression and its C equivalent.

The following is an example of an arithmetic mean (average) of five terms:

Algebra: $m = \dfrac{a + b + c + d + e}{5}$

C: m = (a + b + c + d + e) / 5;

The parentheses are required because division has higher precedence than addition. The entire quantity (a + b + c + d + e) is to be divided by 5. If the parentheses are erroneously omitted, we obtain a + b + c + d + e / 5 which evaluates incorrectly as

$a + b + c + d + \dfrac{e}{5}$

Operator(s)	Operation(s)	Order of evaluation (precedence)
( )	Parentheses	Evaluated first. If the parentheses are nested, the expression in the innermost pair is evaluated first.
*, /, or %	Multiplication Division Modulus	Evaluated second. If there are several, they are evaluated left to right.
+ or –	Addition Subtraction	Evaluated last. If there are several, they are evaluated left to right.

Fig. 2.10 Precedence of arithmetic operators.

The following is an example of the equation of a straight line:

Algebra: $y = mx + b$

C: `y = m * x + b;`

No parentheses are required. The multiplication is evaluated first because multiplication has a higher precedence than addition.

The following example contains modulus (%), multiplication, division, addition, and subtraction operations:

Algebra: $z = pr\%q+w/x–y$

C:

The circled numbers under the statement indicate the order in which C evaluates the operators. The multiplication, modulus, and division are evaluated first in left-to-right order (i.e., they associate from left to right) since they have higher precedence than addition and subtraction. The addition and subtraction are evaluated next. These are also evaluated left to right.

Not all expressions with several pairs of parentheses contain nested parentheses. The expression

```
a * (b + c) + c * (d + e)
```

does not contain nested parentheses. Instead, the parentheses are said to be on the same level. In this situation, C evaluates the parenthesized expressions first and in left-to-right order.

To develop a better understanding of the rules of operator precedence, let us see how C evaluates a second-degree polynomial.

```
y =     a  *  x  *  x  +  b  *  x  +  c;
        1     2     4     3     5
```

The circled numbers under the statement indicate the order in which C performs the operations. There is no arithmetic operator for exponentiation in C, so we have represented x^2 as `x * x`. The C Standard Library does include the `pow` ("power") function to perform exponentiation. Because of some subtle issues related to the data types required by `pow`, we defer a detailed explanation of `pow` until Chapter 4.

Suppose $a = 2$, $b = 3$, $c = 7$, and $x = 5$. Figure 2.11 illustrates how the preceding second degree polynomial is evaluated.

2.6 Decision Making: Equality and Relational Operators

This section introduces a simple version of C's *if structure* that allows a program to make a decision based on the truth or falsity of some *condition*. If the condition is met, i.e., the condition is *true*, the statement in the body of the `if` structure is exe-

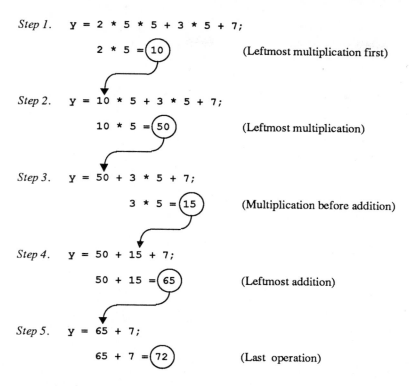

Step 1. y = 2 * 5 * 5 + 3 * 5 + 7;

2 * 5 = ⑩   (Leftmost multiplication first)

Step 2. y = 10 * 5 + 3 * 5 + 7;

10 * 5 = ㊿   (Leftmost multiplication)

Step 3. y = 50 + 3 * 5 + 7;

3 * 5 = ⑮   (Multiplication before addition)

Step 4. y = 50 + 15 + 7;

50 + 15 = ㊻   (Leftmost addition)

Step 5. y = 65 + 7;

65 + 7 = ㊲   (Last operation)

Fig. 2.11 Evaluation of a second degree polynomial.

cuted. If the condition is not met, i.e., the condition is *false*, the other statement is not executed.

Conditions in if structures are formed by using the *equality operators* and *relational operators* summarized in Fig. 2.12. The relational operators have the same level of precedence and associate left to right. The equality operators have a lower level of precedence than the relational operators and also associate left to right.

CPE 2.8
A syntax error will occur if the operators ==, !=, >=, *and* <= *contain spaces.*

CPE 2.9
Reversing the operators !=, >=, *and* <= *as in* =!, =>, *and* =<, *respectively. This causes a syntax error.*

CPE 2.10
Confusing the equality operator == *with the assignment operator* =. *The equality operator is read "is equal to" and the assignment operator is read "gets" or "gets the value of." As we will soon see, confusing these operators may not necessarily cause an easy-to-recognize syntax error, but may cause extremely subtle logic errors.*

Standard algebraic relational operator	C equality or relational operator	Example of C condition	Meaning of C condition
Equality operators			
=	==	x == y	x is equal to y
≠	!=	x != y	x is not equal to y
Relational operators			
>	>	x > y	x is greater than y
<	<	x < y	x is less than y
≥	>=	x >= y	x is greater than or equal to y
≤	<=	x <= y	x is less than or equal to y

Fig. 2.12 Equality and relational operators.

CPE 2.11

Placing a semicolon immediately to the right of the right parenthesis after the condition in an if structure.

The following example uses six if statements to compare two numbers input by the user. If the condition in any of these if statements is satisfied, the printf statement associated with that if is executed. The program and three sample outputs are shown in Fig. 2.13.

Note that the program in Fig. 2.13 uses scanf to input two numbers. Each conversion specifier has a corresponding argument in which a value will be stored. The first %d converts a value to be stored in variable a and the second %d converts a value to be stored in variable b. *Indentation* in if statements enhances program readability. Also, notice that each of the if statements in Fig. 2.13 has a single statement in its body. In Chapter 3 we show how to specify if statements with multiple-statement bodies.

GPP 2.10

Indent the statement in the body of an if structure.

GPP 2.11

There should be no more than one statement per line in a program.

CPE 2.12

Placing commas (when none are needed) between conversion specifiers in the format control string of a scanf statement.

```
/* Using if statements, relational
   operators, and equality operators */

#include <stdio.h>

main()
{
   int a, b;

   printf("Enter two integers, and I will tell you\n");
   printf("the relationships they satisfy: ");
   scanf("%d%d", &a, &b);
   if(a == b)
      printf("%d is equal to %d\n", a, b);

   if(a != b)
      printf("%d is not equal to %d\n", a, b);

   if(a < b)
      printf("%d is less than %d\n", a, b);

   if(a > b)
      printf("%d is greater than %d\n", a, b);

   if(a <= b)
      printf("%d is less than or equal to %d\n", a, b);

   if(a >= b)
      printf("%d is greater than or equal to %d\n", a, b);
}
```

```
Enter two integers, and I will tell you
the relationships they satisfy: 3 7
3 is not equal to 7
3 is less than 7
3 is less than or equal to 7
```

```
Enter two integers, and I will tell you
the relationships they satisfy: 22 12
22 is not equal to 12
22 is greater than 12
22 is greater than or equal to 12
```

```
Enter two integers, and I will tell you
the relationships they satisfy: 7 7
7 is equal to 7
7 is less than or equal to 7
7 is greater than or equal to 7
```

Fig. 2.13 Using equality and relational operators.

Notice that the comment in Fig. 2.13 is split over two lines. In C statements, *white space* characters such as tabs, newlines, and spaces are normally ignored. So, statements may be split over several lines. It is not correct to split identifiers.

GPP 2.12

A lengthy statement may be spread over several lines. If a single statement must be split across lines, choose breaking points that make sense such as after a comma in a comma-separated list. If a statement is split across two or more lines, indent all subsequent lines.

The chart in Fig. 2.14 shows the precedence of the C operators introduced in this chapter. The operators are shown top to bottom in decreasing order of precedence. Notice that all these operators, with the exception of the assignment operator =, associate from left to right. The assignment operator = associates from right to left.

GPP 2.13

Refer to the operator precedence chart when writing expressions containing many operators. Confirm that the operators in the expression are performed in the proper order. If you are uncertain about the order of evaluation in a complex expression, use parentheses to force the order, exactly as you would do in algebraic expressions. Be sure to observe that some of C's operators such as the assignment operator (=) associate from right to left rather than from left to right.

In this chapter, we have introduced many important features of the C programming language, including printing data on the screen, inputting data from the user, performing calculations, and making decisions. In the next chapter, we build upon these techniques as we introduce *structured programming*. The user will become more familiar with indentation techniques. We will study how to specify the order in which statements are executed—this is called *flow of control*.

Summary

- C facilitates a structured and disciplined approach to program design.
- Comments begin with /* and end with */. Programmers insert comments to document programs and improve their readability. Comments do not cause the computer to perform any action when the program is run.
- The line #include <stdio.h> tells the compiler to include the standard input/output header file in the program. This file contains information used by input and output functions such as scanf and printf.
- C programs consist of functions one of which must be main. Every C program begins executing at the function main.
- The printf function can be used to print a string contained in quotation marks, and to print the values of expressions. When printing integer values, the first argument of the printf function —the format control string— contains the conversion

Operators				Associativity
( )				left to right
*	/	%		left to right
+	–			left to right
<	<=	>	>=	left to right
==	!=			left to right
=				right to left

Fig. 2.14 Precedence and associativity of the operators discussed so far.

specifier %d and any other characters that will be printed; the second argument is the expression whose value will be printed. If more than one integer will be printed, then the format control string contains a %d for each integer, and the arguments following the format control string contain the expressions whose values are to be printed.

- The scanf function obtains values the user normally enters at the keyboard. Its first argument is the format control string that tells the computer what type of data should be input by the user. The conversion specifier %d indicates that the data will be an integer. Each of the remaining arguments corresponds to one of the conversion specifiers in the format control string. Each variable name is normally preceded by an ampersand (&), called the address operator in C. The ampersand, when combined with the variable name, tells the computer the location in memory where the value will be stored. The computer then stores the value at that location.

- All variables in a C program must be declared before they can be used in the program.

- A variable name in C is any valid identifier. An identifier is a series of characters consisting of letters, digits, and underscores (_). Identifiers cannot start with a digit. Identifiers can be any length; however, only the first 31 characters are significant according to the ANSI standard.

- C is case sensitive.

- Most calculations are performed in assignment statements.

- Every variable stored in the computer's memory has a name, a value, and a type.

- Whenever a new value is placed in a memory location, it overrides the previous value in that location. Since this previous information is destroyed, the process of reading information into a memory location is called destructive readin.

- When a value is read from memory, the process is referred to as nondestructive readout.

- Arithmetic expressions in C must be written in straight-line form to facilitate entering programs into the computer.

- C evaluates arithmetic expressions in a precise sequence determined by the rules of operator precedence and associativity.
- The `if` statement allows the programmer to make a decision when a certain condition is met. The format for an `if` statement is

```
if (condition)
    statement;
```

If the condition is met, i.e., the condition is true, the `if` statement causes the statement in the body of the `if` to be executed. If the condition is not met, i.e., the condition is false, the other statement is skipped.

- Conditions in if statements are commonly formed by using equality operators and relational operators. The result of using these operators is always simply the observation of "true" or "false." Note that conditions may be any expression that generates a zero (false) or nonzero (true) value.

Terminology

address operator
ampersand (`&`)
arithmetic operators
assignment operator
assignment statement
associativity of operators
asterisk (`*`)
backslash (`\`) escape character
binary operators
body of a function
braces `{}`
C
case sensitive
character string
C keywords
comment
condition
control string
conversational computing
conversion specifier
counter
C preprocessor
C Standard Library
`%d` conversion specifier
decision making
declaration
destructive readin
division by zero assignment operator
embedded parentheses
enter key

equal sign (`=`) assignment operator
equality operators
   `==` "is equal to"
   `!=` "is not equal to"
escape character
escape sequence
false
fatal error
flow of control
format control string
function
highest level of precedence
identifier
`if` structure
indentation
`int`
integer
integer division
interactive computing
left brace (`{`)
left-to-right associativity
literal
location
`main`
`math.h`
memory
memory location
memory location name
memory location value
message

Common Programming Errors

2.1 Placing variable declarations among executable statements.

2.2 Placing a \n outside the format control string of a `printf` statement.

2.3 Forgetting to include in a `printf` that contains conversion specifiers the expressions whose values are to be printed.

2.4 Not providing in a `printf` format control string a conversion specifier when one is needed to print an expression.

2.5 Placing inside the format control string the comma which is supposed to separate the format control string from the expressions to be printed.

2.6 Forgetting to append an `&` to a variable in a `scanf` statement when that variable should, in fact, be preceded by an ampersand.

2.7 Appending an `&` to a variable included in a `printf` statement when, in fact, that variable should not be preceded by an ampersand.

2.8 A syntax error will occur if the operators ==, !=, >=, and <= contain spaces.

2.9 Reversing the operators !=, >=, and <= as in =!, =>, and =< respectively. This causes a syntax error.

2.10 Confusing the equality operator == with the assignment operator =. The equality operator is read "is equal to" and the assignment operator is read "gets" or "gets the value of." As we will soon see, confusing these operators may not necessarily cause an easy-to-recognize syntax error, but may cause extremely subtle logic errors.

2.11   Placing a semicolon immediately to the right of the right parenthesis after the condition in an **if** structure.

2.12   Placing commas (when none are needed) between conversion specifiers in the format control string of a **scanf** statement.

Good Programming Practices

2.1   Every function should be preceded by a comment describing the purpose of the function.

2.2   The last character printed by a function that does any printing should be a newline (\n). This ensures that the function will leave the cursor positioned at the beginning of a new line. Conventions of this nature encourage software reusability—a key goal in software development environments.

2.3   Indent the entire body of each function one level of indentation (three spaces) within the braces that define the body of the function. This indentation makes the functional structure of a program stand out more and helps make programs easier to read.

2.4   Set a convention for the size of indent you prefer and then uniformly apply that convention. The tab key may be used to create indents, but tab stops may vary. We recommend using either 1/4-inch tab stops or hand counting three spaces per level of indent.

2.5   Place a space after each comma (,) to make programs more readable.

2.6   Use identifiers of 31 or fewer characters. This helps ensure portability and can avoid some subtle programming errors.

2.7   Choosing meaningful variable names helps make a program to be more self documenting.

2.8   Separate the declarations and executable statements in a function with one blank line to emphasize where the declarations of the function end and the executable statements begin.

2.9   Place spaces on either side of a binary operator. This makes the operator stand out and makes the program more readable.

2.10   Indent the statement in the body of an **if** structure.

2.11   There should be no more than one statement per line in a program.

2.12   A lengthy statement may be spread over several lines. If a single statement must be split across lines, choose breaking points that make sense such as after a comma in a comma-separated list. If a statement is split across two or more lines, indent all subsequent lines.

2.13   Refer to the operator precedence chart when writing expressions containing many operators. Confirm that the operators in the expression are performed in the proper order. If you are uncertain about the order of evaluation in a complex expression, use parentheses to force the order, exactly as you would do in algebraic expressions. Be sure to observe that some of C's operators such as the assignment operator (=) associate from right to left rather than from left to right.

Self-Review Exercises

2.1   Fill in the blanks in each of the following.
   a) Every C program begins execution at the function _____.
   b) The _____ begins the body of every function and the _____ ends the body of every function.
   c) Every statement ends with a _____.
   d) The _____ standard library function displays information on the screen.
   e) The escape sequence \n represents the _____ character which causes the cursor to position to the beginning of the next line on the screen.
   f) The _____ standard library function is used to obtain data from the keyboard.
   g) The conversion specifier _____ is used in a `scanf` format control string to indicate that an integer will be input and in a `printf` format control string to indicate that an integer will be output.
   h) Whenever a new value is placed in a memory location, that value overrides the previous value in that location. This process is known as _____ readin.
   i) When a value is read out of a memory location the value in that location is preserved; this is called _____ readout.
   j) The _____ statement is used to make decisions.

2.2   State whether each of the following is true or false. If false, explain why.
   a) When the `printf` function is called it always begins printing at the beginning of a new line.
   b) Comments cause the computer to print the text enclosed between /* and */ on the screen when the program is executed.
   c) The escape sequence \n when used in a `printf` format control string causes the cursor to position to the beginning of the next line on the screen.
   d) All variables must be declared before they are used.
   e) All variables must be given a type when they are declared.
   f) C considers the variables `number` and `NuMbEr` to be identical.
   g) Declarations can appear anywhere in the body of a function.
   h) All arguments following the format control string in a `printf` function must be preceded by an ampersand (`&`).
   i) The modulus operator (`%`) can be used only with integer operands.
   j) The arithmetic operators `*`, `/`, `%`, `+`, and `−` all have the same level of precedence.
   k) True or false: The following variable names are identical according to the ANSI C standard.

```
thisisasuperduperlongname1234567
thisisasuperduperlongname1234568
```

   l) True or false: A C program that prints three lines of output must contain three `printf` statements.

2.3   Write a single C statement to accomplish each of the following:
   a) Declare the variables `c`, `thisisavariable`, `q76354`, and `number` to be of type `int`.
   b) Prompt the user to enter an integer. End your prompting message with a colon (`:`) followed by a space and leave the cursor positioned after the space.
   c) Read an integer from the keyboard and store the value entered in integer variable `a`.

d) If the variable **number** is not equal to 7, print **"The variable number is not equal to 7."**

e) Print the message **"This is a C program."** on one line.

f) Print the message **"This is a C program."** on two lines where the first line ends with **C**.

g) Print the message **"This is a C program."** with each word on a separate line.

h) Print the message **"This is a C program."** with each word separated by tabs.

2.4   Write a statement (or comment) to accomplish each of the following:

a) State that a program will calculate the product of three integers.

b) Declare the variables **x**, **y**, **z**, and **result** to be of type **int**.

c) Prompt the user to enter three integers.

d) Read three integers from the keyboard and store them in the variables **x**, **y**, and **z**.

e) Compute the product of the three integers contained in variables **x**, **y**, and **z**, and assign the result to the variable **result**.

f) Print **"The product is"** followed by the value of the variable **result**

2.5   Using the statements you wrote in exercise 2.4, write a complete program that calculates the product of three integers.

2.6   Identify and correct the errors in each of the following statements:

a) `printf("The value is %d\n", &number);`

b) `scanf("%d%d", &number1, number2);`

c) `if (c < 7);`
    `    printf("C is less than 7\n");`

d) `if (c => 7)`
    `    printf("C is equal to or less than 7\n");`

Answers to Self-Review Exercises

2.1   a) **main**. b) Left brace ({), right brace (}). c) Semicolon. d) **printf**. e) Newline. f) **scanf**. g) **%d**. h) Destructive. i) Nondestructive. j) **if**.

2.2   a) False. The **printf** function always begins printing where the cursor is positioned, and this may be anywhere on a line of the screen.

b) False. Comments do not cause any action to be performed when the program is executed. They are used to document programs and improve their readability.

c) True.

d) True.

e) True.

f) False. C is case sensitive, so these variables are unique.

g) False. The declarations must appear after the left brace of the body of a function and before any executable statements.

h) False. Arguments in a **printf** function ordinarily should not be preceded by an ampersand. Arguments following the format control string in a **scanf** function ordinarily should be preceded by an ampersand. We will discuss exceptions in Chapters 6 and 7.

i) True.

j) False. The operators *, /, and % are on the same level of precedence, and the operators + and – are on a lower level of precedence.

k) True, because they are identical in their first 31 characters.

l) False. A single `printf` statement containing multiple \n escape sequences can print several lines.

2.3   a) `int c, thisisavariable, q76354, number;`
      b) `printf("Enter an integer");`
      c) `scanf("%d", &a);`
      d) `if (number != 7)`
         `    printf("The variable number is not equal to 7.\n");`
      e) `printf("This is a C program.\n");`
      f) `printf("This is a C\nprogram.\n");`
      g) `printf("This\nis\na\nC\nprogram.\n");`
      h) `printf("This\tis\ta\tC\tprogram.\n");`

2.4   a) `/* Calculate the product of three integers */`
      b) `int x, y, z, result;`
      c) `printf("Enter three integers: ");`
      d) `scanf("%d%d%d", &x, &y, &z);`
      e) `result = x * y * z;`
      f) `printf("The product is %d\n", result);`

2.5
```
/* Calculate the product of three integers */
#include <stdio.h>

main()
{
    int x, y, z, result;

    printf("Enter three integers: ");
    scanf("%d%d%d", &x, &y, &z);
    result = x * y * z;
    printf("The product is %d\n", result);
}
```

2.6   a) Error: `&number`. Correction: Eliminate the `&`. Later in the text we discuss exceptions that contradict this.

b) Error: `number2` does not have an ampersand. Correction: `number2` should be `&number2`. Later in the text we discuss exceptions that contradict this.

c) Error: Semicolon after the right parenthesis of the condition in the if statement. Correction: Remove the semicolon after the right parenthesis. Note: The result of this error is that the `printf` statement will be executed whether or not the condition in the `if` statement is true. The semicolon after the right parenthesis is considered an empty statement—a statement that does nothing. We will learn more about the empty statement in the next two chapters.

d) Error: The relational operator =>. Correction: Change => to >=.

Exercises

2.7   Fill in the blanks in each of the following:
      a) _____ are used to document a program and improve its readability.
      b) The function used to print information on the screen is _____.

    c)   A C statement that makes a decision is _____.

    d)   Calculations are normally performed by _____ statements.

    e)   The _____ function inputs values from the keyboard.

2.8   Write a single C statement or line that accomplishes each of the following:

    a)   Print the message "`Enter two numbers.`"

    b)   Assign the product of variables **b** and **c** to variable **a**.

    c)   State that a program performs a sample payroll calculation (i.e., use text that helps to document a program).

    d)   Input three integer values from the keyboard and place these values in integer variables **a**, **b**, and **c**.

2.9   State which of the following are true and which are false. Explain your answers.

    a)   C operators are evaluated from left to right.

    b)   The following are all valid variable names: `_under_bar_`, `m928134`, `t5`, `j7`, `her_sales`, `his_account_total`, `a`, `b`, `c`, `z`, `z2`.

    c)   The statement `printf("a = 5;");` is a typical example of an assignment statement.

    d)   A valid C arithmetic expression containing no parentheses is evaluated from left to right.

    e)   The following are all invalid variable names: `3g`, `87`, `67h2`, `h22`, `2h`.

2.10   Fill in the blanks in each of the following:

    a)   What arithmetic operations are on the same level of precedence as multiplication? _____.

    b)   When parentheses are nested, which set of parentheses is evaluated first in an arithmetic expression? _____.

    c)   A location in the computer's memory that may contain different values at various times throughout the execution of a program is called a _____.

2.11   What, if anything, prints when each of the following C statements is performed? If nothing prints, then answer "nothing." Assume **x** = 2 and **y** = 3.

    a)   `printf("%d", x);`

    b)   `printf("%d", x + x);`

    c)   `printf("x=");`

    d)   `printf("x=%d", x);`

    e)   `printf("%d = %d", x + y, y + x);`

    f)   `z = x + y;`

    g)   `scanf("%d%d", &x, &y);`

    h)   `/* printf("x + y = %d", x + y); */`

    i)   `printf("\n");`

2.12   Which, if any, of the following C statements contain variables involved in destructive readin?

    a)   `scanf("%d%d%d%d%d", &b, &c, &d, &e, &f);`

    b)   `p = i + j + k + 7;`

    c)   `printf("Destructive readin");`

    d)   `printf("a = 5");`

2.13   Given the equation $y = ax^3 + 7$, which of the following, if any, are correct C statements for this equation?

    a)   `y = a * x * x * x + 7;`

    b)   `y = a * x * x * (x + 7);`

```
c)  y = (a * x) * x * (x + 7);
d)  y = (a * x) * x * x + 7;
e)  y = a * (x * x * x) + 7;
f)  y = a * x * (x * x + 7);
```

2.14   State the order of evaluation of the operators in each of the following C statements, and show the value of x after each statement is performed.

```
a)  x = 7 + 3 * 6 / 2 - 1;
b)  x = 2 % 2 + 2 * 2 - 2 / 2;
c)  x = (3 * 9 * (3 + (9 * 3/ (3))));
```

2.15   Write a program that asks the user to enter two numbers, obtains the two numbers from the user, and prints the sum, product, difference, and quotient of the two numbers.

2.16   Write a program that prints the numbers 1 to 4 on the same line. Write the program using the following methods.

  a)   Using 1 `printf` statement with no conversion specifiers.
  b)   Using 1 `printf` statement with 4 conversion specifiers.
  c)   Using 4 `printf` statements.

2.17   Write a program that asks the user to enter two integers, obtains the numbers from the user, and then prints the larger number followed by the words "`is larger.`" If the numbers are equal, print the message "`These numbers are equal.`"

2.18   Write a C program that inputs three different integers from the keyboard, and then prints the sum, the average, the product, the smallest, and the largest of these numbers. The screen dialogue should appear as follows:

```
Input three different integers: 13 27 14
Sum is 54
Average is 18
Product is 4914
Smallest is 13
Largest is 27
```

3
Structured Program Development

Objectives

- To understand basic problem solving techniques.
- To understand structured programming.
- To be able to develop algorithms.
- To be able to use the while, for, and do/while structures to execute statements in a program repeatedly.
- To understand the development of structured flowcharts.
- To be able to use the increment, decrement, and assignment operators.

The secret to success is constancy to purpose.
Benjamin Disraeli

Let's all move one place on.
Lewis Carroll

The wheel is come full circle.
William Shakespeare
King Lear

*How many apples fell on Newton's head before
he took the hint!*
Robert Frost
Comment

Outline

3.1 Introduction

Before writing a program to solve a particular problem, it is essential to have a thorough understanding of the problem, and a carefully planned approach to solving the problem. The next two chapters discuss techniques that facilitate the development of structured computer programs. In Section 4.11, we present a wrap up of structured programming that ties together the techniques developed here and in Chapter 4.

3.2 Algorithms

The solution to any computing problem involves performing a series of *steps* (or operations) in a specific *order*. A *procedure* for solving a problem in terms of

1. the *steps* to be executed, and
2. the *order* in which these steps should be executed

is called an *algorithm*. The following example demonstrates that correctly specifying the order in which the steps are to be executed is important.

Consider the "rise and shine algorithm" followed by one junior executive for getting out of bed and going to work:

Get out of bed.
Take off pajamas.
Take a shower.
Get dressed.

Eat breakfast.
Carpool to work.

This routine gets the executive to work well prepared to make critical decisions. Suppose, however, that the same steps are performed in a slightly different order:

Get out of bed.
Take off pajamas.
Get dressed.
Take a shower.
Eat breakfast.
Carpool to work.

In this case, our junior executive shows up for work soaking wet. Specifying the order in which statements are to be executed in a computer program is called *program control*. In this and the next chapter, we investigate the program control capabilities of C.

3.3 Pseudocode

Pseudocode is an artificial and informal language that helps programmers develop algorithms. The pseudocode we present here is particularly useful for developing algorithms that will be converted to C programs. Pseudocode is similar to everyday English; it is convenient and user-friendly although it is not an actual computer programming language.

Pseudocode programs are not actually run on computers. Rather, they merely help the programmer to "think out" a program before attempting to write it in a programming language such as C. In this chapter, we give several examples of how pseudocode may be used effectively in developing structured C programs.

Pseudocode consists purely of characters, and therefore programmers may type pseudocode programs into a computer, edit them, and save them. The computer can display or print a fresh copy of a pseudocode program for us at any time. Many programmers have learned from experience that a carefully prepared pseudocode program may be converted easily to a corresponding C program. This is done in many cases simply by replacing pseudocode statements with their C equivalents. Some pseudocode statements become comments in the resulting C program.

Note: Variable declarations are not a part of pseudocode. Pseudocode consists only of action statements, in other words, those that are executed when the program has been converted from pseudocode to C and is run in C. Declarations are not executable statements. They are messages to the compiler. For example, the declaration

```
int i;
```

simply tells the compiler the type of variable i and instructs the compiler to reserve space in memory for the variable. But this declaration does not cause any action—such as input, output, or a calculation—to occur when the program is run.

3.4 Control Structures

Normally, statements in a program are executed one after the other in the order in which they are written. Various C statements we will soon discuss enable the programmer to specify that the next statement to be executed may be other than the next one in sequence. This is called *transfer of control*.

During the 1960s, it became clear that the indiscriminate use of transfers of control was the root of a great deal of difficulty experienced by software development groups. The finger of blame was pointed at the `goto` statement that allows the programmer to specify a transfer of control to one of a very wide range of possible destinations. The notion of so-called *structured programming* became almost synonymous with "`goto` elimination."

The research of Bohm and Jacopini[1] had demonstrated that programs could be written without any `goto` statements. The challenge of the era became for programmers to shift their styles to "`goto`-less programming." It was not until well into the 1970s that the programming profession at large started taking structured programming seriously. The results have been impressive as software development groups have reported reduced development times, more frequent on-time delivery of systems, and more frequent within-budget completion of software projects. The key to these successes is simply that programs produced with structured techniques are clearer, easier to debug and modify, and more likely to be bug-free in the first place.

Bohm and Jacopini's work demonstrated that all programs could be written in terms of only three *control structures*, namely *sequence, selection,* and *repetition*. The *sequence structure* is essentially built into C. Unless directed otherwise, the computer automatically performs C statements one after the other in the order in which they are written. We continue with discussions of the various C statements used to implement selection structures and repetition structures.

3.5 The If Selection Structure

A *selection structure* is used to choose among alternative courses of action. For example, suppose the passing grade on an exam is 60. The pseudocode statement

> *If student's grade is greater than or equal to 60*
>   *print "Passed"*

determines if the condition (see Section 2.6) "student's grade is greater than or equal to 60" is true or false. If the condition is true, then "Passed" is printed, and the next pseudocode statement in order is performed. If the condition is false, the printing is ignored, and the next pseudocode statement in order is performed. Note that the second line of this selection structure is indented. Such indentation is optional, but it is

---

[1] C. Bohm and G. Jacopini, "Flow Diagrams, Turing Machines, and Languages with Only Two Formation Rules," *Communications of the ACM*, Vol. 9, No. 5 (May 1966), pp. 336-371.

highly recommended as it helps emphasize the inherent structure of structured programs. We will carefully apply indentation conventions throughout this text.

GPP 3.1

Consistently applying responsible indentation conventions greatly improves program readability. We suggest a fixed-size tab of about 1/4 inch or three spaces per indent.

The preceding pseudocode if statement may be written in C as

```
if (grade >= 60)
    printf("Passed\n");
```

Notice that the C statements correspond closely to the pseudocode statements. This is one of the properties of pseudocode that makes it such a useful program development tool.

GPP 3.2

Pseudocode is often used to "think out" a program during the program design process. Then the pseudocode program is converted to C.

3.6 The If/Else Selection Structure

The if selection structure performs an indicated action only when the condition is true. The *if/else selection structure* allows the programmer to specify alternative actions to be performed when the condition is true and when the condition is false. For example, the pseudocode statement

> *If student's grade is greater than or equal to 60*
> > *print "Passed"*
>
> *else*
> > *print "Failed"*

will print "Passed" if the student's grade is greater than or equal to 60 and will print "Failed" if the student's grade is less than 60. In either case, after printing occurs, the next pseudocode statement in sequence is "performed." Note that the body of the else is also indented.

GPP 3.3

Indent the body of an if/else structure.

Whatever indentation convention you choose should be carefully applied throughout your programs. It is difficult to read a program that does not obey uniform spacing conventions. If there are several levels of indentation, each level should be indented the same amount of space.

The preceding if/else structure may be written in C as

```
if (grade >= 60)
   printf("Passed\n");
else
   printf("Failed\n");
```

C also provides a special operator for making decisions known as the *conditional operator (? :)*. The conditional operator is C's only *ternary operator*—it takes three arguments. The first argument is a condition, the second argument is an action to be taken if the condition is true, and the third argument is an action to be taken if the condition is false. The arguments together with the conditional operator are called a *conditional expression*. The conditional expression

```
grade >= 60 ? printf("Passed\n") : printf("Failed\n");
```

is read, "If `grade` is greater than or equal to `60` then print `"Passed\n"`, otherwise print `"Failed\n"`. This is equivalent to the preceding `if/else` structure.

Nested `if/else` structures test for multiple cases by placing `if/else` structures inside `if/else` structures. For example, the following pseudocode statement will print A for grades greater than or equal to `90`, B for grades greater than or equal to `80`, C for grades greater than or equal to `70`, D for grades greater than or equal to `60`, and F for all other grades.

> *If student's grade is greater than or equal to 90*
> 　　*print "A"*
> *else*
> 　　*if student's grade is greater than or equal to 80*
> 　　　　*print "B"*
> 　　*else*
> 　　　　*if student's grade is greater than or equal to 70*
> 　　　　　　*print "C"*
> 　　　　*else*
> 　　　　　　*if student's grade is greater than or equal to 60*
> 　　　　　　　　*print "D"*
> 　　　　　　*else*
> 　　　　　　　　*print "F"*

The preceding pseudocode may be written in C as

```
if (grade >= 90)
    printf("A\n");
else
    if (grade >= 80)
        printf("B\n");
    else
        if (grade >= 70)
            printf("C\n");
        else
            if (grade >= 60)
                printf("D\n");
            else
                printf("F\n");
```

If the variable `grade` is greater than or equal to 90, the first four conditions will be true, but only the `printf` statement after the first test will be executed. Often the preceding `if` structure is written as

```
if (grade >= 90)
    printf("A\n");
else if (grade >= 80)
    printf("B\n");
else if (grade >= 70)
    printf("C\n");
else if (grade >= 60)
    printf("D\n");
else
    printf("F\n");
```

This form is popular among programmers because it avoids deep indentation of the code to the right. Such indentation often leaves little room on a line forcing lines to be split and decreasing program readability.

The `if` selection structure expects only one statement in its body. To include several statements in the body of an `if`, the set of statements is explicitly enclosed in braces ({ and }). A set of statements contained within a pair of braces is called a *compound statement*. A compound statement can be placed anywhere in a program that a single statement can be placed. The following example includes a compound statement in the `else` part of an `if/else` structure.

```
if (grade >= 60)
    printf("Passed.\n");
else {
    printf("Failed.\n");
    printf("You must take this course again.\n");
}
```

In this case, if grade is less than 60, the program will print

```
Failed.
You must take this course again.
```

Notice the braces surrounding the two statements in the `else` clause. These braces are important. Without the braces, the statement

```
printf("You must take this course again.\n");
```

would be outside the body of the `else` part of the `if`, and would execute regardless of whether the grade is less than 60.

CPE 3.1

Forgetting one or both of the braces that delimit a compound statement.

GPP 3.4

Type the beginning and ending braces of compound statements before typing the statements themselves. This prevents omitting one or both of the braces.

Just as a compound statement can be placed anywhere a single statement can be placed, it is also possible to have no statement at all, i.e., the *empty statement*. The empty statement is represented by placing a semicolon (;) where a statement would normally be.

3.7 The While Repetition Structure

A *repetition structure* allows the programmer to specify that an action is to be repeated until some *terminating condition* occurs. The pseudocode statement

> *While there are more items on my shopping list*
> *purchase next item and cross it off my list*

describes the repetition that occurs during a shopping trip. The condition, "there are more items on my shopping list" may be true or false. If it is true, then the action, "purchase next item and cross it off my list" is performed. This action will be performed repeatedly as long as the condition remains true. The statement(s) contained in the *while repetition structure* constitute the *body* of the while. The while structure body may be a single statement or a compound statement.

Eventually, the condition will become false (when the last item on the shopping list has been purchased and crossed off the list). At this point, the repetition terminates, and the first pseudocode statement after the repetition structure is performed.

CPE 3.2

Not providing an action in the body of a **while** *structure that eventually causes the condition in the* **while** *to become false. Otherwise, the loop will never terminate—a common error called an infinite loop.*

As an example of an actual while, consider a structure designed to find the first power of 2 larger than 1000. Suppose the integer variable product has been initialized to 2. When the repetition finishes, product will contain the desired answer:

```
while (product <= 1000)
    product = 2 * product;
```

When the while structure is entered, the value of product is 2. The variable product is repeatedly multiplied by 2, thus taking on the values 4, 8, 16, 32, 64, 128, 256, 512, and 1024. When product becomes 1024, the condition in the while structure, product <= 1000, becomes false. Therefore, repetition terminates and the final value of product is 1024.

The for structure and the do/while structure also provide additional means for specifying repetition. These structures are discussed in Chapter 4.

3.8 Formulating Algorithms

To illustrate how algorithms are developed, we solve several variations of a class averaging problem. Consider the following problem statement:

> *A class of ten students took a quiz. The grades for this quiz are available to you. Determine the class average on the quiz.*

The class average is equal to the sum of the grades divided by the number of students. The algorithm for solving this problem on a computer must input each of the grades, perform the averaging calculation, and print the result. Let us use pseudocode, list the steps, and indicate the order in which these steps should be performed. We use *counter-controlled repetition* to input the grades one at a time. Counter-controlled repetition uses a variable called a *counter* to specify the number of times a set of statements should execute. In this example, the loop terminates when the counter is equal to 11. The pseudocode algorithm is shown in Fig. 3.1.

Note the references in the algorithm to a *total* and a *counter*. A total is a variable used to accumulate the sum of a series of values. A counter is a variable used to count—in this case, to count the number of grades entered. Variables used to store totals should always be initialized to zero before being used in a program; otherwise the sum would include the previous value stored in the total's memory location. Counter variables are usually initialized to one. An uninitialized variable contains a "garbage" value—the value last stored in the memory location reserved for the variable. If a counter or total is not initialized, the results of your program will probably be incorrect.

GPP 3.5

Initialize counters and totals.

3.9 Top-down, Stepwise Refinement

Let us now generalize the class average problem. Consider the following problem statement:

> *Develop a class averaging program that will process an arbitrary number of grades each time the program is run.*

In the first class average example, the number of grades was known in advance. In this example, no indication is given of how many grades are to be entered. The program must process an arbitrary number of grades. How will the program determine when to stop the input of grades? How will it know when to calculate and print the class average?

> *Set total to zero*
> *Set grade counter to one*
>
> *While grade counter is less than or equal to ten*
>   *Input the next grade*
>   *Add the grade into the total*
>   *Add one to the grade counter*
>
> *Set the class average to the total divided by ten*
> *Print the class average*

Fig. 3.1 Pseudocode algorithm that uses counter-controlled looping to solve the class average problem.

One way to solve this problem is to use a special value called a *sentinel value* (or a *signal value*, a *dummy value*, or a *flag value*) to indicate "end of data entry." The user types grades in until all legitimate grades have been entered. The user then types the sentinel value to indicate that the last grade has been entered.

Clearly, the sentinel value must be chosen so that it cannot be confused with an acceptable input value. Since grades on a quiz are normally nonnegative numbers, -1 is an acceptable sentinel value for this problem. Thus, a run of the class average program might process a stream of inputs such as 95, 96, 75, 74, 89, and -1. The program would then compute and print the class average for the grades 95, 96, 75, 74, and 89 (-1 is the sentinel value, so it does not enter into the averaging calculation).

We approach the class average program with a technique called *top-down, stepwise refinement,* a technique that is essential to the development of well-structured programs. We begin with a pseudocode representation of the *top:*

> *Determine the class average for the quiz*

The top is a single statement that conveys the overall function of the program. We now begin the refinement process. We divide the top into a series of smaller tasks. This results in the following *first refinement.*

> *Initialize variables*
> *Input and sum the quiz grades*
> *Calculate and print the class average*

Here, only the sequence structure has been used—the steps listed are to be executed in order, one after the other. It is important to note that each refinement, as well as the top itself, is a complete specification of the algorithm; only the level of detail varies.

To proceed to the next level of refinement, we commit to specific variables. We need a running total of the numbers, a count of how many numbers have been processed, a variable to receive the value of each grade as it is input, and a variable to hold the calculated average. The pseudocode statement

> *Initialize variables*

may be refined as follows:

> *Initialize total to zero*
> *Initialize counter to zero*

Notice that only *total* and *counter* need to be initialized; the variables *average* and *grade* (for the calculated average and the user input, respectively) need not be initialized because their values will be written over by the process of destructive readin discussed in Chapter 2. The pseudocode statement

> *Input and sum the quiz grades*

requires a loop that successively inputs each grade. Since we do not know in advance how many grades are to be processed, we will use a sentinel-controlled loop. The user will type legitimate grades in one at a time. After the last legitimate grade is typed, the user will type the sentinel value. The program will test for this value after each grade is input and will terminate the loop when the sentinel is entered. The refinement of the preceding pseudocode statement is then

> *Input the first grade*
> *While the user has not as yet entered the sentinel*
> > *Add this grade into the running total*
> > *Add one to the grade counter*
> > *Input the next grade (possibly the sentinel)*

The pseudocode statement

> *Calculate and print the class average*

may be refined as follows:

> *Set the average to the total divided by the counter*
> *Print the average*

The complete *second refinement* is shown in Fig. 3.2

In Fig. 3.2, we have included some completely blank lines in the pseudocode for readability. Actually, the blanks separate the various phases of this program by function: an *initialization phase* that clears the program variables, a *processing phase* that inputs each grade and adjusts the program variables accordingly, and a *termination phase* that calculates and prints the final results. Many programs can be divided logically into these three phases.

The algorithm in Fig. 3.2 solves the more general class averaging problem. Once the algorithm has been specified in sufficient detail, the process of implementing a working C program is relatively straightforward. The C program and a sample execution are shown in Fig. 3.3. We will assume that only integer grades are entered. We introduce the C data type `float` and a special operator called a *cast* to handle the average calculation. These features are explained in detail after the program is presented.

> *Initialize total to zero*
> *Initialize counter to zero*
>
> *Input the first grade*
> *While the user has not as yet entered the sentinel*
> > *Add this grade into the running total*
> > *Add one to the grade counter*
> > *Input the next grade (possibly the sentinel)*
>
> *Set the average to the total divided by the counter*
> *Print the average*

Fig. 3.2 Pseudocode algorithm that uses sentinel-controlled repetition to solve the class average problem.

```
/* Class Average Program */
#include <stdio.h>

main()
{
    float average;
    int counter, grade, total;

    /* initialization phase */
    total = 0;
    counter = 0;

    /* processing phase */
    printf("Enter grade, -1 to end: ");
    scanf("%d", &grade);

    while (grade != -1) {
        total = total + grade;
        counter = counter + 1;
        printf("Enter grade, -1 to end: ");
        scanf("%d", &grade);
    }

    /* termination phase */
    average = (float) total / counter;
    printf("Class average is %.2f", average);
}
```

```
Enter grade, -1 to end: 75
Enter grade, -1 to end: 94
Enter grade, -1 to end: 97
Enter grade, -1 to end: 88
Enter grade, -1 to end: 70
Enter grade, -1 to end: 64
Enter grade, -1 to end: 83
Enter grade, -1 to end: 89
Enter grade, -1 to end: -1
Class average is 82.50
```

Fig. 3.3 C program and sample execution for the class average problem.

GPP 3.6

In a sentinel-controlled loop the prompts should explicitly remind the user what the sentinel value is.

Averages are not always whole numbers. Often, an average contains a fractional part. Values containing fractional parts such as 7.2 or 93.5 are referred to as *floating point* numbers and are represented by the data type float. We declare the variable average to be of type float to capture the fractional result in our average calculation. However, our result will still be a whole number because the division total / counter is an integer division. In order to produce a floating point calculation with integer values, we must first convert the values to floating point numbers. C provides the unary *cast operator* to accomplish this task. The statement

```
average = (float) total / counter;
```

includes the cast operator (`float`) which converts the value of its operand, `total`, to a floating point number for the calculation. The value of `counter` is still an integer. In an expression with mixed data types (such as `int` and `float` in the preceding calculation), C automatically converts the values to the same data type then performs the calculation. In a calculation involving integer values and floating point values, the integer values are converted to floating point values. It is important to remember that only *copies* of the variable values are converted for the calculation. The variables are still integers. There is a set of rules in the ANSI standard document that specifies the order in which values are converted. We will discuss these rules throughout the text as they are needed.

The cast operator is created by placing parentheses around a data type. Casts of all data types can be created. The cast operator associates from right to left and has a higher precedence than all the operators introduced so far except parentheses.

The program in Fig. 3.3 prints the value stored in `average` with the conversion specifier `%.2f`. The `f` specifies that a floating point value will be printed. The `.2` is the *precision* with which the value will be displayed. It states that the value will be displayed with 2 decimal digits to the right of the decimal point. If a `%f` conversion specifier is used (without specifying the precision) C will automatically assume a precision of 6—exactly as if the conversion specifier `%.6f` had been used. When a floating point value is printed with a precision, the value is rounded to the indicated number of decimal positions. The value is not rounded in memory. If we execute the statements

```
printf("%.2f\n", 3.446);
printf("%.1f\n", 3.446);
```

the values 3.45 and 3.4 are printed.

CPE 3.3

Using floating point numbers in a manner that assumes they are represented precisely can lead to incorrect results. Floating point numbers are represented approximately by most computers. Therefore, calculations involving floating point numbers are often rounded incorrectly.

GPP 3.7

Do not compare floating point values for equality.

Notice the compound statement contained in the `while` loop. Once again, the braces are necessary for all four statements to be executed within the loop. Without the braces, the last three statements in the body of the loop would fall outside the loop causing the computer to give the following incorrect meaning to the code.

```
while(grade != -1)
    total = total + grade;
counter = counter + 1;
printf("Enter grade? ");
scanf("%f", &grade);
```

This would cause an infinite loop if the user does not input -1 for the first grade.

3.10 Structured Flowcharting

Another useful technique for developing and representing algorithms is called flowcharting. A *flowchart* is a graphical representation of an algorithm. Flowcharts are drawn using certain special symbols such as ovals, diamonds, rectangles, and small circles connected by arrows called *flowlines*. The flowchart symbols indicate the steps to be performed; C-like code for each step is written inside its appropriate symbol. The flowlines indicate the order in which the steps are to be performed. Fig. 3.4 is the flowchart that corresponds to the program of Fig. 3.3. The flowchart of Fig. 3.4 is called a *program flowchart* because it uses of C-like code in the flowchart symbols.

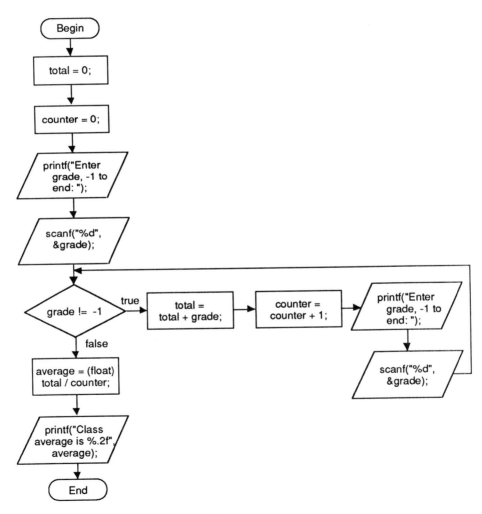

Fig. 3.4 A program flowchart for the sentinel-controlled class average program.

Let us now discuss each of the flowcharting symbols used in Fig. 3.4. The oval symbol (Fig. 3.5), also called the *termination symbol,* is used to indicate the beginning and end of every algorithm. The oval symbol containing the word "Begin" is the first symbol used in a flowchart; the oval symbol containing the word "End" is the last symbol used.

The rectangle symbol (Fig. 3.6), also called the *process symbol,* is used to indicate any type of calculation. Process symbols correspond to the steps that are normally performed by assignment statements in C. Notice that this program flowchart contains many process symbols, each of which indicates some calculation required by the algorithm.

Most algorithms require that information be communicated to the computer in some manner. The parallelogram symbol (Fig. 3.7), also called the *input/output symbol,* is used to indicate that information is to be entered into the computer or that the computer is to output information. Input/output symbols correspond to the steps typically performed by `scanf` and `printf` statements. The program flowchart contains several input/output symbols.

Fig. 3.5 Oval or termination symbols.

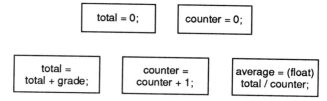

Fig. 3.6 Rectangle or process symbols.

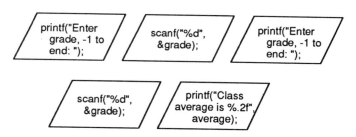

Fig. 3.7 Parallelogram or input/output symbols.

Perhaps the most important flowcharting symbol is the diamond symbol (Fig. 3.8), also called the *decision symbol*, which indicates that a decision is to be made at a certain point in a flowchart. The decision symbol contains a condition that can be either true or false. The decision symbol has two flowlines emerging from it. One indicates the direction to be taken when the condition in the symbol is true; the other indicates the direction to be taken when the condition is false. The program flowchart of Fig. 3.4 contains one decision symbol.

Fig. 3.9 illustrates flowchart segments that correspond to each of the three control structures, namely sequence, selection, and repetition.

3.11 Developing a Program Flowchart

A program flowchart is constructed by replacing the English phrases of pseudocode with the actual statements required in C programs. Once the program flowchart has been constructed, writing the actual C program is usually straightforward. The reader should compare each symbol in the program flowchart of Fig. 3.4 with the corresponding pseudocode of Fig. 3.2. The following points should be considered:

1. The flowchart follows the pseudocode closely and helps illustrate the actual flow of the program.
2. The flowchart uses C-like notations for variables and calculations.
3. The program flowchart uses actual C commands `scanf` and `printf` in input/output symbols.
4. The C program for the class average problem was presented in Fig. 3.3. Each C statement corresponds to a particular symbol in the program flowchart.

In general, to develop a computer solution to any problem, it is useful to perform the following steps:

1. Read the problem statement carefully.
2. Develop an approach to solving the problem, and formulate the algorithm as a series of steps to be performed in a specific order. Some people prefer to use pseudocode for this purpose; others prefer to develop structured flowcharts.
3. Write a C program by carefully referencing either the structured flowchart or the pseudocode.

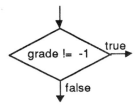

Fig. 3.8 Diamond or decision symbol.

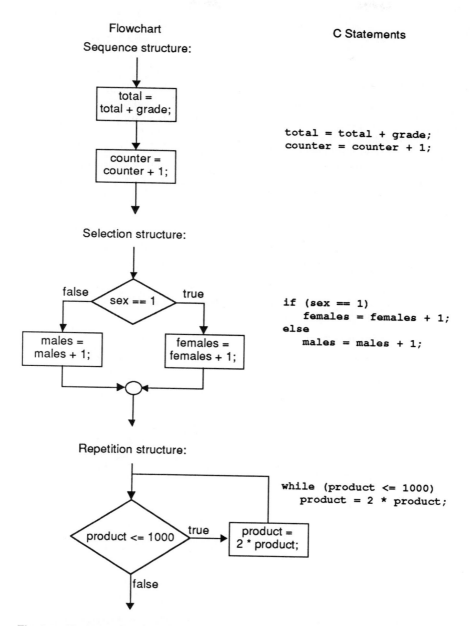

Fig. 3.9 Flowcharting the sequence, selection, and repetition structures.

3.12 Flowcharting: Observations and Guidelines

Experience has shown that the most difficult part of solving a problem on a computer is developing the algorithm for the solution. Once a correct algorithm has been specified, the process of producing a working C program is normally straightforward. Flowcharts help the programmer develop algorithms, particularly those with complex decision making. Flowcharts provide a visual representation of the logic required to solve a problem.

Many programmers write programs without ever writing flowcharts or using pseudocode. They feel that their ultimate goal is to solve the problem on a computer, and that drawing flowcharts merely delays the production of final outputs.

Every flowchart should begin with the oval symbol containing the word Begin. Every flowchart should end with the oval symbol containing the word End. Avoid crossing flowlines. Use a flowcharting template if possible. A flowcharting template is a hard plastic sheet with the flowchart symbols punched out. A particular flowchart symbol is drawn by tracing around the edges of the punched-out shape.

3.13 A Complete Example

Now that we have covered the fundamental principles of algorithms, pseudocode, flowcharting, and top-down, stepwise refinement let us work a complete problem. We will

1. Formulate the algorithm using pseudocode and top-down, stepwise refinement.

2. Draw a program flowchart.

3. Write a C program.

Consider the following problem statement:

A college offers a course that prepares students for the state licensing exam for real estate brokers. Last year, several of the students who completed this course took the licensing examination. Naturally, the college wants to know how well its students did on the exam. A questionnaire has been sent to each of the 10 students who took the exam, and the director of the program has asked you to summarize the results. You have been given a list of these 10 students. Next to each name, one of the following codes has been written:

Code	Meaning
1	Passed the exam
2	Failed the exam

The program should analyze the results of the exam as follows:

1. Input each test result (i.e., a 1 or a 2). Display the message "Enter result" on the screen each time the program requests another test result.

2. Count the number of test results of each type.

3. Display a summary of the test results indicating the number of students who passed and the number of students who failed.

4. If more than 8 students passed the exam, print the message "Raise tuition."

After reading the problem statement carefully, we make the following observations:

1. The program must process 10 test results. A counter-controlled loop will be used.

2. Each test result is simply a number—either a 1 or a 2. Each time the program inputs a test result, the program must determine if the number is a 1 or a 2. We will explicitly test for a 1 in our algorithm. If the number is not a 1, we will assume that it is a 2. (An exercise at the end of the chapter considers the consequences of this assumption.)

3. Two more counters will be used. One will count the number of students who passed the exam; the other will count the number of students who failed the exam.

4. After the program has processed all of the results, it will decide if more than 8 students passed the exam.

Let us proceed with top-down, stepwise refinement. We begin with a pseudocode representation of the top:

Analyze exam results and decide if tuition should be raised

Once again, it is important to emphasize that the top is a complete representation of the program, but several refinements are necessary before the pseudocode naturally evolves into a C program. Our first refinement is

Initialize variables
Input the ten quiz grades and count passes and failures
Print a summary of the exam results and decide if tuition should be raised

Here, too, even though we have a complete representation of the entire program, further refinement is necessary. We now commit to specific variables. Counters are needed to record the passes and failures, a counter will be used to control the looping process, and a variable is needed to store the user input. The pseudocode statement

Initialize variables

may be refined as follows:

Initialize passes to zero
Initialize failures to zero
Initialize student to one

Notice only the counters and totals are initialized. The pseudocode statement

Input the ten quiz grades and count passes and failures

requires a loop that successively inputs the result of each exam. Here it is known in advance that there are precisely ten exam results, so counter-controlled looping is appropriate. Inside the loop, a selection structure will determine whether each exam result is a pass or a failure, and will increment the appropriate counters accordingly. The refinement of the preceding pseudocode statement is then

> *While student counter is less than or equal to ten*
> *Input the next exam result*
>
> *If the student passed*
>   *add one to passes*
> *else*
>   *add one to failures*
>
> *Add one to student counter*

Notice the use of blank lines to set off the `while` and `if/else` control structures to improve program readability. The pseudocode statement

> *Print a summary of the exam results and decide if tuition should be raised*

may be refined as follows:

> *Print the number of passes*
> *Print the number of failures*
> *If eight or more students passed*
>   *print "Raise tuition"*

The complete second refinement appears in Fig. 3.10.

> *Initialize passes to zero*
> *Initialize failures to zero*
> *Initialize student to one*
>
> *While student counter is less than or equal to ten*
> *Input the next exam result*
>
> *If the student passed*
>   *add one to passes*
> *else*
>   *add one to failures*
>
> *Add one to student counter*
>
> *Print the number of passes*
> *Print the number of failures*
> *If eight or more students passed*
>   *print "Raise tuition"*

Fig. 3.10 Pseudocode for examination results problem.

This pseudocode is now sufficiently refined for conversion to C. Fig. 3.11 shows a program flowchart that corresponds to this pseudocode program. The C program and two sample executions are shown in Fig. 3.12. Note that the initialization actions in pseudocode have been incorporated into declarations in the C program.

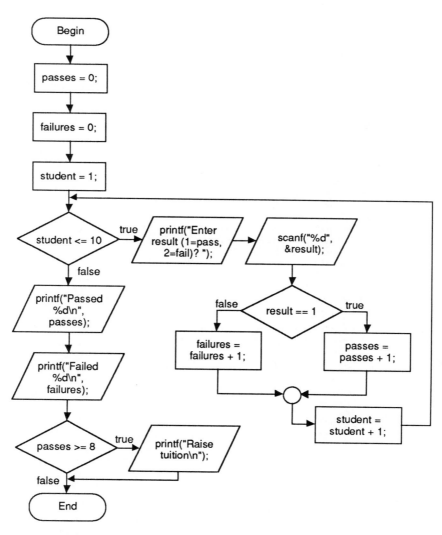

Fig. 3.11 Program flowchart for the examination results program.

```
/* Analysis of examination results */
#include <stdio.h>

main()
{
   int passes = 0, failures = 0, student = 1, result;

   while (student <= 10) {
      printf("Enter result (1=pass,2=fail): ");
      scanf("%d", &result);

      if (result == 1)
         passes = passes + 1;
      else
         failures = failures + 1;

      student = student + 1;
   }

   printf("Passed %d\n", passes);
   printf("Failed %d\n", failures);

   if (passes >= 8)
      printf("Raise tuition\n");
}
```

```
Enter Result (1=pass,2=fail): 1
Enter Result (1=pass,2=fail): 2
Enter Result (1=pass,2=fail): 2
Enter Result (1=pass,2=fail): 1
Enter Result (1=pass,2=fail): 1
Enter Result (1=pass,2=fail): 1
Enter Result (1=pass,2=fail): 2
Enter Result (1=pass,2=fail): 1
Enter Result (1=pass,2=fail): 1
Enter Result (1=pass,2=fail): 2
Passed 6
Failed 4
```

```
Enter Result (1=pass,2=fail): 1
Enter Result (1=pass,2=fail): 1
Enter Result (1=pass,2=fail): 1
Enter Result (1=pass,2=fail): 2
Enter Result (1=pass,2=fail): 1
Enter Result (1=pass,2=fail): 1
Enter Result (1=pass,2=fail): 1
Enter Result (1=pass,2=fail): 1
Enter Result (1=pass,2=fail): 1
Enter Result (1=pass,2=fail): 1
Passed 9
Failed 1
Raise tuition
```

Fig. 3.12 C program and sample executions for examination results problem.

3.14 Increment, Decrement, and Assignment Operators

C provides several *assignment operators* for abbreviating assignment expressions. For example the statement

```
c = c + 3;
```

can be abbreviated with the *assignment operator +=* as

```
c += 3;
```

The += operator adds the value of the expression on the right of the operator to the variable on the left of the operator. In general, any statement of the form

variable = variable `operator` *expression;*

where `operator` is one of the binary operators +, -, *, /, or % (or others we will discuss later), can be written in the form

variable `operator=` *expression;*

In this case, 3 is added to c. Figure 3.13 shows the operators, sample expressions using the operators, and explanations.

   C also provides the unary *increment operator, ++,* and the unary *decrement operator, --* (summarized in Fig. 3.14). If a variable c is incremented by 1, the increment operator ++ can be used rather than the expressions c = c + 1 or c += 1. The increment and decrement operators can be either placed before (*preincrement*) or placed after (*postincrement*) a variable. Preincrementing the variable causes the variable to be incremented by 1, then the new value of the variable is used in the expression in which it appears. Postincrementing the variable causes the current value of the variable to be used in the expression in which it appears, then the variable value is incremented by 1. The program of Fig. 3.15 demonstrates the difference between preincrementing and postincrementing the ++ operator. Postincrementing the variable c causes its value to be incremented after it is used in the `printf` statement. Preincrementing the variable c causes it to be incremented before it is used in the `printf` statement.

Assignment operator	Sample expression	Explanation	Assigns
+=	c += 7	c = c + 7	10 to c
-=	d -= 4	d = d - 4	1 to d
*=	e *= 5	e = e * 5	20 to e
/=	f /= 3	f = f / 3	2 to f
%=	g %= 9	g = g % 9	3 to g
Assume int c = 3, d = 5, e = 4, f = 6, g = 12;			

Fig. 3.13 Arithmetic assignment operators.

The program displays the value of c before and after the ++ operator is used. The decrement operator (--) works similarly.

GPP 3.8
___

Unary operators should be appended to their operands with no intervening spaces.

Using the increment operator, experienced C programmers would write the three assignment statements in Fig 3.12

```
passes = passes + 1;
failures = failures + 1;
students = students + 1;
```

more concisely as

```
++passes;
++failures;
++students;
```

The chart in Fig. 3.16 shows the precedence and associativity of the operators introduced up to this point. They are shown top-to-bottom in decreasing order of precedence. The column to the right of the operators describes the associativity of the operators at each level of precedence. Notice that the unary operators increment (++), decrement (--), and casts and the assignment operators =, +=, -=, *=, /=, and %= associate from right to left. All other operators in Fig. 3.16 associate from left to right.

Summary

- The solution to any computing problem involves performing a series of steps (or operations) in a specific order. A procedure for solving a problem in terms of the steps to be executed and the order in which these steps should be executed is called an algorithm.

- Specifying the order in which statements are to be executed in a computer program is called program control.

- Pseudocode is an artificial and informal language that helps programmers develop algorithms. It is similar to everyday English. Pseudocode programs are not actually run on computers. Rather, they merely help the programmer to "think out" a program before attempting to write it in a programming language such as C.

Operator	Sample expression	Explanation
++	++a or a++	This operator increments the variable to which it is appended by 1
--	--b or b--	This operator decrements the variable to which it is appended by 1

Fig. 3.14 The increment and decrement operators.

```
/* Preincrementing and postincrementing */
#include <stdio.h>

main()
{
    int c;

    c = 5;
    printf("%d\n", c);
    printf("%d\n", c++);        /* postincrement */
    printf("%d\n\n", c);

    c = 5;
    printf("%d\n", c);
    printf("%d\n", ++c);        /* preincrement */
    printf("%d\n", c);
}
```

```
5
5
6

5
6
6
```

Fig. 3.15 Showing the difference between preincrementing and postincrementing.

Pseudocode consists purely of characters, and therefore programmers may type pseudocode programs into the computer, edit them, and save them. Declarations of variables are not part of pseudocode. Pseudocode consists only of executable statements. Declarations are messages to the compiler telling it the attributes of variables and telling it to reserve space for variables.

- A selection structure is used to choose among alternative courses of action.
- The if selection structure performs an indicated action only when the condition is true.
- The if/else selection structure specifies separate actions to be performed when the condition is true and when the condition is false.
- A nested if/else selection structure can test for many different cases. If more than one test is valid, then only the statements after the first valid test will be executed.
- Whenever more than one statement is to be executed within an if statement, these statements must be enclosed in braces forming a compound statement or a block. A block can be placed anywhere a single statement can be placed. An empty statement indicating that no action is to be taken is indicated by placing a semicolon (;) where a statement would normally be.

Operators						Associativity
( )						left to right
++	--	(*type*)				right to left
*	/	%				left to right
+	-					left to right
<	<=	>	>=			left to right
==	!=					left to right
?:						right to left
=	+=	-=	*=	/=	%=	right to left

Fig. 3.16 Precedence of the operators encountered so far in the text.

- A repetition structure specifies that an action is repeated until some terminating condition occurs.
- The format for the `while` repetition structure is

      while (condition)
          statement

  The statement (or compound statement or block) contained in the `while` repetition structure constitutes the body of the loop.
- Some action specified within the body of a `while` must eventually cause the condition to become false. Otherwise, the loop will never terminate—a common programming error called an infinite loop.
- Counter-controlled looping uses a variable as a counter to determine when a loop should terminate.
- A total is a variable that accumulates the sum of a series of numbers. Totals should normally be initialized to zero before a program is run.
- A flowchart is a graphical representation of an algorithm. Flowcharts are drawn using certain special symbols such as ovals, diamonds, rectangles, circles, and others connected together by arrows called flowlines. Flowchart symbols indicate the steps to be performed; C-like code for each step is written inside the corresponding symbol. Flowlines indicate the order in which steps are to be performed.
- The oval symbol, also called the termination symbol, indicates the beginning and end of every algorithm.
- The rectangle symbol, also called the process symbol, indicates any type of calculation. Process symbols correspond to the steps that are normally performed by assignment statements in C.
- The parallelogram symbol, also called the input/output symbol, indicates that information is to be entered into the computer or that information is is to be output by the computer.

- The diamond symbol, also called the decision symbol, indicates that a decision is to be made. The decision symbol contains a condition that can be either true or false. Two flowlines emerge from it. One flowline indicates the direction to be taken when the condition is true; the other indicates the direction to be taken when the condition is false.

- Flowcharts help the programmer develop algorithms, particularly those requiring complex decision making.

- Flowcharts provide visual representations of algorithms.

- C provides various assignment operators that help abbreviate certain common types of assignment expressions. These operators are: +=, -=, *=, /=, and %=. In general, any statement of the form

  variable = variable operator expression;

  where `operator` is one of the binary operators +, -, *, /, or %, can be written in the form

  variable operator= expression;

- C provides the increment operator, ++, and the decrement operator, --, to increment or decrement a variable by 1. These operators can be prefixed or postfixed to a variable. If prefixed, the variable is incremented or decremented by 1 first, then used in its expression. If postfixed, the variable is used in its expression, then incremented or decremented by 1.

Terminology

algorithm
arrow symbol
assignment operators: +=, -=, *=, /=, and
   %=
block
body of a loop
calculation symbol
cast
cast operator
compound statement
control structure
counter
counter-controlled repetition
decision symbol
decrement operator (--)
diamond symbol
double selection
do/while repetition structure
dummy value
empty statement
"end of data entry"

end symbol
flag value
`float`
flowchart
flowcharting template
flowchart symbol
flowline
`goto`
`if/else` selection structure
`if` selection structure
increment operator (++)
infinite loop
initialization
initialization phase
input/output symbol
looping
nested `if/else` structure
order of steps
oval symbol
postdecrement operator
postincrement operator

precision
predecrement operator
preincrement operator
processing phase
process symbol
program flowchart
pseudocode
rectangle symbol
repetition
repetition structures
scope of a loop
selection
selection structures
semicolon (;)
sentinel value

sequence structure
signal value
single selection
steps
stepwise refinement
structured flowchart
structured programming
terminating condition
termination phase
termination symbol
top
top-down, stepwise refinement
total
transfer of control
while repetition structure

Common Programming Errors

3.1   Forgetting one or both of the braces that delimit a compound statement.

3.2   Not providing an action in the body of a **while** structure that eventually causes the condition in the **while** to become false. Otherwise, the loop will never terminate—a common error called an infinite loop.

3.3   Using floating point numbers in a manner that assumes they are represented precisely can lead to incorrect results. Floating point numbers are represented approximately by most computers. Therefore, calculations involving floating point numbers are often rounded incorrectly.

Good Programming Practices

3.1   Consistently applying responsible indentation conventions greatly improves program readability. We suggest a fixed-size tab of about 1/4 inch or three spaces per indent.

3.2   Pseudocode is often used to "think out" a program during the program design process. Then the pseudocode program is converted to C.

3.3   Indent the body of an **if/else** structure.

3.4   Type the beginning and ending braces of compound statements before typing the statements themselves. This prevents omitting one or both of the braces.

3.5   Initialize counters and totals.

3.6   In a sentinel-controlled loop the prompts should explicitly remind the user what the sentinel value is.

3.7   Do not compare floating point values for equality.

3.8   Unary operators should be appended to their operands with no intervening spaces.

Self-Review Exercises

3.1   Answer each of the following questions.
   a)   A procedure for solving a problem in terms of the steps to be executed and the order in which the steps should be executed is called an _____.
   b)   Specifying the order in which statements are to be executed by the computer is called _____.
   c)   All programs can be written in terms of three control structures: _____, _____, and _____.
   d)   The _____ is used to perform one action when a condition is true and another action when that condition is false.
   e)   Several statements grouped together in braces ({ and }) are called a _____.
   f)   The _____ specifies that a statement or group of statements is to be executed repeatedly until some terminating condition occurs.
   g)   Repetition of a set of instructions a specific number of times is called _____ repetition.
   h)   When it is not known in advance how many times a set of statements will be repeated, a _____ can be used to terminate the repetition.
   i)   A _____ is a graphical representation of an algorithm.
   j)   In a structured flowchart, a rectangle can be replaced by _____ or _____ in any order and as often as necessary.

3.2   Write four C statements that each add 1 to the integer variable **x**.

3.3   Write a *single* C statement to accomplish each of the following:
   a)   Assign the sum of **x** and **y** to **z** and increment the value of **x** by 1 after the calculation is performed.
   b)   Multiply the variable **product** by 2 using the ***=** operator.
   c)   Multiply the variable **product** by 2 using the **=** and ***** operators.
   d)   Test if the value of the variable **count** is greater than 10. If it is, print "**Count is greater than 10.**"
   e)   Decrement the variable **x** by 1 then subtract it from the variable **total**.
   f)   Add the variable **x** to the variable **total**, then decrement **x** by 1.
   g)   Calculate the remainder after **q** is divided by **divisor** and assign the result to **q**. Write this statement two different ways.
   h)   Print the value **123.4567** with a precision of **2** decimal positions. What value is displayed on the screen?
   i)   Print the floating point value **3.14159** with three digits to the right of the decimal point.

3.4   Write a C statement to accomplish each of the following tasks.
   a)   Declare variables **sum** and **x** to be of type **int**.
   b)   Initialize variable **x** to **1**.
   c)   Initialize variable **sum** to **0**.
   d)   Add variable **x** to variable **sum** and assign the result to variable **sum**.
   e)   Increment the variable **x** by **1**.
   f)   Print "**The sum is:** " followed by the value of variable **sum**.

3.5.   Combine the statements that you wrote in exercise 3.4 into a program that calculates the sum of the integers from 1 to 10. Use the while structure to loop through the calculation and increment statements. The loop should terminate when the value of **x** becomes 11.

3.6 Determine the values of each variable after the calculation is performed. Assume that all variables begin with the value 5.

a) `product *= x++;`
b) `result = ++x + x;`

3.7 Draw a single flowchart symbol that

a) Shows that an integer variable `x` is being input with `scanf`.
b) Shows that an integer variable `y` is being input with `scanf`.
c) Show that an integer variable `i` is initialized to `1`.
d) Shows that the integer value `power` is initialized to `1`.
e) Shows that the variable `power` is multiplied by `x` and the result is assigned to `power`.
f) Shows that the variable `y` is incremented by `1`.
g) Shows that `y` is being tested to see if it is less than or equal to `x`.
h) Shows that the integer value `power` is output with `printf`.

3.8 Draw a flowchart that uses the symbols in Exercise 3.7 for a program that calculates `x` raised to the `y` power. The flowchart should have a `while` repetition control structure.

3.9 Identify and correct the errors in each of the following:

```
a)  while (c <= 5) {
        product *= c;
        ++c;
b)  while (z >= 0)
        sum += z;
c)  if (x < .5)
        printf("x is less than .5\n");
```

Answers to Self-Review Exercises

3.1 a) Algorithm. b) Program control. c) Sequence, selection, repetition. d) `if/else` selection structure. e) Compound statement. f) `while` repetition structure. g) Counter-controlled repetition. h) Sentinel value. i) Flowchart. j) Two rectangles, any control structure.

3.2
```
x++;
++x;
x += 1;
x = x + 1;
```

3.3
```
a) z = x++ + y;
b) product *= 2;
c) product = product * 2;
d) if (count > 10)
       printf("Count is greater than 10.\n");
e) total -= --x;
f) total -= x--;
g) q %= divisor;
   q = q % divisor;
```

h) `printf("%.2f", 123.4567);`
   `123.46` is displayed.
i) `printf("%.3f\n", 3.14159);`

3.4 a) `int sum, x;`
    b) `x = 1;`
    c) `sum = 0;`
    d) `sum += x;`
    e) `++x;`
    f) `printf("The sum is: %d\n", sum);`

3.5
```
/* Calculate the sum of the integers from 1 to 10 */
#include <stdio.h>

main()
{
   int sum, x;

   x = 1;
   sum = 0;
   while (x <= 10) {
      sum += x;
      ++x;
   }

   printf("The sum is: %d\n", sum);
}
```

3.6 a) `product = 25, x = 6;`
    b) `result = 12, x = 6;`

3.7

a)
```
scanf("%d",
   &x);
```

b)
```
scanf("%d",
   &y);
```

c)
```
i = 1;
```

d)
```
product = 1;
```

e)
```
power *= x;
```

f)
```
y++;
```

g)
```
y <= x
```

h)
```
printf("%d",
   power);
```

3.8

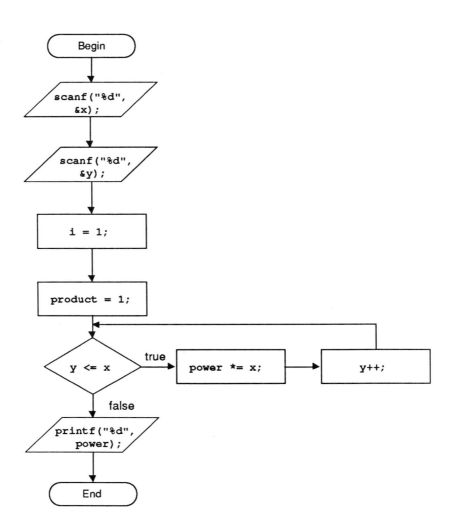

3.9 a) Error: Missing the closing right brace of the **while** body.
Correction: Add closing right brace after the statement **++c;**.
b) Error: No action to cause the loop continuation condition to become false.
Correction: Add the statement **++z;** or postdecrement the variable **z** in the statement in the body of the **while** with the statement **sum += z++;**.
c) Error: Assuming the computer represents floating point numbers precisely.
Correction: Process your values in such a way that integers can be used when precise calculations are required.

Exercises

3.10 Fill in the blanks in each of the following:

a) The solution to any problem involves performing a series of steps in a specific _____.

b) A synonym for procedure is _____.

c) A variable that accumulates the sum of several numbers is a _____.

d) The process of setting certain variables to specific values at the beginning of a program is called _____.

e) A special value used to indicate "end of data entry" is called a _____, a _____, a _____, or a _____ value.

f) A _____ is a graphical representation of an algorithm.

g) In a flowchart, the order in which the steps should be performed is indicated by _____ symbols.

h) A flowchart that uses notations similar to those used in actual programs is called a _____ flowchart.

i) The termination symbol is used to indicate the _____ and _____ of every algorithm.

j) Rectangle symbols correspond to steps that are normally performed by _____ statements in C.

k) The _____ symbol indicates that input or output is to occur.

l) The item written inside a decision symbol is called a _____.

3.11 Draw a single flowchart symbol that indicates each of the following:

a) Display the message `"Enter two numbers"`.

b   Assign the sum of variables `x`, `y`, and `z` to variable `p`.

c) The following condition is to be tested in an `if/else` selection structure: The current value of variable `m` is greater than twice the current value of variable `v`.

d) Obtain values for variables `s`, `r`, and `t` from the keyboard.

e) An algorithm is to terminate.

3.12 For each of the following, formulate the algorithm as a series of steps to be performed in a specific order:

a) Obtain two numbers from the keyboard, compute the sum of the numbers, and display the result.

b) Obtain two numbers from the keyboard, and determine and display which (if either) is the larger of the two numbers.

c) Obtain a series of positive numbers from the keyboard, and determine and display the sum of the numbers. Assume that the user types the sentinel value `-1` to indicate "end of data entry."

3.13 State which of the following are true and which are false. If a statement is false explain why.

a) Experience has shown that the most difficult part of solving a problem on a computer is producing a working C program.

b) A sentinel value must be a value that cannot be confused with a legitimate data value.

c) Flowlines indicate the steps to be performed.

d) Conditions written inside decision symbols always contain arithmetic operators (i.e., `+`, `-`, `*`, `/`, and `%`).

e)   The program flowchart uses C-like notation for variables and arithmetic calcu-
     lations.

f)   In top-down, stepwise refinement, each refinement is a complete representation
     of the algorithm.

For problems 3.14 to 3.18, perform each of these steps:
1.   Read the problem statement.
2.   Formulate the algorithm using pseudocode and top-down, stepwise refine-
     ment.
3.   Draw a program flowchart.
4.   Write a C program.
5.   Test, debug, and execute the C program.

3.14   Because of the high price of gasoline, drivers are concerned with the mileage obtained by their automobiles. One driver has kept track of several tankfuls of gasoline by
recording miles driven and gallons used for each tankful. Develop a C program that will
input the miles driven and gallons used for each tankful. The program should calculate and
display the miles per gallon obtained for each tankful. After processing all input information, the program should calculate and print the combined miles per gallon obtained for all
tankfuls.

3.15   Develop a C program that will determine if a department store customer has exceeded the credit limit on a charge account. For each customer, the following facts are
available:
1.   Account number
2.   Balance at the beginning of the month
3.   Total of all items charged by this customer this month
4.   Total of all credits applied to this customer's account this month
5.   Allowed credit limit

   The program should input each of these facts, calculate the new balance (= beginning balance + charges - credits), and determine if the new balance exceeds the customer's
credit limit. For those customers whose credit limit is exceeded, the program should display
the customer's account number, credit limit, new balance, and the message "Credit limit exceeded."

3.16   One large chemical company pays its salespeople on a commission basis. The salespeople receive $200 per week plus 9 percent of their gross sales for that week. For example,
a salesperson who sells $5000 worth of chemicals in a week receives $200 plus 9 percent of
$5000, or a total of $650. Develop a C program that will input each salesperson's gross sales
for last week and will calculate and display that salesperson's earnings. Process one salesperson's figures at a time.

3.17   The simple interest i on a loan of p dollars at a rate of r percent for a period of t
days is calculated by the formula

```
i = p * r * t / 365
```

   The preceding formula assumes that the rate r is the annual interest rate, and therefore includes the division by 365 (days). Develop a C program that will input p, r, and t
for several loans, and will calculate and display the simple interest for each loan, using the
preceding formula.

3.18   Develop a C program that will determine the gross pay for each of several employees. The company pays "straight-time" for the first 40 hours worked by each employee and pays "time-and-a-half" for all hours worked in excess of 40 hours. You are given a list of the employees of the company, the number of hours each employee worked last week, and the hourly rate of each employee. Your program should input this information for each employee, and should determine and display the employee's gross pay.

3.19   Write a C program that demonstrates the difference between predecrementing and postdecrementing using the decrement operator $--$.

3.20   Write a C program that utilizes looping to print the numbers from 1 to 10 side-by-side on the same line with 3 spaces between each number.

3.21   Write a C program that utilizes looping to print the following table of values:

N	10 * N	100 * N	1000 * N
1	10	100	1000
2	20	200	2000
3	30	300	3000
4	40	400	4000
5	50	500	5000
6	60	600	6000
7	70	700	7000
8	80	800	8000
9	90	900	9000
10	100	1000	10000

The tab character, \t, may be used in the `printf` statement to separate the columns with tabs.

3.22   Write a C program that utilizes looping to produce the following table of values:

A	A + 2	A + 4	A + 6
3	5	7	9
6	8	10	12
9	11	13	15
12	14	16	18
15	17	19	21

3.23   The process of finding the largest number in a group of numbers is used frequently in computer applications. For example, a program that determines the winner of a sales contest would input the number of units sold by each salesperson. The salesperson who sells the most units wins the contest. Write a C program that inputs a series of 10 numbers, and determines and prints the largest of the numbers. *Hint:* Your program should use three variables as follows:

`counter`:   A counter to count to 10 (i.e., to keep track of how many numbers have been input, and to determine when all 10 numbers have been processed).

`number`:   The current number input to the program.

`largest`:   The largest number found so far.

Using these variables, your program should then operate as follows:

Step 1:   Input the first number directly into the variable `largest`. (*Note:* This makes sense, because after you have looked at only the first number, it is perfectly reasonable to say that this is the "largest number found so far.")

Step 2: Set `counter` to `2` (to indicate that you are now going to look at the second number).

Step 3: While `counter` is less than or equal to `10`, input a number into the variable `number`.

Step 4: Compare `number` to `largest` to determine if `number` is larger than `largest`. If it is, replace the value of `largest` with the value of number (i.e., use the C statement `largest = number;`).

Step 5: Add one to `counter`.

Step 6: If `counter` is now `10` (i.e., all 10 numbers have been processed) move on to *Step 7*, otherwise, go back to *Step 3*.

Step 7: At this point, the value in `largest` is the largest of the 10 numbers. Print this value, preceded by the literal `"Largest is."`

Step 8: End of program.

3.24 Using an approach similar to problem 3.23, find the *two* largest values of the 10 numbers input in one pass.

3.25 Modify the program in Fig. 3.12 to validate its inputs. On any input, if the value entered is other than 1 or 2, keep looping until the user enters a correct value.

4

Program Control

Objectives

- To be able to use repetition structures.
- To understand counter-controlled repetition and sentinel-controlled repetition.
- To understand multiple selection using the `switch` selection structure.
- To be able to use the logical operators in C.

Who can control his fate?

William Shakespeare
Othello

The used key is always bright.

Benjamin Franklin

Man is a tool-making animal.

Benjamin Franklin

Intelligence ... is the faculty of making artificial objects,
especially tools to make tools.

Henry Bergson

Outline

4.1 Introduction

At this point , the reader should be comfortable with the process of writing simple but complete C programs. In this chapter, repetition is considered in greater detail, and additional control structures that facilitate repetition are presented. The switch selection structure is introduced. The chapter discusses logical operators used for combining conditions, and concludes with a summary of structured programming.

4.2 The Essentials of Repetition

Most programs involve repetition or *looping*. A *loop* is a group of instructions the computer executes repeatedly until some *terminating condition* is satisfied. We have discussed two means of repetition:

1. Counter-controlled repetition
2. Sentinel-controlled repetition

Counter-controlled repetition is sometimes called *definite repetition* because we know in advance exactly how many times the loop will be executed. Sentinel-controlled repetition is sometimes called *indefinite-repetition* because it is not known in advance how many times the loop will be executed.

In counter-controlled repetition, a *control variable* is used to count the number of repetitions. The control variable is incremented (usually by 1) each time the group of instructions is performed. When the value of the control variable indicates that the correct number of repetitions has been performed, the loop terminates and the computer continues executing with the statement after the repetition structure.

Sentinel values are used to control repetition when:

1. The precise number of repetitions is not known in advance.
2. The loop includes statements that obtain data each time the loop is performed.

The sentinel value indicates "end of data." The sentinel is entered after all regular data items have been supplied to the program. Sentinels must be unique from regular data items.

4.3 Counter-Controlled Repetition

Counter-controlled repetition requires:

1. The *name* of the control variable (or loop counter).
2. The *initial value* of the control variable.
3. The *increment* by which the control variable is modified each time through the loop.
4. The condition that tests for the *final value* of the control variable; i.e., whether looping should continue.

Consider the simple program shown in Fig. 4.1, which prints the numbers from 1 to 10. The declaration

```
int counter = 1;
```

names the control variable (`counter`), declares it to be an integer, reserves space for it, and sets it to an *initial value* of 1. This declaration is not an executable statement.

The declaration and initialization of `counter` could also have been accomplished with the statements

```
int counter;

counter = 1;
```

The declaration is not executable, but the assignment is. We use both methods of initializing variables.

The statement

```
counter++;
```

increments the loop counter by 1 each time the loop is performed. The loop continuation condition in the `while` structure tests if the value of the control variable is less than or equal to 10 (the last value for which the condition is true). Note here the body of this `while` is performed even when the control variable is 10. The loop terminates when the control variable exceeds 10 (i.e., `counter` becomes 11).

```
/* Counter-controlled repetition */
#include <stdio.h>

main()
{
    int counter = 1;

    while (counter <= 10) {
        printf ("%d\n", counter);
        counter++;
    }
}
```

```
1
2
3
4
5
6
7
8
9
10
```

Fig. 4.1 Counter-controlled repetition.

C programmers would normally make the program in Fig. 4.1 more concise by initializing `counter` to 0 and by replacing the `while` structure with

```
while (++counter <= 10)
    printf ("%d\n", counter);
```

This code saves a statement because the incrementing is done directly in the `while` condition before the condition is tested. Also, this code eliminates the braces around the body of the `while` because the `while` now contains only one statement. Coding in such a condensed fashion takes some practice.

CPE 4.1
Since floating point values may be approximate, controlling counting loops with floating point variables may result in imprecise counter values and inaccurate tests for termination.

GPP 4.1
Indent the statements in the body of each control structure.

GPP 4.2
Put a blank line before and after each major control structure to make it stand out in the program.

GPP 4.3

Avoid becoming too deeply nested. This makes the program difficult to understand. As a general rule, no unit should have more than three levels of indentation.

GPP 4.4

The combination of vertical spacing before and after control structures and indentation of the bodies of control structures within the control structure headers gives programs a two-dimensional, flowchart-like appearance that greatly improves program readability.

GPP 4.5

Control counting loops with integer values.

4.4 The For Repetition Structure

Most computer languages provide special statements for implementing repetition. In C, the `for` repetition structure handles all the details of counter-controlled repetition automatically.

To illustrate the power of `for`, let us rewrite the program of Fig. 4.1. The result is shown in Fig. 4.2.

The program operates as follows. The `for` structure is entered, and the control variable `counter` is initialized to 1. Then, the loop continuation condition `counter <= 10` is checked. Since the initial value of `counter` is 1, the condition is satisfied, so the `printf` statement prints the value of `counter`, namely 1. The `counter` control variable is then incremented by the expression `counter++`, and the loop begins again with the loop continuation test. Since the control variable is now equal to 2, the final value is not exceeded, so the program performs the `printf` statement again. This process continues until the control variable `counter` is incremented to its final value of 11—this causes the loop continuation test to fail and the loop terminates. The program continues by performing the first statement after the `for` structure (in this case the end of the program is reached).

Fig. 4.3 takes a closer look at the `for` structure from Fig. 4.2.

```
/* Counter-controlled repetition with the for structure */
#include <stdio.h>

main()
{
   int counter;

   for (counter = 1; counter <= 10; counter++)
      printf("%d\n", counter);
}
```

Fig. 4.2 Counter-controlled repetition with the `for` structure.

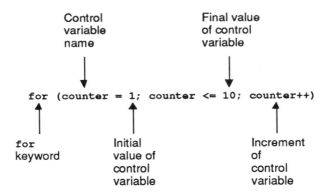

Fig. 4.3 Components of a typical `for` header.

Notice that in a sense the `for` structure "does it all"—it specifies each of the items needed for counter-controlled repetition with a control variable. If there is more than one statement in the body, braces are required to define the body of the loop.

CPE 4.2

Using the incorrect relational operator in the condition of a `while` or `for` structure causes off-by-one errors. An off-by-one error caused when the control variable in a repetition structure is one increment less than or one increment greater than the desired final value.

GPP 4.6

Using the final value in the condition of a `while` or `for` structure, will make off-by-one errors easier to spot during program debugging. For a loop used to print the values 1 to 10, for example, the condition should be `counter <= 10` *rather than* `counter < 11`*.*

The general format of the `for` structure is

```
for (expression1; expression2; expression3)
    statement
```

where *expression1* initializes the loop's control variable, *expression2* is the repetition-continuation condition, and *expression3* increments the control variable. In most cases the `for` structure can be represented with the `while` structure as follows:

```
expression1;
while (expression2) {
    statement
    expression3;
}
```

There is an exception to this rule which we will discuss in Section 4.9.

Often, *expression1* and *expression3* are comma-separated lists of expressions. The *comma operator* guarantees lists of expressions will be evaluated from left to right. The value of the comma expression has the value and type of the rightmost operand in the expression. The comma operator is most often used in a `for` structure. Its primary use is to enable the programmer to use multiple initialization and/or multiple increment expressions. For example, there may be two control variables in a single `for` structure that must be initialized and incremented. The initialization and increment expressions are separated by commas.

GPP 4.7

Only place expressions involving the control variables in the initialization and increment sections of a `for` *structure.*

The three expressions in the `for` structure are optional. If *expression2* is omitted, C assumes that the condition is always true, thus creating an infinite loop. One might omit *expression1* if the control variable is initialized elsewhere in the program, and *expression3* might be omitted if the increment is calculated by statements within the `for` structure. The incrementing expression in the `for` structure acts like a stand-alone C statement at the end of the body of the `for`. Therefore, the expressions

```
++counter
counter++
counter = counter + 1
counter += 1
```

are all equivalent in the incrementing portion of the `for` structure. Many C programmers prefer the form `counter++` because the incrementing does occur after the loop body is executed. So, the post incrementing form seems more natural. The two semicolons in the `for` structure may not be omitted.

4.5 The For Structure: Notes and Observations

1. The initial value, the condition, and the increment can all be arithmetic expressions. If we assume that $x = 2$ and $y = 10$, the statement

    ```
    for (j = x; j <= 4 * x * y; j += y / x)
    ```

    is equivalent to the statement

    ```
    for (j = 2; j <= 80; j += 5)
    ```

2. The increment may be negative (in which case the loop actually counts "backwards").

3. If the condition supplied in the condition section is initially false, the body portion of the loop is not performed. Instead, the computer proceeds to the statement following the `for` structure.

4. The control variable is frequently printed or used in calculations in the body of a loop, but it does not need to be. It is perfectly acceptable to use the control variable for controlling looping while never mentioning it within the body of the loop.

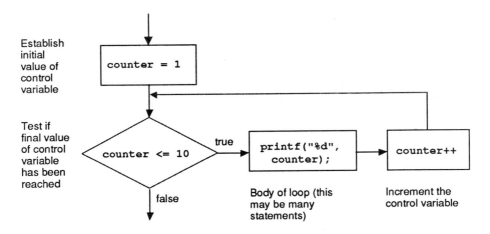

Fig. 4.4 Flowcharting the `for` structure.

5. The `for` structure is flowcharted in much the same manner as the `while` structure discussed in Chapter 3 (see Fig. 4.4).

```
for (counter = 1; counter <= 10; counter++)
    printf("%d", counter);
```

GPP 4.8
_____
Although the value of the control variable can be changed in the body of a loop, do not change it.

4.6 Examples Using the For Structure

The following examples show several ways to vary the control variable in a `for` structure.

a) Vary the control variable from 1 to 100 in increments of 1.

```
for (i = 1; i <= 100; i++)
```

b) Vary the control variable from 100 to 1 in increments of −1 (i.e., decrements of 1).

```
for (i = 100; i >= 1; i--)
```

c) Vary the control variable from 7 to 77 in steps of 7.

```
for (i = 7; i <= 77; i += 7)
```

d) Vary the control variable from 20 to 2 in steps of −2.

```
for (i = 20; i >= 2; i -= 2)
```

e) Vary the control variable over the following sequence of values: 2, 5, 8, 11, 14, 17, 20.

```
for (j = 2; j <= 20; j += 3)
```

f) Vary the control variable over the following sequence of values: $99, 88, 77,$
$66, 55, 44, 33, 22, 11, 0.$

```
for (j = 99; j >= 0; j -= 11)
```

The next two examples provide simple applications of the `for` structure. The program of Fig. 4.5 uses the `for` structure to sum all the even integers from 2 to 100.

Note that the body of the `for` structure in Fig. 4.5 could actually be merged into the rightmost portion of the `for` header by using the comma operator as follows:

```
for (number = 2; number <= 100; sum += number, number += 2)
   ;
```

GPP 4.9

*Although statements preceding a **for** and statements in the body of a **for** can often be merged into the **for** header, avoid doing so because it makes the program more cryptic and difficult to read.*

GPP 4.10

Limit the size of control structure headers to a single line if possible.

The next example computes compound interest using the `for` structure. Consider the following problem statement:

A person invests $1000.00 in a savings account yielding 5 percent interest. Assuming that all interest is left on deposit in the account, calculate and print the amount of money in the account at the end of each year for 10 years. Use the following formula for determining these amounts:

$$a = p(1 + r)^n$$

where

p *is the original amount invested (i.e., the principal)*
r *is the annual interest rate*
n *is the number of years*
a *is the amount on deposit at the end of the nth year.*

```
/* Summation with for */
include <stdio.h>

main()
{
   int sum = 0, number;

   for (number = 2; number <= 100; number += 2)
      sum += number;

   printf("Sum is %d", sum);
}
```

```
Sum is 2550
```

Fig. 4.5 Summation with `for`.

This problem involves a loop that performs the indicated calculation for each of the 10 years the money remains on deposit. The solution is shown in Fig. 4.6.

A `for` structure executes the body of the loop 10 times, varying a control variable from 1 to 10 in increments of 1. Remember that C does not include an exponentiation operator. We can use the Standard Library function `pow` to perform exponentiation. The function `pow(x, y)` calculates the value of x raised to the yth power. It takes two arguments of type `double` and returns a `double` value. The type `double` is a floating point type much like `float`, but a variable of type `double` can store a value of much greater magnitude with greater precision than `float`. Note that the header file `math.h` should be included whenever a math function such as `pow` is used. Actually, this program would malfunction without the inclusion of `math.h`. Function `pow` requires two `double` arguments. Note that `year` is an integer. The `math.h` file includes information that tells the compiler to convert `year` to a `double` representation before calling the function. This information is contained in something called `pow`'s *function prototype*. Function prototypes are an important new feature of ANSI C and are explained in Chapter 5. We will provide a more detailed explanation of the `pow` function and other math library functions in Chapter 5.

```
/* Calculating compound interest */
#include <stdio.h>
#include <math.h>

main()
{
    int year;
    double amount, principal = 1000.0, rate = .05;

    printf("%s%21s\n", "Year", "Amount on deposit");
    for (year = 1; year <= 10; year++) {
        amount = principal * pow(1 + rate, year);
        printf("%4d%21.2f\n", year, amount);
    }
}
```

```
Year      Amount on deposit
 1                1050.00
 2                1102.50
 3                1157.62
 4                1215.51
 5                1276.28
 6                1340.10
 7                1407.10
 8                1477.46
 9                1551.33
10                1628.89
```

Fig. 4.6 Compound interest with `for`.

Notice that we have declared the variables `amount`, `principal`, and `rate` to be of type `double`. We have done this for simplicity because we are dealing with fractional parts of dollars.

GPP 4.11

Do not use variables of type `float` or `double` to perform monetary calculations. The impreciseness of floating point numbers can cause rounding errors that will result in incorrect monetary values. In the exercises we explore the use of integers to perform monetary calculations.

The conversion specifier `%10.2f` is used to print the value of the variable `amount` in the program. The `10` in the conversion specifier denotes the *field width* in which the value will be printed. The field width `10` specifies that the value printed will appear in a field `10` characters wide. The `2` specifies the precision. If the number of characters displayed is less than the field width, then the value will automatically be right justified in the field. This is particularly useful for aligning floating point values with the same precision. To left justify a value in a field, place a – (minus sign) between the `%` and the field width. Note that the minus sign may also be used to left justify integers (such as in `%-6d`) and character strings (such as in `%-8s`). We will discuss `printf`'s powerful formatting capabilities in more detail in Chapter 9.

4.7 The Switch Selection Structure

The `if` statement introduced in Chapter 2 is the primary decision-making structure in C. Occasionally, an algorithm will contain a series of decisions in which a variable or expression is tested for each of the constant integral values it may assume, and different actions are taken. C provides the `switch` selection structure to handle such *multiple-selection decision making*.

The `switch` structure consists of a series of `cases`, and an optional `default` case. The program in Fig. 4.7 uses `switch` to count the number of each different letter grade that students earned on an exam.

In the program, the user enters letter grades for a class. Inside the `while` header,

```
while ((grade = getchar()) != EOF)
```

the assignment `(grade = getchar())` is executed first because it is surrounded by parentheses. The `getchar` function (from the standard input/output library) reads a single character from the keyboard and stores the character in the integer variable `grade`. Characters are normally stored in the data type `char`. However, an important feature of C is that characters can be stored in any integer data type because they are represented as 1 byte integers in the computer. Thus, we can treat a character as either an integer or a character depending on its use. For example, the statement

```
printf("The character (%c) has the value %d.\n", 'a', 'a');
```

uses the conversion specifiers `%c` and `%d` to print the character a and its integer value respectively. The result is

```
/* Counting letter grades */
#include <stdio.h>

main()
{
    int grade;
    int acount = 0, bcount = 0, ccount = 0,
        dcount = 0, fcount = 0;

    printf("Enter the letter grades.\n");
    printf("Enter the EOF character to end input.\n");
    while ((grade = getchar()) != EOF) {

        switch (grade) {
            case 'A': case 'a':
                ++acount;
                break;
            case 'B': case 'b':
                ++bcount;
                break;
            case 'C': case 'c':
                ++ccount;
                break;
            case 'D': case 'd':
                ++dcount;
                break;
            case 'F': case 'f':
                ++fcount;
                break;
            case '\n': case' ':
                break;
            default:
                printf("Incorrect letter grade entered.");
                printf(" Enter a new grade.\n");
                break;
        }
    }

    printf("\nTotals for each letter grade were:\n");
    printf("A: %d\n", acount);
    printf("B: %d\n", bcount);
    printf("C: %d\n", ccount);
    printf("D: %d\n", dcount);
    printf("F: %d\n", fcount);
}
```

Fig. 4.7 An example using `switch` (part 1 of 2).

```
The character (a) has the value 97.
```

The conversion specifier `%c` is also used to read characters with `scanf`. The integer 97 is the character's numerical representation in the computer. Most computers today use the ASCII (American Standard Code for Information Exchange) character set in which 97 represents the lower case letter "a." A list of ASCII values for all characters is presented in Appendix E.

```
Enter the letter grades.
Enter the EOF character to end input.
A
B
C
C
A
D
F
C
E
Incorrect letter grade entered. Enter a new grade.
D
A
B

Totals for each letter grade were:
A: 3
B: 2
C: 3
D: 2
F: 1
```

Fig. 4.7 An example using `switch` (part 2 of 2).

Assignment statements as a whole actually have a value. This is precisely the value that is assigned to the variable on the left side of the =. The value of the assignment grade = getchar() is the character that is returned by getchar and assigned to the variable grade. The fact that assignment statements have values can be useful for initializing several variables to the same value. For example,

        a = b = c = 0;

first evaluates the assignment c = 0. The variable b is assigned the value of the assignment c = 0. Then, the variable a is assigned the value of the assignment b = (c = 0). In the program, the value of the assignement grade = getchar() is compared with the *end-of-file indicator* EOF. We use EOF as the sentinel value. The end-of-file indicator is a symbolic integer constant defined in the <stdio.h> header file. If the value assigned to grade is equal to EOF, the program terminates. We have chosen to represent characters in this program as ints because the EOF indicator is an integer value.

The keystroke combinations for entering the EOF indicator are system dependent. On UNIX systems and many others, the EOF indicator is entered by typing the sequence

        <return> <ctrl-d>

On other systems such as Digital Equipment Corporation's VAX, the EOF indicator can be entered by typing

        <ctrl-z>

The user enters grades at the keyboard. When the return (or enter) key is pressed, the characters are read by the `getchar` function one character at a time. If the character entered is not equal to the `EOF` indicator, the `switch` structure is entered. The keyword `switch` is followed by the variable name `grade` in parentheses. This is called the *controlling expression*. The value of this expression is compared with each of the `case` labels. Assume the user has entered the letter C as a grade. C is compared to each `case` in the `switch`. If a match occurs (`case 'C':`), the statements for that `case` are executed. In the case of the letter C, `ccount` is incremented by 1, and the `switch` structure is exited immediately with the `break` statement. The `break` statement causes program control to continue with the first statement after the `switch` structure. The `break` statement is used because the `case`s in a `switch` statement run together. If `break` is not used anywhere in a `switch` structure, then each time a match occurs in the structure, the statements for all the remaining `case`s will be executed. This feature is rarely useful, although we will use it to our advantage in Chapter 8 when we develop a program that prints the iterative song "The Twelve Days of Christmas." If no match occurs, the `default` case is executed and an error message is printed. The general `switch` multiple-selection structure is flowcharted in Fig. 4.8.

CPE 4.3
---
*Forgetting a **break** statement when one is needed in a **switch** structure.*

GPP 4.12
---
*Provide a **default** case in **switch** statements. As is the case with single selection **if** structures, cases not explicitly tested are ignored. The **default** case helps prevent this by focusing the programmer on the need to process exceptional conditions. There will be cases in which no default processing is needed.*

GPP 4.13
---
*The **break** statement in the **default** case is not required, but some programmers include it for clarity and symmetry with other **case**s.*

In the `switch` structure, the lines

```
case '\n': case ' ':
break;
```

cause the program to skip newline and blank characters without any effect. Reading characters one at a time can cause some problems. To read the characters, they must be sent to the computer by pressing the *return* key on the keyboard. This causes the newline character to be placed in the input as well as the character we wish to process. Often, this newline character must be processed in order to make the program work correctly. By including the preceding cases in our `switch` structure, we prevent the error message in the `default` case from being printed each time a newline or space is encountered in the input.

CPE 4.4

Not processing extra newline characters in the input when processing characters one at a time.

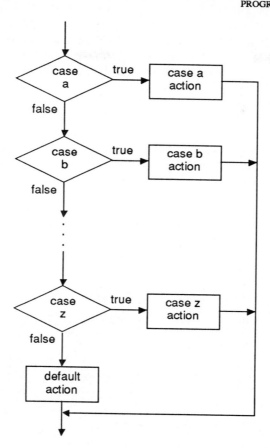

Fig. 4.8 The switch multiple-selection structure.

<u>*GPP 4.14*</u>

Remember to provide processing capabilities for extra newline characters in the input when processing characters one at a time.

Many cases can execute the same statements by listing the cases before the statements as shown in Fig 4.7 for the newline and blank characters and for the other cases as well (the same statements are executed for both the uppercase and lowercase versions of each letter).

When using the switch structure, remember that it can only be used for testing *constant integral expressions*. Constant integral expressions are any combination of character constants and integer constants that evaluates to a constant integer value. Character constants are represented as the specific character in single quotes such as 'A'. Characters must be enclosed within single quotes to be recognized as character constants. Integer constants are simply integer values. In our example we have used character constants. As we stated, characters are actually small integer values.

C provides several different integer sizes which are usually dependent on the computer hardware. To have portable languages like C, there must be flexibility in the size of the data types. Different applications may need many different size integers. In addition to `int`, C provides the integral types `short` (an abbreviation of `short int`) and `long` (an abbreviation of `long int`) for appropriate situations. For example, in performance-oriented situations where memory is at a premium or speed is necessary, it may be desirable to use smaller integer sizes if possible. A `short` integer is stored in 2 bytes of memory and can have values in the range ±32767. For the vast majority of integer calculations, `long` integers (stored in at least 4 bytes of memory) with values in the range ±2147483647 are sufficient. On most systems, `int`s are equivalent either to `short` or to `long`. Since `int`s vary in size between systems, use `long` integers if you expect to process integers outside the range ±32767 and you would like to be able to run the program on several different computer systems. The data type `char` can be used to represent integers in the range ±127 or any of the characters in the computer's character set.

4.8 The Do/While Repetition Structure

The `do/while` repetition structure is similar to the `while` structure. In the `while` structure, the loop continuation condition is tested at the beginning of the loop before the body of the loop is performed. The `do/while` structure tests the loop continuation condition at the end of the loop after the body of the loop is performed. Because the condition is tested at the end of the loop, the statements in the loop will be executed at least once. When a `do/while` terminates, execution continues with the statement after the `while` clause. Note that it is not necessary to use braces in the `do/while` structure if there is only one statement in the body. However, the braces are usually included to avoid confusion between the `while` and `do/while` structures. For example,

        while (*condition*)

is normally regarded as the header to a `while` structure. A `do/while` with no braces around the single statement body appears as

        do
            statement
        while (*condition*) ;

which can be confusing when included in a program. The `while` (*condition*) ; may be regarded as a `while` structure containing an empty statement. Thus, the `do/while` with one statement is written

        do {
            statement
        } **while** (*condition*) ;

_____

GPP 4.15
_____

Always include braces in a do/while structure even if they are not necessary. This will help eliminate ambiguity between the do/while structure containing one statement and the while structure.

CPE 4.5

Infinite loops are caused when the repetition continuation condition in a **while**, **for**, *or* **do/while** *structure never becomes false. To prevent this, make sure there is not a semicolon immediately after the first line of a* **while** *or* **for** *structure. In a counter-controlled loop, make sure the control variable is incremented within the body of the loop. In a sentinel-controlled loop, make sure the sentinel value is eventually input.*

The program in Fig. 4.9 uses a do/while structure to print the numbers from 1 to 10. Note that the control variable counter is pre-incremented in the condition of this do/while repetition structure. The do/while structure is flowcharted in Fig. 4.10.

```
/* Using the do/while repetition structure */
#include <stdio.h>

main()
{
   int counter = 1;

   do {
      printf("%d  ", counter);
   } while (++counter <= 10);
}
```

```
1  2  3  4  5  6  7  8  9  10
```

Fig. 4.9 Using the do/while structure.

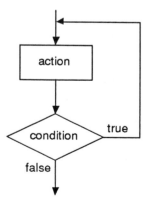

Fig. 4.10 The do/while repetition structure.

4.9 The Break and Continue Statements

The break and continue statements are used to alter the flow of control. The break statement, when executed in the while, for, do/while, or switch structures, causes immediate exit from the structure in which it is contained. Program execution continues with the first statement after the structure. Common uses of the break statement are to escape from an infinite loop, or to skip the remainder of a switch structure as shown in Fig. 4.7. Figure 4.11 demonstrates the break statement in a for repetition structure.

The continue statement, when executed in the while, for, or do/while structures, skips the remaining statements in the body of the structure, and performs the next iteration of the loop. In while and do/while structures, the repetition-continuation test is evaluated immediately after the continue statement is executed. In the for structure, the increment expression is executed, then the repetition-continuation test is evaluated. Earlier in this chapter we stated that the while structure could be used in most cases to represent the for structure. The one exception occurs when the increment expression in the while structure follows the continue statement. In this case, the increment is not executed before the repetition-continuation condition is tested, and the while does not execute in the same manner as the for. Figure 4.12 uses the continue statement in a for structure to skip the printf statement in the structure and begin the next iteration of the loop.

The break and continue statements are usually not required in C. The one exception to this is the use of break with the switch structure.

```
/* Using the break statement in a for structure */
#include <stdio.h>

main()
{
   int x;

   for (x = 1; x <= 10; x++) {

      if (x == 5)
         break;

      printf("%d ", x);
   }

   printf("\nBroke out of loop at x = %d\n", x);
}
```

```
1 2 3 4
Broke out of loop at x = 5
```

Fig. 4.11 Using the break statement in a for structure.

```
/* Using the continue statement in a for structure */
#include <stdio.h>

main()
{
   int x;

   for (x = 1; x <= 10; x++) {
      if (x == 5)
         continue;
      printf("%d ", x);
   }

   printf("\nUsed continue to skip printing the value 5\n");
}
```

```
1 2 3 4 6 7 8 9 10
Used continue to skip printing the value 5
```

Fig. 4.12 Using the `continue` statement in a `for` structure.

4.10 Logical Operators

So far we have studied only *simple conditions* such as `counter <= 10`, `total > 1000`, and `number != sentinelvalue`. We have expressed these conditions in terms of the relational operators `>`, `<`, `>=`, and `<=`, and the equality operators `==`, and `!=`. Each decision tested precisely one condition. If we wanted to test multiple conditions in the process of making a decision, we had to perform these tests in separate statements or in nested `if` structures.

C provides a set of *logical operators* that may be used to form more complex conditions by combining simple conditions. The logical operators are `&&` *(logical AND)*, `||` *(logical OR)*, and `!` *(logical negation)*.

Suppose we wish to ensure at some point in a program that two conditions are *both* true before we choose a certain path of execution. In this case we can use the logical AND operator as follows:

```
if (sex == 1 && age >= 65)
   ++seniorfemales;
```

This `if` statement contains two simple conditions. The condition `sex == 1` is evaluated to determine if the person is a female. The condition `age >= 65` is evaluated to determine if the person is a senior citizen. The two simple conditions are evaluated first because the precedences of `==` and `>=` are both higher than `&&`. The `if` statement then considers the combined condition

```
sex == 1 && age >= 65
```

This condition is true if and only if both of the simple conditions are true. Finally, if this combined condition is indeed true, then the count of `seniorfemales` is incremented by `1`. If either or both of the simple conditions are false (zero), then the program skips the incrementing, and proceeds to the statement following the `if`.

The following table summarizes the `&&` operator. It shows all four possible combinations of zero (false) and nonzero (true) values for expression1 and expression2. Such tables are often called *truth tables*. The reader should remember that C sets a true value to 1, but accepts any nonzero value in an expression as true. All expressions that include the logical operators evaluate to 0 or 1.

expression1	expression2	expression1 `&&` expression2
0	0	0
0	nonzero	0
nonzero	0	0
nonzero	nonzero	1

Now let us consider the logical OR operator. Suppose we wish to ensure at some point in a program that either *or* both of two conditions are true before we choose a certain path of execution. In this case we use the logical OR operator as in the following program segment:

```
if (semesteraverage >= 90 || finalexam >= 90)
    printf("Student grade is A\n");
```

This statement also contains two simple conditions. The variable `semesteraverage >= 90` is evaluated to determine if the student deserves an "A" in the course because of a solid performance throughout the semester. The condition `finalexam >= 90` is evaluated to determine if the student deserves an "A" in the course because of an outstanding performance on the final examination. The `if` statement then considers the combined condition

```
semesteraverage >= 90 || finalexam >= 90
```

and awards the student an "A" if either or both of the simple conditions are true. Note that the message "`Student grade is A`" is not printed only when both of the simple conditions are false. The following is a truth table for the logical OR operator (`||`).

expression1	expression2	expression1 `||` expression2
0	0	0
0	nonzero	1
nonzero	0	1
nonzero	nonzero	1

The `&&` operator has a higher precedence than `||`. Both operators associate from left to right. An expression containing `&&` or `||` operators is evaluated only until truth or falsehood is known. So, in the preceding `if` statement, evaluation of the condition

```
sex == 1 && age >= 65
```

will stop if sex is not equal to 1 (i.e., the entire expression is false), and continue if sex is equal to 1 (i.e., the entire expression could still be true if age >= 65).

C provides the logical negation operator (!) to enable a programmer to "reverse" the meaning of a condition. Unlike the logical AND and logical OR operators, which combine two conditions (and are therefore binary operators), the logical negation operator affects only a single condition, (and is therefore a unary operator). The logical negation operator is placed before a condition when we are interested in choosing a path of execution if the original condition (without the logical negation operator) is false, such as in the following program segment:

```
if (!(grade == sentinelvalue))
    printf("The next grade is %f\n", grade);
```

The parentheses around the condition grade == sentinelvalue are needed because the logical negation operator has a higher precedence than the equality operator. The following is a truth table for the logical negation operator.

expression	!expression
0	1
nonzero	0

In most cases, the programmer can avoid using logical NOT by expressing the condition differently with an appropriate relational operator. For example, the preceding statement may be written without the logical NOT as follows:

```
if (grade != sentinelvalue)
    printf("The next grade is %f", grade);
```

The chart in Fig. 4.13 shows the precedence and associativity of the various C operators introduced up to this point. The operators are shown from top to bottom in decreasing order of precedence.

Operators						Associativity
()						left to right
++	--	(*type*)	!			right to left
*	/	%				left to right
+	-					left to right
<	<=	>	>=			left to right
==	!=					left to right
&&						left to right
||						left to right
?:						right to left
=	+=	-=	*=	/=	%=	right to left
,						left to right

Fig. 4.13 Operator precedence.

4.11 Structured Programming Summary

Just as architects design buildings by employing the collective experience of their profession, so should programmers design programs. Our field is younger than architecture is, and our collective wisdom is considerably sparser. We have learned a great deal in a mere four decades. Perhaps most importantly, we have learned that structured programming produces programs that are easier to understand, and hence easier to test, debug, modify, and even prove correct in a mathematical sense.

Chapters 3 and 4 have concentrated on familiarizing the reader with C's control structures. Each structure has been presented, flowcharted, and discussed separately with examples. Now, we introduce some general insights into the formation and properties of structured programs.

Connecting individual flowchart symbols arbitrarily can lead to unstructured programs. Therefore, the programming profession has chosen to combine flowchart symbols to form control structures, and to build only structured flowcharts by properly combining control structures. For simplicity, only *single entry/single exit* contol structures are used—there is only one way to enter and one way to exit each control structure. Connecting control structures in sequence to form flowcharts is simple—the exit point of one control structure is connected to the entry point of the next control structure. Actually, the rules for forming structured flowcharts are a bit more involved than just connecting control structures in sequence. The rules also allow for nesting of control structures. Figure 4.14 summarizes the control stuctures discussed in Chapters 3 and 4. A small circle is used in the figure to indicate the entry point and the exit point of each structure.

Fig. 4.15 shows the rules for forming structured programs. For simplicity, the rules assume that the rectangle flowchart symbol may be used to indicate any action including input/output. After applying these rules, rectangles in the resulting flowchart may be replaced with parallelograms and the flowchart will still be structured.

Applying the rules of Fig. 4.15 always results in a structured flowchart with a simple, straightforward building-block appearance. Repeatedly applying rule 2 to the simplest flowchart results in a structured flowchart containing many rectangles in sequence (Fig. 4.17).

Repeatedly applying rule 3 to the simplest flowchart results in a flowchart with nested control structures. In Fig. 4.18, the rectangle in the simplest flowchart is first replaced with a double-selection (`if/else`) structure. Then rule 3 is applied again to both rectangles in the double-selection structure, replacing the rectangles with double-selection structures. The dashed boxes around each double selection structure represent the rectangle that was replaced.

Rule 4 generates larger, more involved, and more deeply nested structures. The flowcharts that emerge from applying the rules in Fig. 4.15 constitute the set of all possible structured flowcharts.

Because of the elimination of the `goto` statement, building blocks never overlap one another. The beauty of the structured approach is that we use only a small number of simple single-entry/single-exit pieces, and we put them together in only two simple ways. Figure 4.19 shows the kind of stacked building block that emerge from

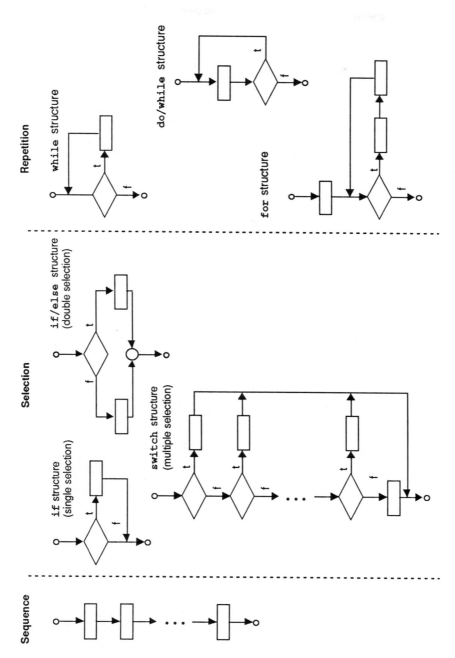

Fig. 4.14 C's single entry/single exit sequence, selection, and repetition structures.

Rules for Forming Structured Programs

1) Begin with the "simplest flowchart" (Fig. 4.16).

2) Any rectangle can be replaced by two rectangles in sequence.

3) Any rectangle can be replaced by any control structure.

4) These rules may be applied as often as you like and in any order.

Fig. 4.15 Rules for forming structured programs.

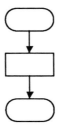

Fig. 4.16 The simplest flowchart.

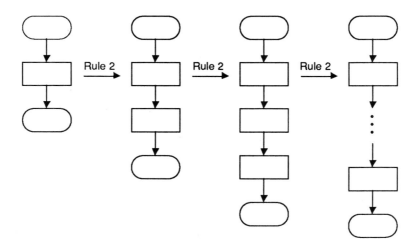

Fig. 4.17 Applying rule 2 of Fig. 4.15 to the simplest flowchart.

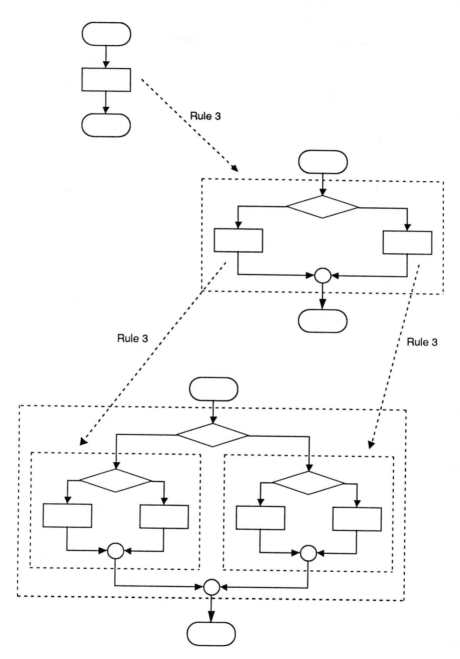

Fig. 4.18 Applying rule 3 of Fig. 4.15 to the simplest flowchart.

applying rule 2, and the kind of nested building blocks, that emerge from applying rule 3. The figure also shows the kind of overlapped building blocks that cannot appear in structured flowcharts (because of the elimination of the `goto` statement).

If the rules in Fig. 4.15 are followed, an unstructured flowchart (such as that in Fig. 4.20) cannot be created. If you are uncertain if a particular flowchart is structured, apply the rules of Fig. 4.15 in reverse to try to reduce the flowchart to the simplest flowchart. If the flowchart does reduce to the simplest flowchart, the original flowchart is structured, otherwise it is not.

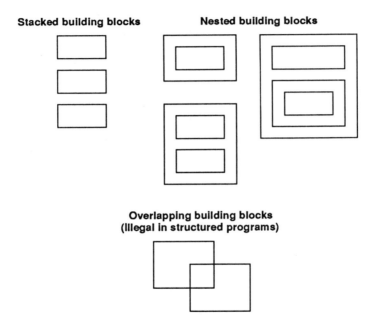

Fig. 4.19 Stacked building blocks, nested building blocks, and overlapped building blocks.

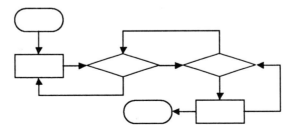

Fig. 4.20 An unstructured flowchart.

Structured programming promotes simplicity. Bohm and Jacopini have given us the result that only three forms of control are needed:

- Sequence
- Selection
- Repetition

Sequence is trivial. Selection is implemented in C in one of three ways:

- `if` structure (single selection)
- `if/else` structure (double selection)
- `switch` structure (multiple selection)

In fact, it is straightforward to prove that the simple `if` structure is sufficient to provide selection. Everything that can be done with the `if/else` structure and the `switch` structure can be implemented with the `if` structure.

Repetition is implemented in C in one of three ways:

- `while` structure
- `do/while` structure
- `for` structure

It is straightforward to prove that the `while` structure is sufficient to provide repetition. Everything that can be done with the `do/while` structure and the `for` structure can be done with the `while` structure.

Combining these results illustrates that any form of control ever needed in a C program can be expressed in terms of only three forms of control:

- sequence
- `if` structure (selection)
- `while` structure (selection)

This confirms that structured programming promotes simplicity.

Summary

- A loop is a group of instructions the computer executes repeatedly until some terminating condition is satisfied. Two forms of repetition are counter-controlled repetition and sentinel-controlled repetition.
- A loop counter is used to count the number of times a group of instructions should be repeated. It is incremented (usually by 1) each time the group of instructions is performed.
- Sentinel values are generally used to control repetition when the precise number of repetitions is not known in advance, or the loop includes statements that obtain data each time the loop is performed.

- The sentinel value is entered after all valid data items have been supplied to the program. Sentinels must be chosen carefully so that there is no possibility of confusing them with valid data items.

- The `for` repetition structure handles all the details of counter-controlled repetition automatically. The general format of the `for` structure is

      for (expression1; expression2; expression3)
          statement

  where *expression1* initializes the loop's *control variable*, *expression2* gives the conditions under which repetition should continue, and *expression3* increments the control variable.

- The `do/while` repetition structure is similar to the `while` repetition structure, but the `do/while` structure tests the repetition continuation condition at the end of the loop. Because the condition is tested at the end of the loop, the block of statements in the loop will be executed at least once. When a `do/while` terminates, execution continues with the statement after the `while` clause. The format for the `do/while` structure is

      do
          statement
      while (condition)

- The `break` statement, when executed in one of the repetition structures (`for`, `while`, and `do/while`), causes immediate exit from the structure. Execution continues with the first statement after the loop.

- The `continue` statement, when executed in one of the repetition structures (`for`, `while`, and `do/while`), skips any remaining statements in the body of the structure, and proceeds with the next iteration of the loop.

- C provides the `switch` statement to handle a series of decisions in which a particular variable or expression is tested for each of the values it may assume, and different actions are taken. Each `case` in a `switch` statement may cause many statements to be performed. It is necessary to include a `break` statement after the statements for each `case`, otherwise the program will execute the statements in each `case` until a `break` statement is encountered, or the end of the `switch` statement is reached. Many `cases` can execute the same statements by listing the `cases` together before the statements. It is important to remember that the `switch` structure can only be used to test constant integral expressions.

- The `getchar` function returns one character from the keyboard (the standard input) as an integer.

- On UNIX systems and many others, the `EOF` character is entered by typing the sequence

      <return> <ctrl-d>

  On other systems such as Digital Equipment Corporation's VMS, the `EOF` character can be entered by typing

      <ctrl-z>

and other systems may have other key combinations.

- C provides a set of logical operators that may be used to form complex conditions by combining conditions. They are && , | | , and ! , meaning logical AND, logical OR, and logical NOT, respectively.
- A true value in C is any nonzero value.
- A false value in C is 0 (zero).

Terminology

binary operator
body of a loop
break
case label
char
continue
control variable
counter-controlled repetition
<ctrl-z>
default case in **switch**
definite repetition
double
do/while repetition structure
end-of-file indicator
EOF
field width final value of control variable
for repetition structure
getchar function
increment of control variable
indefinite repetition
infinite loop
initial value of control variable
logical AND (**&&**)
logical negation (**!**)

logical operators
logical OR (**| |**)
long
loop
loop control variable
loop counter
loop termination
multiple selection
negative increment
nonexecutable statement
positive increment
pow function
repetition
repetition structures
<return><ctrl-d>
scope of the loop
sentinel-controlled repetition
sentinel value
short
simple condition
switch selection structure
terminating condition
truth table
unary operator
while repetition structure

Common Programming Errors

4.1   Since floating point values may be approximate, controlling counting loops with floating point variables may result in imprecise counter values and inaccurate tests for termination.

4.2   Using the incorrect relational operator in the condition of a **while** or **for** structure causes off-by-one errors. An off-by-one error is caused when the control variable in a repetition structure is one increment less than or one increment greater than the desired final value.

4.3 Forgetting a **break** statement when one is needed in a **switch** structure.

4.4 Not processing extra newline characters in the input when processing characters one at a time.

4.5 Infinite loops are caused when the repetition continuation condition in a **while**, **for**, or **do/while** structure never becomes false. To prevent this, make sure there is not a semicolon immediately after the first line of a **while** or **for** structure. In a counter-controlled loop, make sure the control variable is incremented within the body of the loop. In a sentinel-controlled loop, make sure the sentinel value is eventually input.

Good Programming Practices

4.1 Indent the statements in the body of each control structure.

4.2 Put a blank line before and after each major control structure to make it stand out in the program.

4.3 Avoid becoming too deeply nested. This makes the program difficult to understand. As a general rule, no unit should have more than three levels of indentation.

4.4 The combination of vertical spacing before and after control structures and indentation of the bodies of control structures within the control structure headers gives programs a two-dimensional, flowchart-like appearance that greatly improves program readability.

4.5 Control counting loops with integer values.

4.6 Using the final value in the condition of a **while** or **for** structure, will make off-by-one errors easier to spot during program debugging. For a loop used to print the values 1 to 10, for example, the condition should be **counter <= 10** rather than **counter < 11.**

4.7 Only place expressions involving the control variables in the initialization and increment sections of a **for** structure.

4.8 Although the value of the control variable can be changed in the body of a loop, Do not change it.

4.9 Although statements preceding a **for** and statements in the body of a **for** can often be merged into the **for** header, avoid doing so because it makes the program more cryptic and difficult to read.

4.10 Limit the size of control structure headers to a single line if possible.

4.11 Do not use variables of type **float** or **double** to perform monetary calculations. The impreciseness of floating point numbers can cause rounding errors that will result in incorrect monetary values. In the exercises we explore the use of integers to perform monetary calculations.

4.12 Provide a **default** case in **switch** statements. As is the case with single selection **if** structures, cases not explicitly tested are ignored. The **default** case helps prevent this by focusing the programmer on the need to process exceptional conditions. There will be cases in which no default processing is needed.

4.13 The **break** statement in the **default** case is not required, but some programmers include it for clarity and symmetry with other **cases.**

OR

```
x = 1;
while (x <= 20)
   if (x % 5 == 0)
      printf("%d\n", x++);
   else
      printf("%d\t", x++);
```

e)
```
for (x = 1; x <= 20; x++) {
   printf("%d", x);
   if (x % 5 == 0)
      printf("\n");
   else
      printf("\t");
}
```

OR

```
for (x = 1; x <= 20; x++)
   if (x % 5 == 0)
      printf("%d\n", x);
   else
      printf("%d\t", x);
```

4.4   a) Error: Semicolon after the **while** header.
        Correction: Remove the semicolon.
    b) Error: Using a floating point number to control a **for** repetition structure.
        Correction: Use an integer, and perform the proper calculation in order to get the values you desire.
    c) Error: Missing **break** statement in the statements for the first **case**.
        Correction: Add a **break** statement at the end of the statements for the first **case**.
    d) Error: Imporper relational operator used in the while repetition-continuation condition.
        Correction: Use <= rather than <.

Exercises

4.5   State which values of the control variable **x** are printed by each of the following for statements:

    a)
```
for(x = 2; x <= 13; x += 2)
   printf("%d", x);
```
    b)
```
for(x = 5; x <= 22; x += 7)
   printf("%d", x);
```
    c)
```
for(x = 3; x <= 15; x += 3)
   printf("%d", x);
```
    d)
```
for(x = 1; x <= 5; x += 7)
   printf("%d", x);
```

```
e)  for(x = 12; x >= 2; x -= 3)
        printf("%d", x);
```

4.6   Write `for` statements that print the following sequences of values:
a)   1, 2, 3, 4, 5, 6, 7
b)   3, 8, 13, 18, 23
c)   20, 14, 8, 2, -4, -10
d)   19, 27, 35, 43, 51

4.7   Write a C program that sums a sequence of integers. Assume that the first integer read with `scanf` specifies the number of values remaining to be entered. Your program should read only one value each time `scanf` is executed. A typical input sequence might be

        5 100 200 300 400 500

where the 5 indicates that the following 5 values are to be summed.

4.8   Write a C program that calculates and prints the average of several integers. Assume the last value read with `scanf` is the sentinel 9999. A typical input sequence might be

        10 8 11 7 9 9999

indicating that the average of all the values preceding 9999 is to be calculated.

4.9   Write a C program that finds the smallest of several integers. Assume that the first value read specifies the number of values remaining.

4.10   Write a C program that calculates and prints the sum of the even integers from 2 to 30.

4.11   Write a C program that calculates and prints the product of the odd integers from 1 to 15.

4.12   The *factorial* function is used frequently in probability problems. The factorial of a positive integer *n* (written *n!* and pronounced "n factorial") is equal to the product of the positive integers from 1 to *n*. Write a C program that evaluates the factorials of the integers from 1 to 5. Print the results in a neat tabular format. What difficulty might prevent you from calculating the factorial of 20?

4.13   Modify the compound interest problem of Section 4.6 to repeat its steps for interest rates of 5 percent, 6 percent, 7 percent, 8 percent, 9 percent, and 10 percent. Use a `for` loop to vary the interest rate.

4.14   Write a C program that prints the following patterns one below the other. Use `for` loops to generate the patterns. All asterisks (*) should be printed by a single `printf` statement of the form `printf("*");` (this causes the asterisks to print side by side).

```
    (A)             (B)             (C)             (D)

     *          **********      **********            *
    **          *********       *********            **
   ***          ********        ********            ***
  ****          *******         *******            ****
 *****          ******          ******            *****
 ******         *****           *****            ******
 *******        ****            ****            *******
 ********       ***             ***            ********
 *********      **              **            *********
 **********     *               *            **********
```

4.15   Collecting money becomes increasingly difficult during periods of recession, so companies may tighten their credit limits to prevent their accounts receivable (money owed to them) from becoming too large. In response to a prolonged recession, one company has cut its customer's credit limits in half. Thus, if a particular customer had a credit limit of $2000, this customer's credit limit is now $1000. If a customer had a credit limit of $5000, this customer's credit limit is now $2500. Write a C program that analyzes the credit status of three customers of this company. For each customer you are given:

1.   The customer's account number
2.   The customer's credit limit before the recession
3.   The customer's current balance (i.e., the amount the customer owes the company)

Your program should calculate and print the new credit limit for each customer, and should determine (and print) which customers have current balances that exceed their new credit limits.

4.16   One interesting application of computers is drawing graphs and bar charts (sometimes called "histograms"). Write a C program that reads five numbers (each between 1 and 30). For each number read, your program should print a line containing that number of adjacent asterisks. For example, if your program reads the number seven, it should print *******.

4.17   A mail order house sells five different products whose retail prices are shown in the following table:

Product number	Retail price
1	$ 2.98
2	4.50
3	9.98
4	4.49
5	6.87

Write a C program that reads a series of pairs of numbers as follows:

1.   Product number
2.   Quantity sold for one day

Your program should use a **switch** statement to help determine the retail price for each product. Your program should calculate and display the total retail value of all products sold last week.

4.18   Complete the following truth tables by filling in each blank with 0 or 1.

Condition1	Condition2	Condition1 && Condition2
0	0	0
0	nonzero	0
nonzero	0	_____
nonzero	nonzero	_____

Condition1	Condition2	Condition1 || Condition2
0	0	0
0	nonzero	1
nonzero	0	_____
nonzero	nonzero	_____

Condition1	! Condition1
0	1
nonzero	_____

4.19 Rewrite the program of Fig. 4.2 so that the initialization of the variable `counter` is done in the declaration instead of the `for` structure.

4.20 Modify the program of Fig. 4.7 so that it calculates the average grade for the class.

4.21 Modify the program in Fig. 4.6 so that it uses only integers to calculate the compound interest.

5
Functions

Objectives

- To understand how to construct programs from small pieces called functions.
- To introduce the common math functions available in the C standard library.
- To be able to create new functions.
- To understand the mechanisms used to pass information between functions.
- To introduce simulation techniques using random number generation.
- To understand how to write and use functions that call themselves.

Form ever follows function.

Louis Henri Sullivan

E pluribus unus.
(One composed of many.)

Virgil

O! call back yesterday, bid time return.

William Shakespeare
Richard II

Call me Ishmael.

Herman Melville
Moby Dick

When you call me that, smile.

Owen Wister

121

Outline

5.1 Introduction

Most computer programs that solve real-world problems are much larger than the programs presented in the first few chapters. Experience has shown that the best way to develop and maintain a large program is to divide it into smaller pieces or *modules* each of which is more manageable than the original program. This technique is called *divide and conquer*. This chapter describes the features of the C language that facilitate the design, implementation, operation, and maintenance of large programs.

5.2 Program Modules in C

Modules in C are called *functions*. C programs are typically written by combining functions the programmer writes with "pre-packaged" functions available in the *C standard library*. We discuss both kinds of functions in this chapter. The C standard library provides a rich collection of functions for performing common mathematical calculations, string manipulations, character manipulations, input/output, and many other useful operations. This makes the programmer's job easier because these functions provide many of the capabilities programmers need.

> *GPP 5.1*
>
> *Familiarize yourself with the rich collection of functions available in the ANSI C standard library.*

GPP 5.2

Avoid reinventing the wheel. When possible, use ANSI C standard library functions instead of writing new functions. This reduces program development time. It also tends to make programs more portable.

Although the standard library functions are technically not a part of the C language, they are invariably provided with ANSI C systems. The functions `printf`, `scanf`, and `pow` that we have used in previous chapters are standard library functions.

The programmer can write functions to define specific tasks that may be used at many points in a program. These are sometimes referred to as *programmer-defined functions*. The actual statements defining the function are written only once, and the statements are hidden from other functions.

Functions are *invoked* by a *function call*. The function call specifies the function name and provides information (as *arguments*) that the called function needs to perform its designated task. A common analogy for this is the hierarchical form of management. A boss (the *calling function* or *caller*) asks a worker (the *called function*) to perform a task and report back when the task is done. For example, a function that wants to display information on the screen calls the worker function `printf` to perform that task, then `printf` displays the information and reports back—or *returns*—to the calling function when its task is completed. The boss function does not know how the worker function performs its designated tasks. The worker may call other worker functions, and the boss will be unaware of this. We will soon see how this "hiding" of implementation details promotes good software engineering. Figure 5.1 shows the `main` function communicating with several worker functions in a hierarchical manner. Note that `worker1` acts as a boss function to `worker4` and `worker5`. As we will see later in this chapter, the relationships among functions may be other than the hierarchical structure shown here.

5.3 Math Library Functions

Math library functions allow the programmer to perform certain common mathematical calculations. We use various math library functions here to introduce the concept of functions. As we proceed through the book, we will discuss many of the other functions in the C standard library. A complete list of the C standard library functions is provided in Appendix B.

Functions are normally used in a program by writing the name of the function followed by a left parenthesis followed by the *argument* (or a comma separated list of arguments) of the function followed by a right parenthesis. For example, a programmer desiring to calculate and print the square root of `900.0` might write

```
printf("%.2f", sqrt(900.0));
```

When this statement is executed, the math library function `sqrt` is called to calculate the square root of the number contained in the parentheses (`900.0`). The number `900.0` is the argument of the `sqrt` function. The preceding statement would print

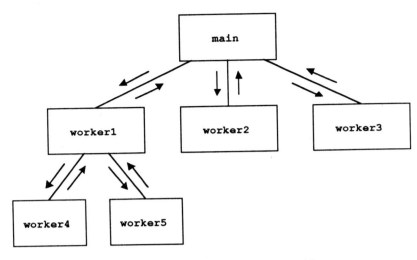

Fig. 5.1 Hierarchical boss function/worker function relationship.

30.00. The sqrt function takes an argument of type double and returns a result of type double. All functions in the math library return the data type double.

GPP 5.3

Include the math header file by using the preprocessor directive #include <math.h> when using functions in the math library.

CPE 5.1

Forgetting to include the math header file when using math library functions can cause strange results.

Function arguments may be constants, variables, or expressions. If c1 = 13.0, d = 3.0, and f = 4.0, then the statement

```
printf("%.2f", sqrt(c1 + d * f));
```

calculates and prints the square root of 13.0 + 3.0 * 4.0 = 25.0, namely 5.00.

Some C math library functions are summarized in Fig. 5.2. In the figure, the variables x and y are of type double. Remember to include <math.h> when using these functions.

5.4 Functions

Functions allow the programmer to modularize a program. All variables declared in function definitions are *local variables*—they are known only in the function in which they are defined. Most functions have a list of *parameters*. The parameters provide the means for communicating information between functions. Parameters are also local variables.

Function	Description	Example
sqrt(x)	square root of x	sqrt(900.0) is 30.0 sqrt(9.0) is 3.0
exp(x)	exponential function e^x	exp(1.0) is 2.718282 exp(2.0) is 7.389056
log(x)	natural logarithm of x (base e)	log(2.718282) is 1.0 log(7.389056) is 2.0
log10(x)	logarithm of x (base 10)	log10(1.0) is 0.0 log10(10.0) is 1.0 log10(100.0) is 2.0
fabs(x)	absolute value of x	if $x > 0$ then fabs(x) is x if $x = 0$ then fabs(x) is 0.0 if $x < 0$ then fabs(x) is $-x$
ceil(x)	rounds x to the smallest integer not less than x	ceil(9.2) is 10.0 ceil(-9.8) is -9.0
floor(x)	rounds x to the largest integer not greater than x	floor(9.2) is 9.0 floor(-9.8) is -10.0
pow(x, y)	x raised to power y (x^y)	pow(2, 7) is 128.0 pow(9, .5) is 3.0
fmod(x, y)	remainder of x/y as a floating point number	fmod(13.657, 2.333) is 2.010
sin(x)	trigonometric sine of x (x in radians)	sin(0.0) is 0.0
cos(x)	trigonometric cosine of x (x in radians)	cos(0.0) is 1.0
tan(x)	trigonometric tangent of x (x in radians)	tan(0.0) is 0.0

Fig. 5.2 Some commonly used math library functions.

GPP 5.4

In programs containing many functions, main should be implemented as a group of calls to functions that perform the bulk of the program's work.

There are several motivations for "functionalizing" a program. The divide and conquer approach makes program development more manageable. Another motivation is *software reusability*—using existing functions as building blocks to create new programs. Software reusability is a major factor in the object-oriented programming movement. With good function naming and definition, programs can be created from standardized functions that accomplish specific tasks rather than from customized code. This technique is known as *abstraction*. We used abstraction each time we wrote programs including standard library functions like printf, scanf, and pow. A third motivation is to avoid repeating code in a program. Packaging code as a function allows the code to be executed from many different locations in a program simply by calling the function.

GPP 5.5

Each function should be limited to performing a single, well-defined task, and the function name should effectively express that task. This facilitates abstraction and promotes software reusability.

5.5 Function Definitions

Each program we have presented has consisted of a function called main that called standard library functions to accomplish its tasks. We now consider how programmers write their own customized functions.

Consider a program that uses a function square to calculate the squares of the integers from 1 to 10 (Fig. 5.3).

GPP 5.6

Place a blank line between function definitions to separate the functions and enhance program readability.

Function square is invoked in main by the statement

```
printf("%d  ", square(x));
```

Function square receives a copy of the value of x in the parameter y. Then square calculates y * y. The result is passed back to the printf function in main where square was invoked, and printf prints the result on the screen. This process is repeated ten times using the for repetition structure.

```
/* A programmer-defined square function */
#include <stdio.h>

main()
{
    int x;
    int square(int); /* function prototype */

    for (x = 1; x <= 10; x++)
        printf("%d  ", square(x));
    printf("\n");
}

int square(int y)
{
    return y * y;
}
```

```
1   4   9   16   25   36   49   64   81   100
```

Fig. 5.3 Using a programmer-defined function.

The definition of `square` shows that `square` expects an integer parameter `y`. The keyword `int` preceding the function name indicates that `square` returns an integer result. The `return` statement in `square` passes the result of the calculation back to the calling function.

The line

```
int square(int);
```

is a *function prototype*. It informs the compiler that `square` expects to receive an integer value from the caller, and that `square` returns an integer result to the caller. The compiler refers to the function prototype to check that calls to `square` contain the correct return type, the correct number of arguments, the correct argument types, and that the arguments are in the correct order. Function prototypes are discussed in detail in Section 5.6.

The format of a function definition is

> *return-value-type function-name* (*parameter-list*)
> {
> > *declarations*
> >
> > *statements*
> }

The *function-name* is any valid identifier. The *return-value-type* is the data type of the result returned to the caller. The *return-value-type* `void` indicates that a function does not return a value. An unspecified *return-value-type* is assumed to be `int`.

CPE 5.2

Omitting the return-value-type causes a syntax error if the function prototype specifies that a type other than `int` is returned.

CPE 5.3

Forgetting to return a value from a function that is supposed to return a value can lead to unexpected errors. The ANSI standard states that the result of this action is undefined.

CPE 5.4

Returning a value from a function whose return type has been declared `void` causes a syntax error.

GPP 5.7

Even though an omitted return type defaults to `int`, always state the return type explicitly. The return type for `main`, however, is normally omitted.

The *parameter-list* is a comma-separated list containing the declarations of the parameters received by the function when it is called. If a function does not receive any values, *parameter-list* is `void`.

CPE 5.5

Placing a semicolon after the right parenthesis enclosing the parameter list of a function definition is a syntax error.

CPE 5.6

Defining a function parameter again as a local variable within the function is a syntax error.

GPP 5.8

Include the type of each parameter in the parameter list, even if that parameter is of the default type `int`*.*

GPP 5.9

Do not use the same names for the arguments passed to a function and the corresponding parameters in the function definition. This helps avoid ambiguity.

The *declarations* and *statements* within braces form the *function body*. The function body is also referred to as a *block*. A block is a compound statement that includes declarations. Variables can be declared in any block, and blocks can be nested. *A function can not be defined inside another function* under any circumstances.

CPE 5.7

Defining a function in another function is a syntax error.

GPP 5.10

Choosing meaningful function names and meaningful parameter names makes programs more readable and helps avoid excessive use of comments.

GPP 5.11

A function should be no longer than one page. Better yet, a function should be no longer than half a page. Small functions promote software reusability.

GPP 5.12

Programs should be written as collections of small functions. This makes programs easier to write, debug, maintain and modify.

GPP 5.13

A function requiring a large number of parameters may be performing too many tasks. Consider dividing the function into smaller functions that perform the separate tasks. The function header should fit on one line if possible.

GPP 5.14

The function prototype, function header, and function calls should all agree in the number, type, and order of arguments and parameters, and in the type of return value.

There are three ways to return control to the point at which a function was invoked. If the function does not return a result, control is returned simply when the function-ending right brace is reached, or by executing the statement

```
return;
```

If the function does return a result, the statement

```
return expression;
```

returns the value of *expression* to the caller.

Our second example uses a programmer-defined function `maximum` to determine and return the largest of three integers (Fig. 5.4). The three integers are input from the user with `scanf`. Next, the integers are passed to `maximum` which determines the largest integer. This value is returned to main with one of the three `return` statements in `maximum`. The value returned is assigned to the variable `largest` which is then printed in the `printf` statement.

5.6 Function Prototypes

One of the most important features of ANSI C is the *function prototype*. A function prototype tells the compiler the type of data returned by the function, the number of parameters the function expects to receive, the types of the parameters, and the order in which these parameters are expected. The compiler uses function prototypes to validate function calls. Previous versions of C did not perform this kind of checking. Function prototypes correct this deficiency.

GPP 5.15

Include function prototypes for all functions to use C's type checking capabilities. Use `#include` preprocessor directives to obtain function prototypes for the standard library functions from the header files for the appropriate libraries. Also use `#include` to obtain header files containing function prototypes used by your group members.

```
/* Finding the maximum of three integers */
#include <stdio.h>

main()
{
    int a, b, c, largest;
    int maximum(int, int, int);    /* function prototype */

    printf("Enter three integers: ");
    scanf("%d%d%d", &a, &b, &c);
    printf("Maximum is: %d\n", maximum(a, b, c));
}

int maximum(int x, int y, int z)
{
    if (x > y && x > z)
        return x;
    else if (y > z)
        return y;
    else
        return z;
}
```

```
Enter three integers: 22 85 17
Maximum is: 85
```

Fig. 5.4 Programmer-defined `maximum` function.

The function prototype for maximum in Fig. 5.4 is

```
int maximum(int, int, int);
```

This function prototype states that maximum takes three arguments of type int, and returns a result of type int. Notice that the function prototype is the same as the first line of the function definition of maximum except the names of the parameters (x, y, and z) are not included.

GPP 5.16

Parameter names are sometimes included in function prototypes for documentation purposes. The compiler ignores these names.

CPE 5.8

Forgetting the semicolon at the end of a function prototype causes a syntax error.

A function call that does not match the function prototype causes a syntax error. An error is also generated if the function prototype and the function definition disagree. For example, in Fig. 5.4, if the function prototype had been written

```
void maximum(int, int, int);
```

the compiler would generate an error because the void return type in the function prototype differs from the int return type in the function header.

Another important feature of function prototypes is the *coercion of arguments*, i.e., the forcing of arguments, to the appropriate type. For example, the math library function sqrt can be called with an integer argument (even though the function expects a double argument), and the function will still work correctly. For example, the statement

```
printf("%.3f\n", sqrt(4));
```

would correctly evaluate sqrt(4), and print the value 2.000. The function prototype causes the integer value 4 to be converted to the double value 4.0 before the value is used in sqrt. C provides a strict set of rules for *promoting* the types of values in automatic conversions. The type of each value in an expression with mixed data types is promoted to the type in the expression that is listed highest (the *higher type*) in Fig. 5.5 in most cases. Expressions containing mixed unsigned int and long int values are handled differently depending on the computer. If the range of values for long int contains all values of unsigned int, the unsigned int value is converted to long int. Otherwise, both values are converted to unsigned long int.

Values may be converted to types listed lower (*lower types*) in Fig. 5.5 either by assigning a value to a variable of lower type, or by using a cast operator. Converting values to lower types usually results in an incorrect value. If our square function that squares an integer is called with a floating point argument, square usually returns an incorrect value. For example, the value of square(4) is 16 and the value of square(4.0) is 16, but the value of square(4.5) is also 16. The method of converting a floating point value to an integer varies between computers. According to

Data types	printf Conversion specifiers	scanf Conversion specifiers
long double	%Lf	%Lf
double	%f	%lf
float	%f	%f
unsigned long int	%lu	%lu
long int	%ld	%ld
unsigned int	%u	%u
int	%d	%d
short	%hd	%hd
char	%c	%c

Fig. 5.5 The data types and their `printf` and `scanf` conversion specifiers.

the ANSI standard, when a floating point value is converted to an integer, the fractional part is discarded. If the integer part cannot be represented, the result is undefined. Often, the conversion is not as simple as truncating the fractional part of the number as in the preceding case. Converting large integer types to small integer types may also present problems.

If the function prototype for a function has not been included in a program, the compiler forms its own function prototype using the first occurrence of the function, either the function definition or a call to the function. By default, the compiler assumes the function returns an `int`, and nothing is assumed about the arguments. Therefore, if the arguments passed to the function are incorrect, the errors are not detected by the compiler. Forgetting a function prototype causes a syntax error if the return type of the function is not `int` and the function definition appears after the function call in the program. Otherwise, forgetting a function prototype may cause a runtime error or an unexpected result.

A function prototype placed outside any function definition applies to all calls to the function appearing after the function prototype in the file. A function prototype placed in a function applies only to calls made in that function.

5.7 Header Files

Each standard library has a corresponding header file containing the function prototypes for all the functions in that library and definitions of various data types and constants needed by those functions. Fig. 5.6 lists alphabetically the standard library header files that may be included in programs. The term "macros" that is used several times in Fig. 5.6 will be discussed in detail in Chapter 13, "Preprocessor."

The programmer can create custom header files. Programmer-defined header files should also end in `.h`. A programmer-defined header file can be included by using the `#include` preprocessor directive. For example, the header file `square.h` can be included in our program by the directive

Standard library header file	Explanation
`<assert.h>`	Contains macros and information for adding diagnostics that aid program debugging.
`<ctype.h>`	Contains function prototypes for functions that test characters for certain properties, and function prototypes for functions that can be used to convert lowercase letters to uppercase letters and vice versa.
`<errno.h>`	Defines macros that are useful for reporting error conditions.
`<float.h>`	Contains the floating point size limits of the system.
`<limits.h>`	Contains the integral size limits of the system.
`<locale.h>`	Contains function prototypes and other information that enables a program to be modified for the current locale on which it is running. The notion of locale enables the computer system to handle different conventions for expressing data like dates, times, dollar amounts, and large numbers in different areas throughout the world.
`<math.h>`	Contains function prototypes for math library functions.
`<setjmp.h>`	Contains function prototypes for functions that allow bypassing of the usual function call and return sequence.
`<signal.h>`	Contains function prototypes and macros to handle various conditions that may arise during program execution.
`<stdarg.h>`	Defines macros for dealing with a list of arguments to a function whose number and types are unknown.
`<stddef.h>`	Contains common definitions of types used by C for performing certain calculations.
`<stdio.h>`	Contains function prototypes for the standard input/output library functions, and information used by them.
`<stdlib.h>`	Contains function prototypes for conversions of numbers to text and text to numbers, memory allocation, random numbers, and other utility functions.
`<string.h>`	Contains function prototypes for string processing functions.
`<time.h>`	Contains function prototypes and types for manipulating the time and date.

Fig. 5.6 The standard library header files.

```
#include "square.h"
```

at the top of the program. Section 13.2 presents additional information on including header files.

5.8 Calling Functions: Call by Value and Call by Reference

Two ways to invoke functions in many programming languages are *call by value* and *call by reference*. When arguments are passed call by value, a *copy* of the argument's value is made and passed to the called function. Changes to the copy do not affect an original variable's value in the caller. When an argument is passed call by reference, the caller actually allows the called function to modify the original variable's value.

Call by value should be used whenever the called function does not need to modify the value of the caller's original variable. This prevents the accidental *side effects* that so greatly hinder the development of correct and reliable software systems. Call by reference should only be used with trusted called functions that need to modify the original variable.

In C, all calls are call by value. As we will see in Chapter 7, it is possible to *simulate* call by reference by using address operators and indirection operators. In Chapter 6, we will see that arrays are automatically passed simulated call by reference. We will have to wait until Chapter 7 for a full understanding of this complex issue. For now, let us concentrate on call by value.

5.9 Random Number Generation

We now take a brief and hopefully entertaining diversion into a popular programming application, namely simulation and game playing. We will develop a nicely structured game-playing program that includes multiple functions.

There is something in the air of a gambling casino that invigorates every type of person from the high-rollers at the plush mahogany-and-felt craps tables to the quarter-poppers at the one-armed bandits. It is the *element of chance,* the possibility that luck will convert a mere pocketful of money into a mountain of wealth.

The element of chance can be introduced into computer applications by the use of the rand function in the C Standard Library. This chapter describes the use of rand for simulating games of chance and other situations characterized by uncertainty.

Consider the following C statement:

```
i = rand();
```

The rand standard library function generates an integer between 0 and RAND_MAX (a symbolic constant defined in the <stdlib.h> header file) and assigns this value to the variable i. The ANSI standard states that the value of RAND_MAX must be at least 32767 which is the maximum value for a two-byte integer. The programs in this section were tested on a C system with a maximum value of 32767 for RAND_MAX. If rand truly produces integers at random, every number between 0 and RAND_MAX has an equal *chance* (or *probability*) of being chosen each time rand is called.

The range of values produced directly by `rand` often is larger or different than what is needed in a specific application. For example, a program that simulates coin tossing might require only 0 for "heads" and 1 for "tails." A program that simulates rolling a six-sided die would require random integers in range 1 to 6.

To demonstrate the use of `rand`, let us develop a program to simulate 20 rolls of a six-sided die and print the value of each roll. The function prototype for the `rand` function can be found in `<stdlib.h>`. Fig. 5.7 uses `rand` directly to confirm the range of values produced.

Notice that these values do fall between 0 and `RAND_MAX` and that they are in fact spread throughout that range. These numbers could be used to simulate the roll of a die by dividing this interval into six equal parts. The number generated by `rand` could then be tested to determine in which of the six intervals it belongs, and an integer from 1 to 6 could then be assigned. All of this can actually be accomplished with a single statement. We use the modulus operator (`%`) in conjunction with `rand` as follows

```
rand() % 6
```

to produce integers in the range 0 to 5. This is called *scaling*. The number 6 is called the *scaling factor*. The program and sample execution of Fig. 5.8 show 20 numbers produced using `rand() % 6`.

The range is 0 to 5 instead of the desired 1 to 6. This problem is easy to correct. We merely *shift* the range of numbers produced by adding 1 to our previous result. Fig. 5.9 confirms that the results are now in the range 1 to 6.

```
/* Random integers produced directly by rand() */
#include <stdio.h>
#include <stdlib.h>

main()
{
    int i;

    for(i = 1; i <= 20; i++) {
        printf("%10d", rand());
        if (i % 4 == 0)
            printf("\n");
    }
}
```

```
    16838       5758      10113      17515
    31051       5627      23010       7419
    16212       4086       2749      12767
     9084      12060      32225      17543
    25089      21183      25137      25566
```

Fig. 5.7 Random integers produced directly by `rand`.

```
/* Scaled integers produced by rand() % 6 */
#include <stdio.h>
#include <stdlib.h>

main()
{
   int i;

   for(i = 1; i <= 20; i++) {
      printf("%10d", rand() % 6);
      if (i % 4 == 0)
         printf("\n");
   }
}
```

2	4	3	1
1	5	0	3
0	0	1	5
0	0	5	5
3	3	3	0

Fig. 5.8 Scaled integers produced by `rand() % 6`.

```
/* Shifted, scaled integers produced by 1 + rand() % 6 */
#include <stdio.h>
#include <stdlib.h>

main()
{
   int i;

   for(i = 1; i <= 20; i++) {
      printf("%10d", 1 + rand() % 6);
      if (i % 4 == 0)
         printf("\n");
   }
}
```

3	5	4	2
2	6	1	4
1	1	2	6
1	1	6	6
4	4	4	1

Fig. 5.9 Shifted, scaled integers produced by `1 + rand() % 6`.

To show that these numbers occur approximately with equal likelihood, let us simulate 6000 rolls of a die. Each integer from 1 to 6 should appear approximately 1000 times (see Fig. 5.10).

```
/* Roll a six-sided die 6000 times */
#include <stdio.h>
#include <stdlib.h>

main()
{
   int face, roll, frequency1 = 0, frequency2 = 0,
      frequency3 = 0, frequency4 = 0,
      frequency5 = 0, frequency6 = 0;

   for (roll = 1; roll <= 6000; roll++) {
      face = rand() % 6 + 1;

      switch (face) {
         case 1:
            ++frequency1;
            break;
         case 2:
            ++frequency2;
            break;
         case 3:
            ++frequency3;
            break;
         case 4:
            ++frequency4;
            break;
         case 5:
            ++frequency5;
            break;
         case 6:
            ++frequency6;
            break;
      }
   }

   printf("%s%13s\n", "Face", "Frequency");
   printf("   1%13d\n", frequency1);
   printf("   2%13d\n", frequency2);
   printf("   3%13d\n", frequency3);
   printf("   4%13d\n", frequency4);
   printf("   5%13d\n", frequency5);
   printf("   6%13d\n", frequency6);
}
```

```
Face    Frequency
  1         945
  2         983
  3        1023
  4        1015
  5        1000
  6        1034
```

Fig. 5.10 Rolling a six-sided die 6000 times.

As the program output in Fig. 5.10 shows, by scaling and shifting we have utilized the `rand` function to simulate realistically the rolling of a six-sided die. Note that *no* `default` case is provided in the `switch` structure. Also note the use of the `%s` conversion specifier to print the strings `"Face"` and `"Frequency"` as column headers. The `%s` conversion specifier is used to print character strings. After we study arrays in Chapter 6, we will be able to write the entire `switch` structure more elegantly with a single statement. Executing the program of Fig. 5.9 again produces

3	5	4	2
2	6	1	4
1	1	2	6
1	1	6	6
4	4	4	1

Notice that exactly the same sequence of values was printed. Can these in fact be random numbers? Ironically, this repeatability is an important characteristic of the `rand` function. When debugging a program, this repeatability is essential for proving that corrections to a program work properly.

The `rand` function actually generates *pseudo-random numbers*. Calling `rand` repeatedly produces a sequence of numbers that appears to be random. However, the sequence repeats itself each time the program is executed. Once a program has been thoroughly debugged, it can be conditioned to produce a different sequence of random numbers for each execution. This is called *randomizing*, and is accomplished with the standard library function `srand`. The `srand` function takes an unsigned integer argument and *seeds* the `rand` function to produce a different sequence of random numbers for each execution of the program.

The use of `srand` is demonstrated in Fig. 5.11. In the program, we use the data type `unsigned` which is short for `unsigned int`. As we have previously stated, an `int` is stored in at least two bytes of memory, and can have positive and negative values. A variable of type `unsigned` can have only positive values in the range representable in two bytes of memory (0 to 65535). The `srand` function takes an unsigned value as an argument. The conversion specifier `%u` is used to read an unsigned value from the user.

Let us run the program several times and observe the results. Notice that a *different* sequence of random numbers is obtained each time the program is run provided a different seed is supplied.

If we wish to randomize without the need for entering a seed each time, we may use a statement like

```
srand(clock());
```

This causes the computer to read its system clock to obtain the value for the seed automatically. The `clock` function returns the amount of processor time used since the program began executing. This value is converted to an unsigned integer and used as the seed to the random number generator. The function prototype for `clock` is in `<time.h>`.

```
/* Randomizing die-rolling program */
#include <stdlib.h>
#include <stdio.h>

main()
{
   int i;
   unsigned seed;

   printf("Enter seed: ");
   scanf("%u", &seed);
   srand(seed);

   for (i = 1; i <= 20; i++) {
      printf("%10d", 1 + (rand() % 6));

      if (i % 4 == 0)
         printf("\n");
   }
}
```

```
Enter seed: 67
        3         1         5         5
        5         3         1         4
        1         2         5         5
        4         1         6         2
        2         5         1         4
```

```
Enter seed: 432
        3         3         3         6
        3         4         6         1
        5         2         1         1
        4         6         4         6
        3         1         3         3
```

Fig. 5.11 Randomizing the die-rolling program.

The values produced directly by rand are always in the range:

```
0 ≤ rand() ≤ RAND_MAX
```

Previously we demonstrated how to write a single C statement to simulate the rolling of a six-sided die:

```
face = 1 + rand() % 6;
```

This statement always assigns an integer value (at random) to the variable face in the range $1 \leq face \leq 6$. Note that the width of this range (i.e., the number of consecutive integers in the range) is 6 and the starting number in the range is 1. Referring to the preceding statement, we see that the width of the range is determined by the number used to scale rand with the modulus operator (i.e., 6), and the starting number of the range is equal to the number (i.e., 1) that is added to `rand % 6`. We can generalize this result as follows

```
n = a + rand() % b;
```

where `a` is the *shifting value* (which is equal to the first number in the desired range of consecutive integers), and `b` is the scaling factor (which is equal to the width of the desired range of consecutive integers). In the exercises, we will see that it is possible to choose integers at random from sets of values other than ranges of consecutive integers.

5.10 Example: A Game of Chance

One of the most popular games of chance is a die game known as "craps," which is played in casinos and back alleys throughout the world. The rules of the game are straightforward:

> *A player rolls two dice. Each die has six faces. These faces contain 1, 2, 3, 4, 5, and 6 spots. After the dice have come to rest, the sum of the spots on the two upward faces is calculated. If the sum is 7 or 11 on the first throw, the player wins. If the sum is 2, 3, or 12 on the first throw (called "craps"), the player loses (i.e., the "house" wins). If the sum is 4, 5, 6, 8, 9, or 10 on the first throw, then that sum becomes the player's "point." To win, you must continue rolling the dice until you "make your point." The player loses by rolling a 7 before making the point.*

The program in Fig. 5.12 simulates the game of craps. Figure 5.13 shows several sample executions.

Notice that the player must roll two dice on the first roll, and must do so later on all subsequent rolls. We define a function `rolldice` to roll the dice and compute and print their sum. Function `rolldice` is defined once, but it is called from two places in the program. Interestingly, `rolldice` takes no arguments, so we have indicated `void` in the parameter list. The function `rolldice` does return the sum of the two dice, so a return type of `int` is indicated in the function header.

The game is reasonably involved. The player may win or lose on the first roll, or may win or lose on any subsequent roll. The variable `gamestatus` is used to keep track of all this.

When the game is won, either on the first roll or on a subsequent roll, `gamestatus` is set to 1. When the game is lost, either on the first roll or on a subsequent roll, `gamestatus` is set to 2.

After the first roll, if the game is over, the `while` is skipped because `gamestatus` is not equal to zero. The program proceeds to the `if/else` structure which prints "`Player wins`" if `gamestatus` is 1 and "`Player loses`" if `gamestatus` is 2.

After the first roll, if the game is not over, then `sum` is saved in `mypoint`. Execution proceeds with the `while` structure because `gamestatus` equals 0. Each time through the `while`, `rolldice` is called to produce a new `sum`. If `sum` matches

```c
/* Craps */
#include <stdio.h>
#include <stdlib.h>
#include <time.h>

int rolldice(void);

main()
{
    int gamestatus, sum, mypoint;

    srand(clock());
    sum = rolldice();

    switch(sum) {

        case 7: case 11:
            gamestatus = 1;
            break;

        case 2: case 3: case 12:
            gamestatus = 2;
            break;

        default:
            gamestatus = 0;
            mypoint = sum;
            printf("Point is %d\n", mypoint);
            break;
    }

    while (gamestatus == 0) {
        sum = rolldice();

        if (sum == mypoint)
            gamestatus = 1;
        else
            if (sum == 7)
                gamestatus = 2;
    }

    if (gamestatus == 1)
        printf("Player wins\n");
    else
        printf("Player loses\n");
}

int rolldice(void)
{
    int die1, die2, worksum;

    die1 = 1 + rand() % 6;
    die2 = 1 + rand() % 6;
    worksum = die1 + die2;
    printf("Player rolled %d + %d = %d\n", die1, die2, worksum);
    return worksum;
}
```

Fig. 5.12 Program to simulate the game of craps.

```
Player rolled 6 + 5 = 11
Player wins
```

```
Player rolled 6 + 6 = 12
Player loses
```

```
Player rolled 4 + 6 = 10
Point is 10
Player rolled 2 + 4 = 6
Player rolled 6 + 5 = 11
Player rolled 3 + 3 = 6
Player rolled 6 + 4 = 10
Player wins
```

```
Player rolled 1 + 3 = 4
Point is 4
Player rolled 1 + 4 = 5
Player rolled 5 + 4 = 9
Player rolled 4 + 6 = 10
Player rolled 6 + 3 = 9
Player rolled 1 + 2 = 3
Player rolled 5 + 2 = 7
Player loses
```

Fig. 5.13 Sample runs for the game of craps.

`mypoint`, `gamestatus` is set to 1 to indicate that the player won, `while`-test fails, the `if/else` structure prints "`Player wins`" and execution terminates. If `sum` is equal to 7, `gamestatus` is set to 2 to indicate that the player lost, the `while`-test fails, the `if/else` statement prints "`Player loses`" and execution terminates.

Note the interesting control structure of the program. We have used several functions, `main` and `rolldice`, and `switch`, `while`, `if/else`, and nested `if` structures. In the exercises, we will investigate various interesting characteristics of the game of craps.

5.11 Storage Classes

A *storage class* determines the duration of a variable in a program. The two basic storage classes in C are *automatic* and *static*. An automatic variable is transient; when the block in which it is defined is entered, the variable is created, and when the block terminates, the variable is discarded. Static variables exist throughout program execution.

C contains four *storage class specifiers*—`auto`, `register`, `extern`, and `static`. Storage class specifiers are placed before the usual variable declaration as in

```
register int total;
```

The storage class specifier `auto` declares an automatic variable. The automatic storage class is the most common of the four storage classes. All local variables are automatic by default. For this reason, the `auto` storage class specifier is rarely used. Automatic variables must be declared in a block or in the parameter list of a function. Unless an automatic variable is explicitly initialized, it contains an undefined ("garbage") value.

The `register` storage class specifier advises the compiler to try to maintain a variable's value in a high-speed register, rather than move the value between memory and a register each time the value is used. The `register` storage class is appropriate for variables used frequently such as loop counters and totals. The compiler may ignore the `register` declaration. For example, the computer may not have sufficient registers available to commit one to a variable. The `register` storage class specifier can only be applied to automatic variables. Variables of storage class `register` contain undefined values unless they are explicitly initialized in the program.

In the past, using the `register` storage class specifier was appropriate for certain variables because computers were much slower than they are today. Now, `register` is rarely needed. Today's *optimizing compilers* are capable of recognizing situations in which registers can be used to speed program execution. *RISC (reduced instruction set computing)* machines provide more registers for optimizing compilers to use. RISC tries to reduce the number of instructions to be executed by placing partial results of calculations in registers.

The storage class specifier `extern` declares an object to be *external*. External objects are either functions or variables. All functions are automatically external because functions can not be defined inside other functions (as is the case in some other languages such as Pascal). A variable is external if it is defined outside any function. An external variable is defined with a type and a name like any other variable, and can be accessed by any function defined after the variable in the file. External variables are normally defined at the beginning of the file. If an external variable is defined between functions, any function defined before the external variable that wishes to refer to the variable must contain an `extern` declaration of the variable. The `extern` declaration makes the variable visible to the function. External variables may be initialized only when the variable is defined. If an external variable is not initialized, it is automatically set to 0.

CPE 5.9

Declaring a variable as external rather than local allows unintended side effects to occur when a function that does not need access to a variable accidentally or maliciously modifies the variable.

GPP 5.17

Variables used only in a particular function should be declared as local variables in that function rather than as external variables.

Static objects are functions or variables. When the keyword `static` is applied to a function or an external variable, the function or external variable may be referred to only by other functions in that file. We will discuss programs containing multiple files in detail in Chapter 13. Local variables declared with `static` retain their values between calls to the function in which they are defined—the first time the function is called a `static` variable contains its initial value, but the next time the function is called, the variable contains the value it had when the function ended previously. Variables declared to be `static` are initialized to 0 by the compiler if they are not explicitly initialized in the program.

5.12 Scope Rules

The *scope* of an identifier is the portion of the program in which the identifier can be referenced. For example, when we declare a local variable in a block, it can only be referenced in that block. The four scopes for an identifier are *function scope*, *file scope*, *block scope*, and *function prototype scope*.

Labels are the only identifiers with *function scope*. Labels can be used anywhere in the function in which they appear, but can not be referenced from outside the function body. Labels are implementation details that functions hide from one another. This hiding—more formally called *information hiding*—is one of the most fundamental principles of good software engineering.

An identifier declared outside any function has file scope. Such an identifier is "known" in all functions from the point at which the identifier declared until the end of the file. External variables, function definitions, and function prototypes placed outside a function all have file scope.

Identifiers declared inside a block have *block scope*. Block scope ends at the terminating right brace (`}`) of the block. Automatic variables declared at the beginning of a function have block scope as do function parameters, which are considered local variables by the function. Any block may contain variable declarations. When blocks are nested, and an identifier in an outer block has the same name as an identifier in an inner block, the identifier in the outer block is "hidden" until the inner block terminates. This means that while executing in the inner block, the inner block sees the value of its own identifier, and not the value of the identically named identifier in the enclosing block.

Figure 5.14 illustrates scoping. The figure shows the values of the variables x and y through a program with nested blocks. The body of `main` is the outer block. Nested block 1 and nested block 2 are "on the same level" inside the body of `main`. Variables x and y are first declared in the body of `main` and initialized with the values 1 and 2 respectively. In the first nested block, the variable x is declared again and initialized with the value 3. At this point the active variables are y in the outer block, and x in nested block 1. When the end of the first nested block is reached, x in nested block 1 is discarded because automatic variables only exist while the block in which they are defined is being executed. Now the active variables are x and y in main. Nested block 2 is then entered, and y is declared and initialized to 4. This declaration hides y in the outer block, so the active variables are x in the outer block and y in nested block 2. When the end of the second nested block is reached, y in nested block 2 is discarded. The active variables are once again x and y in the outer block.

CPE 5.10
_____
Accidentally using the same name for an identifier in an inner block as is used for an identifier in an outer block, when in fact, the programmer wants the identifier in the outer block to be active for the duration of the inner block.

GPP 5.18
_____
Avoid variable names that hide names in other scopes. This can be accomplished simply by avoiding the use of duplicate identifiers in a program.

Identifiers declared in the parameter list of a function prototype have *function prototype scope*. Any identifier with function prototype scope is known only in the function prototype.

5.13 Recursion

The programs we have discussed are generally structured as functions that call one another in a disciplined hierarchical, manner. For some types of problems, it is useful to have functions call themselves. A *recursive function* is a function that calls itself either directly or indirectly. Recursion is a complex topic discussed at length in upper-level computer science courses. In this section and the next, simple examples of recursion are presented.

The factorial of a nonnegative integer *n*, written *n*! (and pronounced "*n* factorial"), is the product

$$n * (n - 1) * (n - 2) * \ldots * 1$$

with 1! equal to 1, and 0! defined to be 1. For example, 5! is the product $5 * 4 * 3 * 2 * 1$, which is equal to 120.

The factorial of an integer, `number`, greater than or equal to 0 can be calculated *iteratively* (nonrecursively) using `for` as follows:

```
factorial = 1;
for(counter = number; counter >= 1; counter--)
    factorial *= counter;
```

A recursive definition of the factorial function is arrived at by observing the relationship

$$n! = n * (n - 1)!$$

For example, 5! is clearly equal to 5 * 4! as is shown by the following:

$$5! = 5 * 4 * 3 * 2 * 1$$
$$5! = 5 * (4 * 3 * 2 * 1)$$
$$5! = 5 * (4!)$$

```
/* An example of scoping */
#include <stdio.h>

main()
{
    int x = 1, y = 2;

    printf("The values printed are:\n");
    printf("x and y in the outer block\n");
    printf("x = %d, y = %d\n\n", x, y);

    {   /* nested block 1 */
        int     x = 3;

        printf("%s\n%s\n",
            "x in the nested block, ",
            "and y in the outer block");
        printf("x = %d, y = %d\n\n", x, y);
    }

    printf("x and y in the outer block\n");
    printf("x = %d, y = %d\n\n", x, y);

    {   /* nested block 2 */
        int y = 4;

        printf("%s\n%s\n",
            "x in the outer block, ",
            "and y in the nested block");
        printf("x = %d, y = %d\n\n", x, y);
    }

    printf("x and y in the outer block\n");
    printf("x = %d, y = %d\n", x, y);
}
```

```
The values printed are:
x and y in the outer block
x = 1, y = 2

x in the nested block,
and y in the outer block
x = 3, y = 2

x and y in the outer block
x = 1, y = 2

x in the outer block,
and y in the nested block
x = 1, y = 4

x and y in the outer block
x = 1, y = 2
```

Fig. 5.14 Hiding identifiers in outer scopes with block scoping.

The evaluation of 5! would proceed as shown in Fig. 5.15. Figure 5.15a shows how the succession of recursive calls proceeds until 1! is evaluated to be 1, which terminates the recursion. Figure 5.15b shows the values returned from each recursive call to its caller until the final value is calculated and returned.

The program of Fig. 5.16 uses recursion to calculate and print the factorials of the integers 0 to 10 (the choice of the data type `long` will be explained momentarily). The recursive function `factorial` first tests to see if a terminating condition is true, i.e., is `number` less than or equal to 1. If `number` is indeed less than or equal to 1, `factorial` returns 1, no further recursion is necessary, and the program terminates. If `number` is greater than 1, the statement

```
return number * factorial(number - 1);
```

expresses the problem as the product of `number` and a recursive call to `factorial` evaluating the factorial of `number - 1`. Note that `factorial(number - 1)` is a slightly simpler problem than the original calculation `factorial(number)`.

Function `factorial` has been declared to receive a parameter of type `long` and return a result of type `long`. This is shorthand notation for `long int`. The ANSI standard specifies that a variable of type `long int` is stored in at least 4 bytes, and thus may hold a value as large as +2147483647. As can be seen in Fig. 5.16, factorial values become large quickly. We have chosen the data type `long` so the program can calculate factorials greater than 7! on computers with small (such as 2 byte) integers. The conversion specifier `%ld` is used to print `long` values. Unfortunately, the `factorial` function produces large values so quickly that even `long int` does not

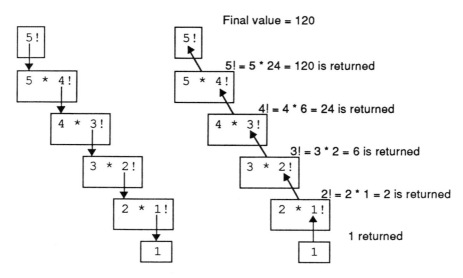

a) Procession of recursive calls.   b) Values returned from each recursive call.

Fig. 5.15 Recursive evaluation of 5!.

help us print many factorial values before the size of a `long int` variable is exceeded. As we will explore in the exercises, `float` and `double` may ultimately be needed by the user desiring to calculate factorials.

There are typically two components to any recursive function, namely the *base case* and the *recursion step*. When the base (or trivial) case is detected, the recursion terminates a result is returned. The recursion step expresses the problem as a recursive call that evaluates a slightly simpler problem. Each time the recursion step is executed, the problem being solved becomes simpler, eventually converging on the base case. In evaluating a factorial, for example, we know that 0! equals 1 and 1! equals 1, so no further recursion is needed, and the result 1 can be returned.

CPE 5.11
_____

Forgetting to return a value from a recursive function when one is needed.

```
/* recursive factorial function */
#include <stdio.h>

long factorial(long);

main()
{
    int i;

    for (i = 0; i <= 10; i++)
        printf("%2d! = %ld\n", i, factorial(i));
}

long factorial(long number)
{
    if (number <= 1)
        return 1;
    else
        return(number * factorial(number - 1));
}
```

```
 0! = 1
 1! = 1
 2! = 2
 3! = 6
 4! = 24
 5! = 120
 6! = 720
 7! = 5040
 8! = 40320
 9! = 362880
10! = 3628800
```

Fig. 5.16 Calculating factorials with a recursive function.

CPE 5.12

Either omitting the base case, or writing the recursion step incorrectly so that it does not converge on the base case will cause infinite recursion, eventually exhausting memory. This is analogous to the problem of an infinite loop in an iterative (nonrecursive) solution.

5.14 Example Using Recursion: The Fibonacci Series

The Fibonacci series

$$0, 1, 1, 2, 3, 5, 8, 13, 21, \ldots$$

begins with 0 and 1 and has the property that each subsequent Fibonacci number is the sum of the previous two Fibonacci numbers.

The series occurs in nature and, in particular, describes a form of Fibonacci spiral. The ratio of successive Fibonacci numbers converges on a constant value of 1.618... This number, too, repeatedly occurs in nature and has been called the *golden ratio* or the *golden mean*. Humans tend to find the golden mean aesthetically pleasing. Architects often design windows, rooms, and buildings whose length and width are in the ratio of the golden mean. Postcards are often designed with a golden mean length/width ratio.

The Fibonacci series may be defined recursively as follows:

fibonacci(0) = 0
fibonacci(1) = 1
fibonacci(n) = fibonacci(n – 1) + fibonacci(n – 2)

The program in Fig. 5.17 calculates the ith Fibonacci number recursively. Notice that Fibonacci numbers tend to become large quickly. Therefore, we have chosen the data type `long` for the parameter type and the return type in function `fibonacci`.

The first call to `fibonacci` from `main` is not a recursive call, but all subsequent calls to `fibonacci` are recursive. Each time `fibonacci` is invoked, it immediately tests for the base case of n being 0 or 1. If this is true, n is returned. If n is greater than 1, the recursion step interestingly generates *two* recursive calls, each of which is for a slightly simpler problem than the original call to `fibonacci`. Figure 5.18 shows how function `fibonacci` would evaluate `fibonacci(3)` —we abbreviate `fibonacci` simply as `f` to make the figure more readable.

Note that the order in which the figure indicates the recursive calls to `fibonacci` are executed may at first seem incorrect. For example, when `f(3)` is evaluated, it generates two calls to evaluate `f(2)` and `f(1)`, so one might expect these calls to be executed left-to-right one immediately after the other. Actually, these calls are executed left-to-right, but while `f(2)` is being executed, the function generates recursive calls to `f(1)` and `f(0)`. Thus, the `f(1)` call "below" `f(2)` in the diagram is executed before the `f(1)` call to the right of `f(2)` in the diagram.

```
#include <stdio.h>

main()
{
    long result, number;
    long fibonacci(long);

    printf("Enter an integer: ");
    scanf("%ld", &number);
    result = fibonacci(number);
    printf("Fibonacci(%ld) = %ld\n", number, result);
}

long fibonacci(long n)
{
    if (n == 0 || n == 1)
        return n;
    else
        return fibonacci(n - 1) + fibonacci(n - 2);
}
```

```
Enter an integer: 0
Fibonacci(0) = 0

Enter an integer: 1
Fibonacci(1) = 1

Enter an integer: 2
Fibonacci(2) = 1

Enter an integer: 3
Fibonacci(3) = 2

Enter an integer: 4
Fibonacci(4) = 3

Enter an integer: 5
Fibonacci(5) = 5

Enter an integer: 6
Fibonacci(6) = 8

Enter an integer: 10
Fibonacci(10) = 55

Enter an integer: 20
Fibonacci(20) = 6765

Enter an integer: 30
Fibonacci(30) = 832040

Enter an integer: 35
Fibonacci(35) = 9227465
```

Fig. 5.17 Recursively generating Fibonacci numbers.

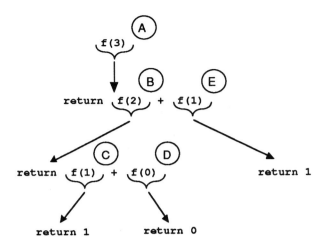

A: Nonrecursive call from **main**. A is only "open" call.

B: First recursive call. A and B calls are "open."

C: Second recursive call. A, B, and C calls are "open."

D: Third recursive call. C has returned a value, and only A, B, and D calls are open.

E: Fourth recursive call. D has returned a value, B has returned a value, and only A and E calls are open.

Finally, E and A return their values and **main** gets back the result 2.

Fig. 5.18 Sequence of recursive calls to function **fibonacci**.

5.15 Recursion vs. Iteration

In the previous sections, we studied two functions that can easily be implemented either recursively or iteratively. Why would the programmer choose one approach over the other?

Recursion has many negatives. It repeatedly invokes the mechanism, and consequently the overhead, of function calls. This can be expensive in both processor time and memory space. Iteration normally occurs within a function so the overhead of repeated function calls is omitted.

In the final analysis, there is one truly significant reason for choosing recursion over iteration as is summarized in GPP 5.19.

GPP 5.19
_____

Any problem that can be solved recursively can also be solved iteratively (nonrecursively). A recursive approach is normally chosen in preference to an iterative approach when the recursive approach more naturally mirrors the problem and results in a program that is easier to understand and debug.

Summary

- The best way to develop and maintain a large program is to divide it into several smaller program modules each of which is more manageable than the original program. Modules are written as functions in C.

- A function is invoked by a function call. The function call mentions the function by name and provides information (as arguments) that the called function needs to perform its task.

- The purpose of information hiding is for functions to have access only to the information they need to complete their tasks. This is a means of implementing the principle of least privilege, one of the most important principles of good software engineering.

- Functions are normally invoked in a program by writing the name of the function followed by a left parenthesis followed by the *argument* (or a comma separated list of arguments) of the function followed by a right parenthesis.

- Data type `double` is a floating point type like `float`. A variable of type `double` can store a value of much greater magnitude and precision than `float` can store.

- Each argument of a function may be a constant, a variable, or an expression.

- A local variable is known only in a function definition. Other functions are not allowed to know the names of a function's local variables, nor is any function allowed to know the implementation details of any other function.

- The general format for a function definition is

    return-value-type function-name (*parameter-list*)
    {
        declarations

        statements
    }

    The *return-value-type* states the type of the value returned to the calling function. If a function does not return a value, the *return-value-type* is declared as `void`. The *function-name* is any valid identifier. The *parameter-list* is a comma-separated list containing the declarations of the variables that will be passed to the function. If a function does not receive any values, *parameter-list* is declared as `void`. The *function-body* is the set of declarations and statements that constitute the function.

- The arguments passed to a function should match in number, type, and order with the parameters in the function definition.

- When a program encounters a function, control is transferred from the point of invocation to the called function, the statements of the called function are executed, and control returns to the caller.

- A called function can return control to the caller in one of three ways. If the function does not return a value, control is returned when the function-ending right brace is reached, or by executing the statement

```
return;
```
If the function does return a value, the statement
```
return expression;
```
returns the value of `expression`.

- A function prototype declares the type of the result returned by the function, and declares the number, the types, and order of the parameters the function expects to receive.
- Function prototypes enable the compiler to verify that functions are called correctly.
- The compiler ignores variable names mentioned in the function prototype.
- Each standard library has a corresponding header file containing the function prototypes for all the functions in that library, as well as definitions of various symbolic constants needed by those functions.
- Programmers can create and include their own header files.
- When an argument is passed call by value, a *copy* of the variable's value is made and the copy is passed to the called function. Changes to the copy in the called function do not affect the original variable's value.
- All calls are call by value.
- The `rand` function generates an integer between 0 and RAND_MAX which is defined by the ANSI C standard to be at least 32767.
- The function prototypes for `rand` and `srand` are contained in `<stdlib.h>`.
- Values produced by `rand` can be scaled and shifted to produce values in a specific range.
- To randomize a program, use the C standard library function `srand`.
- The `srand` statement is ordinarily inserted in a program only after the program has been thoroughly debugged. While debugging, it is better to omit `srand`. This ensures repeatability, which is essential to proving that corrections to a random number generation program work properly.
- To randomize without the need for entering a seed each time, we may use `srand(clock())`. The `clock` function returns the elapsed processor time since program execution began. The `clock` function prototype is located in the header `<time.h>`.
- The general equation for scaling and shifting a random number is
```
n = a + rand() % b;
```
where a is the shifting value (which is equal to the first number in the desired range of consecutive integers), and b is the scaling factor (which is equal to the width of the desired range of consecutive integers).
- A recursive function is a function that calls itself directly or indirectly.
- Recursive functions are implemented as a succession of recursive function calls leading to a base case that terminates the recursion. Each recursive call is designed to solve a slightly simpler version of the problem.

- There are two components to any recursive function. One provides a means for the recursion to terminate by evaluating the simplest case. The other expresses the problem as a recursive call that evaluates a slightly simpler problem. The recursive call with a simpler version of the problem is designed to slice away at the problem gradually until it becomes the base case.

Terminology

abstraction	object-oriented programming
argument in a function call	optimizing compiler
automatic variable	parameter in a function definition
`auto` storage class specifier	pop
base case in recursion	principle of least privilege
block	programmer-defined function
block scope	pseudo-random numbers
C standard library	push
called function	`rand`
caller	`RAND_MAX`
calling function	randomize
call by reference	random number generation
call by value	recursion
`clock`	recursive call
copy of a value	recursive function
divide and conquer	`register` storage class specifier
element of chance	`return`
`extern` storage class specifier	return value type
factorial function	RISC
file scope	scaling
formal parameter	`%s` conversion specifier
function	scope
function call	shifting
function declaration	side effects
function definition	simulation
function prototype	software engineering
function prototype scope	software reusability
function scope	`srand`
global variable	standard library header files
header file	`static` storage class specifier
information hiding	`static` variable
invoke a function	storage classes
iteration	storage class specifier
local variable	`time`
main function	`unsigned`
math library functions	`unsigned int`
modular program	`void`
module	

Common Programming Errors

5.1 Forgetting to include the math header file when using math library functions can cause strange results.

5.2 Omitting the return-value-type causes a syntax error if the function prototype specifies that a type other than `int` is returned.

5.3 Forgetting to return a value from a function that is supposed to return a value can lead to unexpected errors. The ANSI standard states that the result of this action is undefined.

5.4 Returning a value from a function whose return type has been declared `void` causes a syntax error.

5.5 Placing a semicolon after the right parenthesis enclosing the parameter list of a function definition is a syntax error.

5.6 Defining a function parameter again as a local variable within the function is a syntax error.

5.7 Defining a function in another function is a syntax error.

5.8 Forgetting the semicolon at the end of a function prototype causes a syntax error.

5.9 Declaring a variable as external rather than local allows unintended side effects to occur when a function that does not need access to the variable accidentally or maliciously modifies the variable.

5.10 Accidentally using the same name for an identifier in an inner block as is used for an identifier in an outer block, when in fact, the programmer wants the identifier in the outer block to be active for the duration of the inner block.

5.11 Forgetting to return a value from a recursive function when one is needed.

5.12 Either omitting the base case, or writing the recursion step incorrectly so that it does not converge on the base case will cause infinite recursion, eventually exhausting memory. This is analogous to the problem of an infinite loop in an iterative (nonrecursive) solution.

Good Programming Practices

5.1 Familiarize yourself with the rich collection of functions available in the ANSI C standard library.

5.2 Avoid reinventing the wheel. When possible, use ANSI C standard library functions instead of writing new functions. This reduces program development time. It also tends to make programs more portable.

5.3 Include the math header file by using the preprocessor directive `#include <math.h>` when using functions in the math library.

5.4 In programs containing many functions, `main` should be implemented as a group of calls to functions that perform the bulk of the program's work.

5.5 Each function should be limited to performing a single, well-defined task, and the function name should effectively express that task. This facilitates abstraction and promotes software reusability.

5.6   Place a blank line between function definitions to separate the functions and enhance program readability.

5.7   Even though an omitted return type defaults to `int`, always state the return type explicitly. The return type for `main`, however, is normally omitted.

5.8   Include the type of each parameter in the parameter list, even if that parameter is of the default type `int`.

5.9   Do not use the same names for the arguments passed to a function and the corresponding parameters in the function definition. This helps avoid ambiguity.

5.10 Choosing meaningful function names and meaningful parameter names makes programs more readable and helps avoid excessive use of comments.

5.11 A function should be no longer than one page. Better yet, a function should be no longer than half a page. Small functions promote software reusability.

5.12 Programs should be written as collections of small functions. This makes programs easier to write, debug, maintain and modify.

5.13 A function requiring a large number of parameters may be performing too many tasks. Consider dividing the function into smaller functions that perform the separate tasks. The function header should fit on one line if possible.

5.14 The function prototype, function header, and function calls should all agree in the number, type, and order of arguments and parameters, and in the type of return value.

5.15 Include function prototypes for all functions to use C's type checking capabilities. Use `#include` preprocessor directives to obtain function prototypes for the standard library functions from the header files for the appropriate libraries. Also use `#include` to obtain header files containing function prototypes used by your group members.

5.16 Parameter names are sometimes included in function prototypes for documentation purposes. The compiler ignores these names.

5.17 Variables used only in a particular function should be declared as local variables in that function rather than as external variables.

5.18 Avoid variable names that hide names in other scopes. This can be accomplished simply by avoiding the use of duplicate identifiers in a program.

5.19 Any problem that can be solved recursively can also be solved iteratively (nonrecursively). A recursive approach is normally chosen in preference to an iterative approach when the recursive approach more naturally mirrors the problem and results in a program that is easier to understand and debug.

Self-Review Exercises

5.1   Answer each of the following:
   a) A program module in C is called a _____.
   b) A function is invoked with a _____.
   c) A variable that is known only within the function in which it is defined is called a _____.
   d) The _____ statement in a called function is used to pass the value of an expression back to the calling function.

e) The keyword _____ is used in a function header to indicate that a function does not return a value or to indicate that a function contains no parameters.

f) The _____ of an identifier is the portion of the program in which the identifier can be used.

g) The three ways to return control from a called function to a caller are _____, _____, and _____.

h) A _____ allows the compiler to check the number, types, and order of the arguments passed to a function.

i) The _____ function is used to produce random numbers.

j) The _____ function is used to set the random number seed to randomize a program.

k) The four storage class specifiers in C are _____, _____, _____, and _____.

l) Variables declared in a block or in the parameter list of a function are assumed to be of storage class _____ unless specified otherwise.

m) The storage class specifier _____ is a recommendation to the compiler to store a variable in one of the computer's registers.

n) A variable declared outside any block or function is an _____ variable.

o) For a local variable in a function to retain its value between calls to the function, it must be declared with the _____ storage class specifier.

p) The four possible scopes of an identifier are _____, _____, _____, and _____.

q) A function that calls itself either directly or indirectly is a _____ function.

r) A recursive function typically has two components: one that provides a means for the recursion to terminate by testing for a _____ case, and one that expresses the problem as a recursive call that evaluates a slightly simpler problem than in the original call.

5.2 For the following program, state the scope (either function scope, file scope, block scope, or function prototype scope) of each of the following elements.

a) The variable x in **main**.
b) The variable y in **cube**.
c) The function **cube**.
d) The function **main**.
e) The function prototype for **cube**.
f) The identifier y in the function prototype for **cube**.

```
#include <stdio.h>
int cube(int y);

main()
{
    int x;

    for (x = 1; x <= 10; x++)
        printf("%d\n", cube(x));
}

int cube(int y)
{
    return y * y * y;
}
```

5.3   Write a program that tests if the examples of the math library function calls shown in Fig. 5.2 actually produce the indicated results.

5.4   Give the function header for each of the following functions.

    a)   Function `hypotenuse` that takes two double-precision floating point arguments, `side1` and `side2`, and returns a double-precision floating point result.

    b)   Function `power` that takes two integer arguments, `base` and `exponent`, and returns an integer result.

    c)   Function `smallest` that takes three integer arguments, `x`, `y`, `z`, and returns an integer result.

    d)   Function `instructions` that does not receive any arguments and does not return a value. (Note: Such functions are commonly used to display instructions to a user.)

    e)   Function `inttofloat` that takes an integer argument, `number`, and returns a floating point result.

5.5   Give the function prototype for each of the following:

    a)   The function described in 5.4a.

    b)   The function described in 5.4b.

    c)   The function described in 5.4c.

    d)   The function described in 5.4d.

    e)   The function described in 5.4e.

5.6   Write a declaration for each of the following:

    a)   Integer `count` that should be maintained in a register. Initialize `count` to 0.

    b)   Floating point variable `lastval` that is to retain its value between calls to the function in which it is defined.

    c)   External integer `number` whose scope should be restricted to the remainder of the file in which it is defined.

5.7   Find the error in each of the following program segments and explain how the error can be corrected:

    a)
```
int g(void) {
    printf("Inside function g\n");

    int h(void) {
        printf("Inside function h\n");
    }
}
```

    b)
```
int sum(int x, int y) {
    int result;

    result = x + y;
}
```

    c)
```
int sum(int n) {
    if (n == 0)
        return 0;
    else
        n + sum(n - 1);
}
```

    d)
```
void f(float a); {
    float a;

    printf("%f", a);
}
```

```
e)   void product(void) {
         int a, b, c, result;

         printf("Enter three integers: ")
         scanf("%d%d%d", &a, &b, &c);
         result = a * b * c;
         printf("Result is %d", result);
         return result;
     }
f)   int sum(int, int)
```

Answers to Self-Review Exercises

5.1   a) Function. b) Function call. c) Local variable. d) **return**. e) **void**. f) Scope. g) **return;** or **return expression;** or encountering the closing left brace of a function. h) Function prototype. i) **rand**. j) **srand**. k) **auto, register, extern, static**. l) Automatic. m) **register**. n) External, global. o) **static**. p) Function scope, file scope, block scope, function prototype scope. q) Recursive. r) Base case.

5.2   a) Block scope. b) Block Scope. c) File scope. d) File scope. e) File scope. f) Function prototype scope.

5.3

```
/* Testing the math library functions */
#include <stdio.h>
#include <math.h>

main()
{
    printf("sqrt(%.1f) = %.1f\n", 900.0, sqrt(900.0));
    printf("sqrt(%.1f) = %.1f\n", 9.0, sqrt(9.0));
    printf("exp(%.1f) = %f\n", 1.0, exp(1.0));
    printf("exp(%.1f) = %f\n", 2.0, exp(2.0));
    printf("log(%f) = %.1f\n", 2.718282, log(2.718282));
    printf("log(%f) = %.1f\n", 7.389056, log(7.389056));
    printf("log10(%.1f) = %.1f\n", 1.0, log10(1.0));
    printf("log10(%.1f) = %.1f\n", 10.0, log10(10.0));
    printf("log10(%.1f) = %.1f\n", 100.0, log10(100.0));
    printf("fabs(%.1f) = %.1f\n", 13.5, fabs(13.5));
    printf("fabs(%.1f) = %.1f\n", 0.0, fabs(0.0));
    printf("fabs(%.1f) = %.1f\n", -13.5, fabs(-13.5));
    printf("ceil(%.1f) = %.1f\n", 9.2, ceil(9.2));
    printf("ceil(%.1f) = %.1f\n", -9.8, ceil(-9.8));
    printf("floor(%.1f) = %.1f\n", 9.2, floor(9.2));
    printf("floor(%.1f) = %.1f\n", -9.8, floor(-9.8));
    printf("pow(%.1f, %.1f) = %.1f\n", 2.0, 7.0, pow(2.0, 7.0));
    printf("pow(%.1f, %.1f) = %.1f\n", 9.0, 0.5, pow(9.0, 0.5));
    printf("fmod(%.3f/%.3f) = %.3f\n",
        13.675, 2.333, fmod(13.675, 2.333));
    printf("sin(%.1f) = %.1f\n", 0.0, sin(0.0));
    printf("cos(%.1f) = %.1f\n", 0.0, cos(0.0));
    printf("tan(%.1f) = %.1f\n", 0.0, tan(0.0));
}
```

```
sqrt(900.0) = 30.0
sqrt(9.0) = 3.0
exp(1.0) = 2.718282
exp(2.0) = 7.389056
log(2.718282) = 1.0
log(7.389056) = 2.0
log10(1.0) = 0.0
log10(10.0) = 1.0
log10(100.0) = 2.0
fabs(13.5) = 13.5
fabs(0.0) = 0.0
fabs(-13.5) = 13.5
ceil(9.2) = 10.0
ceil(-9.8) = -9.0
floor(9.2) = 9.0
floor(-9.8) = -10.0
pow(2.0, 7.0) = 128.0
pow(9.0, 0.5) = 3.0
fmod(13.675/2.333) = 2.010
sin(0.0) = 0.0
cos(0.0) = 1.0
tan(0.0) = 0.0
```

5.4   a) `double hypotenuse(double side1, double side2)`
      b) `int power(int base, int exponent)`
      c) `int smallest(int x, int y, int z)`
      d) `void instructions(void)`
      e) `float inttofloat(int number)`

5.5   a) `double hypotenuse(double, double);`
      b) `int power(int, int);`
      c) `int smallest(int, int, int);`
      d) `void instructions(void);`
      e) `float inttofloat(int);`

5.6   a) `register int count = 0;`
      b) `extern int done;`
      c) `static float lastval;`
      d) `static int number;`
      Note: This would appear outside any function definition.

5.7   a) Error: Function `h` is defined in function `g`.
      Correction: Move the definition of `h` out of the definition of `g`.
      b) Error: The function is supposed to return an integer, but does not.
      Correction: Eliminate the variable **result** and place the statement

            `return x + y;`

      in the function.
      c) Error: The result of `n + sum(n - 1)` is not returned, therefore the function
will return an improper result.
      Correction: Rewrite the statement in the **else** clause as

            `return n + sum(n - 1);`

      d) Error: Semicolon after the right parenthesis that encloses the parameter list, and
redefining the parameter **a** in the function definition.

Correction: Delete the semicolon after the right parenthesis of the parameter list, and delete the declaration **float a;**.

e) Error: The function returns a value when it is not supposed to.

Correction: Eliminate the **return** statement.

f) Error: Missing a semicolon at the end of the function prototype, or function header missing names and body.

Correction: Add a semicolon to the end of the function prototype, or define function **sum** as follows:

```
int sum(int x, int y)
{
    return x + y;
}
```

Exercises

5.8 Show the value of x after each of the following statements is performed:

a) **x = fabs(7.5)**

b) **x = floor(7.5)**

c) **x = fabs(0.0)**

d) **x = ceil(0.0)**

e) **x = fabs(-6.4)**

f) **x = ceil(-6.4)**

g) **x = ceil(-fabs(-8+floor(-5.5)))**

5.9 A parking garage charges a $2.00 minimum fee to park for up to three hours. The garage charges an additional $0.50 per hour for each hour *or part thereof* in excess of three hours. The maximum charge for any given 24-hour period is $10.00. Assume that no car parks for longer than 24 hours at a time. Write a program that will calculate and print the parking charges for each of 3 customers who parked their cars in this garage yesterday. You should enter the hours parked for each customer. Your program should print the results in a neat tabular format, and should calculate and print the total of yesterday's receipts. The program should use the function **calculatecharges** to determine the charge for each customer. Use the following format for your outputs:

Car	Hours	Charge
1	1.5	2.00
2	4.0	2.50
3	24.0	10.00
TOTAL	29.5	14.50

5.10 One important application of the **floor** function is rounding a number to the nearest integer. The statement

```
y = floor(x + .5);
```

will round the number x to the nearest integer, and assign the result to y. Write a program that reads several numbers and uses the preceding statement to round each of these numbers to the nearest integer. For each number processed, print both the original number and the rounded number.

5.11 The **floor** function may also be used to round a number to a particular decimal place. The statement

```
y = floor(x * 10 + .5) / 10;
```

will round the number **x** to the tenths position (i.e., the first position to the right of the decimal point). The statement

```
y = floor(x * 100 + .5) / 100;
```

will round the number **x** to the hundredths position (i.e., the second position to the right of the decimal point).

Write a program that defines four functions to round a number **x** in various ways

    a)   **roundtointeger(number)**
    b)   **roundtotenths(number)**
    c)   **roundtohundreths(number)**
    d)   **roundtothousandths(number)**

For each value read your program should print the original value, the number rounded to the nearest integer, the number rounded to the nearest tenth, the number rounded to the nearest hundredth, and the number rounded to the nearest thousandth.

5.12   Answer each of the following questions.
    a)   What does it mean to choose numbers "at random?"
    b)   Why is the **rand** function useful for simulating games of chance?
    c)   Why would you randomize a program by using **srand**? Under what circumstances is it desirable not to randomize?
    d)   Why is it often necessary to scale and/or shift the values produced by **rand**?
    e)   Why is computerized simulation of real-world situations a useful technique?

5.13   Write statements that assign an integer (at random) to the variable n in each of the following ranges:
    a) $1 \le n \le 2$
    b) $1 \le n \le 6$
    c) $1 \le n \le 100$
    d) $0 \le n \le 9$
    e) $100 \le n \le 112$
    f) $1000 \le n \le 1112$
    g) $-1 \le n \le 1$
    h) $-3 \le n \le 11$

5.14   For each of the following sets of integers, write a single statement that will print a number at random from the set.
    a)   2, 4, 6, 8, 10.
    b)   3, 5, 7, 9, 11.
    c)   6, 10, 14, 18, 22.

5.15   Define a function **hypotenuse** that calculates the length of the hypotenuse of a right triangle when the other two sides are given. Use this function in a program to determine the length of the hypotenuse for each of the following triangles. The function should take two arguments of type **double** and return the hypotenuse as a **double**.

Triangle	Side 1	Side 2
1	3.0	4.0
2	5.0	12.0
3	8.0	15.0

5.16 Write a function **integerpower(base, exponent)** that returns the value of the expression

$base^{exponent}$

For example, **integerpower(3,4)** = 3 * 3 * 3 * 3. Assume that **exponent** is a positive, nonzero integer, and **base** is an integer. The function **power** should use **for** to control the calculation. Do not use any math library functions.

5.17 Write a function **multiple** that determines for a pair of integers whether the second integer is a multiple of the first. The function should take two integer arguments and return **1** (true) if the second is a multiple of the first, and **0** (false) otherwise. Use this function in a program that inputs a series of pairs of integers.

5.18 Write a program that inputs a series of integers and passes them one at a time to function **even** which uses the modulus operator to determine if an integer is even. The function should take an integer argument and return **1** if the integer is even and **0** otherwise.

5.19 Write a function that will display at the left margin of the screen a solid square of asterisks whose side is specified in integer parameter **side**. For example, if **side** is **4**, the function should display

```
****
****
****
****
```

5.20 Modify the function created in Exercise 5.19 to form the square out of whatever character is contained in character parameter **fillcharacter**. Thus if **side** is 5 and **fillcharacter** is "#" then this function should print

```
#####
#####
#####
#####
#####
```

5.21 Use techniques similar to those developed in Exercises 5.19 and 5.20 to produce a program that graphs a wide range of shapes.

5.22 Write program segments that accomplish each of the following:
    a) Calculate the integer part of the quotient when integer **a** is divided by integer **b**.
    b) Calculate the integer remainder when integer **a** is divided by integer **b**.
    c) Use the program pieces developed in a) and b) to write a function that inputs an integer between **1** and **32767** and prints it as a series of digits, each pair of which is separated by two spaces. For example, if the number **4562** is entered, then your function should print

      4   5   6   2

5.23 Write a function that takes the time as three integer arguments (for hours, minutes, and seconds), and returns the number of seconds since the last time the clock "struck 12." Use this function to calculate the amount of time in seconds between two times, both of which are within one 12-hour cycle of the clock.

5.24 Implement the following integer functions:
    a) Write a function **Celsius** that returns the Celsius equivalent of a Fahrenheit temperature.

b)   Write a function **Fahrenheit** that returns the Fahrenheit equivalent of a Celsius temperature.

c)   Use these functions to write a program that prints charts showing the Fahrenheit equivalents of all Celsius temperatures from 0 to 100 degrees, and the Celsius equivalents of all Fahrenheit temperatures from 32 to 212 degrees. Print the outputs in a condensed neat tabular format that minimizes the number of lines of output while remaining readable.

5.25   Write a function that returns the smallest of three floating point numbers.

5.26   An integer number is said to be a *perfect number* if its factors, including 1 (but not the number itself), sum to the number. For example, 6 is a perfect number because 6 = 1 + 2 + 3. Write a function **perfect** that determines if parameter **number** is a perfect number. Use this function in a program that determines and prints all the perfect numbers between 1 and 1000. Print the factors of each perfect number to confirm that the number is indeed perfect. Challenge the power of your computer by testing numbers much larger than 1000.

5.27   An integer is said to be *prime* if it is divisible only by 1 and itself. For example, 2, 3, 5, and 7 are prime, but 4, 6, 8, and 9 are not.

a)   Write a function that determines if a number is prime.

b)   Use this function in a program that determines and prints all the prime numbers between 1 and 10,000. How many of these 10,000 numbers do you really have to test before being sure that you have found all the primes?

c)   Initially you might think that $n/2$ is the upper limit for which you must test to see if a number is prime, but you need only go as high as the square root of n. Why? Rewrite the program, and run it both ways. Estimate the performance improvement.

5.28   Write a function that takes an integer value and returns the number with its digits reversed. For example, given the number 7631, the function should return 1367.

5.29   The *greatest common divisor (GCD)* of two integers is the largest integer that evenly divides each of the two numbers. Write a function **gcd** that returns the greatest common divisor of two integers.

5.30   Write a function **qualitypoints** that inputs a student's average and returns 4 if a student's average is 90-100, 3 if the average is 80-89, 2 if the average is 70-79, 1 if the average is 60-69, and 0 if the average is lower than 60.

5.31   Write a program that simulates coin tossing. For each toss of the coin the program should print **Heads** or **Tails**. Let the program toss the coin 100 times, and count the number of times each side of the coin appears. Print the results. The program should call a separate function **flip** that takes no arguments and returns **0** for tails and **1** for heads. *Note:* If the program realistically simulates the coin tossing, then each side of the coin should appear approximately half the time for a total of approximately 50 heads and 50 tails.

5.32   Computers are playing an increasing role in education. Write a program that will help an elementary school student learn multiplication. Use **rand** to produce two positive one-digit integers. It should then type a question such as:

   How much is 6 times 7?

The student then types the answer. Your program checks the student's answer. If it is correct, print **"Very good!"** and then ask another multiplication question. If the answer is wrong, print **"No. Please try again."** and then let the student try the same question again repeatedly until the student finally gets it right.

5.33   The use of computers in education is referred to as *computer-assisted instruction* (CAI). One problem that can develop in CAI environments is student fatigue. This can often be eliminated by varying the computer's dialogue to hold the student's attention. Modify the program of Exercise 5.32 so that the computer prints various comments for each correct answer and each incorrect answer as follows:

Responses to a correct answer

```
Very good!
Excellent!
Nice work!
Keep up the good work!
```

Responses to an incorrect answer

```
No. Please try again.
Wrong. Try once more.
Don't give up!
No. Keep trying.
```

Your program should use the random number generator to choose a number from 1 to 4 to select an appropriate response to each answer. Use a `switch` structure with `printf` statements to issue the responses.

5.34   More sophisticated CAI systems monitor the student's performance over a period of time. The decision to begin a new topic is often based on the student's degree of success with previous topics. Modify the program of Exercise 5.33 to count the number of correct and incorrect responses. After the student types 10 answers, your program should calculate the percentage of correct responses. If this is lower than 75 percent, your program should print `"Please ask your instructor for extra help"` and then terminate.

5.35   Write a C program that plays the game of "guess the number" as follows: Your program chooses the number to be guessed by selecting an integer at random in the range 1 to 1000. The program then types:

```
I have a number between 1 and 1000.
Can you guess my number?
Please type your first guess.
```

The player then types a first guess. The program responds with one of the following:

```
1.  Excellent! You guessed the number!
    Would you like to play again?
    Please type "yes" or "no."
2.  Too low. Try again.
3.  Too high. Try again.
```

If the player's guess is incorrect, your program should loop until the player finally gets the number right. Your program should keep telling the player `Too high` or `Too low` to help the player "zero in" on the correct answer. Note: The searching technique employed in this problem is called *binary search*. We will say more about this in the next problem.

5.36   Modify the program of Exercise 5.35 to count the number of guesses the player makes. If the number of guesses is 10 or fewer, print `Either you know the secret or you got lucky!` If the player guesses the number in 10 tries, then print `Ahah! You know the secret!` If the player makes more than 10 guesses, then print `You should be able to do better!` Why should it take no more than 10 guesses? Well with each "good guess" the player should be able to eliminate half of the numbers. Now show why any number 1 to 1000 can be guessed in 10 or fewer tries.

5.37   Write a recursive function `power (base, exponent)` that when invoked returns

$base^{exponent}$

For example, `power(3, 4)` = 3 * 3 * 3 * 3. Assume that `exponent` is an integer greater than or equal to 1. *Hint:* The recursion step would use the relationship

$base^{exponent} = base * base^{exponent - 1}$

and the terminating condition occurs when `exponent` is equal to 1 because

$base^1 = base$

5.38   The Fibonacci series

0, 1, 1, 2, 3, 5, 8, 13, 21, ...

begins with the terms 0 and 1 and has the property that each succeeding term is the sum of the two preceding terms. a) Write a *nonrecursive* function `fibonacci(n)` that calculates the nth Fibonacci number. b) Determine the largest fibonacci number that can be printed on your system. Modify the program of part a) to use `double` instead of `int` to calculate and return Fibonacci numbers. Let the program loop until it fails because of an excessively high value.

5.39   (*Towers of Hanoi*) Every budding computer scientist must grapple with certain classic problems, and the Towers of Hanoi (see Fig. 5.19) is one of the most famous of these. Legend has it that in a temple in the Far East, priests are attempting to move a stack of disks from one peg to another. The initial stack had 64 disks threaded onto one peg and arranged from bottom to top by decreasing size. The priests are attempting to move the stack from this peg to a second peg under the constraints that exactly one disk is moved at a time, and at no time may a larger disk be placed above a smaller disk. A third peg is available for temporarily holding the disks. Supposedly the world will end when the priests complete their task, so there is little incentive for us to facilitate their efforts.

Let us assume that the priests are specifically attempting to move the disks from peg 1 to peg 3. We wish to develop an algorithm that will print the precise sequence of disk-to-disk peg transfers.

If we were to approach this problem with conventional methods, we would rapidly find ourselves hopelessly knotted up in managing the disks. Instead, if we attack the problem with recursion in mind, it immediately becomes tractable. Moving *n* disks can be viewed in terms of moving only *n* - 1 disks (and hence the recursion) as follows:

1.   Move *n* - 1 disks from peg 1 to peg 2, using peg 3 as a temporary holding area.
2.   Move the last disk (the largest) from peg 1 to peg 3.
3.   Move the *n* - 1 disks from peg 2 to peg 3, using peg 1 as a temporary holding area.

The process ends when the last task involves moving *n* = 1 disk, i.e., the base case. This is accomplished by trivially moving the disk without the need for a temporary holding area.

Write a program to solve the Towers of Hanoi problem. Use a recursive function with four parameters:

1.   The number of disks to be moved
2.   The peg on which these disks are initially threaded
3.   The peg to which this stack of disks is to be moved
4.   The peg to be used as a temporary holding area

Your program should print the precise instructions it will take to move the disks from the starting peg to the destination peg. For example, to move a stack of three disks from peg 1 to peg 3, your program should print the following series of moves:

$1 \rightarrow 3$ (This means move one disk from peg 1 to peg 3.)

$1 \rightarrow 2$

$3 \rightarrow 2$

$1 \rightarrow 3$

$2 \rightarrow 1$

$2 \rightarrow 3$

$1 \rightarrow 3$

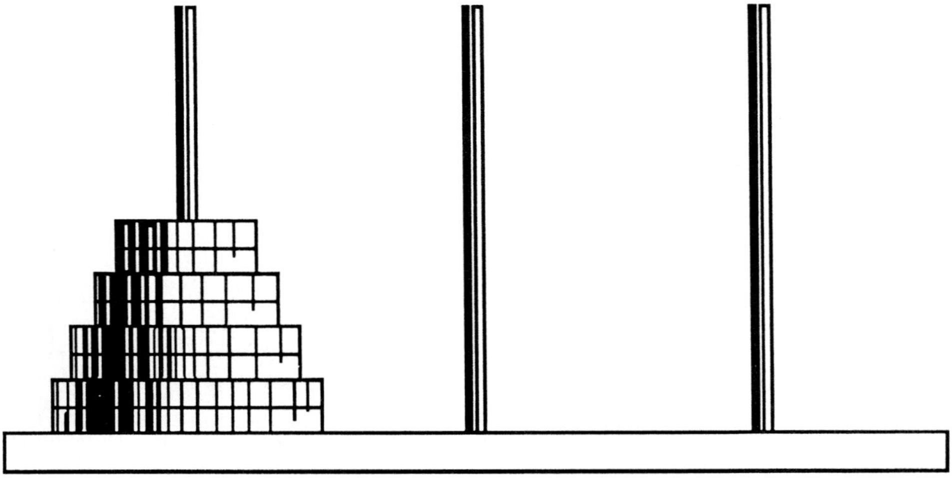

Fig. 5.19 The Towers of Hanoi for the case with four disks.

6
Arrays

Objectives

- To introduce the array data structure.
- To understand the use of arrays to store, sort, and search lists and tables of values.
- To understand how to declare an array, initialize and array, and refer to individual elements of an array.
- To be able to pass arrays to functions.
- To understand basic sorting techniques.
- To be able to declare and manipulate multiple subscript arrays.

With sobs and tears he sorted out
Those of the largest size ...
Lewis Carroll

Attempt the end, and never stand to doubt;
Nothing's so hard, but search will find it out.
Robert Herrick

Now go, write it before them in a table,
and note it in a book.
Isaiah 30:8

'Tis in my memory lock'd,
And you yourself shall keep the key of it.
William Shakespeare

Outline

6.1 Introduction

This chapter serves as an introduction to the important topic of data structures. *Arrays* are data structures consisting of related data items of the same type. In Chapter 10, we discuss `structs` (structures)—data structures consisting of related data items of possibly different types. Arrays and structures are "static" entities in that they remain the same size throughout program execution (they may, of course, be of automatic storage class and hence created and destroyed each time the blocks in which they are defined are entered and exited). In Chapter 12, we introduce dynamic data structures such as lists, queues, stacks, and trees that may grow and shrink as programs execute.

6.2 Arrays

An array is a group of related memory locations. These locations are related by the fact that they all have the same name and the same type. To refer to a particular location or element within the array, we specify the name of the array and the *position number* of the particular element within the array.

Fig. 6.1 shows an integer array called `c`. This array contains twelve *elements*. Any one of these elements may be referred to by giving the name of the array followed by the position number of the particular element in square brackets (`[]`). The first element in every array is the *zeroth element*. Thus, the first element of array `c` is referred to as `c[0]`, the second element of array `c` is referred to as `c[1]`, the seventh element of array `c` is referred to as `c[6]`, and, in general, the ith element of array `c` is referred to as `c[i-1]`. Array names follow the same conventions as other variable names.

The position number contained within square brackets is more formally called a *subscript*. A subscript may be an integer or an integer expression. If a program uses an expression as a subscript, then the expression is evaluated to determine the subscript. For example, if `a = 5` and `b = 6`, then the statement

```
c[a + b] += 2;
```

results in array element c[11] being incremented by 2.

Let us examine array c in Fig. 6.1 more closely. The *name* of the array is c. Its twelve elements are referred to as c[0], c[1], c[2], ..., c[11]. The *value* of c[0] is −45, the value of c[1] is 6, the value of c[2] is 0, the value of c[7] is 62, and the value of c[11] is 78. To print the sum of the values contained in the first three elements of array c, we would write

```
printf("%d", c[0] + c[1] + c[2]);
```

To divide the value of the seventh element of array c by 2 and assign the result to the variable x, we would write

```
x = c[6] / 2;
```

___

CPE 6.1

It is important to note the difference between the "seventh element of the array" and "array element seven." The "seventh element of the array" has a subscript of 6, while "array element seven" has a subscript of 7 and is actually the eighth element of the array. This is a source of many "off-by-one" errors.

Name of array (Note that
all elements of this array
have the same name, c)

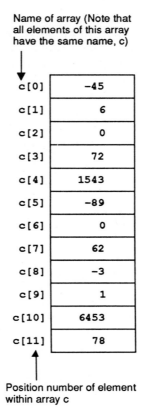

c[0]	−45
c[1]	6
c[2]	0
c[3]	72
c[4]	1543
c[5]	−89
c[6]	0
c[7]	62
c[8]	−3
c[9]	1
c[10]	6453
c[11]	78

Position number of element
within array c

Fig. 6.1 A 12-element array.

The brackets used to enclose the subscript of an array are actually considered to be an operator in C. They have the same level of precedence as parentheses. The chart in Fig. 6.2 shows the precedence and associativity of the various C operators introduced up to this point in the text. They are shown from top to bottom in decreasing order of precedence.

6.3 Declaring Arrays

Arrays occupy space in memory. The programmer specifies the number of locations required by each array so that the computer may reserve the appropriate amount of memory. To tell the computer to reserve 12 elements for integer array c, the declaration

```
int c[12];
```

is used. Memory may be reserved for several arrays with a single declaration. To reserve 100 elements for integer array b and 27 elements for integer array x, the following declaration is used:

```
int b[100], x[27];
```

The elements of the preceding arrays were declared to be of type int. Arrays may be declared to contain other data types. For example, an array of type char can be used to store a *character string*. Character strings and their similarity to arrays are discussed in Chapter 8.

6.4 Examples Using Arrays

The program in Fig. 6.3 uses a for repetition structure to initialize the elements of a ten-element integer array n to zeros, and prints the array in tabular format.

Operators						Associativity
( )	[ ]					left to right
++	--	!	(*type*)			right to left
*	/	%				left to right
+	-					left to right
<	<=	>	>=			left to right
==	!=					left to right
&&						left to right
||						left to right
?:						right to left
=	+=	-=	*=	/=	%=	right to left
,						left to right

Fig. 6.2 Operator precedence.

Note that we chose not to place a blank line between the first `printf` and the `for` structure in Fig. 6.3 because they are closely related. In this case, the `printf` displays the column heads for the two columns that will be printed in the `for`. Programmers often omit the blank line between a `for` structure and a closely related `printf`.

The elements of an array can also be initialized in the array declaration by following the declaration with an equals sign and a comma-separated list (enclosed in braces) of initializers. The program in Fig. 6.4 initializes an integer array with ten values, and prints the array in tabular format.

If there are fewer initializers than elements in the array, ANSI C automatically initializes the remaining elements to zero. For example, the elements of the array n in Fig. 6.3 could have been initialized to zero with the declaration

```
int n[10] = {0};
```

which explicitly initializes the first element to zero, and automatically initializes the remaining nine elements to zero because there are fewer initializers than there are elements in the array. It is important to remember that arrays are not automatically initialized to zero by ANSI C. The programmer must at least initialize the first element to zero in order for ANSI C to initialize the remaining elements as shown in the preced-

```
/* initializing an array */
#include <stdio.h>

main()
{
    int n[10], i;

    for (i = 0; i <= 9; i++)
        n[i] = 0;

    printf("%s%13s\n", "Element", "Value");
    for(i = 0; i <= 9; i++)
        printf("%7d%13d\n", i, n[i]);
}
```

```
Element      Value
      0          0
      1          0
      2          0
      3          0
      4          0
      5          0
      6          0
      7          0
      8          0
      9          0
```

Fig. 6.3 Initializing the elements of an array to zeros.

ing declaration. This method of initializing the array elements to 0 can only be performed once in a program. The method used in Fig. 6.3 can be done repeatedly throughout the program.

CPE 6.2

Forgetting to initialize the elements of an array whose elements are supposed to be initialized.

If an initializer list contains more initializers than the array has elements, an error will occur. For example, the declaration

```
int n[5] = {32, 27, 64, 18, 95, 14};
```

would cause an error message when the program containing the declaration is compiled because there are 6 initializers and only 5 array elements.

If the number of elements in an array is omitted from a declaration that uses an initializer list, the number of elements in the array will be the number of elements in the initializer list. For example,

```
int n[] = {1, 2, 3, 4, 5};
```

would create a five-element array.

The program in Fig. 6.5 initializes the elements of a ten-element array s to the values 2, 4, 6, ..., 20, and prints the array in tabular format. The values are generated by multiplying the loop counter by 2 and adding 2.

```
/* Initializing an array with a declaration */
#include <stdio.h>

main()
{
    int n[10] = {32, 27, 64, 18, 95, 14, 90, 70, 60, 37};
    int i;

    printf("%s%13s\n", "Element", "Value");
    for(i = 0; i <= 9; i++)
        printf("%7d%13d\n", i, n[i]);
}
```

```
Element        Value
      0           32
      1           27
      2           64
      3           18
      4           95
      5           14
      6           90
      7           70
      8           60
      9           37
```

Fig. 6.4 Initializing the elements of an array with a declaration.

The #define preprocessor directive is introduced in this program. The line

    #define SIZE 10

defines a *symbolic constant* SIZE whose value is 10. A symbolic constant is an identifier which is replaced with *replacement text* by the C preprocessor before the program is compiled. So, when the program in Fig. 6.5 is preprocessed, all occurrences of the symbolic constant SIZE will be replaced with the replacement text 10. Using symbolic constants with arrays makes our programs more *scalable*. For example, in the program of Fig. 6.5, the first for loop could be used to fill a 1000-element array by simply changing the value assigned to SIZE in the #define preprocessor directive from 10 to 1000. If we had not used the symbolic constant SIZE, we would have had to change the program in three separate places in order to scale the program to handle 1000 array elements. As your programs get larger, this technique will become more useful in writing clear programs.

CPE 6.3

Ending a **#define** or **#include** preprocessor directive with a semicolon. Remember that preprocessor directives are not C statements.

```
/* initialize the elements of array s to the even integers
      from 2 to 20 */
#include <stdio.h>
#define SIZE 10

main()
{
    int s[SIZE], j;

    for (j = 0; j <= SIZE - 1; j++)
       s[j] = 2 + 2 * j;

    printf("%s%13s\n", "Element", "Value");
    for (j = 0; j <= SIZE - 1; j++)
       printf("%7d%13d\n", j, s[j]);
}
```

```
Element        Value
      0            2
      1            4
      2            6
      3            8
      4           10
      5           12
      6           14
      7           16
      8           18
      9           20
```

Fig. 6.5 Generating the values to be placed into elements of an array.

CPE 6.4

Assigning a value to a symbolic constant in executable statements causes a syntax error. A symbolic constant is not a variable. No space is reserved for it by the compiler as is the case with variables that must hold values at execution time.

GPP 6.1

Define the size of each array as a symbolic constant to make programs more scalable.

GPP 6.2

Use only uppercase letters in the names of symbolic constants. This makes these constants stand out in a program, and reminds the programmer that symbolic constants are not variables.

The program in Fig. 6.6 totals the values contained in the twelve-element integer array a. The statement in the body of the `for` loop does the totaling.

Our next example uses arrays to summarize the results of data collected in a survey. Consider the problem statement.

> *Forty students were asked to rate the quality of the food in the student cafeteria on a scale of 1 to 10 (1 means awful and 10 means excellent). Place the forty responses in an integer array and summarize the results of the poll.*

This is a typical array application (See Fig. 6.7). We wish to summarize the number of responses of each type (i.e., 1 through 10). The array `responses` is a 40-element array of the students' responses. We use an eleven-element array, `frequency` to count the number of occurrences of each response. We ignore the first element, `frequency[0]`, because it is more logical to have the response 1 increment `frequency[1]` than `frequency[0]`. This allows us to use each response directly as the subscript in the `frequency` array.

```
/* compute the sum of the elements of the array */
#include <stdio.h>
#define SIZE 12

main()
{
    int a[SIZE] = {1, 3, 5, 4, 7, 2, 99, 16, 45, 67, 89, 45};
    int i, total = 0;

    for (i = 0; i <= SIZE - 1; i++)
        total += a[i];

    printf("Total of array element values is %d", total);
}
```

```
Total of array element values is 383
```

Fig. 6.6 Computing the sum of the elements of an array.

The first `for` loop takes the responses one at a time from the array `response`
and increments one of the ten counters (`frequency[1]` to `frequency[10]`) in
the `frequency` array. The key statement in the loop is

```
++frequency[responses[answer]];
```

This statement increments the appropriate counter depending on the value of `re-
sponses[answer]`. If `responses[answer]` is 1, then this statement is actu-
ally interpreted as

```
++frequency[1];
```

which increments array element one by 1. If `responses[answer]` is 7, then the
statement is interpreted as

```
++frequency[7];
```

Note that regardless of how many responses are processed in the survey, we still need
only an eleven-element array to summarize the results (assuming that the data consists
only of legitimate values from 1 to 10). If the data contained 13, then the statement
would attempt to add 1 to `frequency[13]`. This would be outside the bounds of
the array. *C has no array bounds checking to prevent the computer from referring to
an element that does not exist.* Thus, an executing program can walk off the end of an
array without warning. The (normally serious) effects of referencing elements outside
the array bounds are system dependent. The programmer should ensure that all array
references remain within the bounds of the array.

```
/* Student poll program */
#include <stdio.h>
#define SIZE1 40
#define SIZE2 11

main()
{
   int answer, rating;
   int responses[SIZE1] = {1, 2, 6, 4, 8, 5, 9, 7, 8, 10, 1,
       6, 3, 8, 6, 10, 3, 8, 2, 7, 6, 5, 7, 6, 8, 6, 7, 5, 6,
       6, 5, 6, 7, 5, 6, 4, 8, 6, 8, 10};
   int frequency[SIZE2] = {0};

   for(answer = 0; answer <= SIZE1 - 1; answer++)
       ++frequency[responses[answer]];

   printf("%s%17s\n", "Rating", "Frequency");
   for(rating = 1; rating <= SIZE2 - 1; rating++)
       printf("%6d%17d\n", rating, frequency[rating]);
}
```

```
Rating        Frequency
   1              2
   2              2
   3              2
   4              2
   5              5
   6             11
   7              5
   8              7
   9              1
  10              3
```

Fig. 6.7 A simple student poll analysis program.

Our next example (Fig. 6.8) reads numbers from an array and graphs the information in the form of a bar chart or histogram—each number is printed, and then a bar consisting of that many asterisks is printed beside the number. (See also Problem 4.16.) The nested `for` loop actually draws the bars. Note the use of `printf("\n")` to end a histogram bar and begin printing on the next line.

In Chapter 5 we stated that we would show a more elegant method of writing the dice rolling program of Fig. 5.9. The problem was to roll a single six sided die 6000 times to test whether the random number generator actually produces random numbers. An array version of this program is shown in Fig. 6.9.

6.5 Passing Arrays to Functions

To pass an array to a function, specify the name of the array without any brackets. For example, if array `hourlytemperatures` has been declared as

```
int hourlytemperatures[24];
```

the statement

```
modifyarray(hourlytemperatures);
```

passes array `hourlytemperatures` to function `modifyarray`.

C passes arrays to functions using simulated call by reference; the called functions may modify the element values in the callers' original arrays.

Passing arrays simulated call by reference makes sense for performance reasons. If arrays were passed call by value, a copy of each element would be passed. For large, frequently passed arrays, this could be quite time consuming and could require considerable additional storage for the extra copies of the arrays. It is possible to pass an array by value by using a simple trick we explain in Chapter 10.

Although entire arrays are passed simulated call by reference, individual array elements are passed call by value. To pass an element of an array to a function, use the subscripted name of the array element as an argument in the function call. In Chapter 7, we show how to simulate call by reference for individual variables and array elements.

```
/* Histogram printing program */
#include <stdio.h>
#define SIZE 10

main()
{
    int n[SIZE] = {19, 3, 15, 7, 11, 9, 13, 5, 17, 1};
    int i, j;

    printf("%s%13s%17s\n", "Element", "Value", "Histogram");
    for (i = 0; i <= SIZE - 1; i++) {
        printf("%7d%13d       ", i, n[i]);
        for(j = 1; j <= n[i]; j++)
            printf("%c", '*');
        printf("\n");
    }
}
```

```
Element       Value       Histogram
      0          19        *******************
      1           3        ***
      2          15        ***************
      3           7        *******
      4          11        ***********
      5           9        *********
      6          13        *************
      7           5        *****
      8          17        *****************
      9           1        *
```

Fig. 6.8 A program that prints histograms.

```
/* Roll a six-sided die 6000 times */
#include <stdio.h>
#include <stdlib.h>
#include <time.h>
#define SIZE 7

main()
{
    int face, roll, frequency[SIZE] = {0};

    srand(clock());

    for (roll = 1; roll <= 6000; roll++) {
        face = rand() % 6 + 1;
        ++frequency[face];
    }

    printf("%s%17s\n", "Face", "Frequency");
    for (face = 1; face <= SIZE - 1; face++)
        printf("%4d%17d\n", face, frequency[face]);
}
```

```
Face        Frequency
   1             1037
   2              987
   3             1013
   4             1028
   5              952
   6              983
```

Fig. 6.9 Dice rolling program using arrays instead of `switch`.

For a function to receive an array as an argument, the function's parameter list must specify that an array will be received. For example, the function header for function `modifyarray`

```
void modifyarray(int b[])
```

indicates that `modifyarray` expects to receive an array of integers in parameter b. Because arrays are automatically passed simulated call by reference, when the called function uses the array name b, it will in fact be referring to the actual array in the caller (array `hourlytemperatures` in the preceding call). In Chapter 7, we introduce other notations for indicating that an array is being received by a function.

The program in Fig. 6.10 demonstrates the difference between passing an entire array and passing a single array element. The program first prints the five elements of integer array a. Next, a is passed to function `modifyarray` where each of a's elements is multiplied by 2. Then a is reprinted in `main`. As the output shows, the elements of a are indeed modified by `modifyarray`. Now the program prints the value of a[3] and passes it to function `modifyelement`. Function `modifyelement` multiplies its argument by 2 and prints the new value. Note that when a[3] is reprinted in `main`, it has not been modified because it was passed call by value.

```
/* Passing arrays and individual array elements to functions */
#include <stdio.h>
#define SIZE 5

main()
{
    int a[SIZE] = {0, 1, 2, 3, 4};
    int i;
    void modifyarray(int []);
    void modifyelement(int);

    printf("%s\n\n",
        "Effects of passing entire array call by reference:");
    printf("The values of the original array are:\n");
    for (i = 0; i <= SIZE - 1; i++)
        printf("%3d", a[i]);
    printf("\n");

    modifyarray(a);
    printf("The values of the modified array are:\n");
    for (i = 0; i <= SIZE - 1; i++)
        printf("%3d", a[i]);

    printf("\n\n\n%s\n\n",
        "Effects of passing array element call by value:");
    printf("The value of a[3] is %d\n", a[3]);
    modifyelement(a[3]);
    printf("The value of a[3] is %d\n", a[3]);
}

void modifyarray(int b[])
{
    int j;

    for (j = 0; j <= SIZE - 1; j++)
        b[j] *= 2;
}

void modifyelement(int e)
{
    printf("Value in modifyelement is %d\n", e *= 2);
}
```

```
Effects of passing entire array call by reference:

The values of the original array are:
  0   1   2   3   4
The values of the modified array are:
  0   2   4   6   8


Effects of passing array element call by value:

The value of a[3] is 6
Value in modifyelement is 12
The value of a[3] is 6
```

Fig. 6.10 Passing arrays and individual array elements to functions.

6.6 Sorting Arrays

Sorting data (i.e., placing the data into some particular order) is one of the most important computing applications. A bank must sort all checks by account number so that it can prepare individual bank statements at the end of each month. Virtually every organization must sort some data to facilitate the processing of information.

The program in Fig. 6.11 sorts the values in the elements of the ten-element array a into ascending order. The technique we use is called the *bubble sort* because the smaller values gradually "bubble" their way upward to the top of the array (like air bubbles rising in water), while the larger values sink to the bottom of the array. The technique is to make several passes through the array. On each pass, successive pairs of elements are compared. If a pair is in increasing order (or if the values are identical), we leave it as it is. If a pair is in decreasing order, we swap the values.

```
/* This program sorts an array's values into
   ascending order */
#include <stdio.h>
#define SIZE 10

main()
{
    int a[SIZE] = {2, 6, 4, 8, 10, 12, 89, 68, 45, 37};
    int i, pass, hold;

    printf("Data items in original order\n");
    for (i = 0; i <= SIZE - 1; i++)
        printf("%4d", a[i]);

    for (pass = 1; pass <= SIZE - 1; pass++)
        for (i = 0; i <= SIZE - 2; i++)
            if (a[i] > a[i + 1]) {
                hold = a[i];
                a[i] = a[i + 1];
                a[i + 1] = hold;
            }

    printf("\nData items in ascending order\n");
    for (i = 0; i <= SIZE - 1; i++)
        printf("%4d", a[i]);
    printf("\n");
}
```

```
Data items in original order
   2   6   4   8  10  12  89  68  45  37
Data items in ascending order
   2   4   6   8  10  12  37  45  68  89
```

Fig. 6.11 Sorting an array with bubble sort.

First the program compares a[0] to a[1], then a[1] to a[2], then a[2] to a[3], and so on until it completes the pass by comparing a[8] to a[9]. Note that although there are 10 elements, only nine comparisons are performed. Because of the way the successive comparisons are made, a large value may move down the array many positions on a single pass, but a small value may move up only one position. On the first pass, the largest value will sink to the bottom element of the array, a[9]. On the second pass, the second largest value is guaranteed to sink to a[8]. On the ninth pass, the ninth largest value will sink to a[1]. This, of course, will leave the smallest value in a[0], so only nine passes of the array are needed to sort the array even though there are ten elements.

The sorting is performed by the nested for loop. If a swap is necessary, it is performed by the three assignments

```
hold = a[i];
a[i] = a[i + 1];
a[i + 1] = hold;
```

where the extra variable hold temporarily stores one of the two values being swapped. The swap cannot be performed with only the two assignments

```
a[i] = a[i + 1];
a[i + 1] = a[i];
```

Let us see why. Suppose a[i] is 7 and a[i + 1] is 5. After the first assignment both values will be 5 and the value 7 will be lost. Hence the need for the extra variable hold.

The chief virtue of the bubble sort is that it is easy to program. However, the bubble sort runs slowly. This becomes apparent when sorting large arrays. In the exercises, we will develop more efficient versions of the bubble sort. Far more efficient sorts than the bubble sort have been developed. We will investigate a few of these later in the text. More advanced courses investigate sorting and searching in greater depth.

6.7 Example: Computing the Mean, Median, and Mode Using Arrays

We now move on to a larger example. Computers are commonly used to compile and analyze the results of surveys and opinion polls. The program in Fig. 6.12 uses an array response that contains 99 responses to a survey. Each of the responses is a number from 1 to 10. The program computes the mean, median, and mode of the 99 values.

The mean is the arithmetic average of the 99 values. The function mean computes the mean by totaling the 99 elements and dividing the result by 99.

The median is the "middle value." The function median determines the median by sorting the array of responses into ascending order, and picking the middle element, workarray[49], of the sorted array. Note that when there is an even number of elements, the median should be calculated as the mean of the two middle elements.

The mode is the value that occurs most frequently among the 99 responses. The function mode determines the mode by first tabulating the number of responses of each type, and then selecting the value that occurred the greatest number of times. Function mode also produces a histogram to aid in determining the mode graphically. Fig. 6.12 contains a sample run of this program. This example includes most of the common manipulations usually required in array problems, including passing arrays to functions.

```c
/* This program introduces the topic of survey data
   analysis. It computes the mean, median, and  mode
   of the survey data */
#include <stdio.h>

main()
{
    int response[99] = {6, 7, 8, 9, 8, 7, 8, 9, 8, 9,
                        7, 8, 9, 5, 9, 8, 7, 8, 7, 8,
                        6, 7, 8, 9, 3, 9, 8, 7, 8, 7,
                        7, 8, 9, 8, 9, 8, 9, 7, 8, 9,
                        6, 7, 8, 7, 8, 7, 9, 8, 9, 2,
                        7, 8, 9, 8, 9, 8, 9, 7, 5, 3,
                        5, 6, 7, 2, 5, 3, 9, 4, 6, 4,
                        7, 8, 9, 6, 8, 7, 8, 9, 7, 8,
                        7, 4, 4, 2, 5, 3, 8, 7, 5, 6,
                        4, 5, 6, 1, 6, 5, 7, 8, 7};
    int frequency[10] = {0};
    int n;
    void mean(int []);
    void median(int []);
    void mode(int [], int []);

    mean(response);
    median(response);
    mode(frequency, response);
}

void mean(int answer[])
{
    int j, total = 0;

    printf("%s\n%s\n%s\n", "******", " Mean", "******");

    for (j = 0; j <= 98; j++)
        total += answer[j];

    printf("The mean is the average value of the data\n");
    printf("items. The mean is equal to the total of\n");
    printf("all the data items divided by the number\n");
    printf("of data items (99). The mean value for\n");
    printf("this run is: ");
    printf("%d / 99 = %.4f\n\n", total, (float) total/99);
}
```

Fig. 6.12 Survey data analysis program (part 1 of 3).

```
void median(int answer[])
{
    int j, pass, hold, firstrow;

    printf("\n%s\n%s\n%s\n", "******", "Median", "******");
    printf("The unsorted array of responses is\n");

    for (j = 0, firstrow = 1; j <= 98; j++) {

        if (j % 20 == 0 && !firstrow)
            printf("\n");

        printf("%2d", answer[j]);
        firstrow = 0;
    }

    printf("\n\n");

    for (pass = 0; pass <= 97; pass++)

        for (j = 0; j <= 97; j++)

            if (answer[j] > answer[j+1]) {
                hold = answer[j];
                answer[j] = answer[j+1];
                answer[j+1] = hold;
            }

    printf("The sorted array is\n");

    for (j = 0, firstrow = 1; j <= 98; j++) {

        if (j % 20 == 0 && !firstrow)
            printf("\n");

        printf("%2d", answer[j]);
        firstrow = 0;
    }
    printf("\n\n");

    printf("The median is the 50th element of\n");
    printf("the sorted 99 element array.\n");
    printf("For this run the median is ");
    printf("%d\n\n", answer[49]);
}
```

Fig. 6.12 Survey data analysis program (part 2 of 3).

```
void mode(int freq[], int answer[])
{
    int rating, j, h, largest = 0, modevalue = 0;

    printf("\n%s\n%s\n%s\n", "******", " Mode", "******");

    for(rating = 1; rating <= 9; rating++)
        freq[rating] = 0;

    for(j = 0; j <= 98; j++)
        ++freq[answer[j]];

    printf("%s%11s%19s\n\n",
        "Response", "Frequency", "Histogram");
    printf("%54s\n", "1    1    2    2");
    printf("%54s\n\n", "5    0    5    0    5");

    for (rating = 1; rating <= 9; rating++) {
        printf("%8d%11d          ", rating, freq[rating]);

        if (freq[rating] > largest) {
            largest = freq[rating];
            modevalue = rating;
        }

        for(h = 1; h <= freq[rating]; h++)
            printf("*");

        printf("\n");
    }

    printf("The mode is the most frequent value.\n");
    printf("For this run the mode is %d ", modevalue);
    printf("which occurred %d times.\n", largest);
}
```

Fig. 6.12 Survey data analysis program (part 3 of 3).

6.8 Searching Arrays

Often, a programmer will be working with large amounts of data stored in arrays. It may be necessary to determine whether an array contains a value that matches a certain *key value*. The process of finding a particular element of an array is called *searching*. In this section we discuss the simple *linear search* technique (Fig. 6.14).

The linear search compares each element of the array with the value being searched for, i.e., the search key. Since the array is not in any particular order, it is just as likely that the value will be found in the first element as the last. On the average, therefore, the program will have to compare the search key with half the elements of the array. This searching method is fine if the array is small. However, for large arrays this method is inefficient. The exercises discuss other important searching methods.

```
******
 Mean
******
The mean is the average value of the data
items. The mean is equal to the total of
all the data items divided by the number
of data items (99). The mean value for
this run is: 681 / 99 = 6.8788


******
Median
******
The unsorted array of responses is
  6 7 8 9 8 7 8 9 8 9 7 8 9 5 9 8 7 8 7 8
  6 7 8 9 3 9 8 7 8 7 7 8 9 8 9 8 9 7 8 9
  6 7 8 7 8 7 9 8 9 2 7 8 9 8 9 8 9 7 5 3
  5 6 7 2 5 3 9 4 6 4 7 8 9 6 8 7 8 9 7 8
  7 4 4 2 5 3 8 7 5 6 4 5 6 1 6 5 7 8 7

The sorted array is
  1 2 2 2 3 3 3 4 4 4 4 4 5 5 5 5 5 5 5
  5 6 6 6 6 6 6 6 6 6 7 7 7 7 7 7 7 7 7
  7 7 7 7 7 7 7 7 7 7 7 7 8 8 8 8 8 8 8
  8 8 8 8 8 8 8 8 8 8 8 8 8 8 8 8 8 8 8
  9 9 9 9 9 9 9 9 9 9 9 9 9 9 9 9 9 9 9

The median is the 50th element of
the sorted 99 element array.
For this run the median is 7


******
 Mode
******
Response    Frequency            Histogram

                                  1     1     2     2
                               5     0     5     0     5

         1            1         *
         2            3         ***
         3            4         ****
         4            5         *****
         5            8         ********
         6            9         *********
         7           23         ***********************
         8           27         ***************************
         9           19         *******************
The mode is the most frequent value.
For this run the mode is 8 which occurred 27 times.
```

Fig. 6.13 Sample run for the survey data analysis program.

```
/* Linear search of an array */
#include <stdio.h>
#define SIZE 100

main()
{
    int a[SIZE], x, searchkey, element;
    int linearsearch(int [], int, int);

    for (x = 0; x <= SIZE - 1; x++)
        a[x] = 2 * x;

    printf("Enter integer search key:\n");
    scanf("%d", &searchkey);
    element = linearsearch(a, searchkey, SIZE);

    if (element != -1)
        printf("Found value in element %d\n", element);
    else
        printf("Value not found\n");
}

int linearsearch(int array[], int key, int size)
{
    int n;

    for (n = 0; n <= size - 1; n++)
        if (array[n] == key)
            return n;

    return -1;
}
```

```
Enter integer search key:
36
Found value in element 18
```

```
Enter integer search key:
37
Value not found
```

Fig. 6.14 Linear search of an array.

6.9 Multiple-Subscripted Arrays

Arrays in C can have multiple subscripts. A common use of arrays is to represent *tables* of values consisting of information arranged in *rows* and *columns*. To identify a particular element of such a table, we must specify two subscripts: the first (by convention) identifies the row in which the element is contained, and the second (by convention) identifies the column in which the element is contained. Tables or arrays that require two subscripts to identify a particular element are called *double-subscripted arrays*. Note that multiple-subscripted arrays can have more than two subscripts.

Fig. 6.15 illustrates a double-subscripted array, a. The array contains three rows and four columns, so it is said to be a "3-by-4" array. In general, an array with *m* rows and *n* columns is called an *m-by-n array*.

Every element in array a is identified in the figure by an element name of the form a[i][j]; a is the name of the array, and i and j are the subscripts that uniquely identify each element in a. Notice that the names of the elements in the first row all have a first subscript of 0; the names of the elements in the fourth column all have a second subscript of 3.

<u>*CPE 6.6*</u>

Referencing a double-subscripted array element a[x][y] *incorrectly as* a[x, y].

A multiple-subscripted array can be initialized in its declaration much like a single subscripted array. For example, a double-subscripted array b[2][2] could be declared and initialized with

```
int b[2][2] = {{1, 2}, {3, 4}};
```

The values are grouped by row in braces. So, 1 and 2 initialize b[0][0] and b[0][1], and 3 and 4 initialize b[1][0] and b[1][1]. If there are not enough initializers for a given row, the remaining elements of that row are initialized to 0. Thus, the declaration

```
int b[2][2] = {{1}, {3, 4}};
```

would initialize b[0][0] to 1, b[0][1] to 0, b[1][0] to 3 and b[1][1] to 4.

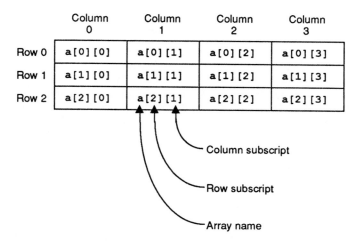

Fig. 6.15 A double-subscripted array with three rows and four columns.

A `for` repetition structure can be used to set all the elements in the third row of array a in Fig. 6.15 to zero as follows:

```
for (column = 0; column <= 3; column++)
    a[2][column] = 0;
```

We specified the *third* row, therefore we know that the first subscript is always 2 (0 is the first row, and 1 is the second row). The `for` loop varies only the second subscript (i.e., the column subscript). The preceding `for` loop is equivalent to the assignment statements:

```
a[2][0] = 0;
a[2][1] = 0;
a[2][2] = 0;
a[2][3] = 0;
```

The following nested `for` structure determines and prints the total of all the elements in array a.

```
total = 0;
for (row = 0; row <= 2; row++)
    for (column = 0; column <= 3; column++)
        total += a[row][column];
printf("Total is %d\n", total);
```

The `for` structure totals the elements of the array one row at a time. The outer `for` structure begins by setting row (i.e., the row subscript) to 0 so that the elements of the first row may be totaled by the inner `for` structure. The outer `for` structure then causes the row subscript to be incremented to 1. The elements of the second row are then totaled. Then the third row is totaled and the result is printed.

When receiving a multiple-subscripted array in a function, it is not necessary to specify the size of the first subscript in the function header, but sizes must be specified for all other subscripts. For example, a 3-by-4 integer array can be received by a function with the formal parameter int a[][4]. The compiler will ignore the size of the first subscript if the size is included in the formal parameter.

Summary

- C stores lists of values in arrays. An array is a group of related memory locations. These locations are related by the fact that they all have the same name and the same type. To refer to a particular location or element within the array, we specify the name of the array and the subscript.

- A subscript may be an integer or an integer expression. If a program uses an expression as a subscript, then the expression is evaluated to determine the particular element of the array.

- It is important to note the difference when referring to the seventh element of the array as opposed to array element seven. The seventh element has a subscript of 6, while array element seven has a subscript of 7 (actually the eighth element of the array). This is a source of "off-by-one" errors.

- Arrays occupy space in memory. To reserve 100 elements for integer array b and 27 elements for integer array x, the programmer writes

```
int b[100], x[27];
```

- An array of type char can be used to store a character string.

- The elements of an array can be initialized three ways: by declaration, by assignment, and by input.

- If there are fewer initializers than elements in the array, C automatically initializes the remaining elements to zero.

- C does not prevent a program from referencing elements beyond the bounds of an array.

- When an array is passed to a function simply by mentioning the array by name, it is automatically passed call by reference. Any array that is passed in this manner to a function may be modified by the function. If a single element of an array is passed to a function, it is passed by value and cannot be modified in the calling environment by the function. In Chapter 7, we will see how to pass individual variables and array elements call by reference.

- To pass an array to a function, the name of the array is passed. For example, the statement

```
modifyarray(a);
```

passes the array a to the function modifyarray. To pass a single element of an array to a function, simply pass the name of the array followed by the subscript (contained in square brackets) of the particular element.

- An array can be sorted using the bubble sort technique. Several passes of the array are made. On each pass, successive pairs of elements are compared. If a pair is in order (or if the values are identical), it is left as is. If a pair is out of order, the values are swapped. For small arrays the bubble sort is acceptable, but for larger arrays it is inefficient compared to other more sophisticated sorting algorithms.

- Arrays may be used to represent tables of values consisting of information arranged in rows and columns. To identify a particular element of a table, two subscripts are specified: the first (by convention) identifies the row in which the element is contained, and the second (by convention) identifies the column in which the element is contained. Tables or arrays that require two subscripts to identify a particular element are called double-subscripted arrays. C also allows for arrays with more than two subscripts.

Terminology

a[i]	bubble sort
a[i][j]	column subscript
array	declare an array
bar chart	#define preprocessor directive
bounds checking	double precision

double-subscripted array
element of an array
expression as a subscript
histogram
initialize an array
linear search
m-by-n array
mean
median
mode
multiple-subscripted array
name of an array
off-by-one error
pass-by-reference
passing arrays to functions
position number
row subscript
scalability

search key
searching an array
single-subscripted array
sorting
sorting pass
sorting the elements of an array
square brackets
string
subscript
survey data analysis
symbolic constant
table of values
tabular format
temporary area for exchange of values
totaling the elements of an array
value of an element
walk off an array
zeroth element

Common Programming Errors

6.1   It is important to note the difference between the "seventh element of the array" and "array element seven." The "seventh element of the array" has a subscript of 6, while "array element seven" has a subscript of 7 and is actually the eighth element of the array. This is a source of many "off-by-one" errors.

6.2   Forgetting to initialize the elements of an array whose elements are supposed to be initialized.

6.3   Ending a `#define` or `#include` preprocessor directive with a semicolon. Remember that preprocessor directives are not C statements.

6.4   Assigning a value to a symbolic constant in executable statements causes a syntax error. A symbolic constant is not a variable. No space is reserved for it by the compiler as is the case with variables that must hold values at execution time.

6.5   Referring to an element outside the array bounds.

6.6   Referencing a double-subscripted array element as `a[x, y]` instead of `a[x][y]`.

Good Programming Practices

6.1   Define the size of your arrays as a symbolic constant to make your programs more scalable.

6.2   Call attention to the use of symbolic constants by using only capital letters in the names of symbolic constants.

6.3   Always strive for clarity in your programs.

6.4   When looping through an array, the array subscript should never go below 0 and should always be less than the total number of elements in the array (size − 1). Make sure the loop terminating condition prevents accessing elements outside this range.

6.5   Mention the high array subscript in a **for** structure to help eliminate off-by-one errors.

6.6   Have programs check all input values for validity so that erroneous information may be rejected before it enters into a program's calculations.

Self-Review Exercises

6.1   Answer each of the following:
   a)   Lists and tables of values are stored in _____.
   b)   The elements of an array are related by the fact that they have the same _____ and _____.
   c)   The number used to refer to a particular element of an array is called its _____.
   d)   A _____ should be used to declare the size of an array because it makes the program more scalable.
   e)   The process of placing the elements of an array in order is called _____ the array.
   f)   The process of determining if an array contains a certain key value is called _____ the array.
   g)   An array that uses two subscripts is referred to as a _____ array.

6.2   State whether the following are true or false. If the answer is false, explain why.
   a)   An array can store many different types of values.
   b)   An array subscript can be of data type **float**.
   c)   If there are fewer initializers in an initializer list than the number of elements in the array, C automatically initializes the remaining elements to the last value in the list of initializers.
   d)   It is an error if an initializer list contains more initializers than there are elements in the array.
   e)   An individual array element that is passed to a function and modified in the called function will contain the modified value in the calling function.

6.3   Answer the following questions regarding the array **fractions**.
   a)   Define a symbolic constant **SIZE** to be replaced with the replacement text 10.
   b)   Declare the array to have **SIZE** elements of type **float** and initialize the elements to 0.
   c)   Name the fourth element from the beginning of the array.
   d)   Refer to array element 4.
   e)   Assign the value **1.667** to array element nine.
   f)   Assign the value **3.333** to the seventh element of the array.
   g)   Print array elements 6 and 9 with two digits of precision to the right of the decimal point, and show the output that is actually displayed on the screen.
   h)   Print all the elements of the array using a **for** repetition structure. Assume the integer variable x has been defined as a control variable for the loop. Show the output.

6.4 Answer the following questions regarding the array `table`.

  a) Declare the array to be an integer array and to have 3 rows and 3 columns. Assume the symbolic constant `SIZE` has been defined to be 3.

  b) How many elements does the array contain?

  c) Use a `for` repetition structure to initialize each element of the array to the sum of its subscripts. Assume the integer variables `x` and `y` have been declared as control variables.

  d) Print the values of each element of array `table`. Assume the array was initialized with the declaration,

```
int table[SIZE][SIZE] = {{1, 8}, {2, 4, 6}, {5}};
```

and that the integer variables `x` and `y` have been declared as control variables. Show the output.

6.5 Find the error in each of the following program segments and explain how the error can be corrected.

  a) `#define SIZE 100;`

  b) `SIZE = 10;`

  c) Assume `int b[10] = {0}, i;`
```
for (i = 0; i <= 10; i++)
    b[i] = 1;
```

  d) `#include <stdio.h>;`

  e) Assume `int a[2][2] = {{1, 2}, {3, 4}};`
```
a[1, 1] = 5;
```

Answers to Self-Review Exercises

6.1 a) Arrays. b) Name, type. c) Subscript. d) Symbolic constant. e) Sorting. f) Searching. g) Double-subscripted.

6.2 a) False. An array can store only values of the same type.

  b) False. An array subscript must be an integer or an integer expression.

  c) False. C automatically initializes the remaining elements to zero.

  d) True.

  e) False. Individual elements of an array are passed call by value. If the entire array is passed to a function, then any modifications will be reflected in the original.

6.3 a) `#define SIZE 10`

  b) `float fractions[SIZE] = {0};`

  c) `fractions[3].`

  d) `fractions[4].`

  e) `fractions[9] = 1.667;`

  f) `fractions[6] = 3.333;`

  g) `printf("%.2f %.2f\n", fractions[6], fractions[9]);`
  Output: 1.67 3.33.

  h) `for (x = 0; x <= SIZE - 1; x++)`
      `printf("fractions[%d] = %f\n", x, fractions[x]);`
  Output:
```
fractions[0] = 0.000000
fractions[1] = 0.000000
fractions[2] = 0.000000
fractions[3] = 0.000000
fractions[4] = 0.000000
```

```
fractions[5] = 0.000000
fractions[6] = 3.333000
fractions[7] = 0.000000
fractions[8] = 0.000000
fractions[9] = 1.667000
```

6.4   a) `int table[SIZE][SIZE];`
      b) Nine elements.
      c)
```
for (x = 0; x <= SIZE - 1; x++)
    for (y = 0; y <= SIZE - 1; y++)
        table[x][y] = x + y;
```
      d)
```
for (x = 0; x <= SIZE - 1; x++)
    for (y = 0; y <= SIZE - 1; y++)
        printf("table[%d][%d] = %d\n", x, y, table[x][y]);
```
      Output:
```
table[0][0] = 1
table[0][1] = 8
table[0][2] = 0
table[1][0] = 2
table[1][1] = 4
table[1][2] = 6
table[2][0] = 5
table[2][1] = 0
table[2][2] = 0
```

6.5   a) Error: Semicolon at end of `#define` preprocessor directive.
         Correction: Eliminate semicolon.
      b) Error: Assigning a value to a symbolic constant using an assignment statement.
         Correction: A symbolic constant can only be assigned a value in a `#define`
preprocessor directive.
      c) Error: Referencing an array element outside the bounds of the array (`b[10]`).
         Correction: Change the final value of the control variable to **9**.
      d) Error: Semicolon at end of `#include` preprocessor directive.
         Correction: Eliminate semicolon.
      e) Error: Array subscripting done incorrectly.
         Correction: Change the statement to `a[1][1] = 5;`

Exercises

6.1   Fill in the blanks in each of the following:
      a)   C stores lists of values in _____.
      b)   The elements of an array are related by the fact that they _____.
      c)   When referring to an array element, the position number contained within
           parentheses is called a _____.
      d)   The names of the five elements of array **p** are _____, _____,
           _____, _____, and _____.
      e)   The contents of a particular element of an array is called the _____ of that
           element.
      f)   Naming an array, stating its type, and specifying the number of elements in the
           array is called _____ the array.

g) The process of placing the elements of an array into either ascending or descending order is called _____.

h) In a double-subscripted array, the first subscript (by convention) identifies the _____ of an element, and the second subscript (by convention) identifies the _____ of an element.

i) An m-by-n array contains _____ rows, _____ columns, and _____ elements.

j) The name of the element in row 3 and column 5 of array **d** is _____.

6.2 State which of the following are true and which are false; for those that are false, explain why.

a) To refer to a particular location or element within an array, we specify the name of the array and the value of the particular element.

b) An array declaration reserves space for the array.

c) To indicate that 100 locations should be reserved for integer array **p**, the programmer writes the declaration

     `p[100];`

d) A C program that initializes the elements of a 15-element array to zero must contain one **for** statement.

e) A C program that totals the elements of a double-subscripted array must contain nested **for** statements.

f) The mean, median, and mode of the following set of values are 5, 6, and 7, respectively: 1, 2, 5, 6, 7, 7, 7.

6.3 Write C statements to accomplish each of the following:

a) Display the value of the seventh element of character array **f**.

b) Input a value into element 4 of single-subscripted floating point array **b**.

c) Initialize each of the 5 elements of single-subscripted integer array **g** to 8.

d) Total the elements of floating point array **c** of 100 elements.

e) Copy array **a** into the first portion of array **b**. Assume **float a[11], b[34];**

f) Determine and print the smallest and largest values contained in 99-element floating point array **w**.

6.4 Consider a 2-by-5 integer array **t**.

a) Write a declaration for **t**.

b) How many rows does **t** have?

c) How many columns does **t** have?

d) How many elements does **t** have?

e) Write the names of all the elements in the second row of **t**.

f) Write the names of all the elements in the third column of **t**.

g) Write a single C statement that sets the element of **t** in row 1 and column 2 to zero.

h) Write a series of C statements that initializes each element of **t** to zero. Do not use a repetition structure.

i) Write a nested **for** structure that initializes each element of **t** to zero. Use **for**.

j) Write a C statement that inputs the values for the elements of **t** from the terminal.

k) Write a series of C statements that determines and prints the smallest value in array **t**.

l) Write a C statement that displays the elements of the first row of **t**.

m) Write a C statement that totals the elements of the fourth column of **t**.

n) Write a series of C statements that prints the array **t** in neat tabular format. List the column subscripts as headings across the top, and list the row subscripts at the left of each row.

6.5   Use a single-subscripted array to solve the following problem. A company pays its salespeople on a commission basis. The salespeople receive $200 per week plus 9 percent of their gross sales for that week. For example, a salesperson who grosses $3000 in sales in a week receives $200 plus 9 percent of $3000, or a total of $470. Write a C program (using an array of counters) that determines how many of the salespeople earned salaries in each of the following ranges (assume that each salesperson's salary is truncated to an integer amount):

1. $200–$299
2. $300–$399
3. $400–$499
4. $500–$599
5. $600–$699
6. $700–$799
7. $800–$899
8. $900–$999
9. $1000 and over

6.6   The bubble sort presented in Fig. 6.11 is inefficient for large arrays. Make the following simple modifications to improve the performance of the bubble sort.

a) After the first pass, the largest number is guaranteed to be in the highest-numbered element of the array; after the second pass, the two highest numbers are "in place," and so on. Therefore, instead of making nine comparisons on every pass, modify the bubble sort to make eight comparisons on the second pass, seven on the third pass, and so on.

b) The data in the array may already be in the proper order or near proper order, so why make nine passes if fewer will suffice? Modify the sort to check at the end of each pass if any swaps have been made. If none has been made, then the data must already be in the proper order, so the program should terminate. If swaps have been made, then at least one more pass is needed.

6.7   Write single statements that perform each of the following single-subscripted array operations:

a) Initialize the 10 elements of integer array **counts** to zeros.

b) Add 1 to each of the 15 elements of integer array **bonus**.

c) Read the 12 values of floating point array **monthlytemperatures** from the keyboard.

d) Print the 5 values of integer array **bestscores** in column format.

6.8   Use a single-subscripted array to solve the following problem. Read in 20 numbers, each of which is between 10 and 100 inclusive. As each number is read, print it only if it is not a duplicate of a number already read. Provide for the "worst case" in which all 20 numbers are different. Use the smallest possible array to solve this problem.

6.9   Label the elements of 3-by-5 double-subscripted array **sales** to indicate the order in which they are set to zero by the following program segment:

```
for (row = 0; row <= 2; row++)
   for (column = 0; column <= 4; column++)
      sales[row][column] = 0;
```

6.10   Write a C program that simulates the rolling of two dice. The program should use `rand` to roll the first die, and should use `rand` again to roll the second die. The sum of the two values should then be calculated. *Note:* Since each die can show an integer value from 1 to 6, then the sum of the two values will vary from 2 to 12 with 7 being the most frequent sum and 2 and 12 being the least frequent sums. Fig. 6.16 shows the 36 possible combinations of the two dice. Your program should roll the two dice 36,000 times. Use a single-subscripted array to tally the numbers of times each possible sum appears. Print the results in a tabular format. Also, determine if the totals are reasonable, i.e., there are six ways to roll a 7, so approximately one sixth of all the rolls should be 7.

6.11   Write a program that runs 1000 games of craps and answers each of the following questions:

   a)   How many games are won on the first roll, second roll, ..., twentieth roll, and after the twentieth roll?

   b)   How many games are lost on the first roll, second roll, ..., twentieth roll, and after the twentieth roll?

   c)   What are the chances of winning at craps? (*Note:* You should discover that craps is one of the fairest casino games. What do you suppose this means?)

   d)   What is the average length of a game of craps?

   e)   Do the chances of winning improve with the length of the game?

6.12   (*Airline Reservations System*) A small airline has just purchased a computer for its new automated reservations system. The president has asked you to program the new system in C. You are to write a program to assign seats on each flight of the airline's only plane (capacity: 10 seats).

Your program should display the following menu of alternatives:

```
Please type 1 for "smoking"
Please type 2 for "nonsmoking"
```

If the person types 1, then your program should assign a seat in the smoking section (seats 1-5). If the person types 2, then your program should assign a seat in the nonsmoking section (seats 5-10). Your program should then print a boarding pass indicating the person's seat number and whether it is in the smoking or nonsmoking section of the plane.

Use a single-subscripted array to represent the seating chart of the plane. Initialize all the elements of the array to 0 to indicate that all seats are empty. As each seat is assigned, set the corresponding elements of the array to 1 to indicate that the seat is no longer available.

	1	2	3	4	5	6
1	2	3	4	5	6	7
2	3	4	5	6	7	8
3	4	5	6	7	8	9
4	5	6	7	8	9	10
5	6	7	8	9	10	11
6	7	8	9	10	11	12

Fig. 6.16 The 36 possible outcomes of rolling two dice.

Your program should, of course, never assign a seat that has already been assigned. When the smoking section is full, your program should ask the person if it is acceptable to be placed in the nonsmoking section (and vice versa). If yes, then make the appropriate seat assignment. If no, then print the message **"Next flight leaves in 3 hours."**

6.13   Use a double-subscripted array to solve the following problem. A company has four salespeople (1 to 4) who sell five different products (1 to 5). Once a day, each salesperson passes in a slip for each different type of product sold. Each slip contains:

1.   The salesperson number
2.   The product number
3.   The total dollar value of that product sold that day

Thus, each salesperson passes in between 0 and 5 sales slips per day. Assume that the information from all of the slips for last month is available. Write a program that will read all this information for last month's sales, and summarize the total sales by salesperson by product. All totals should be stored in the double-subscripted, array `sales`. After processing all the information for last month, print the results in tabular format with each of the columns representing a particular salesperson, and each of the rows representing a particular product. Cross total each row to get the total sales of each product for last month; cross total each column to get the total sales by salesperson for last month. Your tabular printout should include these cross totals to the right of the totaled rows and to the bottom of the totaled columns.

6.14   (*Turtle Graphics*) The Logo language, which is particularly popular among personal computer users, made the concept of *turtle graphics* famous. Imagine a mechanical turtle that walks around the room under the control of a C program. The turtle holds a pen in one of two positions, up or down. While the pen is down, the turtle traces out shapes as it moves; while the pen is up, the turtle moves about freely without writing anything. In this problem you will simulate the operation of the turtle and create a computerized sketchpad as well.

Use a 50-by-50 array `floor` which is initialized to zeros. Read commands from an array that contains them. Keep track of the current position of the turtle at all times and whether the pen is currently up or down. Assume that the turtle always starts at position 1,1 of the floor with its pen up. The set of turtle commands your program must process are as follows:

Command	Meaning
1	Pen up
2	Pen down
3	Turn right
4	Turn left
5,10	Move forward 10 spaces (or a number other than 10)
6	Print the 50-by-50 array
9	End of data (sentinel)

Suppose that the turtle is somewhere near the center of the floor. The following "program" would draw and print a 12-by 12-square:

```
2
5,12
3
5,12
3
5,12
3
5,12
1
6
9
```

As the turtle moves with the pen down, set the appropriate elements of array `floor` to 1s. When the `6` command (print) is given, wherever there is a `1` in the array, display an asterisk, or some other character you choose. Wherever there is a zero display a blank. Write a C program to implement the turtle graphics capabilities discussed here. Write several turtle graphics programs to draw interesting shapes. Add other commands to increase the power of your turtle graphics language.

6.15. (*Knight's Tour*) One of the more interesting puzzlers for chess buffs is the Knight's Tour problem, originally proposed by the mathematician Euler. The question is this: Can the chess piece called the knight move around an empty chessboard and touch each of the 64 squares once and only once? We study this intriguing problem in depth here.

The knight makes L-shaped moves (over two in one direction and then over one in a perpendicular direction). Thus, from a square in the middle of an empty chessboard, the knight can make eight different moves (numbered 0 through 7) as shown in Fig. 6.17.

a) Draw an 8-by-8 chessboard on a sheet of paper and attempt a Knight's Tour by hand. Put a `1` in the first square you move to, a `2` in the second square, a `3` in the third, and so on. Before starting the tour, estimate how far you think you will get, remembering that a full tour consists of 64 moves. How far did you get? Were you even close to your estimate?

b) Now let us develop a program that will move the knight around a chessboard. The board itself is represented by an 8-by-8 double-subscripted array, `board`. Each of the squares is initialized to zero. We describe each of the eight possible moves in terms of both their horizontal and vertical components. For example, a move of type 0 as shown in Fig. 6.17 consists of moving two squares horizontally to the right and one square vertically upward. Move 2 consists of moving one square horizontally to the right and two squares vertically upward. Horizontal moves to the left and vertical moves downward are indicated with negative numbers. The eight moves may be described by two single-subscripted arrays, `horizontal` and `vertical`, as follows:

```
horizontal[0] = 2
horizontal[1] = 1
horizontal[2] = -1
horizontal[3] = -2
horizontal[4] = -2
horizontal[5] = -1
horizontal[6] = 1
horizontal[7] = 2
```

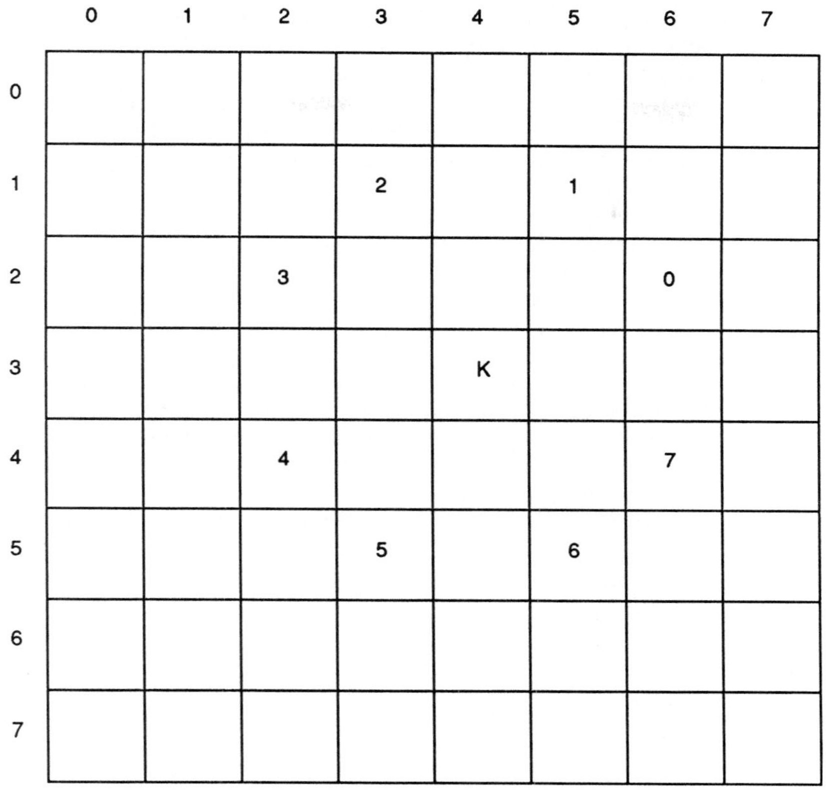

Fig. 6.17 The eight possible moves of the knight.

```
vertical[0] = -1
vertical[1] = -2
vertical[2] = -2
vertical[3] = -1
vertical[4] = 1
vertical[5] = 2
vertical[6] = 2
vertical[7] = 1
```

Let the variables `currentrow` and `currentcolumn` indicate the row and column of the knight's current position. To make a move of type `movenumber`, where movenumber is between 0 and 7; your program uses the statements

```
currentrow += vertical[movenumber];
currentcolumn += horizontal[movenumber];
```

Keep a counter that varies from 1 to 64. Record the latest count in each square the knight moves to. Remember to test each potential move to see if the knight has already visited that square. And, of course, test every potential move to make sure that the knight does not land off the chessboard. Now write a program to move the knight around the chessboard. Run the program. How many moves did the knight make?

c) After attempting to write and run a Knight's Tour program, you have probably developed some valuable insights. We will use these to develop a *heuristic* (or strategy) for moving the knight. Heuristics do not guarantee success, but a carefully developed heuristic greatly improves the chance of success. You may have observed that the outer squares are in some sense more troublesome than the squares nearer the center of the board. In fact, the most troublesome, or inaccessible, squares are the four corners.

Intuition may suggest that you should attempt to move the knight to the most troublesome squares first, and leave open those that are easiest to get to so that when the board gets congested near the end of the tour there will be a greater chance of success.

We may develop an "accessibility heuristic" by classifying each of the squares according to how accessible they are, and then always moving the knight to the square (within the knight's L-shaped moves, of course) that is most inaccessible. We label a double-subscripted array `accessibility` with numbers indicating from how many squares each particular square is accessible. On a blank chessboard, the center squares are therefore rated as 8s, the corner squares are rated as 2s, and the other squares have accessibility numbers of 3, 4, or 6 as follows:

```
2   3   4   4   4   4   3   2
3   4   6   6   6   6   4   3
4   6   8   8   8   8   6   4
4   6   8   8   8   8   6   4
4   6   8   8   8   8   6   4
4   6   8   8   8   8   6   4
3   4   6   6   6   6   4   3
2   3   4   4   4   4   3   2
```

Now write a version of the Knight's Tour program using the accessibility heuristic. At any time, the knight should move to the square with the lowest accessibility number. In case of a tie, the knight may move to any of the tied squares. Therefore, the tour may begin in any of the four corners. (*Note:* As the knight moves around the chessboard, your program should reduce the accessibility numbers as more and more squares become occupied. In this way, at any given time during the tour, each available square's accessibility number will remain equal to precisely the number of squares from which that square may be reached.) Run this version of your program. Did you get a full tour? Now modify the program to run 64 tours, one from each square of the chessboard. How many full tours did you get?

d) Write a version of the Knight's Tour program which, when encountering a tie between two or more squares, decides what square to choose by looking ahead to those squares reachable from the "tied" squares. Your program should move to the square for which the next move would arrive at a square with the lowest accessibility number.

6.16 (*Knight's Tour: Brute Force Approaches*) In problem 6.15 we developed a solution to the Knight's Tour problem. The approach used, called the "accessibility heuristic," generates many solutions and executes efficiently.

As computers continue increasing in power, we will be able to solve many problems with sheer computer power and relatively unsophisticated algorithms. Let us call this approach "brute force" problem solving.

a) Use random number generation to enable the knight to walk around the chess board (in its legitimate L-shaped moves, of course) at random. Your program should run one tour and print the final chessboard. How far did the knight get?

b) Most likely, the preceding program produced a relatively short tour. Now modify your program to attempt 1000 tours. Use a single-subscripted array to keep track of the number of tours of each length. When your program finishes attempting the 1000 tours, it should print this information in neat tabular format. What was the best result?

c) Most likely, the preceding program gave you some "respectable" tours but no full tours. Now "pull all the stops out" and simply let your program run until it produces a full tour. (*Caution.* This version of the program could run for hours on a powerful computer.) Once again, keep a table of the number of tours of each length, and print this table when the first full tour is found. How many tours did your program attempt before producing a full tour? How much time did it take?

d) Compare the brute force version of the Knight's Tour with the accessibility heuristic version. Which required a more careful study of the problem? Which algorithm was more difficult to develop? Which required more computer power? Could we be certain (in advance) of obtaining a full tour with the accessibility heuristic approach? Could we be certain (in advance) of obtaining a full tour with the brute force approach? Argue the pros and cons of brute force problem solving in general.

6.17. (*Eight Queens*) Another puzzler for chess buffs is the Eight Queens problem. Simply stated: Is it possible to place eight queens on an empty chessboard so that no queen is "attacking" any other, that is, so that no two queens are in the same row, the same column, or along the same diagonal? Use the kind of thinking developed in Problem 6.15 to formulate a heuristic for solving the Eight Queens problem. Run your program. (*Hint:* It is possible to assign a numeric value to each square of the chessboard indicating how many squares of an empty chessboard are "eliminated" once a queen is placed in that square. For example, each of the four corners would be assigned the value 22, as in Fig. 6.18.)

Once these "elimination numbers" are placed in all 64 squares, an appropriate heuristic might be: place the next queen in the square with the smallest elimination number. Why is this strategy intuitively appealing?

Fig. 6.18 The 22 squares eliminated by placing a queen in the upper left corner.

6.18 (Eight Queens: Brute Force Approaches) In this problem you will develop several brute force approaches to solving the Eight Queens problem introduced in problem 6.17.

a) Solve the Eight Queens problem, using the random brute force technique developed in Problem 6.16.

b) Use an exhaustive technique, i.e., try all possible positionings of eight queens on the chessboard.

c) Why do you suppose the exhaustive brute force approach may not be appropriate for solving the Knight's Tour problem?

d) Compare and contrast the random brute force and exhaustive brute force approaches in general.

7
Pointers

Objectives

- To be able to use pointers.
- To be able to pass arguments to functions call by reference.
- To understand the similarities between pointers, arrays, and strings.
- To understand the use of pointers to functions.

Addresses are given to us to conceal our whereabouts.
Saki (H. H. Munro)

By indirections find directions out.
William Shakespeare
Hamlet

Many things, having full reference
To one consent, may work contrariously.
William Shakespeare
King Henry V

You will find it a very good practice always to verify your references, sir!
Dr. Routh

You can't trust code that you did not totally create yourself.
(Especially code from companies that employ people like me.)
Ken Thompson
1983 Turing Award Lecture
Association for Computing Machinery, Inc.

Outline

7.1 Introduction

In this chapter, we discuss one of the most powerful features of the C programming language, the *pointer*. Pointers are among C's most difficult capabilities to master. Pointers enable programs to simulate call by reference, and to facilitate the creation and manipulation of dynamic data structures such as linked lists, queues, stacks, and trees. This chapter explains basic pointer concepts. Chapter 10 examines the use of pointers with structures. Chapter 12 presents examples of creating and using dynamic data structures.

7.2 Pointer Variable Declarations and Initialization

Pointers are variables that contain as their values memory addresses. Normally a variable directly contains a specific value. A pointer, on the other hand, contains an address of a variable that contains a specific value. In this sense, a pointer *indirectly* references a value (Fig. 7.1). This style of reference is called *indirection*.

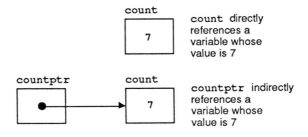

Fig. 7.1 Direct and indirect referencing of a variable.

Pointers, like any other variables, must be declared before they can be used. The declaration

```
int *countptr;
```

declares the variable `countptr` to be a pointer to an integer value, and is read, "`countptr` is a pointer to `int`" or "`countptr` points to an object of type integer." When `*` is used in this fashion in a declaration, it indicates that the variable being declared is a pointer. Pointers can be declared to point to objects of any data type.

GPP 7.1

Include the letters `ptr` in pointer variable names to make it clear that these variables are pointers and need to be handled appropriately.

Pointers should be initialized when they are declared, or in an assignment statement. A pointer may be initialized to 0, NULL, or an address. Initializing a pointer to 0 is equivalent to initializing a pointer to NULL, but NULL is preferred. A NULL pointer points to nothing. NULL is a symbolic constant defined in the `<stdio.h>` header file (and also in several other header files). The only integer that may be assigned to a pointer is 0. Assigning an address to a pointer is discussed in section 7.3.

GPP 7.2

Initialize pointers to prevent unexpected results.

7.3 Pointer Operators

The `&`, or *address, operator* is a unary operator that returns the address of its operand. For example, assuming the declarations

```
int y = 5;
int *yptr;
```

the statement

```
yptr = &y;
```

assigns the address of the variable y to pointer variable `yptr`. Variable `yptr` is then said to "point to" y. Figure 7.2 shows a schematic representation of memory after the preceding statement is executed.

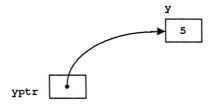

Fig. 7.2 Graphical representation of a pointer pointing to an integer variable in memory.

Figure 7.3 shows the representation of the pointer in memory assuming that integer variable y is stored at location 600000 and pointer variable yptr is stored at location 500000. The operand of the address operator must be a variable; it can not be applied to constants, to expressions, or to variables declared with the storage class register.

The * operator, commonly referred to as the *indirection operator* or *dereferencing operator*, returns the value of the object that its operand (i.e., a pointer) points to. For example, the statement

```
printf("%d", *yptr);
```

prints the value of variable y, namely 5. Using * in this manner is called *dereferencing a pointer*. When * is used in this manner it is referred to as the indirection operator or the dereferencing operator.

> **CPE 7.1**
>
> *Dereferencing a pointer that has not been properly initialized, or that has not been assigned to point to a specific location in memory. This could cause a fatal execution time error, or it could accidentally modify important data and allow the program to run to completion providing incorrect results.*

The program in Fig. 7.4 demonstrates the use of the pointer operators. The conversion specifier %lu prints the memory location as an unsigned long integer. Notice that the address of a and the value of aptr are the same, thus confirming that the address of a is indeed assigned to the pointer variable aptr. The & and * operators are complements of each other. Note that when they are both applied consecutively to aptr in either order, the same result is printed. Pointer values can also be printed using the %p conversion specifier. We discuss this interesting form in Chapter 9. The chart in Fig. 7.5 shows the precedence and associativity of the various operators introduced to this point.

7.4 Calling Functions by Reference

There are two ways to pass arguments to a function—call by value and call by reference. All function calls in C are call by value. As we saw in Chapter 5, return may be used to return one value from a called function to a caller. Often it is necessary for a called function to modify one or more variables in the caller, or to pass a pointer to a large data object to avoid the overhead of passing the object call by value (which, of course, requires making a copy of the object). For these purposes, C provides the capabilities for simulating call by reference.

Fig. 7.3 Representation of y and yptr in memory.

```
/* Using the & and * operators */
#include <stdio.h>

main()
{
    int a;          /* a is an integer */
    int *aptr;      /* aptr is a pointer to an integer */

    a = 7;
    aptr = &a;      /* aptr set to address of a */

    printf("The address of a is %lu\n", &a);
    printf("The value of aptr is %lu\n\n", aptr);

    printf("The value of a is %d\n", a);
    printf("The value of *aptr is %d\n\n", *aptr);

    printf("%s\n",
        "Proving that * and & are complements of each other.");
    printf("&*aptr = %lu\n", &*aptr);
    printf("*&aptr = %lu\n", *&aptr);
}
```

```
The address of a is 2042756
The value of aptr is 2042756

The value of a is 7
The value of *aptr is 7

Proving that * and & are complements of each other.
&*aptr = 2042756
*&aptr = 2042756
```

Fig. 7.4 The & and * pointer operators.

Operators						Associativity
() []						left to right
++ -- ! * & (type)						right to left
* / %						left to right
+ -						left to right
< <= > >=						left to right
== !=						left to right
&&						left to right
||						left to right
?:						right to left
= += -= *= /= %=						right to left
,						left to right

Fig. 7.5 Operator precedence.

In C, programmers use pointers and the indirection operator to simulate call by reference. When calling a function with arguments that should be modified, the addresses of the arguments are passed. This is normally accomplished with the address operator (&). But, as we saw in Chapter 6, when an argument is an array name, C automatically passes the address of array, so the & is not needed. When the address of a variable is passed to a function, the indirection operator (*) may be used in the function to modify the value at that location in memory.

CPE 7.2

Arrays are automatically passed simulated call by reference, so appending the address operator, &, to an array name argument causes incorrect referencing to occur by the called function. This is highly likely to lead to a fatal error, but it is possible that the program could run to completion and yield strange results.

The programs in Fig. 7.6 and Fig. 7.7 present two versions of a function called add1 that increments its argument by 1. The program in Fig. 7.6 passes the variable count using call by value. The function add1 increments its argument and passes the new value back to main using a return statement. The new value is assigned to count in main. The program in Fig. 7.7 passes the variable count using call by reference. The address of count is passed to add1. The function add1 takes a pointer to int called countptr as an argument. The function add1 dereferences the pointer and increments the value pointed to by countptr. This changes the value of count in main. Figures 7.8 and 7.9 analyze graphically the programs in Fig. 7.6 and Fig. 7.7 respectively.

```
/* Incrementing a variable using call by value */
#include <stdio.h>

main()
{
    int count = 7;
    int add1(int);

    printf("The original value of count is %d\n", count);
    count = add1(count);
    printf("The new value of count is %d\n", count);
}

int add1(int c)
{
    return ++c;    /* increments local variable c */
}
```

```
The original value of count is 7
The new value of count is 8
```

Fig. 7.6 Incrementing a variable using call by value.

```
/* Incrementing a variable using call by reference */
#include <stdio.h>

main()
{
    int count = 7;
    void add1(int *);

    printf("The original value of count is %d\n", count);
    add1(&count);
    printf("The new value of count is %d\n", count);
}

void add1(int *countptr)
{
    return ++(*countptr);    /* increments count in main */
}
```

```
The original value of count is 7
The new value of count is 8
```

Fig. 7.7 Incrementing a variable using call by reference.

CPE 7.3

Forgetting to dereference a pointer when it is necessary to do so to obtain the value of the object pointed to.

A function receiving an address as an argument must include a pointer as its corresponding parameter. For example, the header for the add1 function in Fig. 7.6 is

```
void add1(int *countptr)
```

The header states that add1 will receive an address of an integer variable and will store that address in countptr. The header also indicates that the function will not return a value.

The function prototype for add1 in main contains int * in parentheses. As with all other types of variables, it is not necessary to include names of pointers in function prototypes. If names are included for documentation purposes, the names are ignored by the C compiler.

In the function header and in the function prototype for a function that expects a single subscripted array as an argument, the pointer notation used in the parameter list of add1 may be used. The function can not tell the difference between a pointer and a single subscripted array. This, of course, means that the function must "know" when it is receiving an array or simply a single variable for which it is to perform call by reference.

GPP 7.3

Use call by value to pass arguments to a function unless the caller explicitly requires that the called function modify the value of the argument variable in the caller's environment. This is another example of the principle of least privilege.

Before `main` calls `add1`:

```
main()                    count
{                         [  7  ]
    int count = 7;

    count = add1(count);
}
```

```
int add1(int c)          c
{                        [undefined]
    return ++c;
}
```

After `add1` receives the call:

```
main()                    count
{                         [  7  ]
    int count = 7;

    count = add1(count);
}
```

```
int add1(int c)          c
{                        [  7  ]
    return ++c;
}
```

After `add1` increments the counter:

```
main()                    count
{                         [  7  ]
    int count = 7;

    count = add1(count);
}
```

```
int add1(int c)          c
{                        [  8  ]
    return (++c);
}
```

After `add1` returns to `main`:

```
main()                    count
{                         [  7  ]
    int count = 7;

    count = (add1(count));
}
```

```
int add1(int c)          c
{                        [undefined]
    return ++c;
}
```

After `main` completes the assignment to `count`:

```
main()                    count
{                         [  8  ]
    int count = 7;

    count = add1(count);
}
```

```
int add1(int c)          c
{                        [undefined]
    return ++c;
}
```

Fig. 7.8 Analysis of a typical call by value.

Before the call by reference to **add1** :

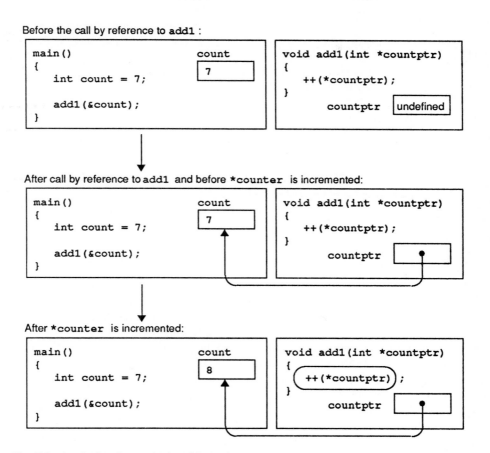

Fig. 7.9 Analysis of a typical call by reference.

7.5 Bubble Sort Using Call by Reference

Let us modify the bubble sort program of Fig. 6.11 to use a separate function, swap, to exchange the array elements a[counter] and a[counter + 1] (See Fig. 7.10). Remember that C enforces information hiding between functions, so swap does not have access to the array elements to be swapped in main. Because main wants swap to have access to the array elements to be swapped, main passes each of these elements call by reference to swap. Although entire arrays are automatically passed call by reference, individual array elements are treated as conventional simple (nonarray) variables, and are ordinarily passed call by value. Therefore, main uses the address operator, &, on each of the array elements in the swap call as follows

```
swap(&a[counter],  &a[counter + 1]);
```

to effect call by reference. Function `swap` receives `&a[counter]` in pointer variable `element1ptr`. Even though `swap`—because of information hiding— is not allowed to know the name `a[counter]`, `swap` may use `*element1ptr` as a synonym for `a[counter]`. Therefore, when `swap` references `*element1ptr` it is actually referencing `a[counter]` in `main`. Similarly, when `swap` references `*element2ptr` it is actually referencing `a[counter + 1]` in `main`. Thus, even though `swap` is not allowed to say

```
temp = a[counter];
a[counter] = a[counter + 1];
a[counter + 1\] = temp;
```

precisely the same effect is achieved by

```
temp = *element1ptr;
*element1ptr = *element2ptr;
*element2ptr = temp;
```

in the `swap` function of Fig. 7.10.

7.6 Pointer Expressions and Pointer Arithmetic

Pointers are valid operands in arithmetic expressions, assignment expressions, and comparison expressions. Not all the operators normally used in these expressions are valid in conjunction with pointer variables. This section describes the operators that can have pointers as operands, and how these operators are used.

A limited set of arithmetic operations may be performed on pointers. A pointer may be incremented (++) or decremented (--), an integer may be added to a pointer (+ or +=), an integer may be subtracted from a pointer (- or -=), or one pointer may be subtracted from another.

Assume that array `v[10]` has been declared, it is of type `int`, and its first element is at location `3000` in memory. Assume pointer `vptr` has been initialized to point to the first element of `v`, i.e., the value of `vptr` is `3000`, thus `vptr` points to `v[0]`. Fig. 7.11 shows a diagram of this situation for a machine that has 4-byte integers. Remember that many machines have 2-byte integers, so the effects we describe could be different on your system. This is another way of saying that pointer arithmetic is *machine dependent*. Note that `vptr` can be initialized to point to array `v` with either of the statements

```
vptr = v;
vptr = &v[0];
```

In straightforward arithmetic, the addition `3000 + 2` yields the value `3002`. This is not necessarily the case in pointer arithmetic. When an integer is added to or subtracted from a pointer, the pointer is not simply incremented or decremented by that integer, but by that integer times the size of the object pointed to. The number of bytes depends on the data type of the object to which the pointer refers. For example, the statement

```
vptr += 2;
```

```
/* This program puts values into an array, sorts
   the values into ascending order, and prints the
   resulting array. */
#include <stdio.h>

main()
{
    int a[10] = {2, 6, 4, 8, 10, 12, 89, 68, 45, 37};
    int counter, pass;
    void swap(int *, int *);

    printf("Data items in original order\n");
    for (counter = 0; counter <= 9; counter++)
        printf("%4d", a[counter]);

    for (pass = 0; pass <= 8; pass++) {
        for (counter = 0; counter <= 8; ++counter) {
            if (a[counter] > a[counter+1])
                swap(&a[counter], &a[counter+1]);
        }
    }

    printf("\nData items in ascending order\n");
    for (counter = 0; counter <= 9; counter++)
        printf("%4d", a[counter]);
    printf("\n");
}

void swap(int *element1ptr, int *element2ptr)
{
    int temp;

    temp = *element1ptr;
    *element1ptr = *element2ptr;
    *element2ptr = temp;
}
```

```
Data items in original order
   2    6    4    8   10   12   89   68   45   37
Data items in ascending order
   2    4    6    8   10   12   37   45   68   89
```

Fig. 7.10 Bubble sort with call by reference.

would produce 3008 ($3000 + 2 * 4$) assuming an integer is stored in 4 bytes of memory. In the array v, vptr would now point to v[2] (Fig. 7.12). If an integer is stored in 2 bytes of memory, then the preceding calculation would result in memory location 3004 ($3000 + 2 * 2$). If the array were of a different data type, the above statement would increment the pointer by the appropriate number of bytes. When performing pointer arithmetic on a character array, the results will appear to be like regular arithmetic because each character is one byte long.

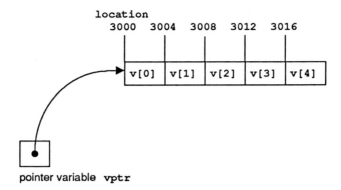

Fig. 7.11 The array **v** and the pointer variable **vptr** that points to **v**.

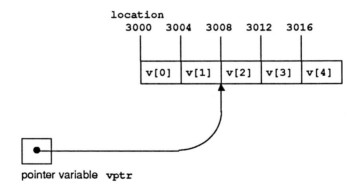

Fig. 7.12 The pointer **vptr** after pointer arithmetic.

If vptr had been incremented to 3016, which points to v[4], the statement

```
vptr -= 4;
```

would set vptr back to 3000—the beginning of the array. If a pointer is only being incremented or decremented by one, the increment (++) and decrement (−−) operators can be used. Either of the statements

```
++vptr;
vptr++;
```

would increment the pointer to point to the next location in the array. Either of the statements

```
--vptr;
vptr--;
```

would decrement the pointer to point to the previous element of the array.

Pointer variables may be subtracted from one another. For example, if vptr contains the location 3000, and v2ptr contains the address 3008, the statement

```
x = v2ptr - vptr;
```

would assign the number of elements from vptr to v2ptr in x. In this case, the variable x would be assigned the value 2. Pointer arithmetic operations are meaningless unless performed on an array. It is not possible to determine the location of a variable in memory before a program is compiled. Therefore, you can not assume that two integer variables are stored in consecutive locations in memory unless they are the elements of an array. Array elements are guaranteed to be stored contiguously in memory.

CPE 7.4
Using pointer arithmetic on a pointer that does not refer to an array of values.

CPE 7.5
Subtracting or comparing two pointers that do not refer to the same array.

CPE 7.6
Running off either end of an array when using pointer arithmetic.

A pointer may be assigned to another pointer only if both pointers are of the same type. Otherwise, a cast operator must be used. The exception to this rule is the pointer to void which is a generic pointer that can hold any pointer type. It can be assigned pointers of other types and can be assigned to pointers of other types without a cast. A pointer of type "pointer to void" (i.e., void *) may not be dereferenced. For example, a pointer to int is known to point to two bytes of memory on a machine with 4 byte integers, but a pointer to void just points to a location without a specific number of bytes. The number of bytes dereferenced is the number of bytes used to store the data type pointed to. In the case of pointer to void, this number of bytes cannot be determined from the type.

CPE 7.7
*Assigning a pointer of one type to a pointer of another type if neither is of type void * causes a syntax error.*

CPE 7.8
Dereferencing a void pointer.

Pointers can be compared using equality and relational operators, but such comparisons are meaningless unless the pointers point to members of the same array. Pointer comparisons compare the addresses stored in the pointers. A comparison of two pointers pointing to the same array could show, for example, that one pointer points to a higher-numbered element of the array than the other pointer does. A common use of pointer comparison is determining whether a pointer is NULL.

7.7 The Relationship between Pointers and Arrays

Arrays and pointers are intimately related in C and may be used *almost* interchangeably. An array name can be thought of as a constant pointer. Pointers can be used to do any operation involving array subscripting. Array subscripting notation is converted to pointer notation during compilation, so writing array subscripting expressions with pointer notation can save compile time.

GPP 7.4

Use array notation instead of pointer notation when manipulating arrays. Although the program may take slightly longer to compile, the it will probably be much clearer.

Assume that integer array b[5] and integer pointer variable bptr have been declared. Since the array name without a subscript is a pointer to the first element of the array, we can set bptr equal to the address of the first element in array b with the statement

```
bptr = b;
```

This statement is equivalent to taking the address of the first element of the array as follows

```
bptr = &b[0];
```

Array element b[3] can alternatively be referenced with the pointer expression

```
*(bptr + 3)
```

The 3 in the above expression is the *offset* to the pointer. When the pointer points to the beginning of an array, the offset indicates which element of the array should be referenced, and the offset is identical to the array subscript. The preceding notation is referred to as *pointer/offset notation*. The parentheses are necessary because the precedence of * is higher than the precedence of +. Without the parentheses, the above expression would add 3 to the value of the expression *bptr (i.e., 3 would be added to b[0] assuming bptr points to the beginning of the array). Just as the array element can be referenced with a pointer expression, the address

```
&b[3]
```

can be written with the pointer expression

```
bptr + 3
```

The array itself can be treated as a pointer and indexed. For example, the expression

```
*(b + 3)
```

also refers to the array element b[3]. In general, all subscripted array expressions can be written with a pointer and an offset. In this case pointer/offset notation was used with the name of the array as a pointer. Note that the preceding statement does not modify the array name in any way; b still points to the first element in the array.

Pointers can also be subscripted exactly as arrays can. For example, the expression

```
bptr[1]
```

refers to the array element b[1]. This is referred to as *pointer/subscript notation.*

Remember that an array name is essentially a constant pointer; it always points to the beginning of the array. Thus, the expression

```
b += 3
```

is invalid because it attempts to modify the value of the array name with pointer arithmetic.

CPE 7.9

Attempting to modify an array name with pointer arithmetic is a syntax error.

The program in Fig. 7.13 uses the four methods we have discussed for referring to array elements discussed above—array subscripting, pointer/offset with the array name as a pointer, pointer subscripting, and pointer/offset with a pointer—to print the four elements of the integer array b.

7.8 Arrays of Pointers

Arrays may contain pointers. A common use of such a data structure is to form an array of strings, referred to simply as a *string array*. Each entry in the array is a string, but in C a string is essentially a pointer to its first element, so each entry in an array of strings is actually a pointer to the first element of a string. Consider the declaration of string array suit that might be useful in representing a deck of cards.

```
char *suit[4] = {"Hearts", "Diamonds", "Clubs", "Spades"};
```

The suit[4] portion of the declaration indicates an array of 4 elements. The char * portion of the declaration indicates that each component of array suit is of type "pointer to char." The four values to be placed in the array are "Hearts", "Diamonds", "Clubs", and "Spades". Each of those is a character string that when stored in memory is one character longer than the number of characters between quotes. This is so because of the NULL character that terminates each string. The four strings are 7, 9, 6, and 7 characters long respectively. Although it appears as though these strings are being placed in the suit array, only pointers are actually stored in the array (Fig 7.14). Each pointer points to the first element of one of the strings. Thus, even though the suit array is fixed in size, it provides access to a set of character strings that can each be of any length. This kind of flexibility is only one example of the power of C's data structuring capabilities.

The suits could have been placed into a double array in which each row would represent one suit, and each column would represent one of the letters of a suit name. Such a data structure would have to have a fixed number of columns per row, and that number would have to be as large as the largest string. Therefore, considerable memory could be wasted when a large number of strings are being stored, with most strings much shorter than the longest string. We will use arrays of strings to help represent a deck of cards in the next section.

```c
/* Using subscripting and pointer notations with arrays */
#include <stdio.h>

main()
{
   int b[] = {10, 20, 30, 40};
   int *b_ptr, i, offset;

   b_ptr = b;  /* set b_ptr to point to array b */

   printf("Array b printed with:\n");
   printf("Array subscript notation\n");
   for (i = 0; i <= 3; i++)
      printf("b[%d] = %d\n", i, b[i]);

   printf("\nPointer/offset notation where \n");
   printf("the pointer is the array name\n");
   for (offset = 0; offset <= 3; offset++)
      printf("*(b + %d) = %d\n", offset, *(b + offset));

   printf("\nPointer subscript notation\n");
   for (i = 0; i <= 3; i++)
      printf("b_ptr[%d] = %d\n", i, b_ptr[i]);

   printf("\nPointer/offset notation\n");
   for (offset = 0; offset <= 3; offset++)
      printf("*(b_ptr + %d) = %d\n", offset,
         *(b_ptr + offset));
}
```

```
Array b printed with:
Array subscript notation
b[0] = 10
b[1] = 20
b[2] = 30
b[3] = 40

Pointer/offset notation where
the pointer is the array name
*(b + 0) = 10
*(b + 1) = 20
*(b + 2) = 30
*(b + 3) = 40

Pointer subscript notation
bptr[0] = 10
bptr[1] = 20
bptr[2] = 30
bptr[3] = 40

Pointer/offset notation
*(bptr + 0) = 10
*(bptr + 1) = 20
*(bptr + 2) = 30
*(bptr + 3) = 40
```

Fig. 7.13 Using the four methods of referencing array elements.

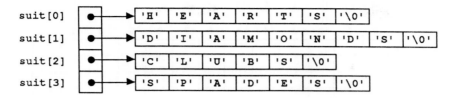

Fig. 7.14 A graphical example of the array `suit`.

7.9 Example: A Card Shuffling and Dealing Simulation

In this section we use random number generation to develop a card shuffling and dealing simulation program. This program can then be used as the root of various programs that play specific card games. We have intentionally used sub-optimal shuffling and dealing algorithms. In the exercises we develop more efficient algorithms.

Using a top-down, stepwise refinement approach, we develop a program that will shuffle a deck of 52 playing cards, and then deal each of the 52 cards. The top-down approach here is particularly useful in attacking larger, more complex problems than we have seen in the early chapters.

We use a 4-by-13 double-subscripted array `deck` to represent the deck of playing cards (Fig. 7.15). The rows correspond to the suits—row 0 corresponds to hearts, row 1 to diamonds, row 2 to clubs, and row 3 to spades. The columns correspond to the face values of the cards—columns 0 through 9 correspond to faces ace through ten respectively, and columns 10 through 12 correspond to jack, queen, and king. We shall load array `suit` with character strings representing the four suits, and array `face` with character strings representing the thirteen face values.

This simulated deck of cards may be shuffled as follows. First the array `deck` is cleared to zeros. Then, a `row` (0–3) and a `column` (0–12) are chosen at random. The number 1 is inserted in array element `deck[row][column]` to indicate that this card is going to be first one dealt from the shuffled deck. This process continues with the numbers 2, 3, ..., 52 being inserted in the `deck` array to indicate which cards are to be placed second, third, ..., and fifty-second in the shuffled deck. As the `deck` array begins to fill with card numbers, it is possible that a card will be selected twice, i.e., `deck[row][column]` will be nonzero when it is selected. This selection is simply ignored and other `rows` and `columns` are repeatedly chosen at random until an unselected card is found. Eventually, the numbers 1 through 52 will occupy the 52 slots of the `deck` array. At this point, the deck of cards is fully shuffled.

This shuffling algorithm could execute indefinitely if cards that have already been shuffled are repeatedly selected at random. This is known as *indefinite postponement*. In the exercises we discuss a better shuffling algorithm that eliminates the possibility of indefinite postponement.

tion `"%5s of %-8s"` will print a character string right-justified in a field of five characters followed by `" of "` and a character string left-justified in a field of eight characters. The minus sign in `%-8s` signifies that the string should be left-justified in the field of width 8.

There is a weakness in the dealing algorithm. Once a match is found, even if it is found on the first try, the two inner `for` structures continue searching the remaining elements of `deck` for a match. We leave it to the exercises to correct this. In Chapter 10, we develop high-performance shuffling and dealing algorithms.

7.10 Pointers to Functions

A pointer to a function contains the address of the function in memory. Pointers to functions can be passed to functions, returned from functions, stored in arrays, and assigned to other function pointers.

To illustrate the use of pointers to functions we have modified the bubble sort program of Fig. 7.10 to form the program of Fig. 7.18. Our new program consists of a `main` function, and the functions `bubble`, `swap`, `ascending`, and `descending`. The bubble sort has been moved into a separate function that receives a pointer to either function `ascending` or function `descending`. The program prompts the user to specify if the array should be sorted in ascending order or in descending order. If the user enters 1, a pointer to function `ascending` is passed to function `bubble` causing the array to be sorted into ascending order. If the user enters 2, a pointer to function `descending` is passed to function `bubble` causing the array to be sorted into descending order.

The following parameter appears in the function header for `bubble`:

```
int (*compare)(int, int)
```

This tells `bubble` to expect a parameter that is a pointer to a function that receives two integer parameters and returns an integer result. Parentheses are needed around `*compare` because `*` has a lower precedence than the parentheses enclosing the function parameters. If we had not included the parentheses, the declaration would have been

```
int *compare(int, int)
```

which declares a function that receives two integers as parameters and returns a pointer to an integer.

The corresponding parameter in the function prototype of `bubble` is

```
int (*)(int, int)
```

Note that only types have been included, but the user may optionally include names that the compiler ignores.

The function passed to `bubble` is called in an `if` statement as follows

```
if ((*compare)(work[count], work[count + 1]))
```

```
/* Card dealing program */

#include <stdio.h>
#include <stdlib.h>
#include <time.h>

void shuffle(int workdeck[4][13]);
void deal(int workdeck2[4][13], char *worksuit[4],
    char *workface[13]);

main()
{
    int card, row, column;
    char *suit[4] = {"Hearts", "Diamonds", "Clubs", "Spades"};
    char *face[13] = {"Ace", "Deuce", "Three", "Four", "Five", "Six",
                      "Seven", "Eight", "Nine", "Ten", "Jack",
                      "Queen", "King"};
    int deck[4][13] = {0};

    srand(clock());

    shuffle(deck);
    deal(deck, face, suit);
}

void shuffle(int workdeck[][13])
{
    int card, row, column;

    for(card = 1; card <= 52; card++) {
        row = rand() % 4;
        column = rand() % 13;
        while(workdeck[row][column] != 0) {
            row = rand() % 4;
            column = rand() % 13;
        }
        workdeck[row][column] = card;
    }
}

void deal(int workdeck2[][13], char *workface[], char *worksuit[])
{
    int card, row, column;

    for (card = 1; card <= 52; card++)
        for (row = 0; row <= 3; row++)
            for (column = 0; column <= 12; column++)
                if (workdeck2[row][column] == card) {
                    printf("%5s of %-8s",
                        workface[column], worksuit[row]);
                    if (card % 2 == 0)
                        putchar('\n');
                    else
                        putchar('\t');
                    break;
                }
}
```

Fig. 7.16 Card dealing program.

```
    Six of Clubs         Seven of Diamonds
    Ace of Spades          Ace of Diamonds
    Ace of Hearts        Queen of Diamonds
  Queen of Clubs         Seven of Hearts
    Ten of Hearts          Deuce of Clubs
    Ten of Spades          Three of Spades
    Ten of Diamonds         Four of Spades
   Four of Diamonds         Ten of Clubs
    Six of Diamonds         Six of Spades
  Eight of Hearts         Three of Diamonds
   Nine of Hearts         Three of Hearts
  Deuce of Spades           Six of Hearts
   Five of Clubs         Eight of Clubs
  Deuce of Diamonds      Eight of Spades
   Five of Spades         King of Clubs
   King of Diamonds       Jack of Spades
  Deuce of Hearts        Queen of Hearts
    Ace of Clubs          King of Spades
  Three of Clubs          King of Hearts
   Nine of Clubs          Nine of Spades
   Four of Hearts        Queen of Spades
  Eight of Diamonds       Nine of Diamonds
   Jack of Diamonds      Seven of Clubs
   Five of Hearts         Five of Diamonds
   Four of Clubs          Jack of Hearts
   Jack of Clubs         Seven of Spades
```

Fig. 7.17 Sample run of card dealing program.

Just as a pointer to a variable must be dereferenced to access the value of the variable, a pointer to a function must be dereferenced to use the function. The call to the function could have been made with

```
        if (compare(work[count], work[count + 1]))
```

which uses the pointer as the function name. We prefer the first method because it explicitly states that `compare` is a pointer to a function, whereas the second method makes it appear as though `compare` is an actual function. The new bubble sort program and its outputs are shown in Fig. 7.18 and Fig. 7.19.

Summary

- Pointers are variables that contain as their values addresses of other variables.

- Pointers must be declared before they can be used.

- The declaration

```
        int *ptr;
```

declares `ptr` to be a pointer to an object of type `int`, and is read, "`ptr` is a pointer to `int`." The `*` as used here in a declaration indicates that the variable is a pointer.

```
/* Multipurpose sorting program with function pointers */

#include <stdio.h>
#define SIZE 10

main()
{
    int a[SIZE] = {2, 6, 4, 8, 10, 12, 89, 68, 45, 37};
    int counter, order;

    void bubble(int *, int, int (*)(int, int));
    void swap(int *, int *);
    int ascending(int, int);
    int descending(int, int);

    printf("Enter 1 to sort in ascending order,\n");
    printf("Enter 2 to sort in descending order:\n");
    scanf("%d", &order);

    printf("\nData items in original order\n");
    for (counter = 0; counter <= SIZE - 1; counter++)
        printf("%4d", a[counter]);

    if (order == 1) {
        bubble(a, SIZE, ascending);
        printf("\nData items in ascending order\n");
    }
    else {
        bubble(a, SIZE, descending);
        printf("\nData items in descending order\n");
    }

    for (counter = 0; counter <= SIZE - 1; counter++)
        printf("%4d", a[counter]);
    printf("\n");
}

void bubble(int *work, int size, int (*compare)(int, int))
{
    int pass, count;

    for (pass = 0; pass <= SIZE - 2; pass++)

        for (count = 0; count <= SIZE - 2; count++)

            if ((*compare)(work[count], work[count + 1]))
                swap(&work[count], &work[count + 1]);
}

void swap(int *element1ptr, int *element2ptr)
{
    int temp;

    temp = *element1ptr;
    *element1ptr = *element2ptr;
    *element2ptr = temp;
}
```

Fig. 7.18 Multipurpose sorting program using function pointers (part 1 of 2).

```
int ascending(int a, int b)
{
    return a > b;
}

int descending(int a, int b)
{
    return a < b;
}
```

Fig. 7.18 Multipurpose sorting program using function pointers (part 2 of 2).

```
Enter 1 to sort in ascending order,
Enter 2 to sort in descending order:
1

Data items in original order
    2   6   4   8  10  12  89  68  45  37
Data items in ascending order
    2   4   6   8  10  12  37  45  68  89
```

```
Enter 1 to sort in ascending order,
Enter 2 to sort in descending order:
2

Data items in original order
    2   6   4   8  10  12  89  68  45  37
Data items in descending order
   89  68  45  37  12  10   8   6   4   2
```

Fig. 7.19 The outputs of the bubble sort program in Fig. 7.18.

- There are three values that can be used to initialize a pointer; 0, NULL, or an address. Initializing a poi nter to 0 and initializing that same pointer to NULL are identical.
- The only integer that can be assigned to a pointer is 0.
- The & (address) operator returns the address of its operand.
- The operand of the address operator must be a variable; the address operator can not be applied to constants, to expressions, or to variables declared with the storage class register.
- The * operator, referred to as the indirection or dereferencing operator, returns the value of the object that its operand points to in memory. This is called dereferencing the pointer.

- When calling a function with an argument that the caller wants the called function to modify, the address of the argument is passed. The called function then uses the indirection operator ($*$) to modify the value of the argument in the calling function.

- A function receiving an address as an argument must include a pointer as its corresponding formal parameter.

- It is not necessary to include the names of pointers in function prototypes; it is only necessary to include the pointer types. Pointer names may be included for documentation reasons, but the compiler ignores them.

- Arrays are automatically passed by reference because the value of the array name is the address of the array.

- To pass a single element of an array call by reference, the address of the specific array element must be passed.

- The arithmetic operations that may be performed on pointers are incrementing (++) a pointer, decrementing (--) a pointer, adding (+ or +=) a pointer and an integer, subtracting (- or -=) a pointer and an integer, and subtracting one pointer from another.

- When an integer is added or subtracted from a pointer, the pointer is incremented or decremented by that integer times the size of the object pointed to.

- Pointer arithmetic operations should only be performed on contiguous portions of memory such as an array. All elements of an array are stored contiguously in memory.

- When performing pointer arithmetic on a character array, the results are like regular arithmetic because each character is stored in one byte of memory.

- Pointers can be assigned to one another if both pointers are of the same type. Otherwise, a cast must be used. The exception to this rule is the pointer to `void` which is a generic pointer type that can hold pointers of any type. Pointers to `void` can be assigned pointers of other types and can be assigned to pointers of other types without a cast.

- A pointer to `void` may not be dereferenced.

- Pointers can be compared using the equality and relational operators. Pointer comparisons are normally meaningful only if the pointers point to members of the same array.

- Pointers can be subscripted exactly as array names can.

- An array name without a subscript is a pointer to the first element of the array.

- In pointer/offset notation, the offset is the same as an array subscript.

- All subscripted array expressions can be written with a pointer and an offset using either the name of the array as a pointer, or a separate pointer that points to the array.

- An array name is a constant pointer that always points to the same location in memory. Array names can not be modified as conventional pointers can.

- It is possible to have arrays of pointers.
- It is possible to have pointers to functions.
- A pointer to a function is the address where the code for the function resides.
- Pointers to functions can be passed to functions, returned from functions, stored in arrays, and assigned to other pointers.

Terminology

adding a pointer and an integer	linked list
address operator (&)	NULL pointer
array of pointers	offset
array of strings	pointer
call by reference	pointer arithmetic
call by value	pointer assignment
character pointer	pointer comparison
constant pointer	pointer expression
decrement a pointer	pointer to a function
dereference a pointer	pointer indexing
dereferencing operator (*)	pointer/offset notation
dynamic memory allocation	pointer subscripting
function pointer	pointer types
increment a pointer	string array
indefinite postponement	subtracting an integer from a pointer
indirection	subtracting two pointers
indirection operator (*)	top-down, stepwise refinement
initializing pointers	void

Common Programming Errors

7.1   Dereferencing a pointer that has not been initialized, or that has not been assigned to point to a specific location in memory.

7.2   Arrays are automatically passed simulated call by reference, so appending the address operator, &, to an array name argument causes incorrect referencing to occur by the called function. This is highly likely to lead to a fatal error, but it is possible that the program could run to completion and yield strange results.

7.3   Not dereferencing a pointer to a value that will be used in a calculation.

7.4   Using pointer arithmetic on a pointer that does not refer to an array of values.

7.5   Subtracting or comparing two pointers that do not refer to the same array.

7.6   Running off either end of an array when using pointer arithmetic.

7.7   Assigning a pointer of one type to a pointer of another type if neither is of type `void *` causes a syntax error.

7.8   Dereferencing a `void` pointer.

7.9   Although array names are pointers to the beginning of the array, and pointers can be modified in arithmetic expressions, array names can not be modified in arithmetic expressions.

Good Programming Practices

7.1   Include the letters `ptr` in pointer variable names to make it clear that these variables are pointers and thus need to be handled appropriately.

7.2   Initialized pointers to prevent unexpected results.

7.3   Use call by value to pass arguments to a function unless the value of the variable must be modified. This is an example of the principle of least privilege. Some people prefer call by reference for performance reasons because the overhead of copying values is avoided.

7.4   Use array notation instead of pointer notation when manipulating arrays. Although the program may take slightly longer to compile, the it will probably be much clearer.

Self-Review Exercises

7.1   Answer each of the following:
  a) A pointer is a variable that contains as its value the _____ of another variable.
  b) The three values that can be used to initialize a pointer are _____, _____, or an _____.
  c) The only integer that can be assigned to a pointer is _____.

7.2   State whether the following are true or false. If the answer is false, explain why.
  a) The address operator `&` can only be applied to constants, to expressions, and to variables declared with the storage class `register`.
  b) A pointer that is declared to be `void` can be dereferenced.
  c) In all cases, pointers of different types may not be assigned to one another without a cast operation.

7.3   Answer each of the following. Assume that single-precision floating point numbers are stored in 4 bytes, and that the starting address of the array is at location 1002500 in memory. Each part of the exercise should use the results of previous parts where appropriate.
  a) Declare an array of type `float` called `numbers` with 10 elements, and initialize the elements to the values `0.0, 1.1, 2.2, ..., 9.9`. Assume the symbolic constant `SIZE` has been defined as `10`.
  b) Declare a pointer `nptr` that points to an object of type `float`.
  c) Print the elements of array `numbers` using array subscript notation. Use a `for` structure, and assume the integer control variable `i` has been declared. Print each number with 1 position of precision to the right of the decimal point.
  d) Give two separate statements that assign the starting address of array `numbers` to the pointer variable `nptr`.
  e) Print the elements of array `numbers` using pointer/offset notation with the pointer `nptr`.

f)   Print the elements of array **numbers** using pointer/offset notation with the array name as the pointer.

g)   Print the elements of array **numbers** by subscripting pointer **nptr**.

h)   Refer to element 4 of array **numbers** using array subscript notation, pointer/offset notation with the array name as the pointer, pointer subscript notation with **nptr**, and pointer/offset notation with **nptr**.

i)   Assuming that **nptr** points to the beginning of array **numbers**, what address is referenced by **nptr + 8**? What value is stored at that location?

j)   Assuming that **nptr** points to **numbers[5]**, what address is referenced by **nptr -= 4**. What is the value stored at that location?

7.4   For each of the following, write a single statement that performs the indicated task. Assume that floating point variables **number1** and **number2** have been declared, and that **number1** has been initialized to **7.3**.

a)   Declare the variable **fptr** to be a pointer to an object of type **float**.

b)   Assign the address of variable **number1** to pointer variable **fptr**.

c)   Print the value of the object pointed to by **fptr**.

d)   Assign the value of the object pointed to by **fptr** to variable **number2**.

e)   Print the value of **number2**.

f)   Print the address of **number1**. Use the **%lu** conversion specifier.

g)   Print the address stored in **fptr**. Use the **%lu** conversion specifier. Is the value printed the same as the address of **number1**?

7.5   Do each of the following.

a)   Write the function header for a function called **exchange** that takes two pointers to floating point numbers **x** and **y** as parameters, and does not return a value.

b)   Write the function prototype for the function in part (a).

c)   Write the function header for a function called **evaluate** that returns an integer and that takes as parameters integer **x** and a pointer to function **poly**. Function **poly** takes an integer parameter and returns an integer.

d)   Write the function prototype for the function in part (c).

7.6   Find the error in each of the following program segments. Assume

```
int *zptr;    /* zptr will reference array z */
int *aptr = NULL;
void *sptr = NULL;
int number, i;
int z[5] = {1, 2, 3, 4, 5};

sptr = z;
```

a)   ++zptr;

b)   /* use pointer to get first value of array */
   number = zptr;

c)   /* assign array element 2 (the value 3) to number */
   number = *zptr[2];

d)   /* print entire array z */
   for (i = 0; i <= 5; i++)
       printf("%d ", zptr[i]);

e)   /* assign the value pointed to by sptr to integer number */
   number = *sptr;

f)   ++z;

Answers to Self-Review Exercises

7.1   a) address. b) 0, NULL, an address. c) 0.

7.2   a) False. The address operator can only be applied to variables, and it can not be applied to variables declared with storage class **register**.

b) False. A pointer to **void** cannot be dereferenced because there is no way to know exactly how many bytes of memory should be dereferenced.

c) False. Pointers of type **void** can be assigned pointers of other types, and pointers of type **void** can be assigned to pointers of other types.

7.3   a) `float numbers[SIZE] = {0.0, 1.1, 2.2, 3.3, 4.4, 5.5,`
`            6.6, 7.7, 8.8, 9.9};`
b) `float *nptr;`
c) `for (i = 0; i <= SIZE - 1; i++)`
`       printf("%.1f ", numbers[i]);`
d) `nptr = numbers;`
`   nptr = &numbers[0];`
e) `for (i = 0; i <= SIZE - 1; i++)`
`       printf("%.1f ", *(nptr + i));`
f) `for (i = 0; i <= SIZE - 1; i++)`
`       printf("%.1f ", *(numbers + i));`
g) `for (i = 0; i <= SIZE - 1; i++)`
`       printf("%.1f ", nptr[i]);`
h) `numbers[4]`
`   *(numbers + 4)`
`   nptr[4]`
`   *(nptr + 4)`
i) The address is `1002500 + 8 * 4 = 1002532`. The value is `8.8`.
j) The address of `numbers[5]` is `1002500 + 5 * 4 = 1002520`.
The address of `nptr -= 4` is `1002520 - 4 * 4 = 1002504`.
The value at that location is `1.1`.

7.4   a) `float *fptr;`
b) `fptr = &number1;`
c) `printf("The value of *fptr is %f\n", *fptr);`
d) `number2 = *fptr;`
e) `printf("The value of number2 is %f\n", number2);`
f) `printf("The address of number1 is %lu\n", &number1);`
g) `printf("The address stored in fptr is %lu\n", fptr);`
Yes, the value is the same.

7.5   a) `void exchange(float *x, float *y)`
b) `void exchange(float *, float *);`
c) `int evaluate(int x, int (*poly)(int))`
d) `int evaluate(int, int (*)(int));`

7.6   a) Error: `zptr` has not been initialized.
Correction: Initialize `zptr` with `zptr = z;`
b) Error: The pointer is not dereferenced.
Correction: Change the statement to `number = *zptr;`
c) Error: `zptr[2]` is not a pointer and should not be dereferenced.
Correction: Change `*zptr[2]` to `zptr[2]`.

d) Error: Referring to an array element outside the array bounds with pointer sub-scripting.

Correction: Change the final value of the control variable in the `for` structure to **4**.

e) Error: Dereferencing a void pointer.

Correction: In order to dereference the pointer, it must first be cast to an integer pointer. Change the above statement to `number = *(int *)sptr;`

f) Error: Trying to modify an array name with pointer arithmetic.

Correction: Use a pointer variable instead of the array name to accomplish pointer arithmetic, or subscript the array name to refer to a specific element.

Exercises

7.7   Answer each of the following:

a) The _____ operator returns the location in memory where its operand is stored.

b) The _____ operator returns the value of the object to which its operand points.

c) To simulate call by reference when passing a non-array variable to a function, it is necessary to pass the _____ of the variable to the function.

7.8   State whether the following are true or false. If false, explain why.

a) Two pointers that point to different arrays cannot be compared meaningfully.

b) Because the name of an array is a pointer to the first element of the array, array names may be manipulated in precisely the same manner as pointers.

7.9   Answer each of the following. Assume that unsigned integers are stored in 2 bytes, and that the starting address of the array is at location 1002500 in memory.

a) Declare an array of type `unsigned int` called `values` with 5 elements, and initialize the elements to the even integers from 2 to 10. Assume the symbolic constant `SIZE` has been defined as **5**.

b) Declare a pointer `vptr` that points to an object of type `unsigned int`.

c) Print the elements of array `values` using array subscript notation. Use a `for` structure, and assume integer control variable `i` has been declared.

d) Give two separate statements that assign the starting address of array `values` to pointer variable `vptr`.

e) Print the elements of array `values` using pointer/offset notation.

f) Print the elements of array `values` using pointer/offset notation with the array name as the pointer.

g) Print the elements of array `values` by subscripting the pointer to the array.

h) Refer to element 5 of array `values` using array subscript notation, pointer/offset notation with the array name as the pointer, pointer subscript notation, and pointer/offset notation.

i) What address is referenced by `vptr + 3`? What value is stored at that location?

j) Assuming `vptr` points to `values[4]`, what address is referenced by `vptr -= 4`. What value is stored at that location?

7.10   For each of the following, write a single statement that performs the indicated task. Assume that long integer variables `value1` and `value2` have been declared, and that `value1` has been initialized to `200000`.

    a)   Declare the variable `lptr` to be a pointer to an object of type `long`.

    b)   Assign the address of variable `value1` to pointer variable `lptr`.

    c)   Print the value of the object pointed to by `lptr`.

    d)   Assign the value of the object pointed to by `lptr` to variable `value2`.

    e)   Print the value of `value2`.

    f)   Print the address of `value1`.

    g)   Print the address stored in `lptr`. Is the value printed the same as the address of `value1`?

7.11   Do each of the following.

    a)   Write the function header for function `zero` which takes a long integer array parameter `bigintegers` and does not return a value.

    b)   Write the function prototype for the function in part **(a)**.

    c)   Write the function header for function `add1andsum` which takes an integer array parameter `onetoosmall` and returns an integer.

    d)   Write the function prototype for the function described in part **(c)**.

Note: Exercises 7.12 through 7.15 are reasonably challenging. Once you have done these problems, you ought to be able to implement most popular card games easily.

7.12   Modify the program in Fig. 7.16 so that the card dealing function deals a five card poker hand. Then write the following additional functions:

    a)   Determine if the hand contains a pair.

    b)   Determine if the hand contains two pairs.

    c)   Determine if the hand contains three of a kind (e.g., three jacks).

    d)   Determine if the hand contains four of a kind (e.g., four aces).

    e)   Determine if the hand contains a flush (i.e., all five cards of the same suit).

    f)   Determine if the hand contains a straight (i.e., five cards of consecutive face values).

7.13   Use the functions developed in Exercise 7.12 to write a program that deals two five-card poker hands, evaluates each hand, and determines which is the better hand.

7.14   Modify the program developed in Exercise 7.13 so that it can simulate the dealer. The dealer's five-card hand is dealt "face down" so the player cannot see it. The program should then evaluate the dealer's hand and, based on the quality of the hand, the dealer should draw one, two, or three more cards to replace the corresponding number of unneeded cards in the original hand. The program should then reevaluate the dealer's hand. (*Caution:* This is a difficult problem!)

7.15   Modify the program developed in Exercise 7.14 so that it can handle the dealer's hand automatically, but the player is allowed to decide which cards of the player's hand to replace. The program should then evaluate both hands and determine who wins. Now use this new program to play 20 games against the computer. Who wins more games, you or the computer? Have one of your friends play 20 games against the computer. Who wins more games? Based on the results of these games, make appropriate modifications to refine your poker playing program (this, too, is a difficult problem). Play 20 more games. Does your modified program play a better game?

7.16   In the card shuffling and dealing program of Fig. 7.16, we intentionally used an inefficient shuffling algorithm that introduced the possibility of indefinite postponement. In this problem, you will create a high-performance shuffling algorithm that avoids indefinite postponement.

Modify the program of Fig. 7.16 as follows. Begin by initializing the **deck** array as shown in Fig. 7.20. Modify the **shuffle** function to loop row-by-row and column-by-column through the array touching every element once. Each element should be swapped with a randomly selected element of the array.

	0	1	2	3	4	5	6	7	8	9	10	11	12
0	1	2	3	4	5	6	7	8	9	10	11	12	13
1	14	15	16	17	18	19	20	21	22	23	24	25	26
2	27	28	29	30	31	32	33	34	35	36	37	38	39
3	40	41	42	43	44	45	46	47	48	49	50	51	52

Fig. 7.20 Unshuffled **deck** array.

Print the resulting array to determine if the deck is satisfactorily shuffled (as in Fig. 7.21, for example). You may want your program to call the **shuffle** function several times to ensure a satisfactory shuffle.

	0	1	2	3	4	5	6	7	8	9	10	11	12
0	19	40	27	25	36	46	10	34	35	41	18	2	44
1	13	28	14	16	21	30	8	11	31	17	24	7	1
2	12	33	15	42	43	23	45	3	29	32	4	47	26
3	50	38	52	39	48	51	9	5	37	49	22	6	20

Fig. 7.21 Sample shuffled **deck** array.

Note that although the approach in this problem improves the shuffling algorithm, the dealing algorithm still requires searching the **deck** array for card 1, then card 2, then card 3, and so on. Worse yet, even after the dealing algorithm locates and deals the card, the algorithm continues searching through the remainder of the deck. Modify the program of Fig. 7.16 so that once a card is dealt, no further attempts are made to match that card number, and the program immediately proceeds with dealing the next card. In Chapter 10, "Structures, Unions, and Enumerations," we develop a dealing algorithm that requires only one operation per card.

7.17 (*Simulation: The Tortoise and the Hare*) In this problem you will recreate one of the truly great moments in history, namely the classical race of the tortoise and the hare. You will use random number generation to develop a simulation of this memorable event.

Our contenders begin the race at "square 1" of 70 squares. Each square represents a possible position along the race course. The finish line is at square 70. The first contender to reach or pass square 70 is rewarded with a pail of fresh carrots and lettuce. The course weaves its way up the side of a slippery mountain, so occasionally the contenders lose ground.

There is a clock that ticks once per second. With each tick of the clock, your program should adjust the position of the animals according to the following rules:

Animal	Move type	Percentage of the time	Actual move
Tortoise	Fast plod	50%	3 squares to the right
	Slip	20%	6 squares to the left
	Slow plod	30%	1 square to the right
Hare	Sleep	20%	No move at all
	Big hop	20%	9 squares to the right
	Big slip	10%	12 squares to the left
	Small hop	30%	1 square to the right
	Small slip	20%	2 squares to the left

Use variables to keep track of the positions of the animals (i.e., position numbers are 1-70). Start each animal at position 1 (i.e., the "starting gate"). If an animal slips left before square 1, move the animal back to square 1.

Generate the percentages in the preceding table by producing a random integer, i, in the range $1 \leq i \leq 10$. For the tortoise, perform a "fast plod" when $1 \leq i \leq 5$, a "slip" when $6 \leq i \leq 7$, or a "slow plod" when $8 \leq i \leq 10$. Use a similar technique to move the hare.

Begin the race by printing

```
BANG !!!!!
AND THEY'RE OFF !!!!!
```

Then, for each tick of the clock (i.e., each repetition of a loop), print a 70 position line showing the letter T in the position of the tortoise and the letter H in the position of the hare. Occasionally, the contenders will land on the same square. In this case, the tortoise bites the hare and your program should print OUCH!!! beginning at that position. All print positions other than the T, the H, or the OUCH!!! (in case of a tie) should be blank.

After each line is printed, test if either animal has reached or passed square 70. If so, then print the winner and terminate the simulation. If the tortoise wins, print TORTOISE WINS!!! YAY!!! If the hare wins, print Hare wins. Yuch. If both animals win on the same tick of the clock, you may want to favor the turtle (the "underdog"), or you may want to print It's a tie. If neither animal wins, perform the loop again to simulate the next tick of the clock. When you are ready to run your program, assemble a group of fans to watch the race. You'll be amazed at how involved your audience gets!

Special Section: Building Your Own Computer

In the next several problems, we take a temporary diversion away from the world of high-level language programming. We "peel open" a computer and look at its internal structure. We introduce machine language programming and write several machine language programs. To make this an especially valuable experience, we then build a computer (through the technique of software-based *simulation)* on which you can execute your machine language programs!

7.18   (*Machine Language Programming*) Let us create a computer we will call the Simpletron. As its name implies, it is a simple machine, but, as we will soon see, a powerful one as well. The Simpletron runs programs written in the only language it directly understands, that is, Simpletron Machine Language, or SML for short.

The Simpletron contains an *accumulator*—a "special register" in which information is put before the Simpletron uses that information in calculations or examines it in various ways. All information in the Simpletron is handled in terms of *words*. A word is a signed four-digit decimal number such as $+3364$, -1293, $+0007$, -0001, etc. The Simpletron is equipped with a 100-word memory, and these words are referenced by their location numbers 00, 01, ..., 99.

Before running an SML program, we must *load* or place the program into memory. The first instruction (or statement) of every SML program is always placed in location 00.

Each instruction written in SML occupies one word of the Simpletron's memory (and hence instructions are signed four-digit decimal numbers). We shall assume that the sign of an SML instruction is always plus, but the sign of a data word may be either plus or minus. Each location in the Simpletron's memory may contain either an instruction, a data value used by a program, or an unused (and hence undefined) area of memory. The first two digits of each SML instruction are the *operation code*, which specifies the operation to be performed. SML operation codes are summarized in Fig. 7.22.

Operation code	Meaning
Input/output operations:	
10	Read a word from the terminal into a specific location in memory.
11	Write a word from a specific location in memory to the terminal.
Load/store operations:	
20	Load a word from a specific location in memory into the accumulator.
21	Store a word from the accumulator into a specific location in memory.
Arithmetic operations:	
30	Add a word from a specific location in memory to the word in the accumulator (leave result in accumulator).
31	Subtract a word from a specific location in memory from the word in the accumulator (leave result in accumulator).
32	Divide a word from a specific location in memory into the word in the accumulator (leave result in accumulator).
33	Multiply a word from a specific location in memory by the word in the accumulator (leave result in accumulator).
Transfer of control operations:	
40	Branch to a specific location in memory.
41	Branch to a specific location in memory if the accumulator is negative.
42	Branch to a specific location in memory if the accumulator is zero.
43	Halt, i.e., the program has completed its task

Fig. 7.22 Simpletron Machine Language (SML) operation codes.

The last two digits of an SML instruction are the *operand*, which is the address of the memory location containing the word to which the operation applies. Now let us consider several simple SML programs.

Example 1

Location	Number	Instruction
00	+1007	(Read A)
01	+1008	(Read B)
02	+2007	(Load A)
03	+3008	(Add B)
04	+2109	(Store C)
05	+1109	(Write C)
06	+4300	(Halt)
07	+0000	(Variable A)
08	+0000	(Variable B)
09	+0000	(Result C)

This SML program reads two numbers from the keyboard and computes and prints their sum. The instruction +1007 reads the first number from the keyboard and places it into location 07 (which has been initialized to zero). Then +1008 reads the next number into location 08. The *load* instruction, +2007, puts the first number into the accumulator, and the *add* instruction, +3008, adds the second number to the number in the accumulator. *All SML arithmetic instructions leave their result in the accumulator.* The *store* instruction, +2109, places the result back into memory location 09 from which the *write* instruction, +1109, takes the number and prints it (as a signed four-digit decimal number). The *halt* instruction, +4300, terminates execution.

Example 2

Location	Number	Instruction
00	+1009	(Read A)
01	+1010	(Read B)
02	+2009	(Load A)
03	+3110	(Subtract B)
04	+4107	(Branch negative to 07)
05	+1109	(Write A)
06	+4300	(Halt)
07	+1110	(Write B)
08	+4300	(Halt)
09	+0000	(Variable A)
10	+0000	(Variable B)

This SML program reads two numbers from the keyboard and determines and prints the larger value. Note the use of the instruction +4107 as a conditional transfer of control, much the same as C's **if** statement. Now write SML programs to accomplish each of the following tasks.

  a) Use a sentinel-controlled loop to read 10 positive numbers and compute and print their sum.

  b) Use a counter-controlled loop to read seven numbers, some positive and some negative, and compute and print their average.

  c) Read a series of numbers and determine and print the largest number. The first number read indicates how many numbers should be processed.

7.19   (*A Computer Simulator*) It may at first seem outrageous, but in this problem you are going to build your own computer. No, you will not be soldering components together. Rather, you will use the powerful technique of software-based simulation to create a *software model* of the Simpletron. You will not be disappointed. Your Simpletron simulator will turn the computer you are using into a Simpletron, and you will actually be able to run, test, and debug the SML programs you wrote in Exercise 7.18.

When you run your Simpletron simulator, it should begin by printing:

```
*** Welcome to Simpletron! ***

*** Please enter your program one instruction ***
*** (or data word) at a time. I will type the ***
*** location number and a question mark (?).  ***
*** You then type the word for that location. ***
*** Type the sentinel -99999 to stop entering ***
*** your program. ***
```

Simulate the memory of the Simpletron with a single-subscripted array **memory** that has 100 elements. Now assume that the simulator is running, and let us examine the dialog as we enter the program of Example 2 of Exercise 7.18:

```
00 ? +1009
01 ? +1010
02 ? +2009
03 ? +3110
04 ? +4107
05 ? +1109
06 ? +4300
07 ? +1110
08 ? +4300
09 ? +0000
10 ? +0000
11 ? -99999

*** Program loading completed ***
*** Program execution begins  ***
```

The SML program has now been placed (or loaded) into the array **memory**. Now the Simpletron executes your SML program. Execution begins with the instruction in location 00 and, like C, continues sequentially, unless directed to some other part of the program by a transfer of control.

Use the variable **accumulator** to represent the accumulator register. Use the variable **instructioncounter** to keep track of the location in memory that contains the instruction being performed. Use the variable **operationcode** to indicate the operation currently being performed, i.e., the left two digits of the instruction word. Use the variable `operand` to indicate the memory location on which the current instruction operates. Thus, `operand` is the rightmost two digits of the instruction currently being performed. Do not execute instructions directly from `memory`. Rather, transfer the next instruction to be performed from `memory` to a variable called `instructionregister`. Then "pick off" the left two digits and place them in `operationcode`, and "pick off" the right two digits and place them in `operand`.

When Simpletron begins execution, the special registers are initialized as follows:

```
accumulator           +0000
instructioncounter      00
instructionregister   +0000
operationcode           00
operand                 00
```

Now let us "walk through" the execution of the first SML instruction, `+1009` in memory location `00`. This is called an *instruction execution cycle*.

The `instructioncounter` tells us the location of the next instruction to be performed. We *fetch* the contents of that location from `memory` by using the C statement

```
instructionregister = memory[instructioncounter];
```

The operation code and the operand are extracted from the instruction register by the statements

```
operationcode = instructionregister / 100;
operand = instructionregister % 100;
```

Now the Simpletron must determine that the operation code is actually a *read* (versus a *write*, a *load*, etc.). A `switch` differentiates among the twelve operations of SML.

In the `switch` structure, the behavior of various SML instructions is simulated as follows (we leave the others to the reader):

read: `scanf("%d", &memory[operand]);`
load: `accumulator = memory[operand];`
add: `accumulator += memory[operand];`
Various branch instructions: We'll discuss these shortly.
halt: This instruction prints the message
          `*** Simpletron execution terminated ***`

and then prints the name and contents of each register as well as the complete contents of memory. Such a printout is often called a *computer dump* (and, no, a computer dump is not a place where old computers go). To help you program your dump function, a sample dump format is shown in Fig. 7.23. Note that a dump after executing a Simpletron program would show the actual values of instructions and data values at the moment execution terminated.

Let us proceed with the execution of our program's first instruction, namely the `+1009` in location `00`. As we have indicated, the `switch` statement simulates this by performing the C statement

```
scanf("%d", &memory[operand]);
```

A question mark (?) should be displayed on the screen before the `scanf` is executed to prompt the user for input. The Simpletron waits for the user to type a value and then press the *Return* key. The value is then read into location `09`.

At this point, simulation of the first instruction is completed. All that remains is to prepare the Simpletron to execute the next instruction. Since the instruction just performed was not a transfer of control, we need merely increment the instruction counter register as follows:

```
REGISTERS:
accumulator              +0000
instructioncounter          00
instructionregister      +0000
operationcode               00
operand                     00

MEMORY:
        0     1     2     3     4     5     6     7     8     9
  0 +0000 +0000 +0000 +0000 +0000 +0000 +0000 +0000 +0000 +0000
 10 +0000 +0000 +0000 +0000 +0000 +0000 +0000 +0000 +0000 +0000
 20 +0000 +0000 +0000 +0000 +0000 +0000 +0000 +0000 +0000 +0000
 30 +0000 +0000 +0000 +0000 +0000 +0000 +0000 +0000 +0000 +0000
 40 +0000 +0000 +0000 +0000 +0000 +0000 +0000 +0000 +0000 +0000
 50 +0000 +0000 +0000 +0000 +0000 +0000 +0000 +0000 +0000 +0000
 60 +0000 +0000 +0000 +0000 +0000 +0000 +0000 +0000 +0000 +0000
 70 +0000 +0000 +0000 +0000 +0000 +0000 +0000 +0000 +0000 +0000
 80 +0000 +0000 +0000 +0000 +0000 +0000 +0000 +0000 +0000 +0000
 90 +0000 +0000 +0000 +0000 +0000 +0000 +0000 +0000 +0000 +0000
```

Fig. 7.23 A sample dump.

```
++instructioncounter;
```

This completes the simulated execution of the first instruction. The entire process, i.e., the instruction execution cycle, begins anew with the fetch of the next instruction to be executed.

Now let us consider how the branching instructions—the transfers of control—are simulated. All we need to do is adjust the value in the instruction counter appropriately. Therefore, the unconditional branch instruction (40) is simulated within the **switch** as

```
instructioncounter = operand;
```

The conditional "branch if accumulator is zero" instruction is simulated as

```
if (accumulator == 0)
    instructioncounter = operand;
```

At this point you should implement your Simpletron simulator and run each of the SML programs you wrote in Exercise 7.18. You may embellish SML with additional features and provide for these in your simulator.

Your simulator should check for various types of errors. During the program loading phase, for example, each number the user types into the Simpletron's **memory** must be in the range -9999 to +9999. Your simulator should use a **while** loop to test that each number entered is in this range, and, if not, keep prompting the user to reenter the number until the user enters a correct number.

During the execution phase, your simulator should check for various serious errors, such as attempts to divide by zero, attempts to execute invalid operation codes, accumulator overflows (i.e., arithmetic operations resulting in values larger than +9999 or smaller than -9999), and the like. Such serious errors are called *fatal errors*. When a fatal error is detected, your simulator should print an error message such as:

```
*** Attempt to divide by zero ***
*** Simpletron execution abnormally terminated ***
```

and should print a full computer dump in the format we have discussed previously.

8

Characters and Strings

Objectives

- To be able to use the functions of the character handling library (`ctype`).
- To be able to use the string and character input/output functions of the standard input/output library (`stdio`).
- To be able to use the string conversion functions of the general utilities library (`stdlib`).
- To be able to use the string processing functions of the string handling library (`string`).

The chief defect of Henry King
Was chewing little bits of string.

Hilaire Belloc

Suit the action to the word, the word to the action.

William Shakespeare

Vigorous writing is concise. A sentence should contain no unnecessary words, a paragraph no unnecessary sentences.

William Strunk, Jr.

In a concatenation accordingly.

Oliver Goldsmith

Outline

8.1 Introduction

In this chapter, we introduce the C standard library functions that facilitate string and character processing. The functions enable programs to process characters, strings, lines of text, and blocks of memory.

The chapter discusses the techniques used to develop editors, word processors, page layout software, and computerized typesetting systems. The kinds of text manipulations performed by formatted input/output functions like `printf` and `scanf` can be implemented using the functions discussed in this chapter.

8.2 Fundamentals of Strings and Characters

Characters are the fundamental building blocks of programs. Every program is composed of a sequence of characters that—when grouped together meaningfully—is interpreted by the computer as a series of instructions used to accomplish a task. A program may contain *character constants*. A character constant is an `int` value represented as a character in single quotes. The value of a character constant is the integer value of the character in the machine's character set. For example, `'z'` represents the integer value of z, and `'\n'` represents the integer value of newline.

A string is a series of characters treated as a single unit. A string may include letters, digits, and various *special characters* such as +, -, *, /, $, and others. *String literals* or *string constants* in C are written in quotation marks as follows:

"John Q. Doe"	(a name)
"99999 Main Street"	(a street address)
"Waltham, Massachusetts"	(a city and state)
"235-27-1752"	(a social security number)

A string in C is an array of characters ending in the *null character (' \ 0 ')*. A string is accessed via a pointer to the first character in the string. The value of a string is the address of its first character. Thus in C it is appropriate to say that *a string is a pointer*—in fact a pointer to the string's first character. In this sense, strings are like arrays, because an array is also a pointer to its first element.

A string may be assigned in a declaration to either a character array or a variable of type char *. The declarations

```
char color[] = "blue";
char *colorptr = "blue";
```

each initialize a variable to the string "blue". The first declaration creates a 5-element array color containing the characters 'b', 'l', 'u', 'e', and '\0'. The second declaration creates pointer variable colorptr that points to the string "blue" somewhere in memory. The preceding array declaration could also have been written

```
char color[] = {'b', 'l', 'u', 'e', '\0'};
```

When declaring a character array to store a string, it is important to remember that the array must be large enough to store the string and its terminating NULL character. The preceding declaration determines the size of the array automatically based on the number of initializers in the initializer list.

CPE 8.1
_____

*Not allocating sufficient space in a character array to store the **NULL** character that terminates a string.*

CPE 8.2
_____

*Printing a string that does not contain a terminating **NULL** character. If this is the case, when the string is printed, an error will occur.*

GPP 8.1
_____

When storing a string of characters in a character array, be sure there are enough elements in the array to hold the largest string that will be stored. C allows strings of any length to be stored. If a string is longer than the character array in which it is stored, characters beyond the end of the array overwrite data in the memory following the array.

A string can be assigned to an array using the scanf function. For example, the following statement assigns a string to character array word[20].

```
scanf("%s", word);
```

The string entered by the user is stored in word. Function scanf will read characters until a space, newline, or end-of-file indicator is encountered. Note that the string should be no longer than 19 characters to leave room for the terminating NULL character. For a character array to be printed as a string, the array must contain a terminating NULL character.

CPE 8.3

Processing a single character as a string. A string is a pointer—probably a respectably large integer. However, a character is a small integer (ASCII values range 0-255). On many systems this causes an error because low memory addresses are reserved for special purposes such as operating system interrupt handlers—so, "access violations" occur.

CPE 8.4

Passing a character as an argument to a function when a string is expected.

CPE 8.5

Passing a string as an argument to a function when a character is expected.

8.3 Character Handling Library

The character handling library includes several functions that perform useful tests and manipulations of character data. The functions take a character—represented as an int—as an argument. The data type int is used to represent the argument rather than char because the character handling functions can be used to test and manipulate character constants, and character constants are of type int. Figure 8.1 summarizes the functions of the character handling library.

GPP 8.2

When using functions from the character handling library, include the <ctype.h> header file.

The program of Fig. 8.2 demonstrates function *isdigit*, function *isalpha*, function *isalnum*, and function *isxdigit*. Function isdigit determines whether its argument is a digit (0-9). Function isalpha determines whether its argument is an uppercase letter (A-Z) or a lowercase letter (a-z). Function isalnum determines whether its argument is an uppercase letter, a lowercase letter, or a digit. Function isxdigit (Fig. 8.12) determines whether its argument is a hexadecimal digit (A-F, a-f, 0-9).

The program of Fig. 8.2 uses the conditional operator (? :) with each function to determine whether the string " is a " or the string " is not a " should be printed in the output for each character tested. For example, the expression

```
isdigit('8') ? " is a " : " is not a "
```

indicates that if '8' is a digit, i.e., isdigit returns a true (nonzero) value, the string " is a " is printed, and if '8' is not a digit, i.e., isdigit returns 0, the string " is not a " is printed.

Prototype	Function description
`int isdigit(int c)`	Returns a true value if `c` is a digit, and 0 (false) otherwise.
`int isalpha(int c)`	Returns a true value if `c` is a letter, and 0 otherwise.
`int isalnum(int c)`	Returns a true value if `c` is a digit or a letter, and 0 otherwise.
`int isxdigit(int c)`	Returns a true value if `c` is a hexadecimal digit character, and 0 otherwise. (See Appendix F, "Number Systems," for a detailed explanation of hexadecimal numbers.)
`int islower(int c)`	Returns a true value if `c` is a lowercase letter, and 0 otherwise.
`int isupper(int c)`	Returns a true value if `c` is an uppercase letter, and 0 otherwise.
`int tolower(int c)`	If `c` is an uppercase letter, `tolower` returns `c` as a lowercase letter. Otherwise, `tolower` returns the argument unchanged.
`int toupper(int c)`	If `c` is a lowercase letter, `toupper` returns `c` as an uppercase letter. Otherwise, `toupper` returns the argument unchanged.
`int isspace(int c)`	Returns a true value if `c` is a white-space character—space (`' '`), form feed (`'\f'`), newline (`'\n'`), carriage return (`'\r'`), horizontal tab (`'\t'`), or vertical tab (`'\v'`)—and 0 otherwise
`int iscntrl(int c)`	Returns a true value if `c` is a control character, and 0 otherwise.
`int ispunct(int c)`	Returns a true value if `c` is a printing character other than a space, a digit, or a letter, and 0 otherwise.
`int isprint(int c)`	Returns a true value if `c` is a printing character including space (`' '`), and 0 otherwise.
`int isgraph(int c)`	Returns a true value if `c` is a printing character other than space (`' '`), and 0 otherwise.

Fig. 8.1 Summary of the character handling library functions.

The program of Fig. 8.3 demonstrates function *islower*, function *isupper*, function *tolower*, and function *toupper*. Function islower determines whether its argument is a lowercase letter (a-z). Function isupper determines whether its argument is an uppercase letter (A-Z). Function tolower converts an uppercase letter to a lowercase letter, and returns the lowercase letter. If the argument is not an uppercase letter, tolower returns the argument unchanged. Function toupper converts a lowercase letter to an uppercase letter, and returns the uppercase letter. If the argument is not a lowercase letter, toupper returns the argument unchanged.

```
/* Using functions isdigit, isalpha, isalnum, and isxdigit */

#include <stdio.h>
#include <ctype.h>

main()
{
    printf("%s\n%c%s%s\n%c%s%s\n\n",
            "According to isdigit:",
            '8', isdigit('8') ? " is a " : " is not a ", "digit",
            '#', isdigit('#') ? " is a " : " is not a ", "digit");
    printf("%s\n%c%s%s\n%c%s%s\n%c%s%s\n%c%s%s\n\n",
            "According to isalpha:",
            'A', isalpha('A') ? " is a " : " is not a ", "letter",
            'b', isalpha('b') ? " is a " : " is not a ", "letter",
            '&', isalpha('&') ? " is a " : " is not a ", "letter",
            '4', isalpha('4') ? " is a " : " is not a ", "letter");
    printf("%s\n%c%s%s\n%c%s%s\n%c%s%s\n\n",
            "According to isalnum:",
            'A', isalnum('A') ? " is a " : " is not a ", "digit or a letter",
            '8', isalnum('8') ? " is a " : " is not a ", "digit or a letter",
            '#', isalnum('#') ? " is a " : " is not a ", "digit or a letter");
    printf("%s\n%c%s%s\n%c%s%s\n%c%s%s\n%c%s%s\n%c%s%s\n",
            "According to isxdigit:",
            'F', isxdigit('F') ? " is a " : " is not a ", "hexadecimal digit",
            'J', isxdigit('J') ? " is a " : " is not a ", "hexadecimal digit",
            '7', isxdigit('7') ? " is a " : " is not a ", "hexadecimal digit",
            '$', isxdigit('$') ? " is a " : " is not a ", "hexadecimal digit",
            'f', isxdigit('f') ? " is a " : " is not a ", "hexadecimal digit");
}
```

```
According to isdigit:
8 is a digit
# is not a digit

According to isalpha:
A is a letter
b is a letter
& is not a letter
4 is not a letter

According to isalnum:
A is a digit or a letter
8 is a digit or a letter
# is not a digit or a letter

According to isxdigit:
F is a hexadecimal digit
J is not a hexadecimal digit
7 is a hexadecimal digit
$ is not a hexadecimal digit
f is a hexadecimal digit
```

Fig. 8.2 Using isdigit, isalpha, isalnum, and isxdigit.

```
/* Using functions islower, isupper, tolower, toupper */
#include <stdio.h>
#include <ctype.h>

main()
{
   printf("%s\n%c%s%s\n%c%s%s\n%c%s%s\n%c%s%s\n\n",
          "According to islower:",
          'p', islower('p') ? " is a " : " is not a ",
          "lowercase letter",
          'P', islower('P') ? " is a " : " is not a ",
          "lowercase letter",
          '5', islower('5') ? " is a " : " is not a ",
          "lowercase letter",
          '!', islower('!') ? " is a " : " is not a ",
          "lowercase letter");
   printf("%s\n%c%s%s\n%c%s%s\n%c%s%s\n%c%s%s\n\n",
          "According to isupper:",
          'D', isupper('D') ? " is a " : " is not a ",
          "uppercase letter",
          'd', isupper('d') ? " is a " : " is not a ",
          "uppercase letter",
          '8', isupper('8') ? " is a " : " is not a ",
          "uppercase letter",
          '$', isupper('$') ? " is a " : " is not a ",
          "uppercase letter");
   printf("%c%s%c\n%c%s%c\n%c%s%c\n%c%s%c\n",
          'u', " converted to uppercase is ", toupper('u'),
          '7', " converted to uppercase is ", toupper('7'),
          '$', " converted to uppercase is ", toupper('$'),
          'L', " converted to lowercase is ", tolower('L'));
}
```

```
According to islower:
p is a lowercase letter
P is not a lowercase letter
5 is not a lowercase letter
! is not a lowercase letter

According to isupper:
D is a uppercase letter
d is not a uppercase letter
8 is not a uppercase letter
$ is not a uppercase letter

u converted to uppercase is U
7 converted to uppercase is 7
$ converted to uppercase is $
L converted to lowercase is l
```

Fig. 8.3 Using `islower`, `isupper`, `tolower`, and `toupper`.

The program of Fig. 8.4 demonstrates function *isspace*, function *iscntrl*, function *ispunct*, function *isprint*, and function *isgraph*. Function iss-pace determines whether its argument is one of the following white-space characters:

space (' '), form feed ('\f'), newline ('\n'), carriage return ('\r'), horizontal tab ('\t'), or vertical tab ('\v'). Function iscntrl determines whether its argument is one of the following control characters: horizontal tab ('\t'), vertical tab ('\v'), form feed ('\f'), alert ('\a'), backspace ('\b'), carriage return ('\r'), or newline ('\n'). Function ispunct determines whether its argument is a punctuation character or a special printing character other than a space, a digit, or a letter such as $, #, (,), [,], {, }, ;, :, %, etc. Function isprint determines whether its argument is a character that can be displayed on the screen (including the space character). Function isgraph tests for the same characters as isprint, however the space character is not included.

```
/* Using functions isspace, iscntrl, ispunct, isprint, isgraph */
#include <stdio.h>
#include <ctype.h>

main()
{
    printf("%s\n%s%s%s\n%s%s%s\n%c%s%s\n\n",
           "According to isspace:",
           "Newline", isspace('\n') ? " is a " : " is not a ",
           "whitespace character",
           "Horizontal tab", isspace('\t') ? " is a " : " is not a ",
           "whitespace character",
           '%', isspace('%') ? " is a " : " is not a ",
           "whitespace character");
    printf("%s\n%s%s%s\n%c%s%s\n\n",
           "According to iscntrl:",
           "Newline", iscntrl('\n') ? " is a " : " is not a ",
           "control character",
           '$', iscntrl('$') ? " is a " : " is not a ",
           "control character");
    printf("%s\n%c%s%s\n%c%s%s\n%c%s%s\n\n",
           "According to ispunct:",
           ';', ispunct(';') ? " is a " : " is not a ",
           "punctuation character",
           'Y', ispunct('Y') ? " is a " : " is not a ",
           "punctuation character",
           '#', ispunct('#') ? " is a " : " is not a ",
           "punctuation character");
    printf("%s\n%c%s%s\n%s%s%s\n\n",
           "According to isprint:",
           '$', isprint('$') ? " is a " : " is not a ",
           "printing character",
           "Alert", isprint('\a') ? " is a " : " is not a ",
           "printing character");
    printf("%s\n%c%s%s\n%s%s%s\n",
           "According to isgraph:",
           'Q', isgraph('Q') ? " is a " : " is not a ",
           "printing character other than a space",
           "Space", isgraph(' ') ? " is a " : " is not a ",
           "printing character other than a space");
}
```

Fig. 8.4 Using isspace, iscntrl, ispunct, isprint, and isgraph (part 1 of 2).

```
According to isspace:
Newline is a whitespace character
Horizontal tab is a whitespace character
% is not a whitespace character

According to iscntrl:
Newline is a control character
$ is not a control character

According to ispunct:
; is a punctuation character
Y is not a punctuation character
# is a punctuation character

According to isprint:
$ is a printing character
Alert is not a printing character

According to isgraph:
Q is a printing character other than a space
Space is not a printing character other than a space
```

Fig. 8.4 Using `isspace`, `iscntrl`, `ispunct`, `isprint`, and `isgraph` (part 2 of 2).

8.4 String Conversion Functions

This section presents the string conversion functions from the general utilities library
(`stdlib`). The functions presented here convert strings of digits to integer and floating point values. Figure 8.5 summarizes the string conversion functions of the general
utilities library. Note the use of the keyword `const` in the function prototypes;
`const` declares that an argument value will not be modified. Compilers vary in their
ability to enforce the `const` modifier.

> *GPP 8.3*
> _____
>
> *When using functions from the general utilities library, include the*
> *`<stdlib.h>` header file.*

     Function `atof` (Fig. 8.6) converts its first argument—a string that represents a
floating point number—to a `double` value. The function returns the `double` value.
If the converted value cannot be represented—for example, if the first character of the
string is not a digit—the behavior of function `atof` is undefined.

     Function `atoi` (Fig. 8.7) converts its argument—a string of digits that repre-
sents an integer—to an `int` value. The function returns the `int` value. If the converted value cannot be represented, the behavior of function `atoi` is undefined.

Prototype	Function Description
`double atof(const char *nptr)`	Converts the string pointed to by `nptr` to `double`.
`int atoi(const char *nptr)`	Converts the string pointed to by `nptr` to `int`.
`long int atol(const char *nptr)`	Converts the string pointed to by `nptr` to `long int`.
`double strtod(const char *nptr, char **endptr)`	Converts the string pointed to by `nptr` to `double`.
`long int strtol(const char *nptr, char **endptr, int base)`	Converts the string pointed to by `nptr` to `long int`.
`unsigned long int strtoul(const char *nptr, char **endptr, int base)`	Converts the string pointed to by `nptr` to `unsigned long int`.

Fig. 8.5 Summary of the string conversion functions of the general utilities library.

```
/* Using atof */
#include <stdio.h>
#include <stdlib.h>

main()
{
    double d;

    d = atof("99.0");
    printf("%s%.3f\n%s%.3f\n",
           "The string \"99.0\" converted to double is ", d,
           "The converted value divided by 2 is ", d / 2);
}
```

```
The string "99.0" converted to double is 99.000
The converted value divided by 2 is 49.500
```

Fig. 8.6 Using `atof`.

Function `atol` (Fig. 8.8) converts its argument—a string of digits that represent a long integer—to a `long` value. The function returns the `long` value. If the converted value cannot be represented, the behavior of function `atol` is undefined. Note that if `int` and `long` are both stored in 4 bytes, function `atoi` and function `atol` work identically.

Function *strtod* converts a sequence of characters representing a floating point value to `double`. The function receives two arguments—a string (`char *`) and a pointer to a string. The string contains the character sequence to be converted to `double`. The pointer is assigned the location of the first character after the converted portion of the string. The statement

```
/* Using atoi */
#include <stdio.h>
#include <stdlib.h>

main()
{
   int i;

   i = atoi("2593");
   printf("%s%d\n%s%d\n",
           "The string \"2593\" converted to int is ", i,
           "The converted value minus 593 is ", i - 593);
}
```

```
The string "2593" converted to int is 2593
The converted value minus 593 is 2000
```

Fig. 8.7 Using `atoi`.

```
/* Using atol */
#include <stdio.h>
#include <stdlib.h>

main()
{
   long l;

   l = atol("1000000");
   printf("%s%ld\n%s%ld\n",
           "The string \"1000000\" converted to long int is ", l,
           "The converted value divided by 2 is ", l / 2);
}
```

```
The string "1000000" converted to long int is 1000000
The converted value divided by 2 is 500000
```

Fig. 8.8 Using `atol`.

```
d = strtod(string, &stringptr);
```

from the program of Fig. 8.9 indicates that d is assigned the double value converted from string, and &stringptr is assigned the location of the first character after the converted value (51.2) in string.

Function *strtol* converts to long a sequence of characters representing an integer. The function receives three arguments—a string (char *), a pointer to a string, and an integer. The string contains the character sequence to be converted. The pointer is assigned the location of the first character after the converted portion of the string. The integer specifies the *base* of the value being converted. The statement

```
x = strtol(string, &remainderptr, 0);
```

in the program of Fig. 8.10 indicates that x is assigned the long value converted from string. The second argument, &remainderptr, is assigned the remainder of string after the conversion. Using NULL for the second argument causes the remainder of the string to be ignored. The third argument, 0, indicates that the value to be converted can be in octal (base 8), decimal (base 10), or hexadecimal (base 16) format. The base can be specified as 0 or any value between 2 and 36. See Appendix F, "Number Systems," for a detailed explanation of the octal, decimal, and hexadecimal number systems.

Function *strtoul* converts to unsigned long a sequence of characters representing an unsigned long integer. The function works identically to function strtol. The statement

```
x = strtoul(string, &remainderptr, 0);
```

```
/* Using strtod */
#include <stdio.h>
#include <stdlib.h>

main()
{
    double d;
    char *string = "51.2% are admitted";
    char *stringptr;

    stringptr = string;
    d = strtod(string, &stringptr);
    printf("The string \"%s\" is converted to the\n", string);
    printf("double value %.2f and the string \"%s\"\n",
            d, stringptr);
}
```

```
The string "51.2% are admitted" is converted to the
double value 51.20 and the string "% are admitted"
```

Fig. 8.9 Using strtod.

in the program of Fig. 8.11 indicates that x is assigned the `unsigned long` value converted from `string`. The second argument, `&remainderptr`, is assigned the remainder of `string` after the conversion. The third argument, 0, indicates that the value to be converted can be in octal, decimal, or hexadecimal format.

```
/* Using strtol */
#include <stdio.h>
#include <stdlib.h>

main()
{
    long x;
    char *string = "-1234567abc", *remainderptr;

    x = strtol(string, &remainderptr, 0);
    printf("%s\"%s\"\n%s%ld\n%s\"%s\"\n%s%ld\n",
           "The original string is ", string,
           "The converted value is ", x,
           "The remainder of the original string is ", remainderptr,
           "The converted value plus 567 is ", x + 567);
}
```

```
The original string is "-1234567abc"
The converted value is -1234567
The remainder of the original string is "abc"
The converted value plus 567 is -1234000
```

Fig. 8.10 Using `strtol`.

```
/* Using strtoul */
#include <stdio.h>
#include <stdlib.h>

main()
{
    unsigned long x;
    char *string = "1234567abc", *remainderptr;

    x = strtoul(string, &remainderptr, 0);
    printf("%s\"%s\"\n%s%lu\n%s\"%s\"\n%s%lu\n",
           "The original string is ", string,
           "The converted value is ", x,
           "The remainder of the original string is ", remainderptr,
           "The converted value minus 567 is ", x - 567);
}
```

```
The original string is "1234567abc"
The converted value is 1234567
The remainder of the original string is "abc"
The converted value minus 567 is 1234000
```

Fig. 8.11 Using `strtoul`.

8.5 Standard Input/Output Library Functions

This section presents several functions from the standard input/output library (stdio) specifically for manipulating character and string data. Figure 8.12 summarizes the character and string input/output functions of the standard input/output library.

GPP 8.4

When using functions from the standard input/output library, include the <stdio.h> *header file.*

The program of Fig. 8.13 uses functions *gets* and *putchar* to read a line of text from the standard input (keyboard), and output the characters of the line in reverse order. Function gets reads characters from the standard input into its argument—an array of type char—until a newline character or the end-of-file indicator is encountered. A NULL character ('\0') is appended to the array when reading terminates. Function putchar prints its character argument. The program calls recursive function reverse to print the line of text backwards. Function reverse prints each character with putchar.

Function prototype	Function description
int getchar(void)	Input the next character from the standard input and return it as an integer.
char *gets(char *s)	Input characters from the standard input into the array pointed to by s until a newline or end-of-file character is encountered. A terminating NULL character is appended to the array.
int putchar(int c)	Print the character stored in c.
int puts(const char *s)	Print the string pointed to by s followed by a newline character.
int sprintf(char *s, const char *format, ...)	Equivalent to printf except the output is stored in the array pointed to by s.
int sscanf(char *s, const char *format, ...)	Equivalent to scanf except the input is read from the array pointed to by s.

Fig. 8.12 The standard input/output library character and string functions.

```
/* Using gets and putchar */
#include <stdio.h>

main()
{
    char sentence[80];
    void reverse(char *);

    printf("Enter a line of text:\n");
    gets(sentence);
    printf("\nThe line printed backwards is:\n");
    reverse(sentence);
}

void reverse(char *s)
{
    int i = 0;

    if (s[i] == '\0')
        return;
    else {
        reverse(&s[i + 1]);
        putchar(s[i]);
    }
}
```

```
Enter a line of text:
Characters and Strings

The line printed backwards is:
sgnirtS dna sretcarahC
```

```
Enter a line of text:
able was I ere I saw elba

The line printed backwards is:
able was I ere I saw elba
```

Fig. 8.13 Using gets and putchar.

The program of Fig. 8.14 uses functions getchar and puts to read characters from the standard input into character array sentence, and print the array of characters as a string. Function getchar reads a single character from the standard input and returns the character as an integer. Function puts takes a string (char *) as an argument and prints the string followed by a newline character.

The program stops inputting characters when getchar reads a newline character. The newline character is entered by the user to end the line of text. A NULL character is appended to array sentence so that the array may be treated as a string. Function puts prints the string contained in sentence.

```
/* Using getchar and puts */
#include <stdio.h>

main()
{
    char c, sentence[80];
    int i = 0;

    printf("Enter a line of text:\n");

    while ((c = getchar()) != '\n')
        sentence[i++] = c;

    sentence[i] = '\0';
    printf("\nThe line entered was:\n");
    puts(sentence);
}
```

```
Enter a line of text:
This is a test.

The line entered was:
This is a test.
```

Fig. 8.14 Using getchar and puts.

The program of Fig. 8.15 uses function *sprintf* to print formatted data into array s—an array of characters. The function uses the same conversion specifications as printf (see Chapter 9 for a detailed discussion of all print formatting features). The program inputs an int value and a float value to be formatted and printed to array s. Note that array s is the first argument of sprintf.

The program of Fig. 8.16 uses function *sscanf* to read formatted data from character array s. The function uses the same conversion specifications as scanf. The program reads an int and a float from array s, and stores the values in variable x and variable y, respectively. The values of variable x and variable y are printed. Note that array s is the first argument of sscanf.

```
/* Using sprintf */
#include <stdio.h>

main()
{
    char s[80];
    int x;
    float y;

    printf("Enter an integer value and a floating point value:\n");
    scanf("%d%f", &x, &y);
    sprintf(s, "Integer:%6d\nFloat:%8.2f", x, y);
    printf("%s\n%s\n",
           "The formatted output stored in array s is:", s);
}
```

```
Enter an integer value and a floating point value:
298 87.375
The formatted output stored in array s is:
Integer:   298
Float:    87.38
```

Fig. 8.15 Using sprintf.

```
/* Using sscanf */
#include <stdio.h>

main()
{
    char s[] = "31298 87.375";
    int x;
    float y;

    sscanf(s, "%d%f", &x, &y);
    printf("%s\n%s%6d\n%s%8.3f\n",
           "The values stored in character array s are:",
           "Integer:", x, "Float:", y);
}
```

```
The values stored in character array s are:
Integer:   298
Float:  87.375
```

Fig. 8.16 Using sscanf.

8.6 String Manipulation Functions of the String Handling Library

The string handling library provides many useful functions for manipulating string data, comparing strings, searching strings for characters and other strings, tokenizing strings (separating strings into logical pieces), and determining the length of strings. This section presents the string manipulation functions of the string handling library. The functions are summarized in Fig. 8.17.

GPP 8.5

When using functions from the string handling library, include the `<string.h>` *header file.*

Function `strcpy` copies its second argument—a string—into its first argument—a character array that must be large enough to store the string and its terminating NULL character which is also copied. Function `strncpy` is equivalent to `strcpy` except that `strncpy` specifies the number of characters to be copied from the string into the array. Note that function `strncpy` does not necessarily copy the terminating NULL character of its second argument. The terminating NULL character will only be copied if the number of characters to be copied is one more than the length of the string. For example, the terminating NULL character of `"test"` is copied only if the third argument to `strncpy` is 5 (4 characters in `"test"` plus 1 terminating NULL character). The program in Fig. 8.18 uses `strcpy` to copy the entire string in array x into array y, and uses `strncpy` to copy the first 14 characters of array x into array z. A NULL character (`'\0'`) is appended to array z because the call to `strncpy` in the program does not copy the terminating NULL character.

Prototype	Function description
`char *strcpy(char *s1, const char *s2)`	Copies the string s2 into the array s1.
`char *strncpy(char *s1, const char *s2, size_t n)`	Copies n characters of the string s2 into the array s1.
`char *strcat(char *s1, const char *s2)`	Appends the string s2 to the array s1. The first character of s2 overwrites the terminating NULL character of s1.
`char *strncat(char *s1, const char *s2, size_t n)`	Appends n characters of the string s2 to the array s1. The first character of s2 overwrites the terminating NULL character of s1.

Fig. 8.17 The string manipulation functions of the string handling library.

```
/* Using strcpy and strncpy */
#include <stdio.h>
#include <string.h>

main()
{
   char x[] = "Happy Birthday to You";
   char y[25], z[15];

   printf("%s%s\n%s%s\n",
          "The string in array x is: ", x,
          "The string in array y is: ", strcpy(y, x));
   strncpy(z, x, 14);
   z[14] = '\0';
   printf("The string in array z is: %s\n", z);
}
```

```
The string in array x is: Happy Birthday to You
The string in array y is: Happy Birthday to You
The string in array z is: Happy Birthday
```

Fig. 8.18 Using `strcpy` and `strncpy`.

Function *strcat* appends its second argument—a string—to its first argument—a character array containing a string. The first character of the second argument replaces the NULL (`'\0'`) that terminates the string in the first argument. The programmer must ensure that the array used to store the first string is large enough to store the first string, the second string, and the terminating NULL character (copied from the second string). Function *strncat* appends a specified number of characters from the second string to the first string. A terminating NULL character is automatically appended to the result. The program of Fig. 8.19 demonstrates function `strcat` and function `strncat`.

String literals may be concatenated at compile-time. For example, the string literals in the following `printf` statement would be concatenated into one string

```
printf("These words are all part"
       " of the same string.");
```

The preceding statement is equivalent to

```
printf("These words are all part of the same string.");
```

This is particularly useful for splitting long strings into multiple lines to make a program more readable.

```
/* Using strcat and strncat */
#include <stdio.h>
#include <string.h>

main()
{
   char s1[20] = "Happy ";
   char s2[] = "New Year ";
   char s3[40] = "";

   printf("s1 = %s\ns2 = %s\n", s1, s2);
   printf("strcat(s1, s2) = %s\n", strcat(s1, s2));
   printf("strncat(s3, s1, 6) = %s\n", strncat(s3, s1, 6));
   printf("strcat(s3, s1) = %s\n", strcat(s3, s1));
}
```

```
s1 = Happy
s2 = New Year
strcat(s1, s2) = Happy New Year
strncat(s3, s1, 6) = Happy
strcat(s3, s1) = Happy Happy New Year
```

Fig. 8.19 Using strcat and strncat.

8.7 Comparison Functions of the String Handling Library

This section presents the comparison functions, strcmp and strncmp, of the string handling library. The functions are summarized in Fig. 8.20.

Prototype	Function Description
int strcmp(const char *s1, const char *s2)	
	Compares the string s1 to the string s2. The function returns 0, less than 0, or greater than 0 if s1 is equal to, less than, or greater than s2, respectively.
int strncmp(const char *s1, const char *s2, size_t n)	
	Compares up to n characters of the string s1 to the string s2. The function returns 0, less than 0, or greater than 0 if s1 is equal to, less than, or greater than s2, respectively.

Fig. 8.20 The string comparison functions of the string handling library.

The program of Fig. 8.21 compares three strings using functions *strcmp* and *strncmp*. Function strcmp compares its first string argument to its second string argument character-by-character. The function returns 0 if the strings are equal, a negative value if the the first string is less than the second string, and a positive value if the first string is greater than the second string. Function strncmp is equivalent to strcmp except that strncmp compares up to a specified number of characters. Function strncmp does not compare characters following a NULL character in a string. The program prints the integer value returned by each function call.

```c
/* Using strcmp and strncmp */
#include <stdio.h>
#include <string.h>

main()
{
    char *s1 = "Happy New Year";
    char *s2 = "Happy New Year";
    char *s3 = "Happy Holidays";

    printf("%s%s\n%s%s\n%s%s\n\n%s%2d\n%s%2d\n%s%2d\n\n",
           "s1 = ", s1, "s2 = ", s2, "s3 = ", s3,
           "strcmp(s1, s2) = ", strcmp(s1, s2),
           "strcmp(s1, s3) = ", strcmp(s1, s3),
           "strcmp(s3, s1) = ", strcmp(s3, s1));

    printf("%s%2d\n%s%2d\n%s%2d\n",
           "strncmp(s1, s3, 6) = ", strncmp(s1, s3, 6),
           "strncmp(s1, s3, 7) = ", strncmp(s1, s3, 7),
           "strncmp(s3, s1, 7) = ", strncmp(s3, s1, 7));
}
```

```
s1 = Happy New Year
s2 = Happy New Year
s3 = Happy Holidays

strcmp(s1, s2) =  0
strcmp(s1, s3) = -1
strcmp(s3, s1) =  1

strncmp(s1, s3, 6) =  0
strncmp(s1, s3, 7) = -1
strncmp(s3, s1, 7) =  1
```

Fig. 8.21 Using strcmp and strncmp.

To understand just what it means for one string to be "greater than" or "less than" another string, consider the process of alphabetizing a series of last names. The reader would, no doubt, place "Jones" before "Smith" because the first letter of "Jones" comes before the first letter of "Smith" in the alphabet. But the alphabet is more than just a list of 26 letters—it is an ordered list of characters. Each letter occurs in a specific position within the list. "Z" is more than merely a letter of the alphabet; "Z" is specifically the twenty-sixth letter of the alphabet.

How does the computer know that one particular letter comes before another? All characters are represented inside the computer as numeric codes; when the computer compares two strings, it actually compares the numeric codes of the characters in the strings.

The internal numeric codes used to represent characters may be different on different computers. In an effort at standardizing character representations, most computer manufacturers have designed their machines to utilize one of two popular coding schemes, namely, *ASCII* or *EBCDIC*. ASCII stands for "American Standard Code for Information Interchange," and EBCDIC stands for "Extended Binary Coded Decimal Interchange Code." There are other coding schemes, but these two are the most popular.

ASCII and EBCDIC are called *character codes* or *character sets*. String and character manipulations actually involve the manipulation of the appropriate numeric codes and not the characters themselves. This explains the interchangeability of characters and small integers in C. Since it is meaningful to say that one numeric code is greater than, less than, or equal to another numeric code, it becomes possible to relate various characters or strings to one another by referring to the character codes. Appendix E contains a list of ASCII character codes.

8.8 Search Functions of the String Handling Library

This section presents the functions of the string handling library used to search strings for characters and other strings. The functions are summarized in Fig. 8.22. The type `size_t` in the prototypes for function `strcspn` and function `strspn` is a synonym for either `unsigned long` or `unsigned int` (varies between systems).

Function `strchr` searches for the first occurrence of a character in a string. If the character is found, `strchr` returns a pointer to the character in the string, otherwise `strchr` returns NULL. The program of Fig. 8.23 uses `strchr` to search for the first occurrences of 'a' and 'z' in the string "This is a test".

Prototype	Function description
`char *strchr(const char *s, int c)`	Locates the first occurrence of character **c** in string **s**. If **c** is found, a pointer to **c** in **s** is returned. Otherwise a **NULL** pointer is returned.
`size_t strcspn(const char *s1, const char *s2)`	Determines and returns the length of the initial segment of string **s1** consisting of characters not contained in string **s2**.
`char *strpbrk(const char *s1, const char *s2)`	Locates the first occurrence in string **s1** of any character in string **s2**. If a character from string **s2** is found, a pointer to the character in string **s1** is returned. Otherwise a **NULL** pointer is returned.
`char *strrchr(const char *s, int c)`	Locates the last occurrence of **c** in string **s**. If **c** is found, a pointer to **c** in string **s** is returned. Otherwise a **NULL** pointer is returned.
`size_t strspn(const char *s1, const char *s2)`	Determines and returns the length of the initial segment of string **s1** consisting only of characters contained in string **s2**.
`char *strstr(const char *s1, const char *s2)`	Locates the first occurrence in string **s1** of string **s2**. If the string is found, a pointer to the string in **s1** is returned. Otherwise a **NULL** pointer is returned.
`char *strtok(char *s1, const char *s2)`	A sequence of calls to **strtok** breaks string **s1** into "tokens"—logical pieces such as words in a line of text—separated by characters contained in string **s2**. The first call contains **s1** as the first argument, and subsequent calls to continue tokenizing the same string contain **NULL** as the first argument. A pointer to the current token is returned by each call. If there are no more tokens when the function is called, **NULL** is returned.

Fig. 8.22 The string manipulation functions of the string handling library.

```
/* Using strchr */
#include <stdio.h>
#include <string.h>

main()
{
    char *string = "This is a test";
    char character1 = 'a', character2 = 'z', *cptr;

    if (strchr(string, character1) != NULL)
        printf("\'%c\' was found in \"%s\".\n",
            character1, string);
    else
        printf("\'%c\' was not found in \"%s\".\n",
            character1, string);

    if (strchr(string, character2) != NULL)
        printf("\'%c\' was found in \"%s\".\n",
            character2, string);
    else
        printf("\'%c\' was not found in \"%s\".\n",
            character2, string);
}
```

```
'a' was found in "This is a test".
'z' was not found in "This is a test".
```

Fig. 8.23 Using `strchr`.

Function `strcspn` (Fig. 8.24) determines the length of the initial part of the string in its first argument that does not contain any characters from the string in its second argument. The function returns the length of the segment.

Function `strpbrk` searches for the first occurrence in its first string argument of any character in its second string argument. If a character from the second argument is found, `strpbrk` returns a pointer to the character in the first argument, otherwise `strpbrk` returns NULL. The program of Fig. 8.25 locates the first occurrence in `string1` of any character from `string2`.

Function `strrchr` searches for the last occurrence of a character in a string. If the character is found, `strrchr` returns a pointer to the character in the string, otherwise `strrchr` returns NULL. The program of Fig. 8.26 locates the last occurrence of `'z'` in the string `"A zoo has many animals including zebras"`.

```
/* Using strcspn */
#include <stdio.h>
#include <string.h>

main()
{
    char *string1 = "The value is 3.14159";
    char *string2 = "1234567890";

    printf("%s%s\n%s%s\n\n%s\n%s%lu",
            "string1 = ", string1, "string2 = ", string2,
            "The length of the initial segment of string1",
            "containing no characters from string2 = ",
            strcspn(string1, string2));
}
```

```
string1 = The value is 3.14159
string2 = 1234567890

The length of the initial segment of string1
containing no characters from string2 = 13
```

Fig. 8.24 Using strcspn.

```
/* Using strpbrk */
#include <stdio.h>
#include <string.h>

main()
{
    char *string1 = "This is a test";
    char *string2 = "beware";
    char *c;

    printf("\'%c\'%s\n\"%s\"%s\"%s\"\n",
            *strpbrk(string1, string2),
            " is the first character to appear in ", string1,
            " of the characters in ", string2);
}
```

```
'a' is the first character to appear in
"This is a test" of the characters in "beware"
```

Fig. 8.25 Using strpbrk.

```
/* Using strrchr */
#include <stdio.h>
#include <string.h>

main()
{
    char *string1 = "A zoo has many animals including zebras";
    int c = 'z';

    printf("%s\n%s\'%c\'%s\"%s\"\n",
           "The remainder of string1 beginning with the",
           "last occurrence of character ", c,
           " is: ", strrchr(string1, c));
}
```

```
The remainder of string1 beginning with the
last occurrence of character 'z' is: "zebras"
```

Fig. 8.26 Using `strrchr`.

Function *strspn* (Fig. 8.27) determines the length of the initial part of the string in its first argument that contains only characters from the string in its second argument. The function returns the length of the segment.

```
/* Using strspn */
#include <stdio.h>
#include <string.h>

main()
{
    char *string1 = "The value is 3.14159";
    char *string2 = "The value is";

    printf("%s%s\n%s%s\n\n%s\n%s%lu",
           "string1 = ", string1, "string2 = ", string2,
           "The length of the initial segment of string1",
           "containing only characters from string2 = ",
           strspn(string1, string2));
}
```

```
string1 = The value is 3.14159
string2 = The value is

The length of the initial segment of string1
containing only characters from string2 = 13
```

Fig. 8.27 Using `strspn`.

Function $strstr$ searches for the first occurrence of its second string argument in its first string argument. If the second string is found in the first string, a pointer to the location of the string in the first argument is returned. The program of Fig. 8.28 uses $strstr$ to find the string "def" in the string "abcdefabcdef".

Function $strtok$ is used to break a string into a series of *tokens*. A token is a sequence of characters separated by delimiting characters (usually spaces or punctuation marks). For example, in a line of text, each word can be considered a token and the spaces separating the words can be considered delimiters.

Multiple calls to $strtok$ are required to break a string into tokens (assuming the string contains more than one token). The first call to $strtok$ contains two arguments, a string to be tokenized, and a string containing characters that separate the tokens. In the program of Fig. 8.29, the statement

```
tokenptr = strtok(string, " ");
```

assigns $tokenptr$ a pointer to the first token in $string$. The second argument of $strtok$, " ", indicates that tokens in $string$ are separated by spaces. Function $strtok$ searches for the first character in $string$ that is not a delimiting character (space). This begins the first token. The function then finds the next delimiting character in the string and replaces it with a null ('\0') character. This terminates the current token. Function $strtok$ saves a pointer to the next character following the token in $string$, and returns a pointer to the current token.

```
/* Using strstr */
#include <stdio.h>
#include <string.h>

main()
{
    char *string1 = "abcdefabcdef";
    char *string2 = "def";

    printf("%s%s\n%s%s\n\n%s\n%s%s\n",
           "string1 = ", string1, "string2 = ", string2,
           "The remainder of string1 beginning with the",
           "first occurrence of string2 is: ",
           strstr(string1, string2));
}
```

```
string1 = abcdefabcdef
string2 = def

The remainder of string1 beginning with the
first occurrence of string2 is: defabcdef
```

Fig. 8.28 Using $strstr$.

Subsequent calls to strtok to continue tokenizing string contain NULL as the first argument. The NULL argument indicates that the call to strtok should continue tokenizing from the location in string saved by the last call to strtok. If no tokens remain when strtok is called, strtok returns NULL. The program of Fig. 8.29 uses strtok to tokenize the string "This is a sentence with 7 tokens". Each token is printed separately. Note that strtok modifies the input string, therefore a copy of the string should be made if the string will be used again in the program after the calls to strtok.

```
/* Using strtok */

#include <stdio.h>
#include <string.h>

main()
{
    char *string = "This is a sentence with 7 tokens";
    char *tokenptr;

    printf("%s\n%s\n\n%s\n",
           "The string to be tokenized is:", string,
           "The tokens are:");

    tokenptr = strtok(string, " ");

    while (tokenptr) {
        printf("%s\n", tokenptr);
        tokenptr = strtok(NULL, " ");
    }
}
```

```
The string to be tokenized is:
This is a sentence with 7 tokens

The tokens are:
This
is
a
sentence
with
7
tokens
```

Fig. 8.29 Using strtok.

8.9 Memory Functions of the String Handling Library

The string handling library functions presented in this section facilitate manipulating, comparing, and searching blocks of memory. The functions treat blocks of memory as character arrays. These functions may be used to manipulate any block of data. For simplicity, the examples in this section manipulate character arrays (blocks of characters). Figure 8.30 summarizes the memory functions of the string handling library. In the function discussions, "object" refers to a block of data.

Function *memcpy* copies a specified number of characters from the object pointed to by its second argument into the object pointed to by its first argument. The function can receive a pointer to any type of object. The program of Fig. 8.31 uses `mem-cpy` to copy the string in array s2 to array s1.

Prototype	Function description
`void *memcpy(void *s1, const void *s2, size_t n)`	Copies **n** characters from the object pointed to by **s2** into the object pointed to by **s1**. A pointer to the resulting object is returned.
`void *memmove(void *s1, const void *s2, size_t n)`	Copies **n** characters from the object pointed to by **s2** into the object pointed to by **s1**. The copy is performed as if the characters are first copied from the object pointed to by **s2** into a temporary array, then from the temporary array into the object pointed to by **s1**. A pointer to the resulting object is returned.
`int memcmp(const void *s1, const void *s2, size_t n)`	Compares the first **n** characters of the object pointed to by **s1** to the first **n** characters of the object pointed to by **s2**. The function returns **0**, less than **0**, or greater than **0** if **s1** is equal to, less than, or greater than **s2**, respectively.
`void *memchr(const void *s, int c, size_t n)`	Locates the first occurrence of **c** (converted to **unsigned char**) in the first **n** characters of the object pointed to by **s**. If **c** is found, a pointer to **c** in the object pointed to by **s** is returned. Otherwise **NULL** is returned.
`void *memset(void *s, int c, size_t n)`	Copies **c** (converted to **unsigned char**) into the first **n** characters of the object pointed to by **s**. A pointer to the resulting object is returned.

Fig. 8.30 The string manipulation functions of the string handling library.

```
/* Using memcpy */
#include <stdio.h>
#include <string.h>

main()
{
    char s1[16], s2[]  = "Copy this string";

    memcpy(s1, s2, 16);
    printf("%s\n%s\"%s\"\n",
           "After s2 is copied into s1 with memcpy,",
           "s1 contains ", s1);
}
```

```
After s2 is copied into s1 with memcpy,
s1 contains "Copy this string"
```

Fig. 8.31 Using memcpy.

Function *memmove*, like function memcpy, copies a specified number of bytes from the object pointed to by its second argument into the object pointed to by its first argument. Copying is accomplished as if the bytes are first copied from the second argument into a temporary array of characters, then copied from the temporary array into the first argument. This allows characters from one part of a string to be copied into another part of the same string. Other string manipulation functions that copy characters have undefined results when copying takes place between parts of the same string. The program in Fig. 8.32 uses memmove to copy the last 10 bytes of array x into the first 10 bytes of array x.

```
/* Using memmove */
#include <stdio.h>
#include <string.h>

main()
{
    char x[] = "Home Sweet Home";

    memmove(x, &x[5], 10);
    printf("%s%s\n%s%s\n",
           "The string in array x before memmove is: ", x,
           "The string in array x after memmove is:  ", x);
}
```

```
The string in array x before memmove is: Home Sweet Home
The string in array x after memmove is:  Sweet Home Home
```

Fig. 8.32 Using memmove.

Function *memcmp* (Fig. 8.33) compares the specified number of characters of its first and second arguments. The function returns a value greater than 0 if the first argument is greater than the second argument, returns 0 if the arguments are equal, and returns a value less than zero if the first argument is less than the second argument.

Function *memchr* searches for the first occurrence of a byte, represented as unsigned char, in the specified number of bytes of an object. If the byte is found, a pointer to the byte in the object is returned, otherwise a NULL pointer is returned. The program of Fig. 8.34 searches for the character (byte) 'r' in the string "This is a string".

```
/* Using memcmp */
#include <stdio.h>
#include <string.h>

main()
{
    char s1[] = "ABCDEFG", s2[] = "ABCDXYZ";

    printf("%s%s\n%s%s\n\n%s%2d\n%s%2d\n%s%2d\n",
            "s1 = ", s1, "s2 = ", s2,
            "memcmp(s1, s2, 4) = ", memcmp(s1, s2, 4),
            "memcmp(s1, s2, 7) = ", memcmp(s1, s2, 7),
            "memcmp(s2, s1, 7) = ", memcmp(s2, s1, 7));
}
```

```
s1 = ABCDEFG
s2 = ABCDXYZ

memcmp(s1, s2, 4) =   0
memcmp(s1, s2, 7) = -1
memcmp(s2, s1, 7) =  1
```

Fig. 8.33 Using memcmp.

```
/* Using memchr */
#include <stdio.h>
#include <string.h>

main()
{
    char *s = "This is a string";

    printf("%s\'%c\'%s\"%s\"\n",
            "The remainder of s after character ", 'r',
            " is found is ", memchr(s, 'r', 27));
}
```

```
The remainder of s after character 'r' is found is "ring"
```

Fig. 8.34 Using memchr.

Function *memset* copies the value of the byte in its second argument into a specified number of bytes of the object pointed to by its first argument. The program in Fig. 8.35 uses memset to copy 'b' into the first 7 bytes of string1.

8.10 Other Functions of the String Handling Library

The two remaining functions of the string handling library are strerror and strlen. Figure 8.36 summarizes the strerror and strlen functions.

Function *strerror* takes an integer error number and creates an error message string. The message generated is system dependent. A pointer to the string is returned. The program of Fig. 8.37 demonstrates strerror.

```
/* Using memset */
#include <stdio.h>
#include <string.h>

main()
{
    char string1[15] = "BBBBBBBBBBBBBBB";

    printf("string1 = %s\n", string1);
    printf("string1 after memset = %s\n", memset(string1, 'b', 7));
}
```

```
string1 = BBBBBBBBBBBBBBB
string1 after memset = bbbbbbbBBBBBBBB
```

Fig. 8.35 Using memset.

Prototype	Function Description
char *strerror(int errornum)	Translates **errornum** into a full text string in a system dependent manner. A pointer to the string is returned.
size_t strlen(const char *s)	Determines the length of string **s**. The number of characters preceding the terminating **NULL** character is returned.

Fig. 8.36 The string manipulation functions of the string handling library.

Function *strlen* takes a string as an argument, and returns the number of characters in a string—the terminating NULL character is not included in the length. The program of Fig. 8.38 demonstrates function strlen.

Summary

- Function isdigit determines whether its argument is a digit (0-9).
- Function isalpha determines whether its argument is an uppercase letter (A-Z) or a lowercase letter (a-z).

```
/* Using strerror */
#include <stdio.h>
#include <string.h>

main()
{
   char error[100];

   printf("%s\n", strerror(2));
}
```

```
Error 2
```

Fig. 8.37 Using strerror.

```
/* Using strlen */
#include <stdio.h>
#include <string.h>

main()
{
   char *string1 = "abcdefghijklmnopqrstuvwxyz";
   char *string2 = "four";
   char *string3 = "Boston";

   printf("%s\"%s\"%s%lu\n%s\"%s\"%s%lu\n%s\"%s\"%s%lu\n",
          "The length of ", string1, " is ", strlen(string1),
          "The length of ", string2, " is ", strlen(string2),
          "The length of ", string3, " is ", strlen(string3));
}
```

```
The length of "abcdefghijklmnopqrstuvwxyz" is 26
The length of "four" is 4
The length of "Boston" is 6
```

Fig. 8.38 Using strlen.

- Function `isalnum` determines whether its argument is an uppercase letter (A-Z), a lowercase letter (a-z), or a digit (0-9).
- Function `isxdigit` determines whether its argument is a hexadecimal digit (A-F, a-f, 0-9).
- Function `islower` determines whether its argument is a lowercase letter (a-z).
- Function `isupper` determines if its argument is an uppercase letter (A-Z).
- Function `toupper` converts a lowercase letter to an uppercase letter, and returns the uppercase letter.
- Function `tolower` converts an uppercase letter to a lowercase letter, and returns the lowercase letter.
- Function `isspace` determines whether its argument is one of the following white-space characters: `' '` (space), `'\f'`, `'\n'`, `'\r'`, `'\t'`, or `'\v'`.
- Function `iscntrl` determines whether its argument is one of the following control characters: `'\t'`, `'\v'`, `'\f'`, `'\a'`, `'\b'`, `'\r'`, or `'\n'`.
- Function `ispunct` determines whether its argument is a printing character other than a space, a digit, or a letter.
- Function `isprint` determines whether its argument is any printing character including the space character.
- Function `isgraph` determines whether its argument is a printing character other than the space character.
- Function `atof` converts its argument—a string beginning with a series of digits that represent a floating point number—to a `double` value.
- Function `atoi` converts its argument—a string beginning with a series of digits that represent an integer—to an `int` value.
- Function `atol` converts its argument—a string beginning with a series of digits that represent a long integer—to a `long` value.
- Function `strtod` converts a sequence of characters representing a floating point value to `double`. The function receives two arguments—a string (`char *`) and a pointer to `char *`. The string contains the character sequence to be converted, and the pointer to `char *` is assigned the remainder of the string after the conversion.
- Function `strtol` converts a sequence of characters representing an integer to `long`. The function receives three arguments—a string (`char *`), a pointer to `char *`, and an integer. The string contains the character sequence to be converted, the pointer to `char *` is assigned the remainder of the string after the conversion, and the integer specifies the base of the value being converted.
- Function `strtoul` converts a sequence of characters representing an integer to `unsigned long`. The function receives three arguments—a string (`char *`), a pointer to `char *`, and an integer. The string contains the character sequence to be converted, the pointer to `char *` is assigned the remainder of the string after the conversion, and the integer specifies the base of the value being converted.

- Function `gets` reads characters from the standard input (keyboard) until a newline character or the end-of-file indicator is encountered. The argument to `gets` is an array of type `char`. A NULL character (`'\0'`) is appended to the array after reading terminates.

- Function `putchar` prints its character argument.

- Function `getchar` reads a single character from the standard input and returns the character as an integer. If the end-of-file indicator is set, `getchar` returns EOF.

- Function `puts` takes a string (`char *`) as an argument and prints the string followed by a newline character.

- Function `sprintf` uses the same conversion specifications as `printf` to print formatted data into an array of type `char`.

- Function `sscanf` uses the same conversion specifications as function `scanf` to read formatted data from a string.

- Function `strcpy` copies its second argument—a string—into its first argument—a character. The programmer must ensure that the array is large enough to store the string and its terminating NULL character.

- Function `strncpy` is equivalent to `strcpy` except that a call to `strncpy` specifies the number of characters to be copied from the string into the array. The terminating NULL character will only be copied if the number of characters to be copied is one more than the length of the string.

- Function `strcat` appends its second string argument—including the terminating NULL character—to its first string argument. The first character of the second string replaces the NULL (`'\0'`) character of the first string. The programmer must ensure that the array used to store the first string is large enough to store both the first string and the second string.

- Function `strncat` appends a specified number of characters from the second string to the first string. A terminating NULL character is appended to the result.

- Function `strcmp` compares its first string argument to its second string argument character-by-character. The function returns 0 if the strings are equal, returns a negative value if the the first string is less than the second string, and returns a positive value if the first string is greater than the second string.

- Function `strncmp` is equivalent to `strcmp` except that `strncmp` compares a specified number of characters. If the number of characters in one of the strings is less than the number of characters specified, `strncmp` compares characters until the NULL character in the shorter string is encountered.

- Function `strchr` searches for the first occurrence of a character in a string. If the character is found, `strchr` returns a pointer to the character in the string, otherwise `strchr` returns NULL.

- Function `strcspn` determines the length of the initial part of the string in its first argument that does not contain any characters from the string in its second argument. The function returns the length of the segment.

- Function `strpbrk` searches for the first occurrence in its first argument of any character in its second argument. If a character from the second argument is found, `strpbrk` returns a pointer to the character, otherwise `strpbrk` returns NULL.

- Function `strrchr` searches for the last occurrence of a character in a string. If the character is found, `strrchr` returns a pointer to the character in the string, otherwise `strrchr` returns NULL.

- Function `strspn` determines the length of the initial part of the string in its first argument that contains only characters from the string in its second argument. The function returns the length of the segment.

- Function `strstr` searches for the first occurrence of its second string argument in its first string argument. If the second string is found in the first string, a pointer to the location of the string in the first argument is returned.

- A sequence of calls to `strtok` breaks the string pointed to by `s1` into tokens that are separated by characters contained in the string pointed to by `s2`. The first call contains `s1` as the first argument, and subsequent calls to continue tokenizing the same string contain NULL as the first argument. A pointer to the current token is returned by each call. If there are no more tokens when the function is called, a NULL pointer is returned.

- Function memcpy copies a specified number of characters from the object to which its second argument points into the object to which its first argument points. The function can receive a pointer to any type of object. The pointers are received by memcpy as `void` pointers, and converted to `char` pointers for use in the function. Function memcpy manipulates the bytes of the object as characters.

- Function memmove, like function memcpy, copies a specified number of bytes from the object pointed to by its second argument into the object pointed to by its first argument. Copying is accomplished as if the bytes are first copied from the second argument into a temporary array of characters, then copied from the temporary array into the first argument.

- Function memcmp compares the specified number of characters of its first and second arguments.

- Function memchr searches for the first occurrence of a byte, represented as `unsigned char`, in the specified number of bytes of an object. If the byte is found, a pointer to the byte is returned, otherwise a NULL pointer is returned.

- Function memset copies the value of the byte in its second argument, treated as an `unsigned char`, into a specified number of bytes of the object pointed to by the first argument.

- Function `strerror` takes an integer error number and creates an error message string. The message generated is system dependent. A pointer to the string is returned.

- Function `strlen` takes a string as an argument, and returns the number of characters in a string—the terminating NULL character is not included in the length of the string.

Terminology

appending strings to other strings	search string
ASCII	`sprintf`
`atof`	`sscanf`
`atoi`	`stdio.h`
`atol`	`stdlib.h`
character code	`strcat`
character constant	`strchr`
character set	`strcmp`
comparing strings	`strcpy`
copying strings	`strcspn`
`ctype.h`	`strerror`
EBCDIC	string
`getchar`	string concatenation
`gets`	string constant
`isalnum`	`string.h`
`isalpha`	string literal
`iscntrl`	string processing
`isdigit`	`strlen`
`isgraph`	`strncat`
`islower`	`strncmp`
`isprint`	`strncpy`
`ispunct`	`strpbrk`
`isspace`	`strrchr`
`isupper`	`strspn`
`isxdigit`	`strstr`
literal	`strtod`
`memchr`	`strtok`
`memcmp`	`strtol`
`memcpy`	`strtoul`
`memmove`	`tolower`
`memset`	token
numeric code representation	tokenizing
of a character	`toupper`
`putchar`	word processing
`puts`	

Common Programming Errors

8.1   Not allocating sufficient space in a character array to store the NULL character that terminates a string.

8.2   Printing a string that does not contain a terminating NULL character. If this is the case, when the string is printed, an error will occur.

8.3   Processing a single character as a string. A string is a pointer—probably a respectably large integer. However, a character is a small integer (ASCII values range 0-255). On many systems this causes an error because low memory addresses are re served for special purposes such as operating system interrupt handlers—so, "access violations" occur.

8.4 Passing a character as an argument to a function when a string is expected.

8.5 Passing a string as an argument to a function when a character is expected.

Good Programming Practices

8.1 When storing a string of characters in a character array, be sure there are enough elements in the array to hold the largest string that will be stored. A string containing more characters than elements in the array may cause unexpected results.

8.2 When using functions from the character handling library, include the `<ctype.h>` header file.

8.3 When using functions from the general utilities library, include the `<stdlib.h>` header file.

8.4 When using functions from the standard input/output library, include the `<stdio.h>` header file.

8.5 When using functions from the string handling library, include the `<string.h>` header file.

Self-Review Exercises

8.1 Write a single statement to accomplish each of the following. Assume that variables **c** (which stores a character), **x**, **y**, and **z** are of type **int**, variables **d**, **e**, and **f** are of type **float**, variable **ptr** is of type **char ***, and arrays **s1[100]** and **s2[100]** are of type **char**.

    a) Convert the character stored in variable **c** to an uppercase letter. Assign the result to variable **c**.

    b) Determine if the value of variable **c** is a digit. Use the conditional operator to print " **is a** " or " **is not a** "—as in Fig. 8.2, 8.3, and 8.4—when the result is displayed.

    c) Convert the string "**1234567**" to **long** and print the value.

    d) Determine if the value of variable **c** is a control character. Use the conditional operator to print " **is a** " or " **is not a** " when the result is displayed.

    e) Read a line of text into array **s1** from the keyboard. Do not use **scanf**.

    f) Print the line of text stored in array **s1**. Do not use **printf**.

    g) Assign **ptr** the location of the last occurrence of **c** in **s1**.

    h) Print the value of variable **c**. Do not use **printf**.

    i) Convert the string "**8.63582**" to **double** and print the value.

    j) Determine if the value of variable **c** is a letter. Use the conditional operator to print " **is a** " or " **is not a** " when the result is displayed.

    k) Read a character from the keyboard and store the character in variable **c**.

    l) Assign **ptr** the location of the first occurrence of **s2** in **s1**.

    m) Determine if the value of variable **c** is a printing character. Use the conditional operator to print " **is a** " or " **is not a** " when the result is displayed.

n) Read three **float** values into variables **d**, **e**, and **f** from the string "1.27 10.3 9.432".

o) Copy the string stored in array **s2** into array **s1**.

p) Assign **ptr** the location of the first occurrence in **s1** of any character from **s2**.

q) Compare the string in **s1** to the string in **s2**. Print the result.

r) Assign **ptr** the location of the first occurrence of **c** in **s1**.

s) Use **sprintf** to print the values of integer variables **x**, **y**, and **z** into array **s1**. Each value should be printed with a field width of 7.

t) Append 10 characters from the string in **s2** to the string in **s1**.

u) Determine the length of the string in **s1**. Print the result.

v) Convert the string "-21" to **int** and print the value.

w) Assign **ptr** to the location of the first token in **s2**. Tokens in **s2** are separated by commas (,).

8.2 Show two different methods of initializing character array **vowel** with the string of vowels, "**AEIOU**".

8.3 What, if anything, prints when each of the following C statements is performed? If the statement contains an error, describe the error and indicate how to correct it. Assume the following variable declarations:

```
char s1[50] = "jack", s2[50] = " jill", s3[50], *sptr;
```

a) `printf("%c%s", toupper(s1[0]), &s1[1]);`

b) `printf("%s", strcpy(s3, s2));`

c) `printf("%s", strcat(strcat(strcpy(s3, s1), " and "), s2));`

d) `printf("%lu", strlen(s1) + strlen(s2));`

e) `printf("%lu", strlen(s3));`

Answers to Self-Review Exercises

8.1   a) `c = toupper(c);`

b) `printf("\'%c\'%sdigit\n",`
        `c, isdigit(c) ? " is a " : " is not a ");`

c) `printf("%ld\n", atol("1234567"));`

d) `printf("\'%c\'%scontrol character\n",`
        `c, iscntrl(c) ? " is a " : " is not a ");`

e) `gets(s1);`

f) `puts(s1);`

g) `ptr = strrchr(s1, c);`

h) `putchar(c);`

i) `printf("%f\n", atof("8.63582"));`

j) `printf("\'%c\'%sletter\n",`
        `c, isalpha(c) ? " is a " : " is not a ");`

k) `c = getchar();`

l) `ptr = strstr(s1, s2);`

m) `printf("\'%c\'%sprinting character\n",`
        `c, isprint(c) ? " is a " : " is not a ");`

n) `sscanf("1.27 10.3 9.432", "%f%f%f", &d, &e, &f);`

o) `strcpy(s1, s2);`

p) `ptr = strpbrk(s1, s2);`

q) `printf("strcmp(s1, s2) = %d\n", strcmp(s1, s2));`

```
r)  ptr = strchr(s1, c);
s)  sprintf(s1, "%7d%7d%7d", x, y, z);
t)  strncat(s1, s2, 10);
u)  printf("strlen(s1) = %lu\n", strlen(s1));
v)  printf("%d\n", atoi("-21"));
w)  ptr = strtok(s2, ",");
```

8.2   ```char vowel[] = "AEIOU";```
```char vowel[] = {'A', 'E', 'I', 'O', 'U', '\0'};```

8.3   a) ```Jack```
b) ```jill```
c) ```jack and jill```
d) ```8```
e) ```13```

Exercises

8.4   Write a program that inputs a character from the keyboard, and tests the character with each of the functions in the character handling library. The program should print the value returned by each function.

8.5   Write a program that inputs a line of text with function ```gets``` into character array ```s[100]```. Output the line in uppercase letters and in lowercase letters.

8.6   Write a program that inputs 4 strings that represent integers, converts the strings to integers, sums the values, and prints the total of the 4 values.

8.7   Write a program that inputs 4 strings that represent floating point values, converts the strings to double values, sums the values, and prints the total of the 4 values.

8.8   Write a program that uses function ```strcmp``` to compare two strings input by the user. The program should state whether the first string is less than, equal to, or greater than the second string.

8.9   Write a program that uses function ```strncmp``` to compare two strings input by the user. The program should input the number of characters to be compared. The program should state whether the first string is less than, equal to, or greater than the second string.

8.10   Write a program that uses random number generation to create sentences. The program should use four arrays of pointers to ```char``` called ```article```, ```noun```, ```verb```, and ```preposition```. The program should create a sentence by selecting a word at random from each array in the following order: ```article```, ```noun```, ```verb```, ```preposition```, ```article```, and ```noun```. As each word is picked, it should be concatenated to the previous words in an array which is large enough to hold the entire sentence. The words should be separated by spaces. When the final sentence is output, it should start with a capital letter and end with a period. The program should generate 20 such sentences.

The arrays should be filled as follows: the ```article``` array should contain the articles ```"the"```, ```"a"```, ```"one"```, ```"some"```, and ```"any"```; the ```noun``` array should contain the nouns ```"boy"```, ```"girl"```, ```"dog"```, ```"town"```, and ```"car"```; the ```verb``` array should contain the verbs ```"drove"```, ```"jumped"```, ```"ran"```, ```"walked"```, and ```"skipped"```; the ```preposition``` array should contain the prepositions ```"to"```, ```"from"```, ```"over"```, ```"under"```, and ```"on"```.
```

After the preceding program is written and working, modify the program to produce a short story consisting of several of these sentences. (How about the possibility of a random term paper writer!)

8.11   *(Limericks)* A limerick is a humorous five-line verse in which the first and second lines rhyme with the fifth, and the third line rhymes with the fourth. Using techniques similar to those developed in Problem 8.10, write a C program that produces random limericks. Polishing this program to produce good limericks is a challenging problem, but the result will be well worth the effort!

8.12   Write a program that encodes English language phrases into pig Latin. Pig Latin is a form of coded language often used for amusement. Many variations exist in the methods used to form pig Latin phrases. For simplicity, use the following algorithm:

To form a pig Latin phrase from an English language phrase, tokenize the phrase into words with function `strtok`. To translate each English word into a pig Latin word, place the first letter of the English word at the end of the English word, and add the letters "ay." Thus the word "jump" becomes "umpjay," the word "the" becomes "hetay," and the word "computer" becomes "omputercay." Blanks between words remain as blanks. Assume the following: the English phrase consists of words separated by blanks, there are no punctuation marks, and all words have two or more letters. Function `printlatinword` should display each word. Hint: Each time a token is found in a call to `strtok`, pass the token pointer to function `printlatinword`, and print the pig Latin word.

8.13   Write a program that inputs a telephone number as a string in the form `(555) 555-5555`. The program should use function `strtok` to extract the area code as a token, the first three digits of the phone number as a token, and the last four digits of the phone number as a token. The seven digits of the phone number should be concatenated into one string. The program should convert the area code string to `int` and convert the phone number string to `long`. Both the area code and the phone number should be printed.

8.14   Write a program that inputs a line of text, tokenizes the line with function `strtok`, and outputs the tokens in reverse order.

8.15   Write a program that inputs a line of text and a search string from the keyboard. Using function `strstr`, locate the first occurrence of the search string in the line of text, and assign the location to variable `searchptr` of type `char *`. If the search string is found, print the remainder of the line of text beginning with the search string. Then, use `strstr` again to locate the next occurrence of the search string in the line of text. If a second occurrence is found, print the remainder of the line of text beginning with the second occurrence. Hint: the second call to `strstr` should contain searchptr + 1 as its first argument.

8.16   Write a program based on the program of Exercise 8.15 that inputs several lines of text and a search string, and uses function `strstr` to determine the total occurrences of the string in the lines of text. Print the result.

8.17   Write a program that inputs several lines of text and a search character, and uses function `strchr` to determine the total occurrences of the character in the lines of text.

8.18   Write a program based on the program of Exercise 8.17 that inputs several lines of text, and uses function `strchr` to determine the total occurrences of each letter of the alphabet in the lines of text. Uppercase and lowercase letters should be counted together. Store the totals for each letter in an array, and print the values in tabular format after the totals have been determined.

8.19   Write a program that inputs several lines of text and uses `strtok` to count the total number of words. Assume that the words are separated by either spaces or newline characters.

8.20   Use the string comparison functions discussed in Section 8.6 and the techniques for sorting arrays developed in Chapter 6 to write a program that alphabetizes a list of strings. Use the names of 10 or 15 towns in your area as data for your program.

8.21   The chart in Appendix E shows the numeric code representations for the characters in the ASCII character set. Study this chart carefully and then state whether each of the following is true or false.
   a)   The letter `"A"` comes before the letter `"B."`
   b)   The digit `"9"` comes before the digit `"0."`
   c)   The commonly used symbols for addition, subtraction, multiplication, and division all come before any of the digits.
   d)   The digits come before the letters.
   e)   If a sort program sorts strings into ascending sequence, then the program will place the symbol for a right parenthesis before the symbol for a left parenthesis.

8.22   Write a program that reads a series of strings prints only those strings beginning with the letter `"b."`

8.23   Write a program that reads a series of strings and prints only those strings that end with the letters `"ED."`

8.24   Write a program that inputs an ASCII code and prints the corresponding character. Modify this program so that it generates all possible three-digit codes in the range 000 to 255 and attempts to print the corresponding characters. What happens when this program is run?

Special Section: Advanced String Manipulation Exercises

The preceding exercises are keyed to the text and designed to test the reader's understanding of fundamental string manipulation concepts. This section includes a collection of intermediate and advanced problems. The reader should find these problems challenging yet enjoyable. The problems vary considerably in difficulty. Some require an hour or two of program writing and implementation. Others are useful for lab assignments that might require two or three weeks of study and implementation. Some are challenging term projects.

8.25   *(Text Analysis)* The availability of computers with string manipulation capabilities has resulted in some rather interesting approaches to analyzing the writings of great authors. Much attention has been focused on whether William Shakespeare ever lived. Some scholars believe there is substantial evidence indicating that Christopher Marlowe actually penned the masterpieces attributed to Shakespeare. Researchers have used computers to find similarities in the writings of these two authors. This exercise examines three methods for analyzing texts with a computer.
   a)   Write a program that reads several lines of text and prints a table indicating the number of occurrences of each letter of the alphabet in the text. For example, the phrase

```
To be, or not to be: that is the question:
```

contains one "a," two "b's," no "c's," etc.

b) Write a program that reads several lines of text and prints a table indicating the number of one-letter words, two-letter words, three-letter words, etc. appearing in the text. For example, the phrase

```
Whether 'tis nobler in the mind to suffer
```

contains

Word length	Occurrences
1	0
2	2
3	2
4	2 (including 'tis)
5	0
6	2
7	1

c) Write a program that reads several lines of text and prints a table indicating the number of occurrences of each different word in the text. The first version of your program should include the words in the table in the same order in which they appear in the text. A more interesting (and useful) printout should then be attempted in which the words are sorted alphabetically. For example, the lines

```
To be, or not to be: that is the question:
Whether 'tis nobler in the mind to suffer
```

contain the words "to" three times, the word "be" two times, the word "or" once, etc.

8.26 *(Word Processing)* The detailed treatment of string manipulation in this text is greatly attributable to the exciting growth in word processing in recent years. One important function in word processing systems is *type-justification*—the alignment of words to both the left and right margins of a page. This generates a professional-looking document that gives the appearance of being set in type rather than prepared on a typewriter. Type-justification can be accomplished on computer systems by inserting one or more blank characters between each of the words in a line so that the rightmost word aligns with the right margin.

Write a program that reads several lines of text and prints this text in type-justified format. Assume that the text is to be printed on 8 1/2-inch-wide paper, and that one-inch margins are to be allowed on both the left and right sides of the printed page. Assume that the computer prints 10 characters to the horizontal inch. Therefore, your program should print 6 1/2 inches of text or 65 characters per line.

8.27 *(Printing Dates in Various Formats)* Dates are commonly printed in several different formats in business correspondence. Two of the more common formats are:

```
07/21/55 and July 21, 1955
```

Write a program that reads a date in the first format and prints that date in the second format.

8.28 *(Check Protection)* Computers are frequently employed in check-writing systems such as payroll and accounts payable applications. Many strange stories circulate regarding weekly paychecks being printed (by mistake) for amounts in excess of $1 million. Weird amounts are printed by computerized check-writing systems because of human error and/or machine failure. Systems designers, of course, make every effort to build controls into their systems to prevent erroneous checks from being issued.

Another serious problem is the intentional alteration of a check amount by someone who intends to cash a check fraudulently. To prevent a dollar amount from being altered, most computerized check-writing systems employ a technique called *check protection*.

Checks designed for imprinting by computer contain a fixed number of spaces in which the computer may print an amount. Suppose a paycheck contains eight blank spaces in which the computer is supposed to print the amount of a weekly paycheck. If the amount is large, then all eight of those spaces will be filled, for example:

```
1,230.60  (check amount)
--------
12345678  (position numbers)
```

On the other hand, if the amount is less than $1000, then several of the spaces would ordinarily be left blank. For example,

```
   99.87
--------
12345678
```

contains three blank spaces. If a check is printed with blank spaces, it is easier for someone to alter the amount of the check. To prevent a check from being altered, many check-writing systems insert *leading asterisks* to protect the amount as follows:

```
***99.87
--------
12345678
```

Write a program that inputs a dollar amount to be printed on a check, and then prints the amount in check-protected format with leading asterisks if necessary. Assume that nine spaces are available for printing an amount.

8.29 *(Writing the Word Equivalent of a Check Amount)* Continuing the discussion of the previous example, we reiterate the importance of designing check-writing systems to prevent alteration of check amounts. One common security method requires that the check amount be written both in numbers, and "spelled out" in words as well. Even if someone is able to alter the numerical amount of the check, it is extremely difficult to change the amount in words.

Many computerized check-writing systems do not print the amount of the check in words. Perhaps the main reason for this omission is the fact that most high-level languages used in commercial applications do not contain adequate string manipulation features. Another reason is that the logic for writing word equivalents of check amounts is somewhat involved.

Write a C program that inputs a numeric check amount and writes the word equivalent of the amount. For example, the amount 112.43 should be written as

ONE HUNDRED TWELVE and 43/100

8.30 *(Morse Code)* Perhaps the most famous of all coding schemes is the Morse code, developed by Samuel Morse in 1832 for use with the telegraph system. The Morse code assigns a series of dots and dashes to each letter of the alphabet, each digit, and a few special characters (such as period, comma, colon, and semicolon). In sound-oriented systems, the dot represents a short sound and the dash represents a long sound. Other representations of dots and dashes are used with light-oriented systems and signal-flag systems.

Separation between words is indicated by a space, or, quite simply, the absence of a dot or dash. In a sound-oriented system, a space is indicated by a short period of time during which no sound is transmitted. The international version of the Morse code appears in Fig. 8.39.

Write a program that reads an English language phrase and encodes the phrase into Morse code. Also write a program that reads a phrase in Morse code and converts the phrase into the English language equivalent. Use one blank between each Morse-coded letter and three blanks between each Morse-coded word.

8.31 *(A Metric Conversion Program)* Write a program that will assist the user with metric conversions. Your program should allow the user to specify the names of the units as strings (i.e., centimeters, liters, grams, etc. for the metric system and inches, quarts, pounds, etc. for the English system) and should respond to simple questions such as

```
"How many inches are in 2 meters?"
"How many liters are in 10 quarts?"
```

Your program should recognize invalid conversions. For example, the question

```
"How many feet in 5 kilograms?"
```

is not meaningful because **"feet"** is a unit of length while a **"kilogram"** is a unit of weight.

Character	Code	Character	Code
A	.–	N	–.
B	–...	O	–––
C	–.–.	P	.––.
D	–..	Q	––.–
E	.	R	.–.
F	..–.	S	...
G	––.	T	–
H	....	U	..–
I	..	V	...–
J	.–––	W	.––
K	–.–	X	–..–
L	.–..	Y	–.––
M	––	Z	––..

Fig. 8.39 The letters of the alphabet as expressed in international Morse code.

8.32 *(Dunning Letters)* Many businesses spend a great deal of time and money collecting overdue debts. *Dunning* is the process of making repeated and insistent demands upon a debtor to attempt to collect a debt.

Computers are often used to generate dunning letters automatically and in increasing degrees of severity as a debt ages. The theory is that as a debt becomes older it becomes more difficult to collect, and therefore the dunning letters must become more threatening.

Write a C program that contains the texts of five dunning letters of increasing severity. Your program should accept as input:

1. Debtor's name
2. Debtor's address
3. Debtor's account
4. Amount owed
5. Age of the amount owed (i.e., one month overdue, two months overdue, etc.).

Use the age of the amount owed to select one of the five message texts, and then print the dunning letter inserting the other user-supplied information where appropriate.

A challenging string manipulation project

8.33 *(A Crossword Puzzle Generator)* Most people have worked a crossword puzzle at one time or another, but few have ever attempted to generate one. Generating a crossword puzzle is a difficult problem. It is suggested here as a string manipulation project requiring substantial sophistication and effort. There are many issues the programmer must resolve to get even the simplest crossword puzzle generator program working. For example, how does one represent the grid of a crossword puzzle inside the computer? Should one use a series of strings, or should double-subscripted arrays be used? The programmer needs a source of words (i.e., a computerized dictionary) that can be directly referenced by the program. In what form should these words be stored to facilitate the complex manipulations required by the program? The really ambitious reader will want to generate the "clues" portion of the puzzle in which the brief hints for each "across" word and each "down" word are printed for the puzzle worker. Merely printing a version of the blank puzzle itself is not a simple problem.

9

Formatted Input/Output

Objectives

- To understand input and output streams.
- To be able to use all print formatting capabilities.
- To be able to use all input formatting capabilities.

All the news that's fit to print.
Adolph S. Ochs

What mad pursuit? What struggle to escape?
John Keats

Remove not the landmark on the boundary of the fields.
Amenemope

The end must justify the means.
Matthew Prior

Outline

9.1 Introduction

An important part of the solution to any problem is the presentation of the results. In this chapter we discuss the formatting features of the `printf` and `scanf` functions in depth. These functions input data from the *standard input stream,* and output data to the *standard output stream.* Four other functions that use the standard input and standard output—`gets`, `puts`, `getchar`, and `putchar`—were discussed Chapter 8. The header file `<stdio.h>` should be included when these functions are called in a program.

Many features of `printf` and `scanf` were discussed earlier in the text. This chapter summarizes those features and introduces many others. Chapter 11 discusses several other functions included in the standard input/output (`stdio`) library.

9.2 Streams

All input and output is performed with *streams*—sequences of characters organized into lines. Each line consists of zero or more characters and ends with the newline character. There can be up to 254 characters on a line (including the newline character).

When program execution begins, three streams are connected to the program automatically. Normally, the standard input stream is connected to the keyboard, and the standard output stream is connected to the computer screen. Operating systems often allow these streams to be redirected to other devices. A third stream, *standard error*, is connected to the computer screen. Error messages are output to the standard error stream. Streams are discussed in detail in Chapter 11, "File Processing."

9.3 Formatting Output with Printf

Precise output formatting is accomplished with the `printf` library function. Every `printf` call contains a *format control string* that describes the output format. The format control string consists of *conversion specifiers, flags, field widths, precisions*, and *literal characters*. Together with the percent sign (%), these form *conversion specifications*. Function `printf` can be used to perform the following useful formatting capabilities:

1. *Rounding* floating point values to an indicated number of decimal places.
2. *Aligning* a column of numbers with decimal points appearing one below the other.
3. *Right-justification* and *left-justification* of outputs.
4. *Inserting literal characters* at precise locations in a line of output.
5. Representing floating point numbers in exponential format.
6. Representing unsigned integers in octal and hexadecimal format (See Appendix E, "Number Systems," for more information on octal and hexadecimal values).
7. Displaying all types of data with fixed-size field widths and precisions.

The `printf` function has the form:

> `printf`(*format-control-string, other-arguments*) ;

The *format-control-string* describes the output format, and *other-arguments* are the arguments that correspond to each conversion specification in the *format-control-string*. Each conversion specification begins with a percent sign and ends with a conversion specifier. There can be many conversion specifications in one format control string. The next several sections discuss all `printf` formatting capabilities.

CPE 9.1
Forgetting to enclose a format control string in quotation marks.

GPP 9.1
Edit outputs neatly for presentation. This makes program outputs more readable and reduces user errors.

9.4 Printing Integers

An integer is a whole number, such as 776, 5, or –72, that contains no decimal point. Integer values are displayed in one of several formats. Figure 9.1 describes each of the integer conversion specifiers. The program in Fig. 9.2 prints an integer using each of the integer conversion specifiers.

CPE 9.2
Printing a negative value with a conversion specifier that expects an unsigned value.

Conversion Specifier	Description
d	Display a signed decimal integer.
i	Display a signed decimal integer. (Note: the i and d specifiers are different when used with scanf.)
o	Display an unsigned octal integer.
u	Display an unsigned decimal integer.
x or X	Display an unsigned hexadecimal integer. X causes the digits 0-9 and the letters A-F to be displayed, and x causes the digits 0-9 and a-f to be displayed.
h or l (letter l)	Place before any integer conversion specifier to indicate that a short or long integer is displayed respectively.

Fig. 9.1 Integer conversion specifiers.

```
/* Using the integer conversion specifiers */
#include <stdio.h>

main()
{
    printf("%d\n", 455);
    printf("%i\n", 455);
    printf("%o\n", 455);
    printf("%u\n", 455);
    printf("%x\n", 455);
    printf("%X\n", 455);
}
```

```
455
455
707
455
1c7
1C7
```

Fig. 9.2 Using integer conversion specifiers.

9.5 Printing Floating Point Numbers

A floating point value contains a decimal point as in 33.5 or 657.983. Floating point values are displayed in one of several formats. Figure 9.3 describes the floating point conversion specifiers.

Conversion specifier	Description
e or E	Display a floating point value in exponential notation.
f	Display floating point values.
g or G	Display a floating point value in either the floating point form f or the exponential form e (or E).
L	Place before any floating point conversion specifier to indicate that a long double floating point value is displayed.

Fig. 9.3 Floating point conversion specifiers.

The conversion specifiers e and E are used to display floating point values in *exponential notation*. Exponential notation is the computer equivalent of *scientific notation* used in mathematics. For example, the value 150.4582 is represented in scientific notation as

$$1.504582 \times 10^2$$

and is represented in exponential notation as

    1.504582E+02

by the computer. This notation indicates that 1.504582 is multiplied by 10 raised to the second power (E+02). The E stands for "exponent."

Values printed with the conversion specifiers e, E, and f are printed with 6 digits of precision to the right of the decimal point by default. The conversion specifiers e and E print lowercase e and uppercase E preceding the exponent respectively and always print 1 digit to the left of the decimal point.

Conversion specifier g (G) prints in either e (E) or f format with no trailing zeros (i.e., 1.234000 is printed as 1.234). Exponential notation is used if the value's exponent, as expressed in scientific notation, is less than −4, or if the exponent is greater than or equal to the specified precision (6 significant digits by default for g and G). Otherwise conversion specifier f is used to print the value . The values 0.0000875, 8750000.0, and 8.75 are printed as 8.75e−05, 8.75e+06, and 8.75 with the %g conversion specification. The value 0.0000875 uses e notation because its exponent in scientific notation is less than −4. The value 8750000.0 uses e notation because its exponent is equal to the default precision.

The precision for conversion specifiers g and G indicates the maximum number of significant digits printed including the digit to the left of the decimal point. The value 1234567.0 is printed as 1.23457e+06 using conversion specification %g. Note that there are 6 significant digits in the result. The difference between g and G is identical to the difference between e and E when the value is printed in exponential notation.

GPP 9.2

Be sure that the user is aware of situations in which data may be imprecise.

The program in Fig. 9.4 displays the floating point number 1234567.89 in each of the three floating point formats. Note that the %E and %g conversion specifications cause the value to be rounded.

9.6 Printing Strings and Characters

The c and s conversion specifiers are used to print individual characters and strings respectively. Conversion specifier c requires a char argument. Conversion specifier s requires a pointer to char as an argument. Conversion specifier s causes characters to be printed until a terminating NULL ('\0') character is encountered.

CPE 9.3

Using %c to print the first character of a string. The conversion specification %c expects a char argument. A string is a pointer to char.

CPE 9.4

Using %s to print a char argument. The conversion specification %s expects an argument of type pointer to char.

CPE 9.5

Using single quotes around character strings. Character strings must be enclosed in double quotes.

CPE 9.6

Using double quotes around a character constant. This actually creates a string consisting of two characters, the second of which is the terminating NULL. A character constant must be enclosed in single quotes.

```
/* Printing floating point numbers with
   floating point conversion specifiers */
#include <stdio.h>

main()
{
    printf("%e\n", 1234567.89);
    printf("%E\n", 1234567.89);
    printf("%f\n", 1234567.89);
    printf("%g\n", 1234567.89);
    printf("%G\n", 1234567.89);
}
```

```
1.234568e+06
1.234568E+06
1234567.890000
1.23457e+06
1.23457E+06
```

Fig. 9.4 Using floating point conversion specifiers.

```
/* Printing strings and characters */
#include <stdio.h>

main()
{
    char character = 'A';
    char string[] = "This is a string";
    char *stringptr = "This is also a string";

    printf("%c\n", character);
    printf("%s\n", "This is a string");
    printf("%s\n", string);
    printf("%s\n", stringptr);
}
```

```
A
This is a string
This is a string
This is also a string
```

Fig. 9.5 Using the character and string conversion specifiers.

The program in Fig. 9.5 displays characters and strings with conversion specifiers c and s.

9.7 Other Conversion Specifiers

The three remaining conversion specifiers are p, n, and % (Fig. 9.6). The conversion specifier p displays a pointer address in an implementation-defined manner (on many systems, hexadecimal notation is used). The conversion specifier n stores the number of characters already output in the current printf statement—the corresponding argument is a pointer to an integer variable in which the value is stored. Nothing is printed when a %n conversion specification is encountered in a format control string. The conversion specifier % causes a percent sign to be output.

In the program of Fig. 9.7, %p prints the value of ptr and the address of x; they are equal because ptr is assigned the address of x. Next, %n stores the number of characters output by the third printf statement in integer variable y, and the value of y is printed. The last printf statement uses %% to print the % character in a character string.

Actually, every printf call returns a value—either the number of characters output or a negative value if an output error occurs. Therefore, it is possible to determine the total number of characters displayed by any call to printf, or if an error occurred.

CPE 9.7

Trying to print a literal percent character using % rather than %% in the format control string. When % appears in a format control string, it must be followed by a conversion specifier.

Conversion specifier	Description
p	Display a pointer value in an implementation defined manner.
n	Store the number of characters already output in the current `printf` statement. A pointer to an integer is supplied as the corresponding argument. Nothing is displayed on the screen.
%	Display the percent character.

Fig. 9.6 Other conversion specifiers.

```
/* Using the p, n, and % conversion specifiers */
#include <stdio.h>

main()
{
    int *ptr;
    int x = 12345, y;

    ptr = &x;
    printf("The value of ptr is %p\n", ptr);
    printf("The address of x is %p\n\n", &x);

    printf("Total characters printed on this line is:%n", &y);
    printf(" %d\n\n", y);

    y = printf("This line has 28 characters\n");
    printf("%d characters were printed\n\n");

    printf("Printing a %% in a format control string\n");
}
```

```
The value of ptr is 001F2BB4
The address of x is 001F2BB4

Total characters printed on this line is: 41

This line has 28 characters
28 characters were printed

Printing a % in a format control string
```

Fig. 9.7 Using the p, n, and % conversion specifiers.

9.8 Printing with Field Widths and Precisions

The exact size of a field in which data is printed is indicated with a *field width*. If the field width is larger than the data being printed, the data will normally be right-justified within that field. An integer representing the field width is inserted between the percent sign (%) and the conversion specifier in the conversion specification. The program in Fig. 9.8 prints five numbers, right-justifying those that contain fewer digits than the field. Note that the last value is larger than the field width. The field width is automatically increased to print objects larger than the field. Field widths can be used with all conversion specifiers.

CPE 9.8

Not providing a sufficiently large field width to handle a value to be printed. This can offset other data being printed and can produce confusing outputs. Know your data!

Function `printf` also provides the ability to specify the precision with which data is printed. Precision has several different meanings. When used with integer conversion specifiers, precision indicates the minimum number of digits to be printed. If the printed value contains fewer digits than the specified precision, zeros are prefixed to the printed value until the total number of digits is equivalent to the precision. The default precision for integers is 1. When used with floating point conversion specifiers e, E, and f, the precision is the number of digits to appear after the decimal point. When used with conversion specifiers g and G, the precision is the maximum number of significant digits to be printed. When used with conversion specifier s, the precision is the maximum number of characters to be written from the string. To use precision, place a decimal point (.) followed by an integer representing the precision between the percent sign and the conversion specifier. The program in Fig. 9.9 demonstrates the use of precision in format control strings. Note that when printing a floating point value with a precision smaller than the original number of decimal places in the value, the value is rounded.

```
/* Printing integers right-justified*/
#include <stdio.h>

main()
{
    printf("%4d\n", 1);
    printf("%4d\n", 12);
    printf("%4d\n", 123);
    printf("%4d\n", 1234);
    printf("%4d\n", 12345);
}
```

```
   1
  12
 123
1234
12345
```

Fig. 9.8 Right-justifying integers in a field.

```
/* Using precision while printing integers,
   floating point numbers, and strings */
#include <stdio.h>

main()
{
    int i = 873;
    float f = 123.94536;
    char s[] = "Happy Birthday";

    printf("Using precision for integers\n");
    printf("\t%.4d\n\t%.9d\n\n", i, i);
    printf("Using precision for floating point numbers\n");
    printf("\t%.3f\n\t%.3e\n\t%.3g\n\n", f, f, f);
    printf("Using precision for strings\n");
    printf("\t%.11s\n", s);
}
```

```
Using precision for integers
        0873
        000000873

Using precision for floating point numbers
        123.945
        1.239e+02
        124

Using precision for strings
        Happy Birth
```

Fig. 9.9 Using precisions to display information of several types.

The field width and the precision can be combined by placing the field width followed by a decimal point followed by a precision between the percent sign and the conversion specifier, as in the statement

```
printf("%9.3f", 123.456789);
```

that displays 123.457 right justified in a 9 digit field.

It is possible to specify the field width and the precision using integer expressions in the argument list following the format control string. To use this feature, insert an * (asterisk) in place of the field width or precision (or both). The matching argument in the argument list is evaluated and used in place of the asterisk. The value of the argument can be negative for the field width, but must be positive for the precision. A negative value for the field width causes the output to be left justified in the field as described in the next section.

9.9 Using Flags in the Printf Format Control String

Function printf also provides flags to supplement its output formatting capabilities. Five flags are available to the user for use in format control strings (Fig. 9.10).

Flag	Description
– (minus sign)	Left-justify the output within the specified field.
+ (plus sign)	Display a plus sign preceding positive values and a minus sign preceding negative values.
space	Print a space before a positive value not printed with the + flag.
#	Prefix 0 to the output value when used with the octal conversion specifier o.
	Prefix 0x or 0X to the output value when used with the hexadecimal conversion specifiers x or X.
	Force a decimal point for a floating point number printed with e, E, f, g, or G that does not contain a fractional part. (Normally the decimal point is only printed if a digit follows it.) For g and G specifiers, trailing zeros are not eliminated.
0 (zero)	Pad a field with leading zeros.

Fig. 9.10 Format control string flags.

To use a flag in a format control string, place the flag immediately to the right of the percent sign. Several flags may be combined in one conversion specification.

The program in Fig. 9.11 left-justifies eight words in fields of length 10. Left-justification can be done with all the conversion specifiers.

The program in Fig. 9.12 prints a positive number and a negative number, each with and without the + flag. Note that the minus sign is displayed in both cases.

```
/* Left-justifying strings */
#include <stdio.h>

main()
{
    printf("%-10s%-10s", "Each", "word");
    printf("%-10s%-10s\n", "is", "left");
    printf("%-10s%-10s", "justified", "within");
    printf("%-10s%-10s\n", "its", "field");
}
```

```
Each      word      is        left
justified within    its       field
```

Fig. 9.11 Left-justifying strings in a field.

```
/* Printing numbers with and without the + flag */
#include <stdio.h>

main()
{
    printf("%d\n%d\n", 786, -786);
    printf("%+d\n%+d\n", 786, -786);
}
```

```
786
-786
+786
-786
```

Fig. 9.12 Printing positive and negative numbers with and without the + flag.

The program in Fig. 9.13 prefixes a space to the positive number with the space flag. This is useful for aligning positive and negative numbers with the same number of digits.

The program in Fig. 9.14 uses the # flag to prefix 0 to the octal value, 0x and 0X to the hexadecimal values, and to force the decimal point on a floating point number printed with g.

The program in Fig. 9.15 combines the + flag and the 0 (zero) flag to print a positive integer in a 9 space field with a + sign and leading zeros.

```
/* Printing a space before signed values
   not preceded by + or - */
#include <stdio.h>

main()
{
    printf("% d\n% d\n", 547, -547);
}
```

```
 547
-547
```

Fig. 9.13 Using the space flag.

```
/* Using the # flag with conversion specifiers
   o, x, X, and any floating point specifier */
#include <stdio.h>

main()
{
   int c = 1427;
   float p = 1427.0;

   printf("%#o\n", c);
   printf("%#x\n", c);
   printf("%#X\n", c);
   printf("\n%g\n", p);
   printf("%#g\n", p);
}
```

```
02623
0x593
0X593

1427
1427.00
```

Fig. 9.14 Using the # flag.

```
/* Printing with the 0(zero) flag fills in
   leading zeros after any sign or prefix */
#include <stdio.h>

main()
{
   printf("%+09d", 452);
}
```

```
+00000452
```

Fig. 9.15 Using the 0 (zero) flag.

9.10 Printing Literals and Escape Sequences

Most literal characters to be printed in a `printf` statement can simply be included in the format control string. However, there are several characters that can not be included normally such as the quotation mark character (") that is used to delimit the format control string. There are also some control characters, such as the newline and tab characters we have discussed previously, that cannot be explicitly included in the format control string. In these cases, *escape sequences* are used to represent the special characters. When an escape sequence is encountered in a format control string, the special character is printed. An escape sequence is represented by a backslash (\) followed by a particular *escape character*. The table in Fig. 9.16 lists all the escape sequences and the results of including them in a format control string.

CPE 9.9

Trying to print a character such as the double quote (") that must be printed with an escape sequence in a format control string.

9.11 Formatting Input with Scanf

Precise input formatting is accomplished with the `scanf` library function. Every `scanf` statement contains a format control string that describes the format of the data to be input. The format control string consists of conversion specifications and literal characters. Function `scanf` has the following input formatting capabilities:

1. Inputting all types of data.
2. Inputting specific characters from an input stream.
3. Skipping specific characters in the input stream.

The `scanf` function is written in the following form:

    `scanf` (*format-control-string, other-arguments*) ;

The *format-control-string* describes the formats of the input, and the *other-arguments* are pointers to variables in which the input will be stored.

GPP 9.3

When inputting data, prompt the user for one piece, or a few pieces, of information at a time. Avoid asking the user many data items in response to a single prompt.

Escape Sequence	Description
\'	Output the single quote (') character.
\"	Output the double quote (") character.
\?	Output the question mark (?) character.
\\	Output the backslash (\) character.
\a	Cause an audible (bell) or visual alert.
\b	Move the cursor back one position on the current line.
\f	Move the cursor to the start of the next logical page.
\n	Move the cursor to the beginning of the next line.
\r	Move the cursor to the beginning of the current line.
\t	Move the cursor to the next horizontal tab position.
\v	Move the cursor to the next vertical tab position.

Fig. 9.16 Escape sequences.

Figure 9.17 summarizes the conversion specifiers used to input all types of data. The rest of this section provides several programs that demonstrate inputting data with the various scanf conversion specifiers.

The program in Fig. 9.18 reads five integers, one with each of the five integer conversion specifiers, and displays them as decimal integers.

Conversion Specifier	Description
Integers	
d	Read an optionally signed decimal integer. The corresponding argument is a pointer to integer.
i	Read an optionally signed decimal, octal, or hexadecimal integer. The corresponding argument is a pointer to integer.
o	Read an octal integer. The corresponding argument is a pointer to unsigned integer.
u	Read an unsigned decimal integer. The corresponding argument is a pointer to unsigned integer.
x or X	Read a hexadecimal integer. The corresponding argument is a pointer to unsigned integer.
h or l	Place before any of the integer conversion specifiers to indicate that a short or long integer is to be input.
Floating point numbers	
e, E, f, g or G	Read a floating point value. The corresponding argument is a pointer to a floating point variable.
l or L	Place before any of the floating point conversion specifiers to indicate that a double or long double value is to be input.
Characters and strings	
c	Read a character. The corresponding argument is a pointer to char, no null ('\0') is added.
s	Read a string. The corresponding argument is a pointer to an array of type char that is large enough to hold the string and a terminating null ('\0') character.
Scan set	
[scan characters]	Scan a string for a set of characters that are stored in an array.
Miscellaneous	
p	Read a pointer address of the same form produced when an address is output with %p in a printf statement.
n	Store the number of characters input so far in this scanf. The corresponding argument is a pointer to integer
%	Skip a percent sign (%) in the input.

Fig. 9.17 Conversion specifiers for scanf.

When inputting floating point numbers, any of the floating point conversion specifiers e, E, f, g, or G, can be used. The program in Fig. 9.19 demonstrates reading three floating point numbers, one with each of the three types of floating conversion specifiers, and displays all three numbers with conversion specifier f. Note that the program output confirms the fact that floating point values are imprecise—this fact is highlighted by the second value printed.

```
/* Reading integers */
#include <stdio.h>

main()
{
    int a, b, c, d, e;

    printf("Enter five integers: ");
    scanf("%d%i%o%u%x", &a, &b, &c, &d, &e);
    printf("The input displayed as decimal integers is:\n");
    printf("%d %d %d %d %d\n", a, b, c, d, e);
}
```

```
Enter five integers: -70 -70 70 70 70
The input displayed as decimal integers is:
-70 -70 56 70 112
```

Fig. 9.18 Reading input with integer conversion specifiers.

```
/* Reading floating point numbers */
#include <stdio.h>

main()
{
    float a, b, c;

    printf("Enter three floating point numbers: \n");
    scanf("%e%f%g", &a, &b, &c);
    printf("Here are the numbers entered in plain\n");
    printf("floating point notation:\n");
    printf("%f\n%f\n%f\n", a, b, c);
}
```

```
Enter three floating point numbers:
1.27987 1.27987e+03 3.38476e-06
Here are the numbers entered in plain
floating point notation:
1.279870
1279.869995
0.000003
```

Fig. 9.19 Reading input with floating point conversion specifiers.

Characters and strings are input using the conversion specifiers c and s respectively. The program in Fig. 9.20 prompts the user to input a string. The program inputs the first character of the string with %c and stores it in the character variable x, then inputs the remainder of the string with %s and stores it in character array y.

A sequence of characters can be input using a *scan set*. A scan set is a set of characters enclosed in square brackets [] and preceded by a percent sign in the format control string. A scan set scans the characters in the input stream looking only for those characters that match characters contained in the scan set. Each time a character is matched, it is stored in the scan set's corresponding argument—a pointer to a character array. The scan set stops inputting characters when a character that is not contained in the scan set is encountered. If the first character in the input stream does not match a character in the scan set, nothing is stored in the array. The program in Fig. 9.21 uses the scan set [aeiou] to scan the input stream for vowels. Notice only the first letter of the input is read because the second letter (1) is not in the scan set and therefore terminates the scanning.

The scan set can also be used to scan for characters not contained in the scan set by using an *inverted scan set*. To create an inverted scan set, place a *caret (^)* in the square brackets before the scan characters. This causes characters not appearing in the scan set to be stored. When a character contained in the inverted scan set is encountered, input terminates. The program in Fig. 9.22 uses the inverted scan set [^aeiou] to search for consonants.

```
/* Reading characters and strings */
#include <stdio.h>

main()
{
    char x, y[9];

    printf("Enter a string: ");
    scanf("%c%s", &x, y);

    printf("The input was:\n");
    printf("the character \"%c\" ", x);
    printf("and the string \"%s\"\n", y);
}
```

```
Enter a string: Sunday
The input was:
the character "S" and the string "unday"
```

Fig. 9.20 Inputting characters and strings.

```
/* Using a scan set */
#include <stdio.h>

main()
{
   char z[9];

   printf("Enter string: ");
   scanf("%[aeiou]", z);
   printf("The input was \"%s\"\n", z);
}
```

```
Enter String: alphabet
The input was "a"
```

Fig. 9.21 Using a scan set.

```
/* Using an inverted scan set */
#include <stdio.h>

main()
{
   char z[9];

   printf("Enter a string: ");
   scanf("%[^aeiou]", z);
   printf("The input was \"%s\"\n", z);
}
```

```
Enter a string: String
The input was "Str"
```

Fig. 9.22 Using an inverted scan set.

A field width can be used in a `scanf` conversion specification to read a specific number of characters from the input stream. The program in Fig. 9.23 inputs a series of consecutive digits as a two digit-integer and an integer consisting of the remaining digits.

Often it is necessary to skip certain characters in the input stream. For example, a date could be entered as

```
7-9-91
```

Each number in the date needs to be stored, but the dashes that separate the numbers can be discarded. To eliminate unnecessary characters, include them as literals in the format control string of `scanf`. For example, to skip the dashes in the input, use the statement

```
/* inputting data with a field width */
#include <stdio.h>

main()
{
    int x, y;

    printf("Enter a six digit integer: ");
    scanf("%2d%d", &x, &y);
    printf("The integers input were %d and %d\n", x, y);
}
```

```
Enter a six digit integer: 123456
The integers input were 12 and 3456
```

Fig. 9.23 Inputting data with a field width.

```
scanf("%d-%d-%d", &month, &day, &year);
```

Although, this `scanf` does eliminate the dashes in the preceding input, it is possible that the date could be entered as

    7/9/91

In this case the preceding `scanf` would not eliminate the unnecessary characters. For this reason, `scanf` provides the *assignment suppression character* `*`. The assignment suppression character enables `scanf` to read data from the input and discard it without assigning it to a variable. The program in Fig. 9.24 uses the assignment suppression character in the `%c` conversion specification to indicate that a character appearing in the input stream should be read and discarded. Only the month, day, and year are stored. The values of the variables are printed to demonstrate that they are in fact input correctly. Note that no variables in the argument list correspond to the conversion specifications that use the assignment suppression character because no assignments are performed for those conversion specifications.

Summary

- All input and output is dealt with in streams—sequences of characters organized into lines. Each line consists of zero or more characters and ends with a newline character.
- Normally, the standard input steam is connected to the keyboard, and the standard output stream is connected to the computer screen.
- Operating systems often allow the standard input and standard output streams to be redirected to other devices.
- The `printf` format control string describes the formats in which the output values appear. The format control string consists of conversion specifiers, flags, field widths, precisions, and literal characters.

```
/* Reading and discarding characters from the input stream */
#include <stdio.h>

main()
{
    int month1, day1, year1, month2, day2, year2;

    printf("Enter a date in the form mm-dd-yy: ");
    scanf("%d%*c%d%*c%d", &month1, &day1, &year1);
    printf("month = %d   day = %d   year = %d\n\n",
        month1, day1, year1);
    printf("Enter a date in the form mm/dd/yy: ");
    scanf("%d%*c%d%*c%d", &month2, &day2, &year2);
    printf("month = %d   day = %d   year = %d\n",
        month2, day2, year2);
}
```

```
Enter a date in the form mm-dd-yy: 11-18-71
month = 11   day = 18   year = 71

Enter a date in the form mm/dd/yy: 11/18/71
month = 11   day = 18   year = 71
```

Fig. 9.24 Reading and discarding characters from the input stream.

- Integers are printed with the following conversion specifiers: d or i for optionally signed integers, o for unsigned integers in octal form, u for unsigned integers in decimal form, and x or X for unsigned integers in hexadecimal form. The modifier h or l is prefixed to the preceding conversion specifiers to indicate a short or long integer respectively.

- Floating point values are printed with the following conversion specifiers: e or E for exponential notation, f for regular floating point notation, and g or G for either e (or E) notation or f notation. When the g (or G) conversion specifier is indicated, the e (or E) conversion specifier is used if the value's exponent is less than −4 or greater than or equal to the precision with which the value is printed.

- The precision for the g and G conversion specifiers indicates the maximum number of significant digits printed.

- The c conversion specifier prints a character.

- The s conversion specifier prints a string of characters ending in the null character ('\0').

- The conversion specifier p displays a pointer address in an implementation-defined manner (on many systems, hexadecimal notation is used).

- The conversion specifier n stores the number of characters already output in the current printf statement. The corresponding argument is a pointer to an integer.

- The conversion specification %% causes a literal % to be output.

- If the field width is larger than the object being printed, the object is normally right-justified in the field.
- Field widths can be used with all conversion specifiers.
- Precision used with integer conversion specifiers indicates the minimum number of digits printed. If the value contains fewer digits than the precision specified, zeros are prefixed to the printed value until the number of digits is equivalent to the precision.
- Precision used with floating point conversion specifiers e, E, and f indicates the number of digits that appear after the decimal point.
- Precision used with floating point conversion specifiers g and G indicates the number of significant digits to appear.
- Precision used with conversion specifier s indicates the number of characters to be printed.
- The field width and the precision can be combined by placing the field width followed by a decimal point followed by the precision between the percent sign and the conversion specifier.
- It is possible to specify the field width and the precision through integer expressions in the argument list following the format control string. To use this feature, insert an * (asterisk) in place of the field width or precision. The matching argument in the argument list is evaluated and used in place of the asterisk. The value of the argument can be negative for the field width, but must be positive for the precision.
- The – flag left-justifies its argument in a field.
- The + flag prints a plus sign for positive values and a minus sign for negative values.
- The space flag prints a space preceding a positive value not displayed with the + flag.
- The # flag prefixes 0 to octal values, 0x or 0X to hexadecimal values, and forces the decimal point to be printed for floating point value printed with e, E, f, g, or G (normally the decimal point is only displayed if the value contains a fractional part).
- The 0 flag prints leading zeros for a value that does not occupy its entire field width.
- Precise input formatting is accomplished with the scanf library function.
- Integers are input with the conversion specifiers: d and i for optionally signed integers, and o, u, x, or X for unsigned integers. The modifiers h and l are placed before any of the integer conversion specifiers to indicate that the input value is a short or long integer respectively.
- Floating point values are input with the conversion specifiers e, E, f, g, or G. The modifiers l and L are placed before any of the floating point conversion specifiers to indicate that the input value is a double or long double value respectively.

- Characters are input with the conversion specifier c.
- Strings are input with the conversion specifier s.
- A scan set scans the characters in the input looking only for those characters that match characters contained in the scan set. When a character is matched, it is stored in a character array. The scan set stops inputting characters when a character not contained in the scan set is encountered.
- To create an inverted scan set, place a caret (^) in the square brackets before the scan characters. This causes characters not appearing in the scan set to be stored until a character contained in the inverted scan set is encountered.
- Address values are input with the conversion specifier p.
- Conversion specifier n stores the number of characters input previously in the current scanf. The corresponding argument is a pointer to int.
- The conversion specification %% matches a single % character in the input.
- The assignment suppression character is used to read data from the input stream and discard the data.
- A field width is used in a scanf to read a specific number of characters from the input stream.

Terminology

flag
% conversion specifier
* in field width
* in precision
+ (plus sign) flag
– (minus sign) flag
0 (zero) flag
<stdio.h>
\" escape sequence
\' escape sequence
\? escape sequence
\\ escape sequence
\a escape sequence
\b escape sequence
\f escape sequence
\n escape sequence
\r escape sequence
\t escape sequence
\v escape sequence
alignment
assignment suppression character (*)
blank insertion
c conversion specifier
caret (^)

conversion specification
conversion specifiers
d conversion specifier
e or E conversion specifier
escape sequence
exponential floating point format
f conversion specifier
field width
flags
floating point
format control string
g or G conversion specifier
h conversion specifier
hexadecimal format
i conversion specifier
integer conversion specifiers
inverted scan set
L conversion specifier
l conversion specifier
left justification
literal characters
long integer
n conversion specifier
o conversion specifier

Common Programming Errors

9.1   Forgetting to enclose a format control string in quotation marks.

9.2   Printing a negative value with a conversion specifier that expects an unsigned value.

9.3   Using **%c** to print the first character of a string. The conversion specification **%c** expects a **char** argument. A string is a pointer to **char**.

9.4   Using **%s** to print a **char** argument. The conversion specification **%s** expects an argument of type pointer to **char**.

9.5   Using single quotes around character strings. Character strings must be enclosed in double quotes.

9.6   Using double quotes around a character constant. This actually creates a string consisting of two characters, the second of which is the terminating **NULL**. A character constant must be enclosed in single quotes.

9.7   Trying to print a literal percent character using **%** rather than **%%** in the format control string. When **%** appears in a format control string, it must be followed by a conversion specifier.

9.8   Not providing a sufficiently large field width to handle a value to be printed. This can offset other data being printed and can produce confusing outputs. Know your data!

9.9   Trying to print a character such as the double quote (") that must be printed with an escape sequence in a format control string.

Good Programming Practices

9.1   Edit outputs neatly for presentation. This makes program outputs more readable and reduces user errors.

9.2   Be sure that the user is aware of situations in which data may be imprecise.

9.3   When inputting data, prompt the user for one piece, or a few pieces, of information at a time. Avoid asking the user many data items in response to a single prompt.

Self-Review Exercises

9.1 Fill in the blanks in each of the following:

a) All input and output is dealt with in the form of _____.

b) The _____ stream is normally connected to the keyboard.

c) The _____ stream is normally connected to the computer screen.

d) Precise output formatting is accomplished with the _____ function.

e) The format control string may contain _____, _____, _____, _____, and _____.

f) The conversion specifier _____ or _____ may be used to output a signed decimal integer.

g) The conversion specifiers _____, _____, and _____ are used to display unsigned integers in octal, decimal, and hexadecimal form respectively.

h) The modifiers _____ and _____ are placed before the integer conversion specifiers to indicate that **short** or **long** integer values are to be displayed.

i) The conversion specifier _____ is used to display a floating point value in exponential notation.

j) The modifier _____ is placed before any floating point conversion specifier to indicate that a **long double** value is to be displayed.

k) The conversion specifiers **e**, **E**, and **f** are displayed with _____ digits of precision to the right of the decimal point if no precision is specified.

l) The conversion specifiers _____ and _____ are used to print strings and characters respectively.

m) All strings end in the _____ character.

n) The field width and precision in a **printf** conversion specification can be controlled with integer expressions by substituting an _____ for the field width or for the precision, and placing an integer expression in the corresponding argument of the argument list.

o) The _____ flag causes output to be left-justified in a field.

p) The _____ flag causes values to be displayed with either a plus sign or a minus sign.

q) Precise input formatting is accomplished with the _____ function.

r) A _____ is used to scan a string for specific characters and store the characters in an array.

s) The conversion specifier _____ can be used to input optionally signed octal, decimal, and hexadecimal integers.

t) The conversion specifier _____ can be used to input a **double** value.

u) The _____ is used to read data from the input stream and discard it without assigning it to a variable.

v) A _____ can be used in a **scanf** conversion specification to indicate that a specific number of characters or digits should be read from the input stream.

9.2 Find the error in each of the following and explain how the error can be corrected.

a) The following statement should print the character **'c'**.

```
printf("%s\n", 'c');
```

b) The following statement should print **9.375%**.

```
printf("%.3f%", 9.375);
```

    c) The following statement should print the first character of the string "Monday".

```
printf("%c\n", "Monday");
```

    d) `printf(""A string in quotes"");`

    e) `printf(%d%d, 12, 20);`

    f) `printf("%c", "x");`

    g) `printf("%s\n", 'Richard');`

9.3   Write a statement for each of the following:

    a) Print `1234` right-justified in a `10` digit field.

    b) Print `123.456789` in exponential notation with a sign (+ or −) and `3` digits of precision.

    c) Read a `double` value into variable `number`.

    d) Print `100` in octal form preceded by `0`.

    e) Read a string into character array `string`.

    f) Read characters into array `n` until a non-digit character is encountered.

    g) Use integer variables `x` and `y` to specify the field width and precision used to display the `double` value `87.4573`.

    h) Read a value of the form `3.5%`. Store the percentage in `float` variable `percent`, and eliminate the `%` from the input stream. Do not use the assignment suppression character.

    i) Print `3.333333` as a `long double` value with a sign (+ or −)in a field of `20` characters with a precision of `3`.

Answers to Self-Review Exercises

9.1   a) Streams. b) Standard input. c) Standard output. d) `printf`. e) Conversion specifiers, flags, field widths, precisions, and literal characters. f) d, i. g) o, u, x (or X). h) h, l. i) e (or E). j) L. k) 6. l) s, c. m) NULL (`'\0'`). n) asterisk (`*`). o) − (minus). p) + (plus). q) `scanf`. r) Scan set. s) i. t) le, lE, lf, lg, or lG. u) Assignment suppression character (`*`). v) Field width.

9.2   a) Error: Conversion specifier `s` expects an argument of type pointer to `char`.

            Correction: To print the character `'c'`, use the conversion specification `%c` or change `'c'` to `"c"`.

    b) Error: Trying to print the literal character `%` without using the conversion specification `%%`.

            Correction: Use `%%` to print a literal `%` character.

    c) Error: Conversion specifier `c` expects an argument of type `char`.

            Correction: To print the first character of `"Monday"` use the conversion specification `%1s`.

    d) Error: Trying to print the literal character `"` without using the `\"` escape sequence.

            Correction: Replace each quote in the inner set of quotes with `\"`.

    e) Error: The format control string is not enclosed in double quotes.

            Correction enclose `%d%d` in double quotes.

    f) Error: The character `x` is enclosed in double quotes.

            Correction: Character constants to be printed with `%c` must be enclosed in single quotes.

g)   Error: The string to be printed is enclosed in single quotes.

        Correction: Use double quotes instead of single quotes to represent a string.

9.3   a) `printf("%10d\n", 1234);`

        b) `printf("%+.3e\n", 123.456789);`

        c) `scanf("%lf", &number);`

        d) `printf("%#o\n", 100);`

        e) `scanf("%s", string);`

        f) `scanf("%[0123456789]", n);`

        g) `printf("%*.*f\n", x, y, 87.4573);`

        h) `scanf("%f%%", &percent);`

        i) `printf("%+20.3Lf\n", 3.333333);`

Exercises

9.4   Write a `printf` or `scanf` statement for each of the following:

    a) Print unsigned integer `40000` left justified in a `15`-digit field with a minimum of `8` digits.

    b) Read a hexadecimal value into variable `hex`.

    c) Print `200` with and without a sign.

    d) Print `100` in hexadecimal form preceded by `0x`.

    e) Read characters into array `s` until the letter `p` is encountered.

    f) Print `1.234` in a `9`-digit field with preceding zeros.

    g) Read a time of the form `hh:mm:ss` storing the parts of the time in the integer variables `hour`, `minute`, and `second`. Skip the `:` characters in the input stream. Use the assignment-suppression character.

    h) Read a string of the form `"characters"` from the standard input. Store the string in character array `s`. Eliminate the quotation marks from the input stream.

    i) Read a time of the form `hh:mm:ss` storing the parts of the time in the integer variables `hour`, `minute`, and `second`. Skip the colons (`:`) in the input stream. Do not use the assignment-suppression character.

9.5   Show what is printed by each of the following statements. If a statement is incorrect, indicate why.

    a) `printf("%-10d\n", 10000);`

    b) `printf("%c\n", "This is a string");`

    c) `printf("%*.*lf\n", 8, 3, 1024.987654);`

    d) `printf("%#o\n%#X\n%#e\n", 17, 17, 1008.83689);`

    e) `printf("% ld\n%+ld\n", 1000000, 1000000);`

    f) `printf("%10.2E\n", 444.93738);`

    g) `printf("%10.2g\n", 444.93738);`

    h) `printf("%d\n", 10.987);`

9.6   Write a program that loads 10-element array `number` with random integers from 1 to 1000. For each value, print the value and a running total of the number of characters printed. Use the `%n` conversion specification to determine the number of characters output for each value. Print the total number of characters output for all values up to and including the current value each time the current value is printed. The output should have the following format:

```
Value        Total characters
 342                3
1000                7
 963               10
   6               11
etc.
```

9.7   Write a program to test the difference between the **%d** and **%i** conversion specifiers when used in **scanf** statements. Use the statements

```
scanf("%i%d", &x, &y);
printf("%d%d\n", x, y);
```

to input and print the values. Test the program with the following sets of input data:

```
  10        10
 -10       -10
 010       010
0x10      0x10
```

9.8   Write a program that prints pointer values using all the integer conversion specifiers and the **%p** conversion specification. Which ones print strange values? Which ones cause errors? In which format does the **%p** conversion specification display the address on your system?

9.9   Write a program to test the results of printing the integer value **12345** and the floating point value **1.2345** in various size fields. What happens when the values are printed in fields containing fewer digits than the values?

9.10   Write a program that prints the value **100.453627** rounded to the nearest digit, tenth, hundredth, thousandth, and ten thousandth.

9.11   Write a program that inputs a string from the keyboard and determines the length of the string. Print the string using twice the length as the field width.

9.12   Write a program that converts integer Fahrenheit temperatures from **0** to **212** degrees to floating point Celsius temperatures with **3** digits of precision. Use the formula

```
celcius = 5.0/9.0 * (fahrenheit - 32);
```

to perform the calculation. The output should be printed in two right-justified columns, and the Celsius temperatures should be preceded by a sign for both positive and negative values.

9.13   Write a program to test all the escape sequences in Fig. 9.16. For the escape sequences that move the cursor, print a character before and after printing the escape sequence so it is clear where the cursor has moved.

9.14   Write a program that determines whether **?** can be printed as part of a **printf** format control string as a literal character rather than using the **\?** escape sequence.

9.15   Write a program that inputs the value **439** using each of the **scanf** integer conversion specifiers. Print each input value using all the integer conversion specifiers.

9.16   Write a program that uses each of the conversion specifiers **e**, **f**, and **g** to input the value **1.2345**. Print the values of each variable to prove that each conversion specifier can be used to input this same value.

9.17   In some programming languages, strings are entered surrounded by either single *or* double quotation marks. Write a program that reads the three strings **suzy**, **"suzy"**, and **'suzy'**. Are the single and double quotes ignored by C or read as part of the string?

10

Structures, Unions, Bit Manipulations, and Enumerations

Objectives

- To be able to create and use structures, unions, and enumerations.
- To be able to pass structures to functions call by value and call by reference.
- To be able to manipulate data with the bitwise operators.
- To be able to create bit fields for storing data compactly.

I could never make out what those damned dots meant.
Winston Churchill

But yet an union in partition;
William Shakespeare

You can include me out.
Samuel Goldwyn

The same old charitable lie
Repeated as the years scoot by
Perpetually makes a hit—
"You really haven't changed a bit!"
Margaret Fishback

Outline

10.1 Introduction

Structures are collections of related variables—sometimes referred to as *aggregates*—under one name. Structures may contain variables of many different data types—in contrast to arrays that contain only elements of the same data type. Structures are commonly used to define records to be stored in files (see Chapter 11, "File Processing). Pointers and structures facilitate the formation of more complex data structures such as linked lists, queues, stacks, and trees (see Chapter 12, "Data Structures").

10.2 Structure Definitions

Structures are *derived data types*—they are constructed using objects of other types. Consider the following structure definition:

```
struct card {
    char *face;
    char *suit;
};
```

The keyword `struct` introduces the structure definition. The identifier `card` is the *structure tag*. The structure tag names the structure definition, and is used with the keyword `struct` to declare variables of the *structure type*. In this example, the structure type is `struct card`. The variables declared in the braces of the structure definition are the structure's *members*. Members of the same structure must have unique names, but two different structures may contain members of the same name without conflict (we will soon see why). Each structure definition must end with a semicolon.

CPE 10.1

Forgetting the semicolon that ends a structure definition.

The definition of `struct card` contains two members of type `char *`—`face` and `suit`. Structure members can be variables of the basic data types (`int`, `float`, etc.), or aggregates, such as arrays and other structures. A structure cannot, however, contain an instance of itself. For example, a variable of type `struct card` cannot be declared in the structure definition for `struct card`. A pointer to `struct card` may be included. A structure containing a member that is a pointer to the same structure type is referred to as a *self-referential structure*. Self-referential structures are discussed in Chapter 12.

The preceding structure definition does not reserve any space in memory, rather the definition creates a new data type that is used to declare variables. Structure variables are declared, like variables of other types. The declaration

```
struct card a, b[52], *c;
```

declares a to be a variable of type `struct card`, declares b to be an array with 52 elements of type `struct card`, and declares c to be a pointer to `struct card`. Variables of a given structure type may also be declared by placing a comma-separated list of the variable names between the closing brace of the structure definition and the semi-colon that ends the structure definition. For example, the preceding declaration could have been incorporated into the `struct card` structure definition as follows:

```
struct card {
   char *face;
   char *suit;
} a, b[52], *c;
```

The structure tag name is optional. If a structure template does not contain a structure tag name, variables of the structure type may be declared only in the structure definition—not in a separate declaration.

GPP 10.1

Always provide a structure tag name when creating a structure type. The structure tag name is convenient for declaring new variables of the structure type later in the program.

GPP 10.2

Choose a meaningful structure tag name. This helps make the program self-documenting.

The only valid operations that may be performed on structures are: assigning structure variables to structure variables of the same type, taking the address (`&`) of a structure variable, and accessing the members of a structure variable (see section 10.4).

CPE 10.2

Assigning a structure of one type to a structure of a different type.

Structures may not be compared because structure members are not necessarily stored in consecutive bytes of memory. Sometimes there are "holes" in a structure because computers may store specific data types only on certain memory boundaries such as halfword, word, or doubleword boundaries. A word is a standard unit used to store data in a computer—usually 2 bytes or 4 bytes. Consider the following structure definition in which the variables `sample1` and `sample2` are declared to be of type `struct example`:

```
struct example {
    char c;
    int i;
} sample1, sample2;
```

A computer with 2-byte words, may require that each of the members of `struct example` be aligned on a word boundary, i.e., at the beginning of a word (this is machine dependent). Fig 10.1 shows a sample storage alignment for a variable of type `struct example` that has been assigned the character `'a'` and the integer 97 (the bit representations of the values are shown). If the members are stored beginning at word boundaries, there is a 1-byte hole (byte 1 in the figure) in the storage for variables of type `struct example`. The value contained in the 1-byte hole is undefined. If the member values of structure variables `sample1` and `sample2` are in fact equal, the structures do not necessarily compare equal because the undefined 1-byte holes are not likely to contain identical values.

CPE 10.3
Comparing structures is a compiler error because of the different alignment requirements on various systems.

10.3 Initializing Structures

Structures can be initialized using initializer lists much like arrays. To initialize a structure, follow the variable name in the structure declaration with an equal sign and a brace-enclosed, comma-separated list of initializers. For example, the declaration

```
struct card a = {"Three", "Hearts"};
```

creates variable a to be of type `struct card` (as defined previously) and initializes member `face` to "Three" and member `suit` to "Hearts". If there are fewer initializers in the list than members in the structure, the remaining members are automati-

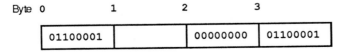

```
Byte  0          1          2          3
     ┌──────────┬──────────┬──────────┬──────────┐
     │ 01100001 │          │ 00000000 │ 01100001 │
     └──────────┴──────────┴──────────┴──────────┘
```

Fig. 10.1 A possible storage alignment for a variable of type `struct example` showing an undefined area in memory.

cally initialized to 0 (or NULL if the member is a pointer). Structure variables declared externally are initialized to 0 or NULL if they are not explicitly initialized in the external declaration. Structure variables may also be initialized in assignment statements by assigning a structure variable of the same type, or by assigning values to the individual members of the structure.

10.4 Accessing Members of Structures

Two operators are used to access members of structures: the *structure member operator* (.)—also called the *dot operator*—and the *structure pointer operator* (->)—also called the *arrow operator*. The structure member operator accesses a structure member via the structure variable name. For example, to print member suit of structure a from the preceding declaration, use the statement

```
printf("%s", a.suit);
```

The structure pointer operator—consisting of a minus (-) sign and a greater than (>) sign with no intervening spaces—accesses a structure member via a pointer to the structure. Assume that the pointer aptr has been declared to point to struct card, and that the address of structure a has been assigned to aptr. To print member suit of structure a with pointer aptr, use the statement

```
printf("%s", aptr->suit);
```

The expression aptr->suit is equivalent to (*aptr).suit which dereferences the pointer and accesses the member suit using the structure member operator. The parentheses are needed here because the structure member operator (.) has a higher precedence than the pointer dereferencing operator (*). The structure pointer operator and structure member operator, along with parentheses and brackets ([ ]) used for array subscripting, have the highest operator precedence and associate from left to right.

GPP 10.3

Avoid using the same names for members of separate structures. This is allowed, but it may cause confusion.

GPP 10.4

Do not put spaces around the -> and . operators. This helps emphasize that the expressions the operators are contained in are essentially single variable names.

CPE 10.4

Inserting space between the - and > components of the structure pointer operator (or inserting spaces between the components of any other multiple keystroke operator except ?:).

CPE 10.5

Forgetting to include the structure variable name when referring to a member of a structure.

CPE 10.6

*Not using parentheses when referring to a structure member using a pointer and the structure member operator (e.g., *aptr.suit).*

The program of Fig 10.2 demonstrates the use of the structure member and structure pointer operators. Using the structure member operator, the members of the structure a are assigned the values "Ace" and "Spades" respectively. Pointer aptr is assigned the address of structure a. A single printf statement prints the members of structure variable a using the structure member operator with variable name a, the structure pointer operator with pointer aptr, and the structure member operator with dereferenced pointer aptr.

10.5 Using Structures with Functions

Structures may be passed to functions by passing individual structure members, by passing an entire structure, or by passing a pointer to a structure. When structures or individual structure members are passed to a function, they are passed call by value. Therefore, the members of a caller's structure cannot be modified by the called function.

To pass a structure call by reference, pass the address of the structure variable. Arrays of structures—like all other arrays—are automatically passed call by reference.

```
/* Using the structure member and structure pointer operators */
#include <stdio.h>

struct card {
    char *face;
    char *suit;
};

main()
{
    struct card a;
    struct card *aptr;

    a.face = "Ace";
    a.suit = "Spades";
    aptr = &a;
    printf("%s%s%s\n%s%s%s\n%s%s%s\n",
            a.face, " of ", a.suit,
            aptr->face, " of ", aptr->suit,
            (*aptr).face, " of ", (*aptr).suit);
}
```

```
Ace of Spades
Ace of Spades
Ace of Spades
```

Fig. 10.2 Using the structure member operator and the structure pointer operator.

In Chapter 6, we stated that an array could be passed call by value using structures. To pass an array call by value, create a structure with the array as a member. Since structures are passed call by value, the array is passed call by value.

CPE 10.7

Assuming that structures, like arrays, are automatically passed simulated call by reference, and trying to modify the caller's structure values in the called function.

PERF 10.1

Passing structures call by reference is more efficient than passing structures call by value (which, of course, requires the entire structure to be copied).

10.6 Typedef

The keyword `typedef` provides a mechanism for creating synonyms for previously defined data types. Names for structure types are often defined with `typedef` to create shorter type names. For example, the statement

```
typedef struct card Card;
```

defines the new type name `Card` as a synonym for type `struct card`.

GPP 10.5

Capitalize `typedef` names to emphasize that these names are synonyms for other variable names.

`Card` can now be used to declare variables of type `struct card`. The declaration

```
Card deck[52];
```

declares an array of 52 `Card` structures (i.e., variables of type `struct card`). Creating a new name with `typedef` does not create a new type; `typedef` simply creates a new type name. A meaningful name helps make the program self documenting. For example, when we read the previous declaration, we know "`deck` is an array of 52 `Card`s."

Often, `typedef` is used to create synonyms for the basic data types. For example, a program requiring 4-byte integers may require type `int` on one system and type `long` on another. A new type name can be created with `typedef`, such as `Integer`, that can be changed once in the program to make the program work on both systems.

PORT 10.1

Use `typedef` to help make a program more portable.

10.7 Example: High-Performance Card Shuffling and Dealing Simulation

The program in Fig. 10.3 is based on the card shuffling and dealing simulation discussed in Chapter 7. The program represents the deck of cards as an array of structures. The program uses a high-performance shuffling algorithm (see Exercise 7.16). The output is shown in Fig. 10.4.

CPE 10.8

Forgetting to include the array subscript when referring to individual structures in an array of structures.

```
/* The card shuffling and dealing program using structures */
#include <stdio.h>
#include <stdlib.h>
#include <time.h>

struct card {
    char *face;
    char *suit;
};

typedef struct card Card;

void filldeck(Card *, char *[], char *[]);
void shuffle(Card *);
void deal(Card *);

main()
{
    Card deck[52];
    char *face[] = {"Ace", "Deuce", "Three", "Four", "Five",
                    "Six", "Seven", "Eight", "Nine", "Ten",
                    "Jack", "Queen", "King"};
    char *suit[] = {"Hearts", "Diamonds", "Clubs", "Spades"};

    srand(clock());

    filldeck(deck, face, suit);
    shuffle(deck);
    deal(deck);
}

void filldeck(Card *wdeck, char *wface[], char *wsuit[])
{
    int i;

    for (i = 0; i <= 51; i++) {
        wdeck[i].face = wface[i % 13];
        wdeck[i].suit = wsuit[i / 13];
    }
}
```

Fig. 10.3 The high-performance card shuffling and dealing simulation (part 1 of 2).

```
void shuffle(Card *wdeck)
{
   int i, j;
   Card temp;

   for (i = 0; i <= 51; i++) {
      j = rand() % 52;

      if (i != j) {
         temp = wdeck[i];
         wdeck[i] = wdeck[j];
         wdeck[j] = temp;
      }
   }
}

void deal(Card *wdeck)
{
   int i;

   for (i = 0; i <= 51; i++) {
      printf("%5s of %-8s", wdeck[i].face, wdeck[i].suit);
      (i + 1) % 2 ? putchar('\t') : putchar('\n');
   }
}
```

Fig. 10.3 The high-performance card shuffling and dealing simulation (part 2 of 2).

```
Eight of Diamonds       Ace of Hearts
Eight of Clubs         Five of Spades
Seven of Hearts       Deuce of Diamonds
  Ace of Clubs          Ten of Diamonds
Deuce of Spades         Six of Diamonds
Seven of Spades       Deuce of Clubs
 Jack of Clubs          Ten of Spades
 King of Hearts        Jack of Diamonds
Three of Hearts       Three of Diamonds
Three of Clubs         Nine of Clubs
  Ten of Hearts       Deuce of Hearts
  Ten of Clubs        Seven of Diamonds
  Six of Clubs        Queen of Spades
  Six of Hearts       Three of Spades
 Nine of Diamonds       Ace of Diamonds
 Jack of Spades        Five of Clubs
 King of Diamonds     Seven of Clubs
 Nine of Spades        Four of Hearts
  Six of Spades       Eight of Spades
Queen of Diamonds      Five of Diamonds
  Ace of Spades        Nine of Hearts
 King of Clubs         Five of Hearts
 King of Spades        Four of Diamonds
Queen of Hearts       Eight of Hearts
 Four of Spades        Jack of Hearts
 Four of Clubs        Queen of Clubs
```

Fig. 10.4 Output for the high-performance card shuffling and dealing simulation.

10.8 Unions

A *union* is a derived data type—like a structure—whose members share the same storage space. For different situations in a program, some variables may not be relevant, but other variables are—so why not share the space instead of wasting storage on variables that are not being used. The members of a union can be of any type. The number of bytes used to store a union is at least enough to hold the largest member. In most cases, unions contain two or more data types. Only one member, and thus one data type, can be referenced at a time.

CPE 10.9

If data is stored in a union as one type and referenced as another type the results are implementation dependent. It is the programmer's responsibility to ensure that the data in a union is referenced with the proper data type.

A union is defined with the `union` keyword in the same format as a structure. The union definition

```
union number {
    int x;
    float y;
};
```

indicates that `number` is a `union` type with members `int x` and `float y`. The union definition normally precedes `main` in a program so the definition can be used to declare variables in all the program's functions.

The operations that can be performed on a union are: assigning a union to another union of the same type, taking the address (`&`) of a union, and accessing union members using the structure member operator and the structure pointer operator. Unions may not be compared for the same reasons that structures cannot be compared.

In a declaration, a union may be initialized only with a value of the same type as the first union member. For example, with reference to the preceding union, the declaration

```
union number value = {10};
```

is a valid initialization of union variable `value` because the union is initialized with an `int`, but the following declaration would be invalid:

```
union number value = {1.43};
```

CPE 10.10

Comparing unions is a compiler error because of the different alignment requirements on various systems.

CPE 10.11

Initializing a union in a declaration with a value whose type is different from the type of the union's first member.

PORT 10.2

The amount of storage required to store a union is implementation-dependent.

PORT 10.3

Some unions may not port easily to other computer systems. Whether a union is portable or not often depends on the storage alignment requirements for the union member data types on a given system.

PERF 10.2

Unions conserve storage.

The program in Fig. 10.5 uses the variable `value` of type `union number` to display the value stored in the union as both an `int` and a `float`. The program output is implementation dependent. Note that the program output helps illustrate the fact that the internal representation of `float` is quite different from the representation of `int`.

```
/* An example of a union */
#include <stdio.h>

union number {
    int x;
    float y;
};

main()
{
    union number value;

    value.x = 100;
    printf("%s\n%s\n%s%d\n%s%f\n\n",
            "Put a value in the integer member",
            "and print both members.",
            "int:    ", value.x,
            "float: ", value.y);

    value.y = 100.0;
    printf("%s\n%s\n%s%d\n%s%f\n",
            "Put a value in the floating member",
            "and print both members.",
            "int:    ", value.x,
            "float: ", value.y);
}
```

```
Put a value in the integer member
and print both members.
int:    100
float: 0.000000

Put a value in the floating member
and print both members.
int:    17096
float: 100.000000
```

Fig. 10.5 Printing the value of a union in both member data types.

10.9 Bitwise Operators

All data is represented internally by computers as sequences of bits. Each bit can assume the value 0 or the value 1. On most systems, a sequence of 8 bits forms a byte—the standard storage unit for a variable of type char. Other data types are stored in larger numbers of bytes. The bitwise operators are used to manipulate the bits of integral operands (char, short, int, and long; both signed and unsigned). Unsigned integers are normally used with the bitwise operators.

PORT 10.4

Bitwise manipulations of data are machine dependent.

Note that the bitwise operator discussions in this section show the binary representations of the integer operands. For a detailed explanation of the binary representation see Appendix E, "Number Systems." Note also that the programs in Sections 10.9 and 10.10 were tested on an Apple Macintosh using Think C and on a PC compatible using Turbo C++. Both systems use 16-bit (2-byte) integers. Because of the machine-dependent nature of bitwise manipulations, these programs may not work on your system.

The six bitwise operators are: *bitwise AND (&), bitwise inclusive OR (|), bitwise exclusive OR (^), left shift (<<), right shift (>>),* and *complement (~).* The bitwise AND, bitwise inclusive OR, and bitwise exclusive OR operators compare their two operands bit-by-bit. The bitwise AND operator sets each bit in the result to 1 if the corresponding bit in both operands is 1. The bitwise inclusive OR operator sets each bit in the result to 1 if the corresponding bit in either operand is 1. The bitwise exclusive OR operator sets each bit in the result to 1 if the corresponding bit in only one operand is 1. The left shift operator shifts the bits of its left operand to the left by the number of bits specified in its right operand. The right shift operator shifts the bits in its left operand to the right by the number of bits specified in its right operand. The bitwise complement operator sets all 0 bits in its operand to 1 in the result and sets all 1 bits to 0 in the result. Detailed discussions of each bitwise operator appear in the following examples. The bitwise operators are summarized in Fig. 10.6.

When using the bitwise operators, it is useful to print values in their binary representation to illustrate the results of applying the bitwise operators to the values. The program of Fig. 10.7 prints an unsigned integer in its binary representation in groups of eight bits each.

Function displaybits uses the bitwise AND operator to combine variable value with variable displaymask. Often, the bitwise AND operator is used with an operand called a *mask*. A mask is an integer value with specific bits set to 1. Masks are used to hide some bits in a value while preserving other bits. In function displaybits, mask variable displaymask is assigned the value 1 << 15 (10000000 00000000). The left shift operator shifts the value 1 from the low order (rightmost) bit to the high order (leftmost) bit in displaymask. The statement

Operator		Description
&	bitwise AND	The bits in the result are set to 1 if the corresponding bits in the two operands are both 1.
|	bitwise inclusive OR	The bits in the result are set to 1 if at least one of the corresponding bits in the two operands is 1.
^	bitwise exclusive OR	The bits in the result are set to 1 if only one of the corresponding bits in the two operands is 1.
<<	left shift	Shifts the bits of the first operand left by the number of bits specified by the second operand.
>>	right shift	Shifts the bits of the first operand right by the number of bits specified by the second operand.
~	one's complement	All 0 bits are set to 1 and all 1 bits are set to 0.

Fig 10.6 The bitwise operators.

```
/* Printing an unsigned integer in bits */
#include <stdio.h>

main()
{
    unsigned x;
    void displaybits(unsigned);

    printf("Enter an unsigned integer: ");
    scanf("%u", &x);
    displaybits(x);
}

void displaybits(unsigned value)
{
    unsigned c, displaymask = 1 << 15;

    printf("%7u = ", value);

    for (c = 1; c <= 16; c++) {
        value & displaymask ? putchar('1') : putchar('0');
        value <<= 1;

        if (c % 8 == 0)
            putchar(' ');
    }

    putchar('\n');
}
```

```
Enter an unsigned integer: 65000
    65000 = 11111101 11101000
```

Fig. 10.7 Printing an unsigned integer in bits.

```
value & displaybits ? putchar('1') : putchar('0');
```

determines whether a 1 or a 0 should be printed for the current leftmost bit of variable `value`. Assume variable `value` contains `65000` (`11111101 11101000`). When `value` and `displaymask` are combined using `&`, all the bits except the high order bit in variable `value` are "masked off" (hidden). If the leftmost bit is 1, `value & displaymask` evaluates to 1, and 1 is printed—otherwise, 0 is printed. Variable `value` is then left shifted 1 bit by the expression `value <<= 1` (this is equivalent to `value = value << 1`). These steps are repeated for each bit in `unsigned` variable `value`. Fig 10.8 summarizes the results of combining two bits with the bitwise AND operator.

CPE 10.12

Using the logical AND operator (&&) for the bitwise AND operator (&) and vice versa.

The program of Fig. 10.9 demonstrates the use of the bitwise AND operator, the bitwise inclusive OR operator, the bitwise exclusive OR operator, and the bitwise complement operator. The program uses function `displaybits` to print the unsigned integer values.

In Fig. 10.9, integer variable `mask` is assigned the value 1 (`00000000 00000001`), and variable `number1` is assigned value `65535` (`11111111 11111111`). When `mask` and `number1` are combined using the bitwise AND operator (`&`) in the expression `number1 & mask`, the result is `00000000 00000001`. All the bits except the low order bit in variable `number1` were "masked off" (hidden) by "ANDing" with variable `mask`.

The bitwise inclusive OR operator is used to set specific bits to 1 in an operand. In Fig. 10.9, variable `number1` is assigned 15 (`00000000 00001111`), and variable `setbits` is assigned `240` (`00000000 11110000`). When `number1` and `setbits` are combined using the bitwise OR operator in the expression `number1 | setbits`, the result is `255` (`00000000 11111111`). Figure 10.11 summarizes the results of combining two bits with the bitwise inclusive OR operator.

CPE 10.13

Using the logical OR operator (||) for the bitwise OR operator (|) and vice versa.

Bit 1	Bit 2	Bit 1 & Bit 2
0	0	0
1	0	0
0	1	0
1	1	1

Fig 10.8 Results of combining two bits with the bitwise AND operator &.

```c
/* Using the bitwise AND, bitwise inclusive OR, bitwise
   exclusive OR, and bitwise complement operators */
#include <stdio.h>

main()
{
    unsigned number1, number2, mask, setbits;
    void displaybits(unsigned);

    number1 = 65535;
    mask = 1;
    printf("The result of combining the following\n");
    displaybits(number1);
    displaybits(mask);
    printf("using the bitwise AND operator & is\n");
    displaybits(number1 & mask);

    number1 = 15;
    setbits = 240;
    printf("\nThe result of combining the following\n");
    displaybits(number1);
    displaybits(setbits);
    printf("using the bitwise inclusive OR operator | is\n");
    displaybits(number1 | setbits);

    number1 = 131;
    number2 = 199;
    printf("\nThe result of combining the following\n");
    displaybits(number1);
    displaybits(number2);
    printf("using the bitwise exclusive OR operator ^ is\n");
    displaybits(number1 ^ number2);

    number1 = 21845;
    printf("\nThe one's complement of\n");
    displaybits(number1);
    printf("is\n");
    displaybits(~number1);
}

void displaybits(unsigned value)
{
    unsigned c, displaymask = 1 << 15;

    printf("%7u = ", value);

    for (c = 1; c <= 16; c++) {
        value & displaymask ? putchar('1') : putchar('0');
        value <<= 1;

        if (c % 8 == 0)
            putchar(' ');
    }

    putchar('\n');
}
```

Fig. 10.9 Using the bitwise AND, bitwise inclusive OR, bitwise exclusive OR, and bitwise complement operators.

```
The result of combining the following
   65535 = 11111111 11111111
       1 = 00000000 00000001
using the bitwise AND operator & is
       1 = 00000000 00000001

The result of combining the following
      15 = 00000000 00001111
     240 = 00000000 11110000
using the bitwise inclusive OR operator | is
     255 = 00000000 11111111

The result of combining the following
     131 = 00000000 10000011
     199 = 00000000 11000111
using the bitwise exclusive OR operator ^ is
      68 = 00000000 01000100

The one's complement of
   21845 = 01010101 01010101
is
   43690 = 10101010 10101010
```

Fig. 10.10 Ouput for the program of Fig. 10.9.

Bit 1	Bit 2	Bit 1 | Bit 2
0	0	0
1	0	1
0	1	1
1	1	1

Fig 10.11 Results of combining two bits with the bitwise inclusive OR operator |.

The bitwise exclusive OR operator (^) sets each bit in the result to 1 if *only* one of the corresponding bits in its two operands is 1. In Fig. 10.9, variables number1 and number2 are assigned the values 131 (00000000 10000011) and 199 (00000000 11000111) respectively. When these variables are combined with the exclusive OR operator in the expression number1 ^ number2, the result is 00000000 01000100. Figure 10.12 summarizes the results of combining two bits with the bitwise exclusive OR operator.

Bit 1	Bit 2	Bit 1 ^ Bit 2
0	0	0
1	0	1
0	1	1
1	1	0

Fig 10.12 Results of combining two bits with the bitwise exclusive OR operator ^.

The *bitw*ise complement operator (~) sets all 1 bits in its operand to 0 in the result and sets all 0 bits to 1 in the result—otherwise referred to as "taking the *one's complement* of the value." In Fig. 10.9, variable `number1` is assigned the value `21845` (01010101 01010101). When the expression `~number1` is evaluated, the result is (10101010 10101010).

The program of Fig 10.13 demonstrates the left shift operator (<<) and the right shift operator (>>). Function `displaybits` is used to print the `unsigned` integer values.

The left shift operator (<<) shifts the bits of its left operand to the left by the number of bits specified in its right operand. Bits vacated to the right are replaced with 0s; 1s shifted off the left are lost. In the program of Fig. 10.13, variable `number1` is assigned the value `960` (00000011 11000000). The result of left shifting variable `number1` 8 bits in the expression `number1 << 8` is `49152` (11000000 00000000).

The right shift operator (>>) shifts the bits of its left operand to the right by the number of bits specified in its right operand. Performing a right shift on an `unsigned` integer causes the vacated bits at the left to be replaced by 0s; 1s shifted off the right are lost. In the program of Fig. 10.13, the result of right shifting `number1` in the expression `number1 >> 8` is `3` (00000000 00000011). The result of shifting a value is undefined if the right operand is negative, or if the right operand is larger than the number of bits in which the left operand is stored. Fig 10.15 summarizes the bitwise operators.

PORT 10.5
───
Right shifting is particularly machine dependent. Right shifting a signed integer fills the vacated bits with 0s on some machines and 1s on others.

Each bitwise operator (except the bitwise complement operator) has a corresponding assignment operator. The bitwise assignment operators are shown in Fig. 10.14.

```
/* Using the bitwise shift operators */
#include <stdio.h>

main()
{
    unsigned number1 = 960;
    void displaybits(unsigned);

    printf("\nThe result of left shifting\n");
    displaybits(number1);
    printf("8 bit positions using the left shift operator << is\n");
    displaybits(number1 << 8);

    printf("\nThe result of right shifting\n");
    displaybits(number1);
    printf("8 bit positions using the right shift operator >> is\n");
    displaybits(number1 >> 8);
}

void displaybits(unsigned value)
{
    unsigned c, displaymask = 1 << 15;

    printf("%7u = ", value);

    for (c = 1; c <= 16; c++) {
        value & displaymask ? putchar('1') : putchar('0');
        value <<= 1;

        if (c % 8 == 0)
            putchar(' ');
    }

    putchar('\n');
}
```

```
The result of left shifting
    960 = 00000011 11000000
8 bit positions using the left shift operator << is
  49152 = 11000000 00000000

The result of right shifting
    960 = 00000011 11000000
8 bit positions using the right shift operator >> is
      3 = 00000000 00000011
```

Fig. 10.13 Using the bitwise shift operators.

Figure 10.15 shows the precedence and associativity of the various operators introduced up to this point in the text. They are shown from top to bottom in decreasing order of precedence.

Bitwise assignment operators	
&=	Bitwise AND assignment operator.
|=	Bitwise inclusive OR assignment operator.
^=	Bitwise exclusive OR assignment operator.
<<=	Left shift assignment operator.
>>=	Right shift assignment operator.

Fig 10.14 The bitwise assignment operators.

Operator	Associativity
() [] . ->	left to right
++ -- ! (*type*) & *	right to left
* / %	left to right
+ -	left to right
<< >>	left to right
< <= > >=	left to right
== !=	left to right
&	left to right
^	left to right
|	left to right
&&	left to right
||	left to right
?:	right to left
= += -= *= /= %= &= != ^= <<= >>=	right to left
	left to right

Fig. 10.15 Operator precedence and associativity.

10.10 Bit Fields

C provides the ability to specify the number of bits in which an `unsigned` or `int` member of a structure or union is stored—referred to as a *bit field*. Bit fields enable better memory utilization by storing data in the minimum number of bits required. Bit field members *must* be declared as `int` or `unsigned`.

__PERF 10.3__

Bit fields help conserve storage.

Consider the following structure definition:

```
struct bitcard {
    unsigned face : 4;
    unsigned suit : 2;
    unsigned color : 1;
};
```

The definition contains three unsigned bit fields—face, suit, and color—used to store a card from a deck of 52 cards. A bit field is declared by following an unsigned or int member name with a colon (:) and an integer constant representing the *width* of the field, i.e., the number of bits in which the member is stored. The constant representing the width must be an integer between 0 and the total number of bits used to store an int variable on your system. Since our examples were tested on a computer with 2-byte (16 bit) integers, the valid width values are 0 to 16.

The preceding structure definition indicates that member face is stored in 4 bits, member suit is stored in 3 bits, and member color is stored in 1 bit. The number of bits is based on the maximum value for each structure member. Member face stores values between 0 (Ace) and 12 (King)—4 bits can store a value between 0 and 15. Member suit stores values between 0 and 3 (0 = Diamonds, 1 = Hearts, 2 = Clubs, 3 = Spades)—2 bits can store a value between 0 and 3. Finally, member color stores either 0 (Red) or 1 (Black)—1 bit can store either 0 or 1.

The program in Fig. 10.16 creates array deck in which 52 structures of type struct bitcard are stored. Function filldeck inserts the 52 cards in the deck array, and function deal prints the values of the 52 cards. Notice that bit field members of structures are accessed exactly as any other structure member. The member color has been included as a means of indicating the card color on a system that allows color displays.

It is possible to specify a bit field without a name in which case the field is used as *padding* in the structure. For example, the structure definition

```
struct example {
    unsigned a : 13;
    unsigned   : 3;
    unsigned b : 4;
};
```

uses an unnamed 3-bit field as padding—nothing can be stored in those three bits. Member b is stored in another storage unit.

An unnamed bit field with a zero width is used to align the next bit field on a new storage unit boundary. For example, the structure definition

```
struct example {
    unsigned a : 13;
    unsigned   : 0;
    unsigned b : 4;
};
```

uses an unnamed 0-bit field to skip the remaining bits of the storage unit in which member a is stored, and align member b on the next storage unit boundary.

PORT 10.6

Bit field manipulations are machine dependent. For example, some computers allow bit fields to cross word boundaries, whereas others do not.

CPE 10.14

Attempting to access individual bits of a bit field as if they were elements of an array. Bit fields are not "arrays of bits."

CPE 10.15

Attempting to take the address of a bit field (the & operator may not be used with bit fields because they do not have addresses).

```c
/* Example using a bit field */
#include <stdio.h>

struct bitcard {
   unsigned face : 4;
   unsigned suit : 2;
   unsigned color : 1;
};

typedef struct bitcard Card;

main()
{
   Card deck[52];
   void filldeck(Card *);
   void deal(Card *);

   filldeck(deck);
   deal(deck);
}

void filldeck(Card *wdeck)
{
   int i, j;

   for (i = 0, j = 1; i <= 51; i++, j++) {

      if (i % 13 == 0)
         j = 0;

      wdeck[i].face = j;
      wdeck[i].suit = i / 13;
      wdeck[i].color = i / 26;
   }
}

void deal(Card *wdeck2)
{
   int k1, k2;

   for (k1 = 0; k1 <= 25; k1++) {
      printf("Card:%3d  Suit:%2d  Color:%2d\t",
            wdeck2[k1].face, wdeck2[k1].suit, wdeck2[k1].color);
      k2 = k1 + 26;
      printf("Card:%3d  Suit:%2d  Color:%2d\n",
            wdeck2[k2].face, wdeck2[k2].suit, wdeck2[k2].color);
   }
}
```

Fig. 10.16 Using bit fields to store a deck of cards.

```
Card:  0  Suit: 1  Color: 0      Card:  0  Suit: 3  Color: 1
Card:  1  Suit: 1  Color: 0      Card:  1  Suit: 3  Color: 1
Card:  2  Suit: 1  Color: 0      Card:  2  Suit: 3  Color: 1
Card:  3  Suit: 1  Color: 0      Card:  3  Suit: 3  Color: 1
Card:  4  Suit: 1  Color: 0      Card:  4  Suit: 3  Color: 1
Card:  5  Suit: 1  Color: 0      Card:  5  Suit: 3  Color: 1
Card:  6  Suit: 1  Color: 0      Card:  6  Suit: 3  Color: 1
Card:  7  Suit: 1  Color: 0      Card:  7  Suit: 3  Color: 1
Card:  8  Suit: 1  Color: 0      Card:  8  Suit: 3  Color: 1
Card:  9  Suit: 1  Color: 0      Card:  9  Suit: 3  Color: 1
Card: 10  Suit: 1  Color: 0      Card: 10  Suit: 3  Color: 1
Card: 11  Suit: 1  Color: 0      Card: 11  Suit: 3  Color: 1
Card: 12  Suit: 1  Color: 0      Card: 12  Suit: 3  Color: 1
Card:  0  Suit: 2  Color: 0      Card:  0  Suit: 4  Color: 1
Card:  1  Suit: 2  Color: 0      Card:  1  Suit: 4  Color: 1
Card:  2  Suit: 2  Color: 0      Card:  2  Suit: 4  Color: 1
Card:  3  Suit: 2  Color: 0      Card:  3  Suit: 4  Color: 1
Card:  4  Suit: 2  Color: 0      Card:  4  Suit: 4  Color: 1
Card:  5  Suit: 2  Color: 0      Card:  5  Suit: 4  Color: 1
Card:  6  Suit: 2  Color: 0      Card:  6  Suit: 4  Color: 1
Card:  7  Suit: 2  Color: 0      Card:  7  Suit: 4  Color: 1
Card:  8  Suit: 2  Color: 0      Card:  8  Suit: 4  Color: 1
Card:  9  Suit: 2  Color: 0      Card:  9  Suit: 4  Color: 1
Card: 10  Suit: 2  Color: 0      Card: 10  Suit: 4  Color: 1
Card: 11  Suit: 2  Color: 0      Card: 11  Suit: 4  Color: 1
Card: 12  Suit: 2  Color: 0      Card: 12  Suit: 4  Color: 1
```

Fig. 10.17 Output of the program in Fig. 10.16.

10.10 Enumeration Constants

C provides one final user-defined type called an *enumeration constant*. An enumeration constant, introduced by the keyword `enum`, is a set of integer constants represented by identifiers. Enumeration constants are, in effect, symbolic constants whose values can be set automatically. The values in an `enum` start with 0, unless specified otherwise, and are incremented by 1. For example, the enumeration constant

```
enum months {JAN, FEB, MAR, APR, MAY, JUN, JUL, AUG, SEP, OCT,
             NOV, DEC};
```

creates a new type, `enum months`, in which the identifiers are set automatically to the integers 0 to 11. To number the months 1 to 12, use the following enumeration:

```
enum months {JAN = 1, FEB, MAR, APR, MAY, JUN, JUL, AUG, SEP,
             OCT, NOV, DEC};
```

Since the first value in the preceding enumeration is explicitly set to 1, the remaining values are incremented from 1 resulting in the values 1 through 12. The identifiers in the enumeration constant must be unique. The value of each member of an enumeration constant can be set explicitly in the definition by assigning a value to the identifier. Multiple members of an enumeration constant can have the same value. In the program of Fig. 10.18, the enumeration variable `month` is used in a `for` structure to print the months of the year from the array `monthname`.

CPE 10.16

Assigning a value to an enumeration constant after it has been defined.

GPP 10.6

Use only uppercase letters in the names of enumeration constants. This makes these constants stand out in a program, and reminds the programmer that enumeration constants are not variables.

Summary

- Structures are collections of related variables, sometimes referred to as aggregates, under one name.

- Structures can contain variables of different data types.

```
/* Using an enumeration type */
#include <stdio.h>

enum months {JAN = 1, FEB, MAR, APR, MAY, JUN,
             JUL, AUG, SEP, OCT, NOV, DEC};

main()
{
   enum months   month;
   char *monthname[] = {"", "January", "February", "March",
                        "April", "May", "June", "July",
                        "August", "September", "October",
                        "November", "December"};

   for (month = JAN; month <= DEC; month++)
      printf("%2d%11s\n", month, monthname[month]);
}
```

```
 1    January
 2   February
 3      March
 4      April
 5        May
 6       June
 7       July
 8     August
 9  September
10    October
11   November
12   December
```

Fig. 10.18 Using an enumeration.

- The keyword `struct` begins every structure definition. Within the braces of the structure definition are the structure member declarations.

- Members of the same structure must have unique names.

- A structure definition creates a new data type that can be used to declare variables.

- There are two methods for declaring structure variables. The first method is to declare the variables in a declaration as is done with variables of other data types using `struct tagname` as the type. The second method is to include the variables between the closing brace of the structure definition and the semi-colon that ends the structure definition.

- The tag name of the structure is optional. If the structure is defined without a tag name, the variables of the derived data type must be declared in the structure definition, and no other variables of the new structure type can be declared.

- A structure can be initialized with an initializer list by following the variable name in the structure declaration with an equal sign and a comma-separated list of initializers enclosed in braces. If there are fewer initializers in the list than members in the structure, the remaining members are automatically initialized to zero (or NULL if the member is a pointer).

- Entire structures may be assigned to structure variables of the same type.

- A structure variable may be initialized by assigning a structure variable of the same type.

- The structure member operator is used when accessing a member of a structure via the structure variable name.

- The structure pointer operator—created with a minus (–) sign and a greater than (>) sign—is used when accessing a member of a structure via a pointer to the structure.

- When structures or individual members of structures are passed to a function, they are passed call by value.

- To pass a structure call by reference, pass the address of the structure variable.

- An array of structures is automatically passed call by reference.

- To pass an array call by value, create a structure with the array as a member.

- Creating a new name with `typedef` does not create a new type; it creates a name that is synonymous to a type defined previously.

- A union is a derived data type whose members share the same storage space. The members can be any type.

- The storage reserved for a union is large enough to store its largest member. In most cases, unions contain two or more data types. Only one member, and thus one data type, can be referenced at a time.

- A union is declared with the `union` keyword in the same format as a structure.

- In a declaration, a union can be initialized only with a value of the type of its first member.

- The bitwise AND operator & takes two integral operands. A bit in the result is set to 1 if the corresponding bits in each of the operands are 1.

- Masks are used to hide some bits while preserving others.

- The bitwise inclusive OR operator | takes two operands. A bit in the result is set to 1 if the corresponding bit in either operand is set to 1.

- Each of the bitwise operators (except the unary bitwise complement operator) has a corresponding assignment operator.

- The bitwise exclusive OR operator ^ takes two operands. A bit in the result is set to 1 if only one of the corresponding bits in the two operands is set to 1.

- The left shift operator << shifts the bits of its left operand left by the number of bits specified by its right operand. Bits vacated to the right are replaced with 0s.

- The right shift operator >> shifts the bits of its left operand right by the number of bits specified in its right operand. Performing a right shift on an unsigned integer causes bits vacated at the left to be replaced by 0s. Vacated bits in signed integers can be replaced with 0s or 1s—this is machine dependent.

- The bitwise complement operator ~ takes one operand and reverses its bits—this produces the one's complement of the operand.

- Bit fields reduce storage use by storing data in the minimum number of bits required.

- Bit field members must be declared as int or unsigned.

- A bit field is declared by following an unsigned or int member name with a colon and the width of the bit field.

- The bit field width must be an integer constant between 0 and the total number of bits used to store an int variable on your system

- If a bit field is specified without a name the field is used as padding in the structure.

- An unnamed bit field with width 0 is used to align the next bit field on a new machine word boundary.

- An enumeration, designated by the keyword enum, is a set of integers that are represented by identifiers. The values in an enum start with 0 unless specified otherwise, and are always incremented by 1.

Terminology

^ bitwise exclusive OR operator
^= bitwise exclusive OR assignment operator
~ one's complement operator
& bitwise AND operator
&= bitwise AND assignment operator
| bitwise inclusive OR operator

|= bitwise inclusive OR assignment operator
<< left shift operator
<<= left shift assignment operator
>> right shift operator
>>= right shift assignment operator
accessing members of structures

aggregates	right shift
array of structures	self-referential structure
bit field	shifting
bitwise operators	**struct**
complementing	structure assignment
derived type	structure definition
enumeration	structure elements
initialization of structures	structure initialization
left shift	structure member (dot) operator (.)
mask	structure name
masking off bits	structure pointer (arrow) operator (->)
member	structure tag
member name	structure template
nested structures	structure type
ones complement	tag name
padding	**typedef**
pointer to a structure	**union**
programmer-defined data types	width of a bit field
record	

Common Programming Errors

10.1   Forgetting the semicolon that ends a structure definition.

10.2   Assigning a structure of one type to a structure of a different type.

10.3   Comparing structures is a compiler error because of the different alignment requirements on various systems.

10.4   Inserting space between the – and > components of the structure pointer operator (or inserting spaces between the components of any other multiple keystroke operator except **?: **).

10.5   Forgetting to include the structure variable name when referring to a member of a structure.

10.6   Not using parentheses when referring to a structure member using a pointer and the structure member operator (e.g., ***aptr.suit**).

10.7   Assuming that structures, like arrays, are automatically passed simulated call by reference, and trying to modify the caller's structure values in the called function.

10.8   Forgetting to include the array subscript when referring to individual structures in an array of structures.

10.9   If data is stored in a union as one type and referenced as another type the results are implementation dependent. It is the programmer's responsibility to ensure that the data in a union is referenced with the proper data type.

10.10 Comparing unions is a compiler error because of the different alignment requirements on various systems.

10.11 Initializing a union in a declaration with a value whose type is different from the type of the union's first member.

10.12 Using the logical AND operator (`&&`) for the bitwise AND operator (`&`) and vice versa.

10.13 Using the logical OR operator (`||`) for the bitwise OR operator (`|`) and vice versa.

10.14 Attempting to access individual bits of a bit field as if they were elements of an array. Bit fields are not "arrays of bits."

10.15 Attempting to take the address of a bit field (the `&` operator may not be used with bit fields because they do not have addresses).

10.16 Assigning a value to an enumeration constant after it has been defined.

Good Programming Practices

10.1 Always provide a structure tag name when creating a structure type. The structure tag name is convenient for declaring new variables of the structure type later in the program.

10.2 Choose a meaningful structure tag name. This helps make the program self-documenting.

10.3 Avoid using the same names for members of separate structures. This is allowed, it may cause confusion.

10.4 Do not put spaces around the `->` and `.` operators. This helps emphasize that the expressions the operators are contained in are essentially single variable names.

10.5 Capitalize `typedef` names to emphasize that these names are synonyms for other variable names.

10.6 Use only uppercase letters in the names of enumeration constants. This makes these constants stand out in a program, and reminds the programmer that enumeration constants are not variables.

Portability Tips

10.1 Use `typedef` to help make a program more portable.

10.2 The amount of storage required to store a union is implementation-dependent.

10.3 Some unions may not port easily to other computer systems. Whether a union is portable or not often depends on the storage alignment requirements for the union member data types on a given system.

10.4 Bitwise manipulations of data are machine dependent.

10.5 Right shifting is particularly machine dependent. Right shifting a signed integer fills the vacated bits with `0`s on some machines and `1`s on others.

10.6 Bit field manipulations are machine dependent. Fields may be assigned either left-to-right or right-to-left depending on the computer. Also, some computers allow bit fields to cross word boundaries, whereas others do not.

Performance Tips

10.1   Passing structures call by reference is more efficient than passing structures call by value (which, of course, requires the entire structure to be copied).

10.2   Unions conserve storage.

10.3   Bit fields help conserve storage.

Self-Review Exercises

10.1   Fill in the blanks in each of the following:
- a)   A _____ is a collection of related variables under one name.
- b)   A _____ is a collection of variables under one name in which the variables share the same storage.
- c)   The bits in the result of an expression using the _____ operator are set to 1 if the corresponding bits in each operand are set to 1. Otherwise, the bits are set to zero.
- d)   The variables declared in a structure definition are called its _____ .
- e)   The bits in the result of an expression using the _____ operator are set to 1 if at least one of the corresponding bits in either operand is set to 1. Otherwise, the bits are set to zero.
- f)   The keyword _____ introduces a structure definition.
- g)   The keyword _____ is used to create a synonym for a previously defined data type.
- h)   The bits in the result of an expression using the _____ operator are set to 1 if only one of the corresponding bits in either operand is set to 1. Otherwise, the bits are set to zero.
- i)   The bitwise AND operator **&** is often used to _____ bits, that is to select certain bits from a bit string while zeroing others.
- j)   The _____ keyword is used to introduce a union definition.
- k)   The name of the structure is referred to as the structure _____ .
- l)   A structure member is accessed with either the _____ operator or the _____ operator.
- m)   The _____ and _____ operators are used to shift the bits of a value to the left or to the right, respectively.
- n)   An _____ is a set of integers represented by identifiers.

10.2   State whether each of the following is true or false. If false, explain why.
- a)   Structures may contain only one data type.
- b)   Two unions can be compared to determine if they are equal.
- c)   The tag name of a structure is optional.
- d)   The members of different structures must have unique names.
- e)   The keyword **typedef** is used to define new data types.
- f)   Structures are always passed to functions call by reference.
- g)   Structures may not be compared.

10.3   Write a single statement or a set of statements to accomplish each of the following:
- a)   Define a structure called **part** containing **int** variable **partnumber**, and **char** array **partname** whose values may be as long as 25 characters.
- b)   Define **Part** to be a synonym for the type **struct part**.

c) Use **Part** to declare variable **a** to be of type **struct part**, array **b[10]** to be of type **struct part**, and variable **ptr** to be of type pointer to **struct part**.

d) Read a part number and a part name from the keyboard into the individual members of variable **a**.

e) Assign the member values of variable a to element 3 of array b.

f) Assign the address of array b to the pointer variable ptr.

g) Print the member values of element 3 of array b using the variable ptr and the structure pointer operator to refer to the members.

10.4   Find the error in each of the following:

a) Assume that **struct card** has been defined containing two pointers to type char, namely **face** and **suit**. Also, the variable **c** has been declared to be of type **struct card** and the variable **cptr** has been declared to be of type pointer to **struct card**. Variable **cptr** has been assigned the address of **c**.

```
printf("%s\n", *cptr->face);
```

b) Assume that **struct card** has been defined containing two pointers to type char, namely **face** and **suit**. Also, the array **hearts[13]** has been declared to be of type **struct card**. The following statement should print the member **face** of element 10 of the array.

```
printf("%s\n", hearts.face);
```

c)
```
union values {
    char w;
    float x;
    double y;
} v = {1.27};
```

d)
```
struct person {
    char lastname[15];
    char firstname[15];
    int age;
}
```

e) Assume **struct person** has been defined as in part (d) but with the appropriate correction.

```
person d;
```

f) Assume variable **p** has been declared as type **struct person**, and variable **c** has been declared as type **struct card**.

```
p = c;
```

Answers to Self-Review Exercises

10.1   a) structure. b) union. c) bitwise AND (**&**). d) members. e) bitwise inclusive OR (**!**). f) **struct**. g) **typedef**. h) bitwise exclusive OR (**^**). i) mask. j) **union**. k) tag. l) structure member, structure pointer. m) left shift operator (**<<**), right shift operator (**>>**). n) enumeration.

10.2   a) False. A structure can contain many data types.

b) False. Unions can not be compared, because of alignment problems.

c) True.

d) False. The members of separate structures can have the same names, but the members of the same structure must have unique names.

e) False. The keyword **typedef** is used to define new names (synonyms) for previously defined data types.

f) False. Structures are always passed to functions call by value.

g) True, because of alignment problems.

10.3 a) ```
struct part {
     int partnumber;
     char partname[25];
};
```
  b) `typedef struct part Part;`
  c) `Part a, b[10], *ptr;`
  d) `scanf("%d%s", &a.partnumber, &a.partname};`
  e) `b[3] = a;`
  f) `ptr = b;`
  g) `printf("%d %s\n", (ptr + 3)->partnumber, (ptr + 3)->partname);`

**10.4**  a) Error: The parentheses that should enclose **\*cptr** have been omitted causing the order of evaluation of the expression to be incorrect.

b) Error: The array subscript has been omitted. The expression should be **hearts[10].face**.

c) Error: A union can only be initialized with a value that has the same type as the union's first member.

d) Error: A semicolon is required to end a structure definition.

e) Error: The **struct** keyword was omitted from the variable declaration.

f) Error: Variables of different structure types cannot be assigned to one another.

## Exercises

**10.5**    Provide the definition for each of the following structures and unions:
  a) Structure **inventory** containing character array **partname[30]**, integer **partnumber**, **float price**, integer **stock**, and integer **reorder**.
  b) Union **data** containing **char c, short s, long l, float f**, and **double d**.
  c) Structure **address** containing character arrays **streetaddress[25]**, **city[20], state[3]**, and **zipcode[6]**.
  d) Structure **student** containing character arrays **firstname[15]** and **lastname[15]**, and variable **homeaddress** of type **struct address** from part (c).
  e) Structure **test** containing 16 bit fields with widths of 1 bit. The names of the bit fields are the letters **a** to **p**.
```

10.6   Given the following structure definitions and variable declarations,

```
struct customer {
    char lastname[15];
    char firstname[15];
    int customernumber;
    struct {
        char phonenumber[11];
        char address[50];
        char city[15];
        char state[3];
        char zipcode[6];
    } personal;
} customerrecord, *customerptr;

customerptr = &customerrecord;
```

write separate expressions that can be used to access each of the following.

a)   Member `lastname` of `customerrecord`.
b)   Member `lastname` of the structure pointed to by `customerptr`.
c)   Member `firstname` of `customerrecord`.
d)   Member `firstname` of the structure pointed to by `customerptr`.
e)   Member `customernumber` of `customerrecord`.
f)   Member `customernumber` of the structure pointed to by `customerptr`.
g)   Member `phonenumber` of member `personal` of `customerrecord`.
h)   Member `phonenumber` of member `personal` of the structure pointed to by `customerptr`.
i)   Member `address` of member `personal` of `customerrecord`.
j)   Member `address` of member `personal` of the structure pointed to by `customerptr`.
k)   Member `city` of member `personal` of `customerrecord`.
l)   Member `city` of member `personal` of the structure pointed to by `customerptr`.
m)   Member `state` of member `personal` of `customerrecord`.
n)   Member `state` of member `personal` of the structure pointed to by `customerptr`.
o)   Member `zipcode` of member `personal` of `customerrecord`.
p)   Member `zipcode` of member `personal` of the structure pointed to by `customerptr`.

10.7   Modify the program of Fig. 10.16 to shuffle the cards using a high performance shuffle (as shown in Fig. 10.3). Print the resulting deck in two column format as in Fig. 10.4. Precede each card with its color.

10.8   Create union `integer` with members `char c`, `short s`, `int i`, and `long l`. Write a program that inputs value of type `char`, `short`, `int` and `long`, and stores the values in union variables of type `union integer`. Each union variable should be printed as a `char`, a `short`, an `int`, and a `long`. Do the values always print correctly?

10.9   Create union `floatingpoint` with members `float f`, `double d`, and `long double l`. Write a program like the one described in Exercise 10.8. Do the values print correctly?

10.10 Write a program that right shifts an integer variable 4 bits. The program should print the integer in bits before and after the shift operation. Does your system place 0s or 1s in the vacated bits.

10.11 If your computer uses 4-byte integers, modify the program of Fig. 10.7 so that it works with 4-byte integers.

10.12 Left shifting an **unsigned** integer by 1 bit is equivalent to multiplying the value 2. Write function **power2** that takes two integer arguments **number** and **pow**, and calculates

number * 2^{pow}

Use the shift operator to calculate the result. The program should print the values as integers and as bits.

10.13 The left shift operator can be used to pack two characters into a 2-byte unsigned integer variable. Write a program that inputs two characters from the user and passes them to function **packcharacters**. To pack two characters into an **unsigned** integer variable, assign the first character to the **unsigned** variable, shift the **unsigned** variable left by 8 bit positions, and combine the **unsigned** variable with the second character using the bitwise inclusive OR operator. The program should print the characters in their bit format before and after they are packed into the **unsigned** integer to prove that the characters are in fact packed correctly.

10.14 Using the right shift operator, the bitwise AND operator, and a mask, write function **unpackcharacters** that takes the **unsigned** integer from Exercise 10.13 and unpacks it into two characters. To unpack two characters from an **unsigned** 2-byte integer, combine the unsigned integer with the mask **32768 (11111111 00000000)** and right shift the result 8 bits. Assign the resulting value to a **char** variable. Then combine the **unsigned** integer with the mask **255 (00000000 11111111)**. Assign the result to another **char** variable. The program should print the **unsigned** integer in bits before it is unpacked, then print the characters in bits to confirm that they were unpacked correctly.

10.15 If your system uses 4-byte integers, rewrite the program of Exercise 10.13 to pack 4 characters.

10.16 If your system uses 4-byte integers, rewrite the program of Exercise 10.14 to unpack 4 characters. Create the masks you need to unpack the 4 characters by left shifting the value 255 in the mask variable by 8 bits 0, 1, 2, or 3 times (depending on the byte you are unpacking).

10.17 Write a program that reverses the order of the bits in an unsigned integer value. The program should input the value from the user and call function **reversebits** to print the bits in reverse order. Print the value in bits both before and after the bits are reversed.

11
File Processing

Objectives

- To be able to create, read, write, and update files.
- To become familiar with sequential access file processing.
- To become familiar with random access file processing.

I read part of it all the way through.
Samuel Goldwyn

Hats off!
The flag is passing by.
Henry Holcomb Bennett

Consciousness ... does not appear to itself chopped up in bits. ... A "river" or a "stream" are the metaphors by which it is most naturally described.
William James

I can only assume that a "Do Not File" document is filed in a "Do Not File" file.
Senator Frank Church
Senate Intelligence Subcommittee Hearing, 1975

Outline

11.1 Introduction

Storage of data in variables and arrays is temporary. *Files* are used for permanent retention of large amounts of data. Computers store files on secondary storage devices, especially disk storage devices. In this chapter, we explain how data files are created, updated, and processed by C programs. We consider both sequential access files and random access files.

11.2 The Data Hierarchy

Ultimately, all data items processed by a computer are reduced to combinations of zeros and ones. This occurs because it is simple and economical to build electronic devices that can assume two stable states—one of the states represents 0 and the other represents 1. It is remarkable that the impressive functions performed by computers involve only the most fundamental manipulations of 0s and 1s.

The smallest data item in a computer can assume the value 0 or the value 1. Such a data item is called a *bit* (short for "*binary digit*"—a digit that can assume one of two values). Computer circuitry performs various simple bit manipulations such as examining the value of a bit, setting the value of a bit, and reversing a bit (from 1 to 0 or from 0 to 1).

It is cumbersome for programmers to work with data in the low-level form of bits. Instead, programmers prefer to work with data in the form of *decimal digits* (i.e., 0, 1, 2, 3, 4, 5, 6, 7, 8, and 9), *letters* (i.e., A through Z, and a through z), and *special symbols* (i.e., $, @, %, &, *, ( ), -, +, ", :, ?, /, and many others). Digits, letters, and special symbols are referred to as *characters*. The set of all characters that may be used to write programs and represent data items on a particular computer is called that computer's *character set*. Since computers can process only 1s and 0s, every character in a computer's character set is represented as a pattern of 1s and 0s (called a *byte*). Today, bytes are most commonly composed of eight bits. Programmers create programs and data items as characters; computers then manipulate and process these characters as patterns of bits.

Just as characters are composed of bits, *fields* are composed of characters. A field is a group of characters that conveys meaning. For example, a field consisting solely of uppercase and lowercase letters can be used to represent a person's name.

Data items processed by computers form a *data hierarchy* in which data items become larger and more complex in structure as we progress from bits, to characters (bytes), to fields, and so on.

A *record* (i.e., a struct in C) is composed of several fields. In a payroll system, for example, a record for a particular employee might consist of the following fields:

1. Social security number
2. Name
3. Address
4. Hourly salary rate
5. Number of exemptions claimed
6. Year-to-date earnings
7. Amount of federal taxes withheld, etc.

Thus, a record is a group of related fields. In the preceding example, each of the fields belongs to the same employee. Of course, a particular company may have many employees, and will have a payroll record for each employee. A *file* is a group of related records. A company's payroll file normally contains one record for each employee. Thus, a payroll file for a small company might contain only 22 records, whereas a payroll file for a large company might contain 100,000 records. It is not unusual for a company to have many files, each containing millions of characters of information. Fig. 11.1 illustrates the data hierarchy.

To facilitate the retrieval of specific records from a file, at least one field in each record is chosen as a *record key*. A record key identifies a record as belonging to a particular person or entity. In the payroll record described in this section, the social security number would normally be chosen as the record key.

There are many ways of organizing records in a file. The most popular type of organization is called a *sequential file* in which records are typically stored in order by the record key field. In a payroll file, records are usually placed in order by social security number. The first employee record in the file contains the lowest social security number, and subsequent records contain increasingly higher social security numbers.

Most businesses utilize many different files to store data. For example, companies may have payroll files, accounts receivable files (listing money due from clients), accounts payable files (listing money due to suppliers), inventory files (listing facts about all the items handled by the business), and many other types of files. A group of related files is sometimes called a *database*. A collection of programs designed to create and manage databases is called a *database management system* (DBMS).

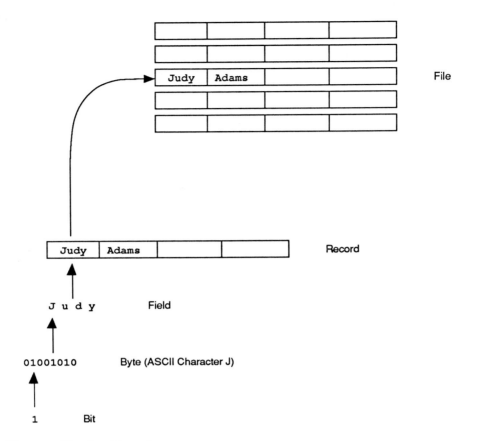

Fig. 11.1 The data hierarchy.

11.3 Files and Streams

C views each file simply as a sequential stream of bytes (Fig. 11.2). Just as each C string ends with the NULL character (' \0 '), each C file ends in EOF—a symbolic constant defined in the stdio.h header file. When a file is *opened*, a stream is associated with the file. Three files and their associated streams are automatically opened when program execution begins—the standard input, the standard output, and the standard error. Streams provide communication channels between files and programs. For example, the standard input stream enables a program to read data from the keyboard, and the standard output stream enables a program to print data on the screen. Opening a file creates a pointer to a structure that contains information used to process the file. The structure is referred to as the *file control block (FCB)*. Each file has a corresponding FCB. File processing functions use the pointer to the FCB to manipulate the file. The standard input, standard output, and standard error are manipulated using the pointers stdin, stdout, and stderr respectively.

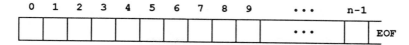

Fig. 11.2 C's view of a file of *n* bytes.

The standard library provides many functions for reading data from files and for writing data to files. Function `fgetc`, like its counterpart `getchar`, reads one character from a file. Function `fgetc` receives as an argument a file pointer to the file from which a character will be read. The function call `fgetc(stdin)` reads one character from the file pointed to by `stdin`—the standard input—so this function call is equivalent to the call `getchar()`. Function `fputc`, like its counterpart `putchar`, writes one character to a file. Function `fputc` receives as arguments a character to be written and a pointer to the file to which the character will be written. The function call `fputc('a', stdout)` writes the character `'a'` to the file pointed to by `stdout`—the standard output—so this function call is equivalent to `putchar('a')`.

Several other functions used to read data from standard input and write data to standard output have similarly named file processing functions. The `fgets` and `fputs` functions, for example, can be used to read a line from a file and write a line to a file, respectively. Their counterparts for reading from standard input and writing to standard output, functions `gets` and `puts`, were discussed in Chapter 8. In this chapter, we introduce the file processing equivalents of functions `scanf` and `printf`—`fscanf` and `fprintf`.

11.4 Creating a Sequential Access File

C imposes no structure on a file. Thus, notions like "record" do not exist in C. Therefore, the programmer must provide any file structure to meet the requirements of a particular application. In the following example, we see how the programmer may impose a simple record structure on a file.

The program of Fig. 11.3 creates a simple sequential access file that might be used in an accounts receivable system to help keep track of the amounts owed by a company's credit clients. For each client, the program obtains an account number, the client's name, and the client's balance (i.e., the amount the client still owes the company for goods and services received in the past). The data obtained for each client constitutes a record for that client. The account number is used as the record key in this application; that is, the file will be created and maintained in account number order. This program assumes the user enters the records in account number order. In a comprehensive accounts receivable system, a sorting capability would be provided so the user could enter the records in any order—the records would then be sorted and written to the file.

```
/* Create a sequential file */
#include <stdio.h>
#include <string.h>

main()
{
    int account;
    char name[10];
    float balance;
    FILE *cfptr;    /* cfptr = clients.dat file pointer */

    if((cfptr = fopen("clients.dat", "w")) == NULL)
        printf("File could not be opened\n");
    else {
        printf("Enter the account, name, and balance.\n");
        printf("Enter EOF to end input.\n");
        printf("? ");
        scanf("%d%s%f", &account, name, &balance);

        while(!feof(stdin)) {
            fprintf(cfptr, "%d %s %.2f\n", account, name, balance);
            printf("? ");
            scanf("%d%s%f", &account, name, &balance);
        }

        fclose(cfptr);
    }
}
```

```
Enter the account, name, and balance.
Enter the EOF character to end input.
? 100 Jones 24.98
? 200 Doe 345.67
? 300 White 0.00
? 400 Stone -42.16
? 500 Rich 224.62
?
```

Fig. 11.3 Creating a sequential file.

Now let us examine this program. The statement

```
FILE *cfptr;
```

states that cfptr is a pointer to a FILE. The type FILE is a structure type defined in the stdio.h header file. The operating system administers each file with a separate FILE structure (file control block or FCB). The FILE structure is operating system dependent (i.e., the members of the structure vary between systems based on how each system handles its files). The programmer need not know the specifics of the FILE structure to use files.

Each open file must have a separately declared pointer of type FILE that is used to refer to the file. The line

```
if((cfptr = fopen("clients.dat", "w")) == NULL)
```

names the file—`"clients.dat"`—to be used by the program, and establishes a "line of communication" with the file. The file pointer `cfptr` is assigned a pointer to the `FILE` structure for the file opened with `fopen`. Function `fopen` takes two arguments: a file name and a *file open mode*. The file open mode `"w"` indicates that the file is to be opened for *writing*. If a file does not exist and it is opened for writing, `fopen` creates the file. If an existing file is opened for writing, the contents of the file are discarded without warning. In the program, the `if` structure is used to determine whether the file pointer `cfptr` is NULL. If it is NULL, an error message is printed and the program ends. Otherwise, the input is processed and written to the file.

CPE 11.1

Opening an existing file for writing ("w") when, in fact, the user wants to preserve the file; the contents of the file are discarded without warning.

CPE 11.2

Forgetting to open a file before attempting to reference it in a program.

The program prompts the user to enter the various fields for each record, or to enter end-of-file when data entry is complete. Figure 11.4 lists the key combinations for entering end-of-file for various computer systems.

The line

```
while(!feof(cfptr))
```

uses function `feof` to determine whether the *end-of-file indicator* has been set. The end-of-file indicator informs the program that there is no more data to be processed. In the program of Fig. 11.3, the end-of-file indicator is set when the end-of-file key combination is entered by the user. Function `feof` receives as an argument a pointer to the file being tested for the end-of-file indicator. The function returns a nonzero value if an attempt is made to access a record once the end-of-file indicator has been set. The `while` structure that includes the `feof` call in this program continues executing while the end-of-file flag is not set.

The statement

```
fprintf(cfptr, "%d %s %.2f\n", account, name, balance);
```

Computer system	Key combination
UNIX systems	*\<return\> \<ctrl\> d*
IBM PC and compatibles	*\<ctrl\> z*
Macintosh	*\<ctrl\> d*
VAX (VMS)	*\<ctrl\> z*

Fig. 11.4 End-of-file key combinations for various popular computer systems.

writes a record to the file `"clients.dat"`. The data may be retrieved later by a program designed to read the file (see Section 11.4). Function `fprintf` is equivalent to `printf` except `fprintf` also receives as an argument a file pointer for the file to which the data will be written.

CPE 11.3

Using an incorrect file pointer to refer to a file.

GPP 11.1

Be sure that calls to file processing functions in a program contain the correct file pointers.

After the user enters end-of-file, the program closes the `clients.dat` file with `fclose` and terminates. Function `fclose` also receives the file pointer (rather than the file name) as an argument. If function `fclose` is not called explicitly, the operating system normally will close the file when program execution terminates. This is an example of operating system "housekeeping."

GPP 11.2

Explicitly close each file as soon as it is known that the program will not reference the file again.

In the sample execution for the program of Fig, 11.3, the user enters information for five accounts, and then signals that data entry is complete by entering end-of-file. Notice that the sample execution does not show how the data records actually appear in the file. To verify that the file has been created successfully, in the next section we create a program to read the file and print its contents.

Figure 11.5 illustrates a group of `FILE` structures (FCBs) on disk. When the file `"clients.dat"` is opened, an FCB for the file is copied into memory. The file pointer `cfptr` is assigned the location of the FCB in memory. All further references to the file use `cfptr` rather that the file name.

Programs may process no files, one file, or several files. Each file has a unique name and is pointed to by a different file pointer returned by `fopen`. All subsequent file processing functions must refer to a file with the appropriate file pointer. Files may be opened in one of several modes. To create a file, or to discard the contents of a file before writing data, open the file for writing (`"w"`). To read an existing file, open it for reading (`"r"`). To add records to the end of an existing file, open the file for appending (`"a"`). To open a file so that it may be written to and read from, open the file for updating in one of the three update modes—`"r+"`, `"w+"`, or `"a+"`. Mode `"r+"` opens a file for reading and writing. Mode `"w+"` creates a file for reading and writing. If the file already exists, the file is opened and the current contents of the file are discarded. Mode `"a+"` opens a file for reading and writing—all writing is done at the end of the file. If the file does not exist, it is created.

If an error occurs while opening a file in any mode, `fopen` returns `NULL`. Some possible errors are: opening a nonexistent file for reading, opening a file for reading without permission, and opening a file for writing when no disk space is available. Figure 11.6 lists the file open modes.

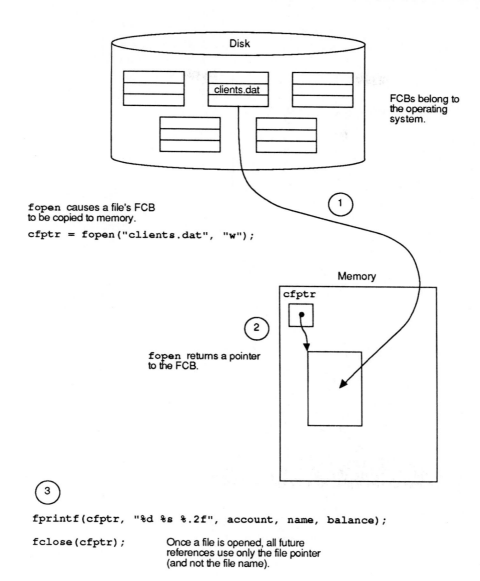

Fig. 11.5 File control blocks and file pointers.

CPE 11.4

Opening a file with the incorrect file mode can lead to devastating errors. For example, opening a file in write mode ("w") when it should be opened in update mode ("r+") causes the contents of the file to be discarded.

GPP 11.3

Open a file only for reading (and not update) if the contents of the file should not be modified. This prevents unintentional modification of the file's contents. This is another example of the principle of least privilege.

11.5 Reading Data from a Sequential Access File

Data are stored in files so that the data may be retrieved for processing when needed. The previous section demonstrated how to create a file for sequential access. In this section, we discuss how to read data sequentially from a file.

The program of Fig. 11.7 reads records from the file "clients.dat" created by the program of Fig. 11.3 and prints the contents of the records. The statement

```
FILE *cfptr;
```

indicates that cfptr is a pointer to a FILE. The line

```
if((cfptr = fopen("clients.dat", "r")) == NULL)
```

attempts to open the file "clients.dat" for reading ("r"), and determines whether the the file is opened successfully (i.e, fopen does not return NULL). The statement

```
fscanf(cfptr, "%d%s%f", &account, name, &balance);
```

reads a record from the file. Function fscanf is equivalent to function scanf except fscanf receives as an argument a file pointer for the file from which the data is read. After the preceding statement is executed the first time, account will have the value 100, name will have the value "Jones", and balance will have the value 24.98. Each time the second fscanf statement is executed, another record is read from the file and account, name, and balance take on new values. When the end of the file has been reached, the file is closed and the program terminates.

Mode	Description
r	Open a file for reading.
w	Create a file for writing. If the file already exists, discard the current contents.
a	Append; open or create a file for writing at end of file.
r+	Open a file for update (reading and writing).
w+	Create a file for update. If the file already exists, discard the current contents.
a+	Append; open or create a file for update; all writing is done at the end of the file.

Fig. 11.6 File open modes.

```
/* Reading and printing a sequential file */
#include <stdio.h>

main()
{
    int account;
    char name[10];
    float balance;
    FILE *cfptr;    /* cfptr = clients.dat file pointer */

    if((cfptr = fopen("clients.dat", "r")) == NULL)
        printf("File could not be opened\n");
    else {
        printf("%-10s%-13s%s\n", "Account", "Name", "Balance");
        fscanf(cfptr, "%d %s %f", &account, name, &balance);

        while(!feof(cfptr)) {
            printf("%-7d    %-13s%7.2f\n", account, name, balance);
            fscanf(cfptr, "%d %s %f", &account, name, &balance);
        }

        fclose(cfptr);
    }

}
```

```
Account   Name         Balance
100       Jones          24.98
200       Doe           345.67
300       White           0.00
400       Stone         -42.16
500       Rich          224.62
```

Fig. 11.7 Reading and printing a sequential file.

To retrieve data sequentially from a file, a program normally starts reading from the beginning of the file, and reads all data consecutively until the desired data are found. It may be desirable to process the data sequentially in a file several times (from the beginning of the file) during the execution of a program. The statement

```
rewind(cfptr);
```

causes the program to reposition the file's *file position pointer*—indicating the number of the next byte in the file to be read or written—to the beginning of the file pointed to by cfptr after each request. The file position pointer is not a pointer. Rather it is an integer value that specifies the location in the file as a number of bytes from the starting location of the file (this is sometimes referred to as the *offset* from the beginning of the file). The file position pointer is a member of the FILE structure (FCB) associated with each file.

We now present a program (Fig. 11.8) that allows a credit manager to obtain lists of those customers with zero balances (i.e., customers who do not owe the company

any money), credit balances (i.e., customers to whom the company owes money), and debit balances (i.e., customers who owe the company money for goods and services received in the past).

The program displays a menu and allows the credit manager to enter one of three options to obtain credit information. Option 1 produces a list of accounts with zero balances. Option 2 produces a list of accounts with credit balances. Option 3 produces a list of accounts with debit balances. Option 4 terminates program execution. A sample output is shown in Fig. 11.9.

```c
/* Credit inquiry program */

#include <stdio.h>

main()
{
    int request, account;
    float balance;
    char name[30];
    FILE *cfptr;

    if ((cfptr = fopen("clients.dat", "r")) == NULL)
        printf("File could not be opened\n");
    else {

        printf("Enter request\n");
        printf(" 1 - List accounts with zero balances\n");
        printf(" 2 - List accounts with credit balances\n");
        printf(" 3 - List accounts with debit balances\n");
        printf(" 4 - End of run\n");
        printf("? ");
        scanf("%d", &request);

        while(request != 4) {
            fscanf(cfptr, "%d%s%f", &account, name, &balance);

            switch(request) {

                case 1:
                    printf("\nAccounts with zero balances:\n");

                    while(!feof(cfptr)) {

                        if (balance == 0)
                            printf("%-7d   %-13s%7.2f\n", account, name,
                                balance);

                        fscanf(cfptr, "%d%s%f", &account, name, &balance);
                    }

                    break;
```

Fig. 11.8 Credit inquiry program (part 1 of 2).

```
             case 2:
                 printf("\nAccounts with credit balances:\n");

                 while(!feof(cfptr)) {
                     if (balance < 0)
                         printf("%-7d    %-13s%7.2f\n", account, name,
                             balance);
                         fscanf(cfptr, "%d%s%f", &account, name, &balance);
                 }

                 break;
             case 3:
                 printf("\nAccounts with debit balances:\n");

                 while(!feof(cfptr)) {
                     if (balance > 0)
                         printf("%-7d    %-13s%7.2f\n", account, name,
                             balance);
                         fscanf(cfptr, "%d%s%f", &account, name, &balance);
                 }

                 break;
         }

         rewind(cfptr);
         printf("\n? ");
         scanf("%d", &request);
     }

     printf("End of run.\n");
     fclose(cfptr);
   }
}
```

Fig. 11.8 Credit inquiry program (part 2 of 2).

Note that data in a sequential file cannot be modified without the risk of destroy-ing other data in the file. For example, if the name "White" needed to be changed to "Worthington," the old name cannot simply be overwritten. The record for White was written to the file as

    300 White 0.00

If the record is rewritten beginning at the same location in the file using the new name, the record would be

    300 Worthington 0.00

The new record contains more characters than the original record. The characters beyond the second "o" in "Worthington" would overwrite the beginning of the next sequential record in the file. The problem here is that in the formatted in-put/output model using fprintf and fscanf, fields—and hence records—can vary in size. For example, 7, 14, -117, 2074, and 27383 are all ints stored in the same number of bytes internally, but they print on the screen or fprintf on the disk as

```
Enter request
 1 - List accounts with zero balances
 2 - List accounts with credit balances
 3 - List accounts with debit balances
 4 - End of run
? 1

Accounts with zero balances:
300        White              0.00

? 2

Accounts with credit balances:
400        Stone            -42.16

? 3

Accounts with debit balances:
100        Jones             24.98
200        Doe              345.67
500        Rich             224.62

? 4
End of run.
```

Fig. 11.9 Sample output of the credit inquiry program of Fig. 11.8.

different-sized fields. Therefore, sequential access is not usually used to update records in place. Instead the entire file is usually rewritten. To make the preceding name change, the records before 300 White 0.00 in a sequential access file would be copied to a new file, the new record would be written, and the records after 300 White 0.00 would be copied to the new file. This requires processing every record in the file to update one record.

11.6 Random Access Files

As we stated previously, records in a file created with the formatted output function fprintf are not necessarily the same length. However, individual records of a *randomly accessed file* are normally fixed in length and may be accessed directly (and thus quickly) without searching through other records. This makes randomly accessed files appropriate for airline reservation systems, banking systems, point-of-sale systems, and other kinds of *transaction processing systems* that require rapid access to specific data.

Since every record in a randomly accessed file is the same length, the computer can quickly calculate (as a function of the record key) the exact location of a record relative to the beginning of the file. We will soon see how this facilitates immediate access to specific records, even in large files.

Figure 11.10 illustrates C's view of a randomly accessed file. A randomly accessed file is like a railroad train with many cars—some empty and some with contents.

Data can be inserted in a randomly accessed file without destroying other data in the file. Data stored previously can also be updated or deleted without rewriting the entire file. In the following sections we explain how to create a randomly accessed file, enter data, read the data both sequentially and randomly, update the data, and delete data no longer needed.

11.7 Creating a Randomly Accessed File

Function `fwrite` transfers a fixed number of bytes beginning at a specified location in memory to a file. The data is written beginning at the location in the file specified by the file position pointer. Function `fread` transfers a fixed number of bytes from the location in the file specified by the file position pointer to an area in memory beginning with a specified address. Now, when writing an integer, instead of using

```
fprintf(fptr, "%d", number);
```

which could print as few as 1 digit or as many as 11 digits (10 digits plus a sign, each of which requires 1 byte of storage) for a 4-byte integer, we can use

```
fwrite(&number, 4, 1, fptr);
```

which always writes 4 bytes. Later, `fread` can be used to read 4 bytes into integer variable `number`. File processing programs rarely write a single field to a file. Normally, they write one `struct` at a time, as we show in the following examples.

Consider the following problem statement:

Create a credit processing system capable of storing up to 100 fixed-length records. Each record should consist of an account number that will be used as the record key, a last name, a first name, and a balance. The resulting program should be able to update an account, insert a new account record, delete an account, and list all the account records in a formatted text file for printing.

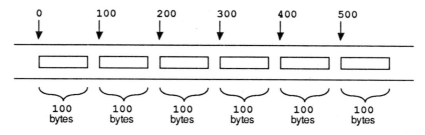

Fig. 11.10 C's view of a randomly accessed file.

The next several sections introduce the techniques necessary to create the credit processing program. The program of Fig. 11.11 shows how to open a randomly accessed file, define the record format using a struct, write data to the disk, and close the file. This program initializes all 100 records of the file "creditaccount.dat" with empty structs using function fwrite. Each empty struct contains 0 for the account number, NULL (represented by empty quotation marks) for the last name, NULL for the first name, and 0.0 for the balance. The file is initialized in this manner to define space on the disk in which the file will be stored, and to make it possible to determine if a record contains data.

Function fwrite writes a block (specific number of bytes) of data to a file. In our program, the statement

```
fwrite(&blankclient, sizeof(struct clientdata), 1, cfptr);
```

causes the structure blankclient of size sizeof(struct clientdata) to be written to the file pointed to by cfptr. The operator sizeof returns the size in bytes of the object contained in parentheses (in this case struct clientdata). The sizeof operator is a compile-time unary operator that returns an unsigned integer. The sizeof operator can be used to determine the size in bytes of any data type or expression. For example, sizeof(int) is used to determine whether an integer is stored in 2 or 4 bytes on a particular computer.

```
/* Creating a randomly accessed file sequentially */
#include <stdio.h>

struct clientdata {
    int acctnum;
    char lastname[15];
    char firstname[10];
    float balance;
};

main()
{
    int i;
    struct clientdata blankclient = {0, "", "", 0.0};
    FILE *cfptr;

    if ((cfptr = fopen("creditaccount.dat", "w")) == NULL)
        printf("File could not be opened.\n");
    else {

        for (i = 1; i <= 100; i++)
            fwrite(&blankclient, sizeof(struct clientdata), 1, cfptr);

        fclose (cfptr);
    }
}
```

Fig. 11.11 Creating a random access file sequentially.

Function `fwrite` can actually be used to write several elements of an array of objects. To write several array elements, the programmer supplies a pointer to an array as the first argument in the call to `fwrite`, and specifies the number of elements to be written as the third argument in the call to `fwrite`. In the preceding statement, `fwrite` was used to write a single object that was not an array element. Writing a single object is equivalent to writing one element of an array.

Figure 11.12 shows the precedence and associativity of the operators introduced to this point. The operators are shown top to bottom in decreasing order of precedence.

11.8 Writing Data Randomly to a Randomly Accessed File

The program of Fig. 11.13 writes data to the file `"creditaccount.dat"`. It uses the combination of `fseek` and `fwrite` to store data at exact locations in the file. Function `fseek` sets the file position pointer to a specific position in the file, then `fwrite` writes the data. A sample execution is shown in Fig. 11.14.

The statement

```
fseek(cfptr, (accountnum - 1) * sizeof(struct clientdata),
    SEEK_SET);
```

positions the file position pointer for the file pointed to by `cfptr` to the byte location calculated by `(accountnum - 1) * sizeof(struct clientdata)`. Since the account number is between 1 and 100, 1 is subtracted from the account

Operator											Associativity
( )	[ ]	->	.								left to right
++	--	!	&	*	~	(*type*)	`sizeof`				right to left
*	/	%									left to right
+	-										left to right
<<	>>										left to right
<	<=	>	>=								left to right
==	!=										left to right
&											left to right
^											left to right
|											left to right
&&											left to right
||											left to right
?:											right to left
=	+=	-=	*=	/=	%=	&=	^=	|=	<<=	>>=	right to left
,											left to right

Fig. 11.12 Operator precedence and associativity.

```
/* Writing to a random access file */
#include <stdio.h>
#include <string.h>

struct clientdata {
    int acctnum;
    char lastname[15];
    char firstname[10];
    float balance;
};

main()
{
    FILE *cfptr;
    struct clientdata client;

    if ((cfptr = fopen("creditaccount.dat", "r+")) == NULL)
        printf("File could not be opened.\n");
    else {
        printf("Enter account number (1 to 100, 0 to end input)\n? ");
        scanf("%d", &client.acctnum);

        while (client.acctnum != 0) {
            printf("Enter lastname, firstname, balance\n? ");
            scanf("%s%s%f",
                &client.lastname, &client.firstname, &client.balance);
            fseek(cfptr, (client.acctnum - 1) * sizeof(struct clientdata),
                SEEK_SET);
            fwrite(&client, sizeof(struct clientdata), 1, cfptr);
            printf("Enter account number\n? ");
            scanf("%d", &client.acctnum);
        }
    }

    fclose(cfptr);
}
```

Fig. 11.13 Writing data randomly to a randomly accessed file.

number when calculating the byte location of the record. Therefore, for record 1, the file position pointer is set to byte 0 of the file. The symbolic constant SEEK_SET indicates that the file position pointer is positioned relative to the beginning of the file. As the above statement indicates, a seek for account number 1 in the file locates the file position pointer at the beginning of the file because the byte location calculated is 0. Figure 11.15 illustrates the file pointer referring to a file control block. The file position pointer indicates that the next byte to be read or written is 5 bytes from the beginning of the file.

```
Enter account number (1 to 100, 0 to end input)
? 37
Enter lastname, firstname, balance
? Barker Doug 0.00
Enter account number
? 29
Enter lastname, firstname, balance
? Brown Nancy -24.54
Enter account number
? 96
Enter lastname, firstname, balance
? Stone Sam 34.98
Enter account number
? 88
Enter lastname, firstname, balance
? Smith Dave 258.34
Enter account number
? 33
Enter lastname, firstname, balance
? Dunn Stacey 314.33
Enter account number
? 0
```

Fig. 11.14 Sample execution of the program in Fig. 11.13.

The function prototype for fseek is

```
int fseek(FILE *stream, long int offset, int whence);
```

where offset is the number of bytes from location whence in the file pointed to by stream. The argument whence can have one of three values—SEEK_SET, SEEK_CUR or SEEK_END—indicating the location in the file from which the seek begins. SEEK_SET indicates that the seek starts at the beginning of the file; SEEK_CUR indicates that the seek starts at the current location in the file; and SEEK_END indicates that the seek starts at the end of the file. These three symbolic constants are defined in the stdio.h header file.

11.9 Reading Data Randomly from a Randomly Accessed File

Function fread reads a specified number of bytes from a file into an object. For example, the statement

```
fread(&client, sizeof(struct clientdata), 1, cfptr);
```

reads the number of bytes determined by sizeof(struct clientdata) from the file pointed to by cfptr and stores the data in the structure client. Function fread can be used to read several fixed size objects by providing a pointer to an array in which the objects will be stored, and by indicating the number of objects to

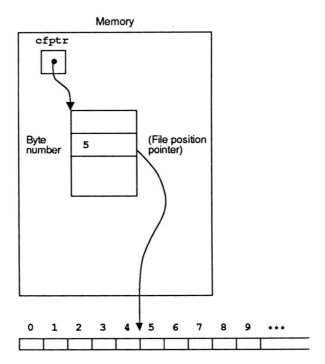

Fig. 11.15 The file position pointer indicating a position 5 bytes from the beginning of the file.

be read. The preceding statement specifies that one object should be read. To read more than one object, specify the number of objects in the third argument of the `fread` statement.

The program of Fig. 11.16 reads sequentially through every record in the `"creditaccount.dat"` file, checks each record to see if it contains data, and prints the formatted data for records containing data. The `feof` function determines when the end of the file is reached, and the `fread` function transfers data from the disk to the `clientdata` structure `client`.

11.10 Example: A Transaction Processing Program

We now present a substantial transaction processing program using randomly accessed files. The program maintains a bank's account information. The program updates existing accounts, adds new accounts, deletes accounts, and stores a listing of all the current accounts in a text file for printing. We assume that the program of Fig. 11.11 has been executed to create the file `creditaccount.dat`.

```
/* Reading a random access file sequentially */
#include <stdio.h>
#include <string.h>

struct clientdata {
   int acctnum;
   char lastname[15];
   char firstname[10];
   float balance;
};

main()
{
   FILE *cfptr;
   struct clientdata client;

   if ((cfptr = fopen("creditaccount.dat", "r")) == NULL)
      printf("File could not be opened.\n");
   else {
      printf("%-6s%-16s%-11s%10s\n", "Acct", "Last Name",
         "First Name", "Balance");

      while (!feof(cfptr)) {
         fread(&client, sizeof(struct clientdata), 1, cfptr);

         if (strcmp(client.lastname, NULL) != 0)
            printf("%-6d%-16s%-11s%10.2f\n",
               client.acctnum, client.lastname,
               client.firstname, client.balance);
      }
   }

   fclose(cfptr);
}
```

```
Acct   Last Name     First Name    Balance
29     Brown         Nancy          -24.54
33     Dunn          Stacey         314.33
37     Barker        Doug             0.00
88     Smith         Dave           258.34
96     Stone         Sam             34.98
```

Fig. 11.16 Reading a random access file sequentially.

The program has five options. Option 1 calls function textfile to store a formatted list of all the accounts in a text file called acctprint.txt that may be printed later. The function uses fread and the sequential file access techniques used in the program of Fig. 11.16. After choosing option 1 the file contains:

```
Acct   Last Name      First Name    Balance
29     Brown          Nancy          -24.54
33     Dunn           Stacey         314.33
37     Barker         Doug             0.00
88     Smith          Dave           258.34
96     Stone          Sam             34.98
```

Option 2 calls the function `updaterecord` to update an account. The function will only update a record that already exists, so the function first checks to see if the record specified by the user is empty. The record is read into structure `client` with `fread`, then `strcmp` is used to determine if the member `lastname` of structure `client` is NULL. If so, the record contains no information, and a message is printed stating that the record is empty. Then, the menu choices are displayed. If the record contains information, function `updaterecord` inputs the transaction amount, calculates the new balance, and rewrites the record to the file. A typical output for option 2 is:

```
Enter account to update (1 - 100): 37
37     Barker         Doug             0.00

Enter charge (+) or payment (-): +87.99
37     Barker         Doug            87.99
```

Option 3 calls the function `newrecord` to add a new account to the file. If the user enters an account number for an account containing data, `newrecord` displays a message that the record contains information, and the menu choices are printed. This function uses the same process to add a new account as does the program in Fig. 11.13. A typical output for option 3 is

```
Enter new account number (1 - 100): 22
Enter lastname, firstname, balance
? Johnston Sarah 247.45
```

Option 4 calls function `deleterecord` to delete a record from the file. Deletion is accomplished by asking the user for the account number and reinitializing the record. Option 5 terminates program execution. The program is shown in Fig. 11.17. Note that the file `"creditaccount.dat"` is opened for update (reading and writing) using `"r+"` mode.

```
/* This program reads a random access file sequentially, *
 * updates data already written to the file, creates new *
 * data to be placed in the file, and deletes data       *
 * already in the file.                                  */

#include <stdio.h>
#include <string.h>

struct clientdata {
   int acctnum;
   char lastname[15];
   char firstname[10];
   float balance;
};

int enterchoice(void);
void textfile(FILE *);
void updaterecord(FILE *);
void newrecord(FILE *);
void deleterecord(FILE *);

main()
{
   FILE *cfptr;
   int choice;

   if ((cfptr = fopen("creditaccount.dat", "r+")) == NULL)
      printf("File could not be opened.\n");
   else {

      while ((choice = enterchoice()) != 5) {

         switch (choice) {

            case 1:
               textfile(cfptr);
               break;

            case 2:
               updaterecord(cfptr);
               break;

            case 3:
               newrecord(cfptr);
               break;

            case 4:
               deleterecord(cfptr);
               break;

         }

      }

      fclose(cfptr);
}
```

Fig. 11.17 Bank account program (part 1 of 3).

```
int enterchoice(void)
{
   int menuchoice;

   printf("%s\n%s\n%s\n%s\n%s\n%s\n%s\n? ",
      "Enter your choice",
      "1 - store a formatted text file of accounts called",
      "    \"acctprint.txt\" for printing",
      "2 - update an account",
      "3 - add a new account",
      "4 - delete an account",
      "5 - end program");
   scanf("%d", &menuchoice);
   return menuchoice;
}

void textfile(FILE *readptr)
{
   FILE *writeptr;
   struct clientdata client;

   if ((writeptr = fopen("acctprint.txt", "w")) == NULL)
      printf("File could not be opened.\n");
   else {
      rewind(readptr);
      fprintf(writeptr, "%-6s%-16s%-11s%10s\n", "Acct", "Last Name",
         "First Name","Balance");

      while (!feof(readptr)) {
         fread(&client, sizeof(struct clientdata), 1, readptr);

         if (strcmp(client.lastname, NULL) != 0)
            fprintf(writeptr, "%-6d%-16s%-11s%10.2f\n",
               client.acctnum, client.lastname,
               client.firstname, client.balance);
      }
   }

   fclose(writeptr);
}
```

Fig. 11.17 Bank account program (part 2 of 3).

Summary

- All data items processed by a computer are reduced to combinations of zeros and ones.

- The smallest data item in a computer can assume the value 0 or the value 1. Such a data item is called a bit (short for "binary digit"—a digit that can assume one of two values).

- Digits, letters, and special symbols are referred to as characters. The set of all characters that may be used to write programs and represent data items on a particular computer is called that computer's character set. Every character in the computer's character set is represented as a pattern of eight 1s and 0s (called a byte).

```c
void updaterecord(FILE *fptr)
{
    int account;
    float transaction;
    struct clientdata client;

    printf("Enter account to update (1 - 100): ");
    scanf("%d", &account);
    fseek(fptr, (account-1) * sizeof(struct clientdata), SEEK_SET);
    fread(&client, sizeof(struct clientdata), 1, fptr);

    if (strcmp(client.lastname, NULL) != 0) {
        printf("%-6d%-16s%-11s%10.2f\n\n", client.acctnum,
            client.lastname, client.firstname, client.balance);
        printf("Enter charge (+) or payment (-): ");
        scanf("%f", &transaction);
        client.balance += transaction;
        printf("%-6d%-16s%-11s%10.2f\n", client.acctnum,
            client.lastname, client.firstname, client.balance);
        fseek(fptr, (account-1) * sizeof(struct clientdata), SEEK_SET);
        fwrite(&client, sizeof(struct clientdata), 1, fptr);
    }
    else
        printf("Account #%d has no information.\n", account);
}

void newrecord(FILE *fptr)
{
    struct clientdata client;
    int accountnum;
    printf("Enter new account number (1 - 100): ");
    scanf("%d", &accountnum);
    fseek(fptr, (accountnum - 1) * sizeof(struct clientdata), SEEK_SET);
    fread(&client, sizeof(struct clientdata), 1, fptr);

    if (strcmp(client.lastname, NULL) == 0) {
        printf("Enter lastname, firstname, balance\n? ");
        scanf("%s%s%f",
            &client.lastname, &client.firstname, &client.balance);
        client.acctnum = accountnum;
        fseek(fptr, (client.acctnum - 1) * sizeof(struct clientdata),
            SEEK_SET);
        fwrite(&client, sizeof(struct clientdata), 1, fptr);
    }
    else
        printf("Account #%d already contains information.\n",
            client.acctnum);
}

void deleterecord(FILE *fptr)
{
    struct clientdata blankclient = {0, "", "", 0};
    int accountnum;

    printf("Enter account number to delete (1 - 100): ");
    scanf("%d", &accountnum);
    fseek(fptr, (accountnum - 1) * sizeof(struct clientdata), SEEK_SET);
    fwrite(&blankclient, sizeof(struct clientdata), 1, fptr);
}
```

Fig. 11.17 Bank account program (part 3 of 3).

- A field is a group of characters that conveys meaning.

- A record is a group of related fields.

- At least one field in each record is normally chosen as a record key. The record key identifies a record as belonging to a particular person or entity.

- The most popular type of organization for records in a file is called a sequential access file in which records are accessed consecutively until the desired data are located.

- A group of related files is sometimes called a database. A collection of programs designed to create and manage databases is called a database management system (DBMS).

- C views each file simply as a sequential stream of bytes.

- C automatically opens three files and their associated streams—standard input, standard output, and standard error—when program execution begins.

- The file pointers assigned to the standard input, standard output, and standard error are stdin, stdout, and stderr, respectively.

- Function fgetc reads a character from a specified file.

- Function fputc writes a character to a specified file.

- Function fgets reads a line from a specified file.

- Function fputs writes a line to a specified file.

- FILE is a structure type defined in the stdio.h header file. The programmer need not know the specifics of this structure to use files. As a file is opened, a pointer to the file's FILE structure is returned.

- Function fopen takes two arguments—a file name and a file open mode—and opens the file. If the file already exists, the contents of the file are discarded without warning. If the file does not exist and the file is being opened for writing, fopen creates the file.

- Function feof determines whether the end-of-file indicator for a file has been set.

- Function fprintf is equivalent to printf except fprintf receives as an argument a pointer to the file (normally other than stdout) to which the data will be written.

- Function fclose closes the file pointed to by its argument.

- To create a file, or to discard the contents of a file before writing data, open the file for writing ("w"). To read an existing file, open it for reading ("r"). To add records to the end of an existing file, open the file for appending ("a"). To open a file so that it may be written to and read from, open the file for updating in one of the three updating modes—"r+", "w+", or "a+". Mode "r+" simply opens the file for reading and writing. Mode "w+" creates the file if it does not exist, and discards the current contents of the file if it does exist. Mode "a+" creates the file if it does not exist, and writing is done at the end of the file.

- Function `fscanf` is equivalent to `scanf` except `fscanf` receives as an argument a pointer to the file (normally other than `stdin`) from which the data will be read.

- Function `rewind` causes the program to reposition the file position pointer for the specified file to the beginning of the file.

- Random access is used to access a record directly without searching through other records.

- To facilitate random access, data is stored in fixed-length records. Since every record is the same length, the computer can quickly calculate (as a function of the record key) the exact location of a record in relation to the beginning of the file.

- Data can be added easily to a random access file without destroying other data in the file. Data stored previously in a file with fixed-length records can also be changed and deleted without rewriting the entire file.

- Function `fwrite` writes a block (specific number of bytes) of data to a file.

- The compile-time operator `sizeof` returns the size in bytes of its operand.

- Function `fseek` sets the file position pointer to a specific position in a file based on the starting location of the seek in the file. The seek can start from one of three locations—`SEEK_SET` is the beginning of the file, `SEEK_CUR` is the current position in the file, and `SEEK_END` is the end of the file.

- Function `fread` reads a block (specific number of bytes) of data from a file.

Terminology

alphabetic field	**fgets**
alphanumeric field	field
alpha order	file
binary digit	file buffer
bit	file name
channel	file pointer
character	file position pointer
character field	**FILE** structure
character set	**fopen**
close a file	formatted input/output
data hierarchy	**fprintf**
database	**fputc**
database management system	**fputs**
DBMS	**fread**
decimal digit	**fscanf**
direct file buffer	**fseek**
double-precision number	**fwrite**
end-of-file	integer number
end-of-file indicator	leading spaces
fclose	letter
feof	long integer number
fgetc	numeric field

open a file	sequential access file
r file open mode	single-precision number
random access	special symbol
random access file	**stderr** (standard error)
record	**stdin** (standard input)
record key	**stdout** (standard output)
record number parameter	stream
rewind	trailing spaces
r+ file open mode	w file open mode
SEEK_CUR	w+ file open mode
SEEK_END	zeros and ones
SEEK_SET	

Common Programming Errors

11.1   Opening an existing file for writing (**"w"**) when, in fact, the user wants to preserve the file; the contents of the file are discarded without warning.

11.2   Forgetting to open a file before attempting to reference it in a program.

11.3   Using an incorrect file pointer to refer to a file.

11.4   Opening a file with the incorrect file mode can lead to devastating errors. For example, opening a file in write mode (**"w"**) when it should be opened in update mode (**"r+"**) causes the contents of the file to be discarded.

Good Programming Practices

11.1   Be sure that calls to file processing functions in a program contain the correct file pointers.

11.2   Explicitly close each file as soon as it is known that the program will not reference the file again.

11.3   Open a file only for reading (and not update) if the contents of the file should not be modified. This prevents unintentional modification of the file's contents. This is another example of the principle of least privilege.

Self-Review Exercises

11.1   Fill in the blanks in each of the following:
   a)   Ultimately, all data items processed by a computer are reduced to combinations of _____ and _____.
   b)   The smallest data item a computer can process is called a _____.
   c)   A _____ is a group of related records.
   d)   Digits, letters, and special symbols are referred to as _____.
   e)   A group of related files is called a _____.
   f)   The _____ function closes a file.
   g)   The _____ statement reads data from a file in a manner similar to how **scanf** reads from **stdin**.

h)   The _____ function reads a character from a specified file.
i)   The _____ function reads a line from a specified file.
j)   The _____ function opens a file.
k)   The _____ function is normally used when reading data from a file in random access applications.
l)   The _____ function repositions the file position pointer to a specific location in the file.

11.2   State which of the following are true and which are false (for those that are false, explain why):

a)   Function `fscanf` cannot be used to read data from the standard input.
b)   The programmer must explicitly use `fopen` to open the standard input, standard output, and standard error streams.
c)   A program must explicitly call function `fclose` to close a file.
d)   If the file position pointer points to a location in a sequential file other than the beginning of the file, the file must be closed and reopened to read from the beginning of the file.
e)   Function `fprintf` can write to the standard output.
f)   Data in sequential access files is always updated without overwriting other data.
g)   It is not necessary to search through all the records in a randomly accessed file to find a specific record.
h)   Records in randomly accessed files are not of uniform length.
i)   Function `fseek` may only seek relative to the beginning of a file.

11.3   Write a single statement to accomplish each of the following. Assume that each of these statements applies to the same program.

a)   Write a statement that opens file `"oldmast.dat"` for reading and assigns the returned file pointer to `ofp`.
b)   Write a statement that opens file `"trans.dat"` for reading and assigns the returned file pointer to `tfp`.
c)   Write a statement that opens file `"newmast.dat"` for writing (and creation) and assigns the returned file pointer to `nfp`.
d)   Write a statement that reads a record from the file `"oldmast.dat"`. The record consists of integer `accountnum`, string `name`, and floating point `current-balance`.
e)   Write a statement that reads a record from the file `"trans.dat"`. The record consists of integer `accountnum` and floating point `dollaramount`.
f)   Write a statement that writes a record to the file `"newmast.dat"`. The record consists of integer `accountnum`, string `name`, and floating point `current-balance`.

11.4   Find the error in each of the following program segments. Explain how the error can be corrected.

a)   The file referred to by `fptr` (`"payables.dat"`) has not been opened.

```
fprintf(fptr, "%d %s %d\n", account, company, amount);
```

b)   `open("receivables.dat", "r+");`

c)   The following statement should read a record from the file `"payables.dat"`. File pointer `payptr` refers to this file, and file pointer `recptr` refers to the file `"receivables.dat"`.

```
fscanf(recptr, "%d %s %d\n", &account, company, &amount);
```

d)   The file `"tools.dat"` should be opened to add data to the file without discarding the current data.

```
if ((tfptr = fopen("tools.dat", "w")) != NULL)
```

e)   The file `"courses.dat"` should be opened for appending without modifying the current contents of the file.

```
if ((cfptr = fopen("courses.dat", "w+")) != NULL)
```

Answers to Self-Review Exercises

11.1   a) 1s, 0s. b) Bit. c) File. d) Characters. e) Database. f) `fclose`. g) `fscanf`. h) `getc`. i) `fgets`. j) `fopen`. k) `fread`. l) `fseek`.

11.2   a) False. Function `fscanf` can be used to read from the standard input by including the pointer to the standard input stream, `stdin`, in the call to `fscanf`.

b) False. These three streams are opened automatically by C when program execution begins.

c) False. The files will be closed when program execution terminates, but all files should be explicitly closed with `fclose`.

d) False. Function `rewind` can be used to reposition the file position pointer to the beginning of the file.

e) True.

f) False. In most cases, sequential file records are not of uniform length. Therefore, it is possible that updating a record will cause other data to be overwritten.

g) True.

h) False. Records in a random access file are normally of uniform length.

i) False. It is possible to seek from the beginning of the file, from the end of the file, and from the current location in the file according to the file position pointer.

11.3   a) `ofp = fopen("oldmast.dat", "r");`

b) `tfp = fopen("trans.dat", "r");`

c) `nfp = fopen("newmast.dat", "w");`

d) `fscanf(ofp, "%d%s%f", &accountnum, name, &currentbalance);`

e) `fscanf(tfp, "%d%f", &accountnum, &dollaramount);`

f) `fprintf(nfp, "%d %s %.2f", accountnum, name, currentbalance);`

11.4   a) Error: The file `"payables.dat"` has not been opened before the reference to its file pointer.

Correction: Use `fopen` to open `"payables.dat"` for writing, appending, or updating.

b) Error: The function open does not exist.

Correction: Use function `fopen`.

c) Error: The `fscanf` statement uses the incorrect file pointer to refer to file `"payables.dat"`.

Correction: Use file pointer `payptr` to refer to `"payables.dat"`.

d) Error: The contents of the file are discarded because the file is opened for writing (**"w"**).

Correction: To add data to the file, either open the file for updating (**"r+"**) or open the file for appending (**"a"**).

e) Error: File **"courses.dat"** is opened for updating in **"w+"** mode which discards the current contents of the file.

Correction: Open the file **"a"** mode.

Exercises

11.5   Fill in the blanks in each of the following:

a) Computers store large amounts of data on secondary storage devices as _____.

b) A _____ is composed of several fields.

c) A field that may contain digits, letters, and blanks is called an _____ field.

d) To facilitate the retrieval of specific records from a file, one field in each record is chosen as a _____.

e) The vast majority of information stored in computer systems is stored in _____ files.

f) A group of related characters that conveys meaning is called a _____.

g) The file pointers for the three files that are opened automatically by C when program execution begins are named _____, _____, and _____.

h) The _____ function writes a character to a specified file.

i) The _____ function writes a line to a specified file.

j) The _____ function is generally used to write data to a randomly accessed file.

k) The _____ function repositions the file position pointer to the beginning of the file.

11.6   State which of the following are true and which are false (for those that are false, explain why):

a) The impressive functions performed by computers essentially involve the manipulation of zeros and ones.

b) People prefer to manipulate bits instead of characters and fields because bits are more compact.

c) People specify programs and data items as characters; computers then manipulate and process these characters as groups of zeros and ones.

d) A person's zip code is an example of a numeric field.

e) A person's street address is generally considered to be an alphabetic field in computer applications.

f) Data items processed by a computer form a data hierarchy in which data items become larger and more complex as we progress from fields to characters to bits, etc.

g) A record key identifies a record as belonging to a particular field.

h) Most organizations store all their information in a single file to facilitate computer processing.

i) Files are always referred to by name in C programs.

j) When a program creates a file, the file is automatically retained by the computer for future reference.

11.7   Problem 11.3 asked the reader to write a series of single statements. Actually, these statements form the core of an important type of file processing program, namely, a file-matching program. In commercial data processing, it is common to have several files in each system. In an accounts receivable system, for example, there is generally a master file containing detailed information about each customer such as the customer's name, address, telephone number, outstanding balance, credit limit, discount terms, contract arrangements, and possibly a condensed history of recent purchases and cash payments.

As transactions occur (i.e., sales are made and cash payments arrive in the mail), they are entered into a file. At the end of each business period (i.e., a month for some companies, a week for others, and a day in some cases) the file of transactions (called `"trans.dat"` in Problem 11.3 is applied to the master file (called `"oldmast.dat"` in Problem 11.3), thus updating each account's record of purchases and payments. After each of these updating runs, the master file is rewritten as a new file (`"newmast.dat"`), which is then used at the end of the next business period to begin the updating process again.

File-matching programs must deal with certain problems that do not exist in single-file programs. For example, a match does not always occur. A customer on the master file may not have made any purchases or cash payments in the current business period, and therefore no record for this customer will appear on the transaction file. Similarly, a customer who did make some purchases or cash payments may have just moved to this community, and the company may not have had a chance to create a master record for this customer.

Use the statements written in Problem 11.3 as a basis for writing a complete file-matching accounts receivable program. Use the account number on each file as the record key for matching purposes. Assume that each file is a sequential file with records stored in increasing account number order.

When a match occurs (i.e., records with the same account number appear on both the master file and the transaction file), add the dollar amount on the transaction file to the current balance on the master file, and write the `"newmast.dat"` record. (Assume that purchases are indicated by positive amounts on the transaction file, and that payments are indicated by negative amounts.) When there is a master record for a particular account but no corresponding transaction record, merely write the master record to `"newmast.dat"`. When there is a transaction record but no corresponding master record, print the message `"Unmatched transaction record for account number ..."` (fill in the account number from the transaction record).

11.8   After writing the program of Problem 11.4, write a simple program to create some test data for checking out the program of Problem 11.4. Use the following sample account data:

Master file:

Account number	Name	Balance
100	Alan Jones	348.17
300	Mary Smith	27.19
500	Sam Sharp	0.00
700	Suzy Green	-14.22

Transaction file:

Account number	Dollar amount
100	27.14
300	62.11
400	100.56
900	82.17

11.9   Run the program of Problem 11.4 using the files of test data created in Problem 11.5. Use the listing program of Section 11.4 to print a new master file. Check the results carefully.

11.10   It is possible (actually common) to have several transaction records with the same record key. This occurs because a particular customer might make several purchases and cash payments during a business period. Rewrite your accounts receivable file-matching program of Problem 11.4 to provide for the possibility of handling several transaction records with the same record key. Modify the test data of Problem 11.5 to include the following additional transaction records:

Account number	Dollar amount
300	83.89
700	80.78
700	1.53

11.11   Write a series of statements that accomplish each of the following. Assume that the structure

```
struct person {
    char lastname[15];
    char firstname[15];
    char age[2];
};
```

has been defined, and that the file is already open for writing.

    a)   Initialize the file `"nameage.dat"` so that there are 100 records with `last-name` = "unassigned", `firstname` = "", and `age` = "0".

    b)   Input 10 last names, first names, and ages, and write them to the file.

    c)   Update a record that has information in it, and if there is none tell the user `"No info"`.

    d)   Delete a record that has information by reinitializing that particular record.

11.12   You are the owner of a hardware store and need to keep an inventory that can tell you what tools you have, how many you have, and the cost of each one. Write a program that initializes the file `"hardwareinventory.dat"` to one hundred empty records, lets you input the data concerning each tool, enables you to list all your tools, lets you delete a record for a tool that you no longer have, and lets you update *any* information in the file. The tool identification number should be the record number. Use the following information to start your file:

Record #	Tool name	Quantity	Cost
3	Electric sander	7	57.98
17	Hammer	76	11.99
24	Jig saw	21	11.00
39	Lawn mower	3	79.50
56	Power saw	18	99.99
68	Screwdriver	106	6.99
77	Sledge hammer	11	21.50
83	Wrench	34	7.50

11.13   Modify the telephone number word generating program you wrote in Exercise 8.22 so that it writes its output to a file. This allows you to read the file at your convenience. If you have a computerized dictionary available, modify your program to look up the words in the dictionary. Some of the interesting seven-letter combinations created by this program may consist of two or more words. For example, the phone number 8432677 produces "THEBOSS."

11.14   Modify the Example of Fig. 8.x to use functions `fgetc` and `fputc` rather than `getchar` and `putchar`. The program should give the user the option to read from the standard input and write to the standard output, or to read from a specified file and write to a specified file. If the user chooses the second option, have the user enter the file names for the input and output files.

11.15   Write a program that uses the `sizeof` operator to determine the sizes in bytes of the various data types on your computer system. Write the results to the file "datasize.dat" so you may print the results later. The format for the results in the file should be:

```
Data type            Size
char                 1
unsigned char        1
short int            2
unsigned short int   2
int                  4
unsigned int         4
long int             4
unsigned long int    4
float                4
double               8
long double          16
```

Note: the type sizes on your computer may not be the same as the ones listed above.

12
Data Structures

Objectives

- To be able to allocate and free memory dynamically for data objects.
- To be able to form linked data structures using pointers, self-referential structures, and recursion.
- To be able to create and manipulate linked lists, queues, stacks, and binary trees.

Much that I bound, I could not free;
Much that I freed returned to me.

Lee Wilson Dodd

'Will you walk a little faster?' said a whiting to a snail,
'There's a porpoise close behind us, and he's treading on my tail.'

Lewis Carroll

There is always room at the top.

Daniel Webster

Push on—keep moving.

Thomas Morton

I think that I shall never see
A poem as lovely as a tree.

Joyce Kilmer

Outline

12.1 Introduction

We have studied fixed-size *data structures* such as arrays, double arrays, and `structs`. This chapter introduces *dynamic* data structures that grow and shrink at execution time. *Linked lists* are collections of data items—insertions and deletions are made anywhere in a linked list. *Stacks* are important in compilers and operating systems—insertions and deletions are made only at one end of a stack—its *top*. *Queues* represent waiting lines; insertions are made at the back of a queue, and deletions are made from the front. *Binary trees* facilitate searching and sorting data, representing file system directories, and compiling expressions into machine language.

12.2 Self-Referential Structures

A *self-referential structure* contains a pointer member that points to a structure of the same structure type. For example, the definition

```
struct node {
   int data;
   struct node *nextptr;
};
```

defines a type, `struct node`. A structure of type `struct node` has two members—integer `data` and pointer `nextptr`. Member `nextptr` points to a structure of type `struct node`—a structure of the same type as the one being declared here, hence the term "self-referential structure." Member `nextptr` is referred to as a *link*—i.e., `nextptr` can be used to link (i.e., tie) a structure of type `struct node` to another structure of the same type. Self-referential structures can be linked together to form useful data structures such as lists, queues, stacks, and trees. Figure 12.1 illustrates two self-referential structures linked together. Note that a slash—representing a `NULL` pointer—is placed in the link member of the second self-referential structure to indicate that the link does not point to another structure. A `NULL` pointer normally indicates the end of the data structure just as the NULL character indicates the end of a string.

12.3 Dynamic Memory Allocation

Creating and maintaining dynamic data structures requires *dynamic memory allocation*—the ability for a program to obtain more memory space at execution time to hold new nodes; programs must also be able to reclaim space no longer needed. The limit for dynamic memory allocation is the amount of available memory in the computer (or the amount of virtual memory available to a user in a virtual memory system).

Functions malloc and free, and operator sizeof, are essential to dynamic memory allocation. Function malloc takes as an argument the number of bytes to be allocated, and returns a pointer of type *pointer to void* (void *) to the allocated memory. A void pointer may be assigned to a variable of any pointer type. Function malloc is normally used with the sizeof operator. For example, the statement

```
newptr = malloc(sizeof(struct node));
```

from the program in section 12.4, evaluates sizeof(struct node) to determine the size in bytes of a structure of type struct node, allocates a new area in memory of sizeof(struct node) bytes, and stores a pointer to the allocated memory in variable newptr. If no memory is available, malloc returns NULL. The free function deallocates memory—i.e., the memory is returned to the system so the memory can be reallocated in the future. To free memory dynamically allocated by the preceding malloc call, use the statement

```
free(newptr);
```

The following sections discuss lists, stacks, queues, and trees. Each of these data structures is created and maintained with dynamic memory allocation and self-referential structures.

GPP 12.1

Use the sizeof operator to determine the size of a structure.

GPP 12.2

When using malloc, test for a NULL return value. Print an error message if the requested memory is not allocated.

GPP 12.3

When memory that was dynamically allocated is no longer needed, use free to return the memory to the system.

Fig. 12.1 Two self-referential structures linked together.

CPE 12.1
_____
Freeing memory not allocated dynamically with `malloc`.

CPE 12.2
_____
Referring to memory that has been freed.

CPE 12.3
_____
Assuming that the size of a structure is simply the sum of the sizes of its members.

PORT 12.1
_____
The structure size is not necessarily the sum of the sizes of its members. This is so because of various machine-dependent boundary alignment requirements.

12.4 Linked Lists

A *linked list* is a collection of self-referential structures, called *nodes*, connected by links—hence, the term "linked" list. A linked list is accessed via a pointer to the first node of the list. Subsequent nodes are accessed via the link pointer stored in each node. The link pointer in the last node of a list is set to NULL to mark the end of the list. Data are stored in a linked list dynamically—each node is created as necessary. A node can contain data of any type including other `struct`s. Stacks and queues, as we will see, are specialized versions of linked lists.

Lists of data can be stored in arrays, but linked lists provide several advantages. Linked lists are used when the number of data elements to be processed is unpredictable. Since linked lists are dynamic, the length of the list can increase or decrease as necessary. On the other hand, the size of an array cannot be altered, because array memory is allocated at compile time. Therefore, arrays can become full. The array can be declared to contain more elements than the number of data items expected, but this may reserve memory that will not be needed.

Linked lists can be maintained in sorted order by always inserting new elements at the appropriate point in the list. Insertion and deletion in a sorted *array* can be time consuming—all the elements following the inserted or deleted element must be shifted appropriately. An advantage of arrays is that the elements of an array are stored contiguously in memory. This allows immediate access to any array element because the address of any element can be calculated quickly. Linked list nodes are normally not stored contiguously in memory. Logically, however, the nodes of a linked list do appear to be contiguous. Figure 12.2 illustrates a linked list with several nodes.

CPE 12.4
_____
Not setting the link in the last node of a list to NULL.

PERF 12.1
_____
Using dynamic memory allocation (instead of arrays) for data structures that grow and shrink at execution time can save memory. Keep in mind, however, that the pointers take up space, and that dynamic memory allocation incurs the overhead of function calls.

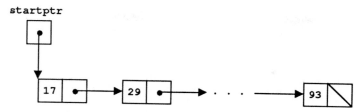

Fig. 12.2 A graphical representation of a linked list.

The program of Fig. 12.3 manipulates a list of characters. The program provides two options: 1) insert a character in the list in alphabetical order (function `insert`), and 2) delete a character from the list (function `delete`). This is a large and complex program. A detailed discussion of the program follows.

The two primary functions associated with linked lists are `insert` and `delete`. These functions are referred to as *constructors*—they are used to build a list. Function `isempty` is referred to as an *observer*—it does not alter the list in any way; rather it looks at the list to determine if the list is empty (i.e., the pointer is `NULL`). If the list is empty, 1 is returned. Otherwise, 0 is returned. Function `print_list` prints the list.

Characters are inserted in the list in alphabetical order. Function `insert` receives the address of the list and a character to be inserted. The address of the list is necessary when a value is to be inserted at the start of the list. Providing the address of the list enables the list (i.e., the pointer) to be modified via a call by reference. Since the list itself is a pointer (to its first element), passing the address of the list creates a *pointer to a pointer* (i.e., *double indirection*). This is a complex notion and requires careful programming. The steps for inserting a character in the list are as follows (see Fig. 12.5):

1) Create node by calling `malloc`, assigning the address of the allocated memory to `newptr`, assigning the character to be inserted to `newptr->data`, and assigning `NULL` to `newptr->nextptr`.

2) Initialize `previousptr` to `NULL`, and `currentptr` to `*sptr` (the pointer to the start of the list). Pointers `previousptr` and `currentptr` are used to store the locations of the node preceding the insertion point and the node after the insertion point.

3) While `currentptr` is not `NULL` and the value to be inserted is greater than `currentptr->data`, store `currentptr` in `previousptr` and advance `currentptr` to the next node in the list. This locates the insertion point.

```
/* Operating and maintaining a list */
#include <stdio.h>
#include <stdlib.h>

struct listnode {
   char data;
   struct listnode *nextptr;
};

typedef struct listnode LISTNODE;
typedef LISTNODE *LISTNODEPTR;

void insert(LISTNODEPTR *, char);
char delete(LISTNODEPTR *, char);
int isempty(LISTNODEPTR);
void print_list(LISTNODEPTR);
void instructions(void);

main()
{
   LISTNODEPTR startptr = NULL;
   int choice = 0;
   char item;

   instructions();

   while (choice != 3) {
      printf("? ");
      scanf("%d", &choice);

      switch (choice) {

         case 1:
            printf("Enter a character: ");
            scanf("\n%c", &item);
            insert(&startptr, item);
            print_list(startptr);
            break;

         case 2:
            if (!isempty(startptr)) {
               printf("Enter character to be deleted: ");
               scanf("\n%c", &item);

               if (delete(&startptr, item)) {
                  printf("\'%c\' deleted.\n", item);
                  print_list(startptr);
               }
               else
                  printf("\'%c\' not found.\n\n");
            }
            else
               printf("List is empty.\n\n");
      }

   }

   printf("End of run.\n");
}
```

Fig. 12.3 Inserting and deleting nodes in a list (part 1 of 3).

```
/* Print the instructions */
void instructions(void)
{
   printf("%s\n%s\n%s\n%s\n",
      "Enter your choice:",
      "   1 to insert an element into the list.",
      "   2 to delete an element from the list.",
      "   3 to end.");
}

/* Insert a new value into the list in sorted order */
void insert(LISTNODEPTR *sptr, char value)
{
   LISTNODEPTR newptr, previousptr, currentptr;

   newptr = malloc(sizeof(LISTNODE));

   if (newptr) {
      newptr->data = value;
      newptr->nextptr = NULL;

      previousptr = NULL;
      currentptr = *sptr;

      while (currentptr != NULL && value > currentptr->data) {
         previousptr = currentptr;
         currentptr = (currentptr)->nextptr;
      }

      if (previousptr == NULL) {
         newptr->nextptr = *sptr;
         *sptr = newptr;
      }
      else {
         previousptr->nextptr = newptr;
         newptr->nextptr = currentptr;
      }

   }
   else
      printf("%c not inserted. No memory available.\n", value);
}
```

Fig. 12.3 Inserting and deleting nodes in a list (part 2 of 3).

4) If `previousptr` is NULL, the new node is inserted as the first node in the list. Assign `*sptr` to `newptr->nextptr` (the new node link points to the former first node), and assign `newptr` to `*sptr` (`*sptr` points to the new node). If `previousptr` is not NULL, the new node is inserted in place. Assign `newptr` to `previousptr->nextptr` (the previous node points to the new node), and assign `currentptr` to `newptr->nextptr` (the new node link points to the current node).

```
/* Delete a list element */
char delete(LISTNODEPTR *sptr, char value)
{
    LISTNODEPTR previousptr, currentptr, tempptr;

    if (value == (*sptr)->data) {
        tempptr = *sptr;
        *sptr = (*sptr)->nextptr;
        free(tempptr);
        return value;
    }
    else {
        previousptr = *sptr;
        currentptr = (*sptr)->nextptr;

        while (currentptr != NULL && currentptr->data != value) {
            previousptr = currentptr;
            currentptr = currentptr->nextptr;
        }

        if (currentptr) {
            tempptr = currentptr;
            previousptr->nextptr = currentptr->nextptr;
            free(tempptr);
            return value;
        }

    }

    return '\0';
}


/* Return 1 if the list is empty, 0 otherwise */
int isempty(LISTNODEPTR sptr)
{
    return !sptr;
}


/* Print the list */
void print_list(LISTNODEPTR currentptr)
{
    if (!currentptr)
        printf("List is empty.\n\n");
    else {
        printf("The list is:\n");

        while (currentptr) {
            printf("%c --> ", currentptr->data);
            currentptr = currentptr->nextptr;
        }

        printf("NULL\n\n");
    }

}
```

Fig. 12.3 Inserting and deleting nodes in a list (part 3 of 3).

```
Enter your choice:
   1 to insert an element into the list.
   2 to delete an element from the list.
   3 to end.
? 1
Enter a character: B
The list is:
B --> NULL

? 1
Enter a character: A
The list is:
A --> B --> NULL

? 1
Enter a character: C
The list is:
A --> B --> C --> NULL

? 2
Enter character to be deleted: D
'D' not found.

? 2
Enter character to be deleted: B
'B' deleted.
The list is:
A --> C --> NULL

? 2
Enter character to be deleted: C
'C' deleted.
The list is:
A --> NULL

? 2
Enter character to be deleted: A
'A' deleted.
List is empty.

? 2
List is empty.

? 3
End of run.
```

Fig. 12.4 Sample output for the program of Fig. 12.3.

GPP 12.4

---

*Assign **NULL** to the link member of a new node. Pointers should be initialized before they are used.*

Fig. 12.5 illustrates the insertion of a node containing the character 'C' into an ordered list. Part a) of the figure shows the list and the new node before the insertion. Part b) of the figure shows the result of inserting the new node. The reassigned pointers are dotted arrows.

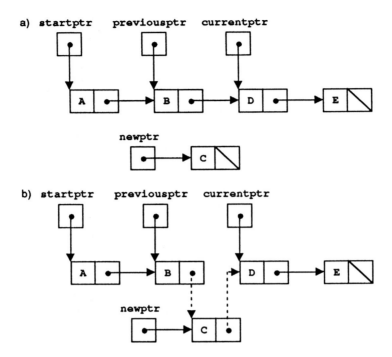

Fig. 12.5 Inserting a node in order in a list.

Function delete receives the address of the pointer to the start of the list and a character to be deleted. The steps for deleting a character from the list are as follows:

1) If the character to be deleted matches the character in the first node of the list, assign * sptr to tmpptr (tmpptr will be used to free the unneeded memory), assign (*sptr) ->nextptr to *sptr (*sptr now points to the second node in the list), free the memory pointed to by tempptr, and return the character that was deleted.

2) Otherwise, initialize previousptr to *sptr and currentptr to (*sptr) ->nextptr.

3) While currentptr is not NULL and the value to be deleted is not equal to currentptr->data, assign currentptr to previousptr, and assign currentptr->next to currentptr. This locates the character to be deleted.

4) If `currentptr` is not `NULL`, assign `currentptr` to `tempptr`, assign
    `currentptr->nextptr` to `previousptr->nextptr`, free the node
    pointed to by `tempptr`, and return the character that was deleted from the
    list. If `currentptr` is `NULL`, return the `NULL` character (`'\0'`) to signify
    that the character to be deleted was not found in the list.

Fig. 12.6 illustrates the deletion of a node from a linked list. Part a) of the figure
shows the linked list after the preceding insert operation. Part b) shows the reassign-
ment of the link element of `previousptr` and the assignment of `currentptr` to
`tempptr`. Pointer `tempptr` will be used to free the memory that was allocated to
store character `'C'`.

Function `print_list` receives a pointer to the start of the list as an argument,
and refers to the pointer as `currentptr`. The function first determines if the list is
empty. If so, `print_list` prints `"The list is empty."` and terminates.
Otherwise, it prints the data in the list. While `currentptr` is not `NULL`, the function prints `currentptr->data`, and assigns `currentptr->nextptr` to
`currentptr`. Note that if the link in the last node of the list is not `NULL`, the
printing algorithm will try to print past the end of the list, and an error will occur.
The printing algorithm is identical for linked lists, stacks, and queues.

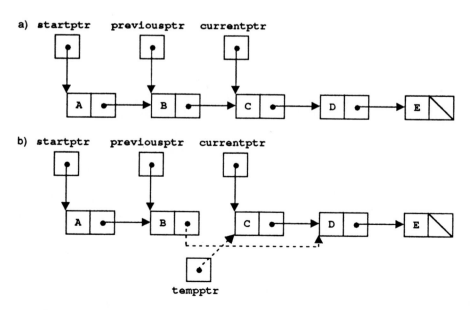

Fig. 12.6 Deleting a node from a list.

12.5 Stacks

A *stack* is a specialized version of a linked list. New nodes are added to a stack and removed from a stack only at the top. For this reason, a stack is referred to as a *last-in first-out (LIFO)* data structure. A stack is referenced via a pointer to the top of the stack. The link member in the last node of the stack is set to NULL to indicate the bottom of the stack. Fig. 12.7 illustrates a stack with several nodes. Note that stacks and linked lists are represented identically. The difference between stacks and linked lists is that insertions and deletions may occur anywhere in a linked list, but only at the top of a stack.

CPE 12.5

Not setting the link in the bottom node of a stack to NULL.

The two primary functions used to manipulate a stack are the constructors *push* and *pop*. Function push creates a new node and places it on top of the stack. Function pop removes a node from the top of the stack, frees the memory that was allocated to the popped node, and returns the popped value.

The program of Fig. 12.8 implements a simple stack that stores integers. The program provides three options: 1) push a node onto the stack (function push), 2) pop a node off the stack (function pop), and 3) terminate the program.

Function push places a new node at the top of the stack. The function consists of three steps:

1) Create a new node by calling malloc, assigning the location of the allocated memory to newptr, assigning the value to be placed on the stack to newptr->data, and assigning NULL to newptr->nextptr.

2) Assign *topptr (the stack top pointer) to newptr->nextptr—the link member of newptr now points to the previous top node.

3) Assign newptr to *topptr—*topptr now points to the new stack top.

Manipulations involving *topptr change the value of stackptr in main. Figure 12.10 illustrates function push. Part a) of the figure shows the stack and the new node before the push operation. The dotted arrows in part b) illustrate steps 2 and 3 of the push operation that enable the node containing 12 to become the new stack top.

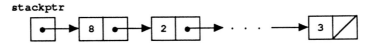

stackptr

Fig. 12.7 Graphical representation of a stack.

```
/* dynamic stack program */
#include <stdio.h>
#include <stdlib.h>

struct stacknode {
    int data;
    struct stacknode *nextptr;
};

typedef struct stacknode STACKNODE;
typedef STACKNODE *STACKNODEPTR;

void push(STACKNODEPTR *, int);
int pop(STACKNODEPTR *);
int isempty(STACKNODEPTR);
void print_stack(STACKNODEPTR);

main()
{
    STACKNODEPTR stackptr = NULL;  /* points to the stack top */
    int choice = 0, value;

    printf("%s\n%s\n%s\n%s\n",
            "Enter choice:",
            "1 to push a value on the stack",
            "2 to pop a value off the stack",
            "3 to end program");

    while (choice != 3) {
        printf("? ");
        scanf("%d", &choice);

        switch (choice) {

            case 1:      /* push onto stack */
                printf("Enter an integer: ");
                scanf("%d", &value);
                push(&stackptr, value);
                print_stack(stackptr);
                break;

            case 2:      /* pop off of stack */

                if (!isempty(stackptr))
                    printf("The popped value is %d.\n", pop(&stackptr));

                print_stack(stackptr);
                break;
        }
    }

    printf("End of run.\n");
}
```

Fig. 12.8 A simple stack program (part 1 of 2).

```
/* Insert a node at the stack top */
void push(STACKNODEPTR *topptr, int info)
{
    STACKNODEPTR newptr;

    newptr = malloc(sizeof(STACKNODE));

    if (newptr) {
        newptr->data = info;
        newptr->nextptr = *topptr;
        *topptr = newptr;
    }
    else
        printf("%d not inserted. No memory available.\n", info);

}


/* Remove a node from the stack top */
int pop(STACKNODEPTR *topptr)
{
    STACKNODEPTR tempptr;
    int popvalue;

    tempptr = *topptr;
    popvalue = (*topptr)->data;
    *topptr = (*topptr)->nextptr;
    free(tempptr);
    return popvalue;
}


/* Is the stack empty? */
int isempty(STACKNODEPTR topptr)
{
    return !topptr;
}


/* Print the stack */
void print_stack(STACKNODEPTR currentptr)
{
    if (currentptr == NULL)
        printf("The stack is empty.\n\n");
    else {
        printf("The stack is:\n");

        while (currentptr != NULL) {
            printf("%d --> ", currentptr->data);
            currentptr = currentptr->nextptr;
        }

        printf("NULL\n\n");
    }

}
```

Fig. 12.8 A simple stack program (part 2 of 2).

```
Enter choice:
1 to push a value on the stack
2 to pop a value off the stack
3 to end program
? 1
Enter an integer: 5
The stack is:
5 --> NULL

? 1
Enter an integer: 6
The stack is:
6 --> 5 --> NULL

? 1
Enter an integer: 4
The stack is:
4 --> 6 --> 5 --> NULL

? 2
The popped value is 4.
The stack is:
6 --> 5 --> NULL

? 2
The popped value is 6.
The stack is:
5 --> NULL

? 2
The popped value is 5.
The stack is empty.

? 2
The stack is empty.

? 3
End of run.
```

Fig. 12.9 Sample output from the program of Fig. 12.8.

Function pop removes a node from the top of the stack. The pop operation consists of five steps:

1) Assign *topptr to tempptr (tempptr will be used to free the unneeded memory).

2) Assign (*topptr)->data to popvalue (save the value stored in the top node).

3) Assign (*topptr)->nextptr to *topptr (assign *topptr the address of the new top node).

4) Free the memory pointed to by tempptr.

5) Return popvalue to the caller (main in the program of Fig. 12.8).

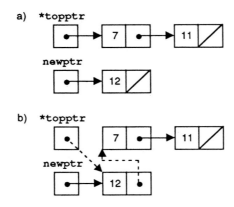

Fig. 12.10 The push operation.

Figure 12.11 illustrates function pop. Part a) shows the stack after the previous push operation. Part b) shows tempptr pointing to the first node of the stack and topptr pointing to the second node of the stack. Function free is used to free the memory pointed to by tempptr.

Stacks have many interesting applications. Whenever a function call is made, the called function must know how to return to its caller, so the return address is pushed onto a stack. If a series of function calls occurs, the successive return values are pushed onto the stack in last-in first-out order so that each function can return to its caller. Stacks support recursive function calls in the same manner as conventional non-recursive calls. Stacks contain the space created for automatic variables on each invocation of a function. When the function returns to its caller, the space for that function's automatic variables is popped off the stack, and these variables no longer are known to the program. Stacks are used by compilers in the process of evaluating expressions and generating machine language code. The exercises explore several applications of stacks.

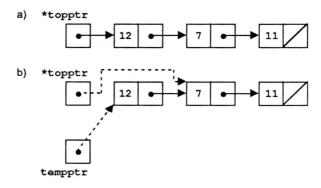

Fig. 12.11 The pop operation.

12.6 Queues

Another common data structures is the *queue*. A queue is similar to a checkout line in a grocery store—the first person in line is serviced first, and other customers enter the line only at the end and wait to be serviced. Queue nodes are removed only from the *head* of the queue, and are inserted only at the *tail* of the queue. For this reason, a queue is referred to as a *first-in first-out (FIFO)* data structure. The insert and remove operations are known as `enqueue` and `dequeue`.

Queues have many applications in computer systems. Most computers have only a single processor, so only one user at a time may be serviced. Entries for the other users are placed in a queue. Each entry gradually advances to the front of the queue as users receive service. The entry at the front of the queue is the next to receive service.

Queues are also used to support print spooling. A multiuser environment may have only a single printer. Many users may be generating outputs to be printed. If the printer is busy, other outputs may still be generated. These are "spooled" to disk where they wait in a queue until the printer becomes available.

Information packets also wait in queues in computer networks. Each time a packet arrives at a network node, it must be routed to the next node on the network along the way to the packet's final destination. The routing node routes one packet at a time, so additional packets are enqueued until the router can route them. Figure 12.12 illustrates a queue with several nodes. Note the pointers to the head and the tail of the queue.

CPE 12.6

Not setting the link in the last node of a queue to ***NULL.***

The program of Fig. 12.13 performs simple queue manipulations. The program provides several options: insert a node in the queue (function `enqueue`), remove a node from the queue (function `dequeue`), and terminate the program.

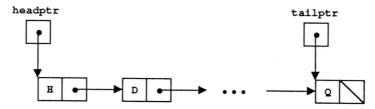

Fig. 12.12 A graphical representation of a queue.

```
/* Operating and maintaining a queue. */
#include <stdio.h>
#include <stdlib.h>

struct queuenode {
   char data;
   struct queuenode *nextptr;
};

typedef struct queuenode QUEUENODE;
typedef QUEUENODE *QUEUENODEPTR;

void print_queue(QUEUENODEPTR);
int isempty(QUEUENODEPTR);
char dequeue(QUEUENODEPTR *);
void enqueue(QUEUENODEPTR *, QUEUENODEPTR *, char);
void instructions(void);

main()
{
   QUEUENODEPTR headptr = NULL, tailptr = NULL;
   int choice = 0;
   char item;

   instructions();

   while (choice != 3) {
      printf("? ");
      scanf("%d", &choice);

      switch(choice) {

         case 1:
            printf("Enter a character: ");
            scanf("\n%c", &item);
            enqueue(&headptr, &tailptr, item);
            print_queue(headptr);
            break;

         case 2:
            if (!isempty(headptr)) {
               item = dequeue(&headptr);
               printf("\'%c\' has been dequeued.\n", item);
            }

            print_queue(headptr);
            break;
      }
   }

   printf("End of run.\n");
}

int isempty(QUEUENODEPTR headptr)
{
   return !headptr;
}
```

Fig. 12.13 Processing a queue (part 1 of 2).

```
void instructions(void)
{
   printf ("%s\n%s\n%s\n%s\n",
           "Enter your choice:",
           "   1 to add an item to the queue",
           "   2 to remove an item from the queue",
           "   3 to end");
}

void enqueue(QUEUENODEPTR *headptr, QUEUENODEPTR *tailptr,
char value)
{
   QUEUENODEPTR newptr;

   newptr = malloc(sizeof(QUEUENODE));

   if (newptr) {
      newptr->data = value;
      newptr->nextptr = NULL;

      if (isempty(*headptr))
         *headptr = newptr;
      else
         (*tailptr)->nextptr = newptr;

      *tailptr = newptr;
   }
   else
      printf("%c not inserted. No memory available.\n", value);
}

char dequeue(QUEUENODEPTR *headptr)
{
   char value;
   QUEUENODEPTR tempptr;

   value = (*headptr)->data;
   tempptr = *headptr;
   *headptr = (*headptr)->nextptr;
   free(tempptr);
   return value;
}

void print_queue(QUEUENODEPTR currentptr)
{
   if (isempty(currentptr))
      printf("Queue is empty.\n\n");
   else {
      printf("The queue is:\n");

      while (currentptr) {
         printf("%c --> ", currentptr->data);
         currentptr = currentptr->nextptr;
      }

      printf("NULL\n\n");
   }
}
```

Fig. 12.13 Processing a queue (part 2 of 2).

```
Enter your choice:
    1 to add an item to the queue
    2 to remove an item from the queue
    3 to end
? 1
Enter a character: A
The queue is:
A --> NULL

? 1
Enter a character: B
The queue is:
A --> B --> NULL

? 1
Enter a character: C
The queue is:
A --> B --> C --> NULL

? 2
'A' has been dequeued.
The queue is:
B --> C --> NULL

? 2
'B' has been dequeued.
The queue is:
C --> NULL

? 2
'C' has been dequeued.
Queue is empty.

? 2
Queue is empty.

? 3
End of run.
```

Fig. 12.14 Sample output from the program in Fig. 12.13.

Function `enqueue` receives three arguments from `main`: the address of the pointer to the head of the queue, the address of the pointer to the tail of the queue, and the value to be inserted in the queue. The function consists of three steps:

1) Create a new node: Call `malloc`, assign the allocated memory location to `newptr`, assign the value to be inserted in the queue to `newptr->data`, and assign NULL to `newptr->nextptr`.

2) If the queue is empty, assign `newptr` to `*headptr`. Otherwise, assign `newptr` to `(*tailptr)->nextptr`.

3) Assign `newptr` to `*tailptr`.

Figure 12.15 illustrates an `enqueue` operation. Part a) of the figure shows the queue and the new node before the operation. The dotted arrows in part b) illustrate steps 2 and 3 of function `enqueue` that enable a new node to be added to the end of a non-empty queue.

Function `dequeue` receives the address of the pointer to the head of the queue as an argument, and removes the first node from the queue. The `dequeue` operation consists of five steps:

1) Assign `(*headptr)->data` to `value` (save the data).

2) Assign `*headptr` to `tempptr` (`tempptr` is used to `free` the unneeded memory).

3) Assign `(*headptr)->nextptr` to `*headptr` (`*headptr` now points to the new first node in the queue).

4) Free the memory pointed to by `tempptr`.

5) Return `value` to the caller (`main` in the program of Fig, 12.13).

Figure 12.16 illustrates function `dequeue`. Part a) shows the queue after the preceding `enqueue` operation. Part b) shows `tempptr` pointing to the dequeued node, and `headptr` pointing to the new first node of the queue. Function `free` is used to reclaim the memory pointed to by `tempptr`.

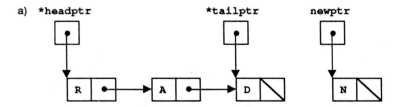

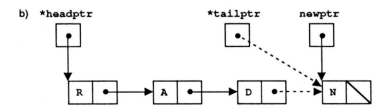

Fig. 12.15 A graphical representation of the `enqueue` operation.

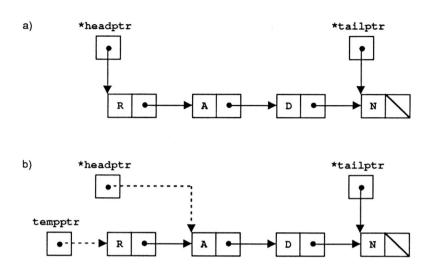

Fig. 12.16 A graphical representation of the `dequeue` operation.

12.7 Trees

Linked lists, stacks, and queues are all *linear data structures*. A tree is a nonlinear, two-dimensional linked data structure with some special properties. Tree nodes contain two or more links. This section discusses *binary trees* (Fig. 12.17)—trees whose nodes all contain two links (none, one, or both of which may be NULL). The *root node* is the first node in a tree. Each link in the root node refers to a *child*. The *left child* is the first node in the *left subtree*, and the *right child* is the first node in the *right subtree*. The children of a node are called *siblings*. If a node does not have any children it is called a *leaf node*. Note that computer scientists normally draw trees from the root node down—exactly the opposite of the way trees appear in nature.

In this section, a special binary tree called a *binary search tree* is created. A binary search tree (with no duplicate node values) has the characteristic that the value in any left child node is less than the value in its parent node, and the value in any right child node is greater than the value in its parent node. Fig. 12.18 illustrates a binary search tree with 15 values. Note that the shape of the binary search tree that corresponds to a particular set of data can vary, depending on the order in which the values are first inserted into the tree.

CPE 12.7
_____
Not setting to NULL the links in leaf nodes of a tree.

The program of Fig. 12.19 creates a binary search tree and traverses it three ways—*inorder*, *preorder*, and *postorder*. The program generates 10 random numbers and inserts each in the tree, with the exception that any duplicate values are discarded.

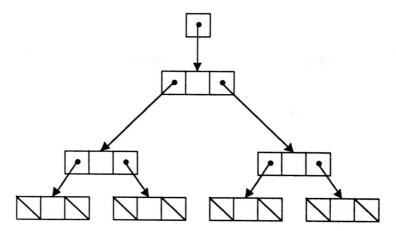

Fig. 12.17 A graphical representation of a binary tree.

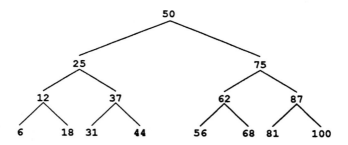

Fig. 12.18 A binary search tree.

The functions used in Fig. 12.19 to create a binary search tree and traverse the tree are recursive. Function `insert_node` receives the address of the tree and an integer to be stored in the tree as arguments. *A node can only be inserted as a leaf node in a binary search tree.* The steps for inserting a node in a binary search tree are as follows:

1) If `*treeptr` is NULL, create a new node. Call `malloc`, assign the allocated memory to `*treeptr`, assign the integer to be stored to `(*treeptr)->data`, assign NULL to `(*treeptr)->leftptr` and `(*treeptr)->rightptr`, and return control to the caller (either `main` or a previous call to `insert_node`).

2) If `*treeptr` is not NULL and the value to be inserted is less than `(*treeptr)->data`, call `insert_node` with the address of `(*treeptr)->leftptr`. Otherwise, call `insert_node` with the address of `(*treeptr)->rightptr`. The recursive steps continue until a NULL pointer is found, then step 1) is executed to insert the new node.

```
/* Create a binary tree and traverse it
   preorder, inorder, and postorder */

#include <stdio.h>
#include <stdlib.h>
#include <time.h>

struct treenode {
   struct treenode *leftptr;
   int data;
   struct treenode *rightptr;
};

typedef struct treenode TREENODE;
typedef TREENODE *TREENODEPTR;

void insert_node(TREENODEPTR *, int);
void inorder(TREENODEPTR);
void preorder(TREENODEPTR);
void postorder(TREENODEPTR);

main()
{
   int i, item;
   TREENODEPTR rootptr = NULL;

   srand(clock());

   /* insert random values between 1 and 15 in the tree */
   printf("The numbers being placed in the tree are:\n");

   for (i = 1; i <= 10; i++) {
      item = rand() % 15;
      printf("%3d", item);
      insert_node(&rootptr, item);
   }


   /* traverse the tree preorder */
   printf("\n\nThe preorder traversal is:\n");
   preorder(rootptr);


   /* traverse the tree inorder */
   printf("\n\nThe inorder traversal is:\n");
   inorder(rootptr);

   /* traverse the tree postorder */
   printf("\n\nThe postorder traversal is:\n");
   postorder(rootptr);
}
```

Fig. 12.19 Creating and traversing a binary tree (part 1 of 2).

```
void insert_node(TREENODEPTR *treeptr, int value)
{
    if (!*treeptr) {    /* treeptr is NULL */
        *treeptr = malloc(sizeof(TREENODE));

        if (*treeptr) {
            (*treeptr)->data = value;
            (*treeptr)->leftptr = NULL;
            (*treeptr)->rightptr = NULL;
        }
        else
            printf("%d not inserted. No memory available.\n", value);

        return;
    }
    else
        if (value < (*treeptr)->data)
            insert_node(&((*treeptr)->leftptr), value);
        else
            if (value > (*treeptr)->data)
                insert_node(&((*treeptr)->rightptr), value);
            else {
              printf("dup");
              return;
              }
}

void inorder(TREENODEPTR treeptr)
{
    if (treeptr) {
        inorder(treeptr->leftptr);
        printf("%3d", treeptr->data);
        inorder(treeptr->rightptr);
    }
}

void preorder(TREENODEPTR treeptr)
{
    if (treeptr) {
        printf("%3d", treeptr->data);
        preorder(treeptr->leftptr);
        preorder(treeptr->rightptr);
    }
}

void postorder(TREENODEPTR treeptr)
{
    if (treeptr) {
        postorder(treeptr->leftptr);
        postorder(treeptr->rightptr);
        printf("%3d", treeptr->data);
    }
}
```

Fig. 12.19 Creating and traversing a binary tree (part 2 of 2).

```
The numbers being placed in the tree are:
   7   8   0   6 14   1   0dup 13   0dup   7dup

The preorder traversal is:
   7   0   6   1   8 14 13

The inorder traversal is:
   0   1   6   7   8 13 14

The postorder traversal is:
   1   6   0 13 14   8   7
```

Fig. 12.20 Sample output from the program of Fig. 12.19.

Functions `inorder`, `preorder`, and `postorder` each receive a tree (i.e., the pointer to the root node of the tree) and traverse the tree.

The steps for an `inorder` traversal are:

1) Traverse the left subtree inorder.
2) Process the value in the node.
3) Traverse the right subtree inorder.

The value in a node is not processed until the values in its left subtree are processed. The `inorder` traversal of the tree in Fig. 12.21 is:

   6 13 17 27 33 42 48

Note that the inorder traversal of a binary search tree prints the node values in ascending order. The process of creating a binary search tree actually sorts the data—and thus this process is called the *binary tree sort*.

The steps for a `preorder` traversal are:

1) Process the value in the node.
2) Traverse the left subtree preorder.
3) Traverse the right subtree preorder.

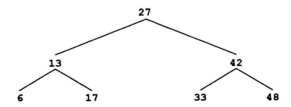

Fig. 12.21 A binary search tree.

The value in each node is processed as the node is visited. After the value in a given node is processed, the values in the left subtree are processed, then the values in the right subtree are processed. The `preorder` traversal of the tree in Fig. 12.21 is:

```
27 13 6 17 42 33 48
```

The steps for a `postorder` traversal are:

1) Traverse the left subtree postorder.
2) Traverse the right subtree postorder.
3) Process the value in the node.

The value in each node is not printed until the values of its children are printed. The `postorder` traversal of the tree in Fig. 12.21 is:

```
6 17 13 33 48 42 27
```

The binary search tree facilitates duplicate elimination. As the tree is being created, an attempt to insert a duplicate value will be recognized because a duplicate will follow the same "go left" or "go right" decisions on each comparison as the original value did. Thus, the dupe will eventually be compared with a node containing the same value. The duplicate value may simply be discarded at this point.

Searching a binary tree for a value that matches a key value is also fast. If the tree is tightly packed, then each level contains about twice as many elements as the previous level. So a binary search tree with n elements would have a maximum of $\log_2 n$ levels, and thus a maximum of $\log_2 n$ comparisons would have to be made either to find a match or to determine that no match exists. This means, for example, that when searching a 1000-element binary search tree, no more than 10 comparisons need to be made because $2^{10} > 1000$. When searching a 1,000,000 element binary search tree, no more than 20 comparisons need to be made because $2^{20} > 1,000,000$.

Summary

- Self-referential structures contain members called links that point to structures of the same structure type.
- Self-referential structures enable many structures to be linked together in stacks, queues, lists, and trees.
- Dynamic memory allocation reserves a block of bytes in memory to store a data object during program execution.
- Function `malloc` takes the number of bytes to be allocated as an argument, and returns a `void` pointer to the allocated memory. Function `malloc` is usually used with the `sizeof` operator. The `sizeof` operator determines the size in bytes of the structure for which memory is being allocated.
- The `free` function deallocates memory.

- A linked list is a collection of data stored in a group of connected self-referential structures.
- A linked list is a dynamic data structure—the length of the list can increase or decrease as necessary.
- Linked lists can continue to grow while memory is available.
- Linked lists provide a mechanism for simple insertion and deletion of data by reassigning pointers.
- Stacks and queues are specialized versions of a linked list.
- New nodes are added to a stack and removed from a stack only at the top. For this reason, a stack is referred to as a last-in first-out (LIFO) data structure.
- The link member in the last node of the stack is set to NULL to indicate the bottom of the stack.
- The two primary operations used to manipulate a stack are push and pop. The push operation creates a new node and places it on the top of the stack. The pop operation removes a node from the top of the stack, frees the memory that was allocated to the popped node, and returns the popped value.
- In a queue data structure, nodes are removed from the head and added to the tail. For this reason, a queue is referred to as a first-in first-out (FIFO) data structure. The add and remove operations are known as enqueue and dequeue.
- Trees are more complex data structures than linked lists, queues, and stacks. Trees are two-dimensional data structures requiring two or more links per node.
- Binary trees contain two links.
- The root node is the first node in the tree.
- Each of the pointers in the root node refers to a child. The left child is the first node in the left subtree, and the right child is the first node in the right subtree. The children of a node are called siblings. If a node does not have any children it is called a leaf node.
- A binary search tree has the characteristic that the value in the left child of a node is less than the parent node value, and the value in the right child of a node is greater than or equal to the parent node value. If it can be determined that there are no duplicate data values, the value in the right child is simply greater than the parent node value.
- An inorder traversal of a binary tree traverses the left subtree inorder, processes the value in the node, and traverses the right subtree inorder. The value in a node is not processed until the values in its left subtree are processed.
- A preorder traversal processes the value in the node, traverses the left subtree preorder, and traverses the right subtree preorder. The value in each node is processed as the node is encountered.
- A postorder traversal traverses the left subtree postorder, traverses the right subtree postorder, and processes the value in the node. The value in each node is not processed until the values in both its subtrees are processed.

Terminology

binary search tree	node
binary tree	nonlinear data structure
binary tree sort	`NULL` pointer
child node	observer function
children	parent node
constructor function	pointer to a pointer
deleting a node	`pop`
`dequeue`	postorder traversal
double indirection	preorder traversal
dynamic memory allocation	`push`
`enqueue`	queue
FIFO (first-in-first-out)	right child
`free`	right subtree
head of a queue	root node
inorder traversal	self-referential structure
inserting a node	siblings
leaf node	`sizeof`
left child	stack
left subtree	subtree
LIFO (last-in-first-out)	tail of a queue
linear data structure	top
link	traversal
linked list	tree
`malloc` (allocate memory)	visit a node

Common Programming Errors

12.1   Freeing memory not allocated dynamically with `malloc`.

12.2   Referring to memory that has been freed.

12.3   Assuming that the size of a structure is simply the sum of the sizes of its members.

12.4   Not setting the link in the last node of a list to `NULL`.

12.5   Not setting the link in the bottom node of a stack to `NULL`.

12.6   Not setting the link in the last node of a queue to `NULL`.

12.7   Not setting to `NULL` the links in leaf nodes of a tree.

Good Programming Practices

12.1   Use the `sizeof` operator to determine the size of a structure.

12.2   When using `malloc`, test for a `NULL` return value. Print an error message if the requested memory is not allocated.

12.3   When memory that was dynamically allocated is no longer needed, use `free` to return the memory to the system.

12.4   Assign `NULL` to the link member of a new node. Pointers should be initialized before they are used.

Performance Tips

12.1   Using dynamic memory allocation (instead of arrays) for data structures that grow and shrink at execution time can save memory. Keep in mind, however, that the pointers take up space, and that dynamic memory allocation incurs the overhead of function calls.

Portability Tips

12.1   The structure size is not necessarily the sum of the sizes of its members. This is so because of various machine-dependent boundary alignment requirements.

Self-Review Exercises

12.1   Fill in the blanks in each of the following:
   a)   A self-_____ structure is used to form dynamic data structures.
   b)   Function _____ is used to dynamically allocate memory.
   c)   A _____ is a specialized version of a linked list in which nodes can be inserted and deleted only from the start of the list.
   d)   Functions used to insert nodes in a linked list and delete nodes from a linked list are referred to as _____.
   e)   Functions that do not alter a linked list, but simply look at the list are referred to as _____.
   f)   A queue is referred to as a _____ data structure because the first nodes inserted are the first nodes removed.
   g)   The pointer to the next node in a linked list is referred to as a _____.
   h)   Function _____ is used to reclaim dynamically allocated memory.
   i)   A _____ is a specialized version of a linked list in which nodes can be inserted only at the start of the list and deleted only from the end of the list.
   j)   A _____ is a nonlinear, two-dimensional data structure that contains nodes with two or more links.
   k)   A stack is referred to as a _____ data structure because the last node inserted is the first node removed.
   l)   The nodes of a _____ tree contain two link members.
   m)   The first node of a tree is the _____ node.
   n)   Each link in a tree node points to a _____ or _____ of that node.
   o)   A tree node that has no children is called a _____ node.
   p)   The three traversal algorithms for a binary tree are _____, _____, and _____.

12.2   What are the differences between a linked list and a stack?

12.3   What are the differences between a stack and a queue?

12.4   Write a statement or set of statements to accomplish each of the following. Assume that all the manipulations occur in **main** (therefore, no addresses of pointer variables are needed), and assume the following definitions:

```
struct gradenode {
   char lastname[20];
   float grade;
   struct gradenode *nextptr;
};

typedef struct gradenode GRADENODE;
typedef GRADENODE *GRADENODEPTR;
```

a) Create a pointer to the start of the list called **startptr**. The list is empty.

b) Create a new node of type GRADENODE that is pointed to by pointer **newptr** of type GRADENODEPTR. Assign "Jones" to member **lastname** and 91.5 to member **grade** (use **strcpy**). Provide any necessary declarations and statements.

c) Assume that the list pointed to by **startptr** currently consists of 2 nodes— one containing "Jones" and one containing "Smith". The nodes are in alphabetical order. Provide the statements necessary to insert in order nodes containing the following data for **lastname** and **grade**:

"Adams"	85.0
"Thompson"	73.5
"Pritchard"	66.5

   Use pointers **previousptr**, **currentptr**, and **newptr** to perform the insertions. State what **previousptr** and **currentptr** point to before each insertion. Assume that **newptr** always points to the new node, and that the new node has already been assigned the data.

d) Write a **while** loop that prints the data in each node of the list. Use pointer **currentptr** to move along the list.

e) Write a **while** loop that deletes all the nodes in the list, and frees the memory associated with each node. Use pointer **currentptr** and pointer **tempptr** to walk along the list and free memory, respectively.

12.5   By hand, provide the inorder, preorder, and postorder traversals of the binary search tree of Fig. 12.22.

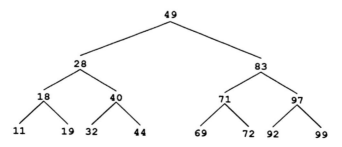

Fig. 12.22 A 15-node binary search tree.

Answers to Self-Review Exercises

12.1   a) referential. b) `malloc`. c) stack. d) constructors. e) observers. f) FIFO. g) link. h) `free`. i) queue. j) tree. k) LIFO. l) binary. m) root. n) child or subtree. o) leaf. p) inorder, preorder, postorder.

12.2   It is possible to insert a node anywhere in a linked list, and remove a node from anywhere in a linked list. Nodes may only be inserted at the top and removed from the top of a stack.

12.3   A queue has pointers to both its head and its tail so that nodes may be inserted at the tail and deleted from the head. A stack has a single pointer to the top of the stack where both insertion and deletion of nodes is performed.

12.4   a) `GRADENODEPTR startptr = NULL;`

b)
```
GRADENODEPTR newptr;
newptr = malloc(sizeof(GRADENODE));
strcpy(newptr->lastname, "Jones");
newptr->grade = 91.5;
newptr->nextptr = NULL;
```

c) To insert `"Adams"`:
previousptr is `NULL`, currentptr points to the first element in the list.
```
newptr->nextptr = currentptr;
startptr = newptr;
```

To insert `"Thompson"`:
previousptr points to the last element in the list (containing `"Smith"`)
currentptr is `NULL`.
```
newptr->nextptr = currentptr;
previousptr->nextptr = newptr;
```

To insert `"Pritchard"`:
previousptr points to the node containing `"Jones"`
currentptr points to the node containing `"Smith"`.
```
newptr->nextptr = currentptr;
previousptr->nextptr = newptr;
```

d)
```
currentptr = startptr;
while (currentptr != NULL) {
    printf("Lastname = %s\nGrade = %6.2f\n",
            currentptr->lastname, currentptr->grade);
    currentptr = currentptr->nextptr;
}
```

e)
```
currentptr = startptr;
while (currentptr != NULL) {
    tempptr = currentptr;
    currentptr = currentptr->nextptr;
    free(tempptr);
}
```

12.5   The inorder traversal is:

   11 18 19 28 32 40 44 49 69 71 72 83 92 97 99

The preorder traversal is:

   49 28 18 11 19 40 32 44 83 71 69 72 97 92 99

The postorder traversal is:

   11 19 18 32 44 40 28 69 72 71 92 99 97 83 49

Exercises

12.6   Write a program that concatenates two linked lists of characters. The program should include function `concatenate` that takes pointers to both lists as arguments and concatenates the second list to the first list.

12.7   Write a program that merges two ordered lists of integers into a single ordered list of integers. Function `merge` should receive pointers to the first node of each of the lists to be merged, and should return a pointer to the first node of the merged list.

12.8   Write a program that inserts 25 random integers between 0 and 100 in order in a linked list. The program should then calculate the sum of the elements, and the floating point average of the elements.

12.9   Write a program that creates a linked list of 10 characters, then creates a copy of the list in reverse order.

12.10   Write a program that inputs a line of text, and uses a stack to print the line reversed.

12.11   Write a program that uses a stack to test whether a string is a palindrome—i.e., the string is spelled identically backward and forward. If the string is a sentence, the program should ignore all spaces or punctuation marks.

12.12   Stacks are used by compilers to help in the process of evaluating expressions and generating machine language code. In this and the next problem, we investigate how compilers evaluate arithmetic expressions consisting only of constants, operators, and parentheses.

Humans generally write expressions like **3 + 4** and **7 / 9** in which the operator (+ or / here) is written between its operands—this is called *infix notation*. Computers "prefer" *postfix notation* in which the operator is written to the right of its two operands. The preceding infix expressions would appear in postfix notation as **3 4 +** and **7 9 /**, respectively.

To evaluate a complex infix expression, a compiler would first convert the expression to postfix notation, and then evaluate the postfix version of the expression. Each of these algorithms requires only a single left-to-right pass of the expression. Each algorithm uses a stack in support of its operation, and in each the stack is used for a different purpose.

In this problem you will write a C version of the infix-to-postfix conversion algorithm. In the next problem you will write a C version of the postfix expression evaluation algorithm.

Write a program that converts an ordinary infix arithmetic expression with single digit integers such as

     (6 + 2) * 5 - 8 / 4

to a postfix expression. The postfix version of the preceding infix expression is

     6 2 + 5 * 8 4 / -

The program should read the expression into character array **infix**, and use modified versions of the stack functions implemented earlier in this chapter to help create the postfix expression. The postfix expression will be written into character array **postfix**. The algorithm for creating a postfix expression is as follows:

   1)   Push a left parenthesis `'('` on the stack.
   2)   Append a right parenthesis `')'` to the end of **infix**.
   3)   While the stack is not empty, read **infix** from left to right and do the following:

If the current character in `infix` is a digit, copy it to the next element of `postfix`.

If the current character in `infix` is a left parenthesis, push it on the stack.

If the current character in `infix` is an operator,

Pop operators (if there are any) at the top of the stack while they have equal or higher precedence than the current operator, and insert the popped operators in `postfix`.

Push the current character in `infix` on the stack.

If the current character in `infix` is a right parenthesis

Pop operators from the top of the stack and insert them in `postfix` until a left parenthesis is at the top of the stack.

Pop (and discard) the left parenthesis from the stack.

The following arithmetic operations are allowed in an expression:

+   addition
−   subtraction
*   multiplication
/   division
^   exponentiation
%   modulus

The stack should be maintained with the following declarations:

```
struct stacknode {
    char data;
    struct stacknode *nextptr;
};

typedef struct stacknode STACKNODE;
typedef STACKNODE *STACKNODEPTR;
```

The program should consist of main and eight other functions with the following function headers:

`void convert_to_postfix(char infix[], char postfix[])`

Convert the infix expression to postfix notation.

`int isoperator(char c)`

Determine if c is an operator.

`int precedence(char operator1, char operator2)`

Determine if the precedence of `operator1` is less that, equal to, or greater than the precedence of `operator2`. The function returns -1, 0, and 1 respectively.

`void push(STACKNODEPTR *topptr, char value)`

Push a value on the stack.

`char pop(STACKNODEPTR *topptr)`

Pop a value off the stack.

`char stacktop(STACKNODEPTR topptr)`

Return the top value of the stack without popping the stack.

`int isempty(STACKNODEPTR topptr)`

Determine if the stack is empty.

```
void print_stack(STACKNODEPTR topptr)
```
   Print the stack.

12.13   Write a program that evaluates a postfix expression such as

```
6 2 + 5 * 8 4 / -
```

The program should read a postfix expression consisting of digits and operators into a character array. Using modified versions of the stack functions implemented earlier in this chapter, the program should scan the expression and evaluate it. The algorithm is as follows:

1) Append the NULL character ('\0') to the end of the postfix expression. When the NULL character is encountered, no further processing is necessary.

2) While the NULL character has not been encountered, read the expression from left to right.

    If the current character is a digit

        push its integer value on the stack (the integer value of a digit character is its value in the computer's character set minus the value of '0' in the computer's character set.

    Otherwise, if the current character is an operator,

        Pop the two top elements of the stack into variables x and y.

        Calculate y operator x.

        Push the result of the calculation on the stack.

3) When the NULL character is encountered in the expression, pop the top value of the stack. This is the result of the postfix expression.

Note that in 2) above, if the operator is '/', the top of the stack is 2, and the next element in the stack is 8, then pop 2 into x, pop 8 into y, evaluate 8 / 2, and push the result, 4, back on the stack. The following arithmetic operations are allowed in an expression:

+   addition
−   subtraction
*   multiplication
/   division
^   exponentiation
%   modulus

The stack should be maintained with the following declarations:

```
struct stacknode {
   int data;
   struct stacknode *nextptr;
};

typedef struct stacknode STACKNODE;
typedef STACKNODE *STACKNODEPTR;
```

The program should consist of main and six other functions with the following function headers:

```
int evaluate_postfix_expression(char *expr)
```
   Evaluate the postfix expression.

```
int calculate(int op1, int op2, char operator)
```
   Evaluate the expression op1 operator op2.

```
void push(STACKNODEPTR *topptr, char value)
```
   Push a value on the stack.

```
int pop(STACKNODEPTR *topptr)
```
Pop a value off the stack.
```
int isempty(STACKNODEPTR topptr)
```
Determine of the stack is empty.
```
void print_stack(STACKNODEPTR topptr)
```
Print the stack.

12.14 Modify the postfix evaluator program of exercise 12.13 so that it can process integer operands larger than 9.

12.15 *(Supermarket simulation)* Write a program that simulates a check-out line at a supermarket. The line is a queue. Customers arrive in random integer intervals of 1 to 4 minutes. Also, each customer is serviced in random integer intervals of 1 to 4 minutes. Obviously, the rates need to be balanced. If the average arrival rate is larger than the average service rate, the queue will grow infinitely. Even with balanced rates, randomness can still cause long lines. Run the supermarket simulation for a 12-hour day (720 minutes) using the following algorithm (the day begins with minute 0):

a) Choose a random integer between 1 and 4 to determine the minute at which the first customer arrives.

b) At the first customer's arrival time
Determine customer's service time (random integer from 1 to 4)
Begin servicing the customer
Schedule the arrival time of the next customer (random integer 1 to 4 added to the current time).

c) For each minute of the day,
If the next customer arrives,
Enqueue the customer
Schedule the arrival time of the next customer
If service was completed for the last customer
Say so
Dequeue next customer to be serviced
Determine customer's service completion time (random integer from 1 to 4 added to the current time).

Now run your simulation for 720 minutes and answer each of the following:

a) What is the maximum number of customers in the queue at any time?

b) What is the longest wait any one customer experienced?

c) What happens if the arrival interval is changed from 1 to 4 minutes to 1 to 3 minutes?

12.16 Modify the definition of a binary search tree to allow the tree to contain duplicate values.

12.17 Write a program based on the program of Fig. 12.17 that inputs a line of text, tokenizes the sentence into separate words, inserts the words in a binary search tree, and prints the inorder, preorder, and postorder traversals of the tree. The program should use the following definitions:

Hint: Read the line of text into an array. Use **strtok** to tokenize the text. When a token is found, create a new node for the tree, assign the pointer returned by **strtok** to member **string** of the new node, and insert the node in the tree.

12.18 In the chapter, we saw that duplicate elimination is straightforward when creating a binary search tree. Describe how you would perform duplicate elimination using only a single subscripted array. Compare the array-based approach with the binary-search-tree-based approach to duplicate elimination.

12.19 Write a function `depth` that receives a binary tree and determines how many levels it has.

13

The Preprocessor

Objectives

- To be able to use #include for developing large programs.
- To be able to use #define to create macros and macros with arguments.
- To understand conditional compilation.
- To be able to display error messages during conditional compilation.
- To be able to use assertions to test if the values of expressions are correct.

Hold thou the good; define it well.
Alfred, Lord Tennyson

I have found you an argument; but I am not obliged to find you an understanding.
Samuel Johnson

A good symbol is the best argument, and is a missionary to persuade thousands.
Ralph Waldo Emerson

Conditions are fundamentally sound.
Herbert Hoover [December 1929]

The partisan, when he is engaged in a dispute, cares nothing about the rights of the question, but is anxious only to convince his hearers of his own assertions.
Plato

Outline

13.1 Introduction

This chapter introduces the *C preprocessor*. Preprocessing occurs before a program is
compiled. Some possible actions are: inclusion of other files in the file being compiled, definition of *symbolic constants* and *macros, conditional compilation* of program code, and *conditional execution of preprocessor directives*. All preprocessor directives begin with #, and only whitespace characters may appear before a preprocessor
directive on a line.

13.2 The #include Preprocessor Directive

The *#include preprocessor directive* has been used throughout this text. The
#include directive causes a copy of a specified file to be included in place of the
directive. The two forms of the #include directive are:

```
#include <filename>
#include "filename"
```

The difference between these is the location the preprocessor searches for the file to be
included. If the file name is enclosed in quotes, the preprocessor searches for the file to
be included in the same directory as the file being compiled. This method is normally
used to include programmer-defined header files. If the file name is enclosed in angle
brackets (< and >)—used for *standard library header files*—the search is performed
in an implementation-dependent manner, normally through predesignated directories.

   The #include directive normally is used to include standard library header files
such as stdio.h and stdlib.h (see Fig. 5.6). The #include directive is also
used with programs consisting of several source files that are to be compiled together.
A *header file* containing declarations common to the separate program files often is

created and included in the file. Examples of such declarations are structure and union declarations, enumerations, and function prototypes.

In UNIX, program files are compiled using the `cc` *command*. For example, to compile and link `main.c` and `square.c` enter the command

```
cc main.c square.c
```

at the UNIX prompt. This produces a single executable file `a.out`. See the reference manuals for your particular system for more information on compiling, linking, and executing programs.

13.3 The #define Preprocessor Directive: Symbolic Constants

The *#define preprocessor directive* is used to create *symbolic constants*—constants represented as symbols—and *macros*—operations defined as symbols. The format for a `#define` directive is

```
#define identifier replacement-text
```

When this line appears in a file, all subsequent occurrences of *identifier* will be replaced by *replacement-text* automatically before the program is compiled. For example, the directive

```
#define PI 3.14159
```

replaces all subsequent occurrences of the symbolic constant `PI` with the numeric constant `3.14159`. Symbolic constants enable the programmer to create a name for a constant, and use the name throughout the program. If the constant needs to be modified throughout the program, it can be modified once in the `#define` directive—and when the program is recompiled, all occurrences of the constant in the program will be modified automatically.

> **GPP 13.1**
> _____
> *Using meaningful names for symbolic constants helps make programs more self-documenting.*

13.4 The #define Preprocessor Directive: Macros

A *macro* is an operation defined in a `#define` preprocessor directive. As with symbolic constants, the *macro-identifier* is replaced in the program with the *replacement-text* before the program is compiled. Macros may be defined with or without *arguments*. A macro without arguments is processed like a symbolic constant. In a macro with arguments, first the arguments are substituted in the replacement text, then the macro is *expanded*—i.e., the replacement-text replaces the identifier and argument list in the program.

Consider the following macro definition with one argument for the area of a circle:

```
#define CIRCLE_AREA(x) PI * (x) * (x)
```

Wherever CIRCLE_AREA(x) appears in the file, the value of x is substituted for x in the replacement text, the symbolic constant PI is replaced by its value (defined previously), and the macro is expanded in the program. For example, the statement

```
area = CIRCLE_AREA(4);
```

is expanded to

```
area = 3.14159 * (4) * (4);
```

Since the expression consists only of constants, at compile time, the value of the expression is evaluated and assigned to variable area. The parentheses around each x in the replacement text force the proper order of evaluation when the macro argument is an expression. For example, the statement

```
area = CIRCLE_AREA(c + 2);
```

is expanded to

```
area = 3.14159 * (c + 2) * (c + 2);
```

which evaluates correctly because the parentheses force the proper order of evaluation. If the parentheses are omitted, the macro expansion is

```
area = 3.14159 * c + 2 * c + 2;
```

which evaluates incorrectly as

```
area = (3.14159 * c) + (2 * c) + 2;
```

because of the rules of operator precedence.

CPE 13.1

Forgetting to enclose macro arguments in parentheses in the replacement text.

Macro CIRCLE_AREA could be defined as a function. Function circle_area

```
double circle_area(double x)
{
   return 3.14159 * x * x;
}
```

performs the same calculation as macro CIRCLE_AREA, but the overhead of a function call is associated with function circle_area. The advantages of macro CIRCLE_AREA are that macros insert code directly in the program—avoiding function overhead—and the program remains readable because the CIRCLE_AREA calculation is defined separately and named meaningfully.

PERF 13.1

Macros can sometimes be used to replace a function call with inline code prior to execution time. This eliminates the overhead of a function call.

The following is a macro definition with 2 arguments for the area of a rectangle:

```
#define RECTANGLE_AREA(x, y)   (x) * (y)
```

Wherever `RECTANGLE_AREA(x, y)` appears in the program, the values of `x` and `y` are substituted in the macro replacement text, and the macro is expanded in place of the macro name. For example, the statement

```
rectarea = RECTANGLE_AREA(a + 4, b + 7);
```

is expanded to

```
rectarea = (a + 4) * (b + 7);
```

The value of the expression is evaluated and assigned to variable `rectarea`.

The replacement text for a macro or symbolic constant is normally any text on the line after the identifier in the `#define` directive. If the replacement text for a macro or symbolic constant is longer than the remainder of the line, a backslash \ must be placed at the end of the line indicating that the replacement text continues on the next line.

Symbolic constants and macros can be discarded using the *#undef preprocessor directive*. Directive `#undef` "undefines" a symbolic constant or macro name. The *scope* of a symbolic constant or macro is from its definition until it is undefined with `#undef`, or until the end of the file.

Functions in the standard library sometimes are defined as macros based on other library functions. An example of a macro that is commonly defined in the `stdio.h` header file is

```
#define getchar()  getc(stdin)
```

The macro definition of `getchar` uses function `getc` to get one character from the standard input stream. Function `putchar` of the `stdio.h` header, and the character handling functions of the `ctype.h` header often are implemented as macros as well.

13.5 Conditional Compilation

Conditional compilation enables the programmer to control the execution of preprocessor directives, and the compilation of program code. Each of the conditional preprocessor directives evaluates a constant integer expression. Cast expressions, `sizeof` expressions, and enumeration constants cannot be evaluated in preprocessor directives.

The conditional preprocessor construct is much like the `if` selection structure. Consider the following preprocessor code:

```
#if !defined(NULL)
    #define NULL 0
#endif
```

The preceding `#if` directive determines if the identifier `NULL` is currently defined. The expression `defined(NULL)` evaluates to 1 if `NULL` is defined and 0 otherwise. If the result is 0, the expression !defined(NULL) evaluates to 1, and symbolic constant NULL is defined. Otherwise, the #define directive is skipped. Every #if construct ends with #endif. Directives *#ifdef* and *#ifndef* are provided as shorthand for #if defined(*name*) and #if !defined(*name*). A multiple-part conditional preprocessor construct may be tested using the #elif (the equivalent of else if in an if structure) and the #else (the equivalent of else in an if structure) directives.

During program development, programmers often find it helpful to "comment out" large portions of code to prevent it from being compiled. If the code contains comments, /* and */ cannot be used to accomplish this task. Instead, the programmer can use the following preprocessor construct

```
#if 0
      code prevented from compiling
#endif
```

To enable the code to be compiled, the 0 in the preceding construct is replaced by 1.

Conditional compilation is commonly used as a debugging aid. Many C implementations provide *debuggers*. However, debuggers often are difficult to use and understand, so they are rarely used by students in a first programming course. Instead, printf statements are used to print variable values and to confirm the flow of control. These printf statements can be enclosed in conditional preprocessor directives so the statements are only compiled while the debugging process is not completed. For example,

```
#ifdef DEBUG
      printf("Variable x = %d\n", x);
#endif
```

causes a printf statement to be compiled in the program if the symbolic constant DEBUG has been defined (#define DEBUG) before directive #ifdef DEBUG. When debugging is completed, the #define directive is removed from the source file, and the printf statements inserted for debugging purposes are ignored during compilation. In larger programs, it may be desirable to define several different symbolic constants that control the conditional compilation of debugging statements in separate sections of the source file.

CPE 13.2

Inserting conditionally compiled **printf** *statements for debugging purposes in locations where C currently expects a single statement. In this case, the conditionally compiled statement should be enclosed in a compound statement. Thus, when the program is compiled with debugging statements the flow of control of the program is not altered.*

13.6 The #error and #pragma Preprocessor Directives

The *#error directive*

```
#error tokens
```

prints an implementation-dependent message that includes the *tokens* specified in the directive. The tokens are sequences of characters separated by spaces. For example, the directive

```
#error 1 - Out of range error
```

contains 6 tokens. In Turbo C for PCs, for example, when a #error directive is processed, the tokens in the directive are displayed as an error message, preprocessing stops, and the program does not compile.

The *#pragma directive*

```
#pragma tokens
```

causes an implementation-defined action. A pragma not recognized by the implementation is ignored. Turbo C, for example, recognizes several pragmas that enable the programmer to take full advantage of the Turbo C implementation. For more information on #error and #pragma, see the documentation for your particular C implementation.

13.7 The # and ## Operators

The # and ## preprocessor operators are available only in ANSI C. The # operator causes a replacement text token to be converted to a string surrounded by quotes. Consider the following macro definition:

```
#define HELLO(x) printf("Hello, " #x "\n");
```

When HELLO(John) appears in a program file, it is expanded to

```
printf("Hello, " "John" "\n");
```

The string "John" replaces #x in the replacement text. Strings separated by white space are concatenated during preprocessing, so the above statement is equivalent to

```
printf("Hello, John\n");
```

Note that the # operator must be used in a macro with arguments because the operand of # refers to an argument of the macro.

The ## operator concatenates two tokens. Consider the following macro definition:

```
#define TOKENCONCAT(x, y)  x ## y
```

When TOKENCONCAT appears in the program, its arguments are concatenated and used to replace the macro. For example, TOKENCONCAT(O, K) is replaced by OK in the program. The ## operator must have two operands.

13.8 Line Numbers

The *#line preprocessor directive* causes the subsequent source code lines to be renumbered starting with the specified constant integer value. The directive

```
#line 100
```

starts line numbering from `100` beginning with the next source code line. A file name can be included in the `#line` directive. The directive

```
#line 100 "file1.c"
```

indicates that lines are numbered from `100` beginning with the next source code line, and that the name of the file for the purpose of any compiler messages is `"file1.c"`. The directive normally is used to help make the messages produced by syntax errors and compiler warnings more meaningful. The line numbers do not appear in the source file.

13.9 Predefined Symbolic Constants

There are five *predefined symbolic constants* (Fig. 13.1). The indentifiers for each of the predefined symbolic constants begin and end with *two* underbars. These identifiers and the `defined` identifier (used in section 13.5) cannot be used in `#define` or `#undef` directives.

13.10 Assertions

The *assert macro*—defined in the `assert.h` header file—tests the value of an expression. If the value of the expression is `0` (false), then `assert` prints an error message and calls function *abort* (of the general utilities library—`stdlib.h`) to terminate program execution. This is a useful debugging tool for testing if a variable

Symbolic constant	Explanation
__LINE__	The line number of the current source code line (an integer constant).
__FILE__	The presumed name of the source file (a string).
__DATE__	The date the source file is compiled (a string of the form "Mmm dd yyyy" such as "Jan 19 1991").
__TIME__	The time the source file is compiled (a string literal of the form "hh:mm:ss").
__STDC__	The integer constant 1. This is intended to indicate that the implementation is ANSI compliant.

Fig. 13.1 The predefined symbolic constants.

has a correct value. For example, suppose variable x should never be larger than 10 in a program. An assertion may be used to test the value of x and print an error message if the value of x is incorrect. The statement would be:

```
assert(x <= 10);
```

If x is greater than 10 when the preceding statement is encountered in a program, an error message containing the line number and file name is printed, and the program terminates. The programmer may then concentrate on this area of the code to find the error. If the symbolic constant NDEBUG is defined, subsequent assertions will be ignored. Thus, when assertions are no longer needed, the line

```
#define NDEBUG
```

is inserted in the program file rather than deleting each assertion manually.

Summary

- All preprocessor directives begin with #.
- Only whitespace characters may appear before a preprocessor directive on a line.
- The #include directive causes a copy of the specified file to be included in place of the directive. If the file name is enclosed in quotes, the preprocessor normally begins searching for the file to be included in the same directory as the file being compiled. If the file name is enclosed in angle brackets (< and >), the search is performed in an implementation-defined manner.
- The #define preprocessor directive is used to create symbolic constants and macros.
- A symbolic constant is a name for a constant.
- A macro is an operation defined in a #define preprocessor directive. Macros may be defined with or without arguments.
- The replacement text for a macro or symbolic constant is normally any text remaining on the line after the identifier in the #define directive. If the replacement text for a macro or symbolic constant is longer than the remainder of the line, a backslash \ must be placed at the end of the line indicating that the replacement text continues on the next line.
- Symbolic constants and macros can be discarded using the #undef preprocessor directive. Directive #undef "undefines" the symbolic constant or macro name.
- The scope of a symbolic constant or macro is from its definition until it is undefined with #undef, or until the end of the file.
- Conditional compilation enables the programmer to control the execution of preprocessor directives and the compilation of program code.
- The conditional preprocessor directives evaluate constant integer expressions. Cast expressions, sizeof expressions, and enumeration constants cannot be evaluated in preprocessor directives.

- Every `#if` construct ends with `#endif`.
- Directives `#ifdef` and `#ifndef` are provided as shorthand for `#if defined(`*name*`)` and `#if !defined(`*name*`)`.
- A multiple-part conditional preprocessor construct may be tested using the `#elif` (the equivalent of `else if` in an `if` structure) and the `#else` (the equivalent of `else` in an `if` structure) directives.
- The `#error` directive prints an implementation-dependent message that includes the tokens specified in the directive.
- The `#pragma` directive causes an implementation-defined action. If the pragma is not recognized by the implementation, the pragma is ignored.
- The `#` operator causes a replacement text token to be converted to a string surrounded by quotes. The `#` operator must be used in a macro with arguments because the operand of `#` must be an argument of the macro.
- The `##` operator concatenates two tokens. The `##` operator must have two operands.
- The `#line` preprocessor directive causes the subsequent source code lines to be renumbered starting with the specified constant integer value.
- There are five predefined symbolic constants. Constant `__LINE__` is the line number of the current source code line (an integer). Constant `__FILE__` is the presumed name of the file (a string). Constant `__DATE__` is the date the source file is compiled (a string). Constant `__TIME__` is the time the source file is compiled (a string). Constant `__STDC__` is 1; it is intended to indicate that the implementation is ANSI compliant. Note that each of the predefined symbolic constants begins and ends with two underbars.
- The `assert` macro—defined in the `assert.h` header file—tests the value of an expression. If the value of the expression is 0 (false), then `assert` prints an error message and calls function `abort` to terminate program execution.

Terminology

`#define`	`__DATE__`
`#elif`	`__FILE__`
`#else`	`__LINE__`
`#endif`	`__STDC__`
`#error`	`__TIME__`
`#if`	`a.out` in UNIX
`#ifdef`	abort
`#ifndef`	argument
`#include <filename>`	assert
`#include "filename"`	`assert.h`
`#line`	C preprocessor
`#pragma`	cc command in UNIX
`#undef`	concatenation preprocessor operator `##`
\ (backslash) continuation character	conditional compilation

conditional execution of preprocessor
   directives
convert-to-string preprocessor operator **#**
debugger
expand a macro
header file
macro
macro with arguments

predefined symbolic constants
preprocessing directive
replacement text
scope of a symbolic constant or macro
standard library header files
stdio.h
stdlib.h
symbolic constant

Common Programming Errors

13.1 Forgetting to enclose macro arguments in parentheses in the replacement text.

13.2 Inserting conditionally compiled **printf** statements for debugging purposes in locations where C currently expects a single statement. In this case, the conditionally compiled statement should be enclosed in a compound statement. Thus, when the program is compiled with debugging statements the flow of control of the program is not altered.

Good Programming Practices

13.1 Using meaningful names for symbolic constants helps make programs more self-documenting.

Performance Tips

13.1 Macros can sometimes be used to replace a function call with inline code prior to execution time. This eliminates the overhead of a function call.

Self-Review Exercises

13.1 Fill in the blanks in each of the following:
a) Every preprocessor directive must begin with _____.
b) The conditional compilation construct may be extended to test for multiple cases by using the _____ and the _____ directives.
c) The _____ directive creates macros and symbolic constants.
d) Only _____ characters may appear before a preprocessor directive on a line.
e) The _____ directive discards symbolic constant and macro names.
f) The _____ and _____ directives are provided as shorthand notation for **#if defined(**_name_**)** and **#if !defined(**_name_**)**.
g) _____ enables the programmer to control the execution of preprocessor directives, and the compilation of program code.
h) The _____ macro prints a message and terminates program execution if the value of the expression the macro evaluates is 0.
i) The _____ directive inserts a file in another file.

j) The _____ operator concatenates its two arguments.

k) The _____ operator converts its operand to a string.

l) The character _____ indicates that the replacement text for a symbolic constant or macro continues on the next line.

m) The _____ directive causes the source code lines to be numbered from the indicated value beginning with the next source code line.

13.2 Write a program that prints the values of the predefined symbolic constants listed in Fig. 13.1.

13.3 Write a preprocessor directive to accomplish each of the following:

a) Define symbolic constant **YES** to have the value **1**.

b) Define symbolic constant **NO** to have the value **0**.

c) Include the header file **common.h**. The header is found in the same directory as the file being compiled.

d) Renumber the remaining lines in the file beginning with line number **3000**.

e) If symbolic constant **TRUE** is defined, undefine it, and redefine it as **1**. Do not use **#ifdef**.

f) If symbolic constant **TRUE** is defined, undefine it, and redefine it as **1**. Use **#ifdef**.

g) If symbolic constant **TRUE** is not equal to **0**, define symbolic constant **FALSE** as **0**. Otherwise define **FALSE** as **1**.

h) Define macro **SQUARE_VOLUME** that computes the volume of a square. The macro takes one argument.

Answers to Self-Review Exercises

13.1 a) **#**. b) **#elif, #else**. c) **#define**. d) whitespace. e) **#undef**. f) **#ifdef**, **#ifndef**. g) Conditional compilation. h) **assert**. i) **#include**. j) **##**. k) **#**. l) ****. m) **#line**.

13.2
```
/* Print the values of the predefined macros */
#include <stdio.h>
main()
{
    printf("__LINE__ = %d\n", __LINE__);
    printf("__FILE__ = %s\n", __FILE__);
    printf("__DATE__ = %s\n", __DATE__);
    printf("__TIME__ = %s\n", __TIME__);
    printf("__STDC__ = %d\n", __STDC__);
}
```

```
__LINE__ = 5
__FILE__ = macros.c
__DATE__ = Nov 08 1991
__TIME__ = 10:23:47
__STDC__ = 1
```

13.3 a) #define YES 1

b) **#define NO 0**

c) **#include "common.h"**

```
d) #line 3000
e) #if defined(TRUE)
       #undef TRUE
       #define TRUE 1
   #endif
f) #ifdef TRUE
       #undef TRUE
       #define TRUE 1
   #endif
g) #if TRUE
       #define FALSE 0
   #else
       #define FALSE 1
   #endif
h) #define SQUARE_VOLUME(x)   x * x * x
```

Exercises

13.4   Write a program that defines a macro with one argument to compute the volume of a sphere. The program should compute the volume for spheres of radius 1 to 10, and print the results in tabular format. The formula for the volume of a sphere is:

$$(4/3) \ * \ \pi \ * \ r^3$$

where π is **3.14159**.

13.5   Write a program that produces the following output:

> The sum of x and y is 13

The program should define macro **SUM** with two arguments, **x** and **y**, and use **SUM** to produce the output.

13.6   Write a program that uses macro **MINIMUM2** to determine the smallest of two numeric values. Input the values from the keyboard.

13.7   Write a program that uses macro **MINIMUM3** to determine the smallest of three numeric values. Macro **MINIMUM3** should use macro **MINIMUM2** defined in Exercise 13.6 to determine the smallest number. Input the values from the keyboard.

13.8   Write a program that uses macro **PRINT** to print a string value.

13.9   Write a program that uses macro **PRINTARRAY** to print an array of integers. The macro should receive the array and the number of elements in the array as arguments.

13.10   Write a program that uses macro **SUMARRAY** to sum the values in a numeric array. The macro should receive the array and the number of elements in the array as arguments.

14

Advanced Topics

Objectives

- To be able to redirect keyboard input to come from a file.
- To be able to redirect screen output to be placed in a file.
- To be able to write functions that use variable-length argument lists.
- To be able to process command-line arguments.
- To be able to assign specific types to numeric constants
- To be able to use temporary files.
- To be able to process unexpected events within a program.
- To be able to allocate memory dynamically for arrays.
- To be able to change the size of memory that was dynamically allocated previously.

*We'll use a signal I have tried and found
far-reaching and easy to yell. Waa-hoo!*
Zane Grey

*Use it up, wear it out;
Make it do, or do without.*
Anonymous

It is quite a three-pipe problem.
Sir Arthur Conan Doyle

Outline

14.1 Introduction

This chapter presents several advanced topics not ordinarily covered in introductory courses. Many of the capabilities discussed here are specific to particular operating systems, especially UNIX and/or DOS.

14.2 Redirecting Input/Output on UNIX and DOS Systems

Normally the input to a program is from the keyboard (standard input), and the output from a program is displayed on the screen (standard output). On most computer systems—UNIX and DOS systems in particular—it is possible to *redirect* inputs to come from a file rather than the keyboard, and redirect outputs to be placed in a file rather than on the screen. Both forms of redirection can be accomplished without using the file processing capabilities of the standard library.

There several ways to redirect input and output from the UNIX command line. Consider the executable file `sum.` that inputs integers one at a time and keeps a running total of the values until the end-of-file indicator is set, then prints the result. Normally the user inputs integers from the keyboard and enters the end-of-file key combination to indicate that no further values will be input. With input redirection, the input can be stored in a file. For example, if the data is stored in file `input`, the command line

```
$ sum < input
```

causes program `sum` to be executed; the *redirect input symbol* `<` indicates that the data in file `input` is to be used as input by the program. Redirecting input on a DOS system is performed identically.

Note that $ is the UNIX command line prompt. Students often find it difficult to understand that redirection is an operating system function, not another C feature.

The second method of redirecting input is *piping*. A *pipe (|)* causes the output of one program to be redirected as the input to another program. Suppose program `random` outputs a series of random integers; the output of `random` can be "piped" directly to program `sum` using the UNIX command line

```
$ random | sum
```

This causes the sum of the integers produced by `random` to be calculated. Piping can be performed in UNIX and DOS.

Program output can be redirected to a file by using the *redirect output symbol >* (the same symbol is used for UNIX and DOS). For example, to redirect the output of program `random` to file `out`, use

```
$ random > out
```

Finally, program output can be appended to the end of an existing file by using the *append output symbol >>* (the same symbol is used for UNIX and DOS). For example, to append the output from program `random` to file `out` created in the preceding command line, use the command line

```
$ random >> out
```

14.3 Variable-Length Argument Lists

It is possible to create functions that receive an unspecified number of arguments. Most of the programs in the text have used the standard library function `printf` which, as you know, takes a variable number of arguments. As a minimum, `printf` must receive a string as its first argument, but `printf` can receive any number of additional arguments. The function prototype for `printf` is

```
int printf(const char *format, ...);
```

The ellipsis (. . .) in the function prototype indicates that the function receives a variable number of arguments of any type. Note that the ellipsis must always be placed at the end of the parameter list.

The macros and definitions of the *variable arguments header `stdarg.h`* (Fig. 14.1) provide the capabilities necessary to build functions with variable length argument lists. The program of Fig. 14.2 demonstrates function `average` that receives a variable number of arguments. The first argument of `average` is always the number of values to be averaged.

Identifier	Explanation
`va_list`	A type suitable for holding information needed by macros `va_start`, `va_arg`, and `va_end`. To access the arguments in a variable-length argument list, an object of type `va_list` must be declared.
`va_start`	A macro that is invoked before the arguments of a variable-length argument list can be accessed. The macro initializes the object declared with `va_list` for use by the `va_arg` and `va_end` macros.
`va_arg`	A macro that expands to an expression of the value and type of the next argument in the variable-length argument list. Each invocation of `va_arg` modifies the object declared with `va_list` so that the object points to the next argument in the list.
`va_end`	A macro that facilitates a normal return from a function whose variable-length argument list was referred to by the `va_start` macro.

Fig. 14.1 The type and the macros defined in header `stdarg.h`.

Function average uses all the definitions and macros of header stdarg.h. Object ap, of type va_list, is used by macros va_start, va_arg, and va_end to process the variable-length argument list of function average. The function begins by invoking macro va_start to initialize object ap for use in va_arg and va_end. The macro receives two arguments—object ap and the identifier of the rightmost argument in the argument list before the ellipsis—i in this case (va_start uses i here to determine where the variable-length argument list begins). Next function average repeatedly adds the arguments in the variable-length argument list to variable total. The value to be added to total is retrieved from the argument list by invoking macro va_arg. Macro va_arg receives two arguments— object ap, and the type of the value expected in the argument list—double in this case. The macro returns the value of the argument. Function average invokes macro va_end with object ap as an argument to facilitate a normal return to main from average. Finally, the average is calculated and returned to main.

CPE 14.1

Placing an ellipsis in the middle of a function parameter list. An ellipsis may only be placed at the end of the parameter list.

The reader may question how printf knows what type to use in each va_arg macro. The answer is that printf scans its format conversion specifiers to determine the type of the next argument to be processed.

```
/* Using variable-length argument lists */
#include <stdio.h>
#include <stdarg.h>

main()
{
    double average(int, ...);
    double w = 37.5, x = 22.5, y = 1.7, z = 10.2;

    printf("%s%.1f\n%s%.1f\n%s%.1f\n%s%.1f\n\n",
           "w = ", w, "x = ", x, "y = ", y, "z = ", z);
    printf("%s%.3f\n%s%.3f\n%s%.3f\n",
           "The average of w and x is ",
           average(2, w, x),
           "The average of w, x, and y is ",
           average(3, w, x, y),
           "The average of w, x, y, and z is ",
           average(4, w, x, y, z));
}

double average(int i, ...)
{
    double total = 0;
    int j;
    va_list ap;

    va_start(ap, i);

    for (j = 1; j <= i; j++)
        total += va_arg(ap, double);

    va_end(ap);
    return total/i;
}
```

```
w = 37.5
x = 22.5
y = 1.7
z = 10.2

The average of w and x is 30.000
The average of w, x, and y is 20.567
The average of w, x, y, and z is 17.975
```

Fig. 14.2 Using variable-length argument lists.

14.4 Using Command-Line Arguments

On many systems—DOS and UNIX in particular—it is possible to pass arguments to main from a command line by including parameters int argc and char *argv[] in the parameter list of main. Parameter argc receives the number of command-line arguments. Parameter argv is an array of strings in which the actual command-line arguments are stored. Common uses of command-line arguments include printing the arguments, passing options to a program, and passing filenames to a program.

The program of Fig. 14.3 copies a file into another file one character at a time. The executable file for the program is called `copy`. A typical command line for the `copy` program on a UNIX system is

```
$ copy input output
```

This command line indicates that file `input` is to be copied to file `output`. When the program is executed, if `argc` is not 3 (`copy` counts as one of the arguments), the program prints an error message, and terminates. Otherwise, array `argv` contains the strings `"copy"`, `"input"`, and `"output"`. The second and third arguments on the command line are used as file names by the program. The files are opened using function `fopen`. If both files are opened successfully, characters are read from file `input` and written to file `output` until the end-of-file indicator for file `input` is set. Then the program terminates. The result is an exact copy of file `input`. Note that not all computer systems support command-line arguments as easily as UNIX and DOS. Macintosh and VMS systems, for example, require special settings for processing command-line arguments. See the manuals for your system for more information on command-line arguments.

14.5 Notes on Compiling Multiple-Source-File Programs

As stated earlier in the text it is possible to build programs that consist of multiple source files. There are several considerations when creating programs that are contained in multiple files. Function definitions cannot be split between two files. For programs compiled in separate source files that contain external variables, it is necessary to declare the external variables in each file in which the variables are used. For exam-

```
/* Using command-line arguments */
#include <stdio.h>

main(int argc, char *argv[])
{
   FILE *infileptr, *outfileptr;
   int c;

   if (argc != 3)
      printf("Usage: copy infile outfile\n");
   else
      if ((infileptr = fopen(argv[1], "r")) != NULL)
         if ((outfileptr = fopen(argv[2], "w")) != NULL)
            while ((c = fgetc(infileptr)) != EOF)
               fputc(c, outfileptr);
         else
            printf("File \"%s\" could not be opened\n", argv[2]);
      else
         printf("File \"%s\" could not be opened\n", argv[1]);
}
```

Fig. 14.3 Using command-line arguments.

ple, if we define external integer variable `flag` in one file, and refer to it in a second file, the second file must contain the declaration

```
extern int flag;
```

before the variable is referred to in that file.

Just as `extern` declarations can be used to declare external variables to other program files, function prototypes enable the scope of a function to be extended beyond the file in which it is defined. This is accomplished by including the function prototype in each file in which the function is invoked, and compiling the files together (see Section 13.2). Note that many systems do not support external variable names or function names of more than 6 characters. This should be considered when writing programs that will be ported to multiple platforms.

When building large programs in multiple source files, compiling the program becomes tedious if small changes are made to one file, and the entire program must be recompiled. Many systems provide special utilities that recompile only the modified program file. On UNIX systems the utility is called *make*. Utility `make` reads a file called *makefile* that contains instructions for compiling and linking the program. Systems such as Turbo C and Turbo C++ for PCs provide `make` utilities as well. For more information on `make` utilities, see the manuals for your particular system.

14.6 Program Termination with Exit and Atexit

The general utilities library (`stdlib.h`) provides methods of terminating program execution other than a conventional return from function `main`. Function *exit* forces a program to terminate as if it executed normally. The function often is used to terminate a program when an error is detected in the input, or if a file to be processed by the program cannot be opened. Function *atexit registers* a function in the program to be called upon successful termination of the program—i.e., either when the program terminates by reaching the end of `main`, or when `exit` is invoked.

Function `atexit` takes a pointer to a function (i.e., the function name) as an argument. Functions called at program termination cannot have arguments, and cannot return a value. Up to 32 functions may be registered for execution at program termination.

Function `exit` takes one argument. The argument is normally the symbolic constant *EXIT_SUCCESS* or the symbolic constant *EXIT_FAILURE*. If `exit` is called with `EXIT_SUCCESS`, the implementation-defined value for successful termination is returned to the calling environment. If `exit` is called with `EXIT_FAILURE`, the implementation-defined value for unsuccessful termination is returned. When function `exit` is invoked, any functions previously registered with `atexit` are invoked in the reverse order of their registration, all streams associated with the program are flushed and closed, and control returns to the host environment. The program of Fig. 14.4 tests functions `exit` and `atexit`. The program prompts the user to determine whether the program should be terminated with `exit` or by reaching the end of `main`. Note that function `print` is executed at program termination in each case.

```
/* Using the exit and atexit functions */

#include <stdio.h>
#include <stdlib.h>

main()
{
   int answer;
   void print(void);

   atexit(print);            /* register function print */
   printf("%s\n%s\n: ",
          "Enter 1 to terminate program with function exit",
          "Enter 2 to terminate program normally");
   scanf("%d", &answer);

   if (answer == 1) {
      printf("\nTerminating program with function exit\n");
      exit(EXIT_SUCCESS);
   }

   printf("\nTerminating program by reaching the end of main\n");
}

void print(void)
{
   printf("Executing function print at program termination\n");
   printf("Program terminated\n");
}
```

```
Enter 1 to terminate program with function exit
Enter 2 to terminate program normally
: 1

Terminating program with function exit
Executing function print at program termination
Program terminated
```

```
Enter 1 to terminate program with function exit
Enter 2 to terminate program normally
: 2

Terminating program by reaching the end of main
Executing function print at program termination
Program terminated
```

Fig. 14.4 Using functions exit and atexit.

14.7 The Const and Volatile Type Qualifiers

The const qualifier indicates that the object to which it is applied is not altered after the object is initialized. Compilers vary in their ability to enforce this. As seen in the function prototypes for many functions in the string handling library, const is often used to indicate that a function does not modify an argument.

The ANSI standard (An90) indicates that when volatile is used to qualify a type, the nature of the access to an object of that type is implementation dependent. Kernighan and Ritchie (Ke88) indicate that the volatile qualifier is used to suppress various kinds of optimizations.

14.8 Suffixes for Integer and Floating Point Constants

C provides integer and floating point suffixes for specifying the types of integer and floating point constants. The integer suffixes are: u or U for an unsigned integer, l or L for a long integer, and ul or UL for an unsigned long integer. The following constants are of type unsigned, long, and unsigned long respectively:

```
174u
8358L
28373ul
```

If an integer constant is not suffixed, its type is determined by the first type capable of storing a value of that size (first int, then long int, then unsigned long int).

The floating point suffixes are: f or F for a float, and l or L for a long double. The following constants are of type float and long double respectively:

```
3.14159L
1.28f
```

A floating point constant that is not suffixed is automatically of type double.

14.9 More on Files

Chapter 11 introduced capabilities for processing text files with sequential access and random access. C also provides capabilities for processing binary files, but some computer systems do not support binary files. If binary files are not supported, and a file is opened in a binary file mode (Fig. 14.5), the file will be processed as a text file. Binary files should be used instead of text files only in situations where rigid speed, storage, and/or compatibility conditions demand binary files. Otherwise, text files are always preferred for their inherent portability, and for the ability to use other standard tools to examine and manipulate the file data.

> **PERF 14.1**
>
> *Consider using binary files instead of text files in applications that demand high performance.*

Mode	Description
rb	Open a binary file for reading.
wb	Create a binary file for writing. If the file already exists, discard the current contents.
ab	Append; open or create a binary file for writing at end-of-file.
rb+	Open a binary file for update (reading and writing).
wb+	Create a binary file for update. If the file already exists, discard the current contents.
ab+	Append; open or create a binary file for update; all writing is done at the end of the file.

Fig. 14.5 Binary file open modes.

PORT 14.1

Use text files when writing portable programs.

In addition to the file processing functions discussed in Chapter 11, the standard library also provides function `tmpfile` that opens a temporary file in mode `"wb+"`. Although this is a binary file mode, some systems process temporary files as text files. A temporary file exists until it is closed with `fclose`, or until the program terminates.

The program of Fig. 14.6 changes the tabs in a file to spaces. The program prompts the user to enter the name of a file to be modified. If the file entered by the user and the temporary file are opened successfully, the program reads characters from the file to be modified, and writes them to the temporary file. If the character read is a tab (`'\t'`), it is replaced by a space and written to the temporary file. When the end of the file being modified is reached, the file pointers for each file are repositioned to the start of each file with `rewind`. Next, the temporary file is copied into the original file one character at a time. The program prints the original file as it copies characters into the temporary file, and prints the new file as it copies characters from the temporary file to the original file to confirm the characters being written.

14.10 Signal Handling

An unexpected event, or *signal*, can cause a program to terminate prematurely. Some unexpected events include *interrupts* (typing `<ctrl> c` on a UNIX or DOS system), *illegal instructions*, *segmentation violations*, *termination orders from the operating system*, and *floating point exceptions* (division by zero or multiplying large floating point values). The *signal handling library* provides the capability to *trap* unexpected events with function *signal*. Function `signal` receives two arguments—an integer signal number and a pointer to the signal handling function. Signals can be generated by function *raise* which takes an integer signal number as an argument. Fig. 14.7 summarizes the standard signals defined in header file *signal.h*. The program of Fig. 14.8 demonstrates functions `signal` and `raise`.

```
/* Using temporary files */
#include <stdio.h>

main()
{
    FILE *fileptr, *tempfileptr;
    int c;
    char filename[30];

    printf("%s\n%s",
            "This program changes tabs to spaces.",
            "Enter a file to be modified: ");
    scanf("%s", filename);

    if ((fileptr = fopen(filename, "r+")) != NULL)
        if ((tempfileptr = tmpfile()) != NULL) {
            printf("\nThe file before modification is:\n");

            while ((c = getc(fileptr)) != EOF) {
                putchar(c);

                if (c == '\t')
                    putc(' ', tempfileptr);
                else
                    putc(c, tempfileptr);

            }

            rewind(tempfileptr);
            rewind(fileptr);
            printf("\n\nThe file after modification is:\n");

            while ((c = getc(tempfileptr)) != EOF) {
                putchar(c);
                putc(c, fileptr);
            }

        } else
            printf("Unable to open temporary file\n");
    else
        printf("Unable to open %s\n", filename);
}
```

```
This program changes tabs to spaces.
Enter a file to be modified: data

The file before modification is:
0       1       2       3       4
        5       6       7       8       9

The file after modification is:
0 1 2 3 4
  5 6 7 8 9
```

Fig. 14.6 Using temporary files.

Signal	Explanation
SIGABRT	Abnormal termination of the program (such as a call to function **abort**).
SIGFPE	An erroneous arithmetic operation, such as a divide by zero or an operation resulting in overflow.
SIGILL	Detection of an illegal instruction.
SIGINT	Receipt of an interactive attention signal.
SIGSEGV	An invalid access to storage.
SIGTERM	A termination request set to the program.

Fig. 14.7 The signals defined in header **signal.h**.

The program of Fig. 14.8 uses function signal to trap an interactive signal (SIGINT). The program begins by calling signal with SIGINT and a pointer to function signal_handler (remember that the name of a function is a pointer to the beginning of the function). When a signal of type SIGINT is generated, control is passed to function signal_handler, a message is printed, and the user is given the option to continue normal execution of the program. If the user wishes to continue execution, the signal handler is reinitialized by calling signal again (some systems require the signal handler to be reinitialized), and control returns to the point in the program at which the signal was detected. In this program, function raise is used to simulate an interactive signal. A random number between 1 and 50 is chosen. If the number is 25, then raise is called to generate the signal. Normally, interactive signals are initiated outside the program. For example, typing <ctrl> c during program execution on a UNIX or DOS system generates an interactive signal that terminates program execution. Signal handling can be used to trap the interactive signal and prevent the program from being terminated.

14.11 Dynamic Memory Allocation: Functions Calloc and Realloc

Chapter 12, "Data Structures," introduced the notion of dynamically allocating memory using the malloc function. As we stated in Chapter 12, arrays are better than linked lists for rapid sorting, searching, and data access. However, arrays are normally *static data structures*. The general utilities library (stdlib.h) provides two other functions for dynamic memory allocation—calloc and realloc. These functions can be used to create and modify *dynamic arrays*. As shown in Chapter 7, "Pointers," a pointer to an array can be subscripted like an array. Thus, a pointer to a contiguous portion of memory created by calloc can be manipulated as an array. Function calloc dynamically allocates memory for an array. The prototype for calloc is

```
void *calloc(size_t nmemb, size_t size);
```

It receives two arguments—the number of elements (nmemb) and the size of each element (size)—and initializes the elements of the array to zero. The function returns a pointer to the allocated memory, or a NULL pointer if the memory is not allocated.

```
/* Using signal handling */

#include <stdio.h>
#include <signal.h>
#include <stdlib.h>
#include <time.h>

void signal_handler(int);

main()
{
   int i, x;

   signal(SIGINT, signal_handler);
   srand(clock());

   for (i = 1; i <= 100; i++) {
      x = 1 + rand() % 50;

      if (x == 25)
         raise(SIGINT);

      printf("%4d", i);

      if (i % 10 == 0)
         printf("\n");

   }
}

void signal_handler(int signalvalue)
{
   int response;

   printf("%s%d%s\n%s",
           "\nInterrupt signal (", signalvalue, ") received.",
           "Do you wish to continue (1 = yes or 2 = no)? ");

   scanf("%d", &response);

   while (response != 1 && response != 2) {
      printf("(1 = yes or 2 = no)? ");
      scanf("%d", &response);
   }

   if (response == 1)
      signal(SIGINT, signal_handler);
   else
      exit(EXIT_SUCCESS);

}
```

Fig. 14.8 Using signal handling (part 1 of 2).

```
    1    2    3    4    5    6    7    8    9   10
   11   12   13   14   15   16   17   18   19   20
   21   22   23   24   25   26   27   28   29   30
   31   32   33   34   35   36   37   38   39   40
   41   42   43   44   45   46   47   48   49   50
   51   52   53   54   55   56   57   58   59   60
   61   62   63   64   65   66   67   68   69   70
   71   72   73   74   75   76   77   78   79   80
   81   82   83   84   85   86   87   88
Interrupt signal (4) received.
Do you wish to continue (1 = yes or 2 = no)? 1
   89   90
   91   92   93   94   95   96   97   98   99  100
```

Fig. 14.8 Using signal handling (part 2 of 2).

Function `realloc` changes the size of an object allocated by a previous call to `malloc`, `calloc`, or `realloc`. The original object's contents are not modified provided that the amount of memory allocated is larger than the amount allocated previously. Otherwise, the contents are unchanged up to the size of the new object. The prototype for `realloc` is

```
void *realloc(void *ptr, size_t size);
```

Function `realloc` takes two arguments—a pointer to the original object (`ptr`) and the new size of the object (`size`). If `ptr` is `NULL`, `realloc` works identically to `malloc`. If `size` is 0 and `ptr` is not `NULL`, the memory for the object is freed. Otherwise, if `ptr` is not `NULL` and size is greater than zero, `realloc` tries to allocate a new block of memory for the object. If the new space can not be allocated, the object pointed to by `ptr` is unchanged. Function `realloc` returns either a pointer to the reallocated memory, or a `NULL` pointer.

Summary

- On many computer systems—UNIX and DOS systems in particular—it is possible to redirect input to a program and output from a program.

- Input is redirected from the UNIX and DOS command lines using the redirect input symbol (<). On a UNIX system, input can also be redirected using a pipe (|).

- Output is redirected from the UNIX and DOS command lines using the redirect output symbol (>) or the append output symbol (>>). The redirect output symbol simply stores the program output in a file, and the append output symbol appends the output to the end of a file.

- The macros and definitions of the variable arguments header `stdarg.h` provide the capabilities necessary to build functions with variable-length argument lists.

- An ellipsis (. . .) in a function prototype indicates that the function receives a variable number of arguments.

- Type `va_list` is suitable for holding information needed by macros `va_start`, `va_arg`, and `va_end`. To access the arguments in a variable-length argument list, an object of type `va_list` must be declared.

- Macro `va_start` is invoked before the arguments of a variable-length argument list can be accessed. The macro initializes the object declared with `va_list` for use by the `va_arg` and `va_end` macros.

- Macro `va_arg` expands to an expression of the value and type of the next argument in the variable length argument list. Each invocation of `va_arg` modifies the object declared with `va_list` so that the object points to the next argument in the list.

- Macro `va_end` facilitates a normal return from a function whose variable argument list was referred to by the `va_start` macro.

- On many systems—DOS and UNIX in particular—it is possible to pass arguments to `main` from the command line by including the parameters `int argc` and `char *argv[]` in the parameter list of `main`. Parameter `argc` receives the number of command-line arguments. Parameter `argv` is an array of strings in which the actual command-line arguments are stored.

- Function definitions cannot be split between files.

- For programs compiled in separate source files that contain external variables, it is necessary to declare external variables in each file in which the variables are used.

- Many systems do not support external variable names or function names of more than 6 characters.

- When building large programs in multiple source files, compiling the program becomes tedious if small changes are made to one file, and the entire program must be recompiled. Some systems provide special utilities that recompile only the modified program file. On UNIX systems the utility is called *make*. The `make` utility reads a file called *makefile* that contains instructions for compiling and linking the program.

- Function `exit` forces a program to terminate as if it executed normally.

- Function `atexit` registers a function in a program to be called upon normal termination of the program—i.e., either when the program terminates by reaching the end of `main`, or when `exit` is invoked.

- Function `atexit` takes a pointer to a function (i.e., the function name) as an argument. Functions called at program termination cannot have arguments, and cannot return a value. Up to 32 functions may be registered for execution at program termination.

- Function `exit` takes one argument. The argument is normally the symbolic constant `EXIT_SUCCESS` or the symbolic constant `EXIT_FAILURE`. If `exit` is called with `EXIT_SUCCESS`, the implementation-defined value for successful termination is returned to the calling environment. If `exit` is called with `EXIT_FAILURE`, the implementation-defined value for unsuccessful termination is returned.

- When function `exit` is invoked, any functions registered with `atexit` are invoked in the reverse order of their registration, all streams associated with the program are flushed and closed, and control returns to the host environment.

- The `const` qualifier indicates that the object to which it is applied is not altered after the object is initialized. Compilers vary in their ability to enforce this.

- The ANSI standard (An90) indicates that when `volatile` is used to qualify a type, the nature of the access to an object of that type is implementation dependent. Kernighan and Ritchie (Ke88) indicate that the `volatile` qualifier is used to suppress various kinds of optimizations.

- C provides integer and floating point suffixes for specifying the types of integer and floating point constants. The integer suffixes are: u or U for an `unsigned` integer, l or L for a `long` integer, and ul or UL for an `unsigned long` integer. If an integer constant is not suffixed, its type is determined by the first type capable of storing a value of that size (first `int`, then `long int`, then `unsigned long int`). The floating point suffixes are: f or F for a `float`, and l or L for a `long double`. A floating point constant that is not suffixed is of type `double`.

- C also provides capabilities for processing binary files, but some computer systems do not support binary files. If binary files are not supported, and a file is opened in a binary file mode, the file will be processed as a text file.

- Function `tmpfile` opens a temporary file in mode `"wb+"`. Although this is a binary file mode, some systems process temporary files as text files. A temporary file exists until it is closed with `fclose`, or until the program terminates.

- The signal handling library provides the capability to trap unexpected events with function `signal`. Function `signal` receives two arguments—an integer signal number and a pointer to the signal handling function.

- Signals can also be generated with function `raise`. Function `raise` takes an integer signal number as an argument.

- The general utilities library (`stdlib.h`) provides two functions for dynamic memory allocation—`calloc` and `realloc`. These functions can be used to create dynamic arrays.

- Function `calloc` receives two arguments—the number of elements (`nmemb`) and the size of each element (`size`)—and initializes the elements of the array to zero. The function returns either a pointer to the allocated memory, or a `NULL` pointer if the memory is not allocated.

- Function `realloc` changes the size of an object allocated by a previous call to `malloc`, `calloc`, or `realloc`. The original object's contents are not modified provided that the amount of memory allocated is larger than the amount allocated previously.

- Function `realloc` takes two arguments—a pointer to the original object (`ptr`) and the new size of the object (`size`). If `ptr` is NULL, `realloc` works identically to `malloc`. If `size` is 0 and the pointer received is not NULL, the memory for the object is freed. Otherwise, if `ptr` is not NULL and size is greater than zero, `realloc` tries to allocate a new block of memory for the object. If the new space cannot be allocated, the object pointed to by `ptr` is unchanged. Function `realloc` returns either a pointer to the reallocated memory, or a NULL pointer.

Terminology

append output symbol `>>`
`argc`
`argv`
`atexit`
`calloc`
command-line arguments
`const`
dynamic arrays
ellipsis (...)
event
`exit`
`EXIT_FAILURE`
`EXIT_SUCCESS`
`float` suffix (`f` or `F`)
floating point constant suffix
floating point exception
I/O redirection
illegal instruction
integer constant suffix
interrupt
`long double` suffix (`l` or `L`)
`long integer` suffix (`l` or `L`)
`make`
`makefile`

pipe `|`
piping
`raise`
redirect input symbol `<`
redirect output symbol `>`
segmentation violation
`signal`
signal handling library
`signal.h`
`stdarg.h`
temporary file
termination order from the operating system
`tmpfile`
trap
`unsigned` integer suffix (`u` or `U`)
`unsigned long` integer suffix (`ul` or `UL`)
`va_arg`
`va_end`
`va_list`
`va_start`
variable-length argument list
`volatile`

Common Programming Errors

14.1   Placing an ellipsis in the middle of a function parameter list. An ellipsis may only be placed at the end of the parameter list.

Portability Tips

14.1   Use text files when writing portable programs.

Performance Tips

14.1 Consider using binary files instead of text files in applications that demand high performance.

Self-Review Exercises

14.1 Fill in the blanks in each of the following:
   a) The _____ symbol is used to redirect input data from the keyboard to come from a file.
   b) The _____ symbol is used to redirect the screen output to be placed in a file.
   c) The _____ symbol is used to append the output of a program to the end of a file.
   d) A _____ is used to direct the output of one program to be the input of another program.
   e) An _____ in the parameter list of a function indicates that the function can receive a variable number of arguments.
   f) Macro _____ must be invoked before the arguments in a variable-length argument list can be accessed.
   g) Macro _____ is used to access the individual arguments of a variable-length argument list.
   h) Macro _____ facilitates a normal return from a function whose variable argument list was referred to by macro **va_start**.
   i) Argument _____ of **main** receives the number of arguments in a command line.
   j) Argument _____ of **main** stores each command-line argument as a character string.
   k) The UNIX utility _____ reads a file called _____ that contains instructions for compiling and linking a program consisting of multiple source files. The utility only recompiles a file if the file has been modified since it was last compiled.
   l) Function _____ forces a program to terminate execution.
   m) Function _____ registers a function to be called upon normal termination of the program.
   n) Type qualifier _____ indicates that an object should not be modified after it is initialized.
   o) An integer or floating-point _____ can be appended to an integer or floating-point constant to specify the exact type of the constant.
   p) Function _____ opens a temporary file that exists until it is closed or program execution terminates.
   q) Function _____ can be used to trap unexpected events.
   r) Function _____ generates a signal from within a program.
   s) Function _____ dynamically allocates memory for an array and initializes the elements to zero.
   t) Function _____ changes the size of a block of memory dynamically allocated previously.

Answers to Self-Review Exercises

14.1   a) redirect input (<). b) redirect output (>). c) append output (>>). d) pipe (|). e) ellipsis (. . .). f) `va_start`. g) `va_arg`. h) `va_end`. i) `argc`. j) `argv`. k) `make, makefile`. l) `exit`. m) `atexit`. n) `const`. o) suffix. p) `tmpfile`. q) `signal`. r) `raise`. s) `calloc`. t) `realloc`.

Exercises

14.2   Write a program that calculates the product of a series of integers that are passed to function `product` using a variable-length argument list. Test your function with several calls each with a different number of arguments.

14.3   Write a program that prints the command-line arguments of the program.

14.4   Write a program that sorts an array of integers into ascending or descending order. The program should use command-line arguments to pass either argument `-a` for ascending order or `-d` for descending order. (Note: this is the standard format for passing options to a program in UNIX.)

14.5   Write a program that places a space between each character in a file. The program should first write the contents of the file being modified into a temporary file with spaces between each character, then copy the file back to the original file. This operation should overwrite the original contents of the file.

14.6   Read the manuals for your system to determine what signals are supported by the signal handling library (`signal.h`). Write a program that contains signal handlers for the standard signals `SIGABRT` and `SIGINT`. The program should test the trapping of these signals by calling function `abort` to generate a `SIGABRT` signal, and by typing <ctrl> c to generate a `SIGINT` signal.

14.7   Write a program that dynamically allocates an array of integers. The size of the array should be input from the keyboard. The elements of the array should be assigned values input from the keyboard. Print the values of the array. Next, reallocate the memory for the array to 1/2 of the current number of elements. Print the values remaining in the array to confirm that they match the first half of the values in the original array.

15

Object-Oriented Programming and C++

Objectives

- To understand what object-oriented programming (OOP) is.
- To appreciate why OOP can improve the software development process.
- To become familiar with C++—the object-oriented variant of C.
- To write object-oriented programs in C++.
- To reexamine C programs from earlier chapters in the context of C++.
- To appreciate why C provides a foundation for further study of programming in general and C++ in particular.

My object all sublime
I shall achieve in time.

W. S. Gilbert

Say not you know another entirely, till you have divided
an inheritance with him.

Johann Kasper Lavater

This method is, to define as the number of a class the
class of all classes similar to the given class.

Bertrand Russell

Outline

15.1 Introduction

Welcome to C++! It may seem unusual for a programming language textbook to end with an introductory chapter on another programming language. But this makes good sense here for several reasons. C's designers and early implementers never anticipated that the language would become such a phenomenon (the same holds true for the UNIX operating system). When a programming language becomes as entrenched as C, new requirements demand that the language evolve rather than simply be displaced by a new language. C++ improves on many of C's features and provides *object-oriented programming (OOP)* capabilities that hold great promise for increasing software productivity and quality.

For many readers, this will be your first exposure to C++ and object-oriented programming. We hope that reading this chapter will encourage you to continue your study of these important topics. The reader is cautioned that our effort here is, at best, an oversimplification of complex subject matter. Our goal is simply to provide a friendly introduction. We have intentionally omitted many important features and subtleties of C++.

C++ was developed by Bjarne Stroustrup at Bell Laboratories (St86), and was originally called "C with classes." The name C++ includes C's increment operator to indicate that C++ is an enhanced version of C.

C++ is a superset of C, so programmers can use a C++ compiler to compile their existing C programs, and then gradually evolve these programs to C++. Already, some leading software suppliers offer C++ compilers and do not offer separate C products.

We show many working C++ programs and their outputs to illustrate key features of the language. * We then present a detailed case study on implementing linked lists, stacks, and queues using object-oriented techniques in C++.

C++ does have some disadvantages (Re91). No ANSI standard exists yet, although an ANSI committee is developing a proposal. C++ program development environments are not as mature as C environments, so program development on significant software projects can be awkward. The language lacks a uniform exception handling methodology and parameterized types, but standards for these have been approved by the ANSI C++ working committee. Despite these problems, it is widely believed that most major C programming environments will convert to C++ by the mid-1990s.

15.2 Object Orientation

Look around you in the real world. Everywhere you look you see them—*objects*! People, animals, plants, cars, planes, buildings, lawnmowers, computers and the like. Humans think in terms of objects. We have the marvelous ability of *abstraction* that enables us to view a screen image of pixels as objects rather than as individual dots of color. We think in terms of beaches rather than grains of sand, forests rather than trees, and houses rather than bricks.

We might be inclined to divide objects into two categories—animate objects and inanimate objects. Animate objects are "alive" in some sense. They move around and do things. Inanimate objects, like towels, seem not to do much at all. They just "sit around." All these objects, however, do have some things in common. They all have *attributes* like size, shape, color, weight, and the like. And they all exhibit various kinds of *behavior*, e.g., a ball rolls, bounces, inflates, deflates, and the like. A baby cries, sleeps, crawls, walks, blinks, and so on.

Humans learn about objects by studying their attributes and observing their behavior. Humans also recognize that different objects can have many of the same attributes and exhibit similar behavior. Such comparisons, for example, can be made be-

---

* *Acknowledgment:* The authors would like to acknowledge the Borland Corporation for their products Turbo C++ and Borland C++, and for the very readable, high-quality documentation supplied by Borland with these products.

tween babies and adults, and between humans and chimpanzees. Cars, trucks, and little red wagons have much in common.

When new objects are created, they often *inherit* many characteristics from "template" objects, even though these new objects may possess unique characteristics of their own. Babies have many characteristics of their parents, yet short parents occasionally have tall children.

Object-oriented programming models real-world objects with software counterparts. It takes advantage of *class* relationships where objects of a certain class have the same characteristics, for example, a class of vehicles. It takes advantage of *inheritance* relationships, and even *multiple inheritance* relationships where newly created objects inherit characteristics of "parents," yet contain unique characteristics of their own. For example, a queue can inherit characteristics and capabilities from a linked list, yet still have its own unique features. OOP also models communication between between objects. Just as people send *messages* to one another (e.g., a sergeant commanding troops to stand at attention), objects also communicate via messages.

Object-oriented programming *encapsulates* data (attributes) and functions (behavior) into packages called *objects*. The data and functions are now intimately tied together. Objects have the property of *information hiding*. This means that although objects may know how to communicate with one another across well-defined *interfaces*, objects normally are not allowed to know how other objects are implemented—implementation details are hidden within the objects themselves.

Object-oriented programming gives us a more natural and intuitive way to view the programming process, namely by modeling real-world objects, their attributes, their behaviors, and their means of communicating, and by viewing software systems as groups of communicating objects. OOP derives from work done in Europe in the 1950s and 1960s that led to the language *Simula67*. Simula67 offered *classes, derived classes,* and *virtual functions*—each capabilities that appear in C++.

15.3 Data Abstraction and Information Hiding

C++ supports the notion of classes. Programmers may define their own classes as user-defined data types in a manner that hides the details of their implementation from the users of the classes. This technique is typically called *information hiding*. Thus, for example, the programmer may create a stack class and hide from its users the way in which the stack is implemented. We can implement stacks using arrays or linked lists. But, a user of a stack should not have to care how the stack is implemented. What the user really cares about is simply that when data items are placed in a stack, the data items will be recalled in last-in-first-out (LIFO) order. This concept is also referred to as *data abstraction*, and C++ classes may be viewed as *abstract data types*. Although users *may* know the details of how a class is implemented, users may not write code that depends on these details. This means that a particular class (such as one that implements a stack and its operations of push and pop) can be replaced with another version at any time without affecting the rest of the system. Once a class is defined, users may create objects that are members of the class. For example, once class stack is created, we can create (or *instantiate*) a new stack object such as functioncallstack by naming the class followed by the name of the object:

```
stack functioncallstack;
```

Classes simplify programming because the user need only be concerned with the operations encapsulated or embedded in them. Such operations are usually closer to the "problem domain" than to the "implementation domain."

Of course, class stack does not have to be created "from scratch." It may be derived from another class, say class linkedlist, that may provide many operations that can be used directly by class stack without having to be rewritten. Such software reuse can greatly enhance productivity, and is a powerful software engineering tool.

15.4 Software Reusability: Class Libraries

People who write object-oriented programs spend lots of time thinking about and implementing useful objects, more precisely *classes* of objects. An object is essentially an *instance of a class* just as two particular people are instances of the class "human," and IBM PCs and Apple Macintoshes are instances of the class "personal computer." An object and its class have essentially the same relationship as a house and its blueprint. Classes model useful, real-world items. There is a tremendous opportunity for us to capture and *catalog* these classes so that they can be accessed by large segments of the programming community. *Class libraries* are being developed worldwide and there are many efforts to make these libraries broadly accessible. Software could then be constructed from existing, well-defined, widely available components. This kind of *software reusability* can speed the development of powerful, high-quality software. *Rapid prototyping* becomes possible—it becomes easy to generate first versions of working software applications quickly. The problems are significant. We need cataloging schemes, licensing schemes, protection to ensure that master "templates" are not corrupted, description schemes so that designers of new systems can determine if existing objects meet their needs, and the like. Many interesting research and development problems need to be solved. These problems *will* be solved because the potential value of their solution is enormous.

C++ provides capabilities for creating classes, for class inheritance, for creating objects (i.e., instances of classes), and for manipulating these objects. We begin with a discussion of C++ features that offer improvements over their C counterparts. We then discuss the object-oriented programming capabilities of C++. We conclude with a detailed case study of OOP in C++.

15.5 C++ Single-Line Comments

Programmers frequently insert a small comment at the end of a line of code. C requires that a comment be delimited by /* and */. C++ allows you to begin a comment with

// and use the remainder of the line for comment text. This saves some keystrokes, but is only applicable for comments that do not continue to the next line.

For example, the C comment

```
/* This is a single-line comment. */
```

requires the use of both the /* and */ delimiters, even for a single-line comment. The C++ single-line version of this is

```
// This is a single-line comment.
```

For multiple-line comments such as

```
/* This is one way to     */
/* write neat multiple-   */
/* line comments.         */
```

the C++ notation may appear to be more concise as in

```
// This is one way to
// write neat multiple-
// line comments.
```

But, remember that C comments may span multiple lines, so only a single pair (rather than the three pairs we have used) of comment delimiters is actually needed as in

```
/* This is one way to
   write neat multiple-
   line comments.        */
```

Remember that C++ is a superset of C, so both forms of comments may be used in a C++ program.

> **GPP 15.1**
> _____
>
> *Using C++-style // comments avoids the unterminated comment errors that occur by forgetting to close C-style comments with */.*

15.6 Declarations in C++

In C, all declarations must appear before any executable statements in a block. C++ allows declarations to appear anywhere an executable statement can appear provided the declarations precede the use of the entities being declared. For example,

```
printf("Enter two integers: ");
int x, y;
scanf("%d%d", &x, &y);
printf("The sum of %d and %d is %d\n", x, y, x + y);
```

declares variables x and y after the executable printf statement. Variable declarations may also appear in the initialization section of a for structure. For example,

```
for (int i = 0; i <= 5; i++)
   printf("%d\n", i);
```

declares variable i to be an integer and initializes it to 0 in the for structure. Note that the scope of a local C++ variable begins with the declaration and extends to the enclosing right brace (}).

GPP 15.2

C++ enables the programmer to place declarations close to the location in the program in which the corresponding variables are used. This can make programs more readable.

15.7 C++ Stream Input/Output

C++ provides an alternative to printf and scanf function calls for handling input/output of the standard C data types and strings. For example, the simple prompting dialog

```
printf("Enter new tag");
scanf("%d", &tag);
```

can be written in C++ as

```
cout << "Enter new tag";
cin >> tag;
```

The first statement mentions the *standard output stream* cout and the operator << (the *stream insertion operator*, pronounced *"put to"*). The statement is read

The string "Enter new tag" is put to the output stream cout.

The second statement mentions the *standard input stream* cin and the operator >> (the *stream extraction operator*, pronounced *"get from"*). This statement is read

"Get a value for tag *from the input stream* cin.*"*

Notice that the stream extraction operator, unlike scanf, does not require the type specifier %d. C++ has many areas like this in which it automatically "knows" what types to use. Note also that tag, when used with stream extraction, does not need to be preceded by the address operator &.

  To use these C++ capabilities properly, the program should include the iostream.h standard header file as follows:

```
#include <iostream.h>
```

The complete C++ program in Fig. 15.1 prompts for the user's age and then determines what the user's age will be in 3 years.

GPP 15.3

Using C++-style stream-oriented input/output makes programs more readable than their counterparts in C written with printf and scanf function calls.

```
// Age calculation
#include <iostream.h>

main()
{
    cout << "Enter your age:  ";
    int age;
    cin >> age;
    cout << "In 3 years you will be " << age + 3 << ".\n";
}
```

```
Enter your age:  22
In 3 years you will be 25.
```

Fig. 15.1 Using C++ comments and stream input/output.

15.8 Inline Functions

Function calls do involve execution-time overhead. C++ *inline functions* can help reduce function-call overhead, especially for small functions. The programmer can explicitly specify the keyword `inline` to "advise" the compiler to generate the function code in line (when possible) to minimize function calls. The tradeoff here is clearly that multiple copies of the function code are inserted in the program, rather than having a single copy of the function to which control is passed each time the function is called. Any change to an `inline` function requires all users of the function to be recompiled. This may be significant in some program development and maintenance situations.

PERF 15.1

*Using **inline** functions can reduce execution-time overhead.*

The program of Fig. 15.2 uses `inline` function `cube` to calculate the volume of a cube of side `s`. The keyword `const` in the parameter list of function cube tells the compiler that the function does not modify variable `s`. Keyword `const` can also be used to create *"constant variables"* (instead of symbolic constants) as in

```
const float PI = 3.14159;
```

This declaration creates "constant variable" (an oxymoron!) `PI` and initializes it to `3.14159`. The variable cannot be modified after it is initialized. "Constant variables" are often called *named constants* or *read-only variables*.

Fig. 15.3 contains a complete list of C++ keywords. Each of the "C++ only" keywords will be explained in the remainder of the chapter.

```
// Using an inline function to calculate the volume of a cube
#include <iostream.h>

inline float cube(const float s) {return s * s * s;}

main()
{
    float side;

    cout << "Enter the length of the side of your cube:   ";
    cin >> side;
    cout << "Volume of cube with side "
         << side << " is " << cube(side) << "\n";
}
```

```
Enter the length of the side of your cube:   3.5
Volume of cube with side 3.5 is 42.875
```

Fig. 15.2 Using an inline function to calculate the volume of a cube.

15.9 Reference Parameters

In C all calls are call-by-value. Normally, call-by-reference in C is simulated by explicitly passing a pointer to an object and then having the called function dereference the pointer to refer to the object. Remember that arrays in C are automatically passed simulated call-by-reference. Other programming languages offer a more direct form of call-by-reference—such as the use of var parameters in Pascal, for example. C++ corrects this weakness of C by offering *reference parameters*.

To indicate that a parameter is a reference parameter, simply follow the parameter's type in the function prototype by an & (exactly as you would follow a parameter's type by * to indicate that a parameter is a "pointer to" a variable of a certain type). Use the same convention when listing the parameter's type in the function header. For example, the declaration int& count in a function header may be pronounced "count is a 'reference to' int." Then, in the function call, simply mention the variable by name and it will automatically be passed call-by-reference. In the called function, mentioning the variable by its local name will actually refer to the original, which may be modified directly from the called function. Some C++ programmers prefer to write int* a rather than int *a, and int& a rather than int &a.

Reference parameters can also be created for local use within a function. For example, a set of declarations and an assignment such as

```
int count = 1;      // declare integer variable count
int& c = count;     // create c as an alias for count

++c;                // increment count (using its alias)
```

would cause variable count to be incremented by using its alias, c. The program of Fig. 15.4 uses call-by-reference parameters to swap the values of two integer variables. Note how straightforward the body of the swap function is.

C++ keywords

C and C++

auto	break	case	char	const
continue	default	do	double	else
enum	extern	float	for	goto
if	int	long	register	return
short	signed	sizeof	static	struct
switch	typedef	union	unsigned	void
while				

C++ only

asm	Implementation-defined means of using assembly language through C++ (see the manuals for your system).
class	Define a new class. Objects of this class may be created.
delete	Destroy a memory object created with **new**.
friend	Declare a function or class to be a "friend" of another class. Friend functions may access all the members (including the **private** members)—both data members and member functions—of a class.
inline	Advise the compiler that a particular function should be generated inline as opposed to requiring a function call.
new	Dynamically allocate a new memory object "on the free store." Automatically deal with how large the object is.
operator	Declare an overloaded operator.
private	A class member accessible to member functions and **friend** functions of the **private** member's class.
protected	An extended form of **private** access; **protected** members may also be accessed by member functions and friends of derived classes, and by objects of a derived class type.
public	A class member accessible to any function.
this	A pointer—implicitly declared in every member function of a class—that points to the object for which this member function has been invoked.
virtual	Declare a virtual function.

Reserved for future use in C++
catch, template, throw, try

Fig. 15.3 The C++ keywords.

GPP 15.4

Using C++-style reference parameters rather than C-style simulated call-by-reference (with pointer passing and dereferencing) makes programs more understandable.

CPE 15.1

Because reference parameters are mentioned only by name in the body of the called function, the programmer might inadvertently treat reference parameters as call-by-value parameters. This can cause unexpected side effects as the original copies of the variables are changed in the calling function.

PERF 15.2

The programmer can use a `const` *reference parameter to simulate the appearance of call-by-value, but avoid the possibly high overhead of passing a copy of the variable.*

15.10 Dynamic Memory Allocation with New and Delete

The *new* and `delete` operators in C++ provide a nicer means of performing dynamic memory allocation than with `malloc` and `free` function calls in C. Consider the following code

```
typename* typenameptr;
```

In ANSI C, to dynamically create an object of type `typename`, you would say

```
typenameptr = malloc(sizeof(typename));
```

```
// An example of true call-by-reference with reference parameters
#include <iostream.h>

main()
{
    void swap(int&, int&);
    int x = 1, y = 2;

    cout << "x before swap is " << x << ".\n";
    cout << "y before swap is " << y << ".\n";
    swap(x, y);
    cout << "x after swap is " << x << ".\n";
    cout << "y after swap is " << y << ".\n";
}

void swap(int& a, int& b)
{
    int temp = a;   // note the declaration for temp
    a = b;          // a and b are aliases for x and y in main
    b = temp;
}
```

```
x before swap is 1.
y before swap is 2.
x after swap is 2.
y after swap is 1.
```

Fig. 15.4 An example of call-by-reference.

This requires a function call to `malloc` and an explicit reference to the `sizeof` operator. In versions of C prior to ANSI C, you would also have to cast the pointer returned by `malloc` with the cast *(typename *)*. In C++, you simply write

```
typenameptr = new typename;
```

The `new` operator automatically creates the object of the proper size, and returns a pointer of the correct type. To free the space for this object in C++ you write

```
delete typenameptr;
```

C++ allows you to provide an *initializer* for a newly created object as follows

```
float* thingptr = new float (3.14159);
```

which in this case initializes a newly created `float` object to `3.14159`.

An array can be created as follows:

```
chessboardptr = new int[8][8];
```

GPP 15.5
Using C++-style dynamic memory allocation with the `new` and `delete` operators makes programs more readable than with the use of C-style `malloc` and `free` function calls.

15.11 Default Arguments

Occasionally one particular value of an argument may be passed to a function the vast majority of the time. To save keystrokes, C++ allows the programmer to indicate that a particular argument is a *default argument*, and that the default argument value is a particular value. Then, if the programmer simply omits that argument in a call to the function, the default value of that argument is automatically used. This feature only works if the default arguments are the rightmost (trailing) arguments in a function. Also, the default arguments must be specified with the first occurrence of the function name—usually the prototype in a header file. The program of Fig. 15.5 demonstrates the use of a default argument in calculating the volume of a box.

GPP15.6
Using default arguments simplifies writing function calls.

CPE 15.2
Specifying and attempting to use a default argument that is not a rightmost (trailing) argument.

15.12 Classes and Objects

A `struct` or `union` in C can contain only data members. C++ introduces the notion of `class` that can contain data members *and* member functions. Instances of a

```
// Using default arguments
#include <iostream.h>

// Function boxvolume calculates the volume of a
// box with a default height of 2
int boxvolume(int length, int width, int height = 2)
{
    return length * width * height;
}

main()
{
    cout << "The volume of a box with length 10\n"
         << "width 5 and default height 2 is: "
         << boxvolume(10, 5)
         << "\n\nThe volume of a box with length 10\n"
         << "width 5 and height 5 is: "
         << boxvolume(10, 5, 5) << "\n";
}
```

```
The volume of a box with length 10
width 5 and default height 2 is: 100

The volume of a box with length 10
width 5 and height 5 is: 250
```

Fig. 15.5 Using default arguments.

class are called *objects*. A class is to an object of that class as a type is to a variable of that type. Member functions are sometimes called *methods* in other object-oriented programming languages. Member functions respond to messages sent to an object.

Classes enable the programmer to model objects that have attributes (described by data members) and behavior or operations (described by member functions). Types containing data members and member functions can be defined in C++ using any of the keywords class, struct, or union, but keyword class is normally used for this purpose. The differences between the notions of struct, union, and class are explained in Section 15.15. Any function *defined* within a class is implicitly an inline function of that class.

Once a class has been defined, the class name can be used to declare objects of that class. For example, a class defined by

```
class thing {
    ...
};
```

can be used in declarations (without using the word class) as

```
thing  thing_item,        // an object of type thing
       array_of_thing[5],  // an array of type thing
       *pointer_to_thing,  // a pointer to thing
       &reference_to_thing; // a reference to thing
```

CPE 15.3
_____
*Forgetting the semicolon at the end of a **class** definition.*

15.13 Scope Resolution Operator

Once a class has been defined and its member functions have been declared, the member functions must be defined (if they were not defined inline in the class definition). When a member function is defined outside its corresponding class definition, the function name is preceded by the class name and the *scope resolution operator (: :)*. This notation specifies the class in which the function is declared. This resolves ambiguity caused by the fact that the same member function name may be used in different class definitions. For example, if function `print` is declared in the definition for class `A`, the function header for the function definition outside the class definition is written

```
void A::print (parameter-list)
```


15.14 Accessing Class Members

Once an object of a class has been instantiated (created), the data members and member functions of the object are referenced through either the object name, through a pointer to the object, or through a reference to the object. The operators used to access the members are identical to the operators used to access structure and union members in C. The *class member operator (.)* is combined with the object name or reference to access object members. The *class pointer operator (->)* is combined with a pointer to an object to access object members. Assume that `class count` has been defined with `public` data member `x` of type `int`, and `public` member function `print`. The definitions

```
count countobject;                     // object
count* countobjectptr = &countobject;  // pointer to object
count& countobjectref = countobject;   // reference to object
```

instantiate an object `countobject` of the class `count`, and create the pointer `countobjectptr` that points to the object `countobject`. The members of object `countobject` can be accessed using the class member operator as follows:

```
countobject.x = 7;        // assign 7 to x (through object)
countobject.print();      // call function print
countobjectref.x = 8;     // assign 8 to x (through alias)
```

The members of `countobject` can be accessed by using the class pointer operator as follows:

```
countobjectptr->x = 10;    // assign 10 to x via a pointer
countobjectptr->print();   // call function print via a pointer
```

15.15 Controlling Access to Data Members and Member Functions

Access to class members is controlled by the *member access specifiers:* `public,` `private,` and `protected`. A `public` member is accessible to any function, including *clients*. The term "client" refers to a function that is not a member of a given class. A client may be a member of another class, or it may be a global function. The listing of member functions of a class is preceded by the word `public:` if the programmer wants to make those functions available across the interface of the object to client functions outside the object. Access to a `private` member is limited to member functions and `friend` functions (see Section 15.16) of the `private` member's class. Access to `protected` members is an extended form of `private` access; `protected` members may be accessed by member functions and `friend` functions of the `protected` member's class, and by member functions and `friend` functions of a class publicly derived (see Section 15.18) from the `protected` member's class.

      The default access for members of a `class` is `private`. Access to members of a `class` may be explicitly changed to `protected` or `public`. The default access for `struct` members and `union` members is `public`. Access to members of a `struct` may be explicitly changed to `protected` or `private`. The member access specifiers may not be used explicitly with a `union`. Normally, data members are declared `private` or `protected` so they may be accessed only by member functions, and member functions are declared `public` so they can be accessed by any function. This supports the concept of information hiding. Utility functions meant to be used only by other members of a class are `private`.

15.16 Friend Functions

A *friend function* of a class is a function defined outside a class that has the right to access `protected` and `private` members of the class. An entire class may be declared to be the `friend` of another class. But, as in real life, if class A is a friend of class B, and class B is a friend of class C, you can not infer any of the following: class B is a friend of class A, class C is a friend of class B, or class A is a friend of class C. Some people in the OOP community feel that "friendship" corrupts information hiding and weakens the value of the object-oriented design approach.

      To declare a function as a `friend` of a class, declare the function in the class and precede the declaration with keyword `friend`. To declare a class as a `friend` of another class, place a declaration of the form

```
friend classname;
```

as a member of the other class.

15.17 Constructor Functions and Destructor Functions

A class may include functions with the same name as the class. These functions are *constructors* for the class. A constructor is a member function that is invoked implicitly each time a new object of the class is to be created. The constructor performs any necessary initialization such as allocating space for data structures and providing initial values. The following is the constructor defined in class `listclass` of Fig. 15.10.

```
listclass() {list = 0;}
```

This constructor—defined inline in the class in this case—simply initializes data member `list` of class `listclass` to zero. A constructor can have arguments if necessary. A class may include more than one constructor, thereby allowing different forms of initialization. If a constructor is not provided by the programmer, C++ automatically creates a default constructor—with no arguments—of the form

```
classname::classname(){};
```

The default constructor does not appear in the source file unless it is provided by the programmer.

Each class may also contain an explicit *destructor* member function that destroys objects of the class. The destructor's name is the class name preceded by the *tilde character (~)*. For example, the destructor function for class `listclass` is `~listclass()`. Destructor functions take no parameters and return no values. If, as is usually the case, a destructor is not provided by the programmer, C++ automatically creates a default destructor. There can be at most one destructor in each class.

15.18 Inheritance and Derived Classes

One of the keys to the power of object-oriented programming is *inheritance*. When creating a new class, instead of having to write completely new data members and member functions, the programmer can designate that the new class is to inherit the data members and member functions of a previously-defined, or *base class*. In this case, the new class is referred to as a *derived class* (Note: other object-oriented languages refer to a derived class as a *subclass* and the base class as a *superclass*). C++ also provides for *multiple inheritance* which allows a derived class to inherit from many base classes, even if these base classes are unrelated. A derived class has a "larger" definition than its base, and represents a smaller set of objects.

To specify that class B is derived from class A, class B would be defined as follows

```
class B : private A {
    ...
};
```

A derived class can access only the `public` and `protected` members of its base class. The preceding class definition specifies that class B inherits the `protected` and `public` members of class A and makes those members `private` to class B. If the keyword `public` is used in place of `private`, the `public` and `protected` members of A are inherited as `public` and `protected` members of B respectively. Base class members that should not be accessible to a derived class via inheritance are declared `private` in the base class. Member functions of a class are normally declared `public` so they may be accessed outside the class. One problem with inheritance is that a derived class can inherit `public` member functions that it should not have. We will see how to deal with this in the case study at the end of the chapter.

The constructor for a derived class always calls the constructor for its base class first to create and initialize the members of its base class. If the constructor for the derived class is omitted, the default constructor for the derived class automatically calls the constructor for the base class.

In the case of single inheritance, the derived class starts out essentially the same as the base class. This is not very interesting! The real strength of inheritance comes from the capabilities in C++ to define, in the derived class, additions, replacements, or refinements over and above the features that are inherited from the base class. The destructor of the derived class is called before the destructor of the base class.

15.19 Operator Overloading

Notice that the operator << is used for multiple purposes in C++, namely as the stream insertion operator ("put to") and as the left-shift operator. This is an example of *operator overloading,* a common phenomenon in C++. Similarly, >> is also overloaded; it is used both as the stream extraction operator ("get from") and as the right-shift operator. C already overloads operators such as + which is used differently depending on its context in integer arithmetic, floating point arithmetic, and pointer arithmetic.

More generally, C++ enables the programmer to redefine the behavior of most operators to be sensitive to the context in which they are used. The compiler generates the appropriate code based on the manner in which the operator is used.

Operators are overloaded by writing a function definition (with a header and body) as you normally would except the function name now becomes the keyword `operator` followed by the symbol for the operator you are overloading. Before writing C++ programs with overloaded operators, the reader should consult the C++ manuals for the reader's system to become aware of various restrictions and requirements unique to particular types of operators. *If you overload* (), [], *or* ->, *the operator overloading function must be declared as a member of a class. For the other operators, the operator overloading functions can be* `friends`. The overloaded modulus operator in Fig. 15.6 can be used to calculate the modulus of two `double` values (remember that the C modulus operator requires integral operands).

```
// Overloaded modulus operator function
double classname::operator %(double a, double b)
{
    while (a > b)
        a -= b;

    return a;
}
```

Fig. 15.6 Overloaded modulus operator function.

15.20 Function Overloading

In C++ it is possible to define several functions with the same name but with different parameter types. This is called *function overloading*. When an overloaded function is called, the C++ compiler automatically selects the proper function by first examining the number and types of arguments in the call. Function overloading can be used, for example, with class constructors to specify several ways to initialize a class object when it is created.

The program of Fig. 15.7 uses overloaded function `square` to calculate the square of an `int` and the square of a `double`. Note that the program does indeed call the appropriate function based on the type of the argument.

Overloaded functions are distinguished by their *signature* which is a combination of the function identifier and the types of all the parameters. *Type-safe linkage* is implemented by using the function signature as the link identifier.

```
// Using overloaded functions
#include <iostream.h>

int square(int x)
{
    return x * x;
}

double square(double y)
{
    return y * y;
}

main()
{
    cout << "The square of integer 7 is " << square(7) << '\n'
    cout << "The square of integer 7.5 is " << square(7.5) << '\n';
}
```

```
The square of integer 7 is 49
The square of double 7.5 is 56.25
```

Fig. 15.7 Using overloaded functions.

15.21 Polymorphism and Virtual Functions

Suppose a set of shapes such as `circle, arc, triangle, rectangle, square,` etc. are all derived from base class `shape`. When drawing a shape, whatever that shape may be, it would be nice to simply call function `draw` of base class `shape`, and let C++ determine which derived class `draw` function to use. The problem is that function `draw` for each of the shapes is quite different. So we define `draw` in the base class as a *virtual function*, and then we *redefine* `draw` in each of the derived classes to draw the appropriate shape. Because function `draw` in the base class has been declared `virtual`, C++ automatically uses the correct `draw` function at execution time. This is called *dynamic binding* because the decision as to which member function to use is delayed until execution time. Redefined functions must have the same return type and signature as the base virtual function.

Note that overloading is resolved at compile time by selecting the function definition with a signature that matches the function call (including implicit type casting). A virtual function is selected by using the definition associated with the class of the object to which the message is sent (all the functions have the same signatures) and only when a pointer or reference is used. If the virtual function is called by referencing a specific object by name, then virtuality plays no part; the reference is resolved at compile time.

C++ enables *polymorphism*, the ability to assume different forms at different times. If, for example, class B is derived from class A, then a B "is" a more specific version of an A. Where an operation is performed on an object of class A, that operation can be performed on an object of class B. Polymorphism is implemented via virtual functions. When a request to use a virtual function is made, C++ chooses the correct redefined function in the appropriate derived class associated with the object.

The program of Fig. 15.8 illustrates polymorphism and virtual functions in C++. The program defines a base class `baseclass` and a derived class `derivedclass`. Class `baseclass` contains integer `x`, constructor `baseclass`, and virtual function `printdata`. Class `derivedclass` inherits the members of class `baseclass`, and redefines function `printdata`. Function `general_printdata` receives a pointer to an object of type `baseclass` and prints the data contained in the object.

Function `main` begins by instantiating object `baseobject` of type `baseclass` and object `derivedobject` of type `derivedclass`. The program passes the address of object `baseobject` to function `general_printdata`, which in turn uses the class pointer operator to call function `printdata` of class `baseclass`. Next the program passes the address of object `derivedobject` to function `general_printdata`, which in turn uses the class pointer operator to call function `printdata` of class `derivedclass`. Function `general_printdata` differentiates between the `printdata` functions based on the object type `general_printdata` receives, not on the type of the pointer.

An important notion in virtual functions and polymorphism is that a pointer to an object of a derived type is compatible with a pointer to an object of the base type. Because these pointers are compatible, the virtual function can be called via a pointer to the base class type. In Fig. 15.8 a pointer to `baseclass` is used to access function `printdata` for both `baseobject` and `derivedobject`. Since pointers to these classes are compatible, function `general_printdata` can receive a pointer to either type. The appropriate function is determined by the type of the object referred to by the pointer.

```
// Using virtual functions
#include <iostream.h>

class baseclass {
protected:
    int x;
public:
    baseclass(int y = 1) { x = y; }
    virtual void printdata()
    {
        cout << "Integer x in this class = " << x << '\n';
    }
};

class derivedclass : public baseclass {
protected:
    char c;
public:
    derivedclass(char d = 'Z') { c = d; }
    void printdata()
    {
        baseclass::printdata();
        cout << "Character c in this class = " << c << '\n';
    }
};

void general_printdata(baseclass* ptr)
{
    ptr->printdata();
}

main()
{
    baseclass baseobject;
    derivedclass derivedobject;

    cout << "First the baseclass's printdata is called.\n";
    general_printdata(&baseobject);    // calls baseclass printdata

    cout << "\nNext the derivedclass's printdata is called.\n";
    general_printdata(&derivedobject); // calls derivedclass printdata
}
```

```
First the baseclass's printdata is called.
Integer x in this class = 1

Next the derivedclass's printdata is called.
Integer x in this class = 1
Character c in this class = Z
```

Fig. 15.8 Using virtual functions.

15.22 Case Study: Software Reusability Using C++ and Object-Oriented Programming

OK, here we go! This is it—the capstone exercise for the entire course. For some of you, this was your first programming experience. For many of you, and probably most of you, this was your first experience using C and your first exposure to both object-oriented programming and C++. Now let us put it all together and wrap up the course with a look at how software is likely to be designed in the future through object-oriented programming with C++.

Is OOP really a better software development methodology? In the following, we will explore how object-orientation changes our view of the world. And we will investigate software reusability via classes and inheritance and see if it really does facilitate rapid prototyping of new software.

We begin by asking the reader to review the list processing program we developed in Chapter 12, "Data Structures." Let us first write a version of this program using some of the C++ enhancements to C discussed in this chapter. In particular, we will

1. Convert C-style comments (delimited by /* and */) to C++ comments (beginning with //) where appropriate.

2. Place variable declarations throughout the program close to where the variables are used.

3. Convert C-style input/output using printf and scanf function calls, to C++-style stream-oriented input/output using cout, cin, and the stream insertion (<<) and stream extraction (>>) operators, respectively.

4. Convert C-style dynamic memory allocation via malloc and free function calls to C++-style dynamic memory allocation with new and delete operators.

5. Convert C-style simulated call-by-reference via pointer passing and pointer dereferencing to C++ style of call-by-reference via reference parameters.

6. Eliminate typedefs because C++ allows types like struct sam—once defined—to be referred to simply as sam, so we do not need to use typedef to squeeze down variable declarations for struct types.

The modified version of the list processing program of Fig. 12.3 is shown in Fig. 15.9. The output is shown in Fig. 12.4.

We would like to demonstrate how OOP promotes software reusability. So, we take our list processing program and "wrap it" as a C++ class. Then, we instantiate (create) an object of this class and show that it does list processing properly. Then, using the similarities between lists, stacks, and queues, we use C++ class inheritance capabilities to create—with very little effort—complete stack-processing and queue-processing programs. Along the way we show the details of many C++ features that we have referred to in the general discussion of the chapter.

```
// Creating and maintaining a list
#include <iostream.h>

struct listnode {
   char data;
   struct listnode *nextptr;
};

void insert(listnode*&, char);
char del(listnode*&, char);
int isempty(listnode*);
void print_list(listnode*);
void instructions(void);

main()
{
   listnode* list = 0;

   instructions();

   int choice = 0;

   while (choice != 3) {
      cout << "? ";
      cin >> choice;

      switch (choice) {
         char item;

         case 1:
            cout << "Enter a character: ";
            cin >> item;
            insert(list, item);
            print_list(list);
            break;

         case 2:
            if (!isempty(list)) {
               cout << "Enter character to be deleted: ";
               cin >> item;

               if (del(list, item)) {
                  cout << "'" << item << "' deleted.\n";
                  print_list(list);
               }
               else
                  cout << "'" << item << "' not found.\n\n";
            }
            else
               cout << "List is empty.\n\n";
      }

   }

   cout << "End of run.\n";
}
```

Fig. 15.9 The modified list processing program (part 1 of 3).

```
// Insert a new value into the list in sorted order
void insert(listnode*& list, char value)
{
    listnode* newptr = new listnode;
    newptr->data = value;
    newptr->nextptr = 0;

    listnode* previousptr = 0;
    listnode* currentptr = list;

    while (currentptr != 0 && value > currentptr->data) {
        previousptr = currentptr;
        currentptr = currentptr->nextptr;
    }

    if (!previousptr) {
        newptr->nextptr = list;
        list = newptr;
    }
    else {
        previousptr->nextptr = newptr;
        newptr->nextptr = currentptr;
    }
}

// Delete a list element
char del(listnode*& list, char value)
{
    listnode* tempptr;

    if (value == list->data) {
        tempptr = list;
        list = list->nextptr;
        delete tempptr;
        return value;
    }
    else {
        listnode* previousptr = list;
        listnode* currentptr = list->nextptr;

        while (currentptr != 0 && currentptr->data != value) {
            previousptr = currentptr;
            currentptr = currentptr->nextptr;
        }

        if (currentptr) {
            tempptr = currentptr;
            previousptr->nextptr = currentptr->nextptr;
            delete tempptr;
            return value;
        }
    }

    return '\0';
}
```

Fig. 15.9 The modified list processing program (part 2 of 3).

```
// Print the instructions
void instructions(void)
{
    cout << "Enter your choice:\n"
         << "    1 to insert an element into the list.\n"
         << "    2 to delete an element from the list.\n"
         << "    3 to end.\n";
}

// Return 1 if the list is empty, 0 otherwise
int isempty(listnode* list)
{
    return !list;
}

// Print the list
void print_list(listnode* currentptr)
{
    if (!currentptr)
        cout << "List is empty.\n\n";
    else {
        cout << "The list is:\n";

        while (currentptr) {
            cout << currentptr->data << " ---> ";
            currentptr = currentptr->nextptr;
        }

        cout << "NULL\n\n";
    }
}
```

Fig. 15.9 The modified list processing program (part 3 of 3).

Our second program wraps the linked list program of Chapter 12 into a new class called `listclass`. The program has been split into three separate files—`list.h`, `listfunc.cpp`, and `listdriv.cpp` (Fig. 15.12). The class is defined in header file `list.h` (Fig. 15.10). The member functions for the class are defined in file `listfunc.cpp` (Fig. 15.11). The list processing driver program (`main` and `instructions`) is contained in file `listdriv.cpp`. Note that C++ program files in Borland C++ end with `.cpp`. Many UNIX systems use the `.C` (as opposed to C's `.c` extension) extension for C++ program files.

Class `listclass` (Fig. 15.10) has been defined to contain the "template" for structures of type `listnode` that will contain the data—pointer `list` of type `listnode*` that points to the first element in the list—and the member functions `listclass`, `insert`, `insertfront`, `print`, `deletenode`, and `isempty`. The member functions of class `listclass` may all access and modify the data members of the class. The data members are declared as `protected` so they may be inherited into classes we will use for defining stacks and queues later in this section. Constructor function `listclass()`, defined inline in the class, initializes pointer `list` to 0 (C++ programmers tend to use 0 instead of `NULL`). File `listfunc.cpp` (Fig. 15.11) defines the remaining member functions.

```
// Definition of class listclass
class listclass {
protected:
   struct listnode {            // a node of the list
      char data;
      listnode* nextptr;
   };

   listnode* list;             // the list
public:
   listclass() {list = 0;}     // constructor
   void insert(char);          // insert in alpha order
   void insertfront(char);     // insert in front (not alpha)
   void print();               // print the linked list
   char deletenode(char);      // delete node given its value
   int isempty();              // test if the list is empty
};
```

Fig. 15.10 Definition of the listclass.

```
// Definitions of class listclass member functions
#include "list.h"
#include <iostream.h>

// Insert a new value into the list in sorted order
void listclass::insert(char value)
{
    listnode *newptr, *previousptr, *currentptr;

    newptr = new listnode;
    newptr->data = value;
    newptr->nextptr = 0;

    previousptr = 0;
    currentptr = list;

    while (currentptr != 0 && value > currentptr->data) {
       previousptr = currentptr;
       currentptr = (currentptr)->nextptr;
    }

    if (previousptr == 0) {
       newptr->nextptr = list;
       list = newptr;
    }
    else {
       previousptr->nextptr = newptr;
       newptr->nextptr = currentptr;
    }
}

// Return 1 if the list is empty, 0 otherwise
int listclass::isempty()
{
    return !list;
}
```

Fig. 15.11 Definitions of class listclass member functions (part 1 of 2).

```cpp
// Insert a new value at the front of the list
void listclass::insertfront(char value)
{
    listnode* newptr = new listnode;
    newptr->data = value;
    newptr->nextptr = list;
    list = newptr;
}

// Delete a list element
char listclass::deletenode(char value)
{
    listnode *previousptr, *currentptr, *tempptr;

    if (value == list->data) {
        tempptr = list;
        list = list->nextptr;
        delete tempptr;
        return value;
    }
    else {
        previousptr = list;
        currentptr = list->nextptr;

        while (currentptr != 0 && currentptr->data != value) {
            previousptr = currentptr;
            currentptr = currentptr->nextptr;
        }

        if (currentptr) {
            tempptr = currentptr;
            previousptr->nextptr = currentptr->nextptr;
            delete tempptr;
            return value;
        }
    }

    return '\0';
}

// Print the list
void listclass::print()
{
    if (!list)
        cout << "Empty.\n\n";
    else {
        listnode* currentptr = list;
        cout << "Front or Top: ";

        while (currentptr) {
            cout << currentptr->data << " ";
            currentptr = currentptr->nextptr;
        }

        cout << "\n\n";
    }
}
```

Fig. 15.11 Definitions of class listclass member functions (part 2 of 2).

The file of Fig. 15.11 `includes` header file `list.h` for its definition of class `listclass`, and file `iostream.h` for its definitions of the stream input and output mechanisms of C++. Since the functions defined in file `listfunc.cpp` are member functions of class `listclass`, and they are not inline functions of the class, the scope resolution operator must be used to indicate that these functions are the member functions of class `listclass`. Therefore, each function name is preceded by `listclass::`. Function `insert` has been modified in this program to use characteristics of the new class. Function `insert` no longer receives a pointer to a pointer to the beginning of the list as it did in Chapter 12 to enable `insert` to modify the beginning of the list. The function now has access to pointer `list` (the pointer to the first element of the list) because the pointer is a member of the same class. Thus, `insert` need only receive the data item to be inserted in the list. Note that the code for the function is easier to read and understand because it is no longer strewn with indirection operators. This is a nice benefit of having objects that encapsulate both functions *and* data. Function `insert` places the item in order in the list.

GPP 15.7

Using an object-oriented programming approach can often simplify function calls by reducing the number of parameters to be passed. This benefit of object-oriented programming derives from the fact that encapsulation of data members and member functions within an object gives the member functions the right to access the data members.

Function `insertfront` has been added to the implementation to enrich the list processing package by enabling the formation of unsorted lists. In the stack example that follows, class `stackclass` (defined later in this section) can inherit function `insertfront` and use it to do the `push` operation. Function `insertfront` receives a data item as an argument and inserts it at the beginning of the list.

Function `deletenode`, like functions `insert` and `insertfront`, no longer receives a pointer to a pointer to the first element in the list as it did in Chapter 12 because it can directly access pointer `list` in an object of type `listclass`. Note once again that the code for the deletion routine has not been modified except that there are no longer any indirection operators, because the function can operate directly on pointer `list` when necessary. Function `deletenode` receives an item to be deleted as an argument, searches for the item, and deletes the item if it is found.

Function `isempty` simply determines if `list` is empty.

Function `print` creates pointer `currentptr` of type `listnode*`, initializes it to pointer `list`, and uses it to walk through the list and print the data elements. Note that `print` no longer receives a pointer to the beginning of the list as an argument, because it, too, can directly reference the pointer in the object.

File `listdriv.cpp` (Fig. 15.12) contains the driver program for processing a list. The file consists of functions `main` and `instructions`. Function `main` begins by declaring object `listobject` of class `listclass`. Note that a pointer to the beginning of the list is no longer declared in `main` because the pointer is a member of the new object and is hidden inside the object. Function `main` processes the list identically to the list processing program of Chapter 12. The only difference is the

```
// Creating and maintaining a list
#include "list.h"
#include <iostream.h>

main()
{
    listclass listobject;        // instantiate a list object
    void instructions(void);

    instructions();

    int choice = 0;

    while (choice != 4) {
        cout << "? ";
        cin >> choice;

        switch (choice) {
            char item;

            case 1:
                cout << "Enter a character: ";
                cin >> item;
                listobject.insert(item);
                listobject.print();
                break;

            case 2:
                cout << "Enter a character: ";
                cin >> item;
                listobject.insertfront(item);
                listobject.print();
                break;
```

Fig. 15.12 Operating and maintaining a list (part 1 of 2).

manner in which the member functions are called. Member function calls are written by preceding the member function name with the object name and a period to specify the object to which the function belongs (remember that many objects of a class may be instantiated). The period is C's member access operator that is used to access the members of structures, unions, and classes. To call function `insert`, the call `listobject.insert(item)` is used. This specifically associates the function call with object `listobject` and gives `insert` access to the data members of `listobject`. The output of the list processing program is shown in Fig. 15.13.

```
            case 3:
               if (!listobject.isempty()) {
                  cout << "Enter character to be deleted: ";
                  cin >> item;

                  if (listobject.deletenode(item)) {
                     cout << "'" << item << "' deleted." << '\n';
                     listobject.print();
                  }
                  else
                     cout << "'" << item << "' not found." << "\n\n";

               }
               else
                  cout << "List is empty.\n\n";

         }

      }

   cout << "End of run.\n";
}

// Print the instructions
void instructions(void)
{
   cout << "Enter your choice:\n"
        << "    1 to insert an element in sorted order.\n"
        << "    2 to insert an element at the front of the list.\n"
        << "    3 to delete an element from the list.\n"
        << "    4 to end.\n";
}
```

Fig. 15.12 Operating and maintaining a list (part 2 of 2).

Our next example, derives a new class, stackclass, from class listclass to help construct a stack processing program. The program is also split into three files—stack.h, stackfnc.cpp, and stackdrv.cpp. Header file stack.h (Fig. 15.14) includes a copy of header file list.h because stackclass is derived from listclass. Our new class does not include any new data members. It does, however, define functions push and pop as member functions of class stackclass, and it redefines functions insert and deletenode (we will see why shortly). It is important to note that class stackclass inherits all the members—data and function—of class listclass. A constructor is not provided for class stackclass because there are no new data members to initialize. C++ will provide a default constructor in this case, and will automatically invoke the listclass constructor of class listclass to initialize inherited pointer list to 0. Function push is also defined inline. Function push calls function insertfront from class listclass to insert value at the top of the stack (the front of the list). The remaining member functions are defined in file stackfnc.cpp (Fig. 15.15).

```
Enter your choice:
   1 to insert an element in sorted order.
   2 to insert an element at the front of the list.
   3 to delete an element from the list.
   4 to end.
? 1
Enter a character: D
Front or Top: D

? 1
Enter a character: B
Front or Top: B D

? 1
Enter a character: F
Front or Top: B D F

? 3
Enter character to be deleted: D
'D' deleted.
Front or Top: B F

? 3
Enter character to be deleted: F
'F' deleted.
Front or Top: B

? 3
Enter character to be deleted: B
'B' deleted.
Empty.

? 2
Enter a character: Z
Front or Top: Z

? 2
Enter a character: P
Front or Top: P Z

? 3
Enter character to be deleted: P
'P' deleted.
Front or Top: Z

? 3
Enter character to be deleted: Z
'Z' deleted.
Empty.

? 3
List is empty.

? 4
End of run.
```

Fig. 15.13 Output for the list processing program.

```
// Definition of class stackclass

#include "list.h"

class stackclass : public listclass {
public:
    void push(char value) { insertfront(value); }
    char pop(void);
    void insert(char);
    char deletenode(char);
};
```

Fig. 15.14 Definition of class `stackclass`.

In the file of Fig. 15.15, function `pop` is defined as it was in the stack processing program of Chapter 12. Again, the difference here is that the pointer to the top of the stack (beginning of the list) is a member of the class, so it is not necessary to pass any pointers. The function modifies pointer `list` each time a value is popped from the stack. Functions `insert` and `deletenode` were inherited from class `listclass`, but they are not needed for stack processing. Since items can only be inserted at the top of a stack and deleted from the top of a stack, we redefined these functions in class `stackclass` so they cannot be used to violate the integrity of the stack. File `stackdrv.cpp` (Fig. 15.16) defines function `main` for controlling stack processing.

GPP 15.8

When inheriting capabilities that are not needed in the derived class, mask those capabilities by redefining the functions.

The file of Fig. 15.16 defines functions `main` and `instructions`. Function `main` begins by declaring object `stackobject` of type `stackclass`. Next, a test is performed to prove that accidental or malicious calls to inherited functions `insert` and `deletenode` will be caught and flagged as errors at execution time. Finally, the program processes object `stackobject`. Note that the code is almost identical to the stack program defined in Chapter 12. Again, the member function names are preceded by the object name and a period to specify the object to which the member functions belong. It is important to remember that file `listfunc.cpp` must be compiled and linked with files `stack.h`, `stackfnc.cpp`, and `stackdrv.cpp` so the entire stack processing program will compile correctly. The output for the stack processing program is shown in Fig. 15.17.

```
// Function definitions for class stackclass

#include <iostream.h>
#include "stack.h"

char stackclass::pop(void)
{
    listnode* tempptr;
    char popvalue;

    tempptr = list;
    popvalue = list->data;
    list = list->nextptr;
    delete tempptr;
    return popvalue;
}

void stackclass::insert(char value)
{
    cout << "ERROR: insert() not a stack function.\n\n";
}

char stackclass::deletenode(char value)
{
    cout << "ERROR: deletenode() not a stack function.\n\n";
    return '\0';
}
```

Fig. 15.15 Function definitions for class `stackclass`.

Our final example creates class `queueclass` that inherits class `stackclass` (which—we recall—inherits class `listclass`). The example also consists of three files—`queue.h`, `queuefnc.cpp`, and `queuedrv.cpp`. Files `listfunc.cpp` and `stackfunc.cpp` must also be compiled and linked with the three files of the example. File `queue.h` (Fig. 15.18) includes `stack.h` because `queueclass` inherits `stackclass`. Class `queueclass` defines new data member `rear`—a pointer to the last element in the queue. Constructor `queueclass()` initializes `rear` to 0 after invoking the constructors for class `stackclass` and class `listclass`. Class `queueclass` also defines member functions `dequeue` and `enqueue`, and redefines function `push`. Member function `dequeue` is defined inline. It calls function `pop` to remove an item from the front of the queue (the top of the stack). The remaining functions are defined in file `stackfnc.cpp` (Fig. 15.19).

In file `queuefnc.cpp` (Fig. 15.19), member function `enqueue` is defined using the same code that was used in the queue processing program of Chapter 12. The function is able to modify directly the pointer to the front of the queue (`list`) and the pointer to the rear of the queue (`rear`) because these pointers are members of class `queueclass`. Function `push` is redefined because it is not needed in queue processing.

```
// Stack processing driver

#include <iostream.h>
#include "stack.h"

main()
{
    stackclass stackobject;    // instantiate a stack object
    void instructions(void);

    cout << "Testing that functions insert and deletenode"
         << "\nfrom class listclass have been overridden.\n\n";
    stackobject.insert('A');
    stackobject.deletenode('A');

    instructions();
    int choice = 0;

    while (choice != 3) {
        cout << "? ";
        cin >> choice;

        switch (choice) {
            char item;

            case 1:
                cout << "Enter a character: ";
                cin >> item;
                stackobject.push(item);
                stackobject.print();
                break;

            case 2:

                if (!stackobject.isempty())
                    cout << "The popped value is "
                         << stackobject.pop() << '\n';

                stackobject.print();
                break;
        }
    }

    cout << "End of run.\n";
}


// Print the instructions
void instructions(void)
{
    cout << "Enter your choice:\n"
    << "   1 to push an item onto the stack.\n"
    << "   2 to pop an item off the stack.\n"
    << "   3 to end.\n";
}
```

Fig. 15.16 Stack processing driver.

```
Testing that functions insert and deletenode
from class listclass have been overridden.

ERROR: insert() not a stack function.

ERROR: deletenode() not a stack function.

Enter your choice:
    1 to push an item onto the stack.
    2 to pop an item off the stack.
    3 to end.
? 1
Enter a character: A
Front or Top: A

? 1
Enter a character: B
Front or Top: B A

? 1
Enter a character: C
Front or Top: C B A

? 2
The popped value is C
Front or Top: B A

? 2
The popped value is B
Front or Top: A

? 1
Enter a character: D
Front or Top: D A

? 2
The popped value is D
Front or Top: A

? 2
The popped value is A
Empty.

? 2
Empty.

? 3
End of run.
```

Fig. 15.17 Output for the stack processing program.

```
// Definition of class queueclass

#include "stack.h"

class queueclass : public stackclass {
    listnode* rear;
public:
    queueclass() {rear = 0;}
    char dequeue(void) {return pop();}
    void enqueue(char);
    void push(char);
};
```

Fig. 15.18 Definition of class queueclass.

```
// Definitions of class queueclass member functions

#include "queue.h"
#include <iostream.h>

void queueclass::enqueue(char value)
{
    listnode* newptr = new listnode;
    newptr->data = value;
    newptr->nextptr = 0;

    if (isempty())
        list = newptr;
    else
        rear->nextptr = newptr;

    rear = newptr;
}

void queueclass::push(char value)
{
    cout << "ERROR: push() not a queue function\n\n";
}
```

Fig. 15.19 Definitions of class queueclass member functions.

File queuedrv.cpp (Fig. 15.19) creates object queueobject for queue processing. Function main first confirms that function push has been redefined so it cannot be used during queue processing. This protects the queue structure from the illegal operation of adding an element at the front of the queue. Function main then controls queue processing. The output for the queue processing program is shown in Fig. 15.21.

```cpp
// Queue processing driver

#include <iostream.h>
#include "queue.h"

main()
{
    queueclass queueobject;         // instantiate a queue object
    void instructions(void);

    cout << "Testing that function push from class"
         << "\nstackclass has been overridden.\n";
    queueobject.push('A');

    instructions();

    int choice = 0;

    while (choice != 3) {
        cout << "? ";
        cin >> choice;

        switch (choice) {
            char item;

            case 1:
                cout << "Enter a character: ";
                cin >> item;
                queueobject.enqueue(item);
                queueobject.print();
                break;

            case 2:

                if (!queueobject.isempty())
                    cout << queueobject.dequeue()
                         << " has been dequeued.\n";

                queueobject.print();
                break;
        }

    }

    cout << "End of run.\n";
}


// Print the instructions
void instructions(void)
{
    cout << "Enter your choice:\n"
         << "   1 to add an item to the queue.\n"
         << "   2 to remove an item from the queue.\n"
         << "   3 to end.\n";
}
```

Fig. 15.20 Queue processing driver.

```
Testing that function push from class
stackclass has been overridden
ERROR: push() not a queue function

Enter your choice:
   1 to add an item to the queue.
   2 to remove an item from the queue.
   3 to end.
? 1
Enter a character: A
Front or Top: A

? 1
Enter a character: B
Front or Top: A B

? 1
Enter a character: C
Front or Top: A B C

? 2
A has been dequeued.
Front or Top: B C

? 2
B has been dequeued.
Front or Top: C

? 1
Enter a character: D
Front or Top: C D

? 2
C has been dequeued.
Front or Top: D

? 2
D has been dequeued.
Empty.

? 2
Empty.

? 3
End of run.
```

Fig. 15.21 Output for the queue processing program.

Notice how little had to be done to create complete stack manipulation and queue manipulation packages. This is an example of software reusability through classes and inheritance, a key benefit of object-oriented programming. This process can promote rapid prototyping, but it is not without its problems.

PERF 15.3
The additional structuring and dynamic binding imposed by object orientation can cause less efficient use of memory and slower execution.

So there are tradeoffs. A big problem in the industry today is meeting the soaring demand for new and more powerful software applications. Hardware technology continues to move at blinding speed—so fast in fact that while we are deliberating how to save a few processor cycles here and there, the technology may actually improve enough to more than make up the difference! Performance issues will always be important. What is needed is the proper use of techniques that facilitate rapid development of high-quality, powerful software in parallel with continuing advances in hardware technology. RISC processors are doubling in speed every 12 to 18 months while maintaining or even reducing costs, and it is widely believed that this phenomenon will continue for the foreseeable future. Hardware technology has been advancing like this for many years. But software technology is only now beginning to realize these kinds of exciting improvements, due in large measure to the potential of object-oriented programming, and software reusability through class libraries.

15.23 Closing Remarks

We sincerely hope you have enjoyed learning C in this course. And we hope you have enjoyed this brief introduction to object-oriented programming in C++. The future seems clear. We wish you great success in pursuing it!

Summary

- C++ is a superset of C, so programmers can use a C++ compiler to compile their existing C programs, and then gradually evolve these programs to C++.
- Object-oriented programming models real-world objects with software counterparts.
- OOP takes advantage of class relationships where objects of a certain class have the same characteristics. OOP also takes advantage of inheritance relationships, and even multiple inheritance relationships where newly created objects inherit characteristics of "parents," yet contain unique characteristics of their own.
- Object-oriented programming encapsulates data (attributes) and functions (behavior) into packages called objects.
- Objects have the property of information hiding. This means that although objects may know how to communicate with one another across well-defined interfaces, objects normally are not allowed to know how other objects are implemented—implementation details are hidden within the objects themselves.
- Data abstraction promotes better software engineering.
- C requires that a comment be delimited by /* and */. C++, in addition, allows you to begin a comment with // and use the remainder of the line for comment text.

- C++ allows declarations to appear anywhere that an executable statement can appear. Variable declarations may also appear in the initialization section of a `for` structure.

- C++ provides an alternative to `printf` and `scanf` function calls for handling input/output of the standard C data types and strings. The output stream `cout`, and the operator `<<` (the stream insertion operator, pronounced "put to") enable data to be output without using `printf`. The input stream `cin` and the operator `>>` (the stream extraction operator, pronounced "get from") enable data to be input without using `scanf`.

- Inline functions help reduce function-call overhead. The programmer can explicitly specify the keyword `inline` to "advise" the compiler to generate function code in line (when possible) to minimize function calls.

- C++ offers a direct form of call-by-reference using reference parameters. To indicate that a parameter is a reference parameter, simply follow the parameter's type in the function prototype by an `&`. In the function call, simply mention the variable by name and it will automatically be passed call-by-reference. In the called function, mentioning the variable by its local name actually refers to the original which may then be modified directly by the called function. Reference parameters can also be created for local use within a function.

- The `new` and `delete` operators in C++ provide a nicer means of performing dynamic memory allocation than with `malloc` and `free` function calls in C. The `new` operator takes a type as an operand, automatically creates an object of the proper size, returns a pointer of the correct type, and runs the associated constructor. The `delete` operator takes a pointer to an object allocated with `new`, runs the destructor, and frees the memory.

- C++ allows the programmer to specify default arguments values. If a default argument is omitted in a call to the function, the default value of that argument is automatically used. This feature only works if the default arguments are the rightmost (trailing) arguments in a function.

- C++ extends the notion of C's `struct`—a `struct` variable can only contain data members—to form new types for holding data members and member functions. The new data types created are referred to as classes. Instances of these types are referred to as objects. Types containing data members and member functions are defined in C++ using the keyword `class`, `struct`, or `union`, but keyword `class` is normally used for this purpose.

- Any function defined within a class is implicitly an inline function of that class.

- When a member function is defined outside the class definition, the function name is preceded by the class name and the scope resolution operator (`::`). This notation is used to specify the class in which the function is declared.

- The listing of member functions of a class is preceded by `public:` if the programmer wants to make those functions available across the interface of the object.

- The data members and member functions of an object are referenced through the object name or references using the class member operator (.), or through a pointer to the object using the class pointer operator (->).

- Access to class members is controlled by the member access specifiers `public`, `private`, and `protected`. A `public` member is accessible to any function. Access to a `private` member is isolated to member functions and `friend` functions of the `private` member's class. Access to `protected` members is an extended form of `private` access; `protected` members may be accessed by member functions and `friend` functions of the `protected` member's class, and by member functions and `friend` functions of a class derived from the `protected` member's class.

- The default access for members of a `class` is `private`. Access to members of a `class` may be explicitly changed to `protected` or `public`. The default access for `struct` members and `union` members is `public`. Access to members of a `struct` may be explicitly changed to `protected` or `private`. The member access specifiers may not be used explicitly with a `union`.

- Normally, data members are declared `private` or `protected` so they may be accessed only by member functions, and member functions are declared `public` so they can be accessed by any function.

- A friend function of a class is a function defined outside that class, that has the right to access `protected` and `private` members of that class. To declare a function as a `friend` of a class, declare the function in the class and precede the declaration with keyword `friend`. To declare a class as a `friend` of another class, place a declaration of the form

      friend *classname;*

  as a member of the other class.

- A class may include a function with the same name as the class. This function is a constructor for the class. The constructor is a member function that is invoked implicitly each time a new object of the class is to be created. The constructor performs any necessary initialization such as allocating space for data structures outside the object and providing initial values. If a constructor is not provided by the programmer, C++ automatically creates a default constructor with no arguments.

- Each class also contains a destructor member function that destroys objects of the class. The destructor's name is the class name preceded by the tilde character (~). Destructor functions take no parameters and return no values. If a destructor is not provided by the programmer (as is normally the case), C++ automatically creates a default destructor.

- When creating a new class, instead of having to write completely new data members and member functions, the programmer can designate that the new class is to inherit the data members and member functions of a previously defined, or base class. In this case, the new class is referred to as a derived class.

- A derived class can access only the `public` and `protected` members of its base class. If a derived class inherits a base class as `public`, all `public` and `protected` members of the base class are inherited as `public` and `protected` members of the derived class. If a derived class inherits a base class as `private`, all `public` and `protected` members of the base class are inherited as `private` members of the derived class.

- The constructor for a derived class always calls the constructor for its base class first to create and initialize the members of its base class. If the constructor for the derived class is omitted, the default constructor for the derived class automatically calls the constructor for the base class.

- The constructors of a base class are invoked before those of a derived class.

- C++ provides for multiple inheritance which allows a derived class to inherit from many base classes, even if these base classes are unrelated.

- The operator `<<` is used for multiple purposes in C++, namely as the stream insertion operator ("put to") and as the left-shift operator. This is an example of operator overloading. C++ enables the programmer to redefine the behavior of most operators to be sensitive to the types of their parameters. The compiler generates the appropriate code based on the manner in which the operator is used.

- Operators are overloaded by writing a function definition (with a header and body) as you normally would, except the name of the function now becomes the keyword `operator` followed by the symbol for the operator being overloaded. Overloaded functions must be members of classes or friends.

- In C++ it is possible to define several functions with the same name but with different parameter types. This is called function overloading. When an overloaded function is called, the C++ compiler automatically selects the proper function by first examining the number and types of arguments in the call.

- The ability to redefine one function to accomplish a similar task for multiple classes is referred to as polymorphism. When a request to use a virtual function is made at execution time, C++ will choose the correct redefined function in the appropriate derived class. Essentially, polymorphism enables an entire set of related classes to be handled as a single class, namely that of the base class.

- An important notion in virtual functions and polymorphism is that a pointer or reference to an object of a derived type is compatible with a pointer or reference to an object of the base type. Because these pointers are compatible, the virtual function can be called via a pointer to the base class type. The appropriate function is determined by the type of the object referred to by the pointer.

Terminology

abstract data type	**asm**
abstraction	AT&T C++
access control	attribute
ampersand (**&**) suffix	base class

Common Programming Errors

15.1   Because reference parameters are mentioned only by name in the body of the called function, the programmer might inadvertently treat reference parameters as call-by-value parameters. This can cause unexpected side effects as the original copies of the variables are changed in the calling function.

15.2   Specifying and attempting to use a default argument that is not a rightmost (trailing) argument.

15.3   Forgetting the semicolon at the end of a `class` definition.

Good Programming Practices

15.1   Using C++-style `//` comments avoids the unterminated comment errors that occur by forgetting to close C-style comments with `*/`.

15.2   C++ enables the programmer to place declarations close to the location in the program in which the corresponding variables are used. This can make programs more readable.

15.3   Using C++-style stream-oriented input/output makes programs more readable than their counterparts in C written with printf and scanf function calls.

15.4   Using C++-style reference parameters rather than C-style simulated call-by-reference (with pointer passing and dereferencing) makes programs more understandable.

15.5   Using C++-style dynamic memory allocation with the `new` and `delete` operators makes programs more readable that with the use of C-style `malloc` and `free` function calls.

15.6   Using default arguments simplifies writing function calls.

15.7   Using an object-oriented programming approach can often simplify function calls by reducing the number of parameters to be passed. This benefit of object-oriented programming derives from the fact that encapsulation of data members and member functions within an object gives the member functions the right to access the data members.

15.8   When inheriting capabilities that are not needed in the derived class, mask those capabilities by redefining the functions.

Performance Tips

15.1   Using `inline` functions can reduce execution-time overhead.

15.2   The programmer can use a `const` reference parameter to simulate the appearance of call-by-value, but avoid the possibly high overhead of passing a copy of the variable.

15.3   The additional structuring and dynamic binding imposed by object orientation can cause less efficient use of memory and slower execution.

Self-Review Exercises

15.1   Fill in the blanks in each of the following:

a) If the class **alpha** inherits from the class **beta**, class **alpha** is called the (base/derived) _____ class and class **beta** is called the (base/derived) _____ class.

b) With _____ inheritance, a derived class can inherit from several base classes.

c) In C++, it is possible to have various functions with the same name that each operate on different types and/or numbers of arguments. This is called function _____.

d) The notion of method in languages like Smalltalk is most like the notion of _____ in C++.

e) The _____ operator informs the compiler the class to which a specified member function belongs.

f) A _____ is a member function that specifies how new objects of a class type are created.

g) Operator _____ dynamically allocates a new object.

h) Class objects are destroyed by member functions called _____.

i) Member functions are normally declared to be (**private/public**)_____, while data members are usually declared to be (**private/public**)_____.

j) In C, suppose **a** and **b** are integer variables and we form the sum **a + b**. Now suppose **c** and **d** are floating point variables and we form the sum **c + d**. The two + operators here are clearly being used for different purposes. This is an example of a property that C++ has, and that C has as well, called function _____.

k) A _____ function is a non-member function that can read or modify data members of a class.

l) The two stream objects we discussed that are predefined in C++ are _____ and _____.

m) C++ provides for _____ which allows a derived class to inherit from many base classes, even if these base classes are unrelated.

n) The destructor function for class C is_____.

15.2   (True/False) When writing a block-style comment that requires many lines of text, it is more concise to use the C++ comment delimiter **//** than the regular C delimiters **/*** and ***/**.

15.3   In C++, why would a function prototype contain a parameter type declaration such as **float&**?

15.4   (True/False) All calls in C++ are call-by-value.

15.5   Explain why the operators **<<** and **>>** are overloaded in C++.

15.6   In what context might the name **operator/** be used in C++?

15.7   (True/False) In C++, you may only overload an existing operator.

15.8   How does the precedence of an overloaded operator in C++ compare with the precedence of the original operator?

15.9   (True/False) The friend relationship in C++, as in life, is generally considered to be a positive one.

15.10   Write segments of C++ programs to accomplish each of the following:

a) Write the string "**Welcome to C!**" to the standard output stream **cout**.

b) Read the value of variable **age** from the standard input stream **cin**.

15.11   Write a complete C++ program that uses stream input/output and an inline function `sphere_volume` to prompt the user for the radius of a sphere, and to calculate and print the volume of that sphere.

15.12   What would happen in C if you declared the same function twice with different argument types? What would happen in C++?

Answers to Self-Review Exercises

15.1   a) derived, base. b) multiple. c) overloading. d) member function. e) scope resolution operator (::). f) constructor. g) **new**. h) destructors. i) **public, private**. j) overloading. k) **friend**. l) **cin, cout**. m) multiple inheritance. n) **~C()**.

15.2   False. The regular C-style delimiters each only need to be written once, whereas the C++ `//` delimiter needs to appear on the beginning of each new line.

15.3   Because the programmer is declaring a reference parameter of type "reference to" `float` to get access to the original argument variable.

15.4   False. C++ allows direct call-by-reference via the use of reference parameters.

15.5   The operator `>>` is both the right-shift operator and the stream extraction operator depending on its context. The operator `<<` is both the left-shift operator and the stream insertion operator depending on its context.

15.6   For function overloading: It would be the name of a function that would provide a new version of the `/` operator.

15.7   True.

15.8   Identical.

15.9   False. Friendship is contrary to important positive attributes of object-oriented programming such as encapsulation.

15.10   a) `cout << "Welcome to C!";`

b) `cin >> age;`

15.11

```
// Inline function that calculates the volume of a sphere
#include <iostream.h>

inline  float sphere_volume(constant float r) {return
                    4/3 * PI * r * r * r;}

main()
{
   float radius;
   const float PI = 3.14159;

   cout << "Enter the length of the radius of your sphere:  ";
   cin >> radius;
   cout << "Volume of sphere with radius " << radius <<
          "is " << sphere_volume(radius) << "\n";
}
```

Fig. 15.22 Using an inline function to calculate the volume of a sphere.

15.12   In C you would get a compilation error indicating that two functions had been given the same name. In C++ this is an example of function overloading—which is allowed—and there would be no error.

Exercises

15.13   Suppose an organization currently emphasizes C programming and wishes to convert to an object-oriented programming environment in C++. What strategy is appropriate for evolving from C environments to C++ environments?

15.14   Consider the class **bicycle**. Given your knowledge of some common components of bicycles, show a class hierarchy in which the class **bicycle** inherits from other classes, which, in turn, inherit from yet other classes. Discuss the instantiation of various objects of class **bicycle**. Discuss inheritance from class **bicycle** for other closely related derived classes.

15.15   Briefly define each of the following terms: class, object, inheritance, multiple inheritance, encapsulation, information hiding, base class, and derived class.

15.16   Explain the concepts of class libraries and software reusability. How will these be used in advancing the state of the practice in software development?

15.17   Write C++-style stream-oriented statements to accomplish each of the following:
   a)   Display "Welcome to C++" on the screen.
   b)   Input a value for **float** variable **temperature** from the keyboard.

15.18   Compare and contrast **printf/scanf**-style input/output with C++-style stream-oriented input/output.

15.19   In the chapter, we mentioned that there are many areas in which C++ automatically "knows" what types to use. List as many of these as you can.

15.20   Write a C++ program that uses stream-oriented input/output to prompt for seven integers, and determine and print their maximum.

15.21   Write a complete C++ program that uses stream input/output and an inline function **circle_area** to prompt the user for the radius of a circle, and to calculate and print the area of that circle.

15.22   Write a complete C++ program with the three alternate functions specified below that each simply add 1 to the variable **count** defined in **main**. The compare and contrast the three alternate approaches. These three functions are
   a)   Function **add1_call_by_value** that passes a copy of **count** call-by-value, adds 1 to the copy, and returns the new value.
   b)   Function **add1_simulated_call_by_reference** that passes access to variable **count** via simulated call-by-reference, and uses the dereferencing operator * to add 1 to the original copy of **count** in **main**.
   c)   Function **add1_by_reference** that passes **count** with true call-by-reference via a reference parameter, and adds 1 to the original copy of **count** through its alias (i.e., the reference parameter).

15.23   What is the purpose of the scope resolution operator?

15.24   Compare and contrast dynamic memory allocation with the C++ operators **new** and **delete**, with dynamic memory allocation with the C Standard Library functions **malloc** and **free**.

15.25   Compare and contrast the notions of **struct**, **union**, and **class** in C++.

15.26   Answer each of the following *true* or *false*. If the answer is *false* state why.
  a)   A **public** member is accessible to any function.
  b)   Access to a **private** member is strictly limited member functions of the **private** member's class.
  c)   Access to **protected** members is strictly limited to member functions and **friend** functions of the **protected** member's class.
  d)   The default access for members of a class is **protected**.
  e)   Member access specifiers may not be used explicitly with a **union**.

15.27   Explain the notion of friendship in C++. Explain the negative aspects of friendship as described in the text.

15.28   What two tasks are ordinarily performed by constructor functions? What is the naming convention for constructor functions? What is the naming convention for destructor functions?

15.29   Give as many examples as you can of operator overloading implicit in C. Give as many examples as you can of operator overloading implicit in C++. Give a reasonable example of a situation in which you might want to overload an operator explicitly in C++.

15.30   What are virtual functions? Describe a circumstance in which virtual functions would be appropriate.

15.31   List the various features of C++ we presented in this chapter that essentially represent non-object-oriented enhancements to C.

15.32   Describe the strategy we used in the case study in this chapter to produce working stack manipulation and queue manipulation programs rapidly from the list processing program we developed in Chapter 12.

15.33   Modify the object-oriented list processing program we created in this chapter to use a more complex **struct**. In particular, enhance the **struct** to include a customer account, customer name, and account balance. Now modify the program to prompt for this information when it creates a new node. Add member functions to **listclass** that list only accounts with zero balances, accounts with negative balances, and accounts with positive balances. Add a member function that sums the balances to determine the total amount of money outstanding to the company.

15.34   Use the class **stackclass** we created in the case study in this chapter to implement the infix-to-postfix conversion algorithm and postfix evaluation algorithm discussed in the Chapter 12 exercises.

15.35   (Defining a String Class) As you know, neither C nor C++ provides a data type for declaring character strings simply and directly. Use the class notion of C++ to form a class **string**. Endow this class with the capabilities to perform the rich set of operations that C and the C Standard Library provide. Use appropriate constructor and destructor functions to create and destroy object of class **string**. The data that represents a string, and the operations that are allowed on strings are encapsulated in the class **string**. Users of the class may not directly manipulate strings; such manipulation is restricted to the members and friend functions of the class. So strings are viewed as an abstract data type.

15.36   (Object-Oriented Queueing Simulation Project) Use the class **queueclass** we created in the case study in this chapter to implement the following discrete-event simulation using object-oriented programming in C++. Customers arrive at a toll plaza on a highway randomly and evenly distributed over the interval 1 through 10 seconds (integers only).

The toll plaza has 10 toll booths numbered 1 through 10. The time it takes for a toll taker to take a toll (phew!) is also randomly and evenly distributed, but over the broader interval 10 through 40 seconds (integers only; the longer time accommodates drivers who use large denomination bills and/or ask for directions). Each time a car arrives at the toll plaza, the driver always decides to get in line at the toll booth with the shortest line. If there is a tie for the shortest line, the driver gets in line behind the lowest-numbered booth. Your simulation is driven by a clock that ticks once per second. Begin by scheduling the first arriving car. Each time the clock ticks, check each toll booth to see if the toll taker is finished taking the toll, and if so remove that car from the line and schedule the next toll to be taken at that booth. Also check if another car has arrived (only one car can arrive in any one second), and if so place the car in the appropriate queue. The turnpike authority opens only one toll booth at the beginning of the day. Toll takers are on call and can arrive to operate another toll booth instantaneously (!) as needed. The turnpike authority guarantees (in its TV commercials) that it will open another toll booth immediately if each open toll booth has three or more cars waiting. The turnpike authority closes down any toll booth (except tollbooth 1, which is always open) once it has not taken a toll within a five-minute interval. Your job is to write a C++ object-oriented program that simulates the operation of the toll plaza for a 6-hour period.

a) Each time the clock ticks, display messages indicating all the activity at the toll plaza including a new car arriving at the toll plaza, cars leaving the toll plaza because the toll takers have finished taking their tolls, the opening of a toll booth (only one can open in any one second), and the closing of one or more toll booths.

b) Once your simulation begins, how long is it until the first car arrives?

c) How long is it until the first additional toll booth has to be opened?

d) How long is it until the first time a toll booth is closed?

e) What is the longest that any one line gets?

f) What is the average number of cars at the toll plaza for the duration of the simulation?

g) What is the maximum number of cars at the toll plaza throughout the simulation.

h) Graphically display the toll plaza at each tick of the clock. The really ambitious reader will animate the simulation and show the car movements.

15.37 (Object-Oriented Sports Simulation Project) Write a complete C++ object-oriented simulation of one of your favorite sports. Use the playing statistics of your favorite players and teams to "tune" your simulation. Develop an appropriate class hierarchy. Use a clock-driven, discrete-event simulation approach.

Recommended Reading

(Ak91)   Aksit, M.; J. W. Dijkstra; and A. Tripathi, "Atomic Delegation: Object-Oriented Transactions," *IEEE Software*, Vol. 8, No. 2, March 1991, pp. 84–92.

(An88)   Anderson, K. J.; R. P. Beck; and T. E. Buonanno, "Reuse of Software Modules," *AT&T Technical Journal*, Vol. 67, No. 4, July/August 1988, pp. 71–76.

(Be91)   Beck, B., "Shared-Memory Parallel Programming in C++," *IEEE Software*, Vol. 7, No. 4, July 1991, pp. 38–48.

(Bl91)   Belcher, K., "Object Orientation—The COBOL Approach," *Object Magazine,*
          Vol. 1, No. 1, May/June 1991, pp. 74–83.

(Bn91)   Bertino, E., and L. Martino, "Object-Oriented Database Management Systems:
          Concepts and Issues," *IEEE Computer,* Vol. 24, No. 4, April 1991, pp. 33–47.

(Bo91)   Booch, G., *Object-Oriented Design with Applications,* Redwood City, CA:
          Benjamin/Cummings, 1991.

(Bo91a)   Booch, G., "Using the Booch OOD Notation," *Object Magazine,* Vol. 1, No. 2,
          July/August 1991, pp. 76–84.

(Br90)   Borland, *Turbo C++ Programmer's Guide,* Part No. 14MN-CPP04-10, Scotts
          Valley, CA: Borland International, Inc., 1990.

(Br90a)   Borland, *Turbo C++ Getting Started,* Part No. 14MN-CPP02-10, Scotts Valley,
          CA: Borland International, Inc., 1990.

(Br91)   Borland, *Borland C++ Programmer's Guide,* Part No. 14MN-TCP04, Scotts
          Valley, CA: Borland International, Inc., 1991.

(Br91a)   Borland, *Borland C++ Getting Started,* Part No. 14MN-TCP02, Scotts Valley,
          CA: Borland International, Inc., 1991.

(Bu91)   Budd, T., *An Introduction to Object-Oriented Programming,* Reading, MA:
          Addison-Wesley, 1991.

(Bw91)   Bowles, A., (moderator), "Evolution vs. Revolution: Should Structured Methods
          be Objectified?" *Object Magazine,* Vol. 1, No. 4, November/December 1991,
          pp. 30–41.

(Ch91)   Chin, R. S., and S. T. Chanson, "Distributed Object-Based Programming
          Systems," *ACM Computing Surveys,* Vol. 23, No. 1, March 1991, pp. 91–124.

(Co91)   Connell, J. L.; L. Shafer; and D. M. Gursky, "Object-Oriented Rapid
          Prototyping," *Embedded Systems,* Vol. 4, No. 9, September 1991, pp. 24–33.

(DP89)   DATAPRO, "C++ and Object-Oriented Programming," *DATAPRO Research,*
          April 1989, pp. UX17-010-101—111.

(De89)   Dewhurst, S. C., and K. T. Stark, *Programming in C++,* Englewood Cliffs, NJ:
          Prentice Hall, 1989.

(El90)   Ellis, M.A. and B. Stroustrup, *The Annotated C++ Reference Manual,* Reading,
          MA: Addison-Wesley, 1990.

(Fr91)   Freburger, E., "Will Object Technology Replace CASE?" *Object Magazine,* Vol.
          1, No. 4, November/December 1991, pp. 60–66.

(Go83)   Goldberg, A., and D. Robson, *Smalltalk-80: The Language and its
          Implementation,* Reading, MA: Addison-Wesley, 1983.

(Ho91)   Horstmann, C. S., *Mastering C++,* New York, NY: John Wiley & Sons, Inc.,
          1991.

(Hu89)   Hu, D., *C/C++ for Expert Systems,* Portland, OR: Management Information
          Source, Inc., 1989.

(Kh90)   Khoshafian, A. and R. Abnous., *Object Orientation: Concepts, Languages, Databases, User Interfaces*, New York, NY: John Wiley, 1990.

(Kl91)   Klausner, S. B., "The V4th Project: A New Foundation for the Computer Software Industry," *Object Magazine*, Vol. 1, No. 2, July/August 1991, pp. 62–75.

(Ko88)   Koenig, A., "What is C++ Anyway?," *Journal of Object-Oriented Programming*, April/May 1991, pp. 48-52.

(La91)   Lane, A., "Demystifying Objects—A Framework for Understanding," *Object Magazine*, Vol. 1, No. 1, May/June 1991, pp. 58–63.

(Li89)   Lippman, S. B., *C++ Primer*, Reading, MA: Addison-Wesley Publishing Company, 1989.

(Li91)   Lippman, S. B., *C++ Primer* (Second Edition), Reading, MA: Addison-Wesley Publishing Company, 1991.

(Li86)   Liskov, B., and J. Guttat, *Abstraction and Specification in Program Development*, Cambridge, MA: MIT Press, 1986.

(Lo91)   Loomis, M. E. S., "Integrating Objects with Relational Technology," *Object Magazine*, Vol. 1, No. 2, July/August 1991, pp. 46–60.

(Lo91a) Loomis, M. E. S., "Objects and SQL: Accessing Relational Databases," *Object Magazine*, Vol. 1, No. 3, September/October 1991, pp. 68–78.

(No91)   Novobilski, A., "From Concept to Code—An Electronic Calendar Application in Objective-C," *Object Magazine*, Vol. 1, No. 1, May/June 1991, pp. 84–91.

(No91a) Novobilski, A., "From Concept to Code—An Electronic Calendar Application in Objective-C (part 2)," *Object Magazine*, Vol. 1, No. 2, July/August 1991, pp. 86–96.

(No91b) Novobilski, A., "From Concept to Code—An Electronic Calendar Application in Objective-C (part 3)," *Object Magazine*, Vol. 1, No. 3, September/October 1991, pp. 80–84.

(Of91)   Offermann, K., and J. Rainmondo, "Objects to the Rescue!" *Personal Workstation*, Vol. 3, No. 6, June 1991, pp. 50–53.

(Os91)   Osher, H., "Distributed Object Management," *Object Magazine*, Vol. 1, No. 3, September/October 1991, pp. 62–66.

(Pa91)   Pappas, C. H., and W. H. Murray, III, *Borland C++ Handbook*, Berkeley, CA: Osborne McGraw-Hill, 1991.

(Po91)   Poole, G. A., "Great Dane," *UNIX World*, Vol. 8, No. 4, April 1991, pp. 47–50.

(Re91)   Reed, D. R., "Moving from C to C++," *Object Magazine*, Vol. 1, No. 3, September/October, 1991, pp. 46–60.

(Ru91)   Rumbaugh, J. and M. Blaha, et al, *Object-Oriented Modeling and Design*, Englewood Cliffs, NJ: Prentice Hall, 1991.

(Sh91)   Shiffman, H., "C++ Object-Oriented Extensions to C," *SunWorld*, Vol. 4, No. 5, May 1991, pp. 63–70.

(St90)   Stevens, A., *Teach Yourself C++*, Portland, OR: Management Information Source, Inc., 1990.

(St84)   Stroustrup, B., "The UNIX System: Data Abstraction in C," *AT&T Bell Laboratories Technical Journal*, Vol. 63, No. 8, Part 2, October 1984, pp. 1701–1732.

(St86)   Stroustrup, B. *The C++ Programming Language*, Reading, MA: Addison-Wesley Series in Computer Science, 1986.

(St88)   Stroustrup, B., "What is Object-Oriented Programming?" *IEEE Software*, Vol. 5, No. 3, May 1988, pp. 10–20.

(St91)   Stroustrup, B. *The C++ Programming Language* (Second Edition), Reading, MA: Addison-Wesley Series in Computer Science, 1991.

(Ta91)   Tasker, D., "Object Lesson," *Computerworld*, April 22, 1991, pp. 79–84.

(Ve91)   Verity, J. W., and E. I. Schwartz; "Software Made Simple: Will Object-Oriented Programming Transform the Computer Industry?" *Business Week*, September 30, 1991, pp. 92–100.

(Wh91)   Whitefield, B., and K. Auer, "You Can't Do That in Smalltalk! Or Can You?" *Object Magazine*, Vol. 1, No. 1, May/June 1991, pp. 64–73.

(Wi88)   Wiener, R. S., and L. J. Pinson, *An Introduction to Object-Oriented Programming and C++*, Reading, MA: Addison-Wesley Publishing Company, 1988.

(Wl91)   Williams, J., "The Object Paradigm Requires Object-Oriented Methods and Tools," *Object Magazine*, Vol. 1, No. 4, November/December 1991, pp. 50–58.

(Wr90)   Wirfs-Brock, R., B. Wilkerson, and L. Wiener, *Designing Object-Oriented Software*, Englewood Cliffs, NJ: Prentice Hall, 1990.

APPENDIX: C++ Resources

Organizations

Object Management Group
492 Old Connecticut Path
Framingham, MA 01701
508-820-4300
Fax: 508-820-4303
3823 Birchwood Drive
Boulder, CO 80304
303-444-8129
Fax: 303-444-8172

Publications

The C Users Journal
1601 West 23rd Street, Ste. 200
Lawrence, KS 66046

C++ Report
Subscriber Services, Dept. CPR
P. O. Box 3000
Denville, NJ
Fax: 212-274-0646

Hotline on Object-Oriented Technology
Sunscriber Services, Dept. HOT
P. O. Box 3000
Denville, New Jersey 07834
212-274-0640
212-274-0646

Journal of Object-Oriented Programming
588 Broadway, Suite 604
New York, New York 10012
212-274-0640

Object Magazine
Sunscriber Services, Dept. OBJ
P. O. Box 3000
Denville, New Jersey 07834-9876

The Smalltalk Report
588 Broadway, Suite 604
New York, New York 10012
212-274-0640
Fax: 212-274-0646

C++ Companies

Borland C++
(Supports Microsoft Windows
applications)
Borland International, Inc.
1800 Green Hills Road
P.O. Box 660001
Scotts Valley, CA 95067-0001
408-439-4825
1-800-331-0877

CNS, Inc.
Software Products, Dept.
1250 Park Road
Chanhassen, MN 55317
612-474-7600
Fax: 612-474-6737

Dyad Software Corporation
16950 151st Avenue Southeast
Renton, WA 98058-8627

Glockenspiel
39 Lower Dominick Street
Dublin 1
Ireland
353 (1) 733166
Fax: 353 (1) 733034

Hewlett-Packard Company
C++ SoftBench
800-752-0900, Ext. 2703

ImageSoft
1-800-245-8840
2 Haven Avenue
Port Washington, New York 11050
Fax: 516-767-9067
516-767-2233
UUCP: mcdhup!image!info

JPI TopSpeed Consortium, Inc.
117 Hunt Hill Road
Rindge, New Hampshire 03461

Liant Software Corporation
959 Concord Street
Framingham, MA 01701
508-872-8700
FAX: 508-626-2221

Microtec Research, Inc.
2350 Mission College Blvd.
Santa Clara, California 95054
408-980-1300

Oasys
One Cranberry Hill
Lexington, MA 02173
617-862-2002
Fax: 617 863-2633

ObjectCraft
2124 Kittredge Street, Suite 118
Berkeley, CA 94704
415-540-4889

Object Design, Inc.
One New England Executive Park
Burlington, MA 01803
617-270-9797
Fax: 617-270-3509

ONTOS
Three Burlington Woods
Burlington, MA 01803
617-272-7110

Oregon Software
7352 S.W. Durham Road
Portland, Oregon 97224
800-874-8501
503-624-6883
Fax: 503-620-6093

Quest Systems Corp.
2700 Augustine Drive
Santa Clara, California 95054
408-496-1900
FAX 408-988-8357
info@quest.com
!questsys!info

Rational
(C++ Booch Components)
3320 Scott Blvd.
Santa Clara, CA 95054-3197
408-496-3700

Rogue Wave
P. O. Box 2328
Corvallis, Oregon 97339
503-754-2311

Saber Software, Inc.
(new name CenterLine Software)
185 Alewife Brook Parkway
Cambridge, Massachusetts 02138
617-876-7636
Fax: 617-547-9011

Sequiter Software Inc.
P. O. Box 5659
Station L
Edmonton, Alberta
Canada T6C 4G1
403-448-0313
Fax: 403-448-0315

Servio Corporation
1420 Harbor Bay Parkway
Alameda, CA 94501
800-243-9369
415-748-6200
415-748-6227

Solution Systems
372 Washington St.
Wellesley, Massachusetts 02181
800-677-0001
617-431-7445

Versant Object Technology
4500 Bohannon Drive
Menlo Park, California 94025
1-800-9-OBJECT
415-325-2300
Fax: 415-325-2380

Zortech Inc.
4-C Gill Street
Woburn, MA 01801
800-848-8408
617-937-0696
Fax: 617-937-0793

Simula

Simula a.s.
Postboks 4403 Torshov
N-0402 Oslo, Norway
473 720530
Fax: 472 720481

Smalltalk

Digitalk, Inc.
9841 Airport Blvd.
Los Angeles, CA 90045
800-922-8255
213-645-1082
Fax: 213-645-1306

Knowledge Systems Corporation
114 MacKenan Drive
Cary, North Carolina 27511
(919) 481-4000

ParcPlace Systems
1550 Plymouth Street
Mountain View, CA 94043

Appendix A[*]
C Syntax

In the syntax notation used, syntactic categories (nonterminals) are indicated by *italic* type, and literal words and character set members (terminals) by **bold** type. A colon (:) following a nonterminal introduces its definition. Alternative definitions are listed on separate lines, except when prefaced by the words "one of." An optional symbol is indicated by the subscript "opt," so that

> { *expression*$_{opt}$ }

indicates an optional expression enclosed in braces.

Language Syntax Summary
A.1 Lexical Grammar
A.1.1 Tokens
token:
 keyword
 identifier
 constant
 string-literal
 operator
 punctuator

preprocessing-token:
 header-name
 identifier
 pp-number
 character-constant
 string-literal
 operator
 punctuator
 each non-white-space character that cannot be one of the above

---

[*] Permissions Acknowledgement: This material has been condensed and adapted from *American National Standard for Information Systems—Programming Language—C, ANSI X3.159-1989*, copyright 1990 by the American National Standards Institute. Copies of this standard may be purchased from the American National Standards Institute, 11 West 42nd Street, New York, NY 10036.

A.1.2 Keywords

keyword: one of

auto	double	int	struct
break	else	long	switch
case	enum	register	typedef
char	extern	return	union
const	float	short	unsigned
continue	for	signed	void
default	goto	sizeof	volatile
do	if	static	while

A.1.3 Identifiers

identifier:
    nondigit
    identifier nondigit
    identifier digit

nondigit: one of

_	a	b	c	d	e	f	g	h	i	j	k	l	m
n	o	p	q	r	s	t	u	v	w	x	y	z
A	B	C	D	E	F	G	H	I	J	K	L	M
N	O	P	Q	R	S	T	U	V	W	X	Y	Z

digit: one of
    0   1   2   3   4   5   6   7   8   9

A.1.4 Constants

constant:
    floating-constant
    integer-constant
    enumeration-constant
    character-constant

floating-constant:
    fractional-constant exponent-part$_{opt}$ floating-suffix$_{opt}$
    digit-sequence exponent-part floating-suffix$_{opt}$

fractional-constant:
    digit-sequence$_{opt}$. digit-sequence
    digit-sequence .

exponent-part:
    e sign$_{opt}$ digit-sequence
    E sign$_{opt}$ digit-sequence

sign: one of
    +   -

digit-sequence:
    digit
    digit-sequence digit

floating-suffix: one of
    f l F L

integer-constant:
    decimal-constant integer-suffix$_{opt}$
    octal-constant integer-suffix$_{opt}$
    hexadecimal-constant integer-suffix$_{opt}$

decimal-constant:
    nonzero-digit
    decimal-constant digit

octal-constant:
    0
    octal-constant octal-digit

hexadecimal-constant:
    0x *hexadecimal-digit*
    0X *hexadecimal-digit*
    hexadecimal-constant hexadecimal-digit

nonzero-digit: one of
    1 2 3 4 5 6 7 8 9

octal-digit: one of
    0 1 2 3 4 5 6 7

hexadecimal-digit: one of
    0 1 2 3 4 5 6 7 8 9
    a b c d e f
    A B C D E F

integer-suffix:
    unsigned-suffix long-suffix$_{opt}$
    long-suffix unsigned-suffix$_{opt}$

unsigned-suffix: one of
    u U

long-suffix: one of
    l L

enumeration-constant:
    identifier

character-constant:
    'c-char-sequence'
    L*'c-char-sequence'*

c-char-sequence:
    c-char
    c-char-sequence c-char

c-char:
    any member of the source character set except the single-quote ', backslash \, or new-
        line character
    escape-sequence

escape-sequence:
    simple-escape-sequence
    octal-escape-sequence
    hexadecimal-escape-sequence

simple-escape-sequence: one of
    \'   \"   \?   \\
    \a   \b   \f   \n   \r   \t   \v

octal-escape-sequence:
    \ *octal-digit*
    \ *octal-digit octal-digit*
    \ *octal-digit octal-digit octal-digit*

hexadecimal-escape-sequence:
    \x *hexadecimal-digit*
    hexadecimal-escape-sequence hexadecimal-digit

A.1.5 String Literals

string-literal:
    "*s-char-sequence*$_{opt}$"
    L"*s-char-sequence*$_{opt}$"

s-char-sequence:
    s-char
    s-char-sequence s-char

s-char:
    any member of the source character set except the double-quote ", backslash \, or new-
        line character
    escape-sequence

A.1.6 Operators

operator: one of

```
[  ]  (  )  .  ->
++  --  &  *  +  -  ~  !  sizeof
/  %  <<  >>  <  >  <=  >=  ==  !=  ^  |  &&  ||
?  :
=  *=  /=  %=  +=  -=  <<=  >>=  &=  ^=  |=
,  #  ##
```

A.1.7 Punctuators

punctuator: one of

```
[  ]  (  )  {  }  *  ,  :  =  ;  ...  #
```

A.1.8 Header Names

header-name:
>   *<h-char-sequence>*
>   *"q-char-sequence"*

h-char-sequence:
>   *h-char*
>   *h-char-sequence h-char*

h-char:
>   any member of the source character set except the new-line character and **>**

q-char-sequence:
>   *q-char*
>   *q-char-sequence q-char*

q-char:
>   any member of the source character set except the new-line character and **"**

A.1.9 Preprocessing Numbers

pp-number:
>   *digit*
>   *. digit*
>   *pp-number digit*
>   *pp-number nondigit*
>   *pp-number e sign*
>   *pp-number* E *sign*
>   *pp-number .*

A.2 Phrase Structure Grammar
A.2.1 Expressions

primary-expression:
>   *identifier*
>   *constant*
>   *string-literal*
>   *(expression)*

postfix-expression:
    primary-expression
    postfix-expression [*expression*]
    postfix-expression (*argument-expression-list*$_{opt}$)
    postfix-expression . *identifier*
    postfix-expression -> *identifier*
    postfix-expression ++
    postfix-expression --

argument-expression-list:
    assignment-expression
    argument-expression-list , *assignment-expression*

unary-expression:
    postfix-expression
    ++ *unary-expression*
    -- *unary-expression*
    unary-operator cast-expression
    sizeof *unary-expression*
    sizeof (*type-name*)

unary-operator: one of
    &   *   +   -   ~   !

cast-expression:
    unary-expression
    (*type-name*) *cast-expression*

multiplicative-expression:
    cast-expression
    multiplicative-expression * *cast-expression*
    multiplicative-expression / *cast-expression*
    multiplicative-expression % *cast-expression*

additive-expression:
    multiplicative-expression
    additive-expression + *multiplicative-expression*
    additive-expression - *multiplicative-expression*

shift-expression:
    additive-expression
    shift-expression << *additive-expression*
    shift-expression >> *additive-expression*

relational-expression:
    shift-expression
    relational-expression < *shift-expression*
    relational-expression > *shift-expression*
    relational-expression <= *shift-expression*
    relational-expression >= *shift-expression*

equality expression:
 relational-expression
 equality-expression == *relational-expression*
 equality-expression != *relational-expression*

AND-expression:
 equality-expression
 AND-expression & *equality-expression*

exclusive-OR-expression:
 AND-expression
 exclusive-OR-expression ^ *AND-expression*

inclusive-OR-expression:
 exclusive-OR-expression
 inclusive-OR-expression | *exclusive-OR-expression*

logical-AND-expression:
 inclusive-OR-expression
 logical-AND-expression && *inclusive-OR-expression*

logical-OR-expression:
 logical-AND-expression
 logical-OR-expression || *logical-AND-expression*

conditional-expression:
 logical-OR-expression
 logical-OR-expression ? *expression* : *conditional-expression*

assignment-expression:
 conditional-expression
 unary-expression assignment-operator assignment-expression

assignment-operator: one of
 = *= /= %= += -= <<= >>= &= ^= |=

expression:
 conditional-expression
 expression , *assignment-expression*

constant-expression:
 conditional-expression

A.2.2 Declarations

declaration:
 declaration-specifiers init-declarator-list$_{opt}$;

declaration-specifiers:
    storage-class-specifier declaration-specifiers$_{opt}$
    type-specifier declaration-specifiers$_{opt}$
    type-qualifier declaration-specifiers$_{opt}$

init-declarator-list:
    init-declarator
    init-declarator-list , init-declarator

init-declarator:
    declarator
    declarator = initializer

storage-class-specifier:
    typedef
    extern
    static
    auto
    register

type-specifier:
    void
    char
    short
    int
    long
    float
    double
    signed
    unsigned
    struct-or-union-specifier
    enum-specifier
    typedef-name

struct-or-union-specifier:
    struct-or-union identifier$_{opt}$ { struct-declaration-list }
    struct-or-union identifier

struct-or-union:
    struct
    union

struct-declaration-list:
    struct-declaration
    struct-declaration-list struct-declaration

struct-declaration:
    specifier-qualifier-list struct-declarator-list ;

specifier-qualifier-list:
    type-specifier specifier-qualifier-list$_{opt}$
    type-qualifier specifier-qualifier-list$_{opt}$

struct-declarator-list:
    struct-declarator
    struct-declarator-list , struct-declarator

struct-declarator:
    declarator
    declarator$_{opt}$ *: constant-expression*

enum-specifier:
    enum *identifier*$_{opt}$ *{ enumerator-list }*
    enum *identifier*

enumerator-list:
    enumerator
    enumerator-list , enumerator

enumerator:
    enumeration-constant
    enumeration-constant = constant-expression

type-qualifier:
    const
    volatile

declarator:
    pointer$_{opt}$ *direct-declarator*

direct-declarator:
    identifier
    (declarator)
    direct-declarator [constant-expression$_{opt}$ *]*
    direct-declarator (*parameter-type-list*)
    direct-declarator (*identifier-list*$_{opt}$)

pointer:
    * *type-qualifier-list*$_{opt}$
    * *type-qualifier-list*$_{opt}$ *pointer*

type-qualifier-list:
    type-qualifier
    type-qualifier-list type-qualifier

parameter-type-list:
    parameter-list
    parameter-list , ...

parameter-list:
    parameter-declaration
    parameter-list , parameter-declaration

parameter-declaration:
    declaration-specifiers declarator
    declaration-specifiers abstract-declarator$_{opt}$

identifier-list:
    identifier
    identifier-list , identifier

type-name:
    specifier-qualifier-list abstract-declarator$_{opt}$

abstract-declarator:
    pointer
    pointer$_{opt}$ *direct-abstract-declarator*

direct-abstract-declarator:
    (abstract-declarator)
    direct-abstract-declarator$_{opt}$ *[constant-expression*$_{opt}$ *]*
    direct-abstract-declarator$_{opt}$ *(parameter-type-list*$_{opt}$ *)*

typedef-name:
    identifier

initializer:
    assignment-expression
    { initializer-list }
    { initializer-list , }

initializer-list:
    initializer
    initializer-list , initializer

A.2.3 Statements

statement:
    labeled-statement
    compound-statement
    expression-statement
    selection-statement
    iteration-statement
    jump-statement

labeled-statement:
    identifier : statement
    case *constant-expression : statement*
    default *: statement*

compound-statement:
    { *declaration-list*$_{opt}$ *statement-list*$_{opt}$ }

declaration-list:
    declaration
    declaration-list declaration

statement-list:
    statement
    statement-list statement

expression-statement:
    expression$_{opt}$;

selection-statement:
    if (*expression*) *statement*
    if (*expression*) *statement* **else** *statement*
    switch (*expression*) *statement*

iteration-statement:
    while (*expression*) *statement*
    do *statement* **while** (*expression*) ;
    for (*expression*$_{opt}$; *expression*$_{opt}$; *expression*$_{opt}$) *statement*

jump-statement:
    goto *identifier* ;
    continue ;
    break ;
    return *expression*$_{opt}$;

A.2.4 External Definitions

translation-unit:
    external-declaration
    translation-unit external-declaration

external-declaration:
    function-definition
    declaration

function-definition:
    declaration-specifiers$_{opt}$ *declarator declaration-list*$_{opt}$ *compound-statement*

A.3 Preprocessing Directives

preprocessing-file:
    group$_{opt}$

group:
    group-part
    group group-part

`size_t`

The unsigned integral type of the result of the `sizeof` operator.

`wchar_t`

An integral type whose range of values can represent distinct codes for all members of the largest extended character set specified among the supported locales; the null character shall have the code value zero and each member of the basic character set shall have a code value equal to its value when used as the lone character in an integer character constant.

B.3 Diagnostics `<assert.h>`
`void assert(int expression);`

Macro `assert` puts diagnostics into programs. When it is executed, if `expression` is false, the `assert` macro writes information about the particular call that failed (including the text of the argument, the name of the source file, and the source line number—the latter are respectively the values of the preprocessing macros `__FILE__` and `__LINE__`) on the standard error file in an implementation-defined format. For example, the message written might be of the form

> `Assertion failed:` *expression,* `file` *xyz,* `line` *nnn*

Macro `assert` then calls function `abort`. If the preprocessor directive

> `#define NDEBUG`

appears in the source file where `assert.h` is included, any assertions in the file are ignored.

B.4 Character Handling `<ctype.h>`
The functions in this section return nonzero (true) if and only if the value of the argument c conforms to that in the description of the function.
`int isalnum(int c);`

Tests for any character for which `isalpha` or `isdigit` is true.

`int isalpha(int c);`

Tests for any character for which `isupper` or `islower` is true.

`int iscntrl(int c);`

Tests for any control character.

`int isdigit(int c);`

Tests for any decimal-digit character.

`int isgraph(int c);`

Tests for any printing character except space (' ').

`int islower(int c);`

Tests for any character that is a lowercase letter.

`int isprint(int c);`

Tests for any printing character including space (' ').

```
int ispunct(int c);
```

Tests for any printing character that is neither space (' ') nor a character for which `isalnum` is true.

```
int isspace(int c);
```

Tests for any character that is a standard white-space character. The standard white-space characters are: space (' '), form feed ('\f'), new-line ('\n'), carriage return ('\r'), horizontal tab ('\t'), and vertical tab ('\v').

```
int isupper(int c);
```

Tests for any character that is an uppercase letter.

```
int isxdigit(int c);
```

Tests for any hexadecimal-digit character.

```
int tolower(int c);
```

Converts an uppercase letter to the corresponding lowercase letter. If the argument is a character for which `isupper` is true and there is a corresponding character for which `islower` is true, the `tolower` function returns the corresponding character; otherwise, the argument is returned unchanged.

```
int toupper(int c);
```

Converts a lowercase letter to the corresponding uppercase letter. If the argument is a character for which `islower` is true and there is a corresponding character for which `isupper` is true, the `toupper` function returns the corresponding character; otherwise, the argument is returned unchanged.

B.5 Localization `<locale.h>`

```
LC_ALL
LC_COLLATE
LC_CTYPE
LC_MONETARY
LC_NUMERIC
LC_TIME
```

These expand to integral constant expressions with distinct values, suitable for use as the first argument to the `setlocale` function.

`NULL`

An implementation-defined null pointer constant.

`struct lconv`

Contains members related to the formatting of numeric values. The structure shall contain at least the following members, in any order. In the "C" locale, the members shall have the values specified in the comments.

```
        char *decimal_point;                /* "." */
        char *thousands-sep;                /* "" */
        char *grouping;                     /* "" */
        char *int_curr_symbol;              /* "" */
        char *currency_symbol;              /* "" */
```

```
char *mon_decimal_point;              /* "" */
char *mon_thousands_sep;              /* "" */
char *mon_grouping;                   /* "" */
char *positive_sign;                  /* "" */
char *negative_sign;                  /* "" */
char int_frac_digits;                 /* CHAR_MAX */
char frac_digits;                     /* CHAR_MAX */
char p_cs_precedes;                   /* CHAR_MAX */
char p_sep_by_space;                  /* CHAR_MAX */
char n_cs_precedes;                   /* CHAR_MAX */
char n_sep_by_space;                  /* CHAR_MAX */
char p_sign_posn;                     /* CHAR_MAX */
char n_sign_posn;                     /* CHAR_MAX */
```

`char *setlocale(int category, const char *locale);`

Function `setlocale` selects the appropriate portion of the program's locale as specified by the `category` and `locale` arguments. Function `setlocale` may be used to change or query the program's entire current locale or portions thereof. The value `LC_ALL` for `category` names the program's entire locale; the other values for `category` name only a portion of the program's locale. `LC_COLLATE` affects the behavior of the `strcoll` and `strxfrm` functions. `LC_CTYPE` affects the behavior of the character handling functions and the multibyte functions. `LC_MONETARY` affects the monetary formatting information returned by the `localeconv` function. `LC_NUMERIC` affects the decimal-point character for the formatted input/output functions and the string conversion functions, as well as the nonmonetary formatting information returned by the `localeconv` function. `LC_TIME` affects the behavior of the `strftime` function.

A value of `"C"` for `locale` specifies the minimal environment for C translation; a value of `""` for `locale` specifies the implementation-defined native environment. Other implementation-defined strings may be passed as the second argument to `setlocale`. At program startup, the equivalent of

```
setlocale(LC_ALL, "C");
```

is executed. If a pointer to a string is given for `locale` and the selection can be honored, the `setlocale` function returns a pointer to the string associated with the specified `category` for the new locale. If the selection cannot be honored, the `setlocale` function returns a null pointer and the program's locale is not changed.

A null pointer for `locale` causes the `setlocale` function to return a pointer to the string associated with the `category` for the program's current locale; the program's locale is not changed.

The pointer to string returned by the `setlocale` function is such that a subsequent call with that string value and its associated category will restore that part of the program's locale. The string pointed to shall be modified by the program, but may be overwritten by a subsequent call to the `setlocale` function.

```
struct lconv *localeconv(void);
```

The `localeconv` function sets the components of an object with type `struct lconv` with values appropriate for the formatting of numeric quantities (monetary and otherwise) according to the rules of the current locale.

The members of the structure with type `char *` are pointers to strings, any of which (except `decimal_point`) can point to `""`, to indicate that the value is not available in the current locale or is of zero length. The members with type `char` are nonnegative numbers, any of which can be `CHAR_MAX` to indicate that the value is not available in the current locale. The members include the following:

```
char *decimal_point
```

The decimal-point character used to format nonmonetary quantities.

```
char *thousands_sep
```

The character used to separate groups of digits before the decimal-point character in formatted nonmonetary quantities.

```
char *grouping
```

A string whose elements indicate the size of each group of digits in formatted nonmonetary quantities.

```
char *int_curr_symbol
```

The international currency symbol applicable to the current locale. The first three characters contain the alphabetic international currency symbol in accordance with those specified in ISO 4217:1987. The fourth character (immediately preceding the null character) is the character used to separate the international currency symbol from the monetary quantity.

```
char *currency_symbol
```

The locale currency symbol applicable to the current locale.

```
char *mon_decimal_point
```

The decimal-point used to format monetary quantities.

```
char *mon_thousands_sep
```

The separator for groups of digits before the decimal-point in formatted monetary quantities.

```
char *mon_grouping
```

A string whose elements indicate the size of each group of digits in formatted monetary quantities.

```
char *positive_sign
```

The string used to indicate a nonnegative-valued formatted monetary quantity.

```
char *negative_sign
```

The string used to indicate a negative-valued formatted monetary quantity.

```
char int_frac_digits
```

The number of fractional digits (those after the decimal-point) to be displayed in a internationally formatted monetary quantity.

`char frac_digits`

The number of fractional digits (those after the decimal-point) to be displayed in a formatted monetary quantity.

`char p_cs_precedes`

Set to 1 or 0 the `currency_symbol` respectively precedes or succeeds the value for a nonnegative formatted monetary quantity.

`char p_sep_by_space`

Set to 1 or 0 the `currency_symbol` respectively is or is not separated by a space from the value for a nonnegative formatted monetary quantity.

`char n_cs_precedes`

Set to 1 or 0 the `currency_symbol` respectively precedes or succeeds the value for a negative formatted monetary quantity.

`char n_sep_by_space`

Set to 1 or 0 the `currency_symbol` respectively is or is not separated by a space from the value for a negative formatted monetary quantity.

`char p_sign_posn`

Set to a value indicating the positioning of the `positive_sign` for a nonnegative formatted monetary quantity.

`char n_sign_posn`

Set to a value indicating the positioning of the `negative_sign` for a negative formatted monetary quantity.

The elements of `grouping` and `mon_grouping` are interpreted according to the following:

`CHAR_MAX`   No further grouping is to be performed.

`0`   The previous element is to be repeatedly used for the remainder of the digits.

other   The integer value is the number of digits that comprise the current group. The next element is examined to determine the size of the next group of digits before the current group.

The value of `p_sign_posn` and `n_sign_posn` is interpreted according to the following:

`0`   Parentheses surround the quantity and `currency_symbol`.

`1`   The sign string precedes the quantity and `currency_symbol`.

`2`   The sign string succeeds the quantity and `currency_symbol`.

`3`   The sign string immediately precedes the `currency_symbol`.

`4`   The sign string immediately succeeds the `currency_symbol`.

The `localeconv` function returns a pointer to the filled-in object. The structure pointed to by the return value shall not be modified by the program, but may be overwritten by a subsequent call to the `localeconv` function. In addition, calls to the `setlocale` function with categories `LC_ALL`, `LC_MONETARY`, or `LC_NUMERIC` may overwrite the contents of the structure.

B.6 Mathematics `<math.h>`

`HUGE_VAL`

A symbolic constant representing a positive **double** expression.

`double acos(double x);`

Computes the principal value of the arc cosine of **x**. A domain error occurs for arguments not in the range [-1, +1]. The **acos** function returns the arc cosine in the range [0, π] radians.

`double asin(double x);`

Computes the principal value of the arc sine of **x**. A domain error occurs for arguments not in the range [-1, +1]. The **asin** function returns the arc sine in the range [-π/2, +π/2] radians.

`double atan(double x);`

Computes the principal value of the arc tangent of **x**. The **atan** function returns the arc tangent in the range [-π/2, +π/2] radians.

`double atan2(double y, double x);`

The **atan2** function computes the principal value of the arc tangent **y/x**, using the signs of both arguments to determine the quandrant of the return value. A domain error may occur if both arguments are zero. The **atan2** function returns the arc tangent of **y/x**, in the range [-π, +π] radians.

`double cos(double x);`

Computes the cosine of **x** (measured in radians).

`double sin(double x);`

Computes the sine of **x** (measured in radians).

`double tan(double x);`

Returns the tangent of **x** (measured in radians).

`double cosh(double x);`

Computes the hyperbolic cosine of **x**. A range error occurs if the magnitude of **x** is too large.

`double sinh(double x);`

Computes the hyperbolic sine of **x**. A range error occurs if the magnitude of **x** is too large.

`double tanh(double x);`

The **tanh** function computes the hyperbolic tangent of **x**.

`double exp(double x);`

Computes the exponential function of **x**. A range error occurs if the magnitude of **x** is too large.

```
double frexp(double value, int *exp);
```

Breaks the floating-point number onto a normalized fraction and an integral power of 2. It stores the integer in the **int** object pointed to by **exp**. The **frexp** function returns the value **x**, such that **x** is a **double** with magnitude in the interval [1/2, 1] or zero, and **value** equals **x** times 2 raised to the power ***exp**. If **value** is zero, both parts of the result are zero.

```
double ldexp(double x, int exp);
```

Multiplies a floating-point number by an integral power of 2. A range error may occur. The **ldexp** function returns the value of **x** times 2 raised to the power **exp**.

```
double log(double x);
```

Computes the natural logarithm of **x**. A domain error occurs if the argument is negative. A range error may occur if the argument is zero.

```
double log10(double x);
```

Computes the base-ten logarithm of **x**. A domain error occurs if the argument is negative. A range error may occur if the argument is zero.

```
double modf(double value, double *iptr);
```

Breaks the argument **value** into integral and fractional parts, each of which has the same sign as the argument. It stores the integral part as a **double** in the object pointed to by **iptr**. The **modf** function returns the signed frantional part of **value**.

```
double pow(double x, double y);
```

Computes **x** raised to the power **y**. A domain error occurs if **x** is negative and **y** is not an integral value. A domain error occurs if the result cannot be represented when **x** is zero and **y** is less than or equal to zero. A range error may occur.

```
double sqrt(double x);
```

Computes the nonnegative square root of **x**. A domain error occurs if the argument is negative.

```
double ceil(double x);
```

Computes the smallest integral value not less than **x**.

```
double fabs(double x);
```

Computes the absolute value of a floating-point number **x**.

```
double floor(double x);
```

Computes the largest integral value not greater than **x**.

```
double fmod(double x, double y);
```

Computes the floating-point remainder of **x/y**.

B.7 Nonlocal Jumps `<setjmp.h>`

```
jmp_buf
```

An array type suitable for holding the information needed to restore a calling environment.

```
int setjmp(jmp_buf env);
```

Saves its calling environment in its `jmp_buf` argument for later use by the `longjmp` function.

If the return is from a direct invocation, the `setjmp` macro returns the value zero. If the return is from a call to the `longjmp` function, the `setjmp` macro returns a nonzero value.

An invocation of the `setjmp` macro shall appear only in one of the following contexts:

- the entire controlling expression of a selection or iteration statement;
- one operand of a relational or equality operator with the other operand an integral constant expression, with the resulting expression being the entire controlling expression of a selection or iteration statement;
- the operand of a unary ! operator with the resulting expression being the entire controlling expression of a selection or iteration statement; or
- the entire expression of an expression statement.

```
void longjmp(jmp_buf env, int val);
```

Restores the environment saved by the most recent invocation of the `setjmp` macro in the same invocation of the program, with the corresponding `jmp_buf` argument. If there has been no such invocation, or if the function containing the invocation of the `setjmp` macro has terminated execution in the interim, the behavior is undefined.

All accessible objects have values as of the time `longjmp` was called, except that the values of objects of automatic storage duration that are local to the function containing the invocation of the corresponding `setjmp` macro that do not have volatile-qualified type and have been changed between the `setjmp` invocation and `longjmp` invocation call are indeterminate.

As it bypasses the usual function call and return mechanisms, the `longjmp` function shall execute correctly in context of interrupts, signals, and any of their associated functions. However, if the `longjmp` function is invoked from a nested signal handler (that is, from a function invoked as a result of a signal raised during the handling of another signal), the behavior is undefined.

After `longjmp` is completed, program execution continues as if the corresponding invocation of the `setjmp` macro had just returned the value specified by `val`. The `longjmp` function cannot cause the `setjmp` macro to return the value 0; if `val` is 0, the `setjmp` macro returns the value 1.

B.8 Signal Handling `<signal.h>`

```
sig_atomic_t
```

The integral type of an object that can be accessed as an atomic entity, even in the presence of asynchronous interrupts.

```
SIG_DFL
SIG_ERR
SIG_IGN
```

These expand to constant expressions with distinct values that have type compatible with the second argument to and the return value of the `signal` function, and whose value compares unequal to the address of any declarable function; and the following, each of which expands to a positive integral constant expression that is the signal number corresponding to the specified condition:

`SIGABRT`	abnormal termination, such as is initiated by the **abort** function
`SIGFPE`	an erroneous arithmetic operation, such as zero divide or an operation resulting in overflow
`SIGILL`	detection of an invalid function image, such as an illegal instruction
`SIGINT`	receipt of an interactive attention signal
`SIGSEGV`	an invalid access to storage
`SIGTERM`	a termination request sent to the program

An implementation need not generate any of these signals, except as a result of explicit calls to the **raise** function.

```
void (*signal(int sig, void (*func)(int)))(int);
```

Chooses one of three ways in which receipt of the signal number **sig** is to be subsequently handled. If the value of **func** is `SIG_DEF`, default handling for that signal will occur. If the value of **func** is `SIG_IGN`, the signal will be ignored. Otherwise, **func** shall point to a function to be called when that signal occurs. Such a function is called a *signal handler*.

When a signal occurs, if **func** points to a function, first the equivalent of **signal(sig, SIG_DFL);** is executed or an implementation-defined blocking of the signal is performed. (If the value of **sig** is `SIGILL`, whether the reset to `SIG_DFL` occurs is implementation-defined.) Next the equivalent of **(*func) (sig);** is executed. The function **func** may terminate by executing a **return** statement or by calling the **abort, exit,** or **longjmp** function. If **func** executes a **return** statement and the value if **sig** was `SIGFPE` or any other implementation-defined value corresponding to a computational exception, the behavior is undefined. Otherwise, the program will resume execution at the point it was interrupted.

If the signal occurs other than as the result of calling the **abort** or **raise** function, the behavior is undefined if the signal handler calls any function in the standard library other than the **signal** function itself (with a first argument of the signal number corresponding to the signal that caused the invocation of the handler) or refers to any object with static storage duration other than by assigning a value to a static storage duration variable of type **volatile sig_atomic_t**. Furthermore, if such a call to the **signal** function results in a `SIG_ERR` return, the value of **errno** in indeterminate.

At program startup, the equivalent of

```
signal(sig, SIG_IGN);
```

may be executed for some signals selected in an implementation-defined manner; the equivalent of

```
signal(sig, SIG_DFL);
```

is executed for all other signals defined by the implementation.

If the request can be honored, the **signal** function returns the value of **func** for the most recent call to **signal** for the specified signal **sig**. Otherwise, a value of `SIG_ERR` is returned and a positive value is stored in **errno**.

```
int raise(int sig);
```

The **raise** function sends the signal **sig** to the executing program The **raise** function returns zero if successful, nonzero if unsuccessful.

B.9 Variable Arguments `<stdarg.h>`

`va_list`

A type suitable for holding information needed by the macros `va_start`, `va_arg`, and `va_end`. If access to the varying arguments is desired, the called function shall declare an object (referred to as `ap` in this section) having type `va_list`. The object `ap` may be passed as an argument to another function; if that function invokes the `va_arg` macro with parameter `ap`, the value of `ap` in the calling function is determinate and shall be passed to the `va_end` macro prior to any further reference to `ap`.

`void va_start(va_list ap, ` *parmN*`);`

Shall be invoked before any access to the unnamed arguments. The `va_start` marco initializes `ap` for subsequent use by `va_arg` and `va_end`. The parameter *parmN* is the identifier of the rightmost parameter in the variable parameter list in the function definition (the one just before the, ...). If the parameter *parmN* is declared with the `register` storage class, with a function or array type, or with a type that is not compatible with the type that results after application of the default argument promotions, the behavior is undefined.

type `va_arg(va_list ap, ` *type*`);`

Expands to an expression that has the type and value of the next argument in the call. The parameter `ap` shall be the same as the `va_list ap` initialized by `va_start`. Each invocation of `va_arg` modifies `ap` so that the values of successive arguments are returned in turn. The parameter *type* is a type name specified such that the type of a pointer to an object that has the specified type can be obtained simply by postfixing a `*` to *type*. If there is no actual next argument, or if *type* is not compatible with the type of the actual next argument (as promoted according to the default argument promotions), the behavior is undefined. The first invocation of the `va_arg` macro after that of the `va_start` macro returns the value of the argument after that specified by *parmN*. Successive invocations return the values of the remaining arguments in succession.

`void va_end(va_list ap);`

Facilitates a normal return from the function whose variable argument list was referred to by the expansion of `va_start` that initialized `va_list` ap. The `va_end` macro may modify `ap` so that it is no longer usable (without an intervening invocation of `va_start`). If there is no corresponding invocation of the `va_start` macro, or if the `va_end` macro is not invoked before the return, the behavior is undefined.

B.10 Input/Output `<stdio.h>`

`_IOFBF`
`_IOLBF`
`_IONBF`

Integral constant expressions with distinct values, suitable for use as the third argument to the `setvbuf` function.

`BUFSIZ`

An integral constant expression, which is the size of the buffer used by the `setbuf` function.

EOF

A negative integral constant expression that is returned by several functions to indicate end-of-file, that is, no more input from a stream.

FILE

An object type capable of recording all the information needed to control a stream, including its file position indicator, a pointer to its associated buffer (if any), an error indicator that records whether a read/write error has occurred, and an end-of-file indicator that records whether the end of the file has been reached.

FILENAME_MAX

An integral constant expression that is the size needed for an array of `char` large enough to hold the longest file name string that the implementation guarantees can be opened.

FOPEN_MAX

An integral constant expression that is the minimum number of files that the implementation guarantees can be open simultaneously.

fpos_t

An object type capable of recording all the information needed to specify uniquely every position within a file.

L_tmpnam

An integral constant expression that is the size needed for an array of `char` large enough to hold a temporary file name string generated by the `tmpnam` function.

NULL

An implementation-defined null pointer constant.

SEEK_CUR
SEEK_END
SEEK_SET

Integral constant expressions with distinct values, suitable for use as the third argument to the `fseek` function.

size_t

The unsigned integral type of the result of the `sizeof` operator.

stderr

Expression of type "pointer to `FILE`" that points to the `FILE` object associated with the standard error stream.

stdin

Expression of type "pointer to `FILE`" that points to the `FILE` object associated with the standard input stream.

stdout

Expression of type "pointer to `FILE`" that points to the `FILE` object associated with the standard output stream.

`TMP_MAX`

An integral constant expression that is the minimum number of unique file names that shall be generated by the `tmpnam` function. The value of the macro `TMP_MAX` shall be at least 25.

`int remove(const char *filename);`

Causes the file whose name is the string pointed to by `filename` to be no longer accessible by that name. A subsequent attempt to open that file using that name will fail, unless it is created anew. If the file is open, the behavior of the `remove` function is implementation-defined. Thr `remove` function returns zero if the operation succeeds, nonzero if it fails.

`int rename(const char *old, const char *new);`

Causes the file whose name is the string pointed to by `old` to be henceforth known by the name given by the string pointed to by `new`. The file named `old` is no longer accessible by that name. If a file named by the string pointed to by `new` exists prior to the call to the `rename` function, the behavior is implementation-defined. The `rename` function returns zero if the operation succeeds, nonzero if it fails, in which case if the file existed previously it is still known by its original name.

`FILE *tmpfile(void);`

Creates a temporary binary file that will automatically be removed when it is closed or at program termination. If the program terminates abnormally, whether an open temporary file is removed is implementation-defined. The file is opened for update with `"wb+"` mode. The `tmpfile` function returns a pointer to the stream of the file that is created. If the file cannot be created, the `tmpfile` function returns a null pointer.

`char *tmpnam(char *s);`

The `tmpnam` function generates a string that is a valid file name and that is not the same as the name of an existing file. The `tmpnam` function generates a different string each time it is called, up to `TMP_MAX` times. If it is called more than `TMP_MAX` times, the behavior is implementation-defined.

   If the argument is a null pointer, the `tmpnam` function leaves its result in an internal static object and returns a pointer to that object. Subsequent calls to the `tmpnam` function may modify the same object. If the argument is not a null pointer, it is assumed to point to an array of at least `L_tmpnam chars`; the `tmpnam` function writes its result in that array and returns the argument as its value.

`int fclose(FILE *stream);`

The `fclose` function causes the stream pointed to by `stream` to be flushed and the associated file to be closed. Any unwritten buffered data for the stream are delivered to the host environment to be written to the file; any unread buffered data are discarded. The stream is disassociated from the file. If the associated buffer was automatically allocated, it is deallocated. The `fclose` function returns zero if the stream was successfully closed, or `EOF` if any errors were detected.

`int fflush(FILE *stream);`

If `stream` points to an output stream or an update stream in which the most recent operation was not input, the `fflush` function causes any unwritten data for that stream to be delivered to the host environment or to be written to the file; otherwise, the behavior is undefined.

If **stream** is a null pointer, the **fflush** function performs this flushing action on all streams for which the behavior is defined above. The **fflush** function returns EOF if a write error occurs, otherwise zero.

FILE *fopen(const char *filename, const char *mode);

The **fopen** function opens the file whose name is the string pointed to by **filename**, and associates a stream with it. The argument **mode** points to a string beginning with one of the following sequences:

r	open text file for reading
w	truncate to zero length or create text file for writing
a	append; open or create text file for writing at end-of-file
rb	open binary file for reading
wb	truncate to zero length or create binary file for writing
ab	append; open or create binary file for writing at end-of-file
r+	open text file for update (reading and writing)
w+	truncate to zero length or create text file for update
a+	append; open or create text file for update, writing at end-of-file
r+b or **rb+**	open binary file for update (reading and writing)
w+b or **wb+**	truncate to zero length or create binary file for update
a+b or **ab+**	append; open or create binary file for update, writing at end-of-file

Opening a file with read mode ('**r**' as the first character in the **mode** argument) fails if the file does not exist or cannot be read. Opening the file with append mode ('**a**' as the first character in the **mode** argument) causes all subsequent writes to the file to be forced to the then current end-of-file, regardless of intervening calls to the **fseek** function. In some implementations, opening a binary file with append mode ('**b**' as the second or third character in the above list of **mode** argument values) may initially position the file position indicator for the stream beyond the last data written, because of null character padding.

When a file is opened with update mode ('**+**' as the second or third character in the above list of **mode** argument values), both input and output may be performed on the associated stream. However, output may not be directly followed by input without an intervening call to the **fflush** function or to a file positioning function (**fseek**, **fsetpos**, or **rewind**), and input may not be directly followed by output without an intervening call to a file positioning function, unless the input operation encounters end-of-file. Opening (or creating) a text file with update mode may instead open (or create) a binary stream in some implementations.

When opened, a stream is fully buffered if and only if it can be determined not to refer to an interactive device. The error and end-of-file indicators for the stream are cleared. The **fopen** function returns a pointer to the object controlling the stream. If the open operation fails, **fopen** returns a null pointer.

```
FILE *freopen(const char *filename, const char *mode, FILE *stream);
```

The `freopen` function opens the file whose name is the string pointed to by `filename` and associates the stream pointed to by `stream` with it. The `mode` argument is used just as in the `fopen` function.

The `freopen` function first attempts to close any file that is associated with the specified stream. Failure to close the file successfully is ignored. The error and end-of-file indicators for the stream are cleared. The `freopen` function returns a null pointer if the open operation fails. Otherwise, `freopen` returns the value of `stream`.

```
void setbuf(FILE *stream, char *buf);
```

The `setbuf` function is equivalent to the `setvbuf` function invoked with the values `_IOFBF` for `mode` and `BUFSIZ` for `size`, or (if `buf` is a null pointer), with the value `_IONBF` for `mode`. The `setbuf` function returns no value.

```
int setvbuf(FILE *stream, char *buf, int mode, size_t size);
```

The `setvbuf` function may be used only after the stream pointed to by `stream` has been associated with an open file and before any other operation is performed on the stream. The argument `mode` determines how `stream` will be buffered, as follows: `_IOFBF` causes input/output to be fully buffered; `_IOLBF` causes input/output to be line buffered; `_IONBF` causes input/output to be unbuffered. If `buf` is not a null pointer, the array it points to may be used instead of a buffer allocated by the `setvbuf` function. The argument `size` specifies the size of the array. The contents of the array at any time are indeterminate. The `setvbuf` function returns zero on success, or nonzero if an invalid value is given for `mode` or if the request cannot be honored.

```
int fprintf(FILE *stream, const char *format, ...);
```

The `fprintf` function writes output to the stream pointed to by `stream`, under control of the string pointed to by `format` that specifies how subsequent arguments are converted for output. If there are insufficient arguments for the format, the behavior is undefined. If the format is exhausted while arguments remain, the excess arguments are evaluated (as always) but are otherwise ignored. The `fprintf` function returns when the end of the format string is encountered. See Chapter 9, "Formatted Input/Output," for a detailed description of the output conversion specifications. The `fprintf` function returns the number of characters transmitted, or a negative value if an output error occurred.

```
int fscanf(FILE *stream, const char *format, ...);
```

The `fscanf` function reads input from the stream pointed to by `stream`, under control of the string pointed to by `format` that specifies the admissible input sequences and how they are to be converted for assignment, using subsequent arguments as pointers to the objects to receive the converted input. If there are insufficient arguments for the format, the behavior is undefined. If the format is exhausted while arguments remain, the excess arguments are evaluated (as always) but are otherwise ignored. See Chapter 9, "Formatted Input/Output," for a detailed description of the input conversion specifications.

The `fscanf` function returns the value of the macro `EOF` if an input failure occurs before any conversion. Otherwise, the `fscanf` function returns the number of input items assigned, which can be fewer than provided for, or even zero, in the event of an early matching failure.

```
int printf(const char *format, ...);
```

The `printf` function is equivalent to `fprintf` with the argument `stdout` interposed before the arguments to `printf`. The `printf` function returns the number of characters transmitted, or a negative value if an output error occurred.

```
int scanf(const char *format, ...);
```

The `scanf` function is equivalent to `fscanf` with the argument `stdin` interposed before the arguments to `scanf`. The `scanf` function returns the value of the macro `EOF` if an input failure occurs before any conversion. Otherwise, the `scanf` function returns the number of input items assigned, which can be fewer than provided for, or even zero, in the event of an early matching failure.

```
int sprintf(char *s, const char *format, ...);
```

The `sprintf` function is equivalent to `fprintf`, except that the argument `s` specifies an array into which the generated output is to be written, rather than to a stream. A null character is written at the end of the characters written; it is not counted as part of the returned sum. If copying takes place between objects that overlap, the behavior is undefined. The `sprintf` function returns the number of characters written by the array, not counting the terminating null character.

```
int sscanf(const char *s, const char *format, ...);
```

The `sscanf` function is equivalent to `fscanf`, except that the argument `s` specifies a string from which the input is to be obtained, rather than from a stream. Reaching the end of the string is equivalent to encountering end-of-file for the `fscanf` function. If copying takes place between objects that overlap, the behavior is undefined.

The `sscanf` function returns the value of the macro `EOF` if an input failure occurs before any conversion. Otherwise, the `sscanf` function returns the number of input items assigned, which can be fewer than provided for, or even zero, in the event of an early matching failure.

```
int vfprintf(FILE *stream, const char *format, va_list arg);
```

The `vfprintf` function is equivalent to `fprintf`, with the variable argument list replaced by `arg`, which shall have been initialized by the `va_start` macro (and possibly subsequent `va_arg` calls). The `vfprintf` function does not invoke the `va_end` macro. The `vfprintf` function returns the number of characters transmitted, or a negative value if an output error occurred.

```
int vprintf(const char *format, va_list arg);
```

The `vprintf` function is equivalent to `printf`, with the variable argument list replaced by `arg`, which shall have been initialized by the `va_start` macro (and possibly subsequent `va_arg` calls). The `vprintf` function does not invoke the `va_end` macro. The `vprintf` function returns the number of characters transmitted, or a negative value if an output error occurred.

```
int vsprintf(char *s, const char *format, va_list arg);
```

The `vsprintf` function is equivalent to `sprintf`, with the variable argument list replaced by `arg`, which shall have been initialized by the `va_start` macro (and possibly subsequent `va_arg` calls). The `vsprintf` function does not invoke the `va_end` macro. If copying takes place between objects that overlap, the behavior is undefined.

The `vsprintf` function returns the number of characters written in the array, not counting the terminating null character.

```
int fgetc(FILE *stream);
```

The `fgetc` function obtains the next character (if present) as an `unsigned char` converted to an `int`, from the input stream pointed to by `stream`, and advances the associated file position indicator for the stream (if defined). The `fgetc` function returns the next character from the input stream pointed to by `stream`. If the stream is at end-of-file, the end-of-file indicator for the stream is set and `fgetc` returns `EOF`. If a read error occurs, the error indicator for the stream is set and `fgetc` returns `EOF`.

```
char *fgets(char *s, int n, FILE *stream);
```

The `fgets` function reads at most one less than the number of characters specified by n from the stream pointed to by `stream` into the array pointed to by `s`. No additional characters are read after a new-line character (which is retained) or after end-of-file. A null character is written immediately after the last character read into the array.

The `fgets` function returns `s` if successful. If end-of-file is encountered and no characters have been read into the array, the contents of the array remain unchanged and a null pointer is returned. If a read error occurs during the operation, the array contents are indeterminate and a null pointer is returned.

```
int fputc(int c, FILE *stream);
```

The `fputc` function writes the character specified by c (converted to an `unsigned char`) to the output stream pointed to by `stream`, at the position indicated by the associated file position indicator for the stream (if defined), and advances the indicator appropriately. If the file cannot support positioning requests, or if the stream was opened with append mode, the character is appended to the output stream. The `fputc` function returns the character written. If a write error occurs, the error indicator for the stream is set and `fputc` returns `EOF`.

```
int fputs(const char *s, FILE *stream);
```

The `fputs` function writes the string pointed to by `s` to the stream pointed to by `stream`. The terminating null character is not written. The `fputs` function returns `EOF` of a write error occurs; otherwise it returns a nonnegative value.

```
int getc(FILE *stream);
```

The `getc` is equivalent to `fgetc`, except that if it is implemented as a macro, it may evaluate `stream` more than once, so the argument should never be an expression with side effects.

The `getc` function returns the next character from the input stream pointed to by `stream`. If the stream is at end-of-file, the end-of-file indicator for the stream is set and `getc` returns `EOF`. If a read error occurs, the error indicator for the stream is set and `getc` returns `EOF`.

```
int getchar(void);
```

The `getchar` function is equivalent to `getc` with the argument `stdin`. The `getchar` function returns the next character from the input stream pointed to by `stdin`. If the stream is at end-of-file, the end-of-file indicator for the stream is set and `getchar` returns `EOF`. If a read error occurs, the error indicator for the stream is set and `getchar` returns `EOF`.

```
char *gets(char *s);
```

The `gets` function reads characters from the input stream pointed to by `stdin`, into the array pointed to by `s`, until end-of-file is encountered or a new-line character is read. Any new-line character is discarded, and a null character is written immediately after the last character read into the array. The `gets` function returns `s` if successful. If end-of-file is encountered and no characters have been read into the array, the contents of the array remain unchanged and a null pointer is returned. If a read error occurs during the operation, the array contents are indeterminate and a null pointer is returned.

```
int putc(int c, FILE *stream);
```

The `putc` function is equivalent to `fputc`, except that if it is implemented as a macro, it may evaluate `stream` more than once, so the argument should never be an expression with side effects. The `putc` function returns the character written. If a write error occurs, the error indicator for the stream is set and `putc` returns `EOF`.

```
int putchar(int c);
```

The `putchar` is equivalent to `putc` with the second argument `stdout`. The `putchar` function returns the character written. If a write error occurs, the error indicator for the stream is set and `putchar` returns `EOF`.

```
int puts(const char *s);
```

The `puts` function writes the string pointed to by `s` to the stream pointed to by `stdout`, and appends a new-line character to the output. The terminating null character is not written. The `puts` function returns `EOF` if a write error occurs; otherwise it returns a nonnegative value.

```
int ungetc(int c, FILE *stream);
```

The `ungetc` function pushes the character specified by `c` (converted to an `unsigned char`) back onto the input stream pointed to by `stream`. The pushed-back characters will be returned by subsequent reads on that stream in the reverse order of their pushing. A successful intervening call (with the stream pointed to by `stream`) to a file positioning function (`fseek`, `fsetpos`, or `rewind`) discards any pushed-back characters for the stream. The external storage corresponding to the stream is unchanged.

One character of pushback is guaranteed. If the `ungetc` function is called too many times on the same stream without an intervening read or file positioning operation on that stream, the operation may fail. If the value of c equals that of the macro `EOF`, the operation fails and the input stream is unchanged.

A successful call to the `ungetc` function clears the end-of-file indicator for the stream. The value of the file position indicator for the stream after reading or discarding all pushed-back characters shall be the same as it was before the characters were pushed back. For a text stream, the value of its file position indicator after a successful call to the `ungetc` function is unspecified until all pushed-back characters are read or discarded. For a binary stream, its file position indicator is determined by each successful call to the `ungetc` function; if its value was zero before a call, it is indeterminate after the call. The `ungetc` function returns the character pushed back after conversion, or `EOF` if the operation fails.

`size_t fread(void *ptr, size_t size, size_t nmemb, FILE *stream);`

The **fread** function reads, into the array pointed to by **ptr**, up to **nmemb** elements whose size is specified by **size**, from the stream pointed to by **stream**. The file position indicator for the stream (if defined) is advanced by the number of characters successfully read. If an error occurs, the resulting value of the file position indicator for the stream is indeterminate. If a partial element is read, its value is indeterminate.

The **fread** function returns the number of elements successfully read, which may be less than **nmemb** if a read error or end-of-file is encountered. If **size** or **nmemb** is zero, **fread** returns zero and the contents of the array and the state of the stream remain unchanged.

`size_t fwrite(const void *ptr, size_t size, size_t nmemb, FILE *stream);`

The **fwrite** function writes, from the array pointed to by **ptr**, up to **nmemb** elements whose size is specified by **size**, to the stream pointed to by **stream**. The file position indicator for the stream (if defined) is advanced by the number of characters successfully written. If an error occurs, the resulting value of the file position for the stream is indeterminate. The **fwrite** function returns the number of elements successfully written, which will be less than **nmemb** only if a write error is encountered.

`int fgetpos(FILE *stream, fpos_t *pos);`

The **fgetpos** function stores the current value of the file position indicator for the stream pointed to by **stream** in the object pointed to by **pos**. The value stored contains unspecified information usable by the **fsetpos** function for repositioning the stream to its position at the time of the call to the **fgetpos** function. If successful, the **fgetpos** function returns zero; on failure, the **fgetpos** function returns nonzero and stores an implementation-defined positive value in **errno**.

`int fseek(FILE *stream, long int offset, int whence);`

The **fseek** function sets the file position indicator for the stream pointed to by **stream**. For a binary stream, the new position, measured in characters from the beginning of the file, is obtained by adding **offset** to the position specified by **whence**. The specified position is the beginning of the file if **whence** is **SEEK_SET**, the current value of the file position indicator if **SEEK_CUR**, or end-of-file if **SEEK_END**. A binary stream need not meaningfully support **fseek** calls with a **whence** value of **SEEK_END**. For a text stream, either **offset** shall be zero, or **offset** shall be a value returned by an earlier call to the **ftell** function on the same stream and **whence** shall be **SEEK_SET**.

A successful call to the **fseek** function clears the end-of-file indicator for the stream and undoes any effects of the **ungetc** function on the same stream. After an **fseek** call, the next operation on an update stream may be either input or output. The **fseek** function returns nonzero only for a request that cannot be satisfied.

`int fsetpos(FILE *stream, const fpos_t *pos);`

The **fsetpos** function sets the file position indicator for the stream pointed to by **stream** according to the value of the object pointed to by **pos**, which shall be a value obtained from an earlier call to the **fgetpos** function on the same stream. A successful call to the **fsetpos** function clears the end-of-file indicator for the stream and undoes any effects of the **ungetc** function on the same stream. After an **fsetpos** call, the next operation on an update stream may be either input or output. If successful, the

fsetpos function returns zero; on failure, the **fsetpos** function returns nonzero and stores an implementation-defined positive value in **errno**.

```
long int ftell(FILE *stream);
```

The **ftell** function obtains the current value of the file position indicator for the stream pointed to by **stream**. For a binary stream, the value is the number of characters from the beginning of the file. For a text stream, its file position indicator contains unspecified information, usable by the **fseek** function for returning the file position indicator for the stream to its position at the time of the **ftell** call; the difference between two such return values is not necessarily a meaningful measure of the number of characters written or read. If successful, the **ftell** function returns the current value of the file position indicator for the stream. On failure, the **ftell** function returns -1L and stores an implementation-defined positive value in **errno**.

```
void rewind(FILE *stream);
```

The **rewind** function sets the file position indicator for the stream pointed to by **stream** to the beginning of the file. It is equivalent to

```
(void)fseek(stream, 0L, SEEK_SET)
```

except that the error indicator for the stream is also cleared.

```
void clearerr(FILE *stream);
```

The **clearerr** function clears the end-of-file and error indicators for the stream pointed to by **stream**.

```
int feof(FILE *stream);
```

The **feof** function tests the end-of-file indicator for the stream pointed to by **stream**. The **feof** function returns nonzero if and only if the end-of-file indicator is set for **stream**.

```
int ferror(FILE *stream);
```

The **ferror** function tests the error indicator for the stream pointed to by **stream**. The **ferror** function returns nonzero if and only if the error indicator is set for **stream**.

```
void perror(const char *s);
```

The **perror** function maps the error number in the integer expression **errno** to an error message. It writes a sequence of characters to the standard error stream thus: first (if s is not a null pointer and the character pointed to by s is not the null character), the string pointed to by s followed by a colon (:) and a space; then an appropriate error message string followed by a new-line character. The contents of the error message strings are the same as those returned by the **strerror** function with argument **errno**, which are implementation-defined.

B.11 General Utilities <stdlib.h>

```
EXIT_FAILURE
EXIT_SUCCESS
```

Integral expressions that may be used as the argument to the **exit** function to return unsuccessful or successful termination status, respectively, to the host environment.

MB_CUR_MAX

A positive integer expression whose value is the maximum number of bytes in a multibyte character for the extended character set specified by the current locale (category LC_CTYPE), and whose value is never greater than MB_LEN_MAX.

NULL

An implementation-defined null pointer constant.

RAND_MAX

An interval constant expression, the value of which is the maximum value returned by the rand function. The value of the RAND_MAX marco shall be at least 32767.

div_t

A structure type that is the type of the value returned by the div function.

ldiv_t

A structure type that is the type of the value returned by the ldiv function.

size_t

The unsigned integral type of the result of the sizeof operator.

wchar_t

An integral type whose range of values can represent distinct codes for all members of the largest extended character set specified among the supported locales; the null character shall have the code value zero and each member of the basic character set shall have a code value equal to its value when used as the lone character in an integer character constant.

double atof(const char *nptr);

Converts the initial portion of the string pointed to by nptr to double representation. The atof function returns the converted value.

int atoi(const char *nptr);

Converts the initial portion of the string pointed to by nptr to int representation. The atoi function returns the converted value.

long int atol(const char *nptr);

Converts the initial portion of the string pointed to by nptr to long representation. The atol function returns the converted value.

double strtod(const char *nptr, char **endptr);

Converts the initial portion of the string pointed to by nptr to double representation. First, it decomposes the input string into three parts: an initial, possibly empty, sequence of white-space characters (as specified by the isspace function), a subject sequence resembling a floating-point constant; and a final string of one or more unrecognized characters, including the terminating null character of the input string. Then, it attempts to convert the subject sequence to a floating-point number, and returns the result.

The expanded form of the subject sequence is an optional plus or minus sign, then a nonempty sequence of digits optionally containing a decimal-point character, then an optional exponent part, but no floating suffix. The subject sequence is defined as the longest initial subsequence of the input string, starting with the first non-white-space character, that is of the expected form. The subject sequence contains no characters if the input string is empty or consists entirely of white space, or if the first non-white-space character is other than a sign, a digit, or a decimal-point character.

If the subject sequence has the expected form, the sequence of characters starting with the first digit or the decimal-point character (whichever occurs first) is interpreted as a floating constant, except that the decimal-point character is used in place of a period, and that if neither an exponent part nor a decimal-point character appears, a decimal point is assumed to follow the last digit in the string. If the subject sequence begins with a minus sign, the value resulting from the conversion is negated. A pointer to the final string is stored in the object pointed to by `endptr`, provided that `endptr` is not a null pointer.

If the subject sequence is empty or does not have the expected form, no conversion is performed; the value of `nptr` is stored in the object pointed to by `endptr`, provided that `endptr` is not a null pointer.

The `strtod` function returns the converted value, if any. If no conversion could be performed, zero is returned. If the correct value is outside the range of representable values, plus or minus `HUGE_VAL` is returned (according to the sign of the value), and the value of the macro `ERANGE` is stored in `errno`. If the correct value would cause underflow, zero is returned and the value of the macro `ERANGE` is stored in `errno`.

`long int strtol(const char *nptr, char **endptr, int base);`

Converts the initial portion of the string pointed to by `nptr` to `long int` representation. First, it decomposes the input string into three parts: an initial, possibly empty, sequence of white-space characters (as specified by the `isspace` function), a subject sequence resembling an integer represented in some radix determined by the value of `base`, and a final string of one or more unrecognized characters, including the terminating null character of the input string. Then, it attempts to convert the subject sequence to an integer, and returns the result.

If the value of `base` is zero, the expected form of the subject sequence is that of an integer constant, optionally preceded by a plus or minus sign, but not including an integer suffix. If the value of `base` is between 2 and 36, the expected form of the subject sequence is a sequence of letters and digits representing an integer with the radix specified by `base`, optionally preceded by a plus or minus sign, but not including an integer suffix. The letters from `a` (or `A`) through `z` (or `Z`) are ascribed the values 10 to 35; only letters whose ascribed values are less than that of `base` are permitted. If the value of `base` is 16, the characters `0x` or `0X` may optionally precede the sequence of letters and digits, following the sign if present.

The subject sequence is defined as the longest initial subsequence of the input string, starting with the first non-white-space character, that is of the expected form. The subject sequence contains no characters if the input string is empty or consists entirely of white space, or if the first non-white-space character is other than a sign or a permissible letter or digit.

If the subject sequence has the expected form and the value of `base` is zero, the sequence of characters starting with the first digit is interpreted as an integer constant. If the subject sequence has the expected form and the value of `base` is between 2 and 36, it is used as the base for conversion, ascribing to each letter its value as given above. If the subject sequence begins with a minus sign, the value resulting from the conversion is negated. A pointer to the final string is stored in the object pointed to by `endptr`, provided that `endptr` is not a null pointer.

If the subject sequence is empty or does not have the expected form, no conversion is performed; the value `nptr` is stored in the object pointed to by `endptr`, provided that `endptr` is not a null pointer.

The `strtol` function returns the converted value, if any. If no conversion could be performed, zero is returned. If the correct value is outside the range of representable values, `LONG_MAX` or `LONG_MIN` is returned (according to the sign of the value), and the value of the macro `ERANGE` is stored in `errno`.

`unsigned long int strtoul(const char *nptr, char **endptr, int base);`

Converts the initial portion of the string pointed to by `nptr` to `unsigned long int` representation. The `strtoul` function works identically to the `strtol` function. The `strtoul` function returns the converted value, if any. If no conversion could be performed, zero is returned. If the correct value is outside the range of representable values, `ULONG_MAX` is returned, and the value of the macro `ERANGE` is stored in `errno`.

`int rand(void);`

The `rand` function computes a sequence of pseudo-random integers in the range 0 to `RAND_MAX`. The `rand` function returns a pseudo-random integer.

`void srand(unsigned int seed);`

Uses the argument as a seed for a new sequence of pseudo-random numbers to be returned by subsequent calls to `rand`. If `srand` is then called with the same seed value, the sequence of pseudo-random numbers shall be repeated. If `rand` is called before any calls to `srand` have been made, the same sequence shall be generated as when `srand` is first called with a seed value of 1. The following functions define a portable implementation of `rand` and `srand`.

```
static unsigned long int next = 1;

int rand(void)    /* RAND_MAX assumed to be 32767 */
{
    next = next * 1103515245 + 12345;
    return (unsigned int) (next/65536) % 32768;
}

void srand(unsigned int seed)
{
    next = seed;
}
```

`void *calloc(size_t nmemb, size_t size);`

Allocates space for an array of `nmemb` objects, each of whose size is `size`. The space is initialized to all bits zero. The `calloc` function returns either a null pointer or a pointer to the allocated space.

`void free(void *ptr);`

Causes the space pointed to by `ptr` to be deallocated, that is, made available for further allocation. If `ptr` is a null pointer, no action occurs. Otherwise, if the argument does not match a pointer earlier returned by the `calloc`, `malloc`, or `realloc` function, or if the space has been deallocated by a call to **free** or **realloc**, the behavior is undefined.

`void *malloc(size_t size);`

Allocates space for an object whose size is specified by **size** and whose value is indeterminate. The **malloc** function returns a null pointer or a pointer to the allocated space.

`void *realloc(void *ptr, size_t size);`

Changes the size of the object pointed to by **ptr** to the size specified by **size**. The contents of the object shall be unchanged up to the lesser of the new and old sizes. If the new size is larger, the value of the newly allocated portion of the object is indeterminate. If **ptr** is a null pointer, the **realloc** function behaves like the **malloc** function for the specified size. Otherwise, if **ptr** does not match a pointer earlier returned by the **calloc, malloc,** or **realloc** function, or if the space has been deallocated by a call to the **free** or **realloc** function, the behavior is undefined. If the space cannot be allocated, the object pointed to by **ptr** is unchanged. If **size** is zero and **ptr** is not a null pointer, the object it points to is freed. The **realloc** function returns either a null pointer or a pointer to the possibly moved allocated space.

`void abort(void);`

Causes abnormal program termination to occur, unless the signal **SIGABRT** is being caught and the signal handler does not return. Whether open output streams are flushed or open streams closed or temporary files removed is implementation-defined. An implementation-defined form of the status *unsuccessful termination* is returned to the host environment by means of the function call **raise(SIGABRT)**. The **abort** function cannot return to its caller.

`int atexit(void (*func)(void));`

Registers the function pointed to by **func**, to be called without arguments at normal program termination. The implementation shall support the registration of at least 32 functions. The **atexit** function returns zero if the registration succeeds, nonzero if it fails.

`void exit(int status);`

Causes normal program termination to occur. If more than one call to the **exit** function is executed by a program, the behavior is undefined. First, all functions registered by the **atexit** function are called, in the reverse order of their registration. Each function is called as many times as it was registered. Next, all open streams with unwritten buffered data are flushed, all open streams are closed, and all files created by the **tmp-file** function are removed.

Finally, control is returned to the host environment. If the value of **status** is zero or **EXIT_SUCCESS**, an implementation-defined form of the status *successful termination* is returned. If the value of **status** is **EXIT_FAILURE**, an implementation-defined form of the status *unsuccessful termination* is returned. Otherwise the status returned is implementation-defined. The **exit** function cannot return to its caller.

`char *getenv(const char *name);`

Searches an *environment list*, provided by the host environment, for a string that matches the string pointed to by **name**. The set of environment names and the method for altering the environment list are implementation-defined. Returns a pointer to a string associated with the matched list member. The string pointed to shall not be modified by the program, but may be overwritten by a subsequent call to the `getenv` function. If the specified `name` cannot be found, a null pointer is returned.

`int system(const char *string);`

Passes the string pointed to by `string` to the host environment to be executed by a *command processor* in an implementation-defined manner. A null pointer may be used for `string` to inquire whether a command processor exists. If the argument is a null pointer, the `system` function returns nonzero only if a command processor is available. If the argument is not a null pointer, the `system` function returns an implementation-defined value.

`void *bsearch(const void *key, const void *base, size_t nmemb, size_t`
`      size, int (*compar)(const void *, const void *));`

Searches an array of `nmemb` objects, the initial element of which is pointed to by `base`, for an element that matches the object pointed to by `key`. The size of each element of the array is specified by `size`. The comparison function pointed to by `compar` is called with two arguments that point to the `key` object and to an array element, in that order. The function shall return an integer less than, equal to, or greater than zero if the `key` object is considered, respectively, to be less than, to match, or to be greater than the array element. The array shall consist of: all the elements that compare less than, all the elements that compare equal to, and all the elements that compare greater than the `key` object, in that order.

The `bsearch` function returns a pointer to a matching element of the array, or a null pointer if no match is found. If two elements compare as equal, which element is matched is unspecified.

`void qsort(void *base, size_t nmemb, size_t size, int (*compar)(const`
`      void *, const void *));`

Sorts an array of `nmemb` objects, the initial element of which is pointed to by `base`. The size of each object is specified by `size`. The contents of the array are sorted into ascending order according to a comparison function pointed to by `compar`, which is called with two arguments that point to the objects being compared. The function shall return an integer less than equal to, or greater than zero if the first argument is considered to be respectively less than, equal to, or greater than the second. If two elements compare as equal, their order in the sorted array is undefined.

`int abs(int j);`

Computes the absolute value of an integer `j`. If the result cannot be represented, the behavior is undefined. The `abs` function returns the absolute value.

`div_t div(int numer, int denom);`

Computes the quotient and remainder of the division of the numerator `numer` by the denominator `denom`. If the division is inexact, the resulting quotient is the integer of lesser magnitude that is the nearest to the algebric quotient. If the result cannot be represented, the behavior is undefined; otherwise, `quot * denom + rem` shall equal numer. The `div` function returns a structure of type `div_t`, comprising both the quotient and the remainder. The structure shall contain the following members, in either order:

```
int quot;     /* quotient */
int rem;      /* remainder */
```

long int labs(long int j);

Similar to the `abs` function, except that the argument and the returned value each have type `long int`.

ldiv_t ldiv(long int numer, long int denom);

Similar to the `div` function, except that the arguments and the members of the returned structure (which has type `ldiv_t`) all have type `long int`.

int mblen(const char *s, size_t n);

If s is not a null pointer, the `mblen` function determines the number of bytes contained in the multibyte character pointed to by s. If s is a null pointer, the `mblen` function returns a nonzero or zero value, if multibyte character encodings, respectively, do or do not have state-dependent encodings. If s is not a null pointer, the `mblen` function either returns 0 (if s points to the null character), or returns the number of bytes that are contained in the multibyte character (if the next n or fewer bytes form a valid multibyte character), or returns -1 (if they do not form a valid multibyte character).

int mbtowc(wchar_t *pwc, const char *s, size_t n);

If s is not a null pointer, the `mbtowc` function determines the number of bytes that are contained in the multibyte character pointed to by s. It then determines the code for the value of type `wchar_t` that corresponds to that multibyte character. (The value of the code corresponding to the null character is zero.) If the multibyte character is valid and `pwc` is not a null pointer, the `mbtowc` function stores the code in the object pointed to by `pwc`. At most n bytes of the array pointed to by s will be examined.

If s is a null pointer, the `mbtowc` function returns a nonzero or zero value, if multibyte character encodings, respectively, do or do not have state-dependent encodings. If s is not a null pointer, the `mbtowc` function either returns 0 (if s points to the null character), or returns the number of bytes that are contained in the converted multibyte character (if the next n or fewer bytes form a valid multibyte character), or returns -1 (if they do not form a valid multibyte character). In no case will the value returned be greater than n or the value of the `MB_CUR_MAX` macro.

int wctomb(char *s, wchar_t wchar);

The `wctomb` function determines the number of bytes needed to represent the multibyte character corresponding to the code whose value is `wchar` (including any change in shift state). It stores the multibyte character representation in the array object pointed to by s (if s is not a null pointer). At most `MB_CUR_MAX` characters are stored. If the value of `wchar` is zero, the `wctomb` function is left in the initial shift state.

If s is a null pointer, the `wctomb` function returns a nonzero or zero value, if multibyte character encodings, respectively, do or do not have state-dependent encodings. If s is not a null pointer, the `wctomb` function returns -1 if the value of `wchar` does not correspond to a valid multibyte character, or returns the number of bytes that are contained in the multibyte character corresponding to the value of `wchar`. In no case will the value returned be greater than the value of the `MB_CUR_MAX` macro.

`size_t mbstowcs(wchar_t *pwcs, const char *s, size_t n);`

The `mbstowcs` function converts a sequence of multibyte characters that begins in the initial shift state from the array pointed to by `s` into a sequence of corresponding codes and stores not more than n codes into the array pointed to by `pwcs`. No multibyte characters that follow a null character (which is converted into a code with value zero) will be examined or converted. Each multibyte character is converted as if by a call to the `mbtowc` function, except that the shift state of the `mbtowc` function is not affected.

No more than n elements will be modified in the array pointed to by `pwcs`. If copying takes place between objects that overlap, the behavior is undefined. If an invalid multibyte character is encountered, the `mbstowcs` function returns `(size_t)-1`. Otherwise, the `mbstowcs` function returns the number of array elements modified, not including a terminating zero code, if any.

`size_t wcstombs(char *s, const wchar_t *pwcs, size_t n);`

The `wcstombs` function converts a sequence of codes that correspond to multibyte characters from the array pointed to by `pwcs` into a sequence of multibyte characters that begins in the initial shift state and stores these multibyte characters into the array pointed to by `s`, stopping if a multibyte character would exceed the limit of n total bytes or if a null character is stored. Each code is converted as if by a call to the `wctomb` function, except that the shift state of the `wctomb` function is not affected.

No more than n bytes will be modified in the array pointed to by `s`. If copying takes place between objects that overlap, the behavior is undefined. If a code is encountered that does not correspond to a valid multibyte character, the `wcstombs` function returns `(size_t)-1`. Otherwise, the `wcstombs` function returns the number of bytes modified, not including a terminating null character, if any.

B.12 String Handling `<string.h>`

NULL

An implementation-defined null pointer constant.

`size_t`

The unsigned integral type of the result of the `sizeof` operator.

`void *memcpy(void *s1, const void *s2, size_t n);`

The `memcpy` function copies n characters from the object pointed to by `s2` into the object pointed to by `s1`. If copying takes place between objects that overlap, the behavior is undefined. The `memcpy` function returns the value of `s1`.

`void *memmove(void *s1, const void *s2, size_t n);`

The `memmove` function copies n characters from the object pointed to by `s2` into the object pointed to by `s1`. Copying takes place as if the n characters from the object pointed to by `s2` are first copied into a temporary array of n characters that does not overlap the objects pointed to by `s1` and `s2`, and then the n characters from the temporary array are copied into the object pointed to by `s1`. The `memmove` function returns the value of `s1`.

```
char *strcpy(char *s1, const char *s2);
```

The `strcpy` function copies the string pointed to by `s2` (including the terminating null character) into the array pointed to by `s1`. If copying takes place between objects that overlap, the behavior is undefined. The `strcpy` function returns the value of `s1`.

```
char *strncpy(char *s1, const char *s2, size_t n);
```

The `strncpy` function copies not more than `n` characters (characters that follow a null character are not copied) from the array pointed to by `s2` to the array pointed to by `s1`. If copying takes place between objects that overlap, the behavior is undefined. If the array pointed to by `s2` is a string that is shorter than `n` characters, null characters are appended to the copy in the array pointed to by `s1`, until `n` characters in all have been written. The `strncpy` function returns the value of `s1`.

```
char *strcat(char *s1, const char *s2);
```

The `strcat` function appends a copy of the string pointed to by `s2` (including the terminating null character) to the end of the string pointed to by `s1`. The initial character of `s2` overwrites the null character at the end of `s1`. If copying takes place between objects that overlap, the behavior is undefined. The `strcat` function returns the value of `s1`.

```
char *strncat(char *s1, const char *s2, size_t n);
```

The `strncat` function appends not more than `n` characters (a null character and characters that follow it are not appended) from the array pointed to by `s2` to the end of the string pointed to by `s1`. The initial character of `s2` overwrites the null character at the end of `s1`. A terminating null character is always appended to the result. If copying takes place between objects that overlap, the behavior is undefined. The `strncat` function returns the value of `s1`.

```
int memcmp(const void *s1, const void *s2, size_t n);
```

The `memcmp` function compares the first `n` characters of the object pointed to by `s1` to the first `n` characters of the object pointed to by `s2` The `memcmp` function returns an integer greater than, equal to, or less than zero, accordingly as the object pointed to by `s1` is greater than, equal to, or less than the object pointed to by `s2`.

```
int strcmp(const char *s1, const char *s2);
```

The `strcmp` function compares the string pointed to by `s1` to the string pointed to by `s2`. The `strcmp` function returns an integer greater than, equal to, or less than zero, accordingly as the string pointed to by `s1` is greater than, equal to, or less than the string pointed to by `s2`.

```
int strcoll(const char *s1, const char *s2);
```

The `strcoll` function compares the string pointed to by `s1` to the string pointed to by `s2`, both interpreted as appropriate to the **LC_COLLATE** category of the current locale. The `strcoll` function returns an integer greater than, equal to, or less than zero, accordingly as the string pointed to by `s1` is greater than, equal to, or less than the string pointed to by `s2` when both are interpreted as appropriate to the current locale.

```
int strncmp(const char *s1, const char *s2, size_t n);
```

The `strncmp` function compares not more than `n` characters (characters that follow a null character are not compared) from the array pointed to by `s1` to the array pointed to by s2. The strncmp function returns an integer greater than, equal to, or less than zero, accordingly as the possibly null-terminated array pointed to by s1 is greater than, equal to, or less than the possibly null-terminated array pointed to by s2.

```
size_t strxfrm(char *s1, const char *s2, size_t n);
```

The strxfrm function transforms the string pointed to by s2 and places the resulting string into the array pointed to by s1. The transformation is such that if the strcmp function is applied to two transformed strings, it returns a value greater than, equal to, or less than zero, corresponding to the result of the strcoll function applied to the same two original strings. No more than n characters are placed into the resulting array pointed to by s1, including the terminating null character. If n is zero, s1 is permitted to be a null pointer. If copying takes place between objects that overlap, the behavior is undefined. The strxfrm function returns the length of the transformed string (not including the terminating null character). If the value is n or more, the contents of the array pointed to by s1 are indeterminate.

```
void *memchr(const void *s, int c, size_t n);
```

The memchr function locates the first occurrence of c (converted to an unsigned char) in the initial n characters (each interpreted as unsigned char) of the object pointed to by s. The memchr function returns a pointer to the located character, or a null pointer if the character does not occur in the object.

```
char *strchr(const char *s, int c);
```

The strchr function locates the first occurrence of c (converted to a char) in the string pointed to by s. The terminating null character is considered to be part of the string. The strchr function returns a pointer to the located character, or a null pointer if the character does not occur in the string.

```
size_t strcspn(const char *s1, const char *s2);
```

The strcspn function computes the length of the maximum initial segment of the string pointed to by s1 which consists entirely of characters not from the string pointed to by s2. The strcspn function returns the length of the segment.

```
char *strpbrk(const char *s1, const char *s2);
```

The strpbrk function locates the first occurrence in the string pointed to by s1 of any character from the string pointed to by s2. The strpbrk function returns a pointer to the character, or a null pointer if no character from s2 occurs in s1.

```
char *strrchr(const char *s, int c);
```

The strrchr function locates the last occurrence of c (converted to a char) in the string pointed to by s. The terminating null character is considered to be part of the string. The strrchr function returns a pointer to the character, or a null pointer if c does not occur in the string.

```
size_t strspn(const char *s1, const char *s2);
```

The strspn function computes the length of the maximum initial segment of the string pointed to by s1 which consists entirely of characters from the string pointed to by s2. The strspn function returns the length of the segment.

```
char *strstr(const char *s1, const char *s2);
```

The `strstr` function locates the first occurrence in the string pointed to by `s1` of the sequence of characters (excluding the terminating null character) in the string pointed to by `s2`. The `strstr` function returns a pointer to the located string, or a null pointer if the string is not found. If `s2` points to a string with zero length, the function returns `s1`.

```
char *strtok(char *s1, const char *s2);
```

A sequence of calls to the `strtok` function breaks the string pointed to by `s1` into a sequence of tokens, each of which is delimited by a character from the string pointed to by `s2`. The first call in the sequence has `s1` as its argument, and is followed by calls with a null pointer as their first argument. The separator string pointed to by `s2` may be different from call to call.

The first call in the sequence searches the string pointed to by `s1` for the first character that is not contained in the current separator string pointed to by `s2`. If no such character is found, then there are no tokens in the string pointed to by `s1` and the `strtok` function returns a null pointer. If such a character is found, it is the start of the first token.

The `strtok` function then searches from there for a character that is contained in the current separator string. If no such character is found, the current token extends to the end of the string pointed to by `s1`, and subsequent searches for a token will return a null pointer. If such a character is found, it is overwritten by a null character, which terminates the current token. The `strtok` function saves a pointer to the following character, from which the next search for a token will start.

Each subsequent call, with a null pointer as the value of the first argument, starts searching from the saved pointer and behaves as described above. The implementation shall behave as if no library function calls the `strtok` function. The `strtok` function returns a pointer to the first character of a token, or a null pointer if there is no token.

```
void *memset(void *s, int c, size_t n);
```

The `memset` function copies the value of `c` (converted to an `unsigned char`) into each of the first `n` characters in the object pointed to by `s`. The `memset` function returns the value of `s`.

```
char *strerror(int errnum);
```

The `strerror` function maps the error number in `errnum` to an error message string. The implementation shall behave as if no library function calls the `strerror` function. The `strerror` function returns a pointer to the string, the contents of which are implementation-defined. The array pointed to shall not be modified by the program, but may be overwritten by a subsequent call to the `strerror` function.

```
size_t strlen(const char *s);
```

The `strlen` function computes the length of the string pointed to by `s`. The `strlen` function returns the number of characters that precede the terminating null character.

B.13 Date and Time <time.h>

CLOCKS_PER_SEC

The number per second of the value returned by the `clock` function.

NULL

An implementation-defined null pointer constant.

clock_t

An arithmetic type capable of representing time.

time_t

An arithmetic type capable of representing time.

size_t

The unsigned integral type of the result of the **sizeof** operator.

struct tm

Holds the components of a calendar time, called the *broken-down time*. The structure shall contain at least the following members, in any order. The semantics of the members and their normal ranges are expressed in the comments.

```
int tm_sec;       /* seconds after the minute—[0, 61] */
int tm_min;       /* minutes after the hour—[0, 59] */
int tm_hour;      /* hours since midnight—[0, 23] */
int tm_mday;      /*  day of the month—[1, 31] */
int tm_mon;       /* months since January—[0, 11] */
int tm_year;      /* years since 1900 */
int tm_wday;      /* days since Sunday—[0, 6] */
int tm_yday;      /* days since January 1—[0, 365] */
int tm_isdst;     /* Daylight Saving Time flag */
```

The value **tm_isdst** is positive if Daylight Saving Time is in effect, zero if Daylight Saving Time is not in effect, and negative if the information is not available.

clock_t clock(void);

The **clock** function determines the processor time used. The **clock** function returns the implementation's best approximation to the processor time used by the program since the beginning of an implementation-defined era related only to the program invocation. To determine the time in seconds, the value returned by the **clock** function should be divided by the value of the macro **CLOCKS_PER_SEC**. If the processor time used is not available or its value cannot be represented, the function returns the value (clock_t)-1.

double difftime(time_t time1, time_t time0);

The **difftime** function computes the difference between two calendar times: time1 - time0. The **difftime** function returns the difference expressed in seconds as a double.

time_t mktime(struct tm *timeptr);

The **mktime** function converts the broken-down time, expressed as local time, in the structure pointed to by **timeptr** into a calendar time value with the same encoding as that of the values returned by the **time** function. The original values of the **tm_wday** and **tm_yday** components of the structure are ignored, and the original values of the other components are not restricted to the ranges indicated above. On successful completion, the values of the `tm_wday` and `tm_yday` components of the structure are set appropriately, and the other components are set to represent the specified calendar time, but with their values forced to the ranges indicated above; the final value of `tm_mday` is not set until `tm_mon` and `tm_year` are determined. The `mktime` function returns the specified calendar time encoded as a value of type `time_t`. If the calendar time cannot be represented, the function returns the value `(time_t)-1`.

`time_t time(time_t *timer);`

The `time` function determines the current calendar time. The `time` function returns the implementation's best approximation to the current calendar time. The value `(time_t)-1` is returned if the calendar time is not available. If `timer` is not a null pointer, the return value is also assigned to the object it points to.

`char *asctime(const struct tm *timeptr);`

The `asctime` function converts the broken-down time in the structure pointed to by `timeptr` into a string in the form

        `Sun Sep 16 01:03:52 1973\n\0`

The `asctime` function returns a pointer to the string.

`char *ctime(const time_t *timer);`

The `ctime` function converts the calendar time pointed to by `timer` to local time in the form of a string. It is equivalent to

        `asctime(localtime(timer))`

The `ctime` function returns the pointer returned by the `asctime` function with that broken-down time as argument.

`struct tm *gmtime(const time_t *timer);`

The `gmtime` function converts the calendar time pointed to by `timer` into a broken-down time, expressed as Coordinated Universal Time (UTC). The `gmtime` function returns a pointer to that object, or a null pointer if UTC is not available.

`struct tm *localtime(const time_t *timer);`

The `localtime` function converts the calendar time pointed to by `timer` into a broken-down time, expressed as local time. The `localtime` function returns a pointer to that object.

`size_t strftime(char *s, size_t maxsize, const char *format, const struct tm *timeptr);`

The `strftime` function places characters into the array pointed to by `s` as controlled by the string pointed to by `format`. The `format` string consists of zero or more conversion specifiers and ordinary multibyte characters. All ordinary characters (including the terminating null character) are copied unchanged into the array. If copying takes place between objects that overlap, the behavior is undefined. No more than `maxsize` characters are placed into the array. Each conversion specifier is replaced by appropriate characters as described in the following list. The appropriate characters are determined by the `LC_TIME` category of the current locale and by the values contained in the structure pointed to by `timeptr`.

%a   is replaced by the locale's abbreviated weekday name.

%A   is replaced by the locale's full weekday name.

%b   is replaced by the locale's abbreviated month name.

%B   is replaced by the locale's full month name.

%c   is replaced by the locale's appropriate date and time representation.

%d   is replaced by the day of the month as a decimal number (01-31).

%H   is replaced by the hour (24-hour clock) as a decimal number (00-23).

%I   is replaced by the hour (12-hour clock) as a decimal number (01-12).

%j   is replaced by the day of the year as a decimal number (001-366).

%m   is replaced by the month as a decimal number (01-12).

%M   is replaced by the minute as a decimal number (00-59).

%p   is replaced by the locale's equivalent of the AM/PM designations associated with a 12-hour clock.

%S   is replaced by the second as a decimal number (00-61).

%U   is replaced by the week number of the year (the first Sunday as the first day of week 1) as a decimal number (00-53).

%w   is replaced by the weekday as a decimal number (0-6), where Sunday is 0.

%W   is replaced by the week number of the year (the first Monday as the first day of week 1) as a decimal number (00-53).

%x   is replaced by the locale's appropriate date representation.

%X   is replaced by the locale's appropriate time representation.

%y   is replaced by the year without century as a decimal number (00-99).

%Y   is replaced by the year with century as a decimal number.

%Z   is replaced by the time zone name or abbreviation, or by no characters if no time zone is determinable.

%%   is replaced by %.

If a conversion specifier is not one of the above, the behavior is undefined. If the total number of resulting characters including the terminating null character is not more than `maxsize`, the `strftime` function returns the number of characters placed into the array pointed to by `s` not including the terminating null character. Otherwise, zero is returned and the contents of the array are indeterminate.

B.14 Implementation Limits
<limits.h>

The following shall be defined equal to or greater than in magnitude (absolute value) to the values below.

```
#define CHAR_BIT                                    8
```

The number of bits for the smallest object that is not a bit-field (byte).

```
#define SCHAR_MIN                                 -127
```

The minimum value for an object of type `signed char`.

```
#define SCHAR_MAX                                 +127
```
The maximum value for an object of type **signed char**.

```
#define UCHAR_MAX                                  255
```
The maximum value for an object of type **unsigned char**.

```
#define CHAR_MIN                          0  or  SCHAR_MIN
```
The minimum value for an object of type **char**.

```
#define CHAR_MAX                  UCHAR_MAX  or  SCHAR_MAX
```
The maximum value for an object of type **char**.

```
#define MB_LEN_MAX                                   1
```
The maximum number of bytes in a multibyte character, for any supported locale.

```
#define SHRT_MIN                               -32767
```
The minimum value for an object of type **short int**.

```
#define SHRT_MAX                               +32767
```
The maximum value for an object of type **short int**.

```
#define USHRT_MAX                               65535
```
The maximum value for an object of type **unsigned short int**.

```
#define INT_MIN                                -32767
```
The minimum value for an object of type **int**.

```
#define INT_MAX                                +32767
```
The maximum value for an object of type **int**.

```
#define UINT_MAX                                65535
```
The maximum value for an object of type **unsigned int**.

```
#define LONG_MIN                           -2147483647
```
The minimum value for an object of type **long int**.

```
#define LONG_MAX                           +2147483647
```
The maximum value for an object of type **long int**.

```
#define ULONG_MAX                           4294967295
```
The maximum value for an object of type **unsigned long int**.

<float.h>

```
#define FLT_ROUNDS
```
The rounding mode for floating-point addition.

-1 indeterminable

 0 toward zero

 1 to nearest

 2 toward positive infinity

 3 toward negative infinity

The following shall be defined equal to or greater than in magnitude (absolute value) to the values below.

```
#define FLT_RADIX                                    2
```

The radix of exponent representation, b.

```
#define FLT_MANT_DIG
#define LDBL_MANT_DIG
#define DBL_MANT_DIG
```

The number of base-**FLT_RADIX** digits in the floating-point significand, p.

```
#define FLT_DIG                                      6
#define DBL_DIG                                      10
#define LDBL_DIG                                     10
```

The number of decimal digits, q, such that any floating-point number with q decimal digits can be rounded into a floating-point number with p radix b digits and back again without change to the q decimal digits.

```
#define FLT_MIN_EXP
#define DBL_MIN_EXP
#define LDBL_MIN_EXP
```

The minimum negative integer such that **FLT_RADIX** raised to that power minus 1 is a normalized floating-point number.

```
#define FLT_MIN_10_EXP                              -37
#define DBL_MIN_10_EXP                              -37
#define LDBL_MIN_10_EXP                             -37
```

The minimum negative integer such that 10 raised to that power is in the range of normalized floating point numbers.

```
#define FLT_MAX_EXP
#define DBL_MAX_EXP
#define LDBL_MAX_EXP
```

The maximum integer such that **FLT_RADIX** raised to that power minus 1 is a representable finite floating-point number.

```
#define FLT_MAX_10_EXP                              +37
#define DBL_MAX_10_EXP                              +37
#define LDBL_MAX_10_EXP                             +37
```

The maximum integer such that 10 raised to that power is in the range of representable finite floating point numbers.

The following shall be defined equal to or greater than the values shown below.

```
#define FLT_MAX                                     1E+37
#define DBL_MAX                                      1E+37
#define LDBL_MAX                                     1E+37
```

The maximum representable finite floating-point number.

The following shall be defined equal to or less than the values shown below.

```
#define FLT_EPSILON                        1E-5
#define DBL_EPSILON                        1E-9
#define LDBL_EPSILON                       1E-9
```

The difference between 1.0 and the least value greater than 1.0 that is representable in the given floating point type.

```
#define FLT_MIN                            1E-37
#define DBL_MIN                            1E-37
#define LDBL_MIN                           1E-37
```

The minimum normalized positive floating-point number.

Appendix C
Operator Precedence and Associativity

Operator												Associativity
( )	[ ]	->	.									left to right
++	--	+	–	!	~	(type)	*	&	sizeof			right to left
*	/	%										left to right
+	–											left to right
<<	>>											left to right
<	<=	>	>=									left to right
==	!=											left to right
&												left to right
^												left to right
|												left to right
&&												left to right
||												left to right
?:												right to left
=	+=	-=	*=	/=	%=	&=	^=	|=	<<=	>>=		right to left
,												left to right

The operators are shown in decreasing order of precedence from top to bottom.

Appendix D
ASCII Character Set

	0	1	2	3	4	5	6	7	8	9
0	nul	soh	stx	etx	eot	enq	ack	bel	bs	ht
1	nl	vt	ff	cr	so	si	dle	dc1	dc2	dc3
2	dc4	nak	syn	etb	can	em	sub	esc	fs	gs
3	rs	us	sp	!	"	#	$	%	&	`
4	(	)	*	+	,	-	.	/	0	1
5	2	3	4	5	6	7	8	9	:	;
6	<	=	>	?	@	A	B	C	D	E
7	F	G	H	I	J	K	L	M	N	O
8	P	Q	R	S	T	U	V	W	X	Y
9	Z	[	\	]	^	_	'	a	b	c
10	d	e	f	g	h	i	j	k	l	m
11	n	o	p	q	r	s	t	u	v	w
12	x	y	z	{	|	}	~	del		

The digits at the left of the table are the left digits of the decimal equivalent (0-127) of the character code, and the digits at the top of the table are the right digits of the character code. For example, the character code for 'F' is 70, and the character code for '&' is 38.

Appendix E
Number Systems

Objectives

Here are only numbers ratified.

William Shakespeare

Nature has some sort of arithmetic-geometrical coordinate system, because nature has all kinds of models. What we experience of nature is in models, and all of nature's models are so beautiful. It struck me that nature's system must be a real beauty, because in chemistry we find that the associations are always in beautiful whole numbers— there are no fractions.

Richard Buckminster Fuller

Outline

E.1 Introduction

In this appendix, we introduce the key number systems that C programmers use, especially when they are working on software projects that require close interaction with "machine-level" hardware. Projects like this include include operating systems, computer networking software, compilers, database systems, and applications requiring high performance.

When we write an integer such as 19 or 227 or -63 in a C program, the number is automatically assumed to be in the *decimal (base 10) number system*. The *digits* in the decimal number system are 0, 1, 2, 3, 4, 5, 6, 7, 8, and 9. The lowest digit is 0 and the highest digit is 9—one less than the *base* of 10. Internally, computers use the *binary (base 2) number system*. The binary number system has only two digits, namely 0 and 1. Its lowest digit is 0 and its highest digit is 1—one less than the base of 2.

As we will soon see, binary numbers tend to be much longer than their decimal equivalents. Programmers who work in assembly languages and in high-level languages like C that enable programmers reach down to the "machine level," find it cumbersome to work with numbers in binary form. So two other number systems, namely the *octal number system (base 8)* and the *hexadecimal number system (base 16),* have become popular primarily because they make it convenient to abbreviate binary numbers.

In the octal number system, the digits range from 0 to 7. Because both the binary number system and the octal number system have fewer digits than the decimal number system, their digits are the same as the corresponding digits in decimal.

The hexadecimal number system poses a problem because it requires sixteen digits—a lowest digit of 0 and a highest digit with a value equivalent to decimal 15 (one less than the base of 16). By convention, we use the letters A through F to represent the hexadecimal digits corresponding to decimal values 10 through 15. Thus in hexadecimal we can have numbers like 876 consisting solely of decimal-like digits, numbers like 8A55F consisting of digits and letters, and numbers like FFE consisting solely of letters. Occasionally, a hexadecimal number spells a common word such as FACE or FEED—this can appear strange to programmers accustomed to working with numbers.

Binary digit	Octal digit	Decimal digit	Hexadecimal digit
0	0	0	0
1	1	1	1
	2	2	2
	3	3	3
	4	4	4
	5	5	5
	6	6	6
	7	7	7
		8	8
		9	9
			A (decimal value of 10)
			B (decimal value of 11)
			C (decimal value of 12)
			D (decimal value of 13)
			E (decimal value of 14)
			F (decimal value of 15)

Fig. E.1 Digits of the binary, octal, decimal, and hexadecimal number systems.

Attribute	Binary	Octal	Decimal	Hexadecimal
Base	2	8	10	16
Lowest Digit	0	0	0	0
Highest Digit	1	7	9	F

Fig. E.2 Comparison of the binary, octal, decimal, and hexadecimal number systems.

Each of these number systems uses *positional notation*—each position in which a digit is written has a different *positional value*. For example, in the decimal number 937 (the 9, the 3, and the 7 are referred to as *symbol values*), we say that the 7 is written in the *ones position*, the 3 is written in the *tens position*, and the 9 is written in the *hundreds position*. Notice that each of these positions is a power of the base (base 10), and that these powers begin at 0 and increase by 1 as we move left in the number (Fig. E.3).

Decimal digit	9	3	7
Position name	Hundreds	Tens	Ones
Positional value	100	10	1
Positional value as a power of the base, 10	10^2	10^1	10^0

Fig. E.3 Positional values in the decimal number system.

For longer decimal numbers, the next positions to the left would be the *thousands position* (10 to the 3rd power), the *ten-thousands position* (10 to the 4th power), the *hundred-thousands position* (10 to the 5th power), the *millions position* (10 to the 6th power), and so on.

In the binary number 101, we say that the rightmost 1 is written in the *ones position*, the 0 is written in the *twos position*, and the leftmost 1 is written in the *fours position*. Notice that each of these positions is a power of the base (base 2), and that these powers begin at 0 and increase by 1 as we move left in the number (Fig E.4).

For longer binary numbers, the next positions to the left would be the *eights position* (2 to the 3rd power), the *sixteens position* (2 to the 4th power), the *thirty-twos position* (2 to the 5th power), the *sixty-fours position* (2 to the 6th power), and so on.

In the octal number 425, we say that the 5 is written in the *ones position*, the 2 is written in the *eights position*, and the 4 is written in the *sixty-fours position*. Notice that each of these positions is a power of the base (base 8), and that these powers begin at 0 and increase by 1 as we move left in the number (Fig. E.5).

Binary digit	1	0	1
Position name	Fours	Twos	Ones
Positional value	4	2	1
Positional value as a power of the base (2)	2^2	2^1	2^0

Fig. E.4 Positional values in the binary number system.

Decimal digit	4	2	5
Position name	Sixty-fours	Eights	Ones
Positional value	64	8	1
Positional value as a power of the base (8)	8^2	8^1	8^0

Fig. E.5 Positional values in the octal number system.

For longer octal numbers, the next positions to the left would be the *five-hundred-and-twelves position* (8 to the 3rd power), the *four-thousand-and-ninety-sixes position* (8 to the 4th power), the *thirty-two-thousand-seven-hundred-and-sixty eights position* (8 to the 5th power), and so on.

In the hexadecimal number 3DA, we say that the A is written in the *ones position,* the D is written in the *sixteens position,* and the 3 is written in the *two-hundred-and-fifty-sixes position.* Notice that each of these positions is a power of the base (base 16), and that these powers begin at 0 and increase by 1 as we move left in the number (Fig. E.6).

For longer hexadecimal numbers, the next positions to the left would be the *four-thousand-and-ninety-sixes position* (16 to the 3rd power), the *thirty-two-thousand-seven-hundred-and-sixty-eights position* (16 to the 4th power), and so on.

E.2 Abbreviating Binary Numbers as Octal Numbers and Hexadecimal Numbers

The main use for octal and hexadecimal numbers in computing is for abbreviating lengthy binary representations. Figure E.7 highlights the fact that lengthy binary numbers can be expressed concisely in number systems with higher bases than the binary number system.

A particularly important relationship that both the octal number system and the hexadecimal number system have to the binary system is that the bases of octal and hexadecimal (8 and 16 respectively) are powers of the base of the binary number system (base 2). Consider the following 12-digit binary number and its octal and hexadecimal equivalents. See if you can determine how this relationship makes it convenient to abbreviate binary numbers in octal or hexadecimal. The answer follows the numbers.

Binary Number	Octal equivalent	Hexadecimal equivalent
100011010001	4321	8D1

To see how the binary number converts easily to octal, simply break the 12-digit binary number into groups of three consecutive bits each, and write those groups over the corresponding digits of the octal number as follows

Decimal digit	3	D	A
Position name	Two-hundred-and-fifty-sixes	Sixteens	Ones
Positional value	256	16	1
Positional value as a power of the base (16)	16^2	16^1	16^0

Fig. E.6 Positional values in the hexadecimal number system.

Decimal Number	Binary representation	Octal representation	Hexadecimal representation
0	0	0	0
1	1	1	1
2	10	2	2
3	11	3	3
4	100	4	4
5	101	5	5
6	110	6	6
7	111	7	7
8	1000	10	8
9	1001	11	9
10	1010	12	A
11	1011	13	B
12	1100	14	C
13	1101	15	D
14	1110	16	E
15	1111	17	F
16	10000	20	10

Fig. E.7 Decimal, binary, octal, and hexadecimal equivalents.

```
100     011     010     001
 4       3       2       1
```

Notice that the octal digit you have written under each group of thee bits corresponds precisely to the octal equivalent of that 3-digit binary number as shown in Fig. E.7.

The same kind of relationship may be observed in converting numbers from binary to hexadecimal. In particular, break the 12-digit binary number into groups of four consecutive bits each and write those groups over the corresponding digits of the hexadecimal number as follows

```
1000    1101    0001
 8       D       1
```

Notice that the hexadecimal digit you have written under each group of four bits corresponds precisely to the hexadecimal equivalent of that 4-digit binary number as shown in Fig. E.7.

E.3 Converting Octal Numbers and Hexadecimal Numbers to Binary Numbers

In the previous section, we saw how to convert binary numbers to their octal and hexadecimal equivalents by forming groups of binary digits and simply rewriting these groups as their equivalent octal digit values or hexadecimal digit values. This process may be used in reverse to produce the binary equivalent of a given octal or hexadecimal number.

For example, the octal number 653 is converted to binary simply by writing the 6 as its 3-digit binary equivalent 110, the 5 as its 3-digit binary equivalent 101, and the 3 as its 3-digit binary equivalent 011 to form the 9-digit binary number 110101011.

The hexadecimal number FAD5 is converted to binary simply by writing the F as its 4-digit binary equivalent 1111, the A as its 4-digit binary equivalent 1010, the D as its 4-digit binary equivalent 1101, and the 5 as its 4-digit binary equivalent 0101 to form the 16-digit 1111101011010101.

E.4 Converting from Binary, Octal, or Hexadecimal to Decimal

Because we are accustomed to working in decimal, it is often convenient to convert a binary, octal, or hexadecimal number to decimal to get a better sense of what the number is "really" worth. Our diagrams in Section E.1 each expressed the positional values in decimal. To convert a number to decimal from another base, multiply the decimal equivalent of each digit by its positional value, and sum these products. For example, the binary number 110101 is converted to decimal 53 as shown in Fig. E.8.

To convert octal 7614 to decimal 3980, we use the same technique, this time using appropriate octal positional values as shown in Fig. E.9.

To convert hexadecimal AD3B to decimal 44347, we use the same technique, this time using appropriate hexadecimal positional values as shown in Fig. E.10.

Positional values:	32	16	8	4	2	1
Symbol values:	1	1	0	1	0	1
Products:	1*32=32	1*16=16	0*8=0	1*4=4	0*2=0	1*1=1
Sum:	= 32 + 16 + 0 + 4 + 0 + 1 = 53					

Fig. E.8 Converting a binary number to decimal.

Positional values:	512	64	8	1
Symbol values:	7	6	1	4
Products	7*512=3584	6*64=384	1*8=8	4*1=4
Sum:	= 3584 + 384 + 8 + 4 = 3980			

Fig. E.9 Converting an octal number to decimal.

Positional values:	4096	256	16	1
Symbol values:	A	D	3	B
Products	A*4096=40960	D*256=3328	3*16=48	B*1=11
Sum:	= 40960 + 3328 + 48 + 11 = 44347			

Fig. E.10   Converting a hexadecimal number to decimal.

E.5 Converting from Decimal to Binary, Octal, or Hexadecimal

The conversions of the previous section follow naturally from the conventions of positional notation. Converting from decimal to binary, octal, or hexadecimal also follows these conventions.

Suppose we wish to convert decimal 57 to binary. We begin by writing the positional values of the columns right to left until we reach a column whose positional value is greater than the decimal number. We do not need that column, so we discard it. Thus, we first write:

Positional values:	64	32	16	8	4	2	1

Then we discard the column with positional value 64 leaving:

Positional values:		32	16	8	4	2	1

Next we work from the leftmost column to the right. We divide 32 into 57 and observe that there is one 32 in 57 with a remainder of 25, so we write 1 in the 32 column. We divide 16 into 25 and observe that there is one 16 in 25 with a remainder of 9 and write 1 in the 16 column. We divide 8 into 9 and observe that there is one 8 in 9 with a remainder of 1. The next two columns each produce quotients of zero when their positional values are divided into 1 so we write 0s in the 4 and 2 columns. Finally, 1 into 1 is 1 so we write 1 in the 1 column. This yields:

Positional values:	32	16	8	4	2	1
Symbol values:	1	1	1	0	0	1

and thus decimal 57 is equivalent to binary 111001.

To convert decimal 103 to octal, we begin by writing the positional values of the columns until we reach a column whose positional value is greater than the decimal number. We do not need that column, so we discard it. Thus, we first write:

Positional values:	512	64	8	1

Then we discard the column with positional value 512, yielding:

Positional values:		64	8	1

Next we work from the leftmost column to the right. We divide 64 into 103 and observe that there is one 64 in 103 with a remainder of 39, so we write 1 in the 64 column. We divide 8 into 39 and observe that there are four 8s in 39 with a remainder of 7 and write 4 in the 8 column. Finally, we divide 1 into 7 and observe that there are seven 1s in 7 with no remainder so we write 7 in the 1 column. This yields:

Positional values:	64	8	1
Symbol values:	1	4	7

and thus decimal 103 is equivalent to octal 147.

To convert decimal 375 to hexadecimal, we begin by writing the positional values of the columns until we reach a column whose positional value is greater than the decimal number. We do not need that column, so we discard it. Thus, we first write

Positional values:	4096	256	16	1

Then we discard the column with positional value 4096, yielding:

Positional values:	256	16	1

Next we work from the leftmost column to the right. We divide 256 into 375 and observe that there is one 256 in 375 with a remainder of 119, so we write 1 in the 256 column. We divide 16 into 119 and observe that there are seven 16s in 119 with a remainder of 7 and write 7 in the 16 column. Finally, we divide 1 into 7 and observe that there are seven 1s in 7 with no remainder so we write 7 in the 1 column. This yields:

Positional values:	256	16	1
Symbol values:	1	7	7

and thus decimal 375 is equivalent to hexadecimal 177.

E.6 Negative Binary Numbers: Two's Complement Notation

The discussion in this appendix has been focussed on positive numbers. In this section, we explain how computers represent negative numbers using *two's complement notation*. First we explain how the two's complement of a binary number is formed, and then we show why it represents the negative value of the given binary number.

Consider a machine with 32-bit integers. Suppose

```
int value = 13;
```

The 32-bit representation of `value` is

```
00000000 00000000 00000000 00001101
```

To form the negative of `value` we first form its one's complement by applying C's bitwise complement operator (~):

```
ones_complement_of_value = ~value;
```

Internally, `~value` is now `value` with each of its bits reversed—ones become zeros and zeros become ones as follows:

```
value:
00000000 00000000 00000000 00001101
```

`~value` (i.e., `value`'s ones complement):
```
11111111 11111111 11111111 11110010
```

To form the two's complement of `value` we simply add one to `value`'s one's complement. Thus

Two's complement of `value`:
```
11111111 11111111 11111111 11110011
```

Now if this is in fact equal to -13, we should be able to add it to binary 13 and obtain a result of 0. Let us try this:

```
 00000000 00000000 00000000 00001101
+11111111 11111111 11111111 11110011
-------------------------------------
 00000000 00000000 00000000 00000000
```

The carry bit coming out of the leftmost column is discarded and we indeed get zero as a result. If we add the one's complement of a number to the number, the result would be all 1s. The key to getting a result of all zeros is that the twos complement is 1 more than the one's complement. The addition of 1 causes each column to add to 0 with a carry of 1. The carry keeps moving leftward until it is discarded from the leftmost bit, and hence the resulting number is all zeros.

Computers actually perform a subtraction such as

```
x = a - value;
```

by adding the two's complement of `value` to `a` as follows:

```
x = a + (~value + 1);
```

Suppose `a` is 27 and `value` is 13 as before. If the two's complement of `value` is actually the negative of `value`, then adding the two's complement of `value` to `a` should produce the result 14. Let us try this:

```
a (i.e., 27)      00000000 00000000 00000000 00011011
+(~value + 1)    +11111111 11111111 11111111 11110011
                 -------------------------------------
                  00000000 00000000 00000000 00001110
```

which is indeed equal to 14.

Summary

• When we write an integer such as 19 or 227 or -63 in a C program, the number is automatically assumed to be in the decimal (base 10) number system. The digits in the decimal number system are 0, 1, 2, 3, 4, 5, 6, 7, 8, and 9. The lowest digit is 0 and the highest digit is 9—one less than the *base* of 10.

- Internally, computers use the binary (base 2) number system. The binary number system has only two digits, namely 0 and 1. Its lowest digit is 0 and its highest digit is 1—one less than the base of 2.

- The octal number system (base 8) and the hexadecimal number system (base 16) have become popular primarily because they make it convenient to abbreviate binary numbers.

- The digits of the octal number system range from 0 to 7.

- The hexadecimal number system poses a problem because it requires sixteen digits—a lowest digit of 0 and a highest digit with a value equivalent to decimal 15 (one less than the base of 16). By convention, we use the letters A through F to represent the hexadecimal digits corresponding to decimal values 10 through 15.

- Each number system uses positional notation—each position in which a digit is written has a different positional value.

- A particularly important relationship that both the octal number system and the hexadecimal number system have to the binary system is that the bases of octal and hexadecimal (8 and 16 respectively) are powers of the base of the binary number system (base 2).

- To convert an octal number to a binary number, simply replace each octal digit with its three-digit binary equivalent.

- To convert a hexadecimal number to a binary number, simply replace each hexadecimal digit with its four-digit binary equivalent.

- Because we are accustomed to working in decimal, it is often convenient to convert a binary, octal, or hexadecimal number to decimal to get a better sense of what the number is "really" worth.

- To convert a number to decimal from another base, multiply the decimal equivalent of each digit by its positional value, and sum these products.

- Computers represent negative numbers using two's complement notation.

- To form the negative of a value in binary, first form its one's complement by applying C's bitwise complement operator (~). This reverses the bits of the value. To form the two's complement of a value, simply add one to the value's one's complement.

Terminology

base	bitwise complement operator (~)
base 2 number system	conversions
base 8 number system	decimal number system
base 10 number system	digit
base 16 number system	hexadecimal number system
binary number system	negative value

octal number system   positional value
one's complement notation   symbol value
positional notation   two's complement notation

Self-Review Exercises

E.1 The bases of the decimal, binary, octal, and hexadecimal number systems are _____, _____, _____, and _____ respectively.

E.2 In general, the decimal, octal, and hexadecimal representations of a given binary number contain (more/fewer) digits than the binary number contains.

E.3 (True/False) A popular reason for using the decimal number system is that it forms a convenient notation for abbreviating binary numbers simply by substituting one decimal digit per group of four binary bits.

E.4 The (octal / hexadecimal / decimal) representation of a very large binary value is the most concise (of the given alternatives).

E.5 (True/False) The highest digit in any base is one more than the base.

E.6 (True/False) The lowest digit in any base is one less than the base.

E.7 The positional value of the rightmost digit of any number in either binary, octal, decimal, or hexadecimal is always _____.

E.8 The positional value of the digit to the left of the rightmost digit of any number in binary, octal, decimal, or hexadecimal is always equal to _____.

E.9 Fill in the missing values in this chart of positional values for the rightmost four positions in each of the indicated number systems:

decimal	1000	100	10	1
hexadecimal	. . .	256	. . .	. . .
binary	. . .	. . .	. . .	. . .
octal	512	. . .	8	. . .

E.10 Convert binary 110101011000 to octal and to hexadecimal.

E.11 Convert hexadecimal **FACE** to binary.

E.12 Convert octal 7316 to binary.

E.13 Convert hexadecimal **4FEC** to octal. (Hint: First convert **4FEC** to binary then convert that binary number to octal.)

E.14 Convert binary 1101110 to decimal.

E.15 Convert octal 317 to decimal.

E.16 Convert hexadecimal **EFD4** to decimal.

E.17 Convert decimal 177 to binary, to octal, and to hexadecimal.

E.18 Show the binary representation of decimal 417. Then show the one's complement of 417, and the two's complement of 417.

E.19 What is the result when the one's complement of a number is added to itself?

Self-Review Answers

E.1   10, 2, 8, 16.

E.2   Fewer.

E.3   False.

E.4   Hexadecimal.

E.5   False—The highest digit in any base is one less than the base.

E.6   False— The lowest digit in any base is zero.

E.7   1 (the base raised to the zero power).

E.8   The base of the number system.

E.9   Fill in the missing values in this chart of positional values for the rightmost four positions in each of the indicated number systems:

decimal	1000	100	10	1
hexadecimal	4096	256	16	1
binary	8	4	2	1
octal	512	64	8	1

E.10   Octal 6530; Hexadecimal D58.

E.11   Binary 1111 1010 1100 1110.

E.12   Binary 111 011 001 110

E.13   Binary 0 100 111 111 101 100; Octal 47754 .

E.14   Decimal 2+4+8+32+64=110.

E.15   Decimal 7+1*8+3*64=7+8+192=207.

E.16   Decimal 4+13*16+15*256+14*4096=61396.

E.17   Decimal 177
        to binary:
            256 128 64 32 16 8 4 2 1
            128 64 32 16 8 4 2 1
            (1*128)+(0*64)+(1*32)+(1*16)+(0*8)+(0*4)+(0*2)+(1*1)
            10110001
        to octal:
            512 64 8 1
            64 8 1
            (2*64)+(6*8)+(1*1)
            261
        to hexadecimal:
            256 16 1
            16 1
            (11*16)+(1*1)
            (B*16)+(1*1)
            B1

E.18   Binary:
        512 256 128 64 32 16 8 4 2 1
        256 128 64 32 16 8 4 2 1
        (1*256)+(1*128)+(0*64)+(1*32)+(0*16)+(0*8)+(0*4)+(0*2)+
        (1*1)
        110100001
    One's complement: 001011110
    Two's complement: 001011111

Check: Original binary number + its two's complement
```
110100001
001011111
---------
000000000
```
E.19   Zero.

Exercises

E.20   Some people argue that many of our calculations would be easier in the base 12 number system because 12 is divisible by so many more numbers than 10 (for base 10). What is the lowest digit in base 12? What might the highest symbol for the digit in base 12 be? What are the positional values of the rightmost four positions of any number in the base 12 number system?

E.21   How is the highest symbol value in the number systems we discussed related to the positional value of the first digit to the left of the rightmost digit of any number in these number systems?

E.22   Complete the following chart of positional values for the rightmost four positions in each of the indicated number systems:

	1000	100	10	1
decimal	1000	100	10	1
base 6	...	...	6	...
base 13	...	169	...	...
base 3	27	...	...	...

E.23   Convert binary 100101111010 to octal and to hexadecimal.

E.24   Convert hexadecimal 3A7D to binary.

E.25   Convert hexadecimal 765F to octal. (Hint: First convert 765F to binary, then convert that binary number to octal.)

E.26   Convert binary 1011110 to decimal.

E.27   Convert octal 426 to decimal.

E.28   Convert hexadecimal FFFF to decimal.

E.29   Convert decimal 299 to binary, to octal, and to hexadecimal.

E.30   Show the binary representation of decimal 779. Then show the one's complement of 779, and the two's complement of 779.

E.31   What is the result when the two's complement of a number is added to itself?

E.32   Show the two's complement of integer value -1 on a machine with 32-bit integers.

Index